RICHARD HOOKER

Prophet of Anglicanism

RICHARD HOOKER

Prophet of Anglicanism

PHILIP B. SECOR

BURNS & OATES

THE ANGLICAN BOOK CENTRE
Toronto • Canada

Dedicated to the late John H. Hallowell,
esteemed scholar, teacher, friend

First published in Great Britain in 1999 by
BURNS & OATES,
Wellwood, North Farm Road,
Tunbridge Wells, Kent TN2 3DR

First published in Canada and the USA in 1999 by
THE ANGLICAN BOOK CENTRE
600 Jarvis Street, Toronto, Ontario,
Canada M4Y 2J6

Reprinted 2000

ISBN 0 86012 289 1

Typeset by Shelleys The Printers, Sherborne
Printed in Great Britain by
MPG Books Limited, Bodmin, Cornwall

Contents

Illustrations

Sources of Illustrations

Frontis., 1, 5, 8, 11, 19 by Courtesy of the National Portrait Gallery, London; 3, Royal Albert Memorial Museum, Exeter; 2, 5, 10, 126, 15, 16, 17, 18, 20, 21, 23, 24, 26, 27, Author; 9, Bridgeman Art Library, London/New York; 4, Thomas Fowler, *History of Corpus Christi College* (Oxford: Clarendon Press, 1893); 12a, Drayton Beauchamp church bulletin, 1985; 14, Middle Temple brochure; 22, H. Henry Meeter Center for Calvin Studies, Calvin College and Seminary, Grand Rapids, Michigan; 25, Enfield parish brochure.

The maps were drawn for this book by the author.
The Coat of Arms was executed by the Revd Canon A. Malcolm MacMillan.

Proem

By the Right Reverend David Stancliffe, Bishop of Salisbury

I am glad to take the opportunity offered to me by Dr Philip Secor to commend the writings of Richard Hooker to the Church in our day.

The fourth centenary of his death in the year 1600 provides a welcome occasion to look again at Hooker's abiding legacy to the Church of England. In Salisbury Cathedral, where his patron, John Jewel, was bishop, there is a tablet erected to his memory in 1836 by an enthusiastic admirer, Canon Bowles. Although Hooker's connections with Salisbury are slight, he was of course a prebend of the cathedral and for a time held the living of Boscombe, some ten miles east up the Bourne Valley. Such enthusiasm for Hooker in the early years of the nineteenth century is testimony to his continuing importance in the theological tradition of the Church of England. Canon Bowles says:

> To the memory of Richard Hooker, Prebendary of this Cathedral and author of a book entitled *Ecclesiastical Polity* who, exhibiting in his writings the Profoundness of a Scholar, and in his life the holy simplicity of an Apostle successfully vindicated the forms and Ordinances of the Episcopal Church of this Nation, and a Primitive usage of the sweetest songs of Sion, Anthems and Antiphonal Harmonies, adapted to the words of the inspired Psalmist he died AD1600. This tribute of Respect and Veneration for so great a name is offered here by W L Bowles, Canon Residentiary, 1836.

Hooker's *apologia* for the Church of England has stood the test of time: a national Church needs a strong ecclesiology if it is not to become the property or puppet of the State. In spite of the very changed social and political circumstances of today, the relationship between the Crown and the Church of England remains unbroken. Hooker's understanding of the Church was rooted in the theology of the Incarnation—that God in Christ first shares our life and then transforms it. For Hooker this meant that the Church must be rooted in the actualities of time and place. The parish priest's pastoral responsibility for his parish was of prime significance, and the Church could no more be divorced from its social context than from its foundation in Christ. That praying community was to be where Christ's presence could be discerned and acclaimed, as the regular worship of the Church of praise and thanksgiving to God and the parish priest's ministry of prayer and pastoral care established a pattern for the life of the community in every place.

Hooker was among the foremost Christian apologists of his day. His conviction that the truth was discerned with reference to revelation, tradition, and reason has frequently been cited as the foundation stone of an Anglicanism that is both Catholic and Reformed. His successors in the Church of England and throughout the Anglican Communion should take the opportunity of Dr Philip Secor's enthusiastic biography to engage again with the seminal thinker who was ready to hold together these three strands not merely in theory but in practice. It is hard work for a Church that is now a world-wide Communion, doing its best to proclaim afresh the truth of Christ in every generation and in every culture, to find coherence in the midst of of such social, political, and cultural diversity. Hooker reminds us of our roots, and Dr Secor's work will encourage those who look for a common ecclesial identity to go back and read again for themselves the works of Richard Hooker.

Foreword

By W. Speed Hill, General Editor
The Folger Library Edition of the Works of Richard Hooker

It is perhaps not so puzzling that Richard Hooker has had to wait nearly four hundred years for a comprehensive biography. First of all he was claimed by Izaak Walton as one of the Church of England's founding saints in a hagiography that has remained a classic in its own right. Walton's Life first appeared in 1665, commissioned as a corrective to Bishop John Gauden's defective one of 1662, and it has prefaced editions of Hooker's works from 1666 to 1890 and has been reprinted in collected editions of Walton's five Lives (those of George Herbert, John Donne, Robert Sanderson, and Sir Henry Cotton being the other four). Earlier scholars such as David Novarr and C. J. Sisson have examined Walton's Life of Hooker in some detail, undermining much of its documentary authority, but no one has undertaken to replace Walton—until now.

A second reason why Hooker has wanted a biographer for so long is that the distinction of his life lies in what he thought and what he wrote, not in what he did. In this he was unlike, for example, Walter Ralegh, whose poems survive as graceful filigree to a life of high adventure. (Ralegh's *History of the World* is substantial enough but no longer read.) By such a measure, Richard's uncle, John Hooker, would make a far better subject for a contemporary biographer in search of an exemplary subject than does his now more famous nephew. As a result, the founding theologian (some would argue the priority of Thomas Cranmer) of the Church of England still survives as a man from whom it would seem impossible that such an ambitious treatise as his *Of the Laws of Ecclesiastical Polity* should ever have emerged—so passive, so un-self-assertive, so physically frail, so put upon by his shrewish wife Joan does Hooker appear in Walton's portrait.

Thus, it is a long-overdue debt that we now see redeemed in Dr Secor's splendid new biography. And while it is true that Hooker's distinction and importance were intellectual, it is also true, as Dr Secor makes abundantly clear, that Hooker was not writing in a historical vacuum—as he would have been had he stayed at Oxford. The 1570s, when he was a student and later a teacher there, the 1580s, after he had been translated from a parish cure at Drayton Beauchamp to London, and the 1590s, when he was composing the *Laws*, were all stirring times for the England of Elizabeth I, and Hooker was, from 1585 on, by his wish and that of others, at the centre of religious politics of the day. The apparent lack of external events in Hooker's life poses a challenge to the biographer of a man who left almost no personal documents behind and whose life would seem to have comprised a series of minor clerical appointments and a modest list of two books published, and some of whose most important writings (Books VI-VIII of the *Laws*) were not published until years after his death.

Marchette Chute, the distinguished biographer of Geoffrey Chaucer, Ben Jonson, and William Shakespeare, spoke of hers as "silhouette" biographies. Where the object himself is opaque, it is the task of the biographer to bring the subject back to life by recreating the contexts in which he lived and wrote and worked. That is certainly what Dr Secor does, as his extensive notes indicate. Whatever documents do survive—and for these early writers, they are overwhelming legal or institutional records, public not private documents—anyone reading the works of Chaucer, Jonson, or Shakespeare comes to know the character of the men who wrote them. The biographical inferences are clear enough, even if they are unsusceptible to empirical localization in the surviving documents. This too is what Dr Secor has done. He has read Hooker; he has come to understand his character as Hooker himself revealed it in his writings; and he has read the events of Hooker's life, in so far as they are recorded in the kind of documents that historians depend upon, in the light of that self-revealed character. The result is a portrait of Hooker restored to the world in which he grew up and in whose intellectual and political battles he was such an active participant.

Hooker's famous appeal to reason, his ecumenical outreach, his irony, his moderation, his scholarship—all these well-known features now have their origins and contexts clearly and concisely set forth. We learn who, for example, stood in as Hooker's surrogate fathers when his own father, as a younger son, abandoned him to pursue a career far from Exeter as steward to the rich and famous (Sir Thomas Challoner and Sir Peter Carew). Roger's replacements constitute a roll-call of Elizabethan Protestantism: John Hooker, Richard's uncle, chamberlain and civic humanist of Exeter; John Jewel, bishop of Salisbury, who helped Hooker attend Oxford; Edwin Sandys, bishop of London and archbishop of York, who suggested Hooker for the post of master of the Temple Church (having earlier sent his son Edwin to Oxford to study with him as his tutor); and, finally, John Whitgift, the archbishop of Canterbury, who saw to it that, through a string of appointments, Hooker had the time and the resources to pursue his *magnum opus*, the *Laws*. One, maybe two, such patrons we can account for as circumstantial. But a string, ending in the patronage of Whitgift, acting on behalf of the queen herself, argues a lively contemporary appreciation of the exceptional nature of Hooker's gifts.

It was these gifts, of intellect and character, that those in power sought to enlist to serve the political goals of the Church of England as it struggled against adversaries from the Genevan left and the Roman right and to carve out its own identity in a Europe defined by ferocious religious conflict. It is not often remembered, for example, in discussions about Richard Hooker that the defeat of the Spanish Armada occurred as he was scarcely three years into his appointment as Master of the Temple Church. It is the special virtue of this biography that it fills out both background and foreground in its portrait of Hooker. Reading it, we come to know far more about the man—and his mother and his father and his wife and his in-laws and his patrons and his associates—whose austere intellect was the efficient cause of the *Laws*, than we had thought possible.

It must be admitted that Hooker was himself, to a degree, responsible for the subsequent attenuation of his reputation, and in this respect Walton's portrait rings true. In the *Laws*, as well as in the sermons and tractates (composed earlier but published posthumously), Hooker's rhetorical persona is that of the distanced and distancing intellectual, the man of trained scholastic reason who would persuade his sceptical auditors—the Puritans in the case of the *Laws*, the lawyers at the Temple Church in the case of the tractate *Of Justification*—by an appeal to reason, evidence, and shared good will. Literary students of Hooker recognize the constructed nature of such a rhetorical appeal, and his annotations on a quarto pamphlet written against him in the year before he died express some not very saintly aggression towards his antagonists, of whom he had a rather low opinion: "You rage yell and bellow as one that were carried beside him self. A great passionate Rhetorique bestowed to little purpose" is a not untypical comment. But the carefully cultivated stance of Olympian detachment has been far more successful than he could ever have dreamed. Successive generations of readers, taking him at his word, have overlooked the polemical skill and controversial force of his writings, elevating him far above his peers into a realm seemingly detached and timeless. Reflecting this, the *Cambridge Bibliography of English Literature* (new and old), taxonomically ranks Hooker with Chaucer, Milton, and Shakespeare and "above" everybody else. Yet, if there is one lesson that his twentieth-century editors have learned, it is that Hooker was a far more engaged polemicist than he has historically been credited with being. Because the issues at stake seem so distant from our own religio-political concerns—the ordination of women, for example, or the sanctioning of same sex relationships—and because Book I of the *Laws* has been read synecdochically, as a part for the whole, Hooker's assertions in Books II-VIII against the Puritans of the 1590s fall on the unheeding ears of the 1990s. This is where modern scholarship, imaginatively employed, is vital to a recovery of just who this "Prophet of Anglicanism" was and why he was so important. In this project, Dr Secor's biography works in tandem with the multi-volume Folger Edition of his *Works* (1977-98), the first a biographical and broadly historical reconstruction, the other a minutely textual and exegetical analysis and commentary, to recover the revivifying contexts in which Hooker lived and wrote.

Given the nature of the surviving documents and given the non-specialist audience intended for this biography, Dr Secor's occasional re-creations of events for which we have no specific evidence seem quite appropriate. Without them, Hooker shrivels up into a dessicated cleric, obsessed to the point of tedium with issues no longer of import to us, the concerns mainly of a few scattered professionals. The invention of such scenes and events, which has a long and honourable history in humanist historiography, are carefully noted, as "fictional", either by a change in typography or by notes or by both, Other reconstructions, such as the text of Hooker's Paul's Cross sermon of 1584, employ related texts to supply on Hooker's behalf the text of the sermon that has come down to us only in a brief summary sentence in Walton. Again, there can be no deception once one accepts the convention, and the scholar-author is ready at hand, in the notes, to alert the reader of the composite nature of the event being so narrated. The aim, to restore Hooker to a more human and less saintly—or merely intellectual—status within the history of the Church of England, warrants such rhetorical resourcefulness. To be sure, it is obviously "interpretive," but so is Georges Edelen's "Chronology" in volume VI of the Folger Edition. Such a listing, by reducing Hooker's life to a c.v. that one would read in a sixteenth-century *Who's Who*, is no less misleading.

As historical and literary scholarship have emerged in the course of the twentieth century from their earlier idealist sponsorship and assumptions, the question becomes, which material remains are relevant historiographically and which are not? The *corpus* that is available to scholarship is so vast that no author can control more than a fraction of it. "New Historicism" has come to emphasize the local, the anecdotal, the non-canonical as offering ways to re-situate the canonical and to interrogate the master narratives governing the history we read, write, and teach. There is nothing self-consciously "new" about Dr Secor's historical scholarship: he has simply read widely and well in the relevant sources, primary and secondary, but he has deployed the materials available in new and insightful ways, so that Hooker rises up, miraculously reborn, from the pages of his biography. As an academic myself, I was particularly persuaded by Dr Secor's account of Hooker's Oxford years and his explanation of why Hooker's academic career never bloomed: like so many impecunious graduate students or overworked junior staff, he never completed his doctorate! Of course! Other readers will have their own moments of illumination, as the narrative re-situates Richard Hooker in the world in which he lived, worked, wrote, and died. Less an account of a "search" for a "prophet" (though it is that), it is Hooker *redivivus*, the man rediscovered for the twentieth century to accompany the work he composed for the sixteenth, the civic humanist whose polis was the institution in which he found his spiritual home and which he devoted his life to defending, the Church of England.

Author's Preface

Though for no other cause but this, that posterity may know we have not loosely through silence permitted things to pass away as in a dream, there shall be . . . surviving this much . . .

(The opening words of Richard Hooker in his *Of the Laws of Ecclesiastical Polity*, 1593)

For centuries after his death in 1600, Richard Hooker had been one of the brightest luminaries of western culture. But then he was gradually forgotten through a kind of benign neglect. So he just wandered off into obscurity—disappeared, "as in a dream."

Richard Hooker is one of the important founders of our so-called modern era, now almost over. Along with the martyred Archbishop Thomas Cranmer, who wrote and compiled the *Book of Common Prayer*, he is the founding intellect and spirit of Anglicanism, an ecumenical cultural strain that has textured the religion, politics, literature, and social fabric of every corner of the earth touched by English language and culture for more than four centuries. Others came after him to define further and expand Anglicanism, including the Caroline Divines of the seventeenth century, the members of the nineteenth-century Oxford Movement, and many more. But it was Hooker on whose shoulders they all stood; and most of them knew it.[1] Hooker is also one of the seminal thinkers influencing the development of modern constitutional government and, for many, the leading exemplar of Elizabethan prose writing.[2]

His great opus, *Of the Laws of Ecclesiastical Polity*, is without equal in the literature explaining and extolling the theory and practice of the many Churches around the globe that have developed from the emergent Anglicanism of the sixteenth century. His theory of law is one of the most eloquent and influential ever conceived. His political and religious ideas are among the most important bridges between medieval and modern thought.

In the broadest sense, Hooker's genius was to make sense out of much of the clamour of a tumultuous formative age in which he too was an important actor. He translated many of the confusing and destructive conflicts of his time into a useful legacy for future generations, a legacy of order, reason, toleration, compromise—a pragmatic and tolerant middle way between the tempting dogmatisms of his day. Both in his writings and in his life he provides an example of how to live intelligently and morally in times of massive social and intellectual disorder. As such, he represents a useful guide for those of us who try to find our way through the wreckage and promise of our own century.

Hooker's life and personality exemplify a little-known Elizabethan archetype—the thoughtful, tolerant, intellectual counterpoint to the more exuberant characters from that incredible era: Ralegh, Drake, Shakespeare, Spenser, Marlowe, Burghley, and, of course, the colourful, enigmatic Virgin Queen who presided over it all.

For all his importance, Hooker is virtually unknown today except to a handful of scholars who still perfunctorily cite him to justify their opinions on a wide range of topics ranging from theology, English literature, classical rhetoric, law and government, to ethics, aesthetics, prayer, liturgy, and even personal morality. With notable exceptions, few of these scholars have read the corpus of Hooker's works or know anything of the man behind the quotations they pluck from his writings and carefully plant in their footnotes. And, as for more popular literature, Hooker has almost disappeared.

There is, of course, always the wonderful exception. After years of searching, usually in vain, for references to Hooker in our popular culture, I was jolted a few years ago by a surprisingly accurate and unselfconscious citation in, of all places, a mystery novel by Margaret Truman Daniels, daughter of former U.S. President Harry Truman.

In one of her popular potboilers, entitled *Murder at the Washington Cathedral*, the dean of the cathedral explains the idiosyncrasies of a liberal cleric to a high-church Anglo-Catholic canon on his staff in the following words: "I know, I know, Paul Singletary has a remarkable gift for . . . self-promotion. He is grandiose at times and seems to have a great deal of trouble practising the sort of humility that we are expected to demonstrate. Still, as Hooker says, let us not attempt to unscrew the inscrutable."

Hurray for Margaret Truman! We can be sure that few of her millions of readers understood her deliciously accurate allusion to Hooker's pleas for calm, patience, and letting sleeping dogs lie—and barking dogs bark. The great man lives on, however precariously, in the popular literature of the late twentieth century.

Worse than obscurity has been the degradation of Hooker's name and fame, resulting naturally enough from centuries of misinformation and ignorance about his life and work. It was, in fact, the corruption more than the neglect of Hooker that drove me at last to search for this remarkable man in order to rescue him from his tormentors.

I suppose it is inevitable that Hooker would be confused, by otherwise literate people, with the prominent English Puritan and founder of Connecticut, Thomas Hooker, or the U.S. civil war general, Joseph Hooker. It is less excusable when Exeter guide books confuse him with his uncle, John Hooker, one-time chamberlain and historian of the city, or when the May 1995 issue of the popular picture magazine,

Heritage/Realm, repeats the slander about Hooker being a foolish man who was trapped into marrying his landlady's shrewish daughter.

Even more shocking to a former academic like me is an entry in a recent issue of *A Concise Guide to Colleges of Oxford University*, promoting Hooker to the position of "Bishop" in its listing of distinguished alumni. The post may or may not be one he coveted, but he certainly never held it. More of a nit-pick, perhaps, is an error in the 1993 edition of the *New Illustrated History of Oxford*, listing Hooker as the "rector of Boscomb in Wiltshire" at a time when it has long been established that he was living in London and Bishopsbourne.

What finally drove me to write this book, however, was not intellectual chagrin but a painful personal experience. It happened this way.

About fifteen years ago, my wife, Anne, and I were in Exeter visiting the magnificent twin-towered fourteenth-century cathedral where Richard Hooker's family took him to services when he was a little boy during the reign of Mary Tudor. We fell in behind a gaggle of British and American tourists in the cathedral close, clustering around a guide in front of the only outdoor statue of Hooker in the world. This life-sized seated figure with book in hand and impassive scholarly aspect towered impressively over us as we looked up at his grand Elizabethan figure.

The guide apparently used the Hooker statue as a convenient landmark to gather her charges for a daily assault on the cathedral. She made no attempt to explain the sculpture before waving her willing troop on toward the church. To my delight, she was arrested in her progress by a Minnesota accent lingering behind with Richard Hooker: "Who's that up there?" Not surprised by what was surely the first question on many of her tours, the guide answered, "Uh, that's Mr Hooker. He's one of our great religious men. Was a slovenly gent. Had a bad marriage, you know. Got her pregnant and her parents made him marry her. Then he was henpecked all his life by her."

A few chuckles from the group and then more history from the guide, warming to her familiar subject. "I'm not saying his wife was a 'hooker' at first, but she was one after she married him," she said, pointing up at that amiable face and pausing for effect.

"You Americans know what a hooker is, don't you? We don't have that word over here. It comes from your civil war general Joe Hooker who encouraged women to follow his troops to improve morale, if you get my meaning. So they called them hookers. And, that General Hooker of yours—he was a direct relative of our Mr Hooker here. So, you see, we have a lot in common."

Then the tourists, only mildly titillated by this tale, but not doubting its accuracy for an instant and prepared to repeat it back home in Chicago, Fort Worth, Cirencester, and Manchester, straggled on into the cathedral to hear God only knows what other tales of wonderful historical connection between English and American heroes.

Izaak Walton, 1593-1683
Oil painting by Jacob Huysmans, c. 1672

I say "God only knows" because I did not continue with that tour. Instead, my wife and I remained at the statue until everyone was gone. Then I looked up again into that benign face and promised the ghost of my old friend Richard Hooker that I would tell his story.

My friendship with Richard Hooker began forty years ago when I joined the small group who comprise the fellowship of Hooker scholars. My tenure in that company was short-lived. As soon as my doctoral thesis had wended its way through Hooker's opus, *Of the Laws of Ecclesiastical Polity*, in search of his theories on church-state relationships, I abandoned my study of Hooker's writings for a lifetime of other pursuits inside and outside the academy.

But over the years I was bothered by the knowledge that this important person never became part of the consciousness of the modern world in the manner of such other founding heroes as Luther, Calvin, Darwin, Marx, Freud. Yet Hooker's contributions to the fabrics of our culture are only slightly less significant than theirs are.

What is more, I have been haunted by the ghost of Richard Hooker himself, who would not rest until I had done my part to lift the obscuring veil from his life and liberate him from the incomplete, inaccurate, and biased—if sometimes charming—tales told about him for centuries.

Most of the picture current until now of Hooker's life and personality comes from a short biography published in 1665 by Izaak Walton, the famed author of *The Compleat Angler*. Although terribly flawed, this bit of hagiography has withstood any complete attempt to take a fresh look at Hooker, partly because Walton has been so respected—even revered—by scholars and churchmen.

Hooker, Walton tells us, was a dutiful son, a brilliant lad, a pious student, a devoted teacher, a self-sacrificing and long-suffering husband, a beleaguered misunderstood preacher, a humble pastor, who gave his life to the tireless labour of writing so that the Church of England would have the spirit he alone could breathe into her.

Not a wart anywhere.

Walton, and later chroniclers who copied and embellished his characterizations of Hooker, gave posterity such an unbelievably sanctified figure that the man became lost behind an icon of dove-like simplicity, personal purity, unimpassioned docility, and unfailing judiciousness. No one could be that perfect and still be real, much less interesting to know. So Hooker ceased to be flesh and blood. He became a frozen symbol. His writings were all that remained alive. As Christopher Morris, a twentieth-century editor of Hooker's works put it, "Hooker . . . is the name of a book rather than the name of a man . . ."[3]

In fairness, Walton's portrayal of Hooker was altogether in keeping with the classical literary form that authorized using the subject being chronicled to exemplify virtue (or evil) and to teach civic and moral values. In a tradition as old and respectable as Homer and the authors of the Bible, biography was a means to promote a particular system of belief. The idea that writing the history of an individual involved discovering and recording the facts of the subject's life through careful empirical research into the conditions of his rearing, education, social relations, individual accomplishments, and character development is a relatively recent understanding of how biography should be done. We can hardly fault Walton for not being ahead of his time. But neither is it necessary to continue to be intimidated by his reputation or to rely exclusively on him as a source.

I have been able to exorcise the intimidating ghost of Izaak Walton by utilizing the research and speculations of John Keble, C. J. Sisson, David Novarr, W. Speed Hill, and others who have either documented Walton's errors or suggested a more believable persona for Mr Hooker, or both. I have allowed Hooker to give me his own clues about his character and personality by a close reading of his words, especially his sermons. Most of all, I have immersed myself in the environments and persons who most closely surrounded his life.

Hooker's relevance for our own time is evident when we see him for the person he really was: a creative, embattled Elizabethan philosopher-polemicist thoroughly engaged in one of the central struggles of his time, which was to discover and construct some religious and intellectual order amidst the apparent chaos of cultural transition from one age to another. He offered a broad and tolerant intellectual framework and religious spirit, which came to be known as Anglicanism—an inclusive middle way through the often violent and destructive thickets of religious and political debate.

More narrowly, but of potential import to millions of Anglicans and Episcopalians in our day, is Hooker's relevance as the prophet of their tradition. The apparent absence of a founding human intellect and spirit for Anglicanism is a serious detriment to the rekindling of popular interest in this useful tradition of thought and practice. Unbeknownst to most of the seventy million members of Anglican Churches spread through thirty-five self-governing church bodies in 164 nations, they are inheritors of legitimating founding stories to which they may turn for authenticity and inspiration. This is one of them. The good news is that Christians who worship within the remarkably broad, tolerant, and welcoming Anglican tradition were not born of the sexual lust and political ambitions of King Henry VIII or the political and economic aspirations of a rising class of English gentry and merchants. Rather, these Christians were bred in that special seedbed of ideas, persons, and events that had its enduring liturgical expression in Archbishop Thomas Cranmer's *Book of Common Prayer* and came to fruition most significantly in the life and writings of a truly prophetic and hitherto largely unknown person named Richard Hooker.

Since so much of Hooker's influence and persona are transmitted only through his own voice, I have allowed him to speak directly throughout the pages of this book. We will see him standing in the pulpits at the Temple Church, and St Paul's Cross in London, and hear again the famous sermons he preached—sermons that helped formulate the spirit of the emerging Church of England. We will follow him into the city streets, along the roads and rivers, and into the churches, homes, and college halls that defined his environment. We will watch him as he discovers his identity and formulates the ideas that were to fill his sermons and longer expository writings.

The Hooker we discover is a "poor boy" from a small village attending grammar school in Exeter in 1562; an Oxford undergraduate living on financial aid and trying to overcome inadequate academic preparation along with the horrific plagues, constant curriculum changes and student-faculty unrest of those years; a gifted teacher and tutor advising ambitious young men from powerful, wealthy families; a famous London cleric living near St Paul's in one of the great merchant houses on Watling Street and walking through tumultuous and dangerous central London each day on his way to and from work; a sensitive husband of the daughter of a wealthy and prominent Londoner with good political connections; a perceptive, introspective person of peaceful disposition finding his way to fame in an age of bluster, extroversion, and novelty; a writer struggling with inner doubts and outer political pressures to write an honest explanation and defence of a new kind of Christian commonwealth—a broad and open community based upon reason, common sense, and toleration.

John Updike's charming description of the process of doing history, especially biography, in his 1992 book entitled *Memories of the Ford Administration,* describes the spirit of my own search for Richard Hooker. "History," he writes, "unlike fiction or physics, never quite jells; it is an armature of rather randomly preserved verbal and physical remains upon which historians slap wads of supposition in hopes of the lumpy statue's coming to life. One of the joys of doing original research is to observe how one's predecessor historians have fudged their way across the very gaps, or fault lines, that one is in turn balked by" (p. 150).

Hooker, although not exactly lumpy, has been a slippery subject. Each time I thought I had hold of him, he escaped into some shrouded byway, away from the light of recorded history. But I was undaunted in my search and eventually found enough of Hooker on which to slap my own wads of supposition.

The Richard Hooker who emerges in these pages is neither the faceless author of a famous and influential book nor the pious sanctified icon of high-church Anglicans but, I trust, a lively and believable Elizabethan personality fully endowed with the characteristics of active men and women of his time: quick-witted, urbane, intellectually acute, politically sophisticated, compassionate, vulnerable, sensitive, adventurous—a man to match the style and power of his words.

Like all writers, I am indebted to many people. To my friend and wife, Anne Secor, I owe the most. She has been my partner for the past fifteen years in research, editing, and a shared intention to bring Mr Hooker to life. To the late John Hallowell, Emeritus Professor of Political Science at Duke University, I dedicate this book as a token of my gratitude for introducing me to Hooker and, while he was about it, teaching me to appreciate the necessary relationship in any culture between religion and politics. I happily express thanks to Robert Smith, emeritus professor at Drew University, who taught me to think critically; to Hooker's seventeenth-century biographer, Izaak Walton, onto whose shaky shoulders I have tried to climb. I offer a very special thank-you to W. Speed Hill, general editor of the *Folger Library Edition of the Works of Richard Hooker*. Dr Hill's patient reading of early versions of the manuscript, his countless helpful suggestions, and his unfailing support when other scholars doubted both the wisdom and efficacy of this effort, place me permanently and happily in his debt. I wish also to thank the eminent Hooker scholar A. S. McGrade and the historian W. B. Patterson, who have been generous in reading and criticising my efforts here and elsewhere to put Hooker's life on to paper. I am also grateful to the Reverend Alan Duke, Hooker's present-day successor at Bishopsbourne in Kent, who has read critically relevant chapters of the manuscript; and to English friends who have made suggestions, including the eminent Exeter University historian Joyce Youings; the Ralegh biographer Reginald Wood; and the Dorset historian Gerald Pitman. Many librarians have been helpful, especially Sheila Sterling of the Devon and Exeter Institution in Exeter, Suzanne Eward at Salisbury Cathedral, and Christine Butler, archivist at the library of Corpus Christi, Oxford. Peter Doyle, formerly head of history at De Montford University, Bedford, read the typescript, saved me from some errors and over-enthusiasms, and made many other helpful suggestions. Other friends who have been generous with their time, advice, and encouragement include the late Revd Canon Frederick Tindal of Salisbury Cathedral, the Revd Canon Malcolm MacMillan, and my special supporters Mary and the Reverend Peter Lewis of Amesbury in Wiltshire. Last, but far from least, I express my lasting gratitude to my editor Paul Burns. Like Hooker himself, I had found it difficult to secure a publisher for a work generally regarded as worthy in itself but a poor commercial prospect. Paul Burns was not only willing to run a risk but to offer the patience and determination required to bring Hooker to life in the late twentieth century. As well, he successfully faced the daunting task of editing a first-time author who was eager to display every person and event even remotely connected to his subject and who suffered the added handicap of being a North American attempting to understand England and the English. All of these wonderful helpers are of course absolved of any responsibility for what follows.

In the final analysis, my principal thanks go to Richard Hooker himself. His footprints have been scarce, his appearances rare and often dimly lit, but he has shown me enough of himself and his great spirit to make this biography possible.

2 November 1998

NOTES

1. My opinion, highlighted in the title of this book, that Hooker was the principal "prophet" rather than, as many claim, the principal "defender" of Anglicanism is based on the fact that Anglicanism was still an emergent phenomenon in Hooker's sixteenth-century England, not defined as such until the next century. Supporting this view is the distinguished Cambridge historian Dairmaid MacCulloch, in his *The Later Reformation in England 1547-1603* (New York: St Martins Press, 1990), 1-8; 97-102. For an exposition of the special problems involved in writing this biography see Philip B. Secor, "Constructing a Biography of Richard Hooker," Arthur Stephen McGrade, ed., *Richard Hooker and the Construction of Christian Community* (Tempe, Arizona: Medieval & Renaissance Texts & Studies, 1997).

2. A complete analysis of Hooker's influence on later religious and political thought is beyond the scope of this book. Hooker's credits range from Izaak Walton's seventeenth-century comment that "He who Praises Richard Hooker praises God," to Samuel Johnson's use of Hooker as a primary source in his famous dictionary, to John Locke's appropriation of him for some of his ideas on modern government. Recent summaries and analyses of the literature on Hooker's influence are essays by W. Speed Hill and Philip B. Secor in *Ibid.*, 3-37.

3. Christopher Morris, *Richard Hooker of the Laws of Ecclesiastical Polity* (London: J. M. Dent & Sons, Ltd, 1907), 3.

About Sources and Citation

The primary sources used for writings by and about Hooker are W. Speed Hill, gen. ed., *The Folger Library Edition of the Works of Richard Hooker*, 1977-98, in seven volumes, cited in this book as *Folger*; John Keble, ed, *Of the Laws of Ecclesiastical Polity*, 7th edition, by R. W. Church and Francis Paget, Oxford: Oxford University Press, 1887, in three volumes, cited in this book as *Works*. The Folger edition is the definitive choice for serious students of Hooker. Both are cited in this work.

I have sometimes modernized the punctuation and grammar of Hooker and his contemporaries when quoting directly in order to make their words more palatable to the modern reader. When paraphrasing from Hooker's writings, I have made every effort to remain faithful to his meaning and to retain the flavour of his writing by using key phrases and maintaining the syntax of the original text. All paraphrases are noted as such.

A full reference is given the first time any source is cited. Thereafter, only the author's or editor's last name is used. A full bibliography of works cited is at the end of the book.

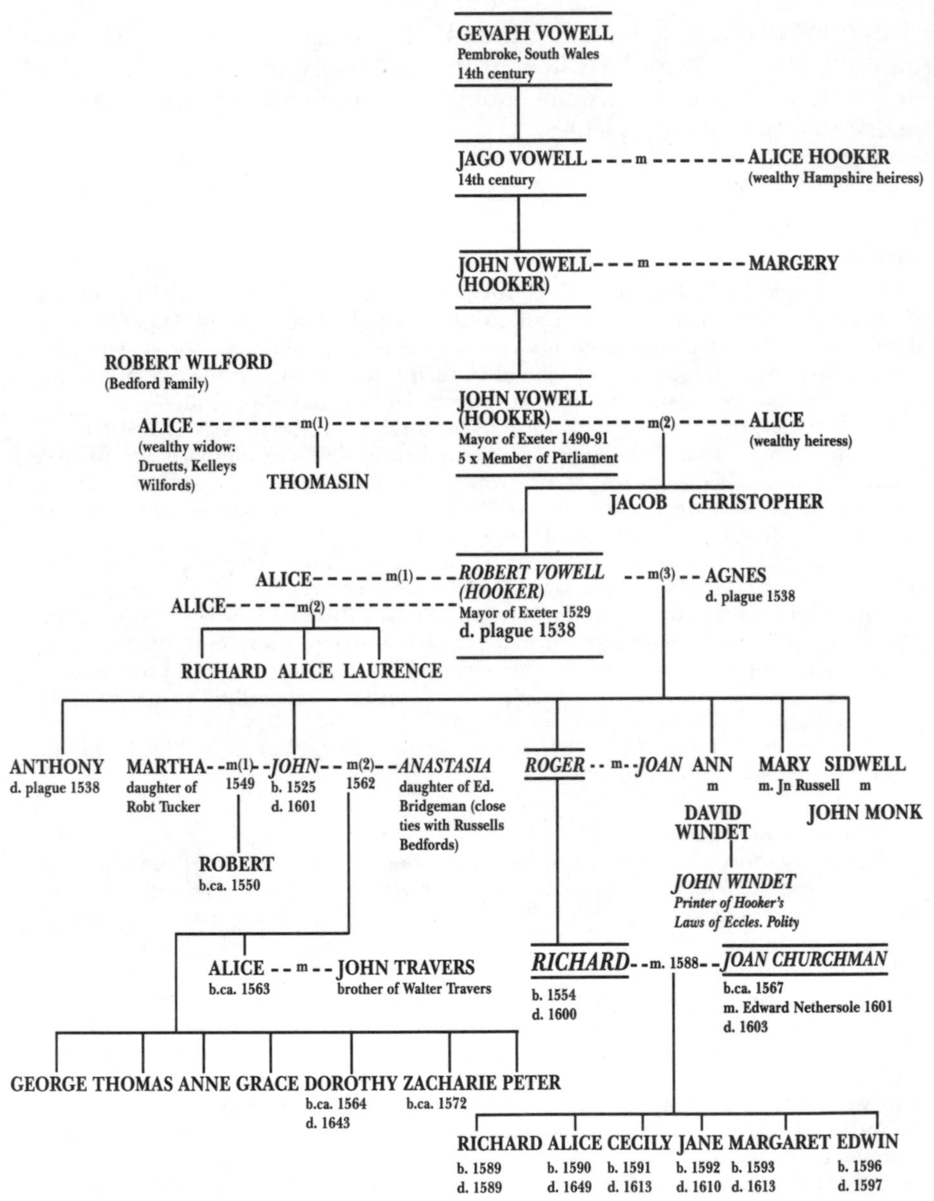
GEVAPH VOWELL
Pembroke, South Wales
14th century
JAGO VOWELL
14th century
m
ALICE HOOKER
(wealthy Hampshire heiress)
JOHN VOWELL
(HOOKER)
m
MARGERY
ROBERT WILFORD
(Bedford Family)
ALICE
(wealthy widow:
Druetts, Kelleys
Wilfords)
m(1)
THOMASIN
JOHN VOWELL
(HOOKER)
Mayor of Exeter 1490-91
5 x Member of Parliament
m(2)
ALICE
(wealthy heiress)
JACOB
CHRISTOPHER
ALICE
m(1)
ALICE
m(2)
ROBERT VOWELL
(HOOKER)
Mayor of Exeter 1529
d. plague 1538
m(3)
AGNES
d. plague 1538
RICHARD
ALICE
LAURENCE
ANTHONY
d. plague 1538
MARTHA
daughter of
Robt Tucker
m(1)
1549
JOHN
b. 1525
d. 1601
m(2)
1562
ANASTASIA
daughter of Ed.
Bridgeman (close
ties with Russells
Bedfords)
ROGER
m
JOAN
ANN
m
DAVID
WINDET
MARY
m. Jn Russell
SIDWELL
m
JOHN MONK
ROBERT
b.ca. 1550
JOHN WINDET
Printer of Hooker's
Laws of Eccles. Polity
ALICE
b.ca. 1563
m
JOHN TRAVERS
brother of Walter Travers
RICHARD
b. 1554
d. 1600
m. 1588
JOAN CHURCHMAN
b.ca. 1567
m. Edward Nethersole 1601
d. 1603
GEORGE
THOMAS
ANNE
GRACE
DOROTHY
b.ca. 1564
d. 1643
ZACHARIE
b.ca. 1572
PETER
RICHARD
b. 1589
d. 1589
ALICE
b. 1590
d. 1649
CECILY
b. 1591
d. 1613
JANE
b. 1592
d. 1610
MARGARET
b. 1593
d. 1613
EDWIN
b. 1596
d. 1597

CHAPTER 1

The Hookers of Exeter

There has never been a birth-story for Richard Hooker. About all that has ever been known of his birth and earliest years is what his seventeenth-century biographer, Izaak Walton, and a few others writing generations after Hooker's death reported: he was born either in Exeter, or in Heavitree, a small village just outside Exeter, in 1554. He had a mother named Joan, a father named Roger, and a well-known uncle named John, who lived in Exeter. That was about it. Hardly an auspicious nativity story for the co-founder of a major religious tradition.

Richard Hooker opened his eyes for the first time in late March or early April 1554, perhaps on Easter Day, 25 March. It is no exaggeration to say that he was born into the midst of one of the most tumultuous, dangerous, confusing, yet formative periods in English history. With the advantage of hindsight and a cool eye on the long-term intellectual and institutional "results" of the period, historians have dubbed the religious changes of this era "The Reformation." But to those who lived through this rapidly changing and violent time, it was no "reformation." It was more like a revolution.[1]

The Hookers had come to Devonshire in south-west England from Wales in the fourteenth century to settle in and around the already ancient town of Exeter. They were descended from Gevaph Vowell of Pembroke in southern Wales. Gevaph's son, Jago, married Alice Hooker, a wealthy heiress from Hampshire, in the fourteenth century. Thereafter, his male heirs, fancying the English name of Hooker, variously styled themselves Vowells, Vowell, alias Hoker, or Hooker.

The Vowell (Hooker) men were prominent in the life of Devon for nearly all of the fifteenth and sixteenth centuries. Richard's great-grandfather, John Vowell, was mayor of Exeter in 1490-91 and five times a member of parliament. His grandfather, Robert Vowell, was the youngest of twenty children but survived them all to inherit the family fortune. Robert was a member of the Exeter ruling oligarchy ("the 24") and was named the first magistrate of the city in 1529. His son, Richard's uncle John, was the most famous Hooker of all, until posterity placed that mantle upon Richard.

Grandfather Robert, along with his third wife, Agnes, and their first son, Anthony, died in a devastating plague that swept through the region in 1537. The seven remaining children were John, only about thirteen at the time, Roger (Richard's father), and five girls: Anne, Sydwell, Mary, Alice, and Juliana[2]. The death of Robert and Agnes put these seven youngsters of one of Exeter's most prominent families in the charge of the orphans' court. Under the prevailing law and custom of the day, guardians for the Hooker children were appointed by the court from among Exeter's best families, who were then responsible for raising and educating the orphans, usually within their own households. The orphans' court made distributions to the guardians from Robert's estate to meet the costs of caring for the children. These were often generous and unmonitored distributions.

Funds not paid out from estates of men like Robert Hooker for child support or "lent" to guardians for their own personal purposes could be made available by the orphans court to the city for public works projects. The Topsham Canal in Exeter was financed, for example, in just this manner. All such loans were to be repaid by the time the orphaned children reached legal maturity. But by that time inheritances were often greatly diminished if not gone altogether—lost by corruption, bankruptcy, and flight by debtors from the jurisdiction of local courts. This problem had become such a scandal by the end of the sixteenth century that national chancery courts and a lord chancellor replaced the local orphans courts in order to create a reliable national system for protecting the assets of legal heirs. Richard Hooker's own children would avail themselves of these very remedies in the next century as they sought to regain their lost inheritances from careless and sometimes unscrupulous guardians.[3]

The details of Robert Hooker's estate and its management are lost. Because of the prominence of the family and its excellent connections in the city, it seems likely that the estate was not abused. It is probable that Robert Hooker's good friend and fellow oligarch, Robert Tucker (Tooker), was named guardian for John, Roger, and the Hooker girls. The mayor of Exeter at the time, John Hunt, may also have shared guardianship responsibilities for one or more of the children.

In about 1549, John Hooker married Robert Tucker's daughter, Martha, thereby merging two of the most powerful and wealthy families in Exeter. The Hooker family crest—a lion holding a battle axe—had been secured originally by Robert Tucker but was adopted by John Hooker as his own after his marriage to Martha. Precisely where Richard Hooker was born and passed his earliest years we cannot know with absolute certainty. But we can assume it was in the environs of Exeter.[4]

In the absence of birth records, it is tempting to adopt a circumstantial case that Richard was raised from infancy and perhaps even born in his uncle's ample homestead in Exeter. After all, the custom in those days often obligated a wealthy sibling who had inherited most of the family fortune to support and even raise one or more of his less fortunate nephews or nieces. True, this social pattern was breaking down about the time of Richard Hooker's birth, but it was still often observed.

Before resting the case for the place of Hooker's birth and childhood on such a slender reed, further probing into ancient records is advisable—this time in civic rather than church archives. The library of the Devon and Exeter Institution furnished a most revealing discovery. In a box of unpublished notes a tiny entry long buried in a list of sixteenth-century Exeter property transactions shines forth to illumine the search for Hooker's birthplace. The notation all but proves that Richard was not born and reared in John Hooker's household.

The record reveals that in 1552, just two years after the death of his first wife, Martha Tucker, and two years before Richard's birth, John leased the family's "mansion house" in which he and Martha had lived, along with the "back houses, stable and cellar and garden . . ." The lease was for ten years at five pounds per year. It included all of the family's substantial holdings on South Street, not only buildings and gardens but household implements and furnishings as well.[5]

Clearly, John did not intend to be burdened with domestic responsibilities after Martha died. He moved into smaller bachelor quarters somewhere near his office in the guildhall and adopted the life of an active provincial townsman, soon to become the most illustrious exemplar of the public life of his native city. By this time John was well launched on his remarkable career. He had already studied abroad and at Oxford, come into his inheritance, and become a freeman of the city. He had assisted Bishop Miles Coverdale in his famous translation of the Bible. In 1553, shortly before his nephew's birth, John was appointed the first chamberlain of the city.

While there is little hard information about John Hooker's activities during the early years of his nephew's life, it is almost certain that he was in no position at that time to assume domestic responsibility for his brother's infant child. The tempting notion that Richard was born and spent his earliest years in Exeter can be put to rest. A decade later, in 1562, when Richard was eight years old and ready for school, his thirty-seven-year-old uncle was comfortably settled again in the historic family home on South Street, married this time to Anastasia Bridgeman, a woman from a prominent family with close ties to those arch-Protestants, the Russells. John was now in a position to welcome his nephew into his substantial care and attention. There is therefore no reason to doubt the tradition that Richard Hooker was born in Heavitree.[6]

HEFA'S TREE

Hooker's birthplace of Heavitree claimed a gently hilly, wooded terrain near the River Exe. For centuries the river teemed with salmon and

2. John Hooker, *c.*1591
Artist unknown

provided easy access to more fish in the sea and to economic and social commerce with the rest of the world. An abundance of fresh water, rich agricultural land, good hunting grounds, and a generous bounty of easily-quarried red-hued limestone ("Heavitree stone") added to Heavitree's importance as a suburb of Exeter. Unfortunately for those searching for Richard Hooker who might like to see Heavitree through his young eyes, only a few churches and other public buildings from his time have survived the ravages of four and a half centuries.[7]

The first Christian church in Heavitree, St Michael and All Angels, was built in the seventh century by the Saxons, who used the area as the capital of their Western Kingdom. They called the area "Wonford" and selected a special tree as a sacred place—a holy tree, "heaford treo" or "hefa's tree"—for proclaiming religious and secular law, issuing judicial pronouncements and executing criminals and enemies. This place, later "heavitrova" and finally Heavitree, eventually replaced Wonford as the name of Hooker's hometown.

In 1531 the Protestant Thomas Benet was put to death in Heavitree at a place called Livery Dole. When Richard was a small boy, he walked by this grisly place on his way to and from school. He knew the story of the anti-papist Benet's public execution here just twenty-three years before his own birth, although he was as yet too young to appreciate Benet's significance as the first Reformation martyr in Exeter and hence a precursor to his own life's work. He was aware that Benet's pro-papist defender at his trial was the renowned Dr John Moreman of Cornwall—the "learned vicar of Menheniot"—who had been the boyhood tutor of his uncle John, and probably of his father as well.[8]

The only hint of Hooker's early life in Heavitree is a street named Hoker Road. It is near St Michael's church—within sight of an ancient yew tree that may have given Heavitree its name—just a short walk from Livery Dole and about two miles from Exeter. Since it has long been a custom in this part of England to name streets for prominent persons and activities, it is plausible, even in the absence of records, to assume that Heavitree's most famous son was born and spent his boyhood in a modest cottage near the place of this present-day street of modest suburban homes.

The exact date of Hooker's birth is as elusive as the precise location. The best surmise, drawn from records at Oxford showing his approximate age at the time of his matriculation there for a master's degree, is that he was born on or about Easter day, 25 March 1554.[9]

Until he was eight years old, in 1562, Richard probably lived in Heavitree with his mother. By then he was old enough to begin school in Exeter and to move, at first probably on a part-time basis, into the ancestral Hooker home in Exeter to live with his uncle John, his new aunt Anastasia, and his two cousins, thirteen-year old Robert and baby Alice. Here he was closer to school and to the protection of his uncle.

As Richard grew from infancy to boyhood during these years of incredibly rapid and dangerous change, his family life was far from stable or secure. His father was absent most of the time. In the midst of instability within his family and in the larger community outside, the boy found one reasonably constant and steady influence in his small world—in addition to his mother. That was the parish church of St Michael and All Angels in Heavitree. From his earliest years, Richard Hooker came to regard the Church as the most reliable safeguard of his well-being. It was a feeling that would grow and sustain him throughout his life.

The historic role of a parish like St Michael's as guardian of public welfare and enforcer of moral probity was being weakened by the eroding force of rapid change in church governance and worship requirements during the English Reformation: Catholic under Henry VIII, Protestant under Edward VI, Catholic under Mary, "Anglican" under Elizabeth—all within three decades—scarcely more than a single generation. Despite the chaos and weakened church loyalty spawned by such confusion, the church remained the single most influential and effective instrument of social control in Heavitree and other extra-mural and rural habitats in England during the middle third of the sixteenth century.[10]

THE FIRST JOAN

Richard Hooker's mother, Joan, is lost to history. Like most ordinary people of her time, she can be viewed only dimly by inference from words and deeds of more famous persons who touched her life and left some record of their own activities.

Joan may be called one of the common people because, although connected by her relationship with Roger—probably as his wife—to the famous Hookers of Exeter, she was most likely a family "accident," the result of an unfortunate but typical liaison between the careless son of a prominent family and an available female of socially inferior status. Had she been a woman of any social standing, that fact would have been recorded in the family genealogy which carefully lists all of the marriages and issues of this long family line. As it is, one genealogical chart shows the mere name "Joan" as Roger's wife, with no surname or family history. In another chart, no wife's name appears at all beside Roger's.[11]

There is no hard evidence that Roger and Joan Hooker were ever officially married. This may be explained by an absence of Heavitree parish records before 1555, or it may be that theirs was a marriage without benefit of clergy and Church. Given the prominence of the Hooker family, if this were a serious relationship with intent by Roger Hooker to marry Joan with the approval of the family, the event would have been marked by at least a modest ceremony at the family homestead and recorded at St Mary Major in Exeter, where church records for this period are extant.

John Hooker, ever the archivist, who carefully recorded every event and person close to his family and career, certainly never mentions such a marriage. Most revealing of all, Joan's famous son, Richard, avoids even the most fleeting reference to his mother. The apparent absence of any other children resulting from the union of Joan and Roger supports the conclusion that the two were not married long enough to produce a family, that she was in fact a poor and largely ignored wife, living for the most part outside the protection and security of the Exeter Hookers, and that she either died or disappeared shortly after Richard's birth or while he was still a small boy. It is, of course, possible that Joan bore the usual child a year, and that none survived. It is also possible that her peripatetic husband simply ignored his conjugal responsibilities.

Some sources have claimed that Joan and Roger did have two other surviving children in addition to Richard: Agnes and Elizabeth. St Mary Major's records show an Agnes Hooker who died in 1590. In the seventeenth century Thomas Fuller mentions a sister for Richard, named Elizabeth, who married a man named Harvey and lived to be 121, conveniently long enough to give Fuller first-hand (but erroneous) information about Richard before her death in 1663![12]

The most plausible conclusion from all of this informed guessing is that, although Richard Hooker may have had siblings, he probably did not, and although he may have been born outside of wedlock, he probably was not. His mother, a skeleton in the Hooker family closet, was doubtless quietly but legally married to Roger. This would have been the respectable thing for the Hookers to do. Joan and her infant son Richard were supported by a largely absent husband until Joan's death, which may have occurred at about the time of Roger's full-time departure from home in about 1560, and John's marriage and return to domesticity in 1562.

This surmise about Joan Hooker's minimal and short-lived relationship with her son makes unlikely Izaak Walton's famous and charming picture of Joan as a loving and doting mother who maintained a nurturing relationship with her son, at least until his young manhood. Walton portrayed Joan Hooker as a concerned mother worrying about and praying for her sick teenage boy far away from Heavitree in college at Oxford. The story is so much a part of Hooker lore that it is worth repeating in its entirety if only as evidence of the desire in Walton's time to create a saintly Hooker.

By the age of eighteen, Walton claims, Richard was "increasing in learning and prudence, and so much in humility and piety, that he seemed to be filled with the Holy Ghost, and even like John the Baptist, to be sanctified from his mother's womb, who did often bless the day in which she bare him".

Walton continues:

About this time of his age he fell into a dangerous sickness [at Oxford], which lasted two months: all which time his mother, having notice of it, did in her hourly prayers as earnestly beg his life of God, as the mother of St Augustine did that he might become a true Christian; and their prayers were both so heard, as to be granted. Which Mr. Hooker would often mention with much joy, and as often pray that he might never live to occasion any sorrow to so good a mother of whom, he would often say, he loved her so dearly, that he would endeavour to be good, even as much for her's as for his own sake.

As soon as he was perfectly recovered from this sickness, he took a journey from Oxford to Exeter, to satisfy and see his good mother, being accompanied with a countryman and companion of his own college, and both on foot; which was then either more in fashion, or for want of money, or their humility made it so: but on foot they went, and took Salisbury in their way, purposely to see the good bishop [Jewel], who made Mr. Hooker and his companion dine with him at his own table; which Mr. Hooker boasted of with much joy and gratitude when he saw his mother and friends: and at the bishop's parting with him, the bishop gave him good counsel, and his benediction, but he forgot to give him money; which when the bishop had considered, he sent a servant in all haste to call Richard back to him: and at Richard's return, the bishop said to him, "Richard, I sent for you back to lend you a horse which has carried me many a mile, and, I thank God, with much ease"; and presently delivered into his hand a walking staff, with which he professed he had travelled through many parts of Germany. And he said, "Richard, I do not give, but lend you my horse; be sure you be honest, and bring my horse back to me at your return to Oxford. And I now give you ten groats to bear your charges to Exeter; and here is ten groats more, which I charge you to deliver to your mother, and tell her, I send the bishop's benediction with it, and beg the continuance of her prayers for me. And if you bring my horse back to me, I will give you ten groats more, to carry you on foot to the college: and so God bless you, good Richard.[13]

This is a wonderful testimonial to maternal affection. One is reluctant to disturb it. Here posterity has been given young Richard at the "temple" in Salisbury to visit, if not to confound his elders. He is charged by the chief elder (Jewel) to be an honest steward of worldly things. More importantly, he is enjoined to honour his mother, whose "sanctified" womb had borne him and whose prayers had led to his conversion. Here, take my own horse and staff, says the elder, and continue your blessed journey to sainthood![14]

A further reason to mistrust Walton's picture of close ties between parent and child, beyond the highly embroidered account itself, is that familial relationships among people of Joan and Roger Hooker's station in mid-sixteenth-century England did not typically display such warmth and affection. In this era, family life tended to be transient, even temporary. Families, in all but the richest classes, were usually small and unstable due to high infant and child mortality, the poor health of one or both parents, and lack of steady employment in the community where the marriage took place.

By twentieth-century standards, childbirth was a horrendous experience for both mother and child. Richard, who was among the fortunate 80 percent of new-borns to survive this trauma, suckled at Joan's breasts, which were probably protected by lead nipple shields. He would have been wrapped tightly in swaddling cloth and perhaps hung on a hook on the wall to be kept out of his mother's way and safely away from household vermin. He probably slept in the same bed with his mother or siblings—if he had any. Even had he lived in his uncle's more commodious household, he would have shared a bed with one or more of his cousins.

Later on, Richard would have joined his mother at meals consisting of an often inadequate diet of spoiled food eaten from poisonous pewter plates (made with lead) and water often polluted by human and animal excrement. They lived in what we would regard as a grim domestic environment where malnutrition, dysentery, rickets, bodily deformities, corporal punishment, and death abounded.

Neither Richard nor his mother bathed, cleaned their teeth, or changed their clothes often. Soap was a luxury. Even by the standards of those days, when cleanliness was not the high virtue it would later become, the English, and especially English women, had a reputation among Europeans (especially the French) for being among the dirtiest and smelliest of God's creatures. There is no reason to think that the modest household in which Richard Hooker was born and where he spent his early years would have exhibited a high standard of domestic health and welfare.[15]

Death, not love, was the most reliable member of the family circle when Hooker was a small boy. The grim reaper visited his cold touch on infants, children, mothers, and fathers. Those children, like Richard, who survived the early years of life—and only about 60 percent lived past the age of five—were usually packed off in their early teens to live and work elsewhere as apprentices, to live with a more affluent relative, or simply to fend for themselves. If Richard had not shown early signs of unusual intellectual promise, he would have been sent away from home to serve as an apprentice in some trade.[16]

Richard's attitude toward his parents and other elders was presumably the normal one of abject obedience. If he displayed any independence of spirit, not to mention rebellion, the custom of the day allowed for whippings and floggings from the earliest age of childhood, both at home and in school. This was the accepted means to break the will of children and civilize them.[17]

Still, in Richard's case there is reason to believe that, owing to the comparatively decent social standing of his father, his childhood was relieved of the more oppressive features of lower-class family life in Heavitree. He may have been that rarity—an only child, in an age when women normally had as many children among whom to divide attention and affection as their health and fecundity permitted. If this were the case, Richard would be the sole recipient of maternal attention.

The only compelling evidence for a close relationship between Joan and her son—and the only reliable image we shall ever have of Joan—is whatever of her may be reflected in her son—in his life and in his writings. There we find warmth, wit, humour, compassion, and grace, which may have been transmitted to him in his earliest years, in the midst of an otherwise harsh environment, by a truly loving mother. To be sure, he may have received this uncritical maternal affection from his aunt in Exeter. More likely, however, his earliest and most significant nurturing came from his mother, Joan.

Although Richard Hooker never mentions his mother in his writings, doubtless because her early death or disappearance left him with no memory of her, he reveals in his life the characteristics of a person who as an infant and small child had been loved and cherished. There was little of the harsh, cruel, loveless, mean-spirited, cynical intolerance in him that characterized so much of the religious and political writing and living of his day and might well have marked the character and style of an unloved or unwanted child.

This, of course, is speculation. But it is a conjecture that helps to explain the exceptional grace and generosity of spirit that overshadows the occasional flash of temper in Hooker's responses to what he saw as religious and political extremism. A tolerant and open spirit is surely his lasting contribution to Western culture.

The first Joan Hooker may not be lost after all.

ROGER HOOKER: "a man very expert & skyllfull"

Richard Hooker's father, Roger, was, for the most part, an absentee parent. But Richard was to have a number of strong and supportive surrogate "fathers" to stand in for his missing birth-father. In his youth, there was his powerful uncle John and his uncle's influential friend, Bishop John Jewel of Salisbury. Later, there was a reliable succession of helpful father figures: his Oxford tutor, John Rainolds; his father-in-law, John Churchman; his ecclesiastical patrons, Archbishops Edwin Sandys and John Whitgift; and, finally, his companion at the end of life, the Dutch theologian, Adrian Saravia.[18]

Roger Hooker was away from home during most of his son's boyhood in Heavitree and Exeter. Later, when Richard was away at college and, later still, residing as an adult in London, Roger was living permanently in Ireland. Despite their lifelong separation, Richard was probably aware of his father's many exploits and accomplishments.

Roger may have had at least an indirect impact on his son's character, even as an absent father.

If we speculate that Richard received his characteristic gentle and compassionate nature from his mother, then in his father he surely had a model for the courageous, self-confident, adventurous, imaginative, and non-parochial spirit apparent at key points in his life and typical in his writing style. The father expressed this liveliness in deeds, the son in words. Not surprisingly, the son's influence upon posterity was the more lasting.

Absentee fatherhood was not unusual in sixteenth-century England. Men like Roger Hooker were forced to seek their fortunes where they could find them—and a host of Devon men found them far from home on the continent or in Ireland. As a son who was not the principal beneficiary of the Hooker family inheritance, Roger had to make do with the leavings of the family estate and the good will of his more fortunate brother, John. In his case, the leavings were modest but not insignificant: one quarter of his father's "goods moveable and not" and a percentage of his father's interests in the local tin works. Tin production was an important and lucrative enterprise. The metal was an essential commodity, used for pewter manufacture and for coin-making. The mining and smelting took place in rural Dartmoor. The workers lived in a section of town called the Stannery, near the Hooker residence.[19]

There is no record to show that Roger took any active part in the Stannery works. Nor is it known how much his inherited financial interest amounted to each year. He was probably only an absentee shareholder. There is evidence, however, that in his young manhood Roger was something of a profligate, or at least a man unable to live within his means. Between 1552 and 1557, the years immediately preceding and following his son's birth, Roger had debts amounting to the then princely sum of £130. His brother covered these for him.[20]

As an orphaned minor, Roger benefited from at least some of the advantages of family wealth. The Exeter orphans court administered and distributed assets from his father's estate to assure him a secure and privileged childhood. Among these privileges was a formal education, at least through grammar school. He probably attended the same school in Cornwall as his brother and thus came under the tutelage of the famous Dr John Moreman. Although he did not attend college, Roger had contacts with some of the leading families in Exeter—people who were among the movers and shakers of Elizabethan England. These were relationships he would use to his advantage throughout his life.

Because so little is recorded about Roger Hooker, we glean what we can about his life by inference from the better-chronicled famous families with whom he found employment after he left Exeter and Heavitree to seek his fortune. These included men and women who played prominent roles in the politics of the age: the Challoners, Blounts, Courtenays, and Carews. A look at the activities of these remarkable families tells us something about Roger Hooker and, at the same time, provides further historical background for his son Richard's life.

Our first glimpse of Richard's father through the veil of nearly half a millennium occurs in 1562, at about the time Richard was probably beginning to live much of the time at his uncle John's house in Exeter. Roger, having left Exeter a short time before, was serving as steward on the staff of Sir Thomas Challoner, a prominent statesman, scholar, and poet. As steward in such a large and important household, Roger held a responsible position, managing the staff, purchasing supplies, keeping inventories of family possessions, often managing finances and serving as secretary to the head of the family.

Roger's employer, a Yorkshireman with extensive family estates in Buckinghamshire, was Queen Elizabeth's ambassador at England's most important diplomatic post, the court of King Philip of Spain, then located in Flanders. Challoner's only surviving son, Thomas, became famous later in the century for introducing into England the use of alum in dyeing wool and leather with madder, a process he had observed in Italy as a young man and that was later to revolutionize the English woollen industry. The discovery of alum on the Challoner's Yorkshire estates not only added lustre to the already shining name of Challoner, but increased the family wealth as well. In 1565, when Sir Thomas died, Roger was a witness to his will and received an inheritance of £20 and a life annuity of £6 13s 4d from family lands in Yorkshire.[21]

That Roger found such respectable employment in so prominent a family as the Challoners reveals much about his ingenuity, talents, and effective use of Hooker family connections. He might not have been the model husband and father, and he may at times have mismanaged his own finances, but he was enterprising when it came to securing good positions for himself.

Sometime after his service with Sir Thomas, probably about 1566, when his son Richard was twelve years old, Roger became steward in one of the most famous and influential families of sixteenth-century England, the Blounts (Barons Mountjoy). Roger's actual employer was not Baron Mountjoy (who had died some years earlier) but his widow, Lady Mountjoy, daughter of Robert Lord Willoughby of Broke and sister-in-law of the stalwart Gertrude Blount Courtenay.

An important episode involving the Mountjoys and their relatives, the Exeters, occurred during Edward VI's reign and came to be known as the Prayer Book, or Western, Rebellion of 1549—called "The Commotion" in Exeter. This unsuccessful armed uprising to overthrow Protestant reforms and restore the Catholic religion was led by prominent families in Devon and the other western counties and was one of the major events in the formative background of Richard Hooker's life, occurring in his own backyard and only a few years before his birth.

Ostensibly, the purpose of the Prayer Book Rebellion was to prevent Protestant reforms, especially the new prayer book, from being instituted by King Edward and his Protestant ministers. In political terms, the Rebellion was yet another attempt by the Exeters, the Mountjoys, and their friends to defeat the Suffolks, Russells, Somersets, Northumberlands, and their allies and to take the crown by rallying deep-seated sympathies for the old religion among peasants and others in the western counties of Devon and Cornwall. The city of Exeter was the key to the rebels' campaign. Inside the city walls were a population and church leadership mostly opposed to the religious changes symbolized by the *First Edwardian Prayer Book*.

On 2 July 1549 a largely peasant army, supported by members of such families as the Blounts and Courtenays, marched on Exeter and laid siege to the city. They hoped Catholic sympathizers would open the gates to them. This did not happen. The city held out for five weeks of severe suffering before it was relieved by the Protector Somerset's man, Lord Russell.[22]

One of the clerical leaders of this anti-Reformation rebellion, Robert Welsh, vicar of St Thomas, the large and powerful extra-mural parish located across the River Exe to the south of the city, was hanged in his Mass vestments from the tower of his church. The reformist Miles Coverdale was installed as bishop of Exeter and remained there until Queen Mary restored Catholicism to England in 1554.[23]

All of this saga and more made up the lives and legends of this highly-charged political family into which Roger Hooker moved in the early 1560s. We know that he actually lived, at least at times, in the household of the widow of the fifth Baron of Mountjoy and not at home with Joan and young Richard during these years from a letter John Hooker wrote in 1568 telling his friend Peter Carew that Roger "dwelleth with Lady Mountjoy."[24]

John was writing to his closest and most influential friend and patron to recommend his brother for what was to be the most dangerous and promising opportunity of Roger's life.

THE HOOKERS IN IRELAND

Roger's new employers, the Carews (often pronounced Carey), were a large and sprawling tribe with several stout branches on their family tree. Some of them were descendants of Normans who had been related since the twelfth century to the Tudors of South Wales. As reward for help in conquering much of Ireland, Henry II had granted the Carews extensive holdings in southern Ireland, in Munster, called the Kingdom of Cork. This grant was the basis for John Hooker's friend Peter Carew's claim to Irish lands eight generations after the fact—a claim that was to shape the life of Richard Hooker's father and, to a lesser extent, his uncle.

The last of the Carews actually to live in Ireland was John, Baron of Carew and Ordone, who served as Edward II's lord justice of Ireland in the mid-fourteenth century at the time of the Black Death. Meantime, back in the west country, the Carews had intermarried with the Mohuns in Devon and eventually had become heirs to Ottery Mohun, their family seat for centuries to come and the place of Peter Carew's birth in 1514.

The Carews were important players in English politics throughout the Tudor period. Peter's grandfather, Sir Edmund, was knighted by Henry VII at Bosworth Field in 1485. When Henry VIII was misbehaving during his youth, as well as during the early years of his reign, another Carew, Nicholas, was a favourite royal companion and fellow-reveller. This Carew was a skilled jouster who had been reproved by no less a person than Cardinal Wolsey in 1519 for roistering in the streets of Paris.[25]

In 1564, at the suggestion of Sir Henry Sidney, who was then the queen's lord deputy of Ireland—the latest in a long line of English governors charged with bringing that rebellious land under Tudor control—Peter Carew began to pursue adventures in Ireland that would consume the rest of his life and that of Roger Hooker as well. In the Spring of 1568 Peter Carew had engaged his friend John Hooker, then chamberlain of Exeter, to come to Ireland as his agent. John had two major assignments. The first was to investigate records in order to substantiate Peter's title to Irish lands. The second was to survey the political and social terrain preparatory to Peter's coming over to set up a permanent household in Ireland. John sat briefly in the Irish parliament of 1568 while he was in Dublin, as a representative for Atheny (Athenry) near Galway Bay in County Galway. He had previously served a term in the English parliament and was appalled by the comparative disorder he found in the Dublin legislative body.

While in Dublin, John wrote to his friend Peter telling him that he would need a reliable steward to manage his household affairs in Ireland. This was not a job that the chamberlain of Exeter coveted for himself but he knew just the right person for the post and would be more than happy not only to recommend him but also to inquire as to his availability. That ideal person was none other than his own enterprising younger brother, Roger. Here are John's words about his brother—Richard Hooker's father:

> And, forasmuch as an expert man in these things may do you pleasure here, I have thought to move you of one who was sometime servant and steward to Sir Thomas Challoner, ambassador in Spain, a man very expert & skilful as also to his said master profitable, and of whose praise

> I would speak as I have heard, if he were not my own brother. He now dwells with the old Lady Mountjoy, and for whose faithfulness I will not refuse to give bond as much as I am able to. If your worship and my lady shall so think it good, I have given order to my wife to send for him. I trust he shall please you both in such sort as to your contentment.[26]

This remarkable letter—one of only two extant contemporary descriptions of Roger Hooker—gives warrant both of John Hooker's affection and regard for his brother and of Roger's considerable experience and talent. Only in his early thirties at the time, and with a son he scarcely knew soon to enter Oxford, Roger Hooker had already served two of England's leading families and was about to enter the service of a third. There is something else of importance about this letter: John Hooker, far from Exeter and needing someone to locate Roger, called not on his brother's wife, Joan, but on his own wife, Anastasia. This may, of course, have been merely the natural response of a man who was not close to his sister-in-law. But it is more likely to have been further indication that Joan simply did not exist within the Hooker family at this time, either because she had died or because she had no continuing relationship of importance with the Hookers.

In short order, Peter Carew hired Roger Hooker for this important post in Ireland. Roger arrived with John shortly after his new employer landed at Waterford in August 1568. He was probably with Sir Peter during meetings later in the year with the constable at Leighlin and Seneschal (Wexford), Thomas Stukeley, and also with chiefs of the Cavenaughs, to lay before them Peter's claims to Irish lands.

Roger quickly passed muster with the Carews. Within a year he was running the family estate at Leighlin and was fairly launched on the final and most successful phase of his eventful career. As the chief manager of Sir Peter Carew's affairs in Ireland, Roger became a minor and altogether unsung figure in Queen Elizabeth's aggressive plans to acquire wealth and political supremacy in Ireland. Roger's first role in this Irish drama was as an actor in the so-called "Butler Wars" of 1569-72. In this drama the queen played her usual game of cat-and-mouse with her agents and enemies, variously approving, disapproving, and remaining marvellously inscrutable concerning her support of activities carried out apparently, but never certainly, in her name. Clearly, she wanted to secure the crown's holdings and increase income flowing from Ireland. To this end she encouraged the likes of Sir Peter Carew. Just as clearly, however, she wanted to distance herself from the significant political or economic costs associated with her ambitions in Ireland.

In due course, Sir Peter's claim was upheld and he was given the title of Baron of Idrone. He was appointed captain of the government's garrison at Leighlin Bridge within his new barony with the understanding that it was his responsibility to provision the fortress and provide most of the soldiers necessary to subdue the barony for himself—and the crown. All that remained for Sir Peter to make good his new legal rights was to settle himself and his household on the land and to defend his holdings with arms if necessary. And it was necessary. In fact, it was during one of the early battles, on 10 August 1569, that Roger wrote the letter that is the only direct word we have from Richard Hooker's father.[27]

Roger had been left in charge of Carew's homestead, called the Queen's House, at Leighlin. Piers Butler was, at the moment of Roger's writing, laying siege to the house with thirty horsemen and carne (foot soldiers) who had just, in Roger's words, "spoiled the whole town of Leighlin, taken one hundred marks in property, burned seventy houses, killed nine men, and burned four children."

Roger writes an appeal for reinforcements to Sir Henry Sidney. He understands that the lord deputy may have some fifty soldiers at Dublin. He requests that they be sent to him as quickly as possible. "My Lord Deputy left about 100 carne to guard the town and county but none to guard the house which has only 12 men among the servants." He says that he cannot get a personal courier out because messengers are captured and killed. "Thus, my Lord, I humbly beseech your honour to consider our estate here, and send us your men that are there, and they shall have victuals provided for them [so] that they shall not want."[28]

His letter is filled with the urgency and immediacy of an event as it is happening. We are there with him as he fights to protect his new master's household from the assault of his arch-enemy, Piers Butler. Roger's assurance of provisions available to supply Sidney's forces shows that he recognized that his master would be obligated to provide supplies (and men) to defend Leighlin and repulse Butler. His pleas for help from Sidney also provide a glimpse of the tenuous, fluid alliance between the west country adventurers like Carew and the queen's policy in Ireland—an ambitious policy of subjugation, with too little commitment of resources to carry it out.

While these battles raged in 1569 and 1570, Roger Hooker was still liable for military service back in Devon. He may have been the man listed as "Roger Hucker" on the muster rolls for Totnes in June 1569, two months before his involvement in the battle of Leighlin Bridge.[29] If this is Roger Hooker on the Totnes muster, then clearly his fortunes at home would be at a low ebb. He was better off staying in Ireland and continuing to seek his fortune there with Sir Peter Carew.

Roger Hooker remained in Ireland for the rest of his life, involved directly and indirectly in many of the adventures that carried his master through so much of the tumultuous history of Ireland in the latter decades of the century. The only view we have of Roger in these later years of his life is in his clerical position of dean of Leighlin parish. He was appointed to that post in 1580. There is no record of his having been ordained. The lord deputy used his broad powers of appointment to reward Roger for faithful service with this clerical living at Leighlin.[30]

At some point while he was dean of Leighlin, Roger was "seized," along with "Master Wood, one of his chapter . . . and carried off with Feagh McHugh as a prisoner by Maurice Kavennaugh of the Garquil." Although the details of this incident are not known, one can easily deduce from it Roger's continued involvement in the Irish wars and the ongoing adventure and danger of his life in Ireland.[31]

Roger Hooker died at Leighlin sometime before Michaelmas in 1582, at about the age of forty-six. His son Richard was still teaching and pursuing his doctorate at Oxford. Given the constant movement of persons close to the Hookers back and forth between Devon, London, Ireland, and Oxford, it is probable that father and son were at least dimly aware of one another's whereabouts and achievements.

We can only lament that Richard Hooker never really knew his father. Roger was a remarkable man—one of a type in Elizabethan England—a man of favoured lineage but essentially disinherited by primogeniture and thereby neither quite a gentleman nor a privileged burgher. He must have been an engaging, enterprising, courageous, quick-witted, risk-taking adventurer. He exploited his family connections and his own good mind to find a place for himself during a long, exciting career as courtier, steward, secretary, aide-de-camp, soldier under arms, and church administrator. His was the life of a sixteenth-century adventurer who ranged far from hearth and home, from wife and son in pursuit of his own destiny.[31]

NOTES

1. Some modern revisionists doubt that the average person was aware of any great movement affecting his daily life. However, like most literate and sensitive persons living through the chaos and violence of our own twentieth century, Hooker and many of his sixteenth-century contemporaries were surely conscious that they were part of a society undergoing rapid and fundamental change in many of the of important aspects of their lives.

Georges Edelen, a close student of the literature of the era, believes that the people of the day were quite conscious that they were living in an age of extraordinary change. Change, he notes, is a "constant of human existence, but the rate of change is not." See Edelen's edition of William Harrison, *Description of England,* 1587 (New York: Dover Publications) 1994, xxix-xxx.

2. *Works* I, 7, n. 3. On the other hand, in a genealogical table on p. cvix of his 1845 edition of the *Laws*, Keble notes only five children, with Alice and Juliana omitted. He also says at p. 7, n. 3 that the "tenor" of Robert's will, registered in 1534, leads him to believe that all of the children, except John, were from previous marriages to Alice (Cole) and Alice (Drake). If this is so, Roger was not only older than John but old enough to have had children before Richard was born, either by Joan or another unknown woman. This surmise flies in the face of too much else that is known about John and Roger to be accepted. See also Thomas Wescote, *A View of Devonshire in MDCXXX*, Exeter, 1845, 526-7.

3. For a useful discussion of orphans court with special attention to the role of John Hooker in its development, see Charles Carlton, *The Court of Orphans* (Leicester: Leicester University Press),1974.

4. Tradition says it was in the village of Heavitree, outside the eastern gate of Exeter and some two miles from the city centre. Some commentators have suggested that he was born and probably raised from infancy in the prosperous and busy household of his famous uncle, John, on South Street in Exeter. This is a convenient surmise for our search for Richard because much more is known about John Hooker and the well-chronicled city of Exeter than will ever be uncovered about Roger Hooker and the hamlet of Heavitree. Which of these was the place of birth is "still a question" wrote John Prince in his *The Worthies of Devon* (London, 1810), 507. Thomas Fuller, *The Worthies of England,* 1662, I, 264, gives Heavitree as the place of birth. John Gauden, in his short biography of the same year (1662), said that Hooker was born either in or near Exeter and cites a Dr Vivian, "an ancient and learned physician in Exeter" who told Gauden that Hooker was born in Southgate Street (the location of the Hooker family residence.) Walton, in his *Life of Hooker* says: "It is not to be doubted, but that Richard Hooker was born at Heavy-tree, near, or within the precincts, or in the city of Exeter." But in an earlier edition Walton had made no mention of Heavitree, saying only that Hooker was born "within the precincts, or in the City of Exeter." *Works* I, 6, n. 5. Walter J. Harte, in his edition of one of John Hooker's writings, says that Richard "was brought up and generously befriended" by his uncle John. See Walter J. Harte, ed., *The Description of the Citie of Excester by John Vowell alias Hoker* (Exeter: Devon and Cornwall Record Society, 1947), 7. There is no record of Richard's birth or baptism in the files of St Mary Major or St Petrarch parish in Exeter where John Hooker was at various times a member. Neither are there such records in Heavitree Parish. (Extant archives there begin in 1555—a near miss!)

5. From research notes of Susan Reece, Card #3539, The Devon and Exeter Institution, 7 The Close, Exeter.

6. Although we do not have the date of his marriage to Anastasia Bridgeman, we do know that their first child, Alice, was born in 1563 and that they had at least nine children in rapid succession. This makes a 1562 or 1563 marriage likely and means that John was a bachelor at the time of Richard's birth and for about eight years thereafter.

7. I have drawn principally on Trevor Falla, "Heavitree," in *Discovering Exeter* (Exeter: Exeter Civic Society, 1983) for information about the history of Heavitree. Also useful on Heavitree is W. G. Hoskins, *Two Thousand years in Exeter* (Chichester: Phillimore and Co., Ltd, 1963).

8. John Hooker told the story of Benet's execution in his *Commonplace Book.* He makes it a point to show that the sheriff in Exeter did not want this kind of execution to take place at the usual spot but ordered it done instead at Livery Dole in Heavitree. See Walter Harte, ed., *Gleanings from the Commonplace Book of John Hooker related to the City of Exeter (1485-1590)* (Exeter: Wheaton & Co. Ltd, n.d.), 12-13.

9. See Corpus Christi College Archives, *Liber Admis 1517-1646* (unnumbered folios). A notation at the top of a page records "Hooker: Disciple" and carries a date of 24 December 1573. In the margin of the same folio is written, "Richd Hooker Disc. Oct 19." The earlier date may be for his "supplication" (application to proceed to an M.A. degree), the latter his admission as "disciple" (a "scholar" and hence a candidate for a baccalaureate degree). A further notation in the archives records that on the following Easter Hooker would be approximately twenty years old. This would put his birth at about Easter of 1554. See also *Works* I, 6, n. 2, and *infra,* 71-73.

10. For a recent analysis of the role of the Church, especially on personal and domestic matters, see Martin Ingram, *Church Courts, Sex and Marraige in England, 1570-1640* (Cambridge: Cambridge University Press, 1987).
11. In the Devon Records Office there is a chart dated 1597, taken from the Office of Arms and edited by Walter J. Harte, J. W. Schopp, and H. Tapley Soper, which names "Joan" as Roger's wife, Exeter Monuments, 52. John Keble, in a family tree included with his notes on Walton's *Life,* shows Roger as Richard's father but gives no name for his wife. *Works* I, cxvi. Walton, although he waxes eloquently about Richard's mother, never gives her a name; but then he does not name Roger either. The probable absence of a formal church wedding also argues for a liaison with less than full family and social approval. Only a public church ceremony would normally serve the requirements of family, Church, and middle-class society. However, younger sons of wealthier families (such as Roger) and members of poorer families were allowed by custom to marry in less formal ways, such as simple co-habitation. See Ralph A. Houlbrooke, *The English Family 1450-1700* (New York: Longmans, 1984), 86-7.
12. John Keble names an Alice as "possibly" Richard's sister. He also has a pedigree chart listing a sister named Elizabeth and noting that she died in 1663 "very aged." There is no mention of Agnes in the chart. See *Works* I, 6, n. 1; cvix. Thomas Fuller, *Worthies*, 424, says that Hooker's sister was "lately living at Hogsden, nigh London." This sister was the person Fuller had cited as the source for correcting his mistake in his earlier *The Church History of Britain from the Birth of Jesus Christ until the Year MDCXLVII,* III (London: John Williams). 1665, to the effect that Hooker was a bachelor without children. Elizabeth also reportedly told Fuller that Hooker, although married, was unhappily so. Neither his wife nor his children, she allegedly reported, brought him "comfort" while he was alive, nor "credit" after his death. Thus began the long tradition of Hooker's unhappy family life, an opinion credited to a woman who may never have existed. If there was an Elizabeth, she could have been born to Roger and Joan as late as 1562 before Roger left home. This would put her age at death at the somewhat more plausible 100 years—still "very aged." If there was a sister named Agnes who died in 1590, as Keble suggests, she could have been born between the early 1550s and the late 1560s after which time it is unlikely that Roger returned from Ireland to share a bed with Joan. This means she was either a near contemporary of Richard or much younger.
13. Walton, *Life,* 11-13.
14. A long history of reliance on and embellishment of such stories by Walton includes Thomas Fuller's, *Worthies,* 507ff; Prince's *Worthies;* and T. L. Pridham's piece on Hooker in *Devonshire Celebrities* (London: Bell & Daldy, 1869). John Keble began a tradition of some scepticism about this Walton/Fuller tradition in his 1836 edition of Hooker's works, picked up in part by Sidney Lee in his article on Hooker in his edition of the *Dictionary of National Biography*, XXVII (London: Macmillan, 1891), 289-95 and accelerated in the next century by the landmark work of C. J. Sisson in his *The Judicious Marriage of Mr. Hooker and The Birth of "The Laws of Ecclesiatical Policy"* (Cambridge: Cambridge University Press, 1940).
15. Lawrence Stone, *The Family, Sex and Marriage in England, 1500-1800* (New York: Harper and Row, 1977) 46. Stone's analysis of living conditions, which I have usually followed, has been criticized for overstating the English disregard for bodily cleanliness. While people of the time did not often bathe their bodies, they did, apparently, wash face and hands daily and before meals. School children were exhorted to arrive with clean shoes, combed hair and clean teeth. People would have been regarded as of the lower class if they were not clean in places where it showed. See Keith Thomas, "Cleanliness and godliness in Early Modern England," in Anthony Fletcher and Peter Roberts, eds., *Religion, Culture and Society in Early Modern Britain: Essays in Honour of Patrick Collinson* (Cambridge: Cambridge University Press, 1994), 56-77.

16. Walton reports that Richard's parents had indeed "intended him for an apprentice." *Life*, 7.
17. Stone, 117ff.
18. Throughout this work I postulate a relationship between Richard Hooker and his uncle characterized by support and concern, if not much affection, by John for his nephew. It is true that in his writings John does little more than acknowledge Richard's existence and even seems to disparage his nephew's great book. See his *Synopsis Corographicall of the Province of Devon* (Devon Records Office, fol. 116, c. 1600). Yet, considerable circumstantial evidence, combined with John's known help with Richard's education at Oxford, argue for a supportive if not intimate relationship. As the distinguished English historian and long-time Exeter resident, Joyce Youings, wrote to the author in a private letter in January 1997, the whole matter of the relationship between the two men "is very tantalizing."
19. *Devon Records Office*, H. H. 3. 55, fol. 39.
20. *Ibid.*, Book 57, 148. Seventeen entries appear in this handwritten list of Roger's debts.
21. Roger is one of the witnesses to Challoner's beautifully handwritten will of 13 October 1565, *Public Records Office*, London, PCC 47, Bakon, 375.
22. See Frances Rose-Troup, *The Western Rebellion 1549* (London: Smith, Elder & Co., 1913), esp. 25-38, for an account of the Mountjoys during the Reformation. A more recent study of Exeter during this period is Wallace T. MacCaffrey, *Exeter 1540-1640* (Cambridge: Harvard University Press, 1958), esp. 20, 185-202. Colourful accounts of the Blounts are in William S. Childe-Pemberton, *Elizabeth Blount and Henry VIII* (London: Eveleigh Nash, 1913).
23. Harte, *Gleanings*, 83-85.
24. See John Maclean, ed., *John Hooker's The Life and Times of Sir Peter Carew* (London: Bill & Daldy, 1857), Appendix H, 202-203.
25. *Ibid.*, xxx-1-2; Appendix I, 299.
26. *Ibid.*, Appendix H, 202-3.
27. We can be sure that this arrangement was clear to Carew from a letter he wrote to the queen's chief minister, Lord Burghley (Cecil) in December of 1568. Peter confirms that this arrangement is in keeping with "the order devised and purposed for the planting of English men in this country for the making and building of towns which shall be replenished with all sorts of English artificers." Letter of 12/26/1568 in *State Papers 63 Ireland to Geo III*, vol. 26, 58, Public Records Office, London.
28. Maclean, Appendix H, 221-2.
29. Devon Records Office, A. J. Howard and T. L. Stoate, eds., *The Devon Muster Role* (Almondsbury, Bristol, 1977), 196, 246. We cannot be certain that "Roger Hucker" is Roger Hooker. Our Roger's family status argues that he would not have been a mere billman. But his record of profligacy and the constant misspelling of the Hooker name suggest that he may have been listed as a low-level foot soldier. In any event, his fortunes were much brighter in Ireland than back home in Devon.
30. John Ossory, "The Father of Richard Hooker," *The Irish Church Quarterly*. VI. Dublin, 1913. 269, speculates that the Carews had ample influence to secure such a post on their lands for Roger without his having attained holy orders. He correctly notes that such practices were not uncommon in Elizabethan England.
31. The wars in Ireland dragged on for two decades after Roger's death. Two of the families with whom his life had been entwined, the Blounts and the Carews, continued to play major roles in Elizabeth's efforts to subject Ireland to her rule.

CHAPTER 2

Growing up in John Hooker's Exeter

LIFE IN THE CITY

Since most remembered experiences begin at about the age of seven or eight, the external environment that first shaped Richard Hooker's lasting consciousness was not the small town of Heavitree where he was born but the bustling urban centre of western England, the ancient cathedral city of Exeter. It was here in his family's historic home—a city in which his uncle John was already a rising star—that Richard had his first taste of the broader world of English life and his first encounter with formal education. These were the childhood experiences that would mark his personality and shape his career.[1]

Visualizing the Exeter of Hooker's day would be easier if German bombers had not obliterated significant parts of the old city in 1942. Fortunately, the Luftwaffe was not successful in destroying the architectural jewel of Hooker's Exeter and ours—the massive twelfth-century Cathedral of St Peter and St Paul. This magnificent pile stands today with the same power and splendour that must have overwhelmed the boy from Heavitree when its majestic towers, great porch doors, vast nave, and towering vaulting first filled his wondering eyes.

A few other fifteenth and sixteenth century city landmarks also remain from Hooker's day, including much of the great Guild Hall on High Street, where his uncle John worked, and Tuckers Hall on Fore Street, home since 1471 to the guild of weavers, fullers (tuckers), and shearmen. Here were regulated the trades so essential to Exeter's production of the rough wool kersey fabric that was the mainstay of western England's cloth production. Others among the earliest guilds in medieval Exeter were the cordwainers, bakers, curriers, and skinners.[2]

Parts of some of the early churches also remain to provide a glimpse of Richard Hooker's Exeter. These include the twelfth-century St Mary Arches and fragments and furnishings of St Mary Steps, St Petrocks (once the largest of the parishes within the city walls), St Martins, St Pancras, St Stephens Bow, and St Sidwells, the large parish church of Heavitree, located outside the eastern gate of the city. Also evident today are examples of the old stone-cobbled streets Richard Hooker

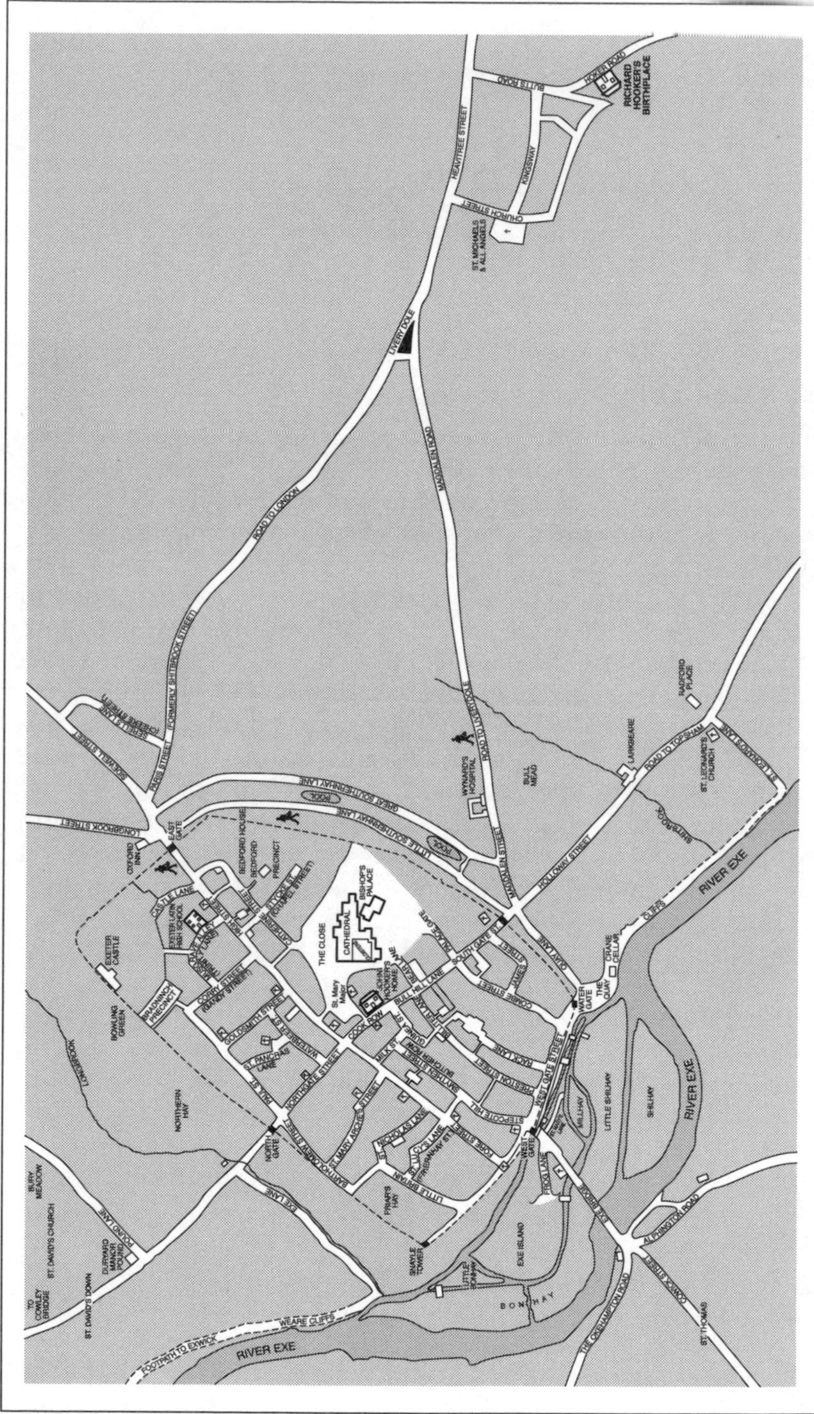
RICHARD HOOKER'S EXETER
RICHARD HOOKER'S BIRTHPLACE
HEAVITREE STREET
MAGDALEN ROAD
ROAD TO LONDON
THE CLOSE
CATHEDRAL
BISHOP'S PALACE
EXETER CASTLE
NORTHERN HAY
EAST GATE
NORTH GATE
WEST GATE
SOUTH GATE ST.
HOLLOWAY STREET
ROAD TO TOPSHAM
RIVER EXE
EXE ISLAND
WEARE CLIFFS
FOOTPATH TO EXWICK
ST. THOMAS

walked, most notably Stepcote Hill, the steep pedestrian extension of Smythen Street running now, as it did in his day, on down the hill past St Mary Steps and through the West Gate to the River Exe. Large sections of the medieval city walls and gates and much of the underground aqueduct, begun in the early thirteenth century and recently uncovered and partially restored, are also visible amidst the commercial bustle of modern Exeter.

Sites from Richard Hooker's Exeter include some remains of the two oldest Norman edifices, which pre-date the cathedral. One is Rougemont Castle, built by William the Conqueror in 1068 shortly after his capture of Exeter. It is constructed on the site of Athelstan's ancient Saxon castle and built with the characteristic local red Heavitree stone that dominated the architectural landscape of Exeter and Heavitree in Hooker's day. The castle stands on high ground overlooking the rest of the city and towering almost directly over the site of Hooker's boyhood grammar school. The other ancient Norman site still showing some of its remains is St Nicholas Benedictine Priory, build later in the eleventh century on the site of St Olaves, which had been the residence of Countess Gytha, the mother of William's defeated Saxon enemy, Harold, and a centre for continuing opposition to the Norman conqueror.

With only about eight thousand souls on ninety acres, Exeter was nevertheless the fifth largest city in England at the time.[3] Imagining Hooker's Exeter, one's twentieth-century sensibilities would be assaulted by the unfamiliar sounds, smells, and sights that Richard would scarcely have noticed: the incessant banging of the giant fullers' hammers at the cloth mills down along the river and on Exe Island as they pounded rough wool into fabric; the putrid odour of tanners' dyes; the clanging, smoking blacksmiths' forges; the bloody, fresh-butchered livestock; the stink of human urine carried through the street in piss-carts on the way to the giant vats where rough wool was scoured for fulling; the endless rows of cloth-drying racks (linhays) lining the banks of the river near the fulling and dyeing mills in the northwestern quarter of the city; the crowded Carfax in the city centre where women filled their water jugs, scrubbed their laundry and gossiped; the busy public stalls with fish, meat, and fowl for sale; the stench of garbage, offal, and human waste in the streets, until all of this debris was cleaned by rain or cleared away by a fresh wind.

The cobbled streets that Richard walked were lined with the shops and stalls of the merchants, tradesmen, and artisans who made Exeter hum with commerce: the taylors, drapers, shoemakers, skinners, smiths, cutlers, wax chandlers, bakers, glovers, cordwinders, glaziers, carpenters, joiners, coopers, weavers, goldsmiths, basket makers, butchers. The city streets and byways were crowded not only with these enterprises but also with the houses (great and small), the gardens, stables, and animal pens of the citizens of the city.

Hooker's Exeter was undergoing rapid transformation from medieval to modern during his years in the city. One of the important changes he watched as a boy was the building of the shipping canal that would one day give the city access to the sea via the river Exe. In the late thirteenth century, the countess of Devon, Elizabeth de Fortibus, had obstructed the waterway between the sea and Exeter by constructing a weir (dam) near Topsham, four miles below Exeter, so that ships would have to use her port. Later, in the early fourteenth century, the Courtenay family, because of a petty quarrel with the city fathers, built a quay at Topsham and required all merchants to use their port and then carry goods overland to Exeter. In subsequent years, other Courtenay earls constructed more weirs and further barred effective trade for the merchants of Exeter. By the early fifteenth century, the Courtenays were effectively controlling most of the trade in and out of Exeter. Despite constant appeals to the crown for relief from this economic tyranny, the kings of England supported their allies the Courtenays until 1538. That was the year in which Henry Courtenay, the Marquis of Exeter, was executed for allegedly conspiring to overthrow Henry VIII. In the event, the king seized the Courtenay's holdings. His successor, Edward VI, rewarded the city for its stand against Catholicism, especially its resistance to the Prayer Book Rebellion, by granting to it the Courtenay lands, including Exe Island.

When Richard was a schoolboy he could have watched the construction of the new city canal. The hated Courteney weirs were pulled down and the dredging operations cleared a new canal all the way to Topsham. In 1566, when Richard was about twelve, construction began on a "pound lock" that could handle ships up to sixteen tons moving in and out of the new Exeter port. In the meanwhile, Queen Elizabeth had authorized the formation of the Society of Merchant Adventurers in Exeter and granted a trading charter to the city.

There was the construction of a new city quay to observe, and a new gate through the city wall providing access to it. The quay was an impressive 150 feet long and eighty feet wide, with a giant crane for loading and unloading ships' cargo. The gate, named "Water Gate," signalled the beginning of a new prosperity for Exeter as a trading and fishing centre. Also in the river and new canal were two large weirs, one the old Callabere Weir, the other a new one called Trew's Weir, named for the designer and builder of the lock and canal system. Richard may have watched it go up in 1564.

All was not industry and commerce in Hooker's Exeter. Along the waterfront near the Callabere Weir stretched a large area with a lovely tree-lined walkway called Bonhay, a favourite recreational expanse. Clambering up the hill behind the castle, just north of his school, young Richard would have found himself in Northern Hay: partly a flat area with bowling greens, partly a rocky area with a steep hill falling away to the north and on down into Longbrook.

Just outside the southern walls of the city was another open area called Southern Hay, a large space where sporting events took place. He may have watched the tilting matches—popular contests in which the participants rode at full speed past a post while trying to detach a ring from it with the points of their lances as they rode by. Another form of the sport involved striking a bag of sand with a cross bar and then trying to avoid the bag as it swung back to knock the careless jouster off his mount.

The city fathers encouraged these and other active sports, including archery and the martial arts. In the robust climate of sixteenth-century Exeter, popular, if more genteel, pastimes such as cards, bowls, tennis, and dice were regarded as frivolous and were prohibited—to little effect. During the 1560s even the bishop, William Alley, enjoyed his game of bowls. The city itself provided some of the public entertainments, especially at festivals when paid musicians, called "waits," performed.

A more important concern of the Exeter city fathers in those days was the public health and safely of residents. Efforts to improve sanitation, for example, led the council to legislate against disposal of household wastes in the streets, especially into those ever-tempting gutters built into the centre of them. (One can still see these "cannells" in today's Stepcote Street.) This sanitary regulation was routinely disregarded.

A more preventable (so it seemed) threat to public safety was crime, a daily occurrence in the rapidly changing social climate of John Hooker's Exeter. Vagrancy was the most common problem; the unemployed and the homeless were everywhere. If apprehended, these poor souls could be banished from the city, and for begging they could be whipped and imprisoned before being tossed out. Some relief was afforded through the workhouse, called Bridewell, where vagrants, along with drunks and assorted vagabonds, were set to work at such tasks as spinning and weaving. Mandated contributions for poor relief, set by quotas given to each parish church, also provided some help for the poor.

Theft, an outgrowth of chronic poverty, was the most troublesome of the serious crimes. Banishment, whipping, and imprisonment were the usual punishments. A strict curfew was the major preventive weapon against thieves. Householders were required to lock and bolt their doors after dark and "to keep all good rule, order, and tranquility." Richard had to be off the streets and either home in Heavitree or at his uncle's by 9 p.m., when the last bell ("bowe bell") sounded.[4]

Growing up in Heavitree and Exeter, Richard would have learned to accept as a matter of course many rules governing personal behaviour that in later generations would be deemed intrusive of individual freedom. Such regulations included required church attendance, receiving the holy Sacrament, and keeping the Sabbath free from all work and play.[5] Living with, or at least being in frequent contact with, an uncle who was simultaneously a pillar of the city's political and economic hierarchies and a working historian bent on recording and explaining the local scene, he would also have come to understand some of the workings of city government and commerce.

Almost every aspect of business and commerce was regulated. No one could buy, sell, or transfer goods or property in the city without approval. Wages were set on a regular basis by the mayor and justices. (Highest paid were master masons and carpenters at six pence per day with meal and ten pence without. Next on the scale came other masons at four pence with meal and eight pence without. Finally, were the apprentices at three pence and six pence respectively.) City government had such extensive power because of Exeter's ancient history as a relatively independent urban centre during Celtic, Roman, and Saxon times. Authority had been specifically conferred by charters granted to the city by a succession of monarchs, from the twelfth century on. In a charter witnessed by Archbishop Thomas Becket in 1150, Henry II granted the city freedom from all tolls, duties, and taxes on merchandise. This freedom was renewed by Richard I in 1190 and Edward III in 1320. Edward's charter also required that all legal pleadings be made before the mayor and city bailiffs and not taken elsewhere to be settled. Henry VIII gave Exeter a constitution with broad powers of self-government in 1509. He appointed a council of twenty-four members with full legislative power within the city. This self-perpetuating oligarchy was appointed for life and had the power to choose the city's two members of Parliament. The council was made up of the leading merchants and wealthiest citizens. Along with a popularly elected mayor, the council was the ruling authority. Council members usually worked co-operatively despite religious, political, and personality differences.

A host of administrative officials executed the laws enacted by the ruling council of twenty-four. These bureaucrats constituted a well-rationalized governing élite at a mature stage of development in modern governmental form and practice. The citizens of Exeter were called "freemen," and they did indeed have the freedom of the city although they had very little real political power. Freemen could elect the city's powerful mayor once a year, although this was usually only a nominal right. The choice was most often between only two nominees selected by the council of twenty-four. Freemen were required to vote, pay some taxes, obey the city ordinances, and remain loyal to the city's leaders. They had the right to own property and to run a business or a trade. Unlike his cousin Robert, Richard's chances of becoming a freeman in Exeter were slim. That status was inherited by the eldest son living inside the city, which ruled out Richard's eligibility. He might purchase the rank if he were a merchant or craftsman doing business in the city or he might acquire it by marrying a freeman's widow. Richard learned early what it meant to be a poor relation.

Those residents who were not freemen were regarded, after the manner of the Greek city-states, as "foreigners." They were without political and economic rights and could neither vote nor hold office. They could not own property or sell goods inside the city walls without a special licence. Exceptions to some of these rules were allowed for the popular market fairs that brought merchants from outside Exeter into the city four times each year to display and sell their wares. The largest and most attractive of these was the London Fair, held once each year. Although the fairs were popular with the city's residents, local merchants were less than enthusiastic about the competition. They did what they could to limit the scope of these "foreign" merchants.

In 1563, Richard may have witnessed a great row during the annual London Fair in Exeter. Jealous local merchants used physical force to prevent their London brothers from setting up their stalls. Some of the goods were then confiscated by city authorities. Undeterred by this interference with their ancient rights, the "foreigners" from London simply moved to a different space near the east gate and set up shop there. The authorities moved in, forcibly removed the Londoners from their stalls, and unceremoniously threw them out of the city.[6]

The most obvious feature of local governance of which Richard was well aware concerned the powerful new post his Uncle John held as chamberlain of the city. As the first chamberlain of Exeter, John Hooker had administrative control over estates of the orphans of deceased freemen, under the direction of the orphans' court. In this position, held for life, John was allowed to retain one third of all money paid out to orphans from their estates. This made him a powerful and wealthy figure in the affairs of the city—so wealthy, in fact, that not long after his death the automatic percentage fees paid to the chamberlain were revoked and his successors received only a fixed salary for their services.

In assuming this new post, John took over one of the three keys to the orphans' chest that held the gold, silver, and other valuables in the care of the orphans' court. (The other keys were held by the mayor and a senior alderman.) He also took on most of the city receiver's former functions of raising taxes, paying wages, and supervising city property and capital improvement projects. In addition, John had a voice in admitting new freemen to the city and in disciplining apprentices. Next to the mayor, Richard's uncle was the leading political figure in the city, a man to be reckoned with in all affairs of consequence. Concerning the position of chamberlain, John wrote:

> His office chiefly and specially concerns the orphans, and then consequently all things concerning the government and estate of the commonwealth; and therefore it is very requisite that he be wise,

learned, and well acquainted in all orders, ordinances, customs, and the whole estate of the commonwealth so that he may advise, instruct, and inform the Mayor and Common Council.[7]

John came under criticism for receiving too much income from this position. In self-defence, he rebuked those who tried to "shake the credit between the city and me." Although he denied taking more than an annual stipend of thirty-two shillings for his work as chamberlain, at least during his early years in office, we may be sure that from this and other preferments of his office, including generous fees for managing city properties, he was handsomely compensated.[8]

At the top of the bureaucratic ladder was the mayor, who actually made laws. His assistants, aldermen, helped with his many duties. Below them were the receiver and the recorder. Then came various wardens and supervisors. At the bottom of the ladder was a group of minor officers whom Richard would have encountered as they went about the city performing their varied duties. These men were responsible in various ways for enforcing laws, keeping the peace, and maintaining city properties. They included sergeants and constables who made arrests, scavengers who cleaned the streets, firemen who provided what little fire protection there was to be had, wardens and watchmen who guarded the city at night, and porters who locked the gates at 10 p.m. in summer and 9 p.m. in winter, and opened them up again at 4 a.m. in summer and 5 a.m. in winter, so that, among many others, boys like Richard Hooker could trudge inside in time for school early in the morning.

Nearly half of the eight thousand inhabitants of Richard Hooker's Exeter lived in poverty and were most probably illiterate. Only about sixty per cent were even listed on the tax rolls, and of these only about five hundred paid more than nominal taxes. Above the mass of uneducated and unskilled workers there were three classes: craftsmen and shopkeepers, merchants, gentry (including the nobility). Approximately twenty per cent of the people might be called middle class, six per cent upper class. Most of the upper class lived in the northern part of the city, near the cathedral, in the parishes of St Mary Major, St Petrock, and St Mary Arches. This is where the Hookers lived.[9]

The Exeter young Richard Hooker knew was a lively place—full of the comings and goings of people and ideas. Young men came to this centre of south-west England to seek fortunes. Political and religious leaders came to try to impose their philosophies and policies. Yet in spite of its burgeoning modernity, Exeter retained much of its medieval character. In the words of one of its modern chroniclers, it was a "miniature world," a self-centred "community" in the medieval sense, even as it was beginning to exhibit the characteristics of a more modern polity. Here in this proud, urbane, growing, rapidly changing city

Richard would have experienced in microcosm many of the problems and challenges awating him at Oxford and in London.[10]

THE REFORMATION IN EXETER

More directly relevant to Hooker's future than the civil and commercial activity of Exeter was its religious life, especially during the early years of the Reformation. As in other areas of Richard's early experience, the influence of the Exeter environment was filtered primarily through the activities and words of his uncle. John Hooker was as involved in and as articulate about religion in Exeter as he was with any aspect of what was, so far as he was concerned, his city. John knew the bishops and deans intimately, used the cathedral library, and chronicled its history. His nephew would certainly recall earnest talk of the great religious issues of the day.

Most of these centred on the cathedral. This and its surrounding parishes were witnesses to dramatic happenings in the decades immediately before Richard's birth. These events were the legacy of the early Reformation to his childhood years in Exeter. Tales about them would have helped to form his adolescent notions about religion and politics, especially his antipathy to confrontation and violent conflict.

We have already noted one local event, close to young Hooker's time and doubtless vivid in his stock of boyhood images. This was the trial for heresy in 1531 of Thomas Benet. A schoolmaster with a Cambridge M.A. and strong Protestant leanings, Benet was arrested for posting anti-Roman doctrines on the Exeter Cathedral door—after the manner of Martin Luther. Benet was subsequently discovered hiding in the Exeter Grammar School, was arrested, and tried for heresy, which at the time was the same as treason. The renowned Dr John Moreman, boyhood teacher of Richard's father and uncle, had defended Benet at the trial. An ardent papist who had spent time in the Tower of London for his convictions, he had to suspend his own beliefs to defend Benet, whose ideas he deplored. In the event, Moreman was unsuccessful in pleading Benet's case. Passions had run too hot. Benet was burned alive at Livery Dole, near Richard's house in Heavitree. When Queen Mary reinstituted Catholicism in England, she named Moreman dean of Exeter Cathedral. But he died before he could assume the post.[11]

In 1535 a piece of Reformation drama unfolded when King Henry's commissioners arrived to inspect the city's two small monasteries, preparatory to taking them over. It seemed that on one fine morning, the commissioners had ordered a workman at St Nicholas Priory to tear down the rood loft (the gallery over a screen that separates the nave from the chancel). Some women, hearing of this, broke open the locked doors of the church and attacked the workman. That frightened fellow fled to the church tower, the angry women in close pursuit. He then jumped out of a window to save himself, nearly breaking his neck in the fall. One of the city aldermen, John Blackaller, heard the commotion and ran to the scene to calm the women. One of them, Elizabeth Glanfeld, attacked him as well. The women then locked themselves in the church as a form of protest (which in the twentieth century would be called a "sit in"). In due course the mayor arrived and had his officers break down the door and arrest the women. The king's commissioners then returned from lunch and asked the mayor to release the women, which he did. Soon after that, in 1536, the crown seized the priory and, in 1538, also took for itself the other small monastery, St Polsloe, just outside the east gate. Both properties were then given to the city—another reward for loyalty to the crown.[12]

An even more striking part of this tapestry of Reformation lore in Exeter that would comprise Richard's store of boyhood memories occurred a few years later when one of Cardinal Wolsey's sons, Thomas Wynter, was given the archdeaconry of nearby Cornwall. He promptly leased the same to one William Body. In 1540 Wynter was called to task for this act when Bishop Veysey, or more probably one of his surrogates, rebuked Wynter for this and other uses of church properties for private gain. The archdeacon was supported by the court of Edward VI and even granted a royal commission to investigate church practices in order to ensure conformity to the new Protestant religious *Injunctions*.

Wynter then convened the clergy and wardens at Penryn and read out to this altogether hostile audience the new Protestant orders forbidding all images, bell ringings, shrines, monuments, altar coverings, pilgrimages, stained-glass windows, candles, and the like. The reactions to this meeting and subsequent attempts by Wynter to enforce the *Injunctions* were so hostile that he was seized and stabbed to death by a crowd at Helston on 5 April 1547, while he was in the act of destroying church images. His murderers and other leaders of the opposition to him and the king were tried for treason and convicted. The penalty for this opposition to King Edward VI and his ministers was to be dragged through the streets of Launceton and then hanged. Before they were quite dead, the offenders were cut down from the gallows, their entrails removed, their heads cut off, and their bodies quartered. Body parts were then displayed in various towns as a warning to others who might resist the king's reformation of religion in England.

Among the colourful figures making up the pantheon of Exeter's religious leaders during the Reformation years none was more enduring or important than Bishop John Veysey. John Hooker, who left posterity his vivid, if opinionated, sketches of the Exeter bishops of his day, did not much care for Bishop Veysey. He characterized him as a learned and cultivated gentleman who played the role of court chaplain and lackey and looked the other way while Henry VIII and his successors plundered the Church.[13]

With hindsight, Veysey can be seen as an astute politician who managed by clever manoeuvering at court—he was rarely in residence at Exeter—to survive both the storms of Henry VIII's and Edward VI's reforms and the bloody persecutions of Queen Mary. Bishop Veysey was a pragmatist—a trait he shared with the city fathers of Exeter, including John Hooker. He believed that doctrinal extremes should be avoided in order to achieve the more vital goals of peace, order, and a measure of independence for the Church. The only safe channel through the dangerous shoals of religious and political conflict was a steady loyalty to the person and religious preference of whoever happened to be monarch at the time. This religious pragmatism was one of the mainstreams of thought and behaviour in a society otherwise defined by violent currents of ideological confrontation.

Evidence of the characteristic religious pragmatism in Exeter—but also, perhaps of its urban opposition to great county families, especially the Courtenays—was the city's reaction to the "Prayer Book Rebellion" of 1549, just five years before Richard's birth. This, as we have seen, was the most potent and disruptive of all Reformation conflicts in western England. Originating some sixty miles south-west of Exeter in Bodmin, Cornwall, a ragged, zealous band of several thousand adherents of traditional Catholicism marched eastward into Devon under a banner displaying the Five Wounds of Christ. They carried before them the consecrated Sacrament under a canopy, along with crosses, candlesticks, and other forbidden items. The rebels captured Plymouth and then moved on to join a larger band of Devon Catholics newly formed in Crediton, the ancient cathedral city north of Exeter.

The principal grievance of the rebels was the Act of Uniformity, which required use of the new English *Book of Common Prayer*, prohibited using Latin in worship, and outlawed many of the traditional liturgical ceremonies. The rebels sought the restoration of virtually all the customary practices that had existed in the earlier days of the reign of Henry VIII, including prayers for those in purgatory, use of holy water, reservation of the Sacrament, images of saints, reinstatement of clerical celibacy, and return of much church property taken by the crown. These demands were sent to the king in a formal petition drawn up in the rebel camps surrounding Exeter during the siege of the cathedral city.

The protestors had good reason to believe that the city gates would open to them and that they would enter as a victorious army to restore the old religion. The church leadership, including such stalwarts as Dr Moreman and Bishop Veysey, was conservative. Most of the common people preferred the old religious forms. Many of the town fathers, including Mayor John Blackaller, were sympathetic to the Catholic cause. Nevertheless, the city held out against the rebels, affirming by its action that its primary loyalty had always been and would remain to the ruling monarch, regardless of the religious policies of whoever wore the crown at the moment. The ensuing five-week siege was devastating. Many of Exeter's poorer inhabitants were on the brink of starvation by the time King Edward VI's forces, commanded by Lord Russell, finally arrived on 6 August to drive off the rebel army and liberate the city. The rebels were driven westward and defeated in several bloody battles, after which their leaders were put to death.[14]

Why did the city fathers not welcome the Catholic rebels? In his history of Exeter, written in 1584, John Hooker presents an eyewitness account of the rebellion and offers his interpretation. He blames the clergy in the city for failing to keep pace with the new religious reforms and for stubbornly clinging to outdated practices, thereby encouraging popular disobedience and rebellion. The only way to assure the health and safety of the Church, he warns, was to move with the times and to affirm loyalty to the English monarch, not to a foreign prince (the pope) who was trying to overthrow the king. It was the duty of the Church to educate the people about the king's Protestant reforms and to encourage them to accept these changes. Instead, John believed, the clergy in Exeter encouraged people to oppose the reformation in religion and to rebel openly against their own sovereign king. Clearly, the pro-Catholic church leadership was at fault for creating a climate that encouraged rebellion. Only the presence of a more pragmatic secular leadership in the city saved the day.

For John Hooker, as for Richard Hooker later, it was the duty of those in charge of Church and State to discourage public disorder and rebellion. Leaders should steer the people in a moderate and pragmatic course marked by toleration, inclusiveness—whenever possible—compromise, and public peace. Only the king could assure God's peace in the Christian commonwealth of England. The self-righteous presumption that each person should follow his own preference in religious matters would lead to anarchy. Now that the king had proclaimed the new form of religious observance, it was the duty of religious and civic leaders to encourage and enforce that line, not to oppose it. With characteristic rhetorical flourish, John Hooker parted company with his famous Catholic tutor, Dr Moreman, and adopted the Reformation—but for something less than purely religious reasons:

> Yet as the old bottles which would not receive new wine but rather wallow in the old dregs and puddles of old superstition than to be filled and refreshed with the wholesome and heavenlie Manna: they [the local church leaders] confederated themselves utterly to renounce, reject and cast off the same, not only to the great offence of God . . . and to the great displeasure of the king whom in all dutifulness they ought to have obeyed, but also to the raising of open rebellion [which is] the cause of the spoil of the whole country and the undoing of themselves, their wives and children, as in sequel and in the end it fell out and came to pass. And here appears what great detriment came . . . to the Church of

> God and what great troubles to the public and commonwealth when learned preachers fail to teach and instruct the people and well-persuaded magistrates to govern the common state; for this people lacking the one and not stored with the other were left to themselves and to their own dispositions; and, thereby, partly of ignorance but more [due to] a forward and rebellious disposition, they do now utterly refuse to accept and resist receiving the reformed religion now put . . . into view and execution.[15]

In his history of Exeter John recounts the events of the rebellion in close detail, with special attention to the role of his friend and patron, Sir Peter Carew, who had aided Lord Russell in defeating the Catholic rebels. Then he proceeds to tell of the danger that exists when people lose all sense of civic loyalty and responsibility in pursuit of religious preference:

> In the city were two sorts of people, the one, and the greater number, were of the old stamp and of the Romish religion; the other, being of lesser number, were of contrary mind and disposition . . . The first were so addicted to their own fantasies and their bottles were so far seasoned with the old wines that they cannot abide to hear of any other religion than that they were first nuzzled in . . . and in respect whereof they regarded no king . . . nor friendship nor country nor commonwealth.

In the face of encouragement of such dangerous public attitudes, by some of the church leadership, the city fathers must assure public order, even if this means acting contrary to their own personal religious preferences:

> The magistrates and chieftans of the city, although not fully resolved and satisfied in religion yet they, not respecting that, but chiefly their dutifulness to the king and commonwealth, did not like the rebellion nor bear with the same but did all things necessary to defend the city and themselves against rebellious attempts. And did likewise give their best endeavour to keep their own citizens in peace and quietness.[16]

Although many of the businessmen and political officeholders leaned toward the old religion and supported the efforts of the rebels to "liberate" their city, John Hooker noted that most remained loyal to the king, despite their distaste for his Protestant religious policies. In so doing, Hooker believed, they were responding to God's will which was that peace and order be maintained in his Christian commonwealth:

> . . . it pleased the Eternal God, so to rule and carry the hearts of the magistrates that although being nuzzled in the Romish religion . . . yet they [so] respected their duty to their prince and the safety of their commonwealth that they openly professed that they would never yield so long as they lived . . . They all with one mind and one voice gave

> a flat answer [to the Catholic rebels] that in the city [where] they had been brought up, had gotten their livings, had sworn their fidelity and allegiance to their king and prince, there they would so continue so long as they could to the uttermost of their powers . . .[17]

Although John Hooker expressed these views many years after the Prayer Book Rebellion, they give some indication of his attitude at a time when he may have had some influence on his teenaged nephew. We need not doubt that certain episodes from the Rebellion, while fresh in the telling, would have found a ready appetite in the imagination of youngsters like Richard. One such story, as we have already seen, told of exploits during the siege of the city by Robert Welsh, vicar of St Thomas, outside the west gate. Welsh had rushed to defend his beloved city against his own religious allies who were trying to break through the gate. Although he was an outspoken opponent of Edward VI's Protestant *Injunctions*, Welsh's daring deeds on top of the city wall at this critical moment almost singlehandedly saved Exeter from being burned. He was a hero in the city's defence. Nevertheless, after Lord Russell's relief of the city, Welsh's heroism was quickly forgotten. He was tried and convicted as a traitor for his papist leanings and for opposing the religious policies of the king.

The account of this episode is recorded in John's written account of the event. The execution of Welsh, John reported, was given over by the sheriff to Barnard Duffield, who,

> being nothing slack in following his commission, caused a pair of gallows to be made and set up on the top of the tower of Walsh's parish church of St Thomas. Everything being ready, Walsh was brought to this place and, by a rope around his waist, was drawn up to the top of the tower. They placed a holy water bucket and sprinkler, a holy bell, pair of beads, and other such popish trash around his neck and waist.

He remained hanging there a long time before he died, John reports, in full sight of the populace. A pity that such a good and loyal saviour of our city should have been so adulterated with the weeds of papism and foul religious practices that it was necessary to treat him so harshly![18]

For John Hooker, primary loyalty for religious and political leaders was always owed to the monarchy because in it resided the only power sufficient to guarantee whatever freedom and security the Church or the city might hope to have. Personal religious convictions were of lesser importance and should be pliant enough to secure the long-term security of the city and the Church. This is the most important single lesson that Richard Hooker would have absorbed from his boyhood experience under the influence of John Hooker. It is an attitude markedly at variance with the stance of those who were the inheritors of the more dogmatic and zealous traditions of the Protestant (Puritan) revolution in both England and America. Those religious zealots followed their consciences, no matter the cost. But there were other Protestants, inheritors of John Hooker, who followed a different path. That way led not so much to America's shores as to a stable and enduring English polity marked by the growth of a broad and accommodating pragmatism in matters both religious and secular. Richard Hooker was to become one of the most important guides along that broad and pragmatic route.

John Hooker's pragmatism was mirrored throughout these Reformation years in Exeter in the behaviour of Bishop Veysey. That prelate remained as aloof as possible from the controversies of the period. He stayed outside the city most of the time, preferring to reside at his sumptuous estate in Warwickshire. He was not present in the 1530s to resist the suppression and despoiling of the Franciscan priory and the new college of anneullars (chantry priests). He was far away from the scene during the Prayer Book Rebellion and conveniently unavailable for providing leadership to the rebels, with whom he may well have sympathized. He was, however, consistently loyal to the crown. While one may fault Veysey for his lack of religious integrity, he and his surrogates epitomized the pragmatism of Church and civic leadership in Exeter.

John Veysey's compromises and accommodations to the shifting claims upon his cathedral's loyalty by the succession of Protestant and Catholic monarchs and prelates who paraded across the English stage during his bishopric left his church in a greatly weakened condition by the time of Elizabeth's ascension. An important result, however, is that the cathedral did survive the dizzying changes of the early Reformation: Henry VIII's break with Rome, the new Prayer Book and liturgical rules of Edward VI, and even the appointment of a dean at the cathedral without the chapter's approval. (This dean was the zealot Simon Heynes, who despoiled many of the beautiful monuments and saints' relics and destroyed valuable books in the cathedral library.)

Veysey was replaced in the last two years of Edward VI's reign by Miles Coverdale, a renowned preacher, famous as the translator of the Bible into English. Coverdale had served as chaplain to Lord Russell's liberating army and had been part of the triumphal entry into Exeter on 6 August 1549. He was a favourite of the more advanced reform element. This group included the influential Peter Martyr, a friend of John Hooker, who wrote from his professorial chair at Oxford to his friend, the Zurich Reformer Heinrich Bullinger, on the occasion of Coverdale's consecration: "Nothing can be more convenient and conducive to the Reformation of religion than the advancement of such men [as Coverdale] to the government of the Church."[19] John Hooker had a favourable opinion of Coverdale as a bishop who had made major efforts to reform the clergy and who exemplified the principles of piety, poverty, and caring commanded by the gospel. John also liked

Coverdale's wholesome, simple family life. He commended such values within his own family and circle of friends.[20]

Unlike Veysey, Coverdale was a bishop in residence who took personal charge of the life of the Church in Exeter. His views were detested by many, especially commoners who preferred the more familiar Catholic religious forms advocated by John Hooker's tutor, John Moreman. John Hooker, who was largely sympathetic to the reform persuasion and probably assisted Coverdale in his great translation of the Bible, spoke of "open railings and false libels and secret backbitings" and even an attempt to murder the good bishop.[21]

Immediately after the death of King Edward VI and the accession of his Catholic half-sister Mary in 1554, Coverdale was removed, and the aging Veysey, who in his earlier years had been a tutor to Princess Mary and a supporter of her mother's claims, was returned to the see at Exeter. The reinstatement of old Catholic liturgical forms and church furnishings began at once. Clerics such as John Moreman were again in favour, and in fact, Moreman was on his way back to Exeter in triumph as new dean of the cathedral when he died in the summer of 1554, shortly after Richard Hooker was born.

When Veysey died a few months later, James Tuberville was named bishop. As resident bishop he oversaw the restoration of Catholic form and practice. Just a few years into his reign at the cathedral, the execution of Exeter's only female Protestant martyr took place. Agnes Prest was a small fifty-four-year-old Cornish woman, one of forty-six females burned for heresy under bloody Mary. Prest was accused by her own husband and children and put to the torch in Southern Hay, just outside the city walls. This took place in November of 1558, when Richard Hooker was just a toddler in Heavitree. Here was another childhood memory for Richard's growing storehouse of examples of religious extremism.[22]

Bishop Tuberville, described by John Hooker as a papist zealot, stayed on until he refused the Oath of Supremacy to Queen Elizabeth. He was removed from office in June of 1559. In that year the new queen dispatched John Jewel, a recently returned Marian exile and the new bishop-elect of Salisbury, as her representative to supervise the reinstitution of Protestant forms and practices at the cathedral and in the Exeter parish churches.

John Hooker knew John Jewel personally and admired in him the same qualities he had liked in Bishop Coverdale: keen intellect, close attention to pastoral duties, and an exemplary personal and family life to serve as an example to his flock. He deemed it a happy day for the city when John Jewel arrived to remove the papist paraphernalia left by Tuberville and to re-establish what Hooker saw as reformed religion and virtue in the churches. Jewel and his commissioners came to town and defaced or pulled down all papist images, which were then brought into the cathedral churchyard and burned in a great fire. Those papal sympathizers who had been most zealous about erecting these romish images were required first to make and then to tend the fire. Bishop Jewel forbade any more Catholic Masses or other Catholic services in either the cathedral or any of the parish churches.[23]

The bishop at Exeter with whom young Richard Hooker may have had a personal relationship—although this is only conjecture—was William Alley (Allen) who took up residence in 1560 and remained until 1570, throughout all the period of Richard's boyhood in Exeter. In 1563 Alley served as a member of the church convocation that developed *The Thirty-Nine Articles of Religion*, soon to become the basic doctrine of the reformed Church of England. His was the voice of moderation on divisive issues of biblical interpretation. According to John Hooker's assessment, Alley was a gentle, affable, lovable man of scholarly inclinations who encouraged students to use his well-stocked library. He was, John claimed, somewhat "credulous . . . loth to offend, ready to forgive, void of malice, full of love, bountiful in hospitality." Hooker faulted Alley, however, for his earlier failure to remain stalwart during Queen Mary's persecutions, either by fleeing to the Continent with his principles intact, or by staying home and accepting martyrdom. Instead, Alley had hidden somewhere in northern England, covering up his religious convictions. Another flaw in Alley, John thought, was that he was too fat.[24]

Withal, William Alley was a better model of episcopal leadership than most bishops of the time. He was a scholar, with a proficiency in Hebrew. His churchmanship and liturgical style were casual, tending to the informal—but not careless. He was committed to the improvement of the clergy. He preached and lectured regularly and was an active pastoral presence in the life of the city and the church. He enjoyed socializing and recreational activities. Not surprisingly, the cathedral began to prosper again under Alley's leadership. His bishopric was an oasis of vitality and growth during an otherwise grim decline in the cathedral's fortunes for most of the century.

JOHN HOOKER'S CHRISTIAN COMMONWEALTH

The religious complexion of Exeter in Hooker's boyhood is not easy to assess because it was in a state of such rapid transformation. Among the more prosperous citizens, including the political and commercial leadership, religious conviction was, as we have seen, less important than loyalty to local civic authority. When push came to shove, as it often did, the *polis* was seen to include and incorporate the Church, not the other way round. Usually this meant that the city went along with the crown, whoever wore it and whatever religion he or she might declare official for the realm. After all, the city's charters and the freedoms that they guaranteed for the citizens had come from Whitehall, not from Canterbury, much less from Rome. Locally, an independent church represented a persistent and annoying threat to the political independence and economic well-being of the city.

Still, many of the people with whom young Richard associated in his boyhood so loved the forms and practices of the old Church that they resisted any changes in this area of their lives, whether such were mandated by Church or State. Exeter was, after all, a provincial centre, removed from much of the radical intellectual and theological ferment of Cambridge, Oxford, and London. In John Hooker's words, most of the people living in Exeter were "of the old stamp, of the Romish religion."[25]

John Hooker's consistent position on matters of Church and State was that a citizen's loyalty was first owed to the polis within which he actually lived, which was the true guarantor of liberty and security, in his case the city of Exeter. From this, it would follow that loyalty to the crown was essential. Ecclesiastical polity was inferior to and subsumed within the civil polis. The Church was to function with whatever degree of independence the crown chose to allow.

In his writings, John cites Cicero, and then goes on to present an essentially Aristotelian philosophy of the state of nature and the social contract:

> And for as much as such is the [natural] state and condition of man, that he was neither born for himself alone, nor yet can live by himself alone, it is most necessary that he do endeavour himself unto those ends for which he was made and created. That is, that he do first and chiefly serve and honour Eternal God . . . and then yield unto man (to whose comfort he was born) those offices of humanity whereby man's society is conserved, which stands and consists in this: that every one [of us] relates to others in all benevolence, generosity, gratefulness, and humanity. For who is not thus affected degenerates from the true nature of man, in his first creation, and becomes worse than the brute-beast. Whereof, in the former ages, not only the children of God, and the professors of His Word . . . but the gentiles also, and the nations which knew not God, have been earnest to maintain the common society, and to perform the offices of humanity.[26]

In John Hooker's view man is, by nature, a political animal destined to civic life. Although John gives lip service to an allegiance to God, his sources are pagan. His philosophy is that of the secular humanist. His strong sense of civic loyalty and of the importance of the commonweal may owe something to his personal history as the orphan who was protected and nurtured by the city, not by the Church. He recalls how he had been a "foster-child to this city and commonwealth," as well as a "free citizen born, and descended of parents who in their times sat in the chiefest seat and chair of government." He is unequivocal in his opinions about the proper relationship between divine and civic authority. It is not the Church alone, or even most importantly, that is responsible for helping citizens to maintain a right relationship with God. The city fathers have a major role to play in passing laws that seek to enforce obedience to God's laws. John goes so far as to claim that ". . . Magistrates are God's ministers, substitutes, and vicars, upon earth from whom all power and authority is ordained."[27]

God's authority on earth need not be filtered through the Church. From this it follows that the first duty of magistrates is "to honour God truely . . . and then in consequence your government must and shall prosper." Richard Hooker's uncle completes his assertion of the pre-eminence of state over church authority:

> Preposterous then is the judgement of those who would have [it] that religion should pertain only to the bishops and the clergy, and the chief magistrates should deal only in matters of policy. But the law of Moses, and the law of the Gospel, doth determine the contrary.

Especially in his time, when religion was in such a shameful condition, it was the duty of civic authorities to enforce true religion. "For atheists," he complains, and "papists, and blasphemers of God's Holy Name, swarm as thick as butterflies without check or containment."[28]

John Hooker, with his characteristic love for agricultural metaphors, exhorts the city fathers to clean up religion in Exeter, which has become "a sour grape" and a "wild olive." He exhorts the city fathers: "you are God's ministers, and he has appointed you to be his Moses unto us, and therefore you must in this dangerous case stand before him between him and the people."[29]

Just how much of John Hooker's philosophy of church-state relations—views shared by most of Exeter's better-educated, wealthier class—rubbed off on young Richard will never be known. It is a good guess that Richard's strong preferences for peace, order, loyalty to civic authority, and compromise and accommodation on troublesome religious quarrels owe something, if only subconsciously, to the strongly held and often expressed views of his uncle John.

NOTES

1. Here I must respectfully disagree with H. G. Hoskins, in whose debt I stand for much of my knowledge of sixteenth-century Exeter and Heavitree. Hoskins, mistakenly I believe, wrote in his history of Devon that "Exeter gave Hooker nothing but the accident of his birth." *History of Devon* (Tiverton, Devon: Devon Books, 1992), 282.
2. For a description of Exeter guilds see Joyce Youings, *Tuckers Hall Exeter* (Exeter: Exeter University Press, 1968), 3-5.
3. Excellent descriptions of Exeter over the centuries are: Hoskin *op. cit.*; Wallace T. MacCaffrey, *op. cit.*; *800 Years of Exeter History, An Exhibition of City Archives* (London, 1962); Bryan Little, *Portrait of Exeter* (London: Robert Hale, 1983).
4. Hoskins, *Exeter*, 62.
5. An excellent source on the function of church courts in this area is Martin Ingram, *op. cit.*

6. Many of the episodes recounted in this chapter are drawn directly from John Hooker's own account of the events as they appear in his later writings, especially in his *Common Place Book*. See Harte, *Gleanings, op. cit.*
7. MacCaffrey, 93; Edward E Freeman and William Hunt, *Historic Towns* (London: Longmans Green and Co., 1906), 154..
8. *John Vowell, alias Hoker, Gent., The Antique Description and Account of the City of Exeter*, dedicated to John Tuckfield and John Rolle by Andrew Brice, 1765, AD/EXE 06 HOO. Another account of Hooker's history is Walter J. Harte, *An Account of the Sieges of Exeter, Foundation of the Cathedral Church and the Disputes Between the Cathedral and City Authorities by John Vowell alias Hoker*, from a manuscript in Exeter Muniment Room, Exeter (James G. Commin, 1911). Excellent contemporary accounts of life in Exeter are in Harrison, 248-9, 366-8, 309-10.
9. MacCaffrey, 249.
10. *Ibid.*, 1-3.
11. Rose-Troup, 108; Vernon F. Snow *Parliament in Elizabethan England, John Hooker's Order and Useage*. (Hartford: Yale University Press, 1977), 5; Harte, *Gleanings*, 12-13. A fine history of the cathedral is Audrey Erskine's edition of Vyvyan Hope and John Lloyd, *Exeter Cathedral* (Exeter, 1988). Other useful sources include Nicholas Orme, *Exeter Cathedral As it Was 1050-1550* (Exeter: Devon Books, 1986); R. J. E. Boggis, *A History of the Diocese of Exeter* (London: William Pollard & Co., 1922).
12. Hoskins, *Exeter*, 56-57.
13. John Vowell, alias Hooker, "Catalogue of the Bishops of Excester," 1584, cited here from the original in the Exeter City Muniments, Book 52, Devon Records Office, Exeter. (The more available edition of this work is Harte, *John Hooker's Description of the Citie of Excester [Antique Description]*(Exeter: Devon and Cornwall Record Society, 1919).
14. Rope-Troup, esp., 185-319.
15. Harte, *Account of the Sieges*, 56.
16. *Ibid.*, 71-2.
17. *Ibid.*, 74.
18. Harte *Antique Description*, 84-5.
19. Boggis, 346.
20. Harte, *Gleanings*, 8.
21. Harte, *Antique Description*, 139.
22. Fuller, *Church History*, 249-50.
23. Harte, *Hooker's Commonplace Book*, 15.
24. Harte, *Antique Description*, 143. Also William Haugaard, *Elizabeth and the English Reformation* (Cambridge: Cambridge University Press, 1968), 57.
25. Harte, *Account of the Sieges*, 71.
26. Hooker, in his"Epistle Dedicatory" to his history of Exeter, Harte, *Antique Description*, 146.
27. *Ibid.*, 150.
28. *Ibid.*
29. *Ibid.*, 157.

CHAPTER 3

School Days

GRAMMAR SCHOOL

By the time Richard entered grammar school in 1562, the violent frenzy of the early Reformation in Exeter and elsewhere in England was subsiding. An astute monarch was safely ensconced and had already begun to affirm her supremacy over all rivals, clerical and secular. For the rest of the century and for all of Hooker's adult life, the political and religious battles of the day would be waged under the visage of this long-lived Renaissance princess. The Machiavellian virgin queen and her superb chief ministers, especially William Cecil and Francis Walsingham, would keep the lid on—or, to use the nautical metaphor Elizabeth would have preferred, provide a stabilizing rudder for the ship of State—so that England might successfully further its tumultuous transition from medieval to modern life.[1]

1562 was a fateful year in Richard's life. His father had, for all intents and purposes, left home for good to find his fortunes elsewhere, having recently begun his peripatetic career by serving as steward to the renowned Sir Thomas Challoner, England's ambassador to Spain. Richard's uncle John, as we have seen, had moved back to Exeter, after sojourns at Oxford and Strasbourg, to take up his family inheritance and assume his position as a leading citizen of Exeter. John had married his second wife, Anastasia Bridgeman, and settled into the family home he had leased a decade earlier. By now Richard's mother may have died, although there are no records to confirm this. It is just as likely that she lived on in modest circumstances in Heavitree, rarely seeing her absent husband and sharing more and more of her young son's life with her prosperous brother-in-law and his family in Exeter.

Each morning, a few minutes before 6, the eight-year-old Richard entered the Exeter City gate after a 20-minute walk from Heavitree. He found his way to his schoolroom, which was a recently-renovated hall of about 400 square feet, located on the ground floor of a building on Trinity Lane (today's Musgrave Alley), just a short distance from St Laurence Church on High Street. Enrollment was low during his years at school, owing to the unfunded scholarships for poor boys. Only about a dozen students spread out comfortably on the benches meant to accommodate nearly three times that number. Most of Richard's classmates had attended the "petty schools" or had enjoyed the benefit of private tutors. Richard's father may have taught him his ABC, but his mother was probably barely literate, and his uncle was not in Exeter during his earliest years.

There has been understandable confusion about the name of Hooker's school. Similar names of various grammar schools in the city from the seventeenth century onward have caused most of the uncertainty. The original church-owned school of ancient lineage dates from about 1050. When the see was moved from Crediton to Exeter, a school was established in the Franciscan Priory of St John the Baptist. Bishop Grandison endowed scholarships for the school as part of his establishment of the St John the Baptist Hospital Foundation in 1332. This school was widely known as the Exeter Grammar School and probably still popularly called this in Hooker's day. However, when Richard was in attendance, the correct name was the Exeter Latin High School, or simply, the Latin High School. In 1630 the city founded a free Latin school, called The Free Grammar School. There was also a Free English School that operated as a part of St John's Orphanage for children between the ages of seven and fourteen and a Dames School for young girls and boys.[2]

At school Richard had to work industriously to overcome his poor academic preparation and prove to Master Williams that he could do the work. Fortunately, he was blessed with an excellent mind and a determined spirit. He was a bright, precocious, even brilliant boy. If we need corroboration of this assessment, we have the testimony of Izaak Walton's inevitable panegyric:

> . . . [as] a school boy he was an early questionist, quietly inquisitive. Why this was and that was not to be remembered? Why was this granted, and that denied? This being mixed with a remarkable modesty, and a sweet serene quietness of nature, and with them a quick apprehension of many perplexing parts of learning . . . made his master and others to believe him to have an inward, blessed divine light, and therefore, to consider him . . . a little wonder.[3]

Overlooking Walton's hyperbolic attributions of sweet serenity, remarkable modesty, and divine light, we may credit—from Hooker's later career and writings—that the boy had a questioning manner and an unusual ability to grasp complex matters.

Young Richard may have been rich in intellectual potential, but otherwise he was a poor boy. Without his uncle's financial support and political influence, he would probably not have entered grammar school. All the costs of education, including books, were supposed to be provided free of charge by the dean and chapter at the cathedral. If this had been so, there would have been more poor boys like Hooker in the school. But the queen's injunctions requiring such support, like those of her royal predecessors, went largely unheeded by the church leaders in Exeter, and it fell to each student's family to pay the schoolmaster from their own pockets. Uncle John not only paid Richard's tuition, but also bought him the cloak, waistcoat, breeches, cap, stockings, shirts, shoes, and handkerchiefs that made up the prescribed attire of an Exeter schoolboy. In later years, John would see to it that his nephew had access to the books, paper, and other supplies he needed to pursue his studies. Some of the books, such as William Lily's *Latin Grammar*, Nicholas Udall's *Flowers of Latin Speaking*, Foxe's *Book of Martyrs*, Erasmus's *Colloquies*, Cicero's *Epistles*, Ovid's *Metamorphoses*, Aesop's *Fables*, various writings by Virgil, Horace, Juvenal and, of course, books by leading reformers like Calvin and Peter Martyr, plus the authorized editions of the Bible and Prayer Book, would probably have been in John's personal library for use by his own children.

Although he may have been poor in his own eyes and those of his peers, Richard was rich indeed to be increasingly under the influence and protection of John Hooker, one of the most important father-figures in his life. Among the attributes he probably absorbed from his uncle's prosperous household were a sense of ease in the presence of rich and powerful people, an interest in the great political and religious issues of the day, a bias in favor of the more moderate, practical, and peaceful—as opposed to ideologically extreme—solutions to the divisive public issues of the day. The most immediate and direct influence of John on Richard was that he rescued his talented nephew from obscure origins in Heavitree and facilitated his formal education, first at school and later at college—an education that would give the final shape and stamp to Richard's character and philosophy.

The Exeter Latin (Grammar) High School had an ancient but not obscure provenance. Earliest records, as we have seen, date it from 1332 when Bishop Grandison endowed a grammar school in Exeter and described how it was to be run. Twelve students were to be chosen, two each from Barnstable, Totnes, Exeter, Cornwall; three from among the choristers at the cathedral and one from Erniscomb parish, whose lands the bishop used to create the scholarship endowment fund. The weekly support of 5d was to be paid from the endowment to support each scholar in the prescribed five-year course of study. The school was originally located in the Franciscan Priory of St John the Baptist on Smythen Street. The monks did not provide instruction or have any role in administration. A secular headmaster was appointed to run the institution under the supervision of the bishop. The master chose the students and hired the teachers and other staff. From its inception, the school was clerical in patronage and control but secular in its management and operation.

The course of studies and academic exercises occupying Richard Hooker—and his fellows at the nearly 350 grammar schools throughout the country in the 1560s—was not much different from the medieval curriculum of two hundred years earlier. Latin was the language of learning, instruction and discourse. At many schools of the day the boys were forbidden to converse in any other language during school hours. Latin was learned as a spoken language by memorization and recitation of the speeches (colloquies) of Erasmus, Vives, and others. Later, students graduated to Cicero's *Epistles*, then on to the works of Ovid, Aesop, Horace, and others, always using only the original Latin.

In time Hooker learned to copy out whole sections of the Latin masters and then incorporate them into his own original Latin compositions. The *trivium* (logic, grammar, rhetoric) was the heart of the curriculum. Even here, Latin was the language for mastering these traditional disciplines. As a consequence of so much emphasis on Latin, the writing and public declamations of literate adults in Elizabethan England would be characterized by their formal, elaborate style, fullness of "rich and copious imagery," "sonorous and stately rhythms," and an "exaggeration and artificiality" that often seem stilted to our ears and eyes.[4]

Apart from Latin, grammar, logic and rhetoric, the primary emphasis of the formal curriculum at Hooker's school was religious study and moral instruction. Unlike a few of the wealthier grammar schools, such as St Paul's or Merchant Taylors in London, which were beginning to offer some Greek and even a bit of Hebrew (along with music, geography, mathematics, history, and some modern foreign language), Richard's school stuck with the traditional medieval curriculum. As its name implied, the Exeter Latin High (Grammar) School emphasized Latin and grammar. Hooker and his classmates learned very little theology. Their readings were intended to sharpen skills in grammar, logic, and rhetoric, not to instruct them on spiritual matters. Religious learning came from a more practical part of the school requirements. Long prayer-times were observed as a part of each school day. Students were expected to copy out and memorize extended sections of Holy Scripture and then recite them in class.

Richard and his fellows were also required to attend church services at the cathedral every Sunday and on all holy days. He took notes during the sermons. On Mondays he might be unfortunate enough to be one of those called on to summarize the sermon and then recite sections verbatim from memory. If he failed to do this to the master's satisfaction, he could be severely punished.

Throughout its history, the Exeter Latin High (Grammar) School was under divided church control. Either the bishop or the archdeacon at Exeter selected, licensed, and paid the salary of the headmaster, but the school building was owned and maintained by the dean and chapter. Since bishop and chapter were usually at odds about this, as about most matters, the question of who really controlled the school was unresolved. In the breach, the headmaster frequently had his own way and operated independently of clerical control. That the school was located outside the cathedral close served further to separate it from church control.

Although surviving records are scarce, it is clear that the school had acquired a good reputation by the time of the Reformation. Over the centuries, through St Johns Hospital Foundation, it was a popular charity in the bequests of wealthy persons. A note in cathedral obit books shows a gift of ten marks in 1457 from one Laurence Bodyngton, who was "late master of the Grammar School of the city of Exeter." A nineteenth-century scholar of English grammar schools doubted "whether there is a single Will . . . in which a legacy to St John's Hospital is not contained."[5]

A severe blow to the school was inflicted in the 1530s when Henry VIII dissolved the local monasteries, taking St John's Foundation endowment, and with it the school's scholarship fund. At the time, there were nine supported students at the school, costing the endowment £15 12s plus 8s per week for each student's maintenance. In its impoverished condition, the school now fell on hard times from which it did not recover until long after Hooker's day.

Many students were undisciplined sons of the nobility and gentry, headed for careers at court, or as landed gentlemen, or as world travellers and soldiers of fortune, or all three. These boys, many of them in their middle to late teens, had neither the need nor the desire to pursue the traditional medieval curriculum of England's better grammar schools. As a result they were often hell-raisers who disrupted the more serious academic pursuits of such classmates as Richard Hooker. Richard, on the other hand, represented the more traditional type of grammar-school student who was headed for university and then a career either in the church, the government, or academic life. Not necessarily of wealthy or noble parentage, his kind of student usually had a patron who recognized his academic potential and covered his costs.

The sharp dichotomy in the student mix, in age and social class, was an accelerating characteristic of education which was to follow Richard Hooker from grammar school in Exeter on into his educational experience at Oxford. The medieval church-supported institution, with its emphasis on training bright young men of modest social backgrounds for careers as clerics, educators, and bureaucrats, was changing during Hooker's life. The emerging pattern was one of secular schools and colleges responding to the career needs of budding merchants, lawyers, doctors, and diplomats who came from families wealthy enough to pay for this more modern and practical course of study.

The disciplinary methods used by Hooker's teachers were, by later standards, severe, regardless of the need to stem the tide of rowdiness among students of such varying ages and interests, all living for ten hours a day in one room. The most common punishment Richard witnessed was when the master laid a rowdy or inattentive boy over a bench or against the back of a classmate and then beat his bare bottom with a bundle of birch branches until he bled. Another typical punishment was to strike the young offender on his hand or mouth with a flat piece of wood that had a hole in the middle of it, called a ferule. This raised a painful blister.

In a day when children were punished severely at home by frequent whippings for even small offences, such treatment at school was not only tolerated but encouraged by parents and community leaders. By early in the next century, however, when pressure was strong in Exeter for a new free school, an exposé of conditions at Hooker's *alma mater* raised an outcry not only against the poor instructional quality there but also against constant beatings of students, as often as "three, four, five and six times in one day" for some boys. Such excessive cruelty, it was charged, encouraged students to truancy so that their parents either had to keep them home or let them run wild in the streets. At a new school, recently opened by one Thomas Spicer, it was said that students "profited more in one quarter of the year than they did in two years at the said Perryman's [Latin] school."[6]

In Edward VI's reign in the late 1540s the bishop and the chapter, financially weakened by the plundering of their resources under the Protestant "reforms" of both Henry and Edward, were failing to provide adequate support either for salaries or building maintenance. In the event, the king issued an injunction requiring the bishop to pay the headmaster a minimum annual wage and provide him with a house. The headmaster would now be permitted to charge his own fees to students in order to supplement his small salary. In return, the master was required to pay the chapter an annual rent of £5 for use of the school building. The chapter was enjoined to support twelve poor students. These royal injunctions were ignored.

Under Queen Mary nothing was done to advance the state of the school. Queen Elizabeth specifically required the cathedral to strengthen the school and expand its service. She ordered that under-educated clergymen enroll at the school. She also commanded that the master and his students attend morning prayer daily. Further, the queen required that the dean and chapter repay the headmaster, William Harte, the money (£3 6s 8d) that he had spent from his own pocket to maintain the school during the years of Queen Mary's reign. Elizabeth was no more obeyed in these matters than Edward had been. On the contrary, beginning in 1561, the dean and chapter actually required headmasters to post a bond of £100 to assure that they would never make any claims against the cathedral under the authority of these royal injunctions.[7]

The once proud Exeter grammar school had indeed fallen on hard days by Richard Hooker's time there. Increasingly, education was regarded as a civic rather than a Church responsibility, especially as the demand rose in the face of declining Church ability (or willingness) to provide education for growing numbers of prospective students. At first, the monarchs, as noted, tried to assume some responsibility for regulation. But their reach was longer than their grasp. By Richard's time, the local city fathers were taking a major interest in education and attempting to wrest control of schools from the cathedral.

An example of this process of change from religious to civic control of education in Exeter occurred in 1561, shortly before Richard was admitted. The school building was in bad repair. Once again, the chapter had failed to heed the demands of parents and city fathers to fix the building. The headmaster, Mr. Williams, had paid the chapter his rent, which was supposed to be used for repairs; but nothing was done. In frustration he appealed to John Hooker, chamberlain of the city, for help. Richard's uncle responded with characteristic alacrity and organized what we would call a capital fund-raising drive. The result was a great success. As John put it, "The high school in this City by a common contribution at the request of Mr. Williams the schoolmaster and by the labour and industry of the writer hereof was rebuilt, sealed, scraped and plastered."[8]

Richard's preparation at the Exeter Latin High School was barely adequate to equip him for Oxford. He attended grammar school at the very end of a long era of church control and medieval curriculum and pedagogy. The new educational era which was to take definite shape in the next century was only beginning to emerge—just strong enough in its earliest impact to disrupt the old educational order but not yet sufficiently clear and authoritative to provide a decent pattern for the new learning and discipline. As in other aspects of Richard Hooker's life, so with his schooling, nothing is more definite than the disorder, change, and decline in quality of the educational institutions on which he and others in his day depended for support and development. Or, at least so it seems with the perspective of four and a half centuries. For Richard himself, attending school in Exeter was simply the first great adventure of his life.

THE BRIDGE TO OXFORD: JOHN JEWEL OF SALISBURY

We know that young Richard Hooker demonstrated promise as a student while at grammar school in Exeter because a leading intellect in the Church of England, Bishop John Jewel, at Salisbury Cathedral some eighty miles to the east, adopted him as one of many talented young men he helped advance educationally.

The celebrated bishop's "discovery" of Richard Hooker came by way of Jewel's association (probably a friendship) with Richard's uncle. These two prominent Devonians had struck up a relationship far from home in Strasbourg during the exile that had seen many such as Jewel flee before the persecutions of Catholic Mary Tudor. Why John Hooker, who was not a cleric or even a devoutly religious person, joined the nearly eight hundred Protestants seeking refuge in Switzerland and along the Rhine in Germany is not at all clear. Perhaps he was just a wealthy young man seeking excitement. Perhaps he had been deeply affected while at Oxford by the teachings of the influential Italian reformer, Peter Martyr (Pietro Martire Vermigli) and subsequently joined other young men in following Martyr into exile. Jewel's motives for flight were not, as we shall see, at all obscure.[9]

When the two men returned from Europe to seek more secure fortunes under the new Protestant queen, their paths may have crossed a number of times. Jewel had visited Exeter in 1560 as head of Elizabeth's commission on religious conformity. No doubt John extended his personal support and hospitality to the queen's emissary on that occasion. Then, sometime in 1567 or 1568 John Hooker had a problem with which he thought his friend the bishop of Salisbury could help. John's nephew, Richard, was doing so well in his studies at the Exeter Latin High School that the headmaster thought he should go on to Oxford University to continue his studies. Which college should he attend? Who would sponsor him for admission and pay for his education? Richard's parents could not help. His father was in Ireland and his mother, assuming she was still alive, had no resources. The boy's future was in his uncle's hands, as it probably had been for years.

John would not have needed any help to secure a place for Richard at Exeter College. Admission there was virtually assured to a recommended student from Exeter. But John probaby preferred to send his promising nephew to Corpus Christi College. This institution, not Exeter, had been endowed with the financial help of Bishop Oldham of Exeter and was well regarded by the Protestant cognoscenti in the city. John also preferred Corpus to Exeter College because of its progressive ("liberal") curriculum and its Calvinist leanings. Most of all, he liked Corpus because his friend John Jewel had spent his own early career there as scholar, fellow, and lecturer. When asked his opinion, the good bishop recommended his own college for Richard. (John later sent his sons Robert, Zachary, and Peter to Corpus Christi, and may have attended there himself for a short time in the early 1550s, though there is no hard evidence for that.)

Izaak Walton reports that John Hooker actually took Richard and headmaster Williams to Salisbury for a private interview with Bishop Jewel to seek his patronage. The bishop was apparently so impressed with Richard that he gave some money to his parents and to the headmaster for the boy's support and promised to keep an eye on him as a candidate for later admission to Corpus Christi. While it is always wise to be sceptical about Walton's accounts of such events, the essentials of this famous story are probably reliable. It is plausible that John Hooker would have asked John Jewel for help in evaluating his nephew's abilities and in assisting with his educational placement and expenses, and it is just as likely that the bishop would have delivered what was asked of him. Jewel was by this time a well-known supporter of promising young men such as Richard Hooker.[10]

Jewel's subsequent request that President William Cole at Corpus Christi take a personal interest in John Hooker's nephew and that John Rainolds, already the most brilliant fellow at Corpus, serve as Richard's tutor, would have fallen on receptive ears at the college. After all, the entreaty came from their most prominent alumnus. The fact that Jewel had been expelled from Corpus for refusing to attend Mass in the college chapel during Queen Mary's reign would only have added to his reputation with the current Puritan régime at the college.[11]

Jewel loved his college but was critical about what he rightly regarded as the deteriorating educational quality there and at Oxford generally. As early as 1560 he wrote to Peter Martyr describing the University as "sadly deserted; without learning, without lectures, without any regard to religion." The colleges at Oxford, he said, were "falling into ruin and decay" and "filled with mere boys and empty of learning." Nonetheless, it is safe to assume that the bishop remained a loyal son of Oxford and was happy to recommend a bright and serious lad like Hooker for admission to his college.

John Jewel was at this time arguably the most influential and respected theological polemicist writing and preaching on behalf of Queen Elizabeth's reformed Church of England. He is important in Richard Hooker's life story not only because he facilitated the beginning of Hooker's career, but also because he was a hero to Hooker and served as a role model for much of his later thinking and writing. In 1547, during the reign of Edward VI, when the renowned Italian Protestant teacher and theologian Peter Martyr came to lecture at Oxford as Regius Professor of Divinity, Jewel, like many young men of his day, fell under the spell of this remarkable man who was to become one of the most influential figures of the English Reformation. Martyr had been brought from Strasbourg to Oxford by Archbishop Cranmer to serve as a major intellectual catalyst for reform at that university. Along with his counterpart Martin Bucer at Cambridge, Martyr's assignment from Cranmer was to stir up religious and intellectual reformation at the colleges, challenge students and fellows to rethink their old theological positions, and bring the colleges and halls into the humanist and Protestant camps. Martyr was hired to be what today might be termed a "liberal," "trouble-making" professor. That is just what he was. Many of his students adored him for giving them new and radical perspectives. For his part, Jewel became such a close disciple that he once called Martyr "my father, my pride, and even the half of my soul."[12]

When Mary Tudor became queen in 1553 Peter Martyr recognized at once the inhospitable climate that this abrupt return to Catholicism would mean for a reformer like himself. He returned to Strasbourg, trailed by a wake of prominent and promising Protestants from the

Church and from both universities. Jewel's loyalty to the new Catholic order was put to the test when he was appointed as the official Oxford orator to prepare and deliver a welcoming address to the new queen. Soon after that event, he accepted the assignment to be the official notary taking testimony at the trials of Archbishop Cranmer and Bishop Ridley in April, 1554. These leading reformers were subsequently martyred for their faith, with some complicity in their executions falling on Jewel. As if these acts did not sufficiently compromise Jewel's integrity as a Protestant reformer, in August of 1554 he went so far as to subscribe in writing to articles that amounted to recanting his Protestant faith and affirming Mary's Catholic position, especially the doctrine on the Blessed Sacrament that he had learned from Martyr to abhor.

Seen in the context of those dangerous days in England, when the price for keeping the Protestant faith was death by burning (some 275 persons suffered this fate under Mary, including one archbishop, three bishops and seventeen other clergy) or flight to a foreign country, we might well sympathize with Jewel for choosing the apparently cowardly route. Perhaps it took more courage to stay at home and equivocate than to flee and leave the battle for reform to those who remained behind and tried to work from within the system. There was also the question of Christian loyalty to the monarch, and it seemed then that the return to Catholicism under Mary would be a lasting one.

Unfortunately—or perhaps fortunately—for Jewel the new pro-Catholic régimes at Oxford, Lambeth, and Whitehall did not believe that his sudden change of heart was sincere. Apparently he had been too clear, too extreme, and too outspoken a Protestant for a sudden change of heart to be accepted at face value. Now Jewel felt that he had no alternative to death or prison but flight. In March 1555, at about the time of Richard Hooker's first birthday, he left England, joining his mentor Peter Martyr and other exiles in Frankfurt. In July 1556 Martyr accepted a post as professor of Hebrew at the university of Zurich and invited Jewel to come with him. During these days with Martyr and other English émigrés at Zurich, Jewel came close to becoming what would be termed a "Puritan."[13]

During the so-called "Elizabethan settlement" of religion, which Jewel would help to forge, there were two major kinds of "Puritan" in England. There were the radical and impatient militants on the far left (Archbishop Parker called them "precisians"), many of whom—whether or not they were open about their true intent—were bent on overthrowing the entire religious establishment, root and branch: bishops, *Book of Common Prayer* and, for some, the queen as head of the Church. These radicals sought to replace the episcopal polity with separate church congregations organized under the presbyterian or congregational models. These were the most advanced Puritans, those who would plague Archbishop Whitgift toward the end of the century—men like John Penry, Job Throckmorton, the author(s) of the infamous *Marprelate Tracts*, and openly separatist leaders such as Robert Browne and Henry Barrow.[14]

Then there were the more moderate Puritans, most of whom I will term "emergent presbyterians." Most of these men sought radical liturgical change and major reform in church polity, but within an established Church of England. Some of them said they would retain the episcopal polity but in truth most in this group preferred, if they did not openly advocate, the presbyterian discipline of consistories of clergy and lay elders. In this group were man like Thomas Cartwright, Walter Travers, John Field, and, perhaps, John Rainolds. What united both types of Puritan was that they were: (1) theologically Calvinist—fired by the Pauline Epistles with their assurance of predestined election and emphasis on redemption, salvation, justification, and "living in the spirit"; (2) believers in the primacy of Scripture as the sole authority for faith and practice; (3) generally advocates of the presbyterian as opposed to the episcopal form of church polity.

Distinguishable from these Puritan Protestants were what I shall call the "emergent Anglicans" such as John Jewel, Edmund Grindal, and Edwin Sandys, who sought further liturgical and theological movement away from Rome within the established episcopal polity, and later, John Whitgift and Richard Bancroft who presaged the high Anglican liturgy and theology of Archbishop Laud and the Caroline Divines in the next century, which moved the church back closer to Rome.

What united the emergent Anglicans and usually distinguished them from most other Protestants was: (1) an insistence on an established Church ruled by bishops and headed by the crown; (2) use of the *Book of Common Prayer* and the *Bishops' Bible* as opposed to the more popular *Geneva Bible*: these "anglican" books expressed a middle-ground in biblical interpretations and liturgical expressions, somewhere between Rome and Geneva; (3) a tendency to view Holy Scripture as the primary but not the only source of faith and practice, holding that reason and religious custom were two other important sources of God's revelation; (4) a preference for the synoptic Gospels rather than Paul's Epistles; (5) an emphasis on the incarnation, the passion and the resurrection as central theological and liturgical themes, with concomitant stress on the importance in worship of the sacraments and common prayer rather than preaching; (6) a tendency to stress human awe and wonder before the holiness of God, and a concomitant aesthetic inclination, as contrasted with the Puritan emphasis on personal sin and God's judgement.

In the dynamic and often confusing drama of emergent Anglicanism—a story with the misleading title "Elizabethan settlement"—John Jewel stood near the beginning. He would not always be comfortable with what was required of him in a Church headed by a monarch and peopled by a citizenry who still had strong preferences for traditional Catholic forms and practices. But he remained loyal to his queen, struggling for all the reform he could get and heading down a pragmatic road that would make Calvin acceptable within the historic established Church of England. In so doing, he presaged Richard Hooker, who was to appear at the end of Elizabeth's reign to clarify, but not settle, the religious divisions in the country.

Elizabeth had scarcely settled herself on the throne when in 1559 she asked Jewel to join Sandys, Grindal, and several other leading Calvinist clerics to engage in a public debate at Westminster with a number of leading Roman-leaning bishops and intellectuals. The conference lasted only a few days, from 31 March to 5 April, and proved abortive. Then in July the queen again called upon Jewel, this time to head a special commission to visit all the dioceses in the western counties and root out papist nonconformity. He subsequently covered some seven hundred miles including stops in Reading, Abington, Gloucester, Bristol, Bath, Wells, Exeter (as we have seen), Cornwall, Dorset, and Salisbury.

During his visit to Salisbury Jewel faced the man who was to become his principal adversary, Thomas Harding. Confronted with Jewel's demand that he subscribe to the queen's new religious orders, Harding, the cathedral treasurer and canon residentiary and a man who had hoped to be named bishop, refused. This meant an end to his career. After being divested of his clerical posts, Harding fled to the Continent, joining the growing number of English Catholic émigrés congregated at the university of Louvain in Belgium. This distinguished group included such luminaries as Nicholas Sanders and William Allen in addition to Harding. They wrote tracts against Elizabeth's Church and schemed, plotted, and waited for the end of her reign and a hoped-for return of the old Catholic faith to the English Church. Jewel's dismissal of Harding from the chapter at Salisbury for holding fast to the very beliefs to which he himself had once sworn allegiance, coupled with this own advancement to the very bishopric that Harding coveted, assured a bitter antagonism between the two men. There is foretaste here of the later controversy between Richard Hooker and Walter Travers, a conflict that also involved the failure of a distinguished scholar to receive the advancement he thought he had been denied at the hands of his rival.

In November of 1559, on the eve of his consecration as bishop of Salisbury, Jewel preached the most famous sermon of his career. This came to be called "The Challenge Sermon" because in it he threw down the gauntlet to Catholics and Catholic-leaning clerics and laity in the English church at home and abroad. He attacked all of the major ingredients in Catholic faith and doctrine, including the supremacy of the pope, the giving of Holy Communion in one kind only to the laity, private Mass, and the doctrine of transubstantiation. His sermon, described as "at once scholarly and reckless, reasonable and foolish," made it clear that the Church of England intended to be a part of the Reformation—a church freed from association with many of the major doctrines and practices of Roman Catholicism.[15] In the spring of 1560 Jewel preached the same sermon at court for Elizabeth and her ministers and courtiers. Shortly thereafter he preached substantially the same message again at Paul's Cross. Clearly, the new bishop of Salisbury was to be the official spokesman for the Church of England during its early anti-Roman phase, as surely as Hooker, later, would be its spokesman for the ages.

In 1561, Jewell fired another and more pointed salvo toward Harding in the *Epistola, or Letter of a Certain Englishman in which is asserted the consensus of true religion, doctrine, and ceremonies in England . . .* In the following year he wrote, or was the principal author of, *The Apology for the Church of England*, and in 1565 he wrote his *Defense of the Apology*. These three works, sponsored by Elizabeth's chief minister, Lord Burghley, became the official theological and scriptural defences of Church doctrine and practice and were regarded, much as Hooker's works would be later, as manuals for instruction to be kept and read in all cathedrals and colleges of the realm. Jewel's *Apology* was immediately regarded as a definitive statement of Church belief and practice. It was placed in every parish and hailed by Calvinists and Lutherans abroad as the hallmark document of English Protestantism.[16]

In his writings against Harding, Jewel relied on Holy Scripture, as well as citations from early Church Fathers and selected philosophers. His arguments against Rome, like Hooker's later polemic against Geneva, were steeped in the humanist traditions of Corpus Christi College, although Jewel depended somewhat more for his authority on Scripture and Hooker somewhat more on church history and the customary practices of Englishmen. Jewel's writings dealt with a variety of theological and liturgical issues separating Catholics from English Protestants. (He was, after all, one of the authors of the official English Calvinist doctrinal canon: *The Thirty-nine Articles*). A major thrust of Jewel's effort was to try to prove by close interpretation of the Bible and citations of the writings of early Church Fathers that the pope was not the legitimate head of the universal Church.

Like John Calvin and his own mentor, Peter Martyr, Jewel saw the prince as God's agent for preserving order on earth and held that he could be resisted when he was tyrannical or anti-Christian, but only in a passive way. Outwardly, full obedience was owed, even to a tyrannical ruler. In expressing this view, Jewel was vindicating his own behaviour in changing his outward obedience to fit changing royal requirements for the Church, while, as he would have it, remaining true inwardly to his basic convictions.

Toward the end of the century, Richard Hooker was to address the same problem in a different guise. This time the issue of disobedience to the monarch was raised by the writings and actions of radical

Puritans and separatists who had become nearly as outspoken as the Catholics had been earlier. Puritans such as Thomas Cartwright would assert, to Hooker's consternation, that obedience to the queen was limited by her obedience to God's Word, which would be interpreted, of course, by the Puritan clergy. In the last analysis, Cartwright wrote, princes are "servants of the church" and must "submit their sceptres" and "throw down their crowns before the church," and "lick the dust at the feet of the church."[17]

Nowhere was Jewel's own loyalty to his prince more evident than in the vestiarian controversy of the mid-1560s. Like the Puritans, he was a staunch opponent of clerics being required to wear the surplice, viewing this adornment as a papist trapping. Nevertheless, since the queen required all her minsters to wear this symbol of office, no doubt because she saw it as a symbol of her own authority over the Church, he vigorously enforced the queen's injunction. His fixed point was loyalty to the crown, even when he disagreed with the queen's orders for the Church. Like his friend John Hooker he was a pragmatist who learned early on that the surest guarantor of his survival—and the survival of a reformed Church of England—was loyalty to the monarch. Also, again like John Hooker, Bishop Jewel understood that he had to play the game of politics to accomplish his ends. Neutrality was rarely an option for an ambitious man in an age that seemed to require the public ideological commitment of choosing sides and then perhaps changing them more than once in a lifetime.

In the final analysis, John Jewel was far more than an influential scholar and cleric who had the political touch to work his way into positions of power and influence in the Elizabethan Church. The John Jewel known to his contemporaries, including, briefly, young Richard Hooker, was a kind, generous, likeable, physically frail man, whose days were filled not only with continuous scholarship, writing, and speaking on behalf of the Church, but also with an exhausting work schedule.[18]

Unlike many of his colleagues, Jewel was not an absentee bishop. He was resident at Salisbury, preaching regularly and working tirelessly to strengthen the performance of the clergy and to reform the worship life at the cathedral and throughout his diocese. He was especially committed to improving the quality of the clergy through better education. To that end, he assisted promising young men like Richard Hooker to find their way to Oxford before ordination.

John Jewel died in the midst of his pastoral rounds on 23 September 1571, at the age of fifty. His legacy to the Church of England is noteworthy. He built the cathedral library at Salisbury, using his own money. This was a fitting reminder of his commitment to the relationship between sound scholarship and Christian faith. He worked tirelessly to improve the performance of the parish clergy, a fitting reminder that the true work of reformation begins and ends at home in the parish church and not in the great halls of civic and religious power. Jewel sought power and influence not for himself but for the Church, a fitting reminder that the Church must live in the world and assert its rights in the midst of an often hostile secular environment. Seen with historical perspective, Jewel was second in importance, in the sixteenth century, only to Cranmer, Hooker, and perhaps Whitgift among the founders of what was later to be called Anglicanism. That he was of such importance was recognized by Hooker himself in one of his rare extant references to any person who had been a part of his own life. He said of his first patron and supporter that bishop Jewel was "the worthiest Divine that Christendom hath bred for the space of some hundreds of years."[19]

NOTES

1. I confess a preference for this traditional view of Elizabeth's influence over "her" age and for the traditional use of the words "Renaissance" and "Reformation," though I am aware of revisionist thinking that casts the queen in a lesser and more indecisive role and deconstructs such potentially obfuscating concepts as "Elizabethan Age," "Renaissance," and "Reformation."
2. Descriptions of the history of these local grammar schools are found in H. Lloyd Parry, *The Founding of Exeter School* (Exeter: James G. Commin, 1913) and MacCaffrey, op. cit. For details about grammar schools in general, see Nicholas Orme, *Education in the West of England 1066-1548* (Exeter: University of Exeter Press, 1976), 2-32, 42-55; Muriel St Clare Byrne, *Elizabethan Life in Town and Country* (Gloucester: Alan Sutton, 1987), 178-95, first published by Methuen & Co., Ltd, 1925; A. H. Dodd, *Life in Elizabethan England* (London: B. T. Batsford, Ltd, 1961), 266-8; Mary Cathcart Borer, *The People of Tudor England* (London: Max Parrish and Co., Ltd., 1966)102-9. For reference to Mr. Williams as headmaster see Francis Paget, *An Introduction to the Fifth Book of the Laws of Ecclesiastical Polity* (Oxford: Clarendon Press, 1899), 79, n. 3.
3. Walton, *Life*, 7.
4. Byrne, 188.
5. Nicholas Carlisle, *A Concise Description of the Endowed Grammar Schools in England and Wales* (London: Baldwin, Cradock & Joy, 1818), 266-7.
6. Parry, 15-18.
7. *Ibid.*, 11-12.
8. Harte, *Hooker's Commonplace Book* , 8; Parry, 13-14; MacCaffrey, 120.
9. For this and other details of Jewel's life and thought, see Anthony Wood, *Athenae Oxoniensis,* (1691-1692), ed. by Philip Bliss (London, 1813), I, 389-96. Jewel's modern biographer is John E. Booty, *John Jewel as Apologist for the Church of England* (London: SPCK, 1963). Also useful is Charles Webb Le Bas, *The Life of Bishop Jewel* (London: J. G. & F. Rivington, 1835).
10. Walton, *Life*, 10-11.
11. According to Thomas Fuller, Jewel was expelled from Corpus Christi during Queen Mary's reign for refusing to attend Mass in the college chapel. See Fuller, *Church History*, II: 378. Letters from Jewel to Peter Martyr in April, 1559 and June 1560, in *Zurich Letters*, Hastings Robinson, ed. (Cambridge: Parker Society, 1845), I: 77, 81.
12. Letter from Jewel to Martyr, April 6, 1559 in *Zurich Letters*, I: 16, 23.
13. The term 'Puritan' first gained currency in about 1567 as part of the vestiarian controversy. Archbishop Whitgift and other church leaders used it later on to describe those who resisted their efforts to maintain conformity to the *Book of*

Common Prayer and the authority of bishops. The term has been both avoided and embraced by students of the English Reformation. Shakespeare exemplified the derisive character of the word, already prevalent in Hooker's day, in *Twelfth Night*, Act II, scene 3, when he had a Puritan challenged with: "Doth thou think because thou art virtuous there shall be no more cakes and ale?"

In the seventeenth century Thomas Fuller regarded the term as already too much abused to be helpful (*Church History*, 474.). C. M. Dent, *Protestant Reformers in Elizabethan Oxford* (Oxford: Oxford University Press, 1983), 2-3, cautions against the term as too pejorative and prefers the phrase "militant protestant reformer." Patrick Collinson uses the term to apply to those particular Calvinist Protestants who opposed the established Anglican Church polity. Collinson, in fact, specifically defines the word (in part) in terms of those who opposed Hooker. See his *The Elizabethan Puritan Movement* (London: Methuen, 1967), 22. I have usually followed Collinson's usage and that of others who apply the term to those more advanced Calvinists who worked within the already reformed Calvinist Church of England to affect further changes in liturgical practice and church polity. See especially, Collinson, *The Religion of Protestants, the Church in English Society 1559-1625* (Oxford: Clarendon Press, 1982); William P. Haugaard, *Elizabeth and the English Reformation* (Cambridge: Cambridge University Press, 1968), 50-1, 53, 228, 258, 339-41; M. M. Knappen, *Tudor Puritanism* (Chicago: University of Chicago Press, 1939); Horton Davies, *Worship and Theology in England from Cranmer to Hooker 1534-1601* (Princeton: Princeton University Press, 1970). Paget, *op. cit.*, 10-13, believes that despite its pejorative connotations, the term "Puritan" is the best word available. His discussion of uses of the word by Thomas Cartwright and Walter Travers is especially useful. I sometimes use the terms "advanced" or "extreme" Calvinist and "Puritan" interchangeably, but only where the context and qualifying adjectives make it clear that I am not referring either to moderate Anglicans or separatists.

14. For these later controversies and a discussion of Browne and Barrow see *infra*, chapter 15.

15. Booty, 29.

16. For an excellent discussion of Jewel's role as theological spokesman for the early phase of the English Reformation see Haugaard, *op. cit.*, 242-5. Harding and his fellow Catholic émigrés were especially angered by the "Challenge Sermon" and *The Apology*. They responded quickly to these works. Of those responding to him, Jewel singled out Harding as the opponent he wished most to engage. In 1564, Harding had written his *Answer to Master Jewel's Challenge*. Jewel responded in 1565 with *A Reply to Mr. Harding's Answer* which was widely distributed at the queen's command. Then came Harding's, *A Reply to Mr. Jewel's Reply* and, following Harding's attack on Jewel's 1562 *Apology*, the latter's massive *Defense of the Apology* in 1567.

17. In citing this quotation from Matthew Parker, *Correspondence* III, 189 (Cambridge: The Parker Society), 1853, Booty, *op. cit.* 201-2, feels that Jewel secretly supported Cartwright's thinking on this matter. If Booty is correct, and I believe that a careful reading of Jewel's correspondence and writings bears out this opinion, then the contrast between Jewel as an advanced Calvinist and Hooker as a moderate one is manifest. Hooker would have had difficulty defending Jewel's position on this issue. Jewel, in fact, had defied Queen Elizabeth's order in the 1560s that crosses and candles be placed on all altars. He had them destroyed and "everywhere broken into pieces" within his diocese and confided to Peter Martyr that this action could cost him his bishopric. *op. cit,* I: 67-8.

18. Anthony Wood, *Athenae Oxonienses, An Exact History of all the Writers and Bishops Who Have Had Their Education in the University of Oxford* (1691-92). ed. by V. I. Philip Bliss. London, 1813, 359.

19. *Folger*, I: 171; *Works*, I: 313-314.

CHAPTER 4

Leaving the Nest

THE ROAD TO OXFORD

In late 1569, at about the time his father was under siege by the troops of Lord Butler at Leighlin Bridge in Ireland, young Richard Hooker was making his way along the old road from Exeter to Sherborne in Dorset, perhaps on a good horse from his uncle's stable.[1] It was the first leg of his long journey to Oxford. Road travel was dangerous. Ever since the monasteries were dissolved back in the 1530s, the roads had been filled with "rufflers." These out-of-work beggars and thieves had once been supported by the monks but now they roamed freely, menacing decent folk. Add to them the roving bands of former soldiers and sailors who had been mustered out with their ragged "uniforms" and little else—rogues who lived now in the forests along the side of the road, coming out at night to prey on travellers. These assorted "footpads" and "high lawyers" were tipped off about good "marks" such as Richard by the ostlers in the stables at roadside inns. The "morts" and "dells" who may have approached him with their offers of adult entertainment—off in the bushes alongside the road right now, or an hour or so later at a nearby inn—were usually unfortunate women, unmarried or abandoned by their husbands. They sold their favours for a few pence, some scraps of food, or a bit of clothing. Some of them, the boy could tell, were true "doxies"—professional whores who enticed for their pimps, "king-of-the-road" rogues. These so-called "upright men" waited at the nearest inn to fleece the latest unsuspecting traveller seduced by their doxies.[2]

The town of Oxford Richard finally reached was not much smaller in population than his native Exeter. But it had a very different tone and texture from his home town. This was a university town, and like all such places before and since, its character was marked, if not dominated, by the needs, serious and frivolous, of those demanding, annoying, and talented prima donnas who inhabit places of higher learning. To be sure, there was an Oxford town before there was an Oxford University; it had been a residence of kings and the setting for important political events; its site on roads and river arteries had assured the town an important place in the history of the nation. Even in the late Middle Ages the town retained a significance in its own right, apart from its growing importance as the seat of one of the two major institutions of English intellectual life.[3]

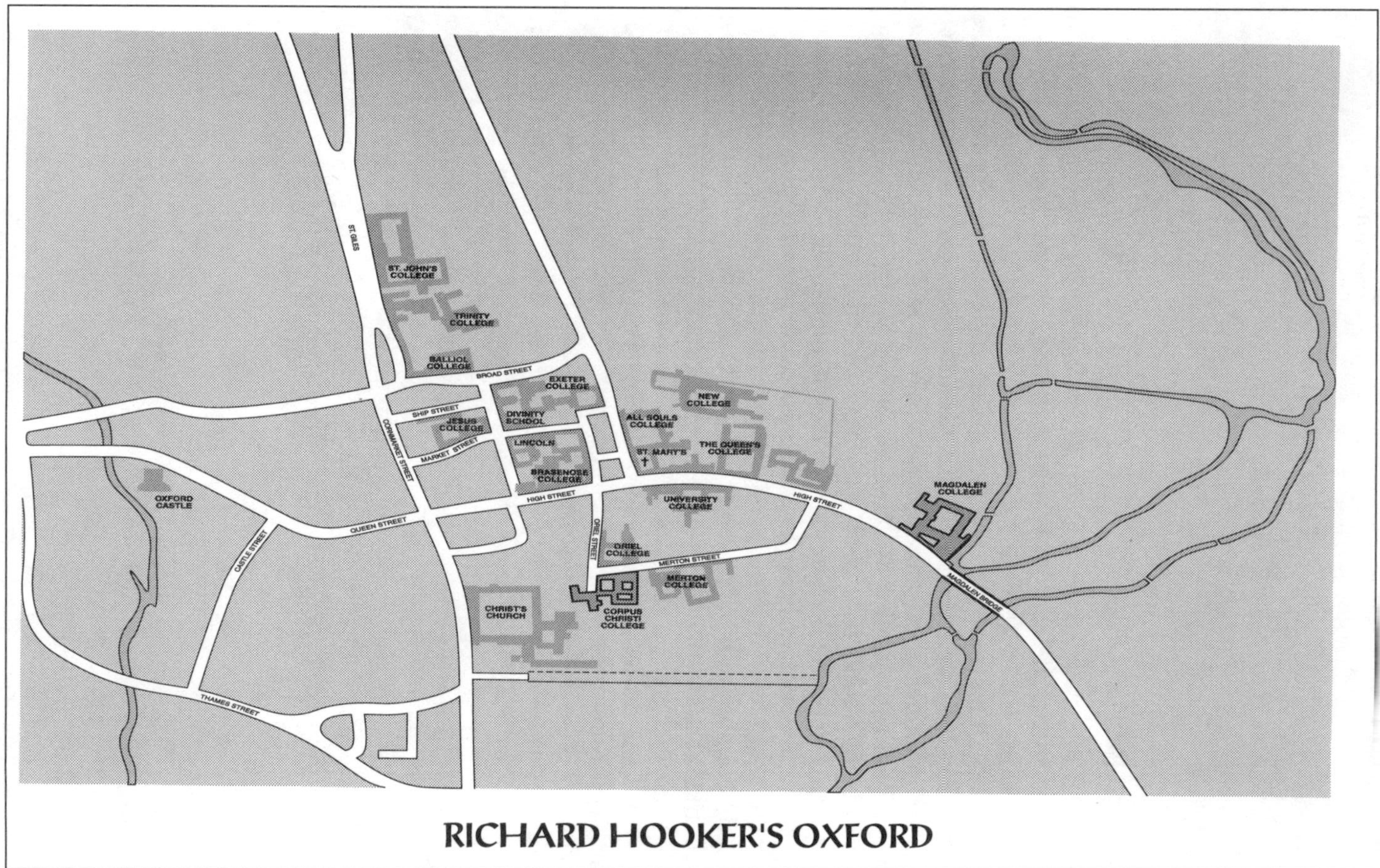

RICHARD HOOKER'S OXFORD

By the time Hooker arrived in 1569 most of Oxford's six thousand residents were actively engaged in supplying goods and services to the colleges. Amidst the impressive academic buildings and tall church steeples there was a working town alive with the sounds and smells of brewers, bakers, butchers, weavers, fishmongers, prostitutes, taverns, haberdashers, masons, carpenters.

Like any student walking the streets of a college town then or now, young Hooker would have observed, in addition to the artisans and shopkeepers, men hurrying about the streets with an air of purpose and dispatch. Later he would learn that these were the so-called "privileged persons" who served as direct suppliers of professional talent and goods and services to the colleges. Principal among them were the provisioners ("manciples") who provided food and other necessaries and the master building contractors. There were also the college stewards, cooks, bailiffs, barber/surgeons, accountants, property managers, rent collectors, and similar persons of professional and administrative skill. These men were usually citizens of the town working at one of the university colleges.

Large college buildings lined the streets and alleys, one after another. In Exeter, the dominant buildings, apart from the churches, had been places of commerce and civic power: Guild Hall, Tucker Hall, Bedford House, the palace. But here the architecture proclaimed learning and study. All along the High Street was a superfluity of impressive collegiate halls: Lincoln, Brasenose, All Souls and, at the end of the street, the magnificent Magdalen College, exemplifying the ornate architectural style of Edward IV's mid-fifteenth-century reign. On the parallel Broad Street were the recently-renovated university buildings: library, law school, and school of theology. Most important, for Hooker, was Corpus Christi College, located on narrow Merton Street, just a short alley below the High Street, next door to fourteenth-century Oriel College.

These great halls of Oxford exuded a dynamic and unsettled spirit charged with the excitement of rapid change and filled with the promise of new ways of living and thinking. This was the Oxford Richard would come to know and draw inspiration from—a centre of learning, teaching, public disputation, writing, and preaching where powerful intellectual and spiritual forces conflicted. The complex, confusing, and sometimes dangerous cross-currents permeating Oxbridge for two centuries we call the "Renaissance" and the "Reformation"—a misleading shorthand for the complicated and intertwined events that historians have often described as "movements" shaping the "modern" era.

Ever since the middle of the fifteenth century English scholars had studied in the Italian scholastic centres at Florence and Venice and then returned to Oxford and Cambridge to spread the new humanism, with its emphasis on Greek and Roman classical language, literature, and philosophy. Such men as William Grocyn, Thomas Linacre, John Colet, and Richard Fox, founder of Corpus Christi College, were the intellectual progenitors of modern Oxford. Their humanistic perspectives represented a major threat to the medieval metaphysical orientation of the academic status quo. These scholars were to be followed by the giants of the English Reformation who came to the universities in the sixteenth century and taught a threatening radical individualism in religion, men such as Peter (Vermigli) Martyr, John Rainolds (Hooker's mentor) at Oxford; William Tyndale, Martin Bucer, and Thomas Cartwright at Cambridge.

To be sure, there had been a temporary setback for these new Protestant emphases at Oxbridge during Queen Mary's reign from 1553 to 1558. Cardinal Pole was installed as chancellor at Oxford. A cohort of Catholic medievalists, mainly Spanish clerics, replaced the Protestants at the universities. The grisly burning to death of the three most famous martyrs of the English Reformation: Bishops Latimer and Ridley and the aged Archbishop Cranmer, in front of Balliol College in 1555 and 1556, brought the agony and danger of this revolutionary age close to home for a generation of Oxford students and fellows. (It was significant that the trial and execution of these prominent Protestants—all Cambridge men—took place not at Cambridge, the university with the more advanced reform tendencies, but at Oxford, where the more conservative climate was less likely to spark disruption over the executions.)

In the generation before Hooker's arrival, Oxford had shown both Protestant and Catholic tendencies, whereas Cambridge had become predominantly Calvinist. There were strong Catholic elements among the fellows at New College, Corpus Christi, Trinity, and St Johns on to the end of the sixteenth century and beyond. In June of 1551, for example, during the heat of Reformation fervour in England, the president of Corpus Christi, Robert Morewent, and two college fellows were imprisoned in the Fleet for continuing to use the traditional Catholic service in the college chapel.[4]

When Queen Mary died and Queen Elizabeth ascended the throne the church bells of Oxford tolled in jubilation. The curriculum increasingly reflected the more humanistic emphases of the Renaissance. The enclosed and self-sufficient secular colleges replaced the medieval religious halls. Education for undergraduates steadily supplanted graduate studies as the major emphasis. In sum, the Reformation and the Renaissance, in somewhat cautious and conservative forms, had returned to Oxford in plenty of time to greet the arrival of Richard Hooker in 1569.[5]

CORPUS CHRISTI COLLEGE

Richard passed through the fortress-like gate tower rising several stories above the crenellated roof line of Corpus Christi College and entered an entirely new world. He carried with him the name of a important Devon family, the blessing and patronage of one of England's most distinguished church leaders, and his own considerable intellectual potential. What he lacked was the close family support, emotional and financial, which would have given him the self-confidence and economic security enjoyed by many of his classmates.

The college gatehouse, with its splendid oriel and fan-vaulted roof, gave him his first glimpse of the quad. But before entering the enclosure, he found the stairs leading up to President Cole's office in the gate tower. He climbed those stairs toward his future, tightly gripping Bishop Jewel's letter of introduction.

There was no minimum age for admission of students; the maximum age was nineteen. So at fifteen he was all right. He intended to complete his B.A. degree in four or five years and then proceed to the M.A. and, perhaps, a doctorate. He planned to seek ordination and a career in the Church. All of this was in line with the college's goals for its students. What may have worried Richard was the adequacy of his preparation in grammar and composition to qualify him for admission as a degree candidate.

He would have had another worry as well, one quite typical for many students in his day and ours—money. He may have been reluctant to express his apprehension out loud for fear of jeopardizing his chance of admission. Richard knew that there was a program of pre-B.A. studies at Corpus Christi designed for younger boys, called "clerks" and "choristers." These students received a small subsistence allowance while they took an advanced grammar-school course at the college or at Magdalen until they were deemed ready to begin regular college studies. This might be the lowly status at which he would have to begin.[6]

President Cole had just completed his first year at Corpus Christi. The queen herself had had to force the fellows to accept him as their head. They were a conservative lot, with strong Catholic sympathies he had not expected. The fellows had gone so far as to defy the queen by electing the papist sympathizer Robert Harrison as their president. The queen had sent for the college Visitor, Bishop Horne of Winchester, who had the authority to force Cole's installation as president.[7] Later that year the queen's favourite, Robert Dudley, Earl of Leicester, had come to the college in his role as university chancellor, examined all the fellows, and dismissed some of them as "romanists." The exodus of college fellows to the Roman Catholic colleges at Louvain, Douai, and Rheims had begun.

An immediate problem faced William Cole with Richard's arrival. He had no openings available for a regular student from Exeter at this time. Only twenty B.A. candidates could be in residence, twenty-seven at most. There was a quota for each of the dioceses and counties named in the statutes of the founder, Bishop Fox: five from Winchester; two each from Exeter, Bath and Wells, Lincoln (Fox's birthplace),

Gloucester, and Kent; one each from Durham, Lancaster (co-founder Bishop Hugh Oldham's birthplace), Wiltshire, Bedford, Oxford; and seven from other counties where the college owned property. Even if the boy in front of him were to pass the qualifying tests, Cole could not admit him officially as a degree candidate because there was simply no opening for Devon at this time.

Even after Richard had completed his degree requirements, four years later, when the college wished to name Hooker a "disciple," an honour reserved for gifted students, it had to use an opening available from Hampshire. Even at that, Hooker was by then over the sacrosanct nineteen-year age limit for matriculation. The only exception to this rule was for older students coming from outside the university who had the special permission of the president. To qualify for that exception, it is likely that Hooker had to withdraw from the university in late 1573, when he had completed his degree requirements, so that he could be re-admitted, probably on Christmas Eve 1573, just a few months short of his twentieth birthday. Almost immediately upon re-admission, he was made a disciple and awarded his B.A. degree. Thus, one of Oxford's most illustrious graduates and one of England's greatest intellectual figures almost failed to get his undergraduate degree.[8]

President Cole had another problem facing him as he considered the qualifications of the fifteen-year-old prospective student. Here was a boy, well-recommended and probably qualified for admission, but without the means to cover the cost of a B.A. degree. This amount could run anywhere from £50 to £100 over the thirteen-term (four-year) period. Although not completely without resources—Corpus rarely admitted the destitute—this boy was clearly not one of that new breed of wealthy full-paying students (commoners) who brought needed revenues with them as they entered their college.

Cole decided to resolve Richard's financial-aid problem by registering him either as a chorister or a clerk. In that way he could admit him on a probationary basis and give him a chorister's clothing allowance. Richard could then study alongside the regular scholars as soon as his tutor stipulated that he was doing well enough in composition and grammar. The college would provide room, board, livery, and a small stipend of one mark (13s 4d) for spending money until Richard finished his B.A. degree, just as it did for the regular scholars. In the meantime, probably on the strength of Bishop Jewel's recommendation, Cole decided he would apply for a Nowell grant for the boy. His friend Alexander Nowell, Dean of St Paul's, administered his (Alexander's) brother Robert's trust fund to support "poor" boys such as Richard. Cole and Nowell, both ardent admirers of John Calvin, had been friends together in exile abroad during Mary Tudor's reign. He would apply to his friend for twenty shillings from the Nowell Trust for Richard's first year at college.[9]

Put in late-twentieth-century terms, the young Richard Hooker sitting in Cole's office in the gate house at Corpus Christi College on that autumn afternoon in 1569, was a rather poor, although not impoverished, boy of promise from the provinces, whose wealthy relatives (and their friends) were using their influence to gain him admission to a good college on a small scholarship. His existence as a student would always be precarious, requiring outstanding academic performance to maintain and secure financial aid from as many sources as possible. He would become what educators in a later century would term an "over-achiever" in order to prove himself worthy to his professors and to the college's "financial aid office," which arranged his package of grants, gifts, work assignments, and loans. His immediate family, as we have seen, gave him little support either financially or emotionally. At a young age, he was largely on his own.

The college quadrangle the young Hooker now entered would become the physical and emotional matrix of his life for the next fifteen years and his intellectual fulcrum until he died in 1600. He was one of those persons who was to find a home at college, whose psyche would be formed primarily by the cloistered academic environment, and who would discover in great literary figures, living and dead, and in fellow-students and scholars the personal relationships and emotional support he often found lacking elsewhere. The comforting enclosure of this monastic-like quadrangle, secure and protected behind the great gate tower and surrounded on all sides by an unbroken inward-facing wall of college buildings, would have been immediately reassuring to him. A young man who had not known the security of a stable family might well hope that here at last was a safe haven. Nor would Hooker's reaction to Corpus Christi College have been unique. The college had been intentionally designed, both architecturally and academically, to create just the effect it was having on him.[10]

It had been founded in 1516 by Richard Fox, bishop of Winchester, with substantial help from his friend, Bishop Oldham of Exeter. Fox was a leading advocate of the new "Renaissance" learning who had studied at both Oxford and Cambridge and held a doctorate in canon law from the university of Paris. At various times in his career he was the bishop of Exeter, Bath, Wells, and Durham, and he was later named Lord Privy Seal. When Henry VIII became king in 1509, only Cardinal Wolsey outranked Fox in power at court.

Bishop Oldham urged Bishop Fox, who had originally intended to found a monastic college for Benedictines at Winchester, to build instead a college that would break the medieval mould and embody the new learning, an educational environment where students would study a more practical (humanistic) curriculum designed to produce an educated clergy. Instead of living in separate halls in town, attending lectures, and then studying in the traditional state of lonely and impoverished isolation, students should reside and study inside college walls where they could have close interaction with one another and their teachers. A free-standing school was envisioned with its own curriculum, faculty, dormitories, library, chapel, and professorial quarters. Bishop Oldham is reported to have said to Fox: "Shall we build houses and provide livelihoods for a company of buzzing monks, whose end and fall we may ourselves live to see? No, it is more meet and a great deal better that we should have care to provide for the increase of learning for such as by their learning shall do good in the church and the Commonwealth."[11] Oldham was as good as his word. He endowed the new foundation with a handsome gift of six thousand marks (£4,000). He had been planning to make a large donation to Exeter College, the traditional beneficiary of the see of Exeter. But he was piqued by a personal affront from college authorities to a friend named Aiken, and so gave his gift to Fox's new venture instead.[12]

Not only did Fox design a college that in its innovative physical layout would invite close interaction between students and their teachers, but he also inaugurated a revised curriculum and a new pedagogy that extended and expanded the radically different style of learning that had been started earlier, in a small way, at Magdalen College. He used the happy metaphor of the "bee garden" to describe the learning environment that he envisioned for Corpus Christi. He referred to his ideal as "a certain bee garden, which we have named the College of Corpus Christi, wherein scholars like ingenious bees are day and night to make wax to the honour of God . . ."

In Fox's garden, the principal "herbalist," was the professor of arts and humanities, who taught Cicero, Horace, Virgil, Pliny, Ovid, Juvenal. The second herbalist was the professor of Greek, who would lecture not only within the college but to the entire university. His task was to introduce the young student "plants" to the ideas of Homer, Aesop, Hesiod, Demosthenes, and, of course, Aristotle and Plato. So important was the study of Greek language and literature in Fox's educational scheme that he established at Corpus Christi Oxford's first endowed professorship in Greek, a complement to his two other endowed professorships in humanities and theology. The "bees" who buzzed about Fox's academic garden carrying life-giving pollen from plant to plant were chosen from among the college fellows. They were called "tutors" and they represented the most important and radical innovation of all. Their task was to assure, by the closest possible interaction with students, the healthy development of the precious seedlings entrusted to their care.[13]

Within a few years Richard Hooker himself would be among the most effective "bees" in Bishop's Fox's collegiate garden, serving as tutor to the grandnephew of the martyred Archbishop Cranmer and the son of no less a personage than Edwin Sandys, archbishop of York. That powerful Elizabethan cleric and his amazing son were each in their turn to have a defining impact on Richard's life and career. But

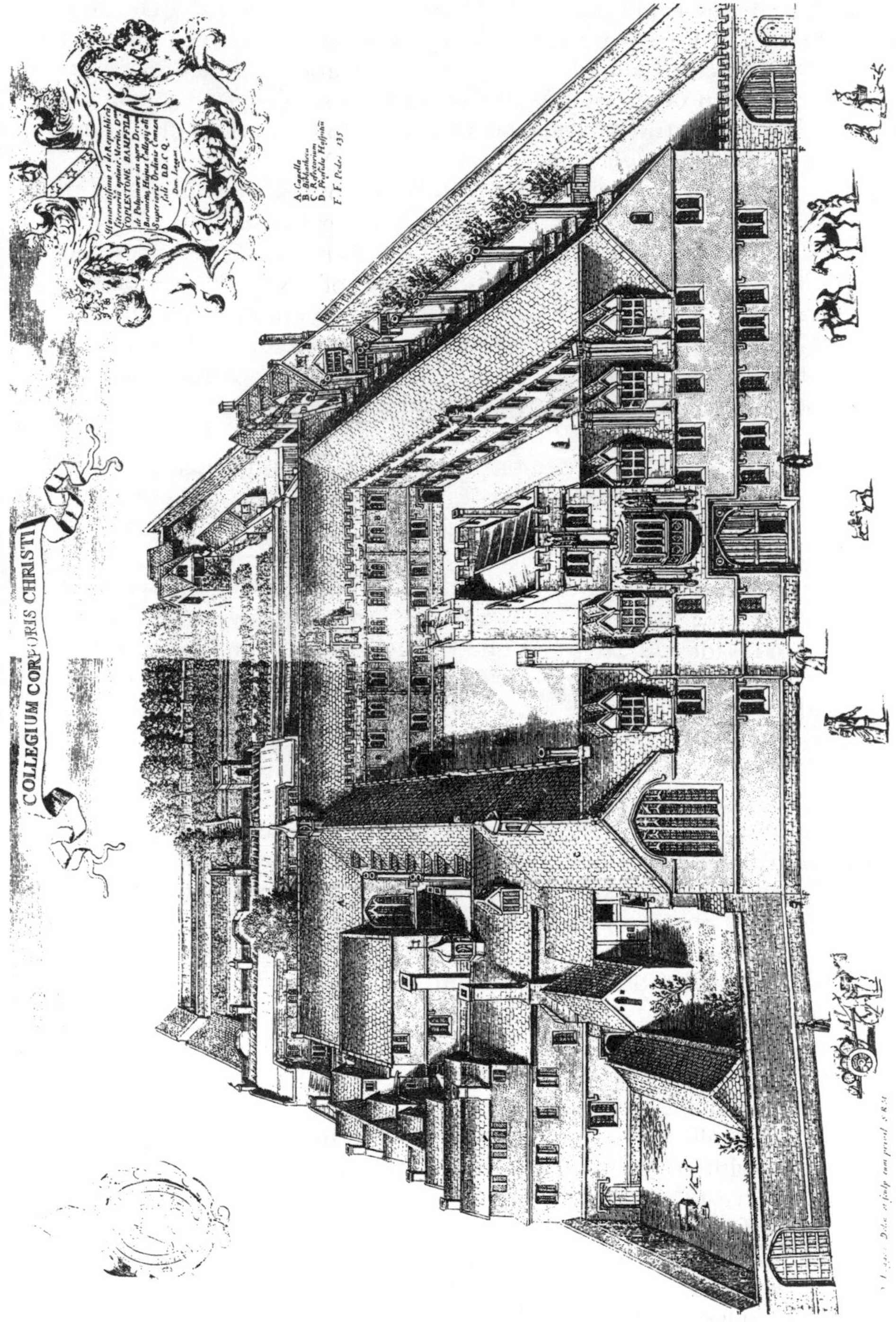

Corpus Christi, Oxford

Loggan's Plan of the College in 1675

today he was looking anxiously for his own tutor, a young man only four years older than himself who had just completed his B.A. degree. His name was John Rainolds. Like John Jewel before him and Richard Hooker after him, he had made the journey up from Devon to be pollinated in Richard Fox's bee garden and then, in turn, had become one of Fox's most prolific bees.

John Rainolds, although not yet twenty, was already one of the most prominent figures at Oxford when Richard Hooker first knocked on his door in the fall of 1569. In securing the precocious and irrepressible Rainolds as Hooker's tutor, Bishop Jewel knew what he was doing. Rainolds had already made a name for himself, not only for his abilities as a scholar and public speaker in the oral disputations that were part of the academic requirements, but also as a thespian. In 1556 he had performed a female role in a play called *Palamon and Arcite*, derived from Chaucer's *The Knight's Tale*, which was performed before the queen. Life at Oxford and Cambridge was regularly enlivened during Elizabeth's reign by such dramatic productions, although stodgy Oxford was less prone than Cambridge to allow the more modern and increasingly popular vernacular plays.

Later in his career, when Rainolds had become a more zealous Puritan, he tangled with the dramatist William Gager concerning morality plays. Rainolds condemned much of contemporary drama and especially the practice of female impersonation. Not surprisingly, his youthful indiscretion was remembered and thrown back in his face. By this time, he had become such a notable Puritan that the queen herself admonished him, in 1592, for what she called his "obstinate preciseness."[14]

By the time Hooker met Rainolds, the tutor's undergraduate high spirits were behind him and he was well on his way to becoming one of Oxford's leading scholars and public figures. Within a few years, he was appointed to the most prestigious faculty post at Corpus, reader in Greek. Four years later, when he presented Richard for a B.A. degree, Rainolds was one of the college's leading orators, debaters, and most outspoken proponents of the Puritan Reformation. He was hard-working and hard-driving—a scholar and a voluminous author.

Rainolds' impact on Hooker cannot be exaggerated. Richard's Protestant theology, although never so rigidly Calvinist as Rainolds', owes much to the influence of his tutor. Under Rainolds' direction, Hooker studied Greek language and literature and—so important for the powerful and persuasive style of his later writings—classical rhetoric. His close familiarity with the great religious reform theologians of the day also owed much to his tutor.

Before his career was over, Rainolds would be Oxford's leading Protestant radical, a key figure along with Hooker's cousin by marriage, Walter Travers, and others, in the important Oxford Presbyterian Conference of 1587. In 1599 he was elected president of Corpus

Christi, and a few years later was the principal initiator of the so-called King James version of the Bible, a project that probably originated in his rooms at Corpus Christi. He would also be a Puritan representative at the important Hampton Court Conference, convened by King James I in 1604, and one of the most widely read and heard Puritan writers and speakers of the day. Oxford might be generally conservative on religious issues compared to Cambridge, and Corpus Christi especially so, but Rainolds was one of the university's few flaming Calvinist radicals.

Rainolds, who made a formidable impression upon his peers, would have seemed an almost overpowering figure to the boy from Exeter. His piercing dark eyes were set in a long thin face that extended from a high forehead down to a short sharply pointed beard, and gave quick evidence that here was a high-strung and brilliant young man who did not suffer fools easily. Hooker would learn soon enough that his tutor was a scholar and teacher nonpareil, a man of immense erudition and massive resources of memory, with an eye for detail and a disposition of high seriousness.[15]

One of Rainolds' first concerns would have been to ascertain if his new charge was ready to begin studying for his degree in the present term. Richard might need remedial work in grammar and composition before he could begin with logic. Rainolds was aware that Hooker's school at Exeter had only a fair reputation. It was no St Paul's or Merchant Taylors'. As soon as Richard was fully qualified in grammar, Rainolds would see to it that he got a spending allowance. In the meantime, Richard's room and meals would be underwritten by the college. Extra money for his support could be had by drawing on the college loan chest. There would probably be at least 100 marks in there at the beginning of the school year. He could borrow from the chest on behalf of Richard and there would be a full year before repayment was due.[16]

In the event, Richard probably roomed for a time with his tutor. Corpus was crowded. As many as twenty-five scholars, about twenty rich commoners and as many as ten younger clerks and choristers like Hooker competed for limited space. Rainolds probably had the larger of two beds, the one nearest the hearth, while assigning Richard a smaller one farther from the fire. Life would be more comfortable for Richard here in this upper floor room with his tutor. It might be draughty and cold in winter, but the small hearth would be some relief. They would not have to endure the awful dampness of the rooms below where there was only a dirt floor and no heat at all. Additionally, Corpus was not so crowded as most of the other colleges where a room this size would have to do for four students, not two or possibly three. Richard would be expected to clean their quarters thoroughly every day. There were no servants to perform this service at Corpus and so the younger students would do the work, just as their tutors and the other fellows had done before them.

There was a long list of the college rules governing most aspects of student life. They had to rise in time for 5 a.m. Matins in the chapel every morning and must never, ever, miss chapel. The penalties for unexcused absence were severe. Required logic classes would start promptly at 6 a.m. Rainolds would give Richard regular and mandatory written and oral examinations on his studies, but he would have to walk over to Magdalen for more preparatory work in grammar and composition. He must, though, never walk out of the college gate to go to Magdalen or anywhere else alone. He must always go with one or more fellow-students. If he disobeyed this, or any other rule, whoever discovered him in the transgression was obliged to report the infraction at the annual Holy Week assembly where all the delations (accusations) were presented. Stiff punishments were administered within two weeks of that assembly.

It was in fact easy to slip in and out of the gate and go into town on one's own. Many of the commoners (rich boys) did just that. They loved to go whoring, drinking, and carousing. Many of them got away with it. In some of the other colleges they even assaulted the college officials who attempted to discipline them. But if any regular Corpus students were caught outside the college on their own they would be in serious trouble. (In a letter written later in life, Rainolds recalled his moral and social prescriptions for Oxford students. He specifically forbade drinking, pleasures of the flesh, card-playing, dancing, football—"a beastly fury"—or lewdness, or any dramatic productions that displayed the foregoing vices, or lovemaking, or violence. Here was a man worthy of the name "Puritan.")[17]

Once he was a scholar (fully matriculated undergraduate), Hooker would attend lectures almost every morning from eight until eleven. Some of the university-wide lectures in Greek, humanity, Hebrew, Latin, and theology were given by Corpus fellows. The lectures in Greek and humanity would introduce him to the important classical philosophers, poets, historians, rhetoricians, and grammarians. Later on, when Richard had his M.A., he would attend afternoon theology lectures on the Old and New Testaments and on the Church Fathers. Many of the lectures would be given in the college hall at Corpus. The humanity lecture was at 8 a.m. every day except Sunday at Magdalen.

Corpus Christi was stricter about class and lecture attendance, participating in disputations, and taking examinations than most of the other colleges. But it was not quite as strict as it had been. Back in Bishop Jewel's day students had to rise at 4 a.m. and missing a lecture or a disputation could mean a loss of meals and a public whipping. Those were harsh days. The health of many a student was wrecked, including, quite possibly, that of the good bishop himself. Nevertheless, Jewel thought Corpus had lost much of its academic and moral discipline in recent years—to such a degree that he worried about the college's loss of quality.[18]

Two meals were served each day. And Hooker would most likely have been one of those who served the meals. Although we have no evidence of the fact, it is not unlikely that Hooker's college job was to join other choristers, clerks, and probationary undergraduates working in the kitchen or dining hall in order to help pay for his expenses. The main meal was dinner at 11 a.m. Supper was at 5 p.m. The food at Corpus, Hooker would soon learn, was plentiful but not much varied and certainly not so fine as at some of the richer colleges, where fellows dined on fish, game, fowl, cream, wine, and good ales. Here, supper would usually consist of cold meats, oatmeal, pottage, bread, and cheese. Dinner might include a piece of mutton or beef at each table along with bread, cheese, butter, and beer.

Corpus Christi was a place where education and moral discipline were serious matters. It was a close-knit community that paid attention to study and was earnest about teaching and learning. They were few in number here, an intimate and well-disciplined society. Most of the teaching fellows had been undergraduates at Corpus, making for an ingrown fellowship. Each student was paired closely with a fellow who had probably once been a student here himself. The older members of the foundation monitored the behaviour, academic and social, of the younger members.[19]

There were philosophical and religious differences among the Corpus men. Some, such as Rainolds and Cole, were completely committed to a strict Calvinist position. Others were more conservative, embracing many features of the old-style religion. After all, the late Cardinal Pole had been one of the earliest graduates. So-called "papists" and "romanists"—those still professing some degree of loyalty to the church of Rome—were no longer tolerated. Their opinions were now regarded as treasonable.

The college buildings were compact and self-contained. The small unobstructed quadrangle was open to the sky but was otherwise a secure enclave surrounded by college buildings. On the west side a two-storey structure housed most of the twenty fellows and twenty regular scholars, usually two to each living chamber. On the east side of the quad was the great hall that housed the refectory and was the setting for all important college events, including the annual reading of the founder's statutes, receptions for visiting dignitaries, major college and university lectures, disciplinary hearings, graduation ceremonies, and any other function requiring a large space.[20]

On the north side of the quad were the tower, containing the entrance gate, the president's quarters, and the rest of the chambers for fellows and scholars. At the far end were the library—the crown jewel of Fox's "bee garden"—and the chapel, with its nave extending well outside the quad itself. Behind the library and chapel was another enclosure that held the president's garden and commons area. No structure marred the open space of the college quad in 1569, and recreational activities were sometimes allowed here. In earlier years of stricter Puritan governance all sporting activity had been forbidden, but Queen Elizabeth was more tolerant, and archery and tennis were allowed. (In fact, the first tennis at Oxford was played in the Corpus quad.) Within a few years, however, by the time Richard had joined his tutor on the staff, they and everyone else at the college would be subjected to a major impediment to tennis or any other sport in this space. A large statue dominating the interior of the quad was erected by one of their colleagues, Charles Trumbell. This unusual structure, just inside the gate, was to become the college landmark. It is a tall pillar with a perpetual calendar and the colourful arms of Bishops Fox and Oldham on its sides, a sundial clock near the apex, and the college emblem—a pelican—at the top. The pelican is pecking its breast for fresh blood to feed her hungry chicks, a symbol of Christ shedding his blood for his children. (There is a replica in the McCosh Quad at Princeton University.)

The security system was tight. The only gate in and out of the college was the main door in the gate tower. The president controlled the keys to this gate which was normally open from 6 a.m. to 8 p.m. In summer it would be open an hour earlier and close an hour later. Furthermore, Richard was told, he could not go into the library or the garden without keys, and only fellows had them. This meant he would need approval to leave the college, enter the library, or stroll in the garden. The library was the showplace of the college and one of the marvels of Oxford. Richard had never before seen its like. No less a person than the leading humanist of the age, Erasmus, who had had a strong impact on the college's founder and whose influence permeated the curriculum, had predicted earlier in the century that the library at Corpus Christi would become one of Oxford's leading attractions. And he was right. By Hooker's time, the college probably had the most complete classical collection at Oxford, one of the best Reformation libraries, and the finest holding of Greek manuscripts.[21]

Many of the books were not chained. This was most unusual at Oxford or anywhere else in those days. Obviously, the intent at Corpus Christi was to allow a freer circulation of books and manuscripts into the rooms of fellows so that they and their undergraduate charges might have convenient access to them at all hours of the day and night. The college founder had contributed over 150 volumes to begin the library, a princely collection in his day. The first president of the college, John Claimond, a prominent scholar lured by Fox from Magdalen, where he had been president, contributed about the same number, mostly valuable Greek and Latin texts and commentaries. Another important donor of books had been Thomas Greneway, the unpopular "papist" president with whom Rainolds had had bitter disagreements during his early student days. Greneway had resigned under fire just a year before Hooker's arrival on campus. He left behind as a gift to the college a fine collection of theology texts. In addition to the nearly four hundred volumes in the college library, many of the fellows had their own personal collections in their chambers, some of which held more than one hundred volumes. These also could be borrowed by students on good terms with the owner.[22]

The chapel, a two-storey structure located directly opposite the library, was one of the original college buildings, dating from 1517. The beloved first president of the college, John Claimond, was buried here. The striking eagle-shaped brass lectern and the beautiful altar-piece, ascribed to Rubens, may have caught Richard's eye. (They can still be seen today.)

The great college hall was the largest room in the college, wider and longer than either the library or the west building. Its beautifully carved hammerbeam six-bay roof was similar to the fan vaulting in the tower entrance. The clean whitewashed plaster walls were adorned with painted hangings, the long trestle tables were arranged neatly around the central hearth, the floor was richly carpeted, and beautiful stained-glass windows commemorated Bishop Fox, various college benefactors, and the queen.

There were rules governing behaviour in the dining hall. One of the most important was that only Greek and Latin would be spoken during the meal. English was strictly prohibited. At some point during the meal one of the fellows would read from the Bible. After the meal, there would be a short homily on the Scripture reading, usually delivered by the president or one of the fellows. Then a large ornamental two-handled silver loving cup would be passed around and all—or at least those at the head table—would share a draught of wine before everyone quietly left the hall. No loitering for conversation was allowed. Eating was not considered a social occasion at Corpus Christi.[23]

This was the college environment into which Richard Hooker took his first tentative steps—a milieu that would nurture his spirit, shape his character, and define most of his intellectual perspectives.

NOTES

1. The traditional story of Richard Hooker's journeys to and from Oxford are contained in Izaak Walton's fanciful tale of the boy's trip on a horse lent to him by Bishop Jewel. While I do not credit all of that story, I see the germ of fact in it to be Jewel's well-known generous disposition toward his fellow-men and particularly the students he helped. See Walton's *Life*, 12. R. J. Schoek is but the latest in a line of scholars stretching back to Walton who credit Jewel with a major influence on Hooker's early education. Schoek goes so far as to suggest that Jewel even arranged for Richard to attend grammar school in Exeter and "sent him back to Exeter" for that schooling. I think it unlikely that Richard lived with Jewel and was

returned to school in Exeter by the bishop. Richard's uncle John was more likely to have played the key role in all this. See R. J. Schoek, "From Erasmus to Hooker," in A. S. McGrade, ed.,*Richard Hooker and the Construction of Christian Community* (Tempe, Arizona: Medieval and Renaissance Studies and Texts, 1997), 68.

2. We are fortunate to have William Harrison's contemporary (1587) account of the distances and typical stopping places ("thoroughfares") for travel in England, including a journey from Exeter to Salisbury. Harrison estimates the trip at 67 miles with possible stopover towns of Honiton, Chard, Crewkerne, Sherborne, and Shaftesbury. *The Description of England, op. cit.* 402. Harrison also describes the inns and innkeepers of the day. 397-399. Good discussions of road travel at this time are in Jasper Ridley, *The Tudor Age* (London: Constable and Company, Ltd, 1988), 74-85; Gamini Salgado, *The Elizabethan Underworld* (Stroud: Alan Sutton Publishing Ltd, 1992), 111-21; A. H. Dodd, *Life in Elizabethan England* (London: B. T. Batsford, Ltd., 1961), 142-7.

3. The primary source used for background on Oxford, especially for the history of Corpus Christi College, during Hooker's time is James McConica, ed., *The History of the University of Oxford,* III (Oxford: Clarendon Press, 1986). This volume covers the period from the end of the Middle Ages to the end of the Tudor period. Good sources on the town of Oxford are: A. L. Rowse, *Oxford in the History of the Nation* (London: Book Club Associates, 1975), esp. 9-54; Carl I. Hammer, Jr., "Oxford Town and Oxford University," in McConica, 69-115. Other important sources include: Thomas Fowler, *The History of Corpus Christi College* (Oxford: Clarendon Press, 1893). (Fowler was president of the College in the late nineteenth century.); Cecil Headlam, *Oxford and Its History* (London: J. M. Dent & Sons, 1926); Mark Curtis, *Oxford and Cambridge in Transition* (Oxford: Clarendon Press, 1959); C. M. Dent, *op. cit.*; J. G. Milne, *The Early History of Corpus Christi College* (Oxford: Basil Blackwell, 1946); Christopher Hobhouse, *Oxford As it Was and As it is Today* (London: B. T. Batsford Ltd., 1939). The classic account of famous graduates is Wood, *op. cit.*

4. Jennifer Loach, "Reformation Controversies," in McConica, 374. For a convincing argument that, with notable exceptions, Oxford was essentially conservative and often pro-Catholic throughout the sixteenth century, see 363-96.

5. A good description of changes at Oxford during this period of transition is McConica, "The Rise of the Undergraduate College," Monica, *op. cit.*, 1-16. 8. *Ibid.*, 666; Curtis, 38-9.

6. Milne, 4-9; Fowler, 147-8.

7. Dent, 42.

8. See Corpus Christi College Archives, *Liber Admis* 1517-1647, (unnumbered folios).

9. Alexander B. Gosart, ed., *The Spending of the Money of Robert Nowell,* The Townley Hall MSS, printed for private circulation in 100 copies (Blackburn, Lancashire, 1877), esp. xiii-xxv; xxxvii-xlii; 206; 220-26; 110, 172. During the history of this trust grants were made to a wide range of people, although most went to university students. Some gifts were whimsical favours to friends, such as money sent to the headmaster of Merchant Taylors school in July 1571 to pay for the marriage of that gentleman's maid! Among the famous persons receiving Nowell grants, in addition to Hooker, were John Field, John Whitgift, Lancelot Andrewes, John Spencer, Richard Hakluyt, Thomas Bilson, and the poet Edmund Spenser. Hooker received five grants from this fund. Folio 108, p. 109 of the Townley Hall MSS records 20s. paid to "Rychard Hoocker" sometime before mid-1570. This is the "admissions" grant to which I refer. Folio 85, p. 115 records payments of ten shillings on 30 January 1571 for a "poor schooler" and 2s 6d on 12 February 1571 to "bring him to Oxford," apparently after a trip home. Folio 86, pp. 117-118 shows 3s 4d on 8 March 1573 to "Rycharde hooker" and 5s on 28 April 1573 to "fr huker," respectively. Many persons figuring directly in Hooker's life also received grants,

including his predecesssor at the Temple, Richard Alvey and John Rainolds' nemesis at Corpus Christi, John Barefoot. See 172; 190. James McConica suggests that Hooker was sufficiently well-off that he never really needed this financial aid and that, by implication, he was but one of many who received help from the fund because of his social and political connections. I agree that Hooker was not impoverished but think he did need the extra funds to meet his living expenses. No doubt his associations with Jewel and Sandys were helpful in securing the grants. See McConica, 725.

10. Monica, "The Collegiate Society" Monica, 666.

11. Milne, 3.

12. Fuller, *Church History*, 11.

13. Curtis, 77-81. Excellent summaries of the founding of Corpus Christi are, Milne, 1-14; McConica, 17-29; Fowler.

14. A. L. Rowse, *Elizabethan Rennaisance*, 8. A good description of Rainolds' life and career is in Dent, esp. 103-10, 115-16, 133-43, 203-4. See also William Ringler, *Stephen Gossen* (Princeton: Princeton University Press, 1942), 2-7.

15. Dent, 103-4. Rainolds' portrait is in the tower of the upper reading room of the Bodleian Library. He was Thomas Bodley's ideal of the Protestant champion at Oxford during the Reformation. Rainolds was, by many accounts, the "most learned man of his generation" at Oxford. Anthony Wood called him "a walking library.' Curtis, 204, 206-7.

16. Milne, 6-9.

17. Fowler, 49-50, describes sleeping arrangements at Corpus. See also Dent, 190.

18. Fowler, 93-5; Dent, 20.

19. McConica, 29.

20. I have drawn descriptions of the buildings and grounds of Corpus from John Newman, "The Physical Setting," in McConica, 607-44, from drawings of college buildings and archival records about them, and from my own visits to the college.

21. Schoeck, 72-73 details Erasmus' influence not only on Fox and Jewel but others at Corpus Christi, including Rainolds, Hooker, and Spencer. He concludes that in the long run, Hooker may have been Erasmus' most important disciple, helped by him toward his key ideas of tolerance, piety, respect for the Church Fathers, and reliance on human reason.

22. N. R. Ker, "On Books at Corpus Christi College," in McConica, 458-77. See also, McConica, "The Collegiate Society," 704-9. Rainolds himself was to give very few books from his own massive library to his alma mater. See Dent, 98.

23. Much of this section, including the background for my speculation that Hooker may have waited on tables, is drawn from Fowler, esp. 46-54.

CHAPTER 5

The Oxford Years

LIFE AS AN UNDERGRADUATE

During Hooker's first few days at Corpus Christi, his tutor examined him in grammar and composition and determined that he was not far enough advanced in these subjects to begin college-level work in logic.[1] Rainolds sent Hooker to Magdalen College each morning, along with several other clerks, choristers, and under-qualified students, to master basic skills that he should have acquired in grammar school.[2]

Although the work in the college preparatory course at Magdalen was similar to what Richard had been studying during his last year at the Exeter Latin High School, the learning environment here was different. The pace was faster, expectations higher, and better discipline was maintained in the classroom—a relief, no doubt, from the near pandemonium that had often reigned in his schoolroom at Exeter.

Before the first term was over, Rainolds probably reassessed the situation and determined that his pupil, ready or not, should proceed with the regular first year in logic. Whatever problems Hooker might be having with his grammar and composition, he would need to get on with the logic if he hoped to move toward his degree in a timely manner.

Writing did not come easily for Richard for some years to come. Putting his carefully-developed thoughts into clear English prose was a struggle. How ironic that this student, who was destined to be an exemplar of English prose, was initially so lacking in basic writing ability that he was not fully certified in composition until the eve of his degree four years later. Even then, Rainolds probably had to look the other way insofar as Hooker's writing skills were concerned in order to recommend him for a degree.

Even when he was a mature writer of masterful sermons and theological works, Hooker's friends often found it necessary to correct his composition and spelling. Probably his mind raced too rapidly for his hand to keep pace. Fortunately, he never lacked friends and admirers willing to help improve his writing, both while he was in the process of composing his major works and after his death. In addition to his tutor and his two prized students, Edwin Sandys and George Cranmer, this small host of sympathetic "editors" would include such notables as Henry Parry, Lancelot Andrewes, Nicholas Eveleigh, Henry Jackson, and John Spenser. All but Andrewes were his contemporaries at Oxford, where a lasting bond was forged between these men and the brilliant if under-prepared young man from Exeter.[3]

The plague ravaged Oxford intermittently for six years beginning in 1571, just two years after Richard's arrival, and ending when it reached its peak in 1577, the year he was made a probationary fellow. In that year, the pestilence infected over six hundred persons in one night, killing some three hundred within a matter of days. This catastrophe was attributed by many pro-Catholic Oxonians to God's retribution for the conviction and punishment of one of their number, a local bookbinder named Rowland Jencks. Jencks was condemned by the Oxford assizes to have his ears cut off for speaking against the queen and the Church. Immediately after the sentence was carried out, the plague struck again and more people began to die. Some Calvinists saw this as a kind of black magic performed by the antichrist as revenge for the just punishment God had meted out to their Catholic foes.[4]

The plague and other epidemics were not merely ingredients in a theological debate between Catholics and Protestants for those who, like the seventeen-year-old Richard Hooker, were struck down by one of these dread diseases. If we may trust Walton's testimony, Hooker was very ill for a time during his undergraduate years. He would have shivered with fever in his small bed in his poorly heated room at Corpus Christi, probably during the early winter of 1571. No doubt, he feared for his life as some of his fellow students sickened and died, their diseased bodies carried off in the city's death carts. During those dark days, Richard remembered that his own father had been orphaned when his grandfather and grandmother had perished in the plague that struck Exeter in 1538.

Once stricken, it was imperative that he leave Oxford as soon as possible. Rainolds could arrange to have him transported as far as Salisbury, where Bishop Jewel would see that he was cared for and, if necessary, returned home to Devon. By the time Richard arrived in Salisbury, Bishop Jewel may have been indisposed himself—too infirm to pay close attention to Hooker and others who came to him from Oxford for safety from the plague. During these final years of his life the bishop was often ailing. He died within the year. Nevertheless, as Walton tells it, the bishop lent Richard a horse and gave him a small purse of two ten-groat pieces (a little less than seven shillings) to cover his expenses for the rest of his trip home to Exeter.

In the event, Hooker made the trip safely back to Exeter, retracing the route he had taken two years earlier. He remained at home, probably at his uncle's house, for several months, recovering from his illness and waiting for word that it was safe to return to Oxford. To finance his trip back, Richard needed help from his uncle, at least in the form of endorsement for another grant from the Nowell Trust.[5]

However upsetting plagues were to the life of an Oxford student in those years, a more fundamental disruption was the rapidly changing composition of the student body. Richard had had evidence of this when he first walked into Oxford and caught sight of those flashy rich boys, some of them with their own servants in tow, and all of them with money to burn. These young men, called "commoners" (to distinguish them from the "scholars"), included his Devon contemporary Walter Ralegh, who was at this time a student just across Merton Street at Oriel College. These sons of wealthy fathers were often glamorously, if not gaudily, attired (contrary to college regulations) in the finery of their social class—a far cry from the traditionally prescribed medieval monastic garb of mendicant scholar-clerks like Hooker.

These new arrivals could break the dress codes and other rules that governed personal expenditures, lecture and chapel attendance, and all the rest with impunity, because the money and influence of their parents protected them from serious punishment. With each passing year, Richard noticed that such rules were being relaxed for everyone in the face of pressure from these new students and their influential parents.[6] Often housed outside college walls and far from depending on scholarships, clerical patrons, and teaching fellowships, as Richard did, they paid their own way for educational costs and room and board. They were a most welcome new source of income for the colleges.

President Cole was as aware as any of his counterparts (then or now) that rich parents meant not only full-paying students but excellent prospects for large capital and endowment gifts. One need only stroke a few parental egos and be careful not to ruffle feathers and plumes by too strict an accounting of infractions of the rules by the progeny of the wealthy.

As long ago as 1458, Magdalen College, with which Corpus Christi had always had close relationships, signalled this radical change in the composition of Oxford's student body by allowing a limited number of the sons of "noble and powerful" persons to be admitted "at their own expense, or that of their friends." But this was viewed as an exception. It was not until shortly before Hooker arrived at Oxford that the practice had spread to most of the colleges and become a trend. By the end of the sixteenth century rich students outnumbered the poorer ones by a six to five margin. The majority of the new students were not being trained for the clergy. Most of them were not even completing their academic work, merely attending university for two or three years to acquire the necessary polish and prestige of having "gone up" to Oxbridge.[7]

Hooker learned how to appreciate and accommodate persons from different social backgrounds who had radically different career aspirations from his own. Within this closed community of shared collegiate experience and tradition, Hooker, as we shall see, was like many poor students in all generations who forge the friendships and acquire the shared bonds of loyalty to their alma mater that provide the contacts with wealth and power necessary to advance their career prospects and move them up the social ladder.

Whenever there are fundamental changes in the social complexion of student populations, challenges to traditional curricular and pedagogical canons and patterns of collegiate governance will not be far behind. This was as true in Hooker's sixteenth-century Oxford as it has been in the schools and colleges of Britain, America, and Europe during the social and political upheavals of the twentieth century. Before Hooker's eyes, the form and content of Oxford—indeed its very mission—was in the process of radical change. The focus was shifting from educating ministers and scholars for the Church to preparing the sons of wealthy and socially important families for careers in government, law, business, trade, natural science, and medicine or simply to providing the broad education in the arts, languages, and sciences deemed necessary for the life of an informed and cultivated gentleman.

Although this change in educational purpose took more than a hundred years to complete, most of it occurred during the sixteenth century. When it was over, nearly every aspect of collegiate life was altered, including the curriculum, teaching methods, governance, and bases of financial support. Nothing less than a revolution in education was underway at Oxford during Hooker's time. All the strain, conflict, and confusion of such change was evident during his fifteen years there as student and professor.

As Richard and John Rainolds planned Hooker's course of study in 1569, they plotted a twelve year academic programme: four years for the undergraduate degree, another three for the M.A., and at least six more for the doctorate. Rainolds told his charge that there would be little he could accomplish during the four year undergraduate programme. The important learning would begin in the masters and doctoral programmes when he studied theology, philosophy, metaphysics, history, and languages. In the meantime, he would do preparatory studies in grammar, logic, rhetoric, geometry, music, history, and astronomy.

Hooker's mentors in grammar were Priscian, Linacre, Virgil, Horace, and Cicero. For rhetoric, Aristotle was his master, along with Quintilian and Cicero. In logic, he drew upon Porphyry, Agricola, Aristotle, and Boethius. For arithmetic, he examined texts by Boethius, as well as two contemporaries: Tunstall and Frisius. He studied geometry in the company of Euclid. For astronomy, there were the writings of Johannes de Sacro Bosco and Ptolemy. He learned his Greek from Homer, Euripedes, and Plato and his history from Plutarch, Sallust, and Caesar's *Commentaries*. In music, he drew, once again, mainly on Boethius. (His *De Institutione Musica* was a somewhat obscure and difficult text that viewed music as a branch of mathematics and, although of no value for practising musicians, was still regarded as useful for learning music theory and may have played a part in stimulating Hooker's life-long interest in music.) In the months and years ahead, Hooker became familiar with these writers and others who comprised the great classical canon of his college, principally Homer, Euripides, Plato, Horace, Pliny, Plutarch, Sallust, Julius Caesar, Virgil, Terence, Plautus, and Ovid.

He took his courses one at a time, spending four to six weeks studying each text and then moving on to another. In this manner, he could concentrate fully on each writer before changing to another subject. Between the readings and examinations on them given by his tutor, Richard attended "disputations" and lectures.[8]

The basic curricular outline into which Rainolds slotted Richard's studies was the time-honoured medieval format consisting of: the *trivium* of grammar, logic, and rhetoric; the *quadrivium* of arithmetic, astronomy, geometry, and music; and the *three philosophies* (reserved largely for the doctoral candidates) of moral philosophy, natural philosophy, and metaphysics. As Rainolds knew, the emphasis was shifting within each of the three main branches of the curriculum toward the more "relevant" subjects. Within the *trivium*, Hooker did most of his work in rhetoric and grammar, although logic was still required for one year. Among the philosophic subjects, metaphysics now received less emphasis than natural and moral philosophy. And the *quadrivium* was now emphasized more than in the past. In later years, Rainolds would urge Hooker to study the "newer" languages of Greek and Hebrew as well as more Latin, still the scholar's choice.

Richard Hooker never satisfied all of the curricular requirements that his tutor laid out for him at the start of his academic career. There was a shocking lack of interest in enforcing the traditional academic canon. The new breed of upper-class students had little interest in studies designed to produce religious scholars. They had no intention of staying in college long enough to complete the curriculum through the doctorate—some twelve years!

Even among the more traditional students such as Hooker, who had to make some effort to take as much of the required curriculum as was available, the standard fare was being modernized. Subjects like logic were generally viewed as less relevant than rhetoric, although Hooker excelled at both. Among Socrates' disciples, the utilitarian Aristippus commanded a more enthusiastic response from staff and students than the idealist, Diogenes. The early church Fathers and medieval theologians were being gradually supplanted by the more exciting modern religious reformers: Luther, Calvin, Theodore Beza, Philip Melanchthon, Huldreich Zwingli, and, of course, the influential Oxford Visiting Professor of Divinity, Peter Martyr (Vermigli).[9]

To one degree or another, everyone at Oxford felt the impact of curricular and pedagogical change. College fellows often failed to deliver the prescribed lectures, preferring to speak on more modern topics or none at all. Students frequently skipped lectures. This did not necessarily mean that serious students like Hooker learned less than their medieval predecessors, only that what they studied and how they did it was often radically different from earlier times. Filling the gap left by fewer lectures was a new pedagogy based on reading books and being examined on their content.

The more affluent students crowding into Oxbridge could afford to buy the books used by their professors as a basis for lectures and tutorial sessions. The students could read the material for themselves, often without benefit of a professorial lecture. At Corpus, Hooker had an excellent library readily at hand for his use, and many of the fellows had their own personal book collections. Passively listening to lectures, taking notes, and then regurgitating professors' ideas in public exercises was a mode of learning being replaced by reading and informal discussion. The eye and the mouth were replacing the ear as primary sensory organs for learning. Nowhere was this trend more advanced than at Corpus Christi.

What the eye and the mind should most importantly fill themselves with, according to Hooker's tutor, were the ideas of John Calvin and his followers. Rainolds advised Hooker that whenever he had any difficulty resolving a theological or moral issue, he should follow the judgement of John Calvin. Peter Martyr was also recommended as a good guide to follow. That dynamic teacher had left Oxford by Hooker's day, but Rainolds probably lent Richard his notes on Martyr's lectures and told his student about Martyr's important ideas. Aristotle was urged on Hooker as the best authority in interpreting the pagan writers. But even here, when in doubt, he should always turn to Master Calvin.

Rainolds urged his students to take careful notes on Calvin's *Institutes*. It would not be sufficent merely to summarize the ideas contained therein; Hooker and his fellow students must also record their own understandings of Calvin's method of thought—the logic of his arguments. Only by learning how to interpret the ancients and the Fathers of the Church in the light of Holy Scripture, and then Scripture in the light of Calvin, could Richard hope to become a wise and learned Christian scholar.[10]

When Hooker and his fellow-students were not reading and analyzing texts and being examined on them, they did attend some lectures. They preferred the intramural presentations given by scholars hired by their own college. These men taught more appealing and immediately relevant subjects, such as law, medicine, and the "Renaissance" languages: Greek and Hebrew. The individual colleges could offer such lectures because their growing affluence provided funds to endow their own professorships. Corpus Christi was in the forefront of this trend with the early establishment of well-endowed lectureships in Hebrew and Greek. Little wonder that students should choose to take these popular subjects rather than attend the often boring and repetitious statutory university lectures.

The lectures Hooker attended supported a host of new courses given outside the statutory curriculum. These included such non-traditional subjects as literature in translation, modern history, geography, biology, magnetism, chronology, practical morality, manners, and courtesy. Among the most popular of the new subjects was modern political theory, including introductions to such works as Machiavelli's *Prince* and *Discourses*, Thomas More's *Utopia*, and Sir Thomas Smith's *De Republica Anglorum*. There is evidence in Hooker's writings that he had become familiar with such thoroughly modern thinkers while a student at Corpus Christi.[11]

An important part of Richard's academic regimen, in addition to lectures, books, and examinations, was participation in periodic public performances called "disputations" and "exercises." These public debates were designed to test abilities in logic, grammar, and metaphysics. Through these oral demonstrations, Hooker gained proficiency in the scholastic mode of argumentation prescribed by Peter Abelard, the early twelfth-century French philosopher, who was still standard fare at Oxford. It was a method that had been used for centuries and would one day be reflected in Hooker's sermons and writings.

The disputations were a cause of daily excitement. The chapel bell heralded each debate and sent students hurrying into the college hall to see and hear their classmates perform. Three or four participants performed in each disputation. A senior student (respondent) would begin the debate by setting forth a proposed subject, presenting the issues involved, and offering an interpretation of the problem. Then one or two other seniors (opponents) would attack this argument. After that, students in the audience (arguers) might join in with their own opinions. Finally, another senior student (replicator or moderator), who had been presiding over the whole affair, would give his analysis, offer conclusions, and either shower abundant praise or heap scorn on the various participants.[12]

During his early years, Hooker, as was the custom, merely attended the disputations as an observer. Because Rainolds was so keenly interested in dramatics and public presentations, he probably required Richard to attend as many of these events as his schedule permitted. The most important disputations in a student's career were called "exercises." For the senior scholars, these were career highlights: formal full-dress affairs attended not only by the fellows but by such dignitaries as the chancellor, members of parliament and the court and, on rare occasions, the queen herself.

Back in 1566, Peter Carew, nephew of Roger Hooker's employer in Ireland, Sir Peter Carew, had performed at just such an Oxford disputation before the queen. Elizabeth was so pleased that she had young Carew present a repeat performance for Lord Burghley. Three years later Peter's older brother, Richard Carew, performed a disputation with Philip Sidney, son of the Lord Deputy of Ireland, Sir Henry Sidney, and nephew of the chancellor of Oxford. This debate took place in the same year that Roger Hooker was sending his urgent plea for help to Lord Sidney from his embattled post at Leighlin Bridge.[13]

Hooker prepared with special care for his "*in parviso*" exercise that took place shortly before he was formally "admitted" to his B.A. degree in early 1574. The nineteen-year-old knew how important this performance was to his future academic career. He was concerned that, since public speaking was not his strongest suit, he would not make a good impression on the senior fellows who would be there to judge him. Rainolds possibly reassured him that, although good preaching was vital to the improved health of the Church, Richard's knowledge of the Greek masters and the reform theologians would shine through his presentation. Furthermore, his ability to persuade (rhetoric) and the clarity of his argument (logic) would more than compensate for any lack in stage presence.

Rainolds, although deeply committed to redressing the sad lack of good preaching in the English church, and so perhaps disappointed that his pupil might never be an outstanding orator from the pulpit, nevertheless appreciated and encouraged Hooker's skills as a scholar and persuasive writer.[14]

At some time between 1573 and 1575, Hooker received news of an event that would fix the course of his career. The bishop of London, Edwin Sandys, wanted him to serve as tutor to his second son, also named Edwin. The boy came up to Oxford at about the age of fourteen and probably moved into Rainolds' room with Hooker for a time. It is safe to assume that, wishing to please the bishop of London, the college soon found Hooker his own room, with adequate space therein for the bishop's son.[15]

Hooker was well aware that this opportunity to become closely involved with the influential Sandys' family could only help his career. He had lost his first clerical patron, Bishop Jewel, to death only two years before. Now, this quickly, he had the prospect of a new supporter at the highest level of the Church. He might dare to hope for a good post if he had to leave Oxford. As bishop of London, Sandys held the third most important post in the Church. He was a prime candidate to replace Edmund Grindal at Canterbury. This was undoubtedly the most exciting news Richard had had since his uncle had first told him he would be attending Oxford.

It is probable that Bishop Jewel had recommended Richard to Bishop Sandys sometime before his death. The two had been close friends and colleagues for many years. John Rainolds, already a well-known scholar and teacher, would probably also have been consulted as to who was best qualified to tutor the bishop's son, and he too would have recommended Hooker. To have so impressed Rainolds that he would make such a recommendation to Bishop Sandys is clear evidence of Hooker's outstanding performance as a student.

This young Edwin Sandys, whom Richard mentored, nurtured, and befriended for the next four years, later became one of Hooker's closest friends, one of the most formative influences on his career, and the most important facilitator of Hooker's reputation as the major apologist for the Anglican reformation of the Church in England.

When Richard had completed nearly all requirements for his undergraduate degree, sometime late in 1574, he participated in a full-dress event, called the "Lenten" or "determination" exercise. Along with other candidates, he presented himself on the Saturday before Ash Wednesday (called "Egg Wednesday") for a disputation in which he was a respondent to propositions presented by a fellow, or an advanced undergraduate, who then evaluated Hooker's performance for intellectual attainment and religious orthodoxy.

When Hooker had finished his presentation, at least nine of the senior bachelors present voted "yes." This was the number required for him to be accepted as an M.A. candidate and allowed to proceed on to a three-year course of study, primarily in moral philosophy, metaphysics, and natural philosophy. Aristotle would be his primary guide for the next few years.

AN OXFORD DON

In 1577, after three years of graduate study, Richard was "incepted" as an M.A. at a public ceremony where he received his degree insignia. He then was admitted by the vice chancellor as one of Oxford's masters of arts. Before the ceremony, he was required to make a scholarly oration called a "declamation" in the hall at Corpus Christi. This requirement, applauded by Erasmus as an excellent means to sharpen rhetorical skills, was an innovation at Oxford in the sixteenth century, taken from an ancient Roman practice.

Unfortunately there is no record of Hooker's oration or of the response to it. Given his rapid rise in the Church shortly thereafter, it is safe to assume that his was a star performance. After the declamation exercise, Richard made a formal "supplication" for his M.A. by visiting the masters at each of the Oxford colleges personally and asking them to certify him as qualified. This was easily accomplished, for he was by then well known throughout the university as a promising candidate. His final step was to make a formal "deposition" to the vice chancellor as to his qualifications.

Why all this fuss to get a master's degree? Because an Oxford master of arts was automatically a voting regent of the university and a junior member of the staff. As such he was expected to enter one of the graduate schools and pursue advanced studies for his doctorate. He was also expected to engage in disputations, tutor undergraduates, accept lecture assignments, preach at Paul's Cross in London, when asked to do so, and generally enter into the full academic life of Oxford as a permanent and responsible member of England's intellectual élite.[16]

The late 1570s were busy times for Hooker. He took his master's degree in 1577 and became a probationary fellow in the same year. Also in that year the son of another distinguished family was entrusted to his tutelage. This was George Cranmer, grand-nephew of Archbishop Cranmer, author/compiler of the *Book of Common Prayer*, who had been martyred outside Balliol College in 1556. George took his B.A. in 1583 at the age of about fifteen—a testimony to his genius and Hooker's ability.[17]

By the end of 1578 Hooker had shepherded Edwin Sandys through the undergraduate requirements at Corpus. In the meantime, Bishop Sandys had been advanced to the post of Archbishop of York. At the age of twenty-four, Hooker had a grateful parent sitting in the second highest seat in the Church of England.

In August of 1579 Hooker took holy orders as a deacon in the Church. The following month he was made a full fellow at the college. These two highlights occurred shortly after an important meeting with President Cole in midsummer of that year. On that occasion, Cole informed Hooker that the university vice chancellor, Leicester, with the approval of Francis Walsingham, would be appointing him to serve as *de facto* Regius Professor of Hebrew at Oxford—a very high honour indeed and eloquent testimony to Hooker's ability and reputation as a scholar and linguist.

Thomas Kingsmill, over at Magdalen, had been the university's Regius Professor of Hebrew ever since Hooker had arrived at Oxford in 1569, but he had been too ill to present lectures for many years. Kingsmill would keep the official title of Regius Professor, but Hooker would deliver the lectures in Hebrew and be designated Deputy Professor of Hebrew. The professorship carried a stipend of £40 a year. Hooker would receive only a small portion of that, £5 6s 8d. The teaching obligation was to deliver four lectures a week beginning at eight in the morning. The topics usually covered Holy Scripture, with a healthy dose of grammar worked in along the way.[18]

Hooker must have exulted in this appointment. What professional academic would not be proud of such an achievement? He was rapidly becoming a star at Oxford. However, Richard may not have felt quite so proud of himself when he read, at about this time, his former student Stephen Gosson's book. The book, published in 1579, was entitled *The*

Sir Edwyn Sandys, Second Son of Archbp. Sandys.
From an Original Picture.
Published Jan.y 1st 1776.

School of Abuse Containing a Pleasant Invective against Poets, Pipers, Plaires, Jesters and such like Caterpillars of a Commonwealth. It recalled Hooker's undergraduate days when he, Gosson, Sandys, and Cranmer—all under the strict disciplinarian influence of John Rainolds—had joined in a self-righteous attack upon much of popular contemporary drama, music, poetry, and other forms of entertainment. On reflection, Hooker may now have thought that those travelling companies of players, jesters, musicians, and jugglers who visited Oxford from time to time were harmless enough. Perhaps some of their performances were not to his taste, but he probably no longer wanted to be counted with Gosson as one of those rigid moralists who would condemn these pleasant diversions.[19]

Earlier in this eventful year of 1579 Richard had the considerable satisfaction of welcoming his cousin Zachary (uncle John's son) as a student at Corpus. The now well-seasoned Oxford don, who had come so far from the poverty of his own beginnings as a poor relation of the Hookers of Exeter, must have felt considerable personal gratification as he showed his fifteen-year-old cousin through the college buildings and, we assume, gave him the inside story on how to succeed at Corpus Christi.[20]

In the following year Hooker, now near the height of his academic career, was summarily tossed out of Corpus Christi. He had committed the crime of supporting the political ambitions of his colleague, friend, and mentor, John Rainolds. One may well wonder what cousin Zachary thought of that. As a Hooker, he was probably as proud of his cousin as his father John would have been. The Hookers seemed to have had a special affinity for taking stands, notable even in those times when it seemed that nearly everyone was in the midst of some kind of public moral posturing.

For Richard to be expelled was not a singular event in those days. Political and religious controversy were regular fare at Oxford throughout the years of the English Reformation. Corpus Christi was scarcely two decades old, for example, when its second president, Robert Morwent, was imprisoned for a short time for his religious beliefs during the reign of Edward VI. Morwent was a diplomat and businessman with a great love of learning who had been selected by Richard Fox himself to head Corpus after Claymond's death in 1537. He successfully steered the College through the dangerous crises occasioned by radical changes in government policies during his twenty-year presidency under Henry VIII, Edward VI, and Mary Tudor.

During the early years of Elizabeth's reign, before Hooker arrived at Oxford, all Corpus Christi's presidents had decidedly Romanist leanings. In 1551, Thomas Morwent and two other fellows of the college were imprisoned in Fleet Street for using the old Catholic service in chapel. William Cheadsey, who served for only a year in

1558-9, was a papal sympathizer who openly challenged Peter Martyr on theological issues.

Thomas Greneway, who headed the college from 1561 to 1568, was also accused of being a romanist. In addition, it was claimed that he was guilty of immoral personal behavior: cavorting with whores, being drunk in public, singing bawdy songs, and stealing college funds. In his defence, Greneway accused others of hiding the chapel vestments and silver from the royal authorities and said that the charges against him were intended to cover up these misdeeds by his accusers. It was a tumultuous era at the college, as elsewhere at Oxford.[21]

By Hooker's time there, the worst features of the political disruption were subsiding, but troubles did not end entirely. President Cole, as already noted, took office the year before Richard arrived only through the forcible intervention of the queen's ministers. He was destined to have a stormy presidency, the event that included Hooker's expulsion being only a minor episode.

The expulsion incident is, however, important to our story. It involved a conflict between John Rainolds and another senior fellow, a Catholic sympathizer named John Barefoot. The two were rivals for the college presidency, a post they had reason to believe William Cole was about to vacate. Each man and his supporters lobbied the university chancellor, the Earl of Leicester, for his support. Barefoot had a good case because he was already vice-president of the college and could expect support from Leicester's older brother, Ambrose Dudley, Earl of Warwick, whom he was serving as chaplain. But Leicester supported Rainolds, a fellow Calvinist of advanced stripe. Cole put an end to the dispute by deciding not to resign the presidency after all. (He remained in office for another tumultuous nineteen years.)

An angered Barefoot then used his authority as vice-president to expel his rival Rainolds from the college, along with four other fellows who supported Rainolds' candidacy. One of these was Richard Hooker. Rainolds wrote to Sir Francis Knollys, in October of 1580, complaining of "the unrighteous dealing of one of our College [Barefoot] who has taken upon himself, against all law and reason, to expel out of our house both me and Mr Hooker, and three other of our fellows, for doing that which by oath we were bound to do."[22]

Within a few weeks of their expulsion, Hooker and his colleagues were restored by the chancellor to their places at the college. In frustration over Cole's failure to leave the presidency, both Barefoot and Rainolds soon departed from Oxford for greener pastures. Barefoot became archdeacon at Lincoln. Rainolds left Corpus in 1586, not to return until he was named president in 1598. In a letter to his old rival Barefoot in 1594, Rainolds said that he had left the college because "dissensions and factions there did make me so weary of the place."[23]

During his nearly eight years as a doctoral candidate, Hooker completed most of the required studies in Hebrew, Bible, Patristics (Church Fathers), the Reformation theologians, and, of course, Greek. Despite the fact that many of the statutory requirements could easily be waived, because required lectures were frequently not even offered, it is safe to assume that Richard attended and participated in all courses available to him. He listened to lectures in theology based not only on the traditional texts but also on Luther's treatments of Genesis, Habakkuk, Psalms, Galatians, and Corinthians, as well as Philip Melanchthon on Genesis, Proverbs, and Romans, and Martin Bucer on many books of the Bible.

Although Hooker arrived too late at Oxford to hear the famed lectures of Peter Martyr on Corinthians and other topics, he did listen to Martyr's learned successor, Lawrence Humphrey, who held the Divinity chair from 1560 to 1589. These two men had begun the tradition of beginning sermons and lectures with a biblical text and proceeding from there with their discourse. This was a change in homiletic practice soon to be followed by most preachers, including Hooker.

Throughout her reign Queen Elizabeth and her high-ranking ministerial "scouts" at Oxford were on the lookout for promising candidates to preach at Paul's Cross in London and to fill the important clerical posts of the realm. They were looking for men who could express with force and conviction the emergent middle-of-the-road position of the Church of England. Hooker displayed the desired qualities in his lectures and disputations: a sound grounding in classical, biblical, and modern thought (the attributes of a Renaissance scholar); a capacity for making an argument and defending it; a homiletic talent; and, what the queen prized above all, a predilection for moderate reformation in religious practice within the established Church headed by the crown—a church to be marked not so much by purity of doctrine as by a welcoming spirit of compromise, inclusion, and accommodation among a variety of acceptable religious positions.

The day was not far off when Hooker would be on his way to London to preach at Paul's Cross, and, later, to accept the queen's appointment as the Master of the Temple Church at the Inns of Court. He might never have received such preferment, despite his connection to Bishop Sandys, had he not been regarded by his peers and betters at Oxford as a man of special talent and promise. As his colleagues and students encountered Richard performing in a public disputation or debate, delivering a formal lecture in Hebrew, teasing and testing them with drills in logic—his favourite subject—informally discussing a Greek writer, arguing with them about what he saw as the excessive claims of some of Calvin's English disciples, or simply listening patiently to their own ideas, they recognized in him exceptional qualities of mind and spirit.

What were these attributes that the professors, students, and colleagues who lived and studied with Hooker on a daily basis at Corpus Christi found so appealing? He had an uncommon ability to see beyond the immediate issue at hand to the more important and enduring truths at stake amidst the passionate polemic that characterized most of the intellectual discourse of the day. He also had the capacity to organize vast quantities of disparate and apparently confusing material into a clear and convincing synthesis. He had a knack for avoiding the academic pedantry so common at the time. He was already proficient at seeing the practical truth of a matter. He could argue convincingly, even passionately, for broad common-sense accommodation of apparently conflicting views. Perhaps most attractive was his moderate tone in argument, and his modest, even shy, personality—most appealing at a time when nearly everyone around him was howling with such passionate intensity! Little wonder that his intellect was admired and his counsel sought.

Another quality that endeared Hooker to many of his academic colleagues was that he posed no real threat to anyone. His relative poverty and lack of social polish meant that he probably could not compete effectively for the best positions outside the university. How easy to befriend, support, and admire this brilliant but reticent academic who was blessed with a sharp wit, a rhetorical flair, and a grand passion for order and rationality. Noblesse oblige!

As Hooker moved beyond his master's degree toward a career as an Oxford fellow and don, he knew well that the apogee of his university career, the goal toward which he was expected to strive, the meal-ticket that would eventually assure him of promotion, was the doctorate in divinity. He had already spent seven years at Oxford and looked forward to at least seven more years of tutoring undergraduates, reading, taking notes, attending lectures, engaging in disputations, and presenting formal lectures of his own, before earning his final degree.

Hooker never received his doctorate. This failure was, for him as it has always been for career academics, a defining fact of life. He remained at Oxford for almost eight years after receiving his M.A. These were probably the happiest years of his life. He fully intended to earn his doctorate and spend all of his career at the university. When he left, it was probably not because he disliked the professorial life. There can be little doubt that he abandoned Oxford primarily for financial reasons. He simply lacked the independent means to continue his studies and to survive at a suitable standard of living in an environment that could not—or would not—provide decent salaries for most of its professors.

Like most of his M.A. colleagues, Hooker was stymied in his quest for a doctorate by the distraction of having to earn his keep by tutoring and lecturing, when he should have been doing his own scholarly work. Eventually, he was lured away from the university by the promise of preferment outside the academic world. Hooker's stipend as a university fellow was only 50 per cent more than the pittance he had received as an undergraduate, 3 marks (£2), rather than 2. His clothing allowance was only slightly higher. Even as a senior (doctoral) fellow he could earn only 4 marks per year. As a university lecturer, the most he could hope to make was a total of about £10, including all stipends and allowances. If he were fortunate enough to secure another position outside the university or to be offered a clerical benefice that could earn him a total of more than £5 a year, he would have been required to resign his fellowship altogether.

In the face of what must have seemed a financial conspiracy ranged against him, it is not at all surprising that Hooker, like most of his pre-doctoral colleagues, did not remain at the university long enough to complete his final degree. The average tenure of a fellow at Corpus Christi in Hooker's time was only about five years.[24]

To say that Hooker had financial needs as a graduate student is not to say that he was destitute. Certainly there were scholars at Oxford in more dire financial straits than he. He had been fortunate to have received a number of grants from the Nowell Trust administered by the Dean of St Paul's in London.[25]

In a special gesture of support, which demonstrates the continuing interest of John Hooker in his nephew's well-being, Richard received from the city of Exeter an annual sum of £4, beginning on 29 September (Michaelmas) 1582. By formal resolution, the mayor and chamber, "Agreed that Richard Hooker, the son of Roger Hooker deceased, and now a student of Corpus Christi College in Oxford shall have the yearly pension or annuity of four pounds to be paid quarterly, and the said payment to continue as long as it shall please this house, and the first payment to begin at Michaelmas next."[26]

This generous financial assistance from home more than doubled Hooker's stipend as a college fellow. But it came late in his Oxford career, after he had already suffered years of genteel (at best) academic poverty. Even with his stipend as Deputy Professor of Hebrew and funds earned as a tutor, Hooker's financial situation was far from enviable. His only recourse was to cut back on his study time and earn extra money by tutoring undergraduates, thereby delaying progress on his doctorate.

Tutoring undergraduates was not merely a matter of supervising studies. It also involved serving as guardians, responsible for overseeing all aspects of students' lives, *in loco parentis*. The tutors, often called "creancers," were employed by the colleges, not the university. One of their most important functions was to assure that allowances and other funds coming to their student charges were deposited in their accounts, paid to the colleges for fees, and doled out as periodic allowances. The tutor was the parents' agent at the college for watching over most of the personal affairs of their sons—their own private "dean of students."

Fathers and patrons usually selected a tutor with the same care they applied to picking a college. Each college understandably took similar care to offer its best fellows to serve in this role. So when John Jewel helped his friend John Hooker choose a college for Richard, his first concern was to select what he felt to be the best one—Corpus Christi, Oxford. His second consideration was to identify the prime tutor. He chose that already famous young Puritan scholar, John Rainolds. A generation later, when Edwin Sandys, bishop of London, wanted the finest possible tutor for his son, he chose Richard Hooker, by then one of the outstanding fellows at Corpus.

Tutoring was a demanding role that left less time and energy for pursuing one's own studies. However unfortunate this diversion to undergraduate mentoring may have been for the scholarly attainment of many graduate students at Oxbridge, it did produce the most profound change in teaching and learning methods taking place in Hooker's Oxford years: the transition from the lonely-scholar mode of the medieval clerk-student to the tutorial mode characterized by personal interaction between a student and his mentor. By 1576, every student at Oxford was required to be registered in a particular college and to be under the tutelage of a fellow.

Nowhere at Oxford was the tutorial method more integral to a reformed undergraduate education than at Corpus Christi College. As one of the "bees" in Bishop Fox's "garden," Hooker was aware of his role as a facilitator of a new pedagogy that focused on improving undergraduate learning, rather than on promoting advanced scholarly attainment. In addition to a strong tutorial relationship, Fox's pedagogy called upon tutors such as Hooker to administer written examinations covering lectures and readings. This in itself was a radical departure from earlier tradition and another example of the replacement of eye for ear in the learning process. Book reading, note taking, and exam writing, instead of listening to lectures and taking public oral examinations, were becoming the stuff of academic life. This change put a heavy burden on the tutors.[27]

From the perspective of college bursars, the tutorial system presented both a problem and an opportunity. The problem was to find an adequate supply of qualified tutors to manage this labour-intensive one-on-one tutor-student relationship. The opportunity was to tempt the needy graduate students with small stipends for teaching and superintending undergraduates. Here was a ready supply of cheap labour. Graduate students, then as now, were willing to toil for a pittance as tutors, graders, lecturers, counsellors, and house proctors. Administrators could then spend their available funds to attract and hold senior lecturers and scholars who were too important to "waste" on undergraduate teaching.

Almost everyone benefited from this new system. Undergraduate students received better instruction from readily available and personally involved tutors than they had under the old system where they sat in large lecture halls listening impassively to scholars who often did not even know their names. Colleges could admit and effectively educate larger numbers of full-paying students. Only the tutors—the graduate students who would never have the time to complete their studies and become full professors—were the losers. Even they might be better off, in the long run, by being forced out of the academy into more rewarding careers in other fields of endeavour.

Along with these fundamental alterations in the social and economic complexion of the student, parent, professor constituency in Hooker's Oxford came pressure not only for curricular change but also for transformation in university governance. Not surprisingly, the fulcrum of control over the university shifted from the church hierarchy to the economic and political leadership within the secular society, principally to the queen and her ministers.

Until the break with Rome in 1533, the pope, as head of the English Church, had been, if very indirectly, the ruler of the Church's principal institutions, including the universities. Thereafter, the crown became head of Church and university, and the secular nobility replaced the church hierarchy as directors of the colleges. For a time, certain church leaders remained of importance to the governance of Oxford and Cambridge. The bishops of Lincoln and Ely retained their historic roles as overseers with the historic right to grant teaching licenses. The chancellors, whom the bishops appointed to run the universities, derived their important judicial and legal power from the crown, to whom they felt primary loyalty. Soon the monarch began to appoint chancellors without reference to the bishops. Although crown and Canterbury shared influence and control over Oxbridge during most of the sixteenth century, by Hooker's day the queen had largely achieved her headship of the Church and so the distinction was fast becoming moot.

In 1571, early in Hooker's student years at Corpus, the official separation of university from church was accomplished by an act of parliament which incorporated Oxford and Cambridge as civil institutions. Oxford's new name was entirely secular: "Chancellor, Masters, Scholars of the University of Oxford." A seal was granted, the considerable historic academic independence of the universities reaffirmed, the authority of crown (and parliament) in matters of governance asserted. Efforts by the Church to thwart this secular control proved fruitless. Lord Burghley simply asserted the queen's right to appoint chancellors and heads of colleges. Beginning in 1559, with his own selection as chancellor at Cambridge and Sir John Mason's at Oxford, Burghley and his successor (his son) assured that no cleric was ever again appointed to run either university during the rest of Elizabeth's long reign.

Of course, the ancient ties with the Church were changed rather than severed. The Church continued to claim Oxbridge as its own and used the universities as the principal intellectual battlegrounds for its struggles against Catholic and Protestant extremist alike as well as for training its clergy. Oxbridge was in practice still clerically dominated. Particular clerics such as John Whitgift, the future archbishop of Canterbury, had enormous influence in the governance of certain colleges, as they did within the queen's court. This authority was no longer wielded as a matter of right, but only at the sufferance of the queen and her chief ministers. (The last high-church official to claim independent rights against Elizabeth was Archbishop Grindal in 1575, and he paid the price of ostracism from court and loss of all real power within the Church.)

Even as Elizabeth and her ministers increased their control over governance and finance at Oxbridge, primarily through their appointment powers, so they used their authority to affect changes in curriculum, student admission policies, and professorial assignments. Elizabeth, ever the Renaissance prince, was soon able to chart the direction of higher education within her realm, with very little regard for the historic role of the Church in university affairs. Her chief agent at Oxford was the chancellor, her favourite courtier, Robert Dudley, Earl of Leicester.

From the time of his appointment in 1564 Dudley was an active participant in the life of the university. For example, he promoted the lively interest in the sometime raucous theatrical productions at Oxford—which Elizabeth so loved and which were later to be the scandal of the Puritans at Oxford. It was near Oxford, at their home at Cumnor Place, that Dudley's wife had been allegedly murdered back in 1560 to make way for his marriage to the virgin queen. (The charge was never proven and was probably false, the most likely cause of her death being suicide.) Dudley promoted the independence of the colleges from university control and asserted the power of the crown in many matters of management and curriculum. The chancellor was a staunch anti-Catholic who instituted an oath of allegiance to the *Thirty-nine Articles* and to the *Oath of Supremacy* to be taken by all students who were over sixteen years old.[28]

Until the days of Elizabeth and Dudley, the individual colleges had enjoyed only limited independent authority. In part, this was because students had taken most of their studies not at the colleges but from a university-wide curriculum. The importance of the colleges had been further weakened by students not living within college walls but in inns, hostels, and "halls" located in town. Life in these cramped, often unpleasant, quarters was part of Oxford's medieval character. It was not supposed that students (clerks) in training for the ministry needed much by way of creature comforts to sustain them. Scholarship was a serious and self-abnegating discipline, as was the profession to which it led. However, for the new breed of rich students now coming to Oxford for professional training, intellectual polish, and social networking, these miserable residences were completely unacceptable. Expansion in enrollment was outstripping the capacity of the town's halls and inns, necessitating the construction of residential colleges.

The colleges, with their newly-found political independence and their coffers stuffed with moneys coming in from paying students and new endowments in land and crops, were able to build facilities to house and feed their own students intramurally. This soon led to the vacating and demolishing of university-owned halls and hostels in town. Courses and lectures were offered within the colleges, quite independently of the university.

By the time Hooker arrived at Oxford, the old medieval guild system, through which the senior university professors, acting as a "Society of Masters," ruled the collegiate halls and hence the university, had been replaced. Now there was a university board, composed of the heads of the colleges, which appointed the operational head of the university (the vice-chancellor), as well as the doctors and masters. An unspoken alliance had been formed between the crown, the landed aristocracy, and the rising merchant and professional classes to wrest control of Oxford and Cambridge from the Church and vest it in their campus surrogates, the heads of the individual colleges. Like their mother, the Church, the universities and their colleges ceased to be ordered by an external universal authority (the pope) and became an integral part of the queen's new English commonwealth, accountable to the authority of English law. Just as the medieval Church had lost most of its wealth in land and buildings to the Reformation princes of Tudor England (and their friends), so it lost control of its academic and intellectual centres to the Renaissance princes of Tudor England (and their friends) who changed them into proper secular schools for their sons.

Queen Elizabeth, as head of the universities, made numerous "visitations," trying to calm troubled waters and root out the extremes, as she saw it, of both Catholicism and Protestantism. During the early part of her reign, the emphasis was on eliminating the so-called papists and Romanists. Between 1559 and 1572, her visitors found eleven officials and fellows at Oxford guilty of Catholic leanings. They were expelled, some of them during Hooker's student days, as examples to the many students and faculty with similar inclinations. During this same period, a few of the more extreme Puritans, such as Whitgift's later protagonist, Thomas Cartwright, were also removed. The moderate Protestants and Catholics were usually left alone.[29]

The full weight of royal displeasure at Protestant disloyalty in Oxford did not fall until later in Elizabeth's reign, when Hooker was a senior fellow and professor. This was the era of outspoken challenges to the queen's established Church by such Protestant intellectuals as Hooker's former tutor and now colleague, John Rainolds, and Hooker's cousin, Walter Travers, at Cambridge. Most Protestant leaders, like these two, were not immediately expelled from their academic posts. Unlike the more outspoken Thomas Cartwright, they felt it expedient to take the *Oath of Supremacy* to the queen and then work behind the scenes to accomplish their reforms, with the help of sympathetic politicians like the queen's own Lord Burghley. The growing power of these more advanced Calvinists, in parliament and within the universities and the church hierarchy, opened avenues for more public and vigorous efforts to undermine the liturgy, theology, and, most importantly, the polity of the established Church of England.

Exactly where Hooker's own religious preferences lay during his years at Oxford is hard to determine with certainty. His ideas, like those of most students and fellows, were in process of development and subject to change, mirroring the age in which he lived. The circumstantial evidence is strong that his sympathies were, for the most part, with the reformers. His family background, although pragmatic, was clearly Calvinist. His first patron and supporter was no less a Puritan stalwart than Bishop Jewel of Salisbury. His tutor at college, who had taught him to follow Calvin's example in all religious matters and whom he supported to the point of being expelled, was the renowned Calvinist, John Rainolds.

Perhaps most telling about Hooker's theological and political leanings, at least early in his years at Oxford, is the fact that the influential bishop of London, the renowned Calvinist Edwin Sandys, had chosen Hooker as mentor for his young son Edwin. Bishop Sandys had suffered much during the reign of Catholic Mary and had been exiled in Zurich with Peter Martyr and in Strasbourg with his long-time friend, John Jewel. He would not have selected Hooker for such a trust unless he were convinced that Richard was a reliable Calvinist—and Sandys had had ample opportunity to verify Jewel's evaluation of Hooker for himself while he was bishop of London.

Despite the Calvinist influence of Rainolds, Cole, and a few of the senior fellows, the religious leaning at Corpus and at Oxford generally during Hooker's years was Catholic. Repeated efforts by the queen and her ministers to root out Catholics were only partially successful despite strict requirements, including the 1578 Convocation that specifically required all undergraduates to receive instruction in the reformed faith and mandated study of Calvin's *Institutes*, the *Heidelberg Catechism of 1563*, and Jewel's *Apology*.

Chancellor Dudley continued to talk of "secret and lurking papists" who "seduce your youth and carry them over by flocks to the [Catholic] seminaries beyond the Seas." The problem, he felt, was the lack of enough required instruction in the reformed faith. In 1586 a new lectureship in theology was created to remedy this default. None other than John Rainolds was appointed to fill the chair.[30]

Hooker was surely influenced by this strong residual Catholic presence at Oxford. His earliest extant sermons and most of his later writings show a tolerant attitude toward Roman Catholics, an emphasis on free will as opposed to Calvin's rigid determinism, and a balancing of Scripture with reason and the patristic tradition as sources of God's divine revelation—all debts to Catholic humanism. Oxford's basic religious conservatism (and Hooker's) in the face of the more radical elements of the Reformation should come as no surprise. After all, one of the founding spirits of sixteenth-century Oxford, and especially Corpus Christi, was the Catholic humanist Erasmus, as his work was filtered through his friend Bishop Fox. This brand of Christian humanism was conservative and quite comfortable with a reformed Roman Catholic theology.

It is not mere speculation to see Oxford as the seedbed for Hooker's later opposition to Calvinist extremists. There was a specific influence that may have moved his ideas away from Rainolds and toward a more moderate position. This was the Spanish theologian, Antonio (del Corro) Corrano, who lectured and served as a catechist in many of Oxford's colleges and halls between 1579 and 1591. Corro was a former Catholic monk who had come to England to preach to Spanish Protestants in London. Both Cecil and Leicester were early patrons and secured him the post of lecturer at the Temple Church in London, where Hooker would one day serve as master. While at the Temple, from 1571 to 1579, Corro was castigated by Hooker's immediate predecessor, Master Richard Alvey, for preaching free will and for "speaking not wisely about predestination." Corro presaged Hooker in such ideas, and in preaching tolerance for Roman Catholics, from this influential London pulpit.[31]

Corro found his theological hero in the anti-Calvinst writings of the influential Danish Lutheran, Nels Hemmingsen. Following Hemmingsen's *Tableau de l'oeuvre de Dieu* (1565), and *Dialogus Theologicus* (1574), Corro questioned the twin pillars of Calvinism: predestination and justification by faith alone. He advocated toleration and reasonableness in resolving religious differences. For his ideas he was accused of heresy and denied a doctorate of divinity at Oxford in 1576, owing largely to the strong opposition of Hooker's mentor—by now Oxford's arch-Puritan—John Rainolds, who accused Corro of being a hypocrite for subscribing to the *Thirty-nine Articles*.[32]

Controversy followed the Spaniard wherever he went. While in London, running afoul of Master Alvey at the Temple, he was roundly attacked for criticizing the darling of French émigré Calvinists in the city, Pierre L'Oiseleur de Villiers, minister of the French Calvinist Church. Villiers had been a personal friend of Calvin. With the help of

Laurence Tomson (a future Puritan nemesis of Hooker's), the Frenchman published an English translation of Theodore Beza's annotations of the *Geneva Bible* in 1576. Renewing their earlier clash in London, Corro and Villiers disputed publicly at Oxford. The more militant young Calvinists at the university sided with the Frenchman, the more moderate and conservative fellows with the Spaniard. Rainolds was among those who most vehemently opposed Corro.

In his teaching and writing Corro stressed human free will and natural reason. He argued against what he saw as the extreme determinism and judgementalism of many Calvinists. He urged brotherly love and compassion, rather than creedal confessions and strict biblical interpretations. His ideas are clearly reflected in Hooker's later sermons at Paul's Cross and the Temple Church. In fact, Hooker's opponent, Walter Travers, accused Hooker specifically of promoting a doctrine "not unlike that wherewith Corranus sometimes troubled the church."[33]

Hooker no doubt spent hours with Corro discussing these issues in his chambers at Corpus Christi and elsewhere at the university. Oxford's new deputy professor of Hebrew, troubled by what he saw as the excesses of Catholics and Calvinist extremists alike, found welcome balm in the sweet reasonableness of the Spaniard. It is tantalizing to speculate as to with whom Hooker sided when John Rainolds urged his friend, Lawrence Humphrey, president of Magdalen, to oppose the move then afoot to grant a degree to Corro. Rainolds told Humphrey that he was afraid that Corro would "raise such flames in our University as [only] the Lord knows whether these shall be quenched."[34]

Another moderate at Oxford who probably influenced Hooker, and who was also opposed by Rainolds, was Corro's fellow Spanish scholar, Francesco Pucci (1540-1593). Pucci earned his M.A. at Oxford in 1574. In his teaching, he flirted with the idea of universal salvation for all who believed in God. He professed the same sort of broad tolerance and brotherly love that Corro taught. Like Corro, Pucci had the kind of winning personality that led such scholars as Rainolds to fear that he was gaining the hearts of too many students. Hooker's tutor was influential in having Pucci expelled from the university in 1576.[35]

Rainolds' influence on Hooker was moderated by the ideas of Corro and Pucci. In turn, Hooker passed on his own more conservative brand of Calvinism to his pupils, Sandys and Cranmer. They became even more ecumenical than Hooker. In his *A Relation to the State of Religion*, (1605) Sandys would one day argue that the Roman Church had so many positive features that it might even serve as a model for Christian unity and, furthermore, that even the pope might be saved.

During Hooker's years at Oxford the university was debating, accommodating, and absorbing the vast intellectual and social challenges represented to traditional learning, piety, and social order by the twin influences of the Renaissance and the Reformation. Individual colleges often differed sharply from one another in religious and intellectual tone, Corpus Christi being among the more humanistic and Puritan. But even at Corpus, the agents of change, exemplified by men such as John Rainolds, did not go unchallenged by the voices of traditional Catholic learning and piety.

With hindsight, a convincing case can be made that during this period Oxford was the seedbed for an emergent middle theological ground between Puritanism and Catholicism. Advanced forms of Calvinism provided the leaven which worked the old patristic system into a new synthesis. Richard Hooker, a son of Oxford, was destined to provide the most complete and influential formulation of that via media we call Anglicanism.[36]

It may also be said, with even less fear of contradiction, that during Richard Hooker's fifteen years in residence Oxford was an altogether noisy, dangerous, dynamic, volatile, fluid, politically-charged, unpredictable place. Izaak Walton was never more misled or misleading about Hooker's life than when he characterized Richard's departure from Oxford by saying that, he passed "from that garden of piety, of pleasure, of peace, and sweet conversation, into the thorny wilderness of a busy world . . ."[37]

NOTES

1. My sense that Hooker had trouble with his grammar and composition is based on circumstantial evidence: (1) the probable poor quality of his grammar-school education at Exeter Latin High School; (2) the fact that he was not certified as a degree candidate until he had satisfied requirements in grammar, which did not occur until he had been in residence for four years, on the eve of his "admission" as a B.A.—and even then he was probably not up to speed in the subject. Milne, 26-27; Fowler, 148; (3) his difficulty in making progress in logic (his best subject) as late as 1576, on the eve of his supplication as an M.A., when he was in the "inferior classis" probably because of poor progress in grammar and compostion; ill health may also have been a factor. Milne, *op. cit.*; (4) the fact that the Nowell Trust initially listed him in his award level as a student who had passed in grammar but not composition (i.e., he received commons only); (5) Sandys' and Cranmer's critical comments on his composition skills as shown in their notes on his draft of Book VI of the *Laws*, Folger, III, 107-40; (6) the way in which rhetoric and logic often overwhelm grammatical construction in his writings. Laetitia Yeandle of the *Folger* Shakepeare Library, who edited Hooker's sermons and tractates for the *Folger* edition of his works, describes Hooker's mature writing as, on the whole, "clear" but often difficult to decipher because of his carelessness with the letters a, e, o, m, n, i, u, s, t, and c. See Folger, V, 308. I have found Hooker's hand more difficult than some of his contemporaries whom I have read. His penmanship is often cramped and careless. For examples of his writing, see Folger, III, xxii-xxiii; IV: 54, 56; V: 330.

2. During Hooker's years at Oxford, Magdalen College was not only the locus for some of Corpus Christi's pre-college remedial work but, more importantly, the centre of radical Puritanism. Magdalen was larger, richer, and more Protestant than any other college. Under the long presidency of Lawrence Humphrey (1561-1589) it was home for many Calvinist theologians from the continent who came to lecture,

study, take degrees, and promote the presbyterian discipline. In fact, the queen regarded the moderate but tolerant Humphrey as her principal ambassador to Protestant reformers abroad. See Dent, 6, 47-73.

3. See *infra*, "Epilogue,"

4. Headlam, 250-4. Not only plagues but an earthquake, in April of 1580, seems to have disrupted Hooker's Oxford. Dent, 126, n. 1.

5. *Works*, I, 12-13. Walton's account of Hooker's illness and return home, like most of his tales, is probably a mixture of fact and fancy. I believe that either Jewel's gift of travel money was insufficient to cover a round trip from Oxford, or that Walton gilded his tale by a groat or two. The Nowell Trust records an award of 2s 6d on 12 February 1572 to "bring him to Oxford," presumably *back* to Oxford from the trip home, which may have been paid for by Jewel. See Gosart, 220.

6. On one of his visitations to Oxford, the Earl of Leicester, as chancellor of the university, described the raucous student life there as comparable to what went on next door to his London palace at the Inns of Court, with ale houses, gambling establishments, and all manner of rowdy "disorders" taking up students' time and energy. Dent, 126-7. See also McConica, 664-6; Curtis, 55-6.

7. McConica, 668-93; Curtis, 38-40, 77-8.

8. Descriptions of the curriculum and pedagogy at the time are drawn from McConica, 701-9; J. M. Fletcher, "The Faculty of Arts," in McConica, 157-199; Curtis, 75-93.

9. Curtis, 160-5.

10. Rainolds' recommendation of Aristotle, Calvin, and Martyr as primary guides for his students is well documented. He specifically mentions Calvin and Martyr in a letter written late in life. See, Dent, 184-190. There is evidence that Rainolds was never so much a Renaissance humanist as he was a Calvinist enthusiast. His strong dislike of much of the contemporary drama, literature, and poetry of his day and some of his criticisms of Aristotle simply for being a pagan philosopher are reflected in his writings, as well as in those of his prominent student, Stephen Gosson. See William Ringler, *Stephen Gosson* (Princeton: Princeton University Press, 1942), 12-14; Curtis, 106.

11. Curtis, 126-64

12. McConica, 24; Fletcher, *op. cit.*, 168-70. An extant copy of one of John Rainolds' disputations as an Oxford student, in which he was the "respondent," provides a clear picture of what Hooker strove to achieve in these exercises. Rainolds begins: "Though my inexperience in this sort of speaking and my fear of betraying the great confidence that you repose in me dissuade me from my task, the burning zeal of my desire and the exceptional pleasure which I find in your presence urge me on with equal force, so that I am the rather urged to speak by the admirable grandeur of poetry than held firm by design by the awkward[ness] and poverty of my oratory." This and the rest of the speech display rhetorical ability and facility in Latin and grammar more than concern for the content of the argument. Ringler, 27, citing Rainolds' *Oratio in Lauden*, edited by Henry Jackson, the same scholar at Corpus Christi who edited and published several of Hooker's sermons and tracts. Ringler has an excellent description of the disputation as a pedagogical form, 8-16. Brian Vickers sees three evidences of Hooker as rhetorician: his style, his strategy, and his use of certain polemical tools. Hooker's rhetorical skills were honed under Rainolds at Corpus Christi, where his student notebooks would have been filled with lists of similes, metaphors and techniques for opening and closing arguments. Vickers argues convincingly that Hooker used rhetoric to teach and persuade his audiences, despite his condemnation of his opponents for doing the same. "Public and Private Rhetoric in Hooker's *Lawes*", McGrade, *Richard Hooker and the Construction of Christian Community*, 95-9, 145.

13. See *supra*, Chapter 1, 15-16.

14. Dent, 203-4. Later in his life, Hooker would take issue with the idea that preaching was the most important part of the liturgy. This can be deduced from his statements in Book V of the *Laws*. See esp. *Folger*, II, 83-110; *Works*, II, 84-115.
15. Sandys was born in 1561 and admitted as a *discipulus* on 16 September 1577. Since he received his M.A. in 1579 and since it is probable that he began his studies at the usual age of thirteen to fifteen, we can assume that he entered sometime between 1573 and 1575. McConica notes that, like Hooker, Sandys was "on the foundation," meaning that he was a serious student and not one of the wealthy "commoners" who were at Oxford primarily for a bit of polish. McConica, 672; 677. The first full account of Sandys' life and career is Theodore K. Rabb, *Jacobean Genteleman, Sir Edwin Sandys, 1561-1629* (Princeton: Princeton U.P., 1998). Throughout his work Rabb underscores Hooker's influence on Sandys' career as writer, parliamentary leader, and merchant adventurer in colonial Virginia. The broad, tolerant, essentially conservative pragmatism of Sandys owed much to the tutelage of Hooker.
16. Fowler, 148; Milne, 9; Fletcher, 181-4.Corpus Christi College archives, *Liber admis*, gives Hooker's date of admission as *discipulus* and hence his eligibility (at last) to receive his undergraduate degree and proceed toward the M.A. as 24 December 1573. But this date has been over-written as 19 October. (In the margin of the folio is written: "Rich Hooker, Disc. Oct 19.").
17. Probationary fellows were designated "scholars." Cranmer's admission as *discipulus* is recorded on an unnumbered folio as 10 January 1577. *Liber admis*.
18. Patrick Collinson sees the appointment as an example of pressure on Hooker to maintain in his sermons and lectures a consistent anti-papal posture. He was expected, Collinson says, "to sing for his supper." See "Hooker and the Elizabethan Establishment," McGrade, *op. cit.*, 156. Kingmill had offended Queen Elizabeth in 1566 in a welcoming speech to her in which he spoke favourably of extremist Protestants at Oxford. See Eleanor Rosenberg, *Leicester Patron of Letters* (New York: Columbia University Press, 1955), 129. See C. D. Duncan, "Public Lectures and Professorial Chairs," in McConica, 356-7, for details of the professorship. Hooker held the position from 14 July 1579 until he left Oxford in 1584 or 1585. Walton, *Life*, 19.
19. I am speculating about Hooker's attitude here. Gosson entered Corpus Christi in 1572 and probably learned his logic from Hooker, who may have been his tutor, and his friend as well. It is as likely that Rainolds was his tutor. His fascinating career as critic of Elizabethan drama, music, and poetry, and as preacher—in 1598 he preached a sermon at Paul's Cross entitled *The Trumpet of Warre*, in which he attacked Puritan extremists, calling them "vermin"—is set forth in Ringler, esp. 8-12, 46-9, 64-5. See also, Dent, 189-90. An excellent discussion of Rainolds' relationship with Gosson, and other aspects of Rainolds' career at Oxford, especially his movement from moderate to more extreme Calvinism is in Dent, 103-10.
20. *Liber admis*, recorded in the margin of a folio as "Zachary Hoker" admitted February 6, 1579.
21. Milne, 23; Jennifer Loach, "Reformation Controversies," in McConica, 374.
22. Walton, *Life*, 19-21; Fowler, 140-1. One reason for Rainolds' expulsion was that, by this time, he, along with President Cole at Corpus and Magdalen President Lawrence Humphrey, was the leading radical Calvinist at Oxford and a primary contact for Protestants abroad hoping to come to study and teach at Oxford. Dent, 74-80.
23. It is noteworthy that Rainolds' bitterness never quite abated. At his death, he failed to follow the custom of his predecessor presidents at Corpus Christi and leave his library to the college. He had a large collection of some 1600 volumes which he gave to his students, except perhaps for a hundred or so books that did go to the college. Dent, 98.

24. Milne 9-10. The financial crunch for Oxford fellows was so acute that, between 1571 and 1580, while undergraduate enrollment was on the rise, only sixty-nine advanced degrees were awarded, and of these only twenty-two were doctorates of divinity. Most fellows, like Hooker, were obliged to leave the University to find gainful employment. Dent, 165. One of the more prominent students who left for financial reasons was Hooker's contemporary at Corpus Christi, the enigmatic poet, critic, and preacher, Stephen Gosson. See Ringler, 17.
25. See *supra*, chapter 4, p. 62 and n. 9.
26. Devon Records Office, *Act Book 4, 1581-1588* (21 December 1582), 399. Here is one of the few occasions in contemporary records when Hooker's name is spelled correctly: "Richard Hooker." See also Fowler, 150.
27. Curtis, 79-81, 105-6
28. *Ibid.*, 45-9. For Leicester's role at Oxford, see Rosenberg, 124-51. For an excellent discussion of Elizabeth's policies at Oxford, including Leicester's role, see Penry Williams' "Elizabethan Oxford: State, Church and University," McConica, *op. cit.*, 397-440.
29. *Ibid.*, 167-8; Curtis, 37-43.
30. Loach, 389.
31. Matthew Parker, *Correspondence* (Cambridge: The Parker Society, 1853), 476. Corro's tenure as reader at the Temple between 1571 and 1579 is recorded in J. Bruce Williamson, ed., *The Middle Temple Bench Book*, 2nd ed., (London: Chancery, 1937), 307. Corro, born about 1527, was a Spanish monk originally from Seville. He was drawn to the Reformation by way of Luther rather than Calvin. Hence, the likes of Bullinger rather than Beza were his heroes and guides. Corro was protected by Leicester despite attacks on him by Oxford's more militant Calvinists. Rosenberg, 135-6. See Dent, 110-25 for a good discussion of Corro's career in England. See also Curtis, 212-13, 222.
32. Nicholas Tyacke, *Anti-Calvinists and the Rise of Arminianism 1590-1640* (Oxford: Clarendon Press, 1987), 59, 23. Tyacke argues that the controversy over Hooker's supposed anti-Calvinst views on predestination should be seen in the light of Corro's influence on him. See also Loach, 390-1.
33. From Travers, *Supplication Works*, III, 558-9; *Folger*, V, 198.
34. Loach, 390.
35. Dent, 109-10.
36. McConica, 732; Rowse, 75; S. L. Greenslade, "The Faculty of Theology," in Monica, 329-34.
37. Walton, *Life*, 25.

CHAPTER 6

Leaving the Academic Cloister

BISHOP SANDYS

There were six "father figures" in Richard Hooker's life. Each had a profound influence by appearing at a critical stage to rescue him from current predicaments and send him forth in new and more promising directions. Three of them, John Hooker, John Jewel, and John Rainolds, had seen him through childhood and college. The fourth was the powerful archbishop of York, Edwin Sandys, who first touched Richard's life when he sent his son to live and study under his guidance in about 1574. In placing such trust in young Hooker, Sandys had acted on the advice of his friend, Bishop Jewel. Once again, friendship among powerful men had formed a network of support for Hooker, as one handed him on to the patronage of another. Sandys was so pleased with Hooker during the years of his tutelage of Edwin that he facilitated offers of advancement for the Oxford don. The first of these came in 1584 when the thirty-year old Hooker had been a fellow for about seven years and Sandys had been archbishop of York for nearly a decade.[1]

By this time, despite the recent largess of the Exeter city fathers, Hooker was probably feeling the pinch of a tight personal budget and the fatigue of his long struggle to finish his doctorate while tutoring undergraduates. The offer of a living at Drayton Beauchamp parish in nearby Buckinghamshire was welcome indeed, as was the opportunity presented at about the same time to preach at Paul's Cross in London and thereby to taste the promising world of church politics on a national level. Bishop Sandys, who was a great favourite of the queen, and her chief minister, Lord Burghley, were most probably behind these early extra-mural appointments. With such friends in high places, Hooker's future seemed bright.

Few Elizabethan clerics cut such a colourful figure in the saga of the English Reformation as the surprisingly unsung Edwin Sandys. Hooker's first clerical patron, John Jewel, had been at heart an intellectual—delicate, sensitive, sometimes indecisive, often enigmatic. Jewel's friend and fellow Calvinist, the robust, courageous, straightforward, and altogether unbending Edwin Sandys, was a very different character.

The archbishop was cut from the same cloth as other heroes during the saga of the English Reformation on both sides of the religious divide. Some of these stalwarts—the Protestants Cranmer, Ridley, and Latimer, and the Catholic Thomas More—went to the stake for their faith. Sandys himself, as we shall see, came close to being martyred under Queen Mary. Queen Elizabeth found him a bit too warm-tempered and cocksure for her Machiavellian tastes. Possessed as he was of intemperate proclivities and, at the same time, being married (perish the thought!) probably stayed the queen from naming this remarkable man archbishop of Canterbury in 1575. Even so, she did give him both of the other two most powerful posts in the church: bishop of London and archbishop of York.

During the reign of King Edward VI Sandys' star had been in the ascendancy, a sure sign of his advanced Calvinist positions. When the sickly king died on 4 July 1553, Sandys went so far as to preach and write against Mary Tudor's succession and to support the efforts of Lord Northumberland and others to seat the Protestant Lady Jane Grey on the throne. Jane was crowned queen in London on 10th July. For his support of her cause, Sandys was made a bishop. Within days, however, the tide turned for Mary Tudor, not so much, perhaps, for her Catholic religion as because she was the rightful heir. Northumberland turned coat and declared for Mary. He was imprisoned just the same, as were Lady Jane and many other Protestant leaders. Both Northumberland and the erstwhile Queen Jane were subsequently executed.

Sandys was arrested almost at once and taken off to be imprisoned in the Tower of London. On Mary's coronation day, his jail door was left open and he was encouraged to walk out. He refused, saying that to do so would be a tacit admission of guilt. He remained in the Tower for twenty-nine weeks before he was removed to the Marshalsea to make room for other notable traitors, including Ridley and Cranmer. While in the Marshalsea, Sandys received an offer to be forcibly liberated by Sir Thomas Wyatt, son of the poet of the same name, who was then leading a rebellion against Mary in the streets of London, a rebellion that represented the only serious armed threat Mary ever faced. Fortunately for Sandys, and for the later career of Richard Hooker, the bishop had the good judgement to decline Wyatt's offer of rescue. He was not convinced, he said, that the rebellion was really God's will. After Sandys spent another two months in prison, his friends convinced the lord chancellor, Stephen Gardiner (who was also Bishop of Winchester) to support his release so long as he agreed not to leave the country. Ever firm in his convictions, Sandys declined the offer and was set at liberty to go free immediately and unconditionally. Gardiner, who obviously had approved no such arrangement, sent constables in pursuit of him. Sandys had many adventures as he made his escape, now hiding, now running, almost being captured after betrayal by supposed friends. At last, in May of 1554, with his would-be captors in hot pursuit, he made his way to Antwerp, just about the time of

Hooker's birth in far-off Devon. Sandys was not safe even in Antwerp. Philip of Spain (Mary's betrothed) had agents there who were just a step or two behind the bishop as he made his final escape to the safety of Strasbourg and, after a year there, to the home of Peter Martyr in Zurich.

When Elizabeth ascended the throne, Sandys returned to England at once, arriving in London on the day of her coronation. She put him to work on a commission to review and reform the Prayer Book. By the end of 1559, he was installed at Hartlebury Castle as bishop of Worcester, quickly becoming a leading figure in the queen's campaign to root out Catholicism in England. At Hartlebury, Cicely Sandys gave birth to a second son, Edwin, who would be Richard Hooker's lifelong associate and friend. In 1570, the queen installed Sandys in the third most powerful clerical post in the realm, the see of London. His friend and fellow-exile, Edmund Grindal, had held that post and now was promoted to archbishop of York. In just five years Queen Elizabeth's first archbishop of Canterbury, Matthew Parker, would die leaving vacant the number one see. Grindal would move there and Sandys would go to York. Ecclesiastical musical chairs.

As soon as he was in the highly political and visible bishop's chair in London, Sandys set about with his usual energy to enforce the queen's reformation of the Church. He issued injunctions requiring use of the *Second Edwardian Prayer Book* and wearing of the prescribed clerical garb. With less enthusiasm, he proscribed preaching and conducting worship in places other than church buildings and holding clerical office without a license from a bishop. These regulations were designed to curb growing disobedience by Calvinist extremists. Some ministers were preaching and administering the sacraments without benefit of ordination by Elizabeth's bishops; they were refusing to wear vestments; they were preaching and conducting services in locations other than churches in order to circumvent what they regarded as the insufficiently reformed features of Elizabeth's Church. Calvin's Genevan Church was their model.

The Church in England was still much too Catholic—"papist" the Puritans called it—for the tastes of a growing number of Protestant intellectuals and clergy. If they could not practise their brand of Calvinism in official church services, they would give religious speeches and hold educational training meetings, which they called "prophesyings."[2] This subterfuge was transparent but difficult to stamp out. To go after the Calvinist extremists was hard for Sandys not only for logistical reasons but also because to do so offended his conscience. Like Jewel before him, he had been thoroughly imbued with the more radical stream of Calvinist thought. He sympathized with most of the arguments against Elizabeth's requirements. His heart was in the battle to root out the vestiges of Roman Catholicism, not to oppose his fellow Calvinists. Nevertheless, like his friend Jewel, Sandys was a faithful and vigorous leader of the Elizabethan reformation—that effort to plant the established English Church in some middle ground between Roman Catholicism and Genevan Protestantism. Unlike Elizabeth or her later archbishop John Whitgift, however, Jewel and Sandys would have seen reformation in more radical terms.

At York, as at London, Sandys was in constant conflict with ministers and other church officials, as well as with powerful figures outside the Church, as he struggled to establish some measure of order and discipline. Aggressive in his efforts to root out "popery," he was less vigorous in exercising his responsibility to eliminate the scourge of the forbidden clergy Bible-study and discussion groups. In 1584 he actually supported in parliament these extra-mural "prophesyings" and so-called worship "exercises" by disaffected Calvinists, so long as they were carried out in an "orderly" manner and showed no overt disloyalty to the established liturgy or to the queen. It is clear that Sandys' instinctive preference was always for the more advanced forms of Protestantism.

Sandys was one of the more powerful preachers among the Elizabethan bishops. His sermons at Paul's Cross, while Bishop of London and later when he was archbishop of York, reveal a strong, clear, and convincing rhetoric. His theology was biblically-grounded but not extreme. He did not avoid the highly divisive issues of the day but was usually moderate in tone rather than inflammatory. He preached tolerance rather than suppression and punishment but was a staunch advocate of doctrinal and liturgical unity within a single national Church headed by the queen and her bishops. In one of his sermons, he exhorted: "The bond of unity is verity; neither can they be truly one which are not one in truth."[3]

Throughout these troubled times in his life, Sandys' attention remained fixed on the major priority of his vocation as a bishop: the improvement of the clergy. Too many ministers were poorly educated, inadequate as preachers, and careless in their conduct of worship services. The bishop's attraction to Hooker and his advancement of him in the Church was born primarily of his zeal to find men of such high quality and see that they were placed in important clerical positions. Sandys was also responsible for his son Edwin's being made a prebend at York and probably wished him to pursue a clerical career. If so, he would be disappointed. It is likely, however, that young Edwin urged his father to look instead at his own teacher, Richard Hooker, as a more likely prospect for advancement in the church. His own interests lie elsewhere: in the law, politics, and world commerce. Before long, Bishop Sandys' influence would see Hooker into a parish church, preaching a controversial sermon at Paul's Cross in London and, finally, into the prestigious post of Master of the Temple Church in London.[4]

PASTOR AT DRAYTON BEAUCHAMP

In the summer of 1584 Richard Hooker, having proved himself to Archbishop Sandys as a promising candidate for preferment in the Church, was offered the living at St Mary's parish in the village of Drayton Beauchamp, near Aylesbury in the shadow of the forested Chiltern hills, amidst the sheep-grazing fields of central Buckinghamshire—a scant twenty-five miles east and slightly north of Oxford.

Izaak Walton reports that, contrary to the practice of many clergymen of the day, Hooker actually resided in the parish and lived the life of a country parson. This is probably so, but Walton's account is not sufficient warrant for the fact. His tale of Hooker's tenure at Drayton Beauchamp is too full of error and hyperbole to serve as a reliable guide to much more than his own continuing effort to sanctify Hooker and vilify certain others, particularly Hooker's wife Joan.[5]

However flawed, Walton's charming story of Richard and Joan's supposedly unhappy domestic life at Drayton and the timely rescue of Hooker from the torment of this supposedly shrewish woman is so ingrained in Hooker lore that it needs to be lifted up and examined one more time. Here is how the great angler wanted posterity to see Hooker at Drayton Beauchamp:

> Now the wife . . . Joan . . . brought him neither beauty nor portion . . . so that this good man had no reason to rejoice . . .
>
> And by this marriage the good man was drawn from the tranquillity of his college, from that garden of piety, of pleasure, of peace . . . into the wilderness of a busy world; into those cares that attend a married priest, and a country parsonage . . . where he behaved himself so as to give no occasion of evil, but (as St. Paul adviseth a minister of God) 'in much patience, in afflictions, in anguishes, in necessities; in poverty, and no doubt in long-suffering;' yet troubling no man with his discontents and wants.
>
> And in this condition he continued about a year, in which time his two pupils, Edwin Sandys and George Cranmer . . . found him with a book in his hand . . . tending his small allotment of sheep in a common field, which he told his pupils he was forced to do then, for his servant was gone home to dine, and assist his wife to do some necessary household business. When his servant returned and released him, then his two pupils attended him into his house, where their best entertainment was his quiet company, which was presently denied them; for 'Richard was called to rock the cradle;' and the rest of their welcome was so like this that they stayed but till next morning, which was time enough to discover and pity their tutor's condition; and they . . . were forced to leave him to the company of his wife Joan, and seek themselves a quieter lodging for next night. But at their parting from him, Mr. Cranmer said, 'Good tutor, I am sorry your lot is fallen in no better ground as to your parsonage: and more sorry that your wife proves not a more comfortable companion after you have wearied yourself in your restless

> studies.' To which the good man replied, 'My dear George, if saints have usually a double share in the miseries of this life, I that am none, ought not to repine at what my wise Creator has appointed for me, but labour (as indeed I do daily) to submit my will to his will, and possess my soul in patience and peace.'[6]

In contrast to this noisy long-suffering state of marital unbliss, Walton describes the heavenly camaraderie of teacher and pupils:

> Betwixt Mr. Hooker, and these his two pupils, there was a sacred friendship; a friendship made up of religious principles, which increased daily by a similitude of inclinations to the same recreations and studies; a friendship elemented in youth, and in a university, free from self-ends, which the friendships of age usually are not: and in this sweet, this blessed, this spiritual amity they went on for many years: and as the holy Prophet says, so 'they took sweet counsel together, and walked in the house of God as friends.' By which means they improved this friendship to such a degree of holy amity as bordered upon heaven: a friendship so sacred, that when it ended in this world, it began in that next, where it shall have no end.[7]

How was a wife, much less crying children and a demanding parish, supposed to compete with such heavenly masculine bliss? When this account of a distracted husband and father is stripped of its beatific glow, what remains is inaccurate, even in its principal factual claim that Hooker was a husband and father at Drayton. In fact, he was not married at the time. That happy event was still three and half years away. His first surviving child was born when he and Joan lived in London, nearly six years after he had left Drayton Beauchamp.

However biased, maudlin, and inaccurate Walton's account of Hooker at Drayton Beauchamp may seem, it is so definite in locating Hooker at Drayton that we take his word as partial evidence that Hooker was in residence there for at least part of his tenure as rector. More convincing is the fact that in its historical literature and archives, St Mary's celebrates the presence of Hooker in the parish for much of that year, before he accepted the prestigious post of Master of the Temple Church in London in March of 1585. He is listed as rector in 1584 on the boards in the south aisle where the names of the church's rectors are inscribed, dating from the thirteenth century. Many years later, the lawyers at the Middle Temple Inn, whose predecessors had attended the Temple Church and heard Hooker preach there, erected a carved pulpit and had a stained-glass window installed in Hooker's honour, not at the Temple Church, but at St Mary's in Drayton Beauchamp. Clearly, they also had reason to believe that an important part of Hooker's life had been spent there.

The most persuasive argument for placing Hooker in residence at Drayton Beauchamp, failing any hard contemporary evidence, is that his latest "father" and patron, Archbishop Sandys, strongly disapproved of absentee appointments and would probably not have allowed his protégé to have one if he could prevent it.[8]

Assuming that Hooker actually resided, if only occasionally, at Drayton Beauchamp, what can be said of his life there? To begin with, it was quiet and peaceful—a dramatic change from the noisy, crowded, contentious, and sometimes violent way of life in Oxford. The new rector was unused to rural living. Now a mature man of thirty, he had spent all of his life—save perhaps his early childhood at Heavitree—in urban environments, surrounded by the human chatter and colour of intellectuals, clerics, merchants, artisans, and politicians. Now his companions were a few farmers and shepherds, a handful of landed gentlemen, some occasional drovers driving flocks to London from as far away as Wales or the border lands along the Severn, and flocks and flocks of sheep. His surroundings were bucolic, restful, conducive to contemplation, prayer, writing.

The commodious rectory at St Mary's was more than adequate for the needs of the young bachelor, who spent at least some of his time away from the parish, in London and Oxford. Richard probably endured at least one of the annual "stephening" celebrations held at the rectory. This local custom required that on St Stephen's day the minister welcome his parishioners into his house for a feast, at his expense, of all the cheese and ale they could consume. (This tradition at St Mary's lasted into the nineteenth century.)

While at Drayton, Hooker had a brief opportunity, immediately before entering the hectic and intensely political phase of his career as master of the Temple Church in London, to clarify and organize his thinking on a number of important controversial subjects. Here at peaceful Drayton he could try out his ideas in sermons, some original and some refined from lectures and sermons previously delivered at Oxford. We may see what Sisson describes as "the beloved figure" of Hooker "stooping in the pulpit to say his word to the congregation, turning from one group to another in intimate address, from the young men to the fathers, to the matrons, to the sisters, and to the little ones too, with great tenderness [when he says]: 'Sweet Babes, I speake it even to you also.' "[9] From his extant writings dating from this time—especially those using a favourite sermon text, the Letter of Jude—it is possible to reconstruct an outline of Hooker's emergent thinking on some important issues of the day. The following are some typical extracts:[10]

How We Know Our Enemies

Let us first examine the description of the worldly and carnal men, the reprobates, who wrongly honour and dishonour, credit and discredit the words and deeds of others according to what they have or what they lack. If a rich and well-attired man comes among us, though he be a thief or murderer or whatever the condition of his heart, so long as his coat be purple or velvet, everyone rises up and all of our reverent solemnities are to little effect. Even among us, a person who truly serves God will be condemned and despised if he is poor.

We know the righteous by their admiration for Christ's Apostles. These were men not only of poverty but of little learning. Yet how fully replenished they were with understanding. They were few in number yet how great in power. They were contemptible in worldly goods yet how strong in spirit, how wonderful.

If I wish to gain true understanding, whom shall I seek to teach me? Shall I get me to the schools of the Greeks? Why? These men who have worldly wisdom are dumb because they have rejected the wisdom of God. Shall I beseech the scribes and interpreters of the law to be my teachers? How can they be wise when they are offended by the cross of Christ? I must have a true teacher because it is death for me to be ignorant of the great mystery of the Son of God. Yet I would have always been ignorant were it not for one of these Apostles of Jesus, a poor fisherman, unknown, unlearned, recently emerging from out of his boat with clothes wringing wet, who opened his inspired mouth and taught me: 'In the beginning was the word, and the word was with God and the word was God.' These Apostles, these poor silly creatures have made us rich in the knowledge of the mysteries of Christ.

Solomon took it as evident proof that a woman cannot have a motherly affection for her child if she agrees to have it cut into parts. You cannot love the Lord Jesus with all your heart if you lend one ear to His Apostles and another to false apostles. This carries us to a mingle-mangle of religion and superstition. Ministers and priests, light and darkness, truth and error, traditions and Scripture. No. We have no Lord but Jesus; no doctrine but the Gospel; no teachers but His Apostles.

Do not marvel if in the last days you see people with whom you live and they walk arm-in-arm laughing at your religion and blaspheming that glorious Name whereto you are called. Thus it was in the days of the patriarchs and prophets. Are we better than they?

These mockers among us are those who use religion as a cloak to put off and on as the weather requires, those who shall hear the preaching of John the Baptist today, and tomorrow agree to Herod's decision to have him beheaded; those who will worship Christ while all the time planning some massacre in their hearts; those who kiss Christ with Judas and betray Christ with Judas. These are the mockers. As Ishmael the son of Hagar laughed at Isaac who was the heir to God's promise to Israel, so shall these mockers laugh at you as the maddest people under the sun if you, like Moses, choose to suffer affliction with the people of God rather than enjoy the pleasures of sin for a season. And why do they mock you so? Because, unlike you, God has not given them the eyes to see nor the hearts to conceive the abundant rewards awaiting you in the promise of salvation.

As atheists, these mockers cannot help but be beasts in conversation. Why do they remove themselves from God's love in this way? Why do they take such pains to abandon and put out of their hearts all taste, all feeling, of religion? They do so because only thus can they give themselves over to lust and unclean behaviour without feelings of inner remorse or guilt. Being mockers of God, these people are of necessity followers of their own ungodly lusts.

How We Know Our Friends
So that you may better see what all this division and separation among members of the Church means, we must understand that the great multitude of true believers, however dispersed they may be from one another, are all of one body, of which Christ is the head, one building, of which He is the cornerstone. As members of this body, they are knit together. They grow into men of perfect stature. As stones of the building they are coupled and used to become the temple of the Lord. They [are that] which joins Christ to us is His mercy and love towards us. That which ties us to Him is our faith in the salvation revealed to us in the Scripture—the word of truth—that which unites and joins us to one another so that we have but one heart and soul in our love.

Thus, those who are inwardly in their hearts lively members of this body and polished stones of this building, coupled and joined to Christ as flesh of His flesh and bones of His bones are linked and fastened to each other by the mutual bond of His unspeakable love towards them and their uncontrived faith in Him. No one can tell, of course, if another is deceitful in his profession. No one can tell who is a true believer and who is inwardly unbelieving; no one can tell, except God Whose eyes alone behold the secret disposition of all men's hearts.

Hooker would preach this message again and again throughout his life: only God can tell who among us is righteous and saved. We have no right to judge one another.

Why We Must Not Judge One Another
We whose eyes are too dim to behold the inner person must leave the secret judgement of each to the Lord, taking everyone as he presents himself and accounting all as brothers and sisters, assuming that Christ loves them tenderly so long as they continue to profess the Gospel and to join outwardly in the communion of the saints. At any time that they outwardly fall away from and forsake either the Gospel or their church membership, then there is no harm in calling them what they are. When they separate themselves from us, they are judged not by us but by their own actions.

Men separate themselves from the church in several ways: heresy, schism, or apostasy. If they forwardly oppose any principal point of Christian doctrine, they have separated themselves by heresy. If they willfully forsake the holy exercises established in the Church, they have separated themselves by schism. If they cast off and forsake both profession of Christ and communion with Christians and take leave of all religion, they have separated themselves by apostasy. It was, St Jude tells us, by apostasy that the mockers who pursued ungodly lusts separated themselves from the Church by determining never again to name Jesus as their Lord or to have fellowship with His Saints.

Such divisions and separations among us harden the hearts and trouble the minds of the weaker brethren. When simple folks observe such backsliding in their midst they are amazed and offended by the fall. They wonder how such apostasy and unrestrained departure can occur if Christ is indeed the Son of the living God who has the words of eternal life and is able to bring salvation to all men who come to Him. Do not be deceived, my children. Those who separate themselves from us were never truly children of God. They lived among us, as St John says, but they were not of us. And St Jude proves this by noticing that their behavior showed them to be carnal and not spiritual in nature. Would you judge wheat by the chaff that the wind scatters from it? Do your children have no bread because the dogs have not tasted it? Are Christians to be deceived in their hope for salvation because non-Christians are denied this joy?

So what if these evil ones seemed to be the pillars and principal upholders of our faith! What is that to us? We already know that angels have fallen down from heaven. If these men had been truly of us, they would have stood more certain than the angels and never departed from their place. As it is, we should not marvel at their departure at all. Nor should we be weakened in our faith by their falling away.

I have already told you that we must beware not to presume to sit as little gods in judgement upon others and, as our mere opinion or fancy leads us, rashly to determine if this man is sincere or that man is a hypocrite. They themselves make it known by actually separating themselves from us. Who are you that you take it upon yourself to judge another beforehand? Judge yourself! God gave you the infallible evidence whereby you may at any time give true and righteous sentence upon yourself. We cannot examine the hearts of others. We may, however, examine our own hearts.

An issue that Hooker could not avoid as his career moved into its public, political phase was the status of Roman Catholics in England, the theology of the Roman Church, and the status of the pope. His stand on these issues, beginning to take shape during his later years at Oxford and his time as rector at Drayton Beauchamp, would become one that was too sympathetic toward Rome to win him much favour with church authorities, and would, in fact, become a major impediment to his advancement to high positions in the Church. But at this point in his career Hooker was still as staunchly anti "Romanist" as the most advanced Calvinists in the Queen's Church, although his tone suggests a merciful response to Catholic excesses and a defensive stance regards Rome's attacks on the reformers rather than a frontal assault of his own on Catholic doctrine. Commentators who have seen these sermons as an example of Hooker's early anti-Romanism and, therefore, of his belated move to an anti-Puritan position exaggerate the point. A careful reading of the Jude sermons shows that the extreme positions of some Puritans was at least as troubling to him as claims of papal supremacy. His attacks on Rome in the early 1580s reflected more his concern about the immediate political threat to the security of the queen and nation than any deep-seated theological and liturgical antipathy to the Roman Church, although he clearly did reject the Roman notion of papal supremacy and any idea that salvation might be earned through one's works.

> *On Papists*
> Here I must, as an aside, advertise to all people who have the certainty of God's holy love within their breasts, how unkindly and injuriously our own countrymen and brethren [the Roman Catholics] have dealt with us. They have acted as if we were the evil-doers of whom St Jude speaks. They never cease charging us with either schism or heresy or plain and clear apostasy, as though we were the ones who had separated ourselves from Christ, utterly forsaken God, quite renounced heaven, and trampled all truth and all religion under our feet. For the charge of apostasy God himself will plead our cause in that day when they shall answer us for these words and we have no need to answer them.
>
> To those who accuse us of schism and heresy, we have often shown that our Church is founded on what is written in law and the prophets and that we are obedient to God's voice telling us to leave sinful Babylon [Rome] and cleave to the everlasting covenant of God with His people. You Jesuits and papists listen to me. You ought to know that the only head of God's Church is His Son. Of course it is true that He is the mystical and unseen Head of the Church. But so is it true that Christ has given the visible headship of each congregation of His Church to whomever of David's sons the Holy Ghost selects to go before them and lead them into their several pastures, one in this congregation, another in that one.

Clearly Hooker toyed with the notion that the head of State is the head of a national Church, to which all citizens must belong. In this he was a medieval thinker, unable to grasp, much less adopt, the emerging modern idea of separation of Church and State. For him the only viable question was which prince should govern the English Church. The answer was clear. It could not be a foreign prince, the pope or any other. It must be the head of the English State. This is not to say that Hooker was uncritical of the idea or practice of national royal church headship. He did not, for example, hold that in all circumstances a national prince should govern the Church in every country. If tradition and custom indicated a different form of church governance, as in Geneva, this was all right with Hooker. But in England custom dictated that once the pope was removed, the governance of the Church was the business of the crown. Furthermore, Hooker was acutely aware of the abuses of kings and queens in the exercise of their governance of national churches. He consistently urged a high degree of independence for the Church from civil authority and, as we shall see, flirted with the idea of passive resistance to monarchs who abused their authority. Hooker sought his authority in these matters in tradition, reason, and of course Scripture.

> No pope or papist will ever be able to prove that these Romish bishops had supremacy over all churches by any word that is in scripture. Even the children in our streets laugh them to scorn when they use the phrase, "thou art Peter" to prove their case. Yet this is the sole basis for the opinion held throughout the world that the pope is the universal head of all churches. But Jesus never said this. All He said was *Tu es Petrus*, You are Peter. But, not being able to overcome the words of Christ which forbid His disciples from behaving like worldly princes, this man of sin has risen up and rebelled against his Lord and to strengthen himself has crept into the house of most of the noble families in his country and taken their children from infancy to be his cardinals. He has fawned on the kings and princes of the earth and by a kind of spiritual blackmail has established, through them, lawful jurisdictions with such titles as *Catholicus, Christianissimus*, *Defensor fidei* and such like. He has sold pardons to entrap the ignorant, built seminaries to lure young men desirous of learning. This, my friends, is the rock upon which his Church is built!
>
> If I should here uncover the cup of those deadly and ugly abominations with which this pope has made the earth so drunk that it has reeled under us, I know your godly hearts would be loath to see them. For my own part, I take no delight to rake in such filth. I would rather take a garment and cover them while my face is turned away. Lord, open their eyes and, if possible, cause them to see how wretched, miserable, poor, blind, and naked they are. Put it, Lord, in their hearts to seek white raiment to cover themselves, so that their filthy nakedness may no longer be visible.
>
> Beloved in Christ, let us hourly and heartily bend our knees and lift up our hands to heaven, each in his own chamber and all of us together openly in our churches, and pray for this pope. Let us do this even though he has laid a solemn sentence of excommunication against our country, even though he and his scholars, whom he has stolen from our very midst, have falsely charged our gracious Lady, the Queen, and the rest of us with abolishing prayers within the realm, allowing sacrilege in God's service, being unfaithful to God by putting a strumpet in place of a virtuous ruler, abandoning fasting, abhorring confession, disliking penance, liking usury, finding no good in celibacy. According to these charges, all who are under our religious care are not only worse off than when we received them, but corrupted as well.

How much of all this theology Hooker's rural flock at Drayton Beachamp understood is a matter for conjecture. At Oxford such fare was simple enough. At London's Paul's Cross, where Hooker would soon employ some of the same ideas, his sermons would stir up a nest of hornets—mostly the Calvinist variety—and launch his career as a controversialist. The folk at Drayton would at least have caught Hooker's anguish over the divisions in the English Church. One of his favourite texts was from the Old Testament prophet, Habakkuk, who expressed so well his own discomfort over the hatred and judgementalism that marked much of church life in his day. Hooker saw Habakkuk as a kindred spirit. He often cited him in his sermons and tracts. He found some consolation in recalling the ancient but oh so timely words of this prophet:

> How long, O Lord, have I cried to thee unanswered? I cry violence!, but thou dost not save. Why dost thou let me see such misery, why countenance wrongdoing? Devastation and violence confront me; strife breaks out, discord raises its head, and so law grows effete; justice does not come forth victorious; for the wicked outwit the righteous, and so justice comes out perverted.
>
> I will stand at my post, I will take up my position on the watch-tower, I will watch to learn what he will say through me, and what I shall reply when I am challenged. Then the Lord made answer: Write down the vision, inscribe it on tablets . . . The reckless will be unsure of himself, while the righteous man will live by being faithful; as for the traitor in his over-confidence, still less will he ride out the storm, for all his bragging.[11]

Self-righteousness, prideful certainty, noisy confrontation, condemnation of those who in other times and other places practise their faith differently from us, judging who is saved and who is not—these, for Hooker, were the threats to Christ's Church. Those who speak and act thusly, he believed, do so contrary to the spirit of Scripture, the dictates of reason and the accumulated wisdom of Christ's Apostles and the Fathers of the Church.

By the time Hooker left Drayton Beachamp for London in 1585, his ideas on the issues of the day were not yet fully formed, especially those concerning the Roman Catholics. But he had the essentials well in mind. And the fire was lit in his spirit.

NOTES

1. Much of my account of Bishop Sandys is drawn from John Ayre, ed., *The Sermons of Edwin Sandys, D.D.* (Cambridge: Parker Society, 1841).
2. These "prophesyings" were usually a well-ordered and strictly-controlled form of training for the clergy rather than alternative services. Grindal and many other bishops supported them not because they were radical or in some sense presbyterian but because they wanted a better-educated clergy and could not wait for new men to come from the universities. Some of the "prophesyings" were taken over by extremists, which is what Elizabeth feared.
3. For two good examples of his sermons, see Ayre, 418-29 and 233-55.
4. I am not the first since Izaak Walton to see Hooker's appointment at the Temple as resulting from a conversation between Bishop Sandys and his son. See Paget, 82. That Edwin, although presumably not ordained, was made a prebend at York in 1581 is recorded by John Hutchinson, *A Catalogue of Notable Middle Templars* (London: Society of the Middle Temple, 1902), 215. It was not unusual for unordained persons with political connections to receive church appointments in

the Elizabethan Church. As we have seen, Hooker's father received such an appointment in Ireland.

5. For early scepticism about Walton's account see R. W. Church, ed., *Hooker, Of the Laws of Ecclesiastical Polity, Book I* (Oxford: Clarendon Press, 1896), vii-ix. Sisson, 20-21, doubts that Hooker actually resided at Drayton. In a recent essay, Patrick Collinson shares this opinion. See note 8 below. I see no reason to be so sceptical, especially since much of the negative argument depends on dating Hooker's Paul's Cross sermon to 1581 rather than the more likely 1584. (Hooker was probably resident in London at about the time of the Paul's Cross sermon.) I would give Walton the benefit of some doubt and place Hooker in at least part-time residence (although certainly not with wife and children) from about October of 1584 until March of 1585 when he was appointed Master of the Temple Church in London.

In a rather harsh review of David Novarr's important book on Walton's writings, *op. cit.*, John Butt and Peter Ure correctly note that the Lincolnshire archives record Hooker's holding the benefice at Drayton Beauchamp during this period. That, of course, does not prove that he was actually in residence there. See *Modern Language Review*, 54, 1959, 588-89.

6. Walton, *Life*, 24-26.

7. *Ibid.*, 18.

8. Collinson, to the contrary, doubts that Hooker ever actually lived at Drayton Beauchamp. "Hooker and the Elizabethan Establishment," McGrade, *op. cit.*, 150.

9. Sisson, 110.

10. Hooker's earliest extant sermons were preached on St Jude's Epistle and probably date from 1582-83. The excerpts presented here are my own editing and modernization of his text as found in *Folger*, V, 13-57. (At Hooker's death, Edwin Sandys came into possession of the sermons on Jude from whence they passed into the hands of Sandys' steward, Nicholas Eveleigh and thence to Henry Jackson who edited and published them on behalf of John Spencer (President of Corpus Christi College and an executor of Hooker's literary estate) in 1614. For a discussion of the provenance of these sermons see Laetitia Yeandle's "Textual Introductions", *Ibid.*, 1-7. Sisson, 103, 108-111, 140.)

For a well-reasoned argument that Hooker was an early anti-Romanist who later took on the role of establishment apologist against the Puritans, see Richard Bauckham, "Hooker, Travers and the Church of Rome in the 1580's," *Journal of Ecclesiastical History,* Vol. 29, 1978, 37-50. See also William Haugaard's excellent introductory chapter in *Folger*, VI, 51, esp. n. 102 and Patrick Collinson's essay, in McGrade, *op. cit.*, 160. It is noteworthy that some of the recent "revisionist" historians of the English Reformation have pushed the thesis that support for Catholicism in England remained strong among the people throughout the sixteenth century despite the supposed "rise" of Protestantism. This view positions Hooker's conciliatory tone toward Catholics as less startling and more in keeping with general sentiment than has previously been supposed by more traditional historians of the Reformation. See Christopher Haigh, ed., *The Reformation Revised* (Cambridge: Cambridge University Press, 1987), 2. One of the "revisionists" has actually placed Hooker in this light: Anthony Milton, *Catholic and Reformed: The Roman and Protestant Churches in English Protestant Thought 1600-1640* (Cambridge: Cambridge University Press, 1995), 146-7. For a lively and helpful discussion of the varying interpretations of the English Reformation, see Rosemary O'Day, *The Debate on the English Reformation* (London and New York: Methuen, 1986.)

11. Habakkuk I: 2-4, *The New English Bible* (Oxford: Oxford University Press, 1970.) For commentary on and text of Hooker's sermons from Habakkuk (delivered at the Temple Church in the Spring of 1585), see *Folger,* V, 59-68.

CHAPTER 7

Debut in London

ST PAUL'S CROSS

Richard Hooker had every reason to be nervous on the Sunday morning in the late summer of 1584 as he walked, possibly in the company of young Edwin Sandys, the short distance from the Churchmans' front door, past neighbouring St Augustine Church and St Paul's School, and on to the churchyard of St Paul's Cathedral. This was the most important day thus far in Hooker's professional career, the day for which all else may be seen as prologue. In just a few minutes, he would stand alone on the Paul's Cross platform and look out upon an audience of some of the most powerful people in England. They would listen to him speak on a controversial subject. (What subject in those days was not controversial?) They would take his measure and then his future might well hang in the balance.[1]

Paul's Cross was nothing less than the national platform for exposition and discussion of public policy and religious doctrine, especially from the viewpoint of the crown and the established Church. From this place, royal proclamations were intoned, new sovereigns welcomed, heretics and traitors condemned, military victories and royal marriages celebrated, and important sermons preached. It was here, on public festival days, that the cathedral clergy, regaled in all the pomp and colour of their various offices, read prayers and preached before a mixed audience of royalty, nobility, and commoners. Paul's Cross was what Thomas Carlyle called "The Times newspaper of the Middle Ages." At the end of the twentieth century we would see it as a media centre, a marketing mecca, the source of the latest offical news, the TV cable news network of Hooker's day.

It could be risky preaching here at the Cross. Hooker would have heard tales of that infamous Sunday in 1558, just two weeks after the queen's ascension, when Bishop Christopherson of Winchester, a renowned papal sympathizer, had preached a sermon here that had angered the new queen. He was brought before her and examined on his sermon. Not satisfied with the bishop's responses to her questions, Elizabeth had him summarily imprisoned in the Tower of London. Clearly, this could be a dangerous pulpit.[2]

Despite any such danger associated with preaching at the Cross, Hooker must have been delighted at the opportunity to speak from this famous pulpit. He would now have wide public exposure for his ideas.

And he would enjoy the opportunity to see a bit of London at the bishop of London's expense. The free lodging at John Churchman's house near St Paul's in Watling St, provided at Bishop Aylmer's request, and the forty-five shilling preacher's stipend, made for a welcome holiday. Hooker was probably pleased that Bishop Aylmer had chosen the Churchmans' as the place to put up his guest preachers this year. Staying here provided an opportunity to talk with Mr and Mrs Churchman about their poor William's brief time with him at Oxford. How tragic to lose their son to sickness, possibly the plague, and so soon after the deaths of their little girls, Katherine and Sara.[3]

Edwin Sandys and George Cranmer were among the lawyers, clerics, and politicians who visited frequently at the Churchmans' when they had business in London. Sandys, as we shall see, was later a permanent resident for years at a time. Clearly, John Churchman was eager, or at least willing, to play the genial host to those reformers and politicians who advocated moderate change within the established order of things in Church and State. His home became, in fact, a kind of boarding house for an array of visiting luminaries. How nice for him to play the Thomas More. But no easier on his Alice than it had been for Dame Alice More a half century earlier. That John probably did not even accept the bishop of London's payment for putting up the visiting preachers at Paul's Cross, or if he did, deposited the money straight away into the alms box at St Augustine's, might not have pleased his harried wife either.[4]

Richard Hooker stood in front of the octagonal wooden structure, with the huge wooden cross atop its lead-covered roof. The Cross had witnessed some dramatic events: the very first sermon on record was in 1330 when the chancellor of St Paul's, William de Renham, preached on the excommunication of Lewis of Bavaria. This was followed by the selling of indulgences by Archbishop Courtenay in 1387 to finance the rebuilding of Paul's Cross; the great day when Thomas Cranmer defended the proclamation declaiming Henry VIII to be the rightful replacement for the pope as head of the Church in England; the unforgettable "Of the Plough" sermon denouncing the greed of the rich and mistreatment of the poor by that Reformation firebrand, Hugh Latimer—the same man who had once preached at Exeter and stayed in uncle John's house. Then there was the day in late November of 1553 when Elizabeth Barton, the "holy maid of Kent," along with a small group of friars and priests, was tied onto a scaffold high above the Cross and forced to listen to a sermon condemning her supposed revelation from God of the king's misdeeds, including his divorce from his most Catholic Queen Catherine, before the maid and her little band were executed at Tyburn a few months later.

Not everyone present on the morning of Hooker's sermon was pleased to see Bishop Aylmer on the dais. His reputation was disreputable among many church and government officials, owing not a little to his penchant for making outlandish and intemperate statements. For example, when criticized for his high living and reminded that he had once advocated modest life-styles for clerics, Aylmer had replied, "When I was a child I spoke as a child, I thought as a child, but now I have put away childish things."[5]

From the time of Henry VIII, this open-air pulpit had been the most rudely disrupted and confrontational public platform in the realm. Here, Sunday after Sunday, ordinary people had mingled with the powerful and the literati to hear a preacher like Hooker proclaim religious doctrine and policy. The crown's policy was supposed to be pronounced from here. But often a nonconforming preacher would slip through the scrutiny of the bishop of London. More often, the official position espoused from the pulpit would be hooted down by jeers from a disapproving crowd or disrupted by loud uninvited rebuttals from someone on the benches or even in the galleries. At the very least, a preacher at Paul's Cross could expect responses in speeches, sermons, and written publications following his sermon, no matter how well prepared he was or how careful he tried to be in his research and argumentation.

No doubt Hooker hoped that his own remarks would not provoke too much controversy. After all, his intent was to plead for an end to conflict in the Church. He would condemn only those who sought to make trouble. In fact, much of what he had to say had been pronounced from this very pulpit by Archbishop Whitgift less than two years earlier.[6] Certainly, Hooker's preaching style would not normally provoke antagonism in his listeners. He is not known to have embellished his thoughts with much oratorical flair. His sermons stood on their own internal logic and were persuasive on their merits—aided only by the use of rhetorical devices woven into the written composition. He rarely employed either dramatic gesture of hand and head or excessive modulation of voice. To be well rewarded, a listener would have to give attentive ear to Hooker's carefully chosen words.[7]

"This morning, I take as my text the Prophet Habakkuk," Hooker began, in a firm voice, looking straight down at the prominent and powerful men in front of him.[8] There is no surviving text of Hooker's Paul's Cross sermon, but it is quite certain that its central theme, or at least the part that most bothered his cousin Walter Travers, dealt with predestination, as preached by English Calvinists of the day. Calvinists such as William Perkins, John Rainolds, Lancelot Andrewes, Travers himself, and others drew on Calvin's successor, Theodore Beza, to answer the burning question of how one could prove to oneself that he was in fact one of the "elect." Once it had been affirmed that Christ died only for those "elected" (supralapsarianism, drawn from 2 Peter 1:10) it became essential to be one of those predestined to salvation. Hooker's view on this subject was closer to that of the Dutchman, Jacobus Arminius (1559-1606), a student of Beza, who opposed his teacher's doctrines and asserted that, if a man believes in his heart, that is proof sufficient that he was predestined to do so and hence he is saved. This more inclusive view of election was the friendlier brand of Calvinism preferred by Hooker.

On this issue Hooker broke with his mentor, John Rainolds, and actually went so far as to aid Whitgift in preventing Rainolds from publishing one of his books. Hooker's view of predestination was based on the distinction between "necessary" and "contingent" events. God has foreknowledge of both types of events but does not interfere with contingent events which therefore may occur or not. Thus, the foreknowledge God has of all things does not prove that he predetermines all things because He foresees both what might have happened and what does happen: God's "prescience", said Hooker, "does not overwhelm contingency, so neither does His will overwhelm freedom [man's or God's]."

"Devastation and violence confront me," Hooker read from his copy of the authorized *Bishop's Bible*. "Strife breaks out, discord raises its head, and so law grows effete; justice does not come forth victorious, for the wicked outwit the righteous and so justice comes out perverted . . ."

"Who is responsible for the strife, the controversy, the disorder, the dishonesty, the hatred, the violence that threaten to destroy all law and justice and all peace in our country? Are you? Am I? Is Rome? Is Mr Calvin? Is the Church? Is God? Who is at fault here?" This would not have sounded like the usual fare from Oxford: a dry recitation of theological axioms and proofs, or the endless citation of scriptural texts to support the charges and countercharges of religious opponents. Maybe there would be some excitement this morning after all.

Hooker continued to read out his sermon from his manuscript. He was no extemporaneous spellbinder like Walter Travers. Hooker knew that Travers had made a name for himself as an exciting and compelling preacher at the nearby Temple Church. Travers employed the new "London" style of preaching so popular among Puritans. These preachers memorized their sermons so that they would appear to be speaking extemporaneously. They made generous use of gestures and voice inflections, as if they were actors in one of the stage plays then popular in the city. Hooker disdained this sort of staged performance from the pulpit. He thought it was better suited for children in the nursery than for instructing adults. He was confident about his own preaching style. His material was organized and well-documented. More importantly, he was sanguine about his ability to move others with the logic of his argument and the power of his words. His rhetorical flair had been well honed in all of those Oxford disputations where he had sharpened his use of metaphor, simile, epigram, and a host of other rhetorical aids. He had had wonderful models at Oxford, including John Rainolds' famed lectures on Aristotle. He was no newcomer to the public platform. He had mastered the art of persuasion.[9]

He continued to preach:

> The fault for all of this terrible conflict and chaos among us lies in our zeal to set ourselves up as judges of one another. In the name of Holy Scripture, in the name of the Fathers of the Church, in the name of Master Calvin, in the name of God himself, some of us condemn others of us as predestined for damnation, as cut off from salvation. We proclaim ourselves to be elected for righteousness, to be saved by God's predetermined election of us.
>
> Who are we to know what God has pre-ordained? By what awful authority do we declare that God had by His pre-election cut off all of our Christian forebears who lived and worshipped in the only Church they knew, the Catholic church of Rome, and then condemned them to a certain damnation?

He continued to elaborate an irenical message of toleration, cooperation, and inclusiveness, which he would expand and develop for the rest of his life. He supported his arguments with generous references to church Fathers, ancient philosophers and Holy Scripture.

> Because the church of Rome is corrupt and mistaken in many of its teachings does not mean that all members of that church today or in past generations are cut off from God's tender mercies because of God's supposed pre-ordination of their damnation. Is it not more reasonable for us to assume that by their ignorance of the Holy Word, which a corrupt church had withheld from them, and by even that small portion of true faith given to them, they are by God's grace, saved?
>
> Wherever we differ strongly on matters of God's plan and intention for His people, to the point of disrupting the public peace and order of our realm and Church, and where the Holy Scripture is silent or unclear, should we not use the light of our God-given reason to point us toward His intention for us? And do we not have evidence that we are close to that divine intention when discord ceases and a tolerant and accepting accord prevails in our mutual relations?
>
> A reasonable interpretation of Scripture and an examination of the history of what God had revealed to His Church throughout the ages has shown us how wrong we are to presume to judge one another. We are asked to forgive and accept as we have been forgiven and accepted. We proclaim the damnation of other men at the peril of our own souls. We must stop this judging and damning one another in God's name, as though it were His eternal will we are proclaiming and not our own presumptuous self-righteousness.
>
> Some among us have based their condemnation of our Roman brothers and others with whom they find fault, including the Galatians of old who practised circumcision, on God's eternal decree of reprobation which they believe predetermined the damnation of such persons. Then they look to the same high place to find the cause of their own pre-election to salvation and blessedness.

> Granted that both the Galatians and the papists were and are in error. From this does it follow that God ordained such error, that He is the author of evil and sin in the world? We mistake Holy Scripture if we find therein the proof that our God is the cause of our ignorance and sin.
>
> Rather, God's will for man is conditional, not absolute. His will is to permit us the freedom to disobey His original intention for us, which is that by His grace we should be saved. When we exercise our free will and deny Him, we cause our own ruin. He has not pre-ordained that we be thus cut off from Him and be damned. No more has He pre-ordained that if we choose, by His Grace, to affirm his Lordship, we have been thereby elected by Him for salvation.
>
> Master Calvin's opinion to the contrary notwithstanding, we may say that there are, with God, two wills. The first is an antecedent will which is that all of us should be saved. The second is a consequent will, which is that those who live, by his Grace, a life which freely responds to God's commands, are in fact saved.

Such words must have made his audience restless. Some may have begun arguing among themselves, as was the custom during sermons at Paul's Cross.

Hooker continued:

> Surely, Holy Scripture does not teach that God wants us to destroy His Church by condemning or electing one another in His name. Is it God's will that we go on fighting about merely accidental historical or regional outward features of our various religious beliefs and practices, such as which vestments, if any, to wear, or whether to stand or kneel at prayer?
>
> We in this realm are one Christian commonwealth with one sovereign prince as head. As citizens of this commonwealth we are all members of one English Church. That Church is founded upon God's truths as revealed in His Holy Scriptures and to His Church over the ages.
>
> Our religion is reformed in the spirit of Master Calvin, but not in slavish obedience to him or his followers. Rather we join his reformed and scripture-based theology with our traditional liturgical practices.
>
> All English men and women are welcomed as members of the Church so long as they conform outwardly to the forms and customs of our religious practice. We do not presume to search the hearts and souls of church members to discern their innermost thoughts and intentions. That is the providence of God alone.
>
> Certainly we should not, in the name of Calvin, sow disorder in our realm, by tempting simple common folks with the belief that many of those with more education, wealth and power than themselves—men they are naturally disposed to envy and dislike—are damned, while they as simple, poor and ignorant people have been elected and blessed by the Holy Spirit as God's special chosen children.
>
> To win converts to any sect by such pandering to common human weakness is not a reformation but a corruption of religion. It is, as well, a threat to the peace and order of our commonweal and the safety of our sovereign queen.

It is not our right to declare the preordained will of God on any subject. When we cease from this practice, we may hope for a return of peace, order and civility in our Church and nation.

God save our gracious queen. God save us all.

Hooker was probably greeted with a mixture of cheers and boos, with the latter no doubt predominating. He was learning a hard lesson. Those who attack the status quo are always welcomed to the speaker's platform and the printer's shop, no matter how intemperate or outlandish their attacks on present institutions and practices might be. Those who take the more temperate course, counselling moderation and support for traditional patterns, can expect only lukewarm response from their audiences, at best. Later on in his life, he expressed this painful lesson in what were to become the oft-quoted opening lines from Book I of his *magnum opus*.

> He that goeth about to persuade a multitude, that they are not so well governed as they ought to be, shall never want attentive and favourable hearers; because they know the manifold defects whereunto every kind of regiment is subject . . . And because such as openly reprove supposed disorders of state are taken for principal friends to the common benefit of all . . . whatsoever they utter passes for good . . . Whereas, on the other side, if we maintain things that are established, we have not only to strive with a number of heavy prejudices deeply rooted in the hearts of men, who think that herein we . . . speak in favour of the present state, because thereby we either hold or seek preferment; but also to bear such exceptions as minds so averted beforehand usually take against that which they are loath should be poured into them.[10]

Hooker was discovering, possibly to his pain, that, by nature, humans resent authority and suspect those who defend it, no matter how nobly. Humankind loves the rebel who breaks the law and threatens order in the name of freedom. Instinctively, most of us resist those who argue against the purity of revolutionary ideals. It is an uphill struggle to convince us of the wisdom of choosing to submit to the ordering established values of the commonwealth.

THE CHURCHMANS OF LONDON

John Churchman was one of London's leading citizens, with friends in high places. He was descended from a long line of successful London officials and merchants, including one of the sheriffs of London, who in 1378 had been instrumental in rebuilding the ancient customs house on Lower Thames Street.[11] His ancestors had been prominent in the powerful Merchant Taylors' guild since the fourteenth century. Like his father-in-law, Robert Hulson, who was master of the company in 1569, John was to rise through the warden's chairs to become master in 1594.

He also served as chamberlain of the city, an office reflecting the highest level of confidence in his financial acumen and reliability—a fitting climax to a long and distinguished career in business and public service.[12]

Churchman probably endorsed Hooker's call for moderation and an end to reckless intemperance in political discourse. So far as we know, he was a moderate Calvinist, not kindly disposed to extreme changes in church polity or, for that matter, to anything that smacked of a threat to the peace and order of the realm—or, more directly, to the city and his business interests therein. He may have told Hooker of Archbishop Sandys' difficulties, when he was the bishop of London, in keeping radical Puritans from using Paul's Cross as a forum for their treason. The bishop would appoint apparently sound men to preach and then they would reveal their true colours, hitherto well-disguised, as soon as they climbed into the pulpit.[13]

When Richard Hooker finally put his tired body to rest on that autumn night in 1584, following his sermon at Paul's Cross, he had no idea that Churchman's large half-timbered house on Watling Street would be his home for the next decade. By January, he would move in and commute to Drayton Beauchamp as necessary. By March, he would be master of the prestigious Temple Church and walk each day the short distance between the Churchman house and the Inns of Court on Fleet Street. Nor did he know what an important role the Churchman family would soon begin to play in his life.

At the time of Hooker's first overnight stay in his house, Churchman was a man of about fifty, nearing the height of his influence and considerable personal wealth. By trade, he was a merchant tailor, dealing primarily in large wholesale transactions for finished woollen cloth in London, throughout England, and overseas, especially in Ireland. In addition to his imposing house on Watling Street, a frequent gathering place for many of the most prominent clerical and business supporters of the queen's policies, John had a summer home in Enfield, a prosperous suburban town just twenty miles up the river Ware, north of the city.

Churchman and his wife, Alice, lived in this fine townhouse with their teenage children, Joan and Robert, and four younger children, John, Mary, Ann, and Elizabeth. They were still grieving the loss of their son William, a student at Corpus Christi, Oxford, who had died just a year earlier during the summer break from college, and two young daughters, Sara and Katherine, who had died shortly thereafter. Hooker gave them some consolation during his few days with them. He had known William as a student at Corpus Christi during his own final years as a senior fellow and professor there.[14]

A typical prosperous merchant's house in London at the time would have been built on four floors, its front door opening on to a great hall, in which the family ate dinner and entertained guests. This would have

RICHARD HOOKER'S LONDON
THE TOWER
LONDON WALL
BISHOP GATE STREET
LEADEN HALL STREET
TOWER STREET
THAMES STREET
MERCHANT TAYLORS
GRACE CHURCH STREET
LONDON BRIDGE
THREADNEEDLE STREET
CORN HILL
LOMBARD STREET
CANDLEWICK STREET
LOTHBURY STREET
OLD JEWERY
OLD FISH STREET
BOWE LANE
MILK STREET
CHEAPSIDE
WATLING STREET
BREAD STREET
FRIDAY STREET
ST. AUGUSTINE
CHURCHMAN HOUSE
OLD CHANGE STREET
PAUL'S CROSS
ST. PAULS
ALDERSGATE
ST. MARTINS
RIVER THAMES
PATERNOSTER ROW
BISHOP'S PLACE
STATIONERS HALL
NEWGATE
ADDLE HILL
BURGHLEY HOUSE
OLD BAILEY
WATER LANE
LUDGATE HILL
FLEET DITCH
FLEET RIVER
SHOE LANE
FLEET STREET
TEMPLE CHURCH
INNER TEMPLE
TEMPLE GARDEN
FLEET LANE
HOLBORNE
CLIFFORD'S INN
CHANCERY LANE
TEMPLE LANE
TEMPLE STAIRS
LINCOLN'S INN
TEMPLE BAR
MIDDLE TEMPLE

had oak panelled walls, a tiled floor, and an elaborately plastered ceiling. Bay windows giving on to the street would have been an extra sign of opulence. All the major pieces of furniture would have been of oak, many with geometrical carvings.

London at the time was a compact but bustling and growing city of about 75,000 restless, striving souls. Watling Street, where the Churchmans lived, was near the Royal Exchange, less than fifteen years old and already the showplace of commercial London. It was a three-sided, four-storey brick edifice built in the high Renaissance style, with a grand marble-columned arcade around the perimeter of a great open courtyard, and a magnificent tiered bell tower rising high above the centre wing. The bell rang twice each day, at noon and six p.m., calling merchants to hear the latest business news from the markets of the world. This great Exchange, John knew, as he passed by it each day on his way to the Merchant Taylors guild on Threadneedle Street, stood as a testimony to the greatness of London among the cities of the world.

Around the Exchange were streets bustling with markets, with wagons and carts laden with wine, beer, coal, fish, combs, fruit, needles, music boxes, toys, and just about every product imaginable, except foodstuffs. John and his wife could find food at markets in nearby streets: vegetables and dairy products at the great Cheapside market; meat and grains along Leadenhall; more butchers on Eastcheap, at the St Nicholas shambles and the stock market next to St Mary Wool church. Dried fish could be found along Thames Street and an abundance of fresh fish, whether perch, trout, smelt, shrimp, eels, or others, from fishmongers on Bridge Street down near the river.[15]

During these first few days with the Churchman family, Hooker had an opportunity to meet his future wife, Joan. She was about seventeen when she joined her parents in welcoming Richard to the house. She was often at family meals where he was present. As the oldest Churchman daughter, rapidly approaching marriageable age, Joan was interested in the young bachelors who frequented the Churchman house. Hers would be a handsome dowry, sufficient to assure a match with someone far more promising than this struggling cleric whom she watched as he talked with her parents. She would have thought him uncommonly quiet and polite—a bit nervous perhaps, and not so polished as other men she had observed, clearly not a sophisticated London man.

Richard's first impressions of Joan were no doubt a mixture of disinterest and fascination. He had had precious little experience with women, and, at the age of thirty, had probably resigned himself to (or been comfortable with) bachelorhood. On the other hand, here was a young woman, readily at hand, who may have seemed self-confident for her age—even somewhat assertive. This meeting of an older man of intellectual bent and limited resources from the provinces who was on his way up in his profession, and a young city woman of privileged economic circumstance, assertive temperament, and urbane tastes, was fraught with possibilities.

Young Robert Churchman, John's fifteen-year-old son, may have made himself available to give the provincial cleric a guided tour of the city, which would have taken in "old" St Paul's, then a Gothic church, not the classical Wren building familiar today, and, outside the city walls, relatively distant Westminster Abbey.[16] Secular sights would have included John Churchman's Merchant Taylors Hall, home to the powerful guild that had become the legal authority overseeing all dealings in cloth, which made it not only an economic but a political power to be reckoned with. Merchant Taylors, like all the guilds, provided not only employment but also an important network of mutual assistance designed to secure desirable schools, lives, houses, political position, child-care—whatever one's fellows might need. Members socialized with one another, worshipped together, attended one another's weddings and funerals, and were welcome guests in each other's homes.[17] The Guild supported its own school, Merchant Taylors School, second only to St Pauls in reputation. Most of the Churchman and Sandys boys attended there.[18]

In London Hooker was introduced to a complex way of life for which his academic and clerical career so far had not prepared him. The city, with its twenty-six wards crowded into a square mile, was, he learned, governed by aldermen, to whom the queen, residing outside the city in Westminster, left its affairs. A short way down the river from Merchant Taylors Hall, the Tower still held Mary Stewart's Jesuit conspirators. To the north and east of St Paul's, Cheapside was the widest and best-paved street of the city, boasting some of its most elegant inhabitants and shops. A short walk along Holborn led to Tyburn, with its "tree," the gallows at which traitors had been hanged for hundreds of years. The permanent triangular structure put up in 1571 had recently been the scene of the death of the Jesuit Edmund Campion and many other Catholic priests who attempted to "reconcile" the queen's subjects to the "old religion."[19] Less grisly were the city's three great schools: St Paul's, founded early in the century by the great humanist scholar John Colet; Merchant Taylors, supported by the guild; St Anthony's, founded in the middle of the previous century, where both Thomas More and Whitgift had studied. The immediate environs of St Paul's housed dozens of booksellers, each advertising their speciality with an appropriate sign: Bible, gun, rose—and cross-keys, which would one day produce Hooker's great opus.

In the cathedral itself, as well as in its external precincts, were the chief employment centres and major spots for hawking cheap, often stolen, merchandise. Here could be found everything from feathers, pins, dog-collars, and earrings to furniture and window-glass. The central aisle was one of London's chief meeting-places for business and social gossip. It was also a place to beware of conmen and pickpockets. Beggars abounded inside and outside the cathedral, as did poets singing their odes, painters adorning and selling their canvases, and musicians performing.

Between the City of London and Westminster were the Inns of Court, the centre of the legal profession, effectively a specialized university. Its thousands of law students, then, as now, saw the law as a ladder to politics and many other positions of influence. By the Inns of Court stood the imposing Temple Church, at which Hooker would soon preside.

NOTES

1. There is no recorded date for Hooker's sermon at Paul's Cross. Most reputable scholars, including C. J. Sisson and W. Speed Hill, have followed Izaak Walton's chronology and put him there in 1581. This is plausible, since preachers were regularly drawn from Oxford and Hooker was a fellow there at that time. However, I prefer the later 1584 date, suggested by Georges Edelen, because it fits better with other developments in Hooker's life at about this time. See Walton, *Life*, 22; Sisson, 25; W. Speed Hill, *Studies in Richard Hooker: Essays Preliminary to an Edition of His Works* (Cleveland and London: The Press of Case Western Reserve University, 1972), 124; Georges Edelen, "A Chronology of Richard Hooker's Life," in *Folger* VI, xxii. For background information on the Cross, see Millar Maclure, *The Pauls Cross Sermons* (Toronto: University of Toronto Press, 1958); P. J. Chandlery, *The Tower to Tyburn* (London: Sands & Co.,1924),113-15.
2. For an account of this incident, see Booty, *Jewel*, 28.
3. John Churchman's son William was a freshman at Corpus Christi in 1581 and died in 1583. Katherine and Sara Churchman, at ages nine and three respectively, died in the early months of 1584, at about the same time as William, presumably from a contagious disease which swept through the family in a matter of months. The connection between the Churchmans and Sandys, and hence between Hooker and both families, was very close, if not always amicable. The fullest account of this association and its consequences for Hooker and his own family is in Sisson, especially 25-44; 188.

Like most of the city, the Churchman house was destroyed in the fire of 1666. We know, however, that it was located on Watling Street, very close to St Paul's. Their parish church, St Augustine's, was also on Watling Street, at the intersection with Old Change Street and just across that street from St Paul's churchyard. The church was also destroyed in the fire and, after being rebuilt, was destroyed again by German bombs in 1940. This was where Hooker and Joan were married in 1588 and where four of their children: Richard, Alice, Cecily, and Edwin were subsequently christened. I believe that the Churchman home was next door to St Augustine Church, about where a modern seven-storey brick and stone office/apartment building now stands. The evidence for selecting this location, although not conclusive, is compelling. According to the antiquarian John Stow (himself a working tailor and member of the Merchant Taylors Company), in his 1598 survey of Tudor London, St Augustine's was "by Paules gate," in "Farrington ward within." There was also a Farrington Ward outside the city limits. (The ward was named for the thirteenth-century goldsmith and alderman whose descendant, in the next century, built the arch-gate near St Augustine's into St Paul's churchyard.) It is likely that the Churchmans, as members of St Augustine parish, lived within Farrington Ward. Since Stow records that there was only one house on

Watling Street within the limits of that ward, namely the house next to the church, we can make a good guess that the Churchmans, and, later, Richard Hooker and his family, lived in that house. See John Stow, *A Survey of London* (Stroud, Gloucester: Publishing Limited, 1994), 298-9. (Reprinted from the 1603 edition by Alan Sutton.)

4. Sisson makes a good case that John Churchman was not, as Walton alleged, so poor and desperate at this time as to need this small stipend. Furthermore, Sisson argues, less convincingly, that the practice of housing Paul's Cross preachers at boarding houses probably postdates Hooker's time. It suited Walton's purpose to depict John Churchman as a man down on his luck—"sometime a draper of good note in Watling Street, upon whom poverty had at last come like an armed man, and brought him into a necessitous condition . . ." This picture provided Walton with another bit of evidence for his own spurious, if innocent, case against the Churchmans and what he regarded as Hooker's unfortunate marriage into that family. I accept Sisson's argument that John Churchman was still a prosperous and important figure in London at the time of Hooker's years in the city. But I see no reason to doubt that the bishop of London was offering a stipend to host his preachers at this time. To this extent I accept Walton's account. See Sisson, 26-9, and Walton, *Life,* 22.

5. An engraving from a painting of Aylmer from about this period reveals a man with a long beard, handlebar mustache, and high forehead shadowing shrewd, keen eyes. See frontispiece in John Strype, *Historical Collections of the Life and Acts of John Aylmer Lord Bishop of London in the Reign of Queen Elizabeth* (Oxford: Oxford University Press, 1821). Original edition, 1700. An authoritative treatment of the religious politics of the English Church in this period is Collinson, *Religion of Protestants*. See esp. 23, 36, 63, 75.

6. Archbishop Whitgift preached at the Cross on 17 November 1583 from Paul's Letter to Titus in which troublemakers are warned to be subject to their rulers and do good works. In a preface to this sermon, written at the time of publication in 1589, Whitgift calls those who attack him and other church leaders "lewd," "shameless," "vile" men who "seek their own glory, rather than the peace of the Church: for every small cause they divide and cut in sunder the glorious body of Christ . . ." He says that these "vicious and intemperate" preachers "straine at a knat and swallow a camel" as they pretend peace but make war on the Church. Copy of this sermon is in the Lambeth Palace Library, 1589.22.

7. As Thomas Fuller said in his oft-quoted characterization of Hooker's preaching style: "Hooker his style was prolixe, but not tedious, and such who would patiently attend and give him credit at the reading and hearing of his Sentences, had their expectation ever paid at the close thereof. He may be said to have made good Musick with his fiddle and stick alone, without any Rosen, having neither Pronunciation nor gesture to grace his matter." Fuller, *Worthies*, I, 264

8. Since there is no surviving text of Hooker's sermon, I have presumed to invent this plausible summary from comments regarding its content by Travers, in his *Supplication to the Privy Council* and Hooker, in his *Answer to the Supplication*. See Folger, V, 198; 235-6. I have also used texts of contemporaneous sermons by Hooker, especially *Certainty and Perpetuity of Faith in the Elect* and *A Discourse of Justification and How the Foundation of Faith is Overthrown. Ibid*, 69-82; 105-169.

A fine summary of the doctrine of predestination, as preached by English Calvinists of the day, is R. T. Kendall, *Calvin and English Calvinism to 1649* (Oxford: Oxford University Press, 1979), 13-31, 141-50. See also Patrick Collinson, "Hooker and the Elizabethan Establishment," McGrade, *Richard Hooker and the Construction of Christian Community*, 156-61. See also Hooker's so-called "Dublin Fragments," *Folger*, IV, 123-133; *Works,* II, 562; also Paget, 217.

9. For an excellent discussion of Hooker's preaching style, see P. E. Forte, "Richard Hooker as Preacher," Folger, V, 658-63; 674-82. See also Lee W. Gibbs,

"Theology, Logic and Rhetoric in the Temple Controversy between Richard Hooker and Walter Travers," *Anglican Theological Review*, 65:2, 1983, 177-188; Brian Vickers, "Hooker's Prose Style," in A. S. McGrade and Brian Vickers, eds., *Richard Hooker: Of the Laws of Ecclesiastical Polity* (New York: St. Martin's Press, 1975), 41-59; Georges Edelen, "Hooker's Style," in Hill, *Studies*, 241-77. Hooker's biting comment about the difference between appropriate teaching styles for children and mature adults is from his sermon *Of the Nature of Pride*, Folger, V, 310.; *Works*, I, 198.
10. *Folger*, I, 56; *Works*, I, 198.
11. Stow, 157.
12. The dates of Churchman's service as city chamberlain are unrecorded. See Sisson, 24; 184, n.1. For detailed accounts of the power and influence of the guilds (companies), especially the Merchant Taylors, in virtually all aspects of community life during these years, see Steve Rappaport, *Worlds Within Worlds: Structures of Life in Sixteenth Century London* (New York: Cambridge University Press, 1989) and Susan Brigden, *London and the Reformation* (Oxford: Clarendon Press, 1989).
13. Bishop Sandys wrote to Burghley and Leicester about his frustration when two ministers he had chosen to preach revealed their true sympathies only after they were in the pulpit: "I do what I can to procure fit men to preach at the Cross; but I cannot know their hearts, and these times have altered opinions. Such as preached discreetly last year now labour by railing to feed the fancies of the people . . . Such men must be restrained if the state shall stand safe. Truly, my Lords, I have dealt so carefully as I can to keep such fanatical spirits from the Cross; but the deceitful devil enemy to religion has so poured out the poison of sedition and so suddenly changed these wavering minds, that it is hard to tell whom a man may trust." Cited in W. H. Fere and C. E. Douglas, eds., *Puritan Manifestoes,* (London, 1954), xxii-xxiii, original edition 1907. See also, Strype, *Whitgift,* 19.
14. Sisson, 124-5.
15. For contemporary descriptions of sixteenth-century London, which complement Stow's *Survey* see Harrison, *The Description of England* (1583). Excellent modern accounts include Roy Porter, *London, A Social History* (Cambridge: Harvard University Press, 1995). Porter's Tudor London is "a bustling, bursting city" filled not only with "sumptuous halls," "gracious residences," "elegant shops," and "majestic manors," but also with masses of people "jostling wherever mazes of backyards and blind alleys led off main streets," "dissolute, loose and insolent people" living in "festering slums." Also useful are A. L. Beir and Roger Finlay, *The Making of the Metropolis: London 1500-1700* (London & New York: Longmans, 1986) and Rosemary Weinstein *Tudor London* (London: Museum of London, 1994). For a detailed description of the streets, buildings and principal events in London the best source is, *The London Encyclopedia*, edited by Ben Weinreb and Christopher Hibbert (London: Macmillan, 1983).
16. We know that Robert Churchman was about fourteen or fifteen because his age is given as about 45 in a 1613 court deposition cited in Sisson, 148. As for Joan, we can only join Sisson, the closest scholar of such Hooker family matters, and "wonder" at her age when Hooker first met her. *Ibid.*, 20. Seventeen is a very good guess.
17. For accounts of some of the more ribald aspects of social life in the guild hall at Merchant Taylors, see William Winstanley, *The Hounour of Merchant Taylors* (London, 1668), esp. 30-31. (Copy in British Museum Library.)
18. See H. B. Wilson, *The History of the Merchant Taylors School* (London: 1812), esp. 11-21.
19. Tyburn, referred to in those days as "Tyburn Tree," was near the site of today's Marble Arch, at the northeast corner of Hyde Park.

CHAPTER 8
Introduction to Church Politics

COUSIN WALTER

1584 was a landmark year in Hooker's life. There had been other important years: 1562, when as an eight-year-old boy he moved from the shelter of his mother's protection in rural Heavitree into the busy life of his uncle's Exeter and began his formal schooling; 1569, when the fifteen-year-old entered Corpus Christi, Oxford as an underprepared, underfunded undergraduate; 1574, when he entered into the life of an Oxford tutor with the auspicious charge to his care of Edwin Sandys, son of the bishop of London; 1579, when his career as a twenty-five year-old Oxford don blossomed with important appointments and challenges.

What marks 1584 is that it signals Hooker's entry into national religious politics and so into the mainstream of the later stage of the Protestant Reformation in England. Hooker's baptism in the national political arena came at a time of rising hysteria over threats of foreign invasion and reinstitution of the Catholic religion. Memories of Catholic Mary Tudor were still vivid, and fears of Catholic Mary Stewart, the current catalyst for foreign and domestic plots against Queen Elizabeth and her brand of Protestantism, were in the forefront of political discourse.

Just as important as the real and imagined threats from Catholics to the queen's safety, and to her style of reformed religion, were challenges to the established Church from the radical Calvinists, many of whom sought not only further reform in theology and liturgy but fundamental changes in church polity as well. It was, in fact, these alterations in the governance of the Church, especially the threatened replacement of queen and bishops by a largely decentralized structure with significant lay control, that most concerned the queen and her chief ministers in these later years of the century. And, of course, once the decision was taken to execute Mary Stewart, and the Spanish invasion had failed, the Catholic threat was significantly diminished and the chief remaining enemies to established authority were perceived to be the radical Calvinists and church separatists, although these groups were, in fact, also much weakened by this time.

The political battles between the queen's emergent Anglican Church and its Catholic and radical Protestant enemies were waged in various locales throughout the later years of the sixteenth century: parliament, the royal court, the church hierarchy, the pulpits of the land, the universities, the streets of London, the printing presses.

Hooker's first entry into the political cauldron was his sermon at Paul's Cross and his meeting, at about that time, with his cousin Walter Travers. Travers was one of the two or three leading exponents of radical Calvinism in England. He set forth his explosive doctrines in writings that were already being seen as basic documents of emergent English presbyterianism, as well as through revolutionary sermons that he preached regularly at the Temple Church where he held the position of reader—a kind of assistant minister.

The first meeting of these two men, soon to become principal protagonists in the English Reformation, took place at about the time of Hooker's Paul's Cross sermon. It may have been Edwin Sandys, Hooker's former student and good friend—now a first-year law student at the Inns of Court and soon to be a member at Middle Temple Inn—who introduced the two men. Certainly, Edwin's stature as the son of the now archbishop of York and nephew of Miles Sandys, who was member of parliament, one of England's leading jurists, and prominent member of Middle Temple about to be elected its treasurer, gave Edwin social and political standing sufficient to make such an introduction.[1]

Young Edwin Sandys no doubt considered his former tutor to be a promising gladiator to challenge Travers at the Temple. Hooker's Paul's Cross sermon and his lectures and talks at Oxford seemed to the moderate Sandys a welcome antidote to the threatening rhetoric of the arch-presbyterian, Travers. Edwin applauded Hooker's uncharacteristic voice of moderation and common sense, his preference for tradition and public order, and his ability to organize and set forth convincing arguments drawn persuasively from first principles. Hooker represented a needed relief from the tedious line-by-line refutations that characterized so much of the Church's apologetic writing. Far more urbane and sophisticated than his Oxford mentor, Sandys was able, even eager, to acquaint Hooker with the dangers inherent in Travers' sermons at the Temple Church, addressing week after week, as he did, an often captive audience of influential lawyers, barristers, judges, and politicians in this, one of England's most important churches.

Sandys would have been among the first to congratulate Hooker on his Paul's Cross sermon and to mention to him the possibility, already under discussion by his father and others in the church leadership, that he, Richard Hooker, might be chosen to replace Travers at the Temple. For his part, Hooker was aware that success at the Cross would lead to more public attention than he had received to date. Part of him must have longed for such notice and the higher position in the Church that might follow from it. Some of his genes, after all, came from those prominent and very public Hookers of Exeter; and, he certainly could use the security of a higher standard of living than that afforded at Drayton Beauchamp parish. There was also much to be said for the opportunity to try out his ideas in the political arena.

Hooker knew that, as reader at the Temple Church, Travers was an important part of the strategy of the radical Calvinists for taking control of the Church of England. The extremist ideas Richard had excoriated in his Paul's Cross sermon were openly expounded at the Temple by Travers and dozens of other Puritan readers, or "lecturers" as they were sometimes called, at the most politically sensitive churches in London.[2]

These readers, in fact, occupied about a quarter of the pulpits in London. When they preached, they drew larger crowds than most sporting and cultural events in town. They were resident in many of the leading churches throughout the country, their number having doubled in recent years. Altogether, they represented as serious a threat to the established Church from within as the Roman Catholics did from without.

It was undoubtedly the tolerant attitude toward "prophesyings" (informal discussion and Bible-study carried on by many of the lecturers and readers) that had allowed this presbyterian movement to take hold so rapidly. With Archbishop John Whitgift now in charge, armed with his *Articles of Subscription* and his episcopal visitations to individual parishes, these radical practices were slowly being exorcised. At about the time of Hooker's sermon at Paul's Cross, Whitgift had removed one of the major Puritan ringleaders, John Field, from his post at St Mary Aldermary. Not long before, the queen herself had said, with some exasperation, to the then Archbishop Edmund Grindal that "it was good for the Church to have few preachers . . . three or four might suffice for the country."[3]

Hooker agreed that a little preaching went a long way. He usually preferred to emphasize common (corporate) prayers, the Sacraments, reading of Scripture, and delivery of prepared homilies. Too much preaching could breed trouble. Nowhere would the danger of undisciplined preaching be more apparent than at the Temple Church, where so many of England's present and future political leaders attended services regularly. Despite efforts by archbishops and many bishops to deny most of the radical Calvinists decent clerical appointments and remove those who persisted in non-conformist practices, they could not easily prevent sympathetic gentry and merchants in London and elsewhere from endowing lectureships and readerships for presbyterian troublemakers. Among the most prominent examples of this practice, as Hooker knew, were, in addition to Walter Travers and John Field, Robert Crowley at St Giles Cripplegate, and William Charke at nearby Lincolns Inn.[4]

When a wealthy layman paid the stipend for a lectureship, he would claim the right to select the reader who filled that pulpit. For decades the gentry had had the gift of parishes within their domains, in many instances replacing the monasteries' appointment rights of earlier centuries. Now they often filled these pulpits with radical Puritan lecturers. To a degree, this was the situation that prevailed at the Temple Church. Although the queen made the clerical appointments here, salaries and benefits were paid (or not) by the lay barristers at Middle and Inner Temple Inns, whose approval for appointment and removal was, therefore, customary, if not legally required. Not surprisingly, the lawyers at the Inns felt that the decision was theirs and not the archbishop's, or the lord treasurer's, as to whether Travers should stay on as reader, be promoted to master, or be replaced altogether.

Advocates of the presbyterian discipline, such as Walter Travers and Thomas Cartwright, claimed scriptural warrant for the use of lecturers and readers. There were four "orders" of ministry, as they saw it: pastor, doctor, elder, and deacon. Of the two professional orders, pastor and doctor, the role of pastor was to exhort the flock, principally through his sermons, to follow Christ. The doctor's function was to interpret Scripture and assure sound doctrine. His pronouncements should be communicated through his sermons, lectures, or readings, hence the terms "lecturer" and "reader."

Hooker quickly learned from his own experiences that bishops often had mixed motives concerning these readers. Since the dioceses usually lacked sufficient funds to staff the churches, they might be glad to have this new source of manpower. The bishops may have disliked the theology of most of the readers and abhorred their churchmanship, yet they could admire their learning and the excellent preaching abilities that drew people into their churches. The Puritan lecturers, including most prominently Walter Travers, were often among the best educated and most effective ministers in the Church.[5]

Hooker knew a good deal about Travers even before their first meeting in 1584. His cousin, by marriage, was, after all, one of the most famous radical Puritans in England, some would say second only in importance, among the emerging Presbyterians, to Archbishop Whitgift's other longtime nemesis, Thomas Cartwright. Although both Travers and Cartwright had sprung from the hotbed of extreme Calvinism at Cambridge, Hooker, as an Oxford man, was familiar with their writings and their general reputation. His own mentor, John Rainolds, a Calvinist who was sympathetic to both men, had made sure of that.

Walter Travers was born in Nottingham in 1548. He had a sister, Anne, and three brothers: Robert, John, and Humphrey. Robert, the eldest, was a prominent Puritan scholar at Cambridge whose career paralleled Walter's. John, the next oldest, who was a near contemporary of Hooker's at Oxford, married Hooker's cousin Alice. Humphrey, the youngest, earned an M.A. at Cambridge in 1574 and served as a priest in Lincolnshire.

Richard had some ambivalence about Walter. Who was he, really, and what did he represent? Was he the brilliant paragon of Protestant reform in England as some, like his own tutor, John Rainolds, seemed to think? Or was he the scourge of Elizabeth's hoped-for Anglican religious consensus, as others, like Whitgift, asserted? Hooker was familiar with the man's writings. He knew that Travers was the most influential architect of the highly-touted presbyterian form of church government. Travers' important book, written in Latin and published at Cambridge in 1574, was titled *Ecclesiasticae Discipline et Anglicanae Explicatio*. Known simply as the *Explicatio*, it was translated into English by Thomas Cartwright and quickly took its place as the authoritative guidebook for church organization among the more advanced Calvinists.

The major points in the *Explicatio* were familiar to Hooker: the Bible is to be taken more literally as the Word of God than Hooker liked. Holy Scripture is the sole authority for determining the correct form (discipline) for church organization; the presbyterian polity, in which clergy are elected by congregations first and later ordained, if at all, by bishops, is the only correct form of governance; each congregation is independent of the others and of any central authority, save a national system of councils with no binding authority; all ministers in each order of ministry are equal to one another. Such a doctrine could lead to a separation of the Church from the crown, an intolerable concept for Hooker and for Anglicanism.

Richard was aware of Travers' brilliant early career at Trinity College, Cambridge, in the 1560s. While a senior fellow there Travers had been highly regarded as one of the most promising among more advanced Calvinist thinkers. He had received his fellowship with the approval of John Whitgift, who was vice-chancellor at the time. Soon after, in 1572, Whitgift had regretted that appointment and expelled Walter and his brother John, also a well-known Puritan scholar, along with Thomas Cartwright (for the second time), for their refusal to abjure dangerous ideas about church discipline and to accept the polity of the established church.[6]

Hooker knew also that after Travers had been expelled from Cambridge, he had left the country to seek more congenial employment in Geneva, the city of Walter's hero, John Calvin, who had died six years earlier. While there, Travers become acquainted with Calvin's ardent disciple and successor, Theodore Beza. The two quickly became colleagues and friends. Cartwright was also in Geneva at the time. In 1578, Travers moved to Antwerp to accept the call to minister to the English company of wool merchants. He was soon in trouble with the Antwerp congregation for such radical actions as his refusal to use the *Book of Common Prayer*. The nature of Travers' ordination at Antwerp (congregational election) would later provide Whitgift with his argument for denying Travers a clerical post in England.

When Travers came home from Antwerp in 1580, he was a virtual outcast from the established Church, apparently with little hope of finding employment in England. He was offered a professorship at St Mary's College in St Andrew's University in 1580, but turned it down—too far from the center of presbyterian politics in London, no doubt. Then his old patron Lord Burghley, ever the protector of radical Calvinists, convinced the queen to appoint Walter as reader at the Temple Church, where Whitgift's approval was not required. If Richard Alvey had not been so ill that he needed help at the Temple, there would probably not have been an opening there. As it was, Travers just moved in and took over most of the master's duties and prerogatives. He was an excellent preacher who quickly won the hearts and the fierce loyalty of many, if not most, of the lawyers and students at the Middle and Inner Temple Inns.

When apprised of the problem Travers was posing for church authorities by his presence at the Temple Church, Richard wondered why the queen, who made all clerical appointments at this prestigious church, did not simply remove him. As he learned the answer to that question, Hooker had his first real education in the subtleties of public policy formation in late Elizabethan England.

A major controlling factor in royal decision-making was that the queen was largely dependent on her chief minister, the lord treasurer, William Cecil (Lord Burghley), to run the country for her. And Burghley was a consistent sympathizer and protector of the more radical Calvinist leaders in the government and in the Church. More to the point, Burghley was the very one who had arranged for Travers' appointment as Temple reader back in 1581, and was now urging the queen to appoint him master of the Temple following Richard Alvey's recent death. During Alvey's illness, Travers had begun living in the master's house and serving as *de facto* master. If the queen were to follow her usual practice and accept Burghley's advice, there would be no hand left to restrain the radical activities of Travers and his allies. He would be free to turn the Temple into a national model for his presbyterian polity.

Much as the queen leaned upon Burghley, she disliked his support of the more extreme Calvinist practitioners in her realm. She was well aware that presbyterianism struck at the very root of her episcopal church polity, and ultimately threatened her own authority as ruler of both State and Church. She turned to her new archbishop, John Whitgift, to stamp out the dissident Puritan voices in the Church. In so doing, she set up an antagonism between her chief advisors—not for the first or last time, for this was a favourite ploy of this machiavellian monarch: divide and conquer or at least divide and survive.

Whitgift was a worthy opponent for the powerful lord treasurer. He offered his own candidate for the Temple post, Dr Nicholas Bond, one of the queen's own chaplains. Bond's theology and churchmanship were to the queen's liking, but she judged her chaplain's health not sturdy enough to withstand the pressures of this tumultuous pulpit.

In pressing his case to the queen against appointing Travers to the Temple post, the archbishop had ample evidence to offer. Travers' own writing convicted him of disloyalty and disobedience to church regulations as promulgated by the archbishop. His *Explicatio*, just released in a new English edition at Cambridge, was so offensive to the church establishment that Whitgift had as many copies as he could find seized and burned immediately.[7]

Whitgift knew that to base his case against Travers primarily on the grounds of Walter's advocacy of a presbyterian polity would produce the very sort of controversy at court and in the country that Elizabeth abhorred. Above all, this queen prized policies that limited conflict and offered promise of as much public peace and tranquillity as possible. The archbishop needed a less divisive ground for his case against lord Burghley's candidate. And it was readily at hand.

The very practical, non-ideological (and so, to Elizabeth, eminently acceptable) reason why Mr Travers could not be master at the Temple, or the incumbent of any other church in the realm, was that he had never been properly ordained. He had, in fact, explicitly denied the efficacy of episcopal ordination, and his doing so had formed part of the heresy for which he had been expelled from Cambridge in 1571. Then, while in exile in Antwerp, he had been ordained according to the presbyterian manner, which required only selection by elders and approval by the congregation to be served. Now he was claiming that that spurious "ordination" qualified him to hold clerical office in the Church of England. Whitgift had a strong case against him on this point alone and could probably make it stick with the queen, if not with Burghley.

Unbeknownst to Hooker or anyone else outside the queen's inner circle, Whitgift had recently written Elizabeth a letter in which he condemned Travers in the strongest terms, describing him as one of the principal authors of dissension in the Church, an open opponent of the *Book of Common Prayer*, an avowed foe of episcopacy, a person not properly ordained to serve in any English parish, and a fomenter of religious discontent, whose placement in a high post would do immeasurable damage to the peace and quiet of the realm. The archbishop's blistering attack left no doubt that Travers was a menace whom the queen could not possibly appoint to the Temple post, regardless of Lord Burghley's partiality toward him.[8]

So as not to appear to be going behind Burghley's back to the queen, Whitgift also wrote to the lord treasurer. In that letter the archbishop asserted his ecclesiastical authority and stated directly that Travers had never been properly ordained and had, in fact, resisted that process. The head of the queen's Church said, in this letter to the queen's chief minister of State, that he would never consent to Burghley's favorite presbyterian (Travers) holding any position of any kind whatsoever in the Church of England.[9]

The stage was now set for Hooker's entry into the firestorm of church politics as it flared at the Temple Church in London.

AN IMPORTANT PROPOSAL

During his brief stay with the Churchman family, at the time of his Paul's Cross sermon, Richard enjoyed his first opportunity to experience some of the warmth and fellowship of a close-knit, prosperous, merchant family in London. After so many years of solitary living as an academic, it must have been a delight to be in the bosom of such a family. While one can only conjecture about the details of his involvement in the Churchmans' life, it is fair to imagine from what is known of the behaviour of such families, that Hooker witnessed and participated in the typical devotional practices of the day. He would have watched appreciatively as John Churchman began an evening meal with a generous reading from his well-worn copy of John Daye's *A Book of Christian Prayers*. Since he had spent so little time in family domestic settings, Hooker had probably not seen that book before but would have been aware of its wide use for family devotions and that is was popular both for its dramatic marginal illustrations and for the variety of prayers it contained, designed to meet any occasion of family life, from birth to death.

As Hooker observed this London family at prayer, he might have pondered once again, in a different context this time, how foolish were the quarrels within the Church—Catholics, Puritans, and emergent Anglicans waging such terrible warfare over the details of church services and governance. Yet, all could agree that the salvation of individuals was the purpose of it all, and that private family prayer and devotional exercises like these were essential to renewal of faith. Was John Churchman aware, Hooker may have wondered, that the book from which he now read was adapted by Puritan writers from devotional books by such brilliant Catholic humanists as Erasmus, Juan Luis Vives, and even that despised Jesuit Robert Persons? How ironic!

Hooker may have had his own "illegal" copy of Persons' *First Book of Christian Exercise*, which had appeared just two years ago and was intended to show English Protestants the errors of their ways. Regardless of its political purpose, Hooker would have found it a useful aid to his own devotional life, as did many moderate Protestant scholars. Persons' work was so good, in fact, that it had come out this very year in an expurgated, puritanized form by Edmund Bunney, the minister at Bolton Percy. Richard may have carried a copy of that bowdlerized version of Persons with him to London. But he could not know that his "Bunney Club" edition of Persons' devotional masterpiece would go through nine printings by the end of the century and would have a profound impact not only on English family and private devotional life but on later generations of church leaders—including the influential seventeenth-century Puritan divine, Richard Baxter. Hooker no doubt also had a copy of Henry Bull's *Christian Prayers and Holy Meditations*, the scholar's devotional companion and perhaps his own favourite. Not only did it contain a virtual theology of prayer, but it had the most complete compendium of the best prayers on every subject.[10]

Hooker's candidacy as master of the Temple Church was probably put forward by Archbishop Sandys. While there is no proof of this, the circumstantial evidence is compelling. A powerful advocate was necessary to secure Richard this high post, since his own reputation was too slim to carry him forward on his own. Whitgift could have advanced Hooker's cause, without benefit of any recommendations. But, since the new archbishop had stormy relations with Burghley, especially over this issue of the Temple Church appointment, an intermediary such as Sandys was in the best position to offer a compromise candidate acceptable to each of the two men—Burghley and Whitgift—upon whom the queen was relying for advice.[11]

Sandys' credentials were good with both Burghley and Whitgift. As bishop of Worcester, London, and now archbishop of York, he was a true brother in the episcopacy to Whitgift. The two had fought the hard fight together and had mutual respect for one another's arduous labours to establish a viable, reformed, episcopal Church in England. Each, in his own way, had played an important role in building the emergent Anglican polity.

As for Burghley, he was far more likely to take advice from Sandys than from Whitgift. The archbishop of York was, as we have seen, a purer Protestant, less pragmatic than the archbishop of Canterbury. He was more in the camp of those advanced Calvinists admired by Burghley, men such as Bishop Jewel and John Rainolds, than he was of those of a harsher political stamp, such as Whitgift and Richard Bancroft. And we may assume that Sandys was pleased with Hooker's sermon at St Paul's Cross, especially for its attacks on the more extreme Calvinist doctrines.

Travers was totally unacceptable to both Sandys and Whitgift as a candidate for the post. Although he was still making the requisite obeisances to royal authority and the established Church, Travers' ideas promoted a church polity in which bishops would have little or no control. Furthermore, Travers was inclined to elevate personal religious conviction and practice above the historic wisdom and experience of the Church. He was so insistent on biblical authority that, as Hooker was later to say of such Protestant extremists, he ran the risk of turning each man (with his own Bible) into a miniature pope of Rome. As Elizabeth's church leaders saw it, Travers' thinking would lead to anarchy in Church and State.[12]

When Hooker learned that he was to be put forward as a candidate for master of the Temple, he did not object. He was possessed of no more than the natural predisposition of any sensitive intellectual to doubt his suitability for such a high post. Despite what may have been a temperamental aversion to public life, born of long experience with happy productivity in the academic world, the honour, the prestige, the financial rewards, the opportunity to try out his ideas and himself in the arena of politics and power were all compelling. He was a Hooker, after all. He could hardly resist the thought that the archbishop of Canterbury, the lord treasurer of England, and the queen herself would all soon have his name on their lips as a man qualified for high office in the Church.

Still, he must have wondered what Whitgift would think of him. Would he indeed be acceptable to the formidable archbishop? Had Whitgift ever even heard of him? In fact, we may be sure that Whitgift knew all about Richard Hooker. He had the best network of informers in the land (save only Burghley and Walsingham). His agents supplied him with information about who was doing and saying what in the Church and the government. His right arm, Richard Bancroft, who would one day be the Bishop of London and later Archbishop of Canterbury, had probably already briefed him on Hooker's sermons at the Cross and elsewhere. The archbishop would have been pleased by Hooker's attacks on extremists.

As Hooker would soon learn, Whitgift was as smooth, shrewd, and politically astute as Burghley or any of his other Puritan foes in high places. The archbishop had a reputation for listening sympathetically to the petitions of any well placed lord or lady who might entreat him on behalf of a religious nonconformist. He could be all grace and charm, seeming to agree with them by his demeanour. He could please one and all with general reassurances and rarely was known to deny any important person's specific desires to his or her face. Yet, by promising little that was specific in regard to the case at hand, he remained free to deliver virtually nothing at all and so pursue his own preferred course of action. He made a very good friend—and a very bad enemy. Richard was glad to be among those who might count the archbishop of Canterbury as his supporter.[13]

An example of what was involved in being on the bad side of Whitgift occurred at about this time. Lord Burghley had protested to the archbishop in the strongest terms over the primate's dismissal of two nonconforming ministers. These clerics had not only refused to subscribe to the oath affirming the queen's supremacy over the church, but had also performed services according to the Genevan form—quite out of step with what was prescribed in the *Book of Common Prayer*.

6 (a). Richard Hooker's statue in Exeter Cathedral Close

6 (b). Stepcote Hill, Exeter

7. Arms of Richard Hooker
Master of the Temple, London

Rendered for the author, exclusively for use in this book, by the Revd. Canon A. Malcolm MacMillan from the official blazon of the arms of Richard Hooker.

The Coat of Arms:
Or a fess vair between two leopards sable, a crescent for candency
(Gold, a band of fur of a conventional pattern of blue and silver, between two leopards)

The Crest:
A hind passant or, in the mouth a branch vert, flowered argent
(A young deer gold, standing on all four feet, holding a green branch, with silver flowers in its mouth)

Allowed at the Visitation of Devon, 1572, to John Vowell, alias Hooker, of Exeter

8. Portait of Bishop John Jewel, 1522-71.
Artist unknown. National Portrait Gallery, London.

9. Portrait of John Rainolds, 1549-1607,
president of Corpus Christi College and co-editor of
the Authorized version of the Bible.
Oil on panel. Corpus Christi College, Oxford

10. Corpus Christi College quad today

11. Archbishop Edwin Sandys, *c.*1518-1588. Artist unknown. National Portrait Gallery, London

12 (a). Drayton Beauchamp church and parsonage, as at the time of Hooker's incumbency, 1585

12 (b). Drayton Beauchamp church today

13. Dr King preaching at Old St Paul's before James I.
J. Stow (seventeenth century). Society of Antiquaries, London

14. Middle Temple Hall, interior

15. Middle Temple Hall, exterior

16. "Round Church," Temple church, exterior

17. Temple church, exterior

18. Temple church, interior, the nave from the Round Church

19. Archbishop John Whitgift, *c.*1530-1604
Artist unknown. National Portrait Gallery, London

20. Paul's Cross today

21. Salisbury Cathedral Chapter House, interior

22. John Calvin, 1509-1564
Artist unknown

23. St Andrew's, Boscombe

24. Netheravon parish church

25. St Andrew's, Enfield

26. St Mary's, Bishopsbourne

27. Graveyard at St Mary's

These were blatant cases of nonconformity. In his written responses to Burghley's complaint against him, Whitgift began by reminding the lord treasurer that he had kept him closely informed on all of his activities so that the two men could work out any disagreements on particular cases before these became public arguments. It was regrettable, Whitgift said, that Burghley saw fit to chastise him solely on the grounds of the charges of others without first checking the facts with him. Whitgift said that he had bent over backwards to give all benefit of doubt to Burghley's nonconformist friends. If he had committed any offence, it had been his leniency toward these conceited, contentious lawbreakers. Whitgift also took offence at the lord treasurer's repeating, with apparent approbation, unfounded charges against the archbishop of being a papist sympathizer, when he (Burghley) knew full well that the archbishop of Canterbury had been one of the strongest enemies of the Church of Rome throughout his career.

Whitgift went on, in this letter, to remind Cecil that the queen herself had charged the archbishop to suppress nonconformity and maintain order in Church and State. Next only to the queen, Whitgift asserted, the chief responsibility for assuring order belonged to him. The lord treasurer should cease being "carried away" by the pressure of his friends to the point where he abandoned the archbishop and his great cause, "lest one day you will be sorry for" it. People like you, he told Burghley, who have great responsibility for the care of our commonwealth, are obligated to join, not to hinder me in my work.[14]

In response to this threat to his authority, Burghley, with support from the Earl of Leicester and other members of the Privy Council, summoned Whitgift to answer charges that he was removing "good" ministers (nonconformists) while leaving alone "ignorant, filthy, and drunken" ministers (conformists). He pressured Whitgift into holding a public disputation in which Whitgift would have to defend himself from Puritan criticisms that would be presented by none other than Walter Travers! In the event, the wily archbishop saw to it that the conference was held at his palace at Lambeth and that he presided over it and controlled the agenda. It was no easy matter to trap this political genius, not even if you were the queen's brilliant chief minister.

Still, Whitgift would never completely thwart the efforts of Burghley and his friends to interfere with his efforts to put a stop to clerical disobedience. They repeatedly went around the archbishop's back to his bishops, urging them to allow, if not encourage, such nonconforming practices as holding prophesyings.[15]

Hooker would soon be aware that all of these political machinations simply to find a master for the Temple Church were in reality but an episode in the larger struggle going on inside the established Church between the lord treasurer and his Puritan allies on the one hand, and the archbishop of Canterbury and his emergent Anglican friends on the other—a fight for control of the Church of England.

There was one especially important qualification that had commended Hooker to Whitgift's attention in addition to his already well-demonstrated abilities and persuasions. That was the simple but crucial fact that he was not married. The queen of England did not look with favour on married clerics and rarely appointed them to high posts if she could avoid it. Some believed that Bishop Sandys had been denied the ultimate post at Canterbury in large part because, unlike Whitgift, he had not remained celibate.

Number twenty-nine of the queen's *Injunctions to the Clergy* was reportedly her favourite. Roughly translated, it said: "You may marry an honest and sober wife if you must marry at all; but only if you feel you cannot resist the temptation and only then if your bishop approves of the lady." Shortly after Elizabeth became queen, she ordered married men at the colleges to keep their wives at home. Richard remembered that Dr Cole had had to move his quarters out of Corpus Christi for just that reason.[16]

If Hooker could continue to avoid the marriage bed, he might look forward not only to the Temple post, but later on, to a deanship or even a bishopric. Whitgift and his queen were always on the lookout for promising new talent to fill vacant sees. If Whitgift were impressed with Richard's performance at the Temple, he might at least have a chance for episcopal appointment. After all, his pedigree was not altogether unimpressive: good family connections in the west country; John Jewel as an early patron; Rainolds as a tutor; the archbishop of York as a supporter. But he would need to perform well at the Temple—defend the establishment but not make political waves of his own—and he would need to remain celibate.

JOHN WHITGIFT: DEFENDER OF THE CHURCH

Whitgift, who would soon become Hooker's latest patron, had begun life with all of the advantages of a wealthy merchant family in the north-eastern port city of Grimsby, proceeded to St Anthony's School in London, then gone up to Queens' College and then Pembroke Hall at Cambridge, where he received his B.A. in 1554, the year of Hooker's birth. The following year he transferred to Peterhouse, where he was elected a fellow. He received his M.A. in 1557 and B.D. in 1563, the same year he was named Lady Margaret Professor in Divinity. In 1567, he earned his doctorate and returned to Pembroke as master of that college.[17]

Whitgift had made his mark, his enemies were fond of saying, by doing Queen Elizabeth's dirty work. He was, many felt, the one who had stayed at home in England and feathered his own nest under the wing of the hated Queen Mary. Many of those who had been exiled and returned in the late 1550s were nevertheless pleased to find that, in their absence, Whitgift and others had assured that good jobs were waiting for them. What did not please many of the purists among the returning Calvinists was that their new twenty-five year old Protestant queen did not share some of their more radical ideas about church governance. In England there would be one national Church with a uniform practice to be governed by the queen and her bishops. No one would preach in this realm without a license from the queen's bishops. There would be no congregational or presbterian church polity. The theology would be moderately reformed and the queen would be head of the Church. The 1559 *Act of Uniformity* mandated use of a common liturgy as contained in the *Second Book Prayer Book of Edward VI*, with alterations, and a theology that affirmed that the real presence of Christ, and not merely a memorial, was transmitted to the believer through the Eucharistic Sacrament.

Of all the unreformed characteristics of Elizabeth's Church, including kneeling at prayer, use of religious images, stained glass, organ music, and the like, none rankled with the returning Protestants more than the requirement that they must don clerical vestments. Consequently, many of them had refused to wear vestments in the parish churches, college chapels, and private chapels of the realm. Many of the bishops looked the other way. Such notables of the realm as the queen's own favourite, Lord Dudley, openly supported the disobedience. The Queen was furious. This was nothing less than a challenge to her authority as head of the Church. In 1565 she ordered her first archbishop of Canterbury, Matthew Parker, himself a strong Calvinist with much sympathy for the anti-vestiarian sentiments of the clergy, to put a stop to the disobedience and enforce conformity to all her ordinances for the church. Thus began the first great test of Elizabeth's rule over the Church—and the beginning of John Whitgift's rapid climb to power.

From the beginning of Elizabeth's reign, Whitgift had been an outspokenly loyal supporter at Cambridge of her religious injunctions. Unlike his classmate Thomas Cartwright, who almost immediately opposed the Elizabethan religious settlement, and John Jewel, who rankled under what he thought to be the queen's Catholic leanings, Whitgift accepted the new order of things happily and completely. To the embattled Archbishop Parker, Whitgift's was a clear and welcome voice crying out in the dangerous wilderness of Cambridge. Edmund Grindal, bishop of London at the time, knew of Whitgift's loyalty and recommended him to fill his own former chair as master at Pembroke. This was a favour Whitgift never forgot. Years later he refused to accept the queen's offer to replace his old patron when she wanted to remove Grindal as archbishop of Canterbury.

Lord Burghley, who had learned in 1567 of this new champion of the establishment at Cambridge, arranged to have Whitgift preach before the queen. She was so pleased by what she heard that within about a year Whitgift was made a royal chaplain, prebend at Ely Cathedral, Regius Professor of Divinity, and master of Trinity College.

Throughout his successful tenure as the virtual head of Cambridge, Whitgift had no use for religious nonconformists. He demanded a strict conformity to established church discipline. The brilliant Thomas Cartwright, darling of Calvinist radicals at Cambridge, quickly ran afoul of Whitgift's restrictions at the college. (Hooker knew all about Thomas Cartwright, having been encouraged by his tutor to admire him as a brilliant scholar and sincere Calvinist, one of the brightest lights of the Protestant Reformation in England.) Cartwright had gone far beyond openly denouncing Parker's vestiarian rules. He condemned the entire system of church government in England and enjoined a return to what he saw as the church polity described in the Book of Acts, a "primitive" presbyterianism.

The future archbishop had steadfastly fought the fight of Elizabeth's Church against Catholics as well as against radical Protestants. Responding to Pope Pius V's 1570 Bull, *Regnans in Excelsis*, which excommunicated the queen and commanded her subjects to cease obeying her on pain of like sentence, Whitgift, as vice-chancellor at Cambridge and, later, as dean of Lincoln and bishop of Worcester, acted vigorously, under the authority of parliament's *Treasons Act* of 1571, to hunt down Catholics and their sympathizers. He became adept at developing and utilizing effective networks of diocesan and university informers.

The Church still needed this kind of energetic defence, Hooker would have thought, as he reflected on current threats from papist conspirators. Catholic students at William Allen's College at Douai were being trained to serve in England as missionary priests. Smuggled into the country, some of them, it had been rumoured, were specially trained to assassinate the queen.

But Whitgift's major foes, Hooker knew, were not Catholics but the Calvinist extremists, especially such men as Cartwright and his fellow presbyterians, including his own kinsman, Walter Travers. It was well-known that Whitgift had played the major role in denying Cartwright his doctorate of divinity at Cambridge. Whitgift later had expelled Cartwright from the university on two separate occasions for his continued expression of what the archbishop regarded as treasonable positions. After all, opposing the wearing of vestments, kneeling at prayer, and the using of unauthorized versions of the Eucharistic service were troublesome, but seeking to undermine the very structure and authority of the established Church, with reference to nothing more than one man's particular interpretation of Holy Scripture, was quite another matter.

Frustrated by their efforts to reform the English Church from within, the Puritans had turned to parliament. Here they received favourable response from the increasing number of members who had economic or political, as well as religious, reasons for wishing to weaken the power of the established Church, end the monarchy's supremacy over the Church, or both. The queen, however, "vetoed" legislation to reform church structure and worship and punished the parliamentary sponsors. In response, the Puritan radicals launched an all-out attack on Elizabeth's Church in their *First* and *Second Admonitions* in 1571 and 1572. These were a battlecry for the Puritans of England and were regarded by many at Oxford and elsewhere as seditious. These papers, as well as subsequent sermons and speeches, had attacked every aspect of the Church of England, root and branch, condemning the entire episcopal polity and insisting on a presbyterian substitute. *The Book of Common Prayer* was called "an imperfect book, culled and picked out of the popish dunghill, the mass-book, full of all abominations."[18]

Cartwright had been suspected of being the primary instigator, if not the actual author, of the *Second Admonition*, but that could not be proved. The authors of the *First Admonition*, John Field and Thomas Wilcox, had been immediately imprisoned. Even advanced Calvinists such as John Rainolds and William Cole at Hooker's Corpus Christi College had distanced themselves from the treatises. Such notable moderate Calvinist bishops as Sandys, now at London, Grindal at York, and Pilkington at Durham were appalled at the radicalism of the *Admonitions* and publicly condemned their sponsors.

Hooker would have remembered the intensity of the religious and political controversy that had permeated university circles. The *Admonition* had stirred up much more than a public debate between two famous sons of Trinity College, Cambridge: Whitgift, a staunch defender of the established Church and Cartwright, its leading Protestant opponent. The more important consequence of the *Admonition* and of the queen's inflexible response to it was to plunge the Church and much of the government into turmoil. Public outcry, seditious preaching, and open disobedience were rampant in London. Shockwaves of discontent were quickly felt up at Oxford and wherever the Puritans and their political supporters were active.

Bishop Sandys' more radical ministers in London were in open rebellion. Preachers he selected to speak at Paul's Cross defied his direct instructions and used the great pulpit to attack the orders of the queen and support the *Admonition*. Some Puritans had gone so far in their hatred of bishops as to attack some of them physically. When Sandys had complained to Burghley or Leicester that unless Cartwright and his cohorts, Field, Wilcox, and others of their party were apprehended, the rebellion would spread from the Church into the country at large, he had been met with silence.

Hooker knew that Archbishop Parker had commissioned Whitgift to respond to the *Admonition*. Contained in two tracts, the first response was *An Answer to a Certain Libel Entitled An Admonition to Parliament*, published in February 1573. Later that year Thomas Cartwright responded in *A Reply to An Answer Made of Dr Whitgift Against the Admonition to the Parliament*. Then in 1574 Whitgift published his *Admonition Against the Reply of T. C.* Despite efforts by the government to suppress Cartwright's writings, they appeared throughout the country in several editions and were avidly read. Conversely, Whitgift's tracts had rather less appeal.

One reason for this disparity in readership was that, as always, people were more attracted to the rebel than the defender of the status quo. Even at Whitgift's own Trinity College, his *Answer* was attacked, while both the *Admonition* and its defender, Cartwright, were applauded. Another problem with Whitgift's tracts was that his style of writing was pedantic. Instead of setting forth his own reasoned argument, defending the Church on biblical and historical grounds, he answered the *Admonition* and Cartwright with an often tedious line-by-line refutation. This was typical of the academic style of religious tracts of the day and was one reason why they were so little read outside the scholarly community. (An incredible irony of Whitgift's *Answer* is that he actually incorporated all of Cartwright's *Admonition*—which had been banned—into his own work in order to demonstrate his refutation of it.)[19]

Hooker would have found much to admire in Whitgift's writings. He surely appreciated the future archbishop's forcible rejection of Cartwright's insistence that the Bible offered an infallible model for the polity of the Church. He would also have applauded Whitgift's rejection of the idea that anything not specifically commanded in Holy Scripture was forbidden. That notion had doubtless struck him as nonsensical the first time he read it. He would also have admired the occasional flash of satire in Whitgift's response to Cartwright. As though exhausted by the tedium of responding to his foe's criticism of almost every detail of the polity and liturgy of the English church, Whitgift reacted sharply to the argument that worshippers should not kneel at Holy Communion because sitting was the more natural posture when eating a meal—or as Cartwright put the matter, "sitting agreeth better with the action of supper." By this logic, Whitgift said, Communion should be held at night because that is when we have supper. Answering the silly objection to kneeling because it is not as restful a state as sitting and that Christ's work of redemption has given us perfect rest, Whitgift was fairly launched. If you are going to start using allegories for arguments, you are surely following the papists, he charged with glee. Anyway, if you like allegories, let us have one for standing at Communion—for surely standing signifies our readiness. Or what about kneeling? Does not that posture signify our submission and humility? If you insist that we should sit because you suppose Christ sat at the Last Supper, I suppose we will have to sit too. Only twelve may be served the meal and all must be men and one a traitor.

We must meet only in the parlour of some private house on the Thursday night before Easter. "Who sees not the absurdity of such reasoning?" the future archbishop of Canterbury had written.[20]

Whitgift's defence of singing in church services would also have struck an answering chord in Hooker, as would his satire on Cartwright's objection to women wearing veils in church. This issue is but a "scare crow," Whitgift had written. By insisting that women bare their faces in church, these Puritans, he said, show that they are so "preoccupied with women and their innermost feelings and they enter so profoundly into women's covert feelings (in very deed altogether unfitting and unmeet to common speech, much more [sic] for preacher's utterance) that chaste ears can hardly above the vanity of their curious and uncivil [remarks] understand."[21]

Hooker was indebted to the archbishop as a source for many of his own thoughts on important issues. Whitgift's preference for common sense and tradition as guides to church practice, whenever Scripture was silent on some particular matter, appealed to him. Controversial issues, on which Scripture was either silent or ambiguous, were "things indifferent," to our salvation rather than essential to it, Whitgift had argued. These matters might well vary from time to time and place to place according to local dictates of custom and common sense. God had not ordained a single model for church governance or worship practices.

In the event, a singular and dramatic episode had done more than all the writings and speeches of the antagonists to clarify issues and turn the tide against the Puritans. The defining event had been an attempt, in 1573, on the life of one of the queen's leading supporters, Sir Christopher Hatton. At the time, Hatton was captain of the queen's guard. An agitated Puritan extremist named Peter Burchet succeeded only in wounding Sir Christopher, mistaking John Hawkins for his intended victim. In the event, both Hatton and Hawkins survived to serve their country well, Hatton as lord chancellor and chancellor of Oxford University, and Hawkins as hero of the Armada battles and one of the most gifted sea captains in English history. But the attempted assassination had horrified moderate Calvinists and hardened the resolve of the queen and her allies. The radicals had overplayed their hand. Moderates in parliament, the universities, and the Church moved to the right for cover. Conservatives carried the field. Arrests were swift and punishments severe. The Church was purged of some of its most radical elements. Many Puritan ministers were deprived of their positions. Cartwright and other radicals fled to avoid arrest.

Clearly this was a turning point for radical Calvinism in England, and Whitgift had been poised to be a beneficiary of the change in climate. For the rest of the century, and well into the next, the Puritan movement gradually lost influential advocates and social respectability among most of the leadership in Church and State. Although

Puritanism's popular appeal and political influence were far from ended, it would be another fifty years before presbyterianism would seriously threaten the established Church of England, and then it would bring with it the political revolution that many of its opponents had forecast—a revolt provoked by Stuart monarchs who were not nearly so astute as Elizabeth and an archbishop, William Laud, who was more intransigent and less politically skillful than Whitgift.

In the critical years from 1573 to 1584, Whitgift emerged as the queen's chief champion. It was he, not her civil ministers Burghley and Leicester, nor even her Puritan-leaning bishops like Sandys and Grindal, who had stood without wavering or equivocating against rebellious extremists. Ever after, whether deserved or not, the queen's unwavering affection and frequent support would go to Whitgift. Still, the queen was a practical woman. She had to keep Burghley and his powerful Calvinist friends in line. When they urged their champion, Edmund Grindal, as new archbishop of Canterbury, she passed over her friend Whitgift and gave the more radical Calvinist the nod in 1575. She was soon to regret this appointment. When she ordered Grindal to suppress the illegal "prophesyings," which she saw as a threat to her authority in the Church, the new archbishop steadfastly refused. Grindal's letter to the queen of December of 1576, though expressed in quite reverential tones, effectively said that she should do as he (Grindal) thought best on this issue. Not surprisingly, the queen had been furious. She was too wise to risk making a martyr of Grindal by sacking him, or worse, but she did put him under virtual house arrest for six months and then proceeded to govern the Church through others, as though he did not exist.[22]

By this time Whitgift was clearly the queen's favourite in the Church. She never forgot his stalwart loyalty. He became her "little black husband," as she affectionately called him. When she was in need of a confessor, she would often call upon him. She was reported to have said that she pitied him because she laid upon him all the burdens of her Church. When Elizabeth was on her deathbed in 1603, she would have no one but him at her side to see her into the next life.[23]

In 1577 the grateful queen had made Whitgift bishop of Worcester. There he continued for six years, defending her emergent Anglican Church from papists and Puritans alike. Then in 1583, as soon as Grindal was dead, the queen was finally free to name her loyal clerical champion eccesiastical head of the Church, archbishop of Canterbury. She did this despite Burghley's recommendation for the post—so it was widely rumoured—of none other than Hooker's patron, Bishop Sandys.

Hooker, like everyone else in the Church, was aware that Whitgift, immediately on taking office at Lambeth, had launched a systematic suppression of Puritan practices. His *Articles* of September 1583 ordained that there would be no preaching in homes or other private places, no avoiding wearing of vestments, no conducting of services by unordained persons, no using of such unapproved versions of Scripture as the *Geneva Bible*, no ordaining of ministers outside the dioceses in which they resided or without pastoral positions. All ministers would be required to swear allegiance to the queen as supreme governor of the Church, to subscribe to the 1563 *Articles of Religion*, and to promise to use only the authorized *Book of Common Prayer*. Richard Bancroft was appointed to the see of London as a replacement for John Aylmer. Hooker knew that Bancroft was personally visiting parishes in the city and elsewhere in order to assure conformity among the clergy and to root out "prophesyings."

In November 1583, on the anniversary of the queen's accession, Whitgift, as we have noted previously, had preached at St Paul's Cross on Paul's Epistle to Titus, where the Apostle says: "Put them in remembrance to be subject unto principalities and powers, to obey magistrates, and to be ready to do every good work." This message had been no more to the liking of Protestant extremists than Richard's sermon there was to be. But everyone needed to know that the archbishop, and those who supported him, would have order in the Church, along with reformation.[24]

He had written to the queen urging her not to turn over any more church properties to her wealthy Protestant supporters but to keep the income for the church, as donors had originally intended. He no doubt had feared that, if he did not speak plainly to the queen, the wealthy friends of the Calvinist reformers, including the Queen's favourite, the Earl of Leicester, would seize for their own gain and pleasure what little was left of the Church's wealth. He needed these dwindling resources for improved training and supervision of clergy. It was not enough to root out and punish the radical dissidents if the queen would not help him correct the abuses of which they correctly complained, especially the unacceptable presence of far too many under-educated, corrupt, slovenly and irresponsible clergy.[25]

Hooker would have seen clearly just why Whitgift was currently so influential with Queen Elizabeth. This was the man who had cleaned up her favourite university in the 1560s and, in her hours of greatest peril from a restive parliament in the early 1570s, had entered the lists to defend her Church from its most dangerous foes, Calvinist and Catholic. If this man wanted the queen to appoint him, Richard Hooker, master of the Temple Church, she would probably do as he asked.

NOTES

1. Although Edwin Sandys was not formally admitted to the Middle Temple Inn as a law student until 11 February 1590, it is fair to assume that he followed the practice of other wealthy students and lived either in one of the lesser Inns, or

shared space with residents of the major "societies" for a number of years, before he was deemed qualified for full admission. Edwin's older brother, Samuel, had been admitted in 1579. His cousins, William and Miles, were moving in at just about the time of Hooker's Paul's Cross sermon. These facts, coupled with the fact that Edwin's uncle Miles was one of the most powerful members of Middle Temple and soon to be named to the highest post of treasurer, lend credence to the possibility that Edwin had some living space at the Middle Temple at this time, either with his brother or his cousins. For admission dates of various members of the Sandys' family to the Middle Temple, see *Register of Admissions to the Honourable Society of the Middle Temple*, compiled by H. A. C. Sturgess (London: Butterworth & Co. Ltd, 1949), I, 45-70. Miles Sandys' election in 1588 to the post of treasurer, succeeding John Popham, is recorded at 301.

2. Some of Travers' sermons are preserved at Trinity College, Dublin, though in scarcely legible form. One may be sure from the documents and reactions to them that they were indeed provocative. Paul S. Seaver, *The Puritan Lectureships, The Politics of Regligious Dissent, 1560-1662* (Stanford: Stanford University Press, 1970) is an excellent source for data and analyses on the lecturers, despite Seaver's minor error at p. 216 describing Travers as Hooker's brother-in-law. For a more sympathetic treatment of preaching and "prophesying" which argues that there was no necessary connection between the increased emphasis on preaching and rising presbyterianism, see Irvonwy Morgan, *The Godly Preachers of the Elizabethan Church* (London: The Epworth Press, 1965).

3. Seaver, 17-18. Richard Bancroft, Whitgift's strong arm in rooting out non-conformity and, later, his successor as archbishop of Canterbury, shared the view that these lecturers represented a serious danger to the realm. Bancroft was suspicious of a presbyterian conspiracy to place the readers not where they were most needed but in politically sensitive areas like the Temple Church. "They not only creep into noble and gentlemen's bosoms in the Country . . . but also thrust themselves forward by all the power of their friends to be as they term it Readers, but I fear Seducers in the Inns of Court. For it is very probable (as they well know) that the . . . flower of the Gentility of England being by that means trained up in a disobedient misliking of the present state of the Church, if occasion serve to show themselves good scholars, they will bring forth corrupt fruit of so contentious an education." *Ibid.*, 64-5.

4. For brief descriptions of the careers of these three men and other leading Puritan lecturers during Hooker's era, see *Ibid.*, 171-239. Another prominent lecturer was William Perkins (1558-1602) at Great St Andrews Church. Less interested in questions of church polity than Travers and other advanced Calvinists, Perkins focused his preaching and writing on advocating Calvin's and Beza's doctrines of double predestination (supralapsarianism). His principal writings, *Whether A Man* . . . (1589) and *Golden Chaine* (1591) were influential and far more popular at the time than Hooker's *Laws* would be when published just a few years later. See R. T. Kendall, *Calvin and English Calvinism to 1649* (Oxford: Oxford University Press, 1979), 53-54; 29-31.

5. Bishop John Gauden of Exeter, Hooker's first serious biographer, whose "errors" Izaak Walton had been commissioned to correct, had been a "preacher"—a term replacing "reader" or "lecturer"—at the Temple in 1660 at the end of the Puritan-dominated commonwealth period. In those years there was no master at the Temple, only a "preacher." Little wonder that Gauden was suspected of unorthodoxy by the conservative church hierarchy after the Restoration.

6. My principal source for Travers' life is S. J. Knox, *Walter Travers: Paragon of Elizabethan Puritanism* (London: Methuen & Co., Ltd), 1962.

7. Knox, 65.

8. For a summary of Whitgift's letters to the queen and Lord Burghley, about the Temple appointment, see John Strype, *The Life and Acts of the Most Reverend Father in God, John Whitgift, D.D.* (London, 1718), 173-5.
9. *Ibid.*, 179; Knox, 51.
10. An invaluable source on spiritual life in Elizabethan England is Horton Davies, *Worship and Theology in England 1534-1603* (Princeton: Princeton University Press, 1970), esp. chapters XI and XII.
11. Rabb, *op. cit.*, 10, describes Archbishop Sandys as "securing" the post for Hooker.
12. Travers (and Cartwright) never quite advocated a disestablished Church. Their desire was to replace episcopal governance with a presbyterian polity. On this important distinction from the Protestant separatists see A. F. Scott Pearson, *Thomas Cartwright and Elizabethan Puritanism* (Cambridge: C.U.P, 1925), 301-11. For my view of the emerging Protestant Church of England, as for most of my perspective of the English Reformation, I have leaned heavily on the works of Patrick Collinson and William Haugaard, especially Collinson's *Religion of Protestants, op. cit.* William Haugaard sees an "emergent Anglicanism" earlier in the English Reformation than most other historians. Those at the time who opposed both the "erratic pressures for conformity" from the bishops and the "zealot's demand for the presbytery" from "militant reformers," marked off this new middle ground of Anglicanism. Haugaard believes that Hooker was the first to express clearly the spirit of Anglican theology, but that he was writing to explain what others had already created. See Haugaard's, *Elizabeth and the English Reformation* (Cambridge: Cambridge University Press, 1968), 339-44. For an opinion that Whitgift and Travers were both "Anglo-Puritans" and that only in the next century was a new middle ground asserted, see A. G. Dickens, *The English Reformation*, rev. ed., Glasgow: Fontana Press, 1967.
13. I have drawn this characterization of Whitgift from Fuller, *Church History* III, 131.
14. For Whitgift's letter to Burghley on this occasion, see John Ayre, ed., *The Works of John Whitgift D.D.* (Cambridge: The Parker Society, 1853), III, 603-9.
15. Knappen, 275-6. See also, Knox, 64-5. For an opinion that Whitgift and Burghley were friends, despite their lifelong conflicts, see V. J. K. Brook, *Whitgift and the English Church* (London: The English University Press, 1957), 87. I disagree with this assessment of the relationship principally because it gives too much credence to the formal protestations of friendship and respect adorning Whitgift's prose.
16. An expression of the queen's strong antipathy to clerical marriage and her attempts to restrict the activities of the wives of clergy is seen in *Correspondence of Matthew Parker*, John Bruce and Thomas Perowne, eds. (Cambridge, 1853), 148-9. Bishop Sandys' letter to Archbishop Parker of 30th April 1589 expresses some anger at the queen's attitude on clerical celibacy. *Ibid.*, 66. See also Haugaard, *Elizabeth and the Reformation*, 200-5.
17. The source used here for Whitgift's writings is Ayre, *op. cit.* As sources for his life, I have used Strype, *op. cit.*; Brook, *op. cit.*, and Powell Mills Dawley, *John Whitgift and the Reformation* (London: Adam and Charles Black), 1955. Perhaps it is not surprising that I take issue with Dawley's assertion, at p. x, that it is Whitgift and not Hooker who deserves the accolade of number one Elizabethan churchman. Dawley claims that Whitgift did the hard work of defending a besieged Church from virulent Calvinist enemies whereas Hooker merely "distill(ed) out the useful spiritual and intellectual" essence of the new Church, while ignoring the hard political realities of the era. Surely each man makes his own legitimate claim to greatness with his own distinctive role in the formation of Anglicanism: Whitgift, by defending politically the established Church in the face of anarchistic religious and political attacks upon it by congregationally-orientated radical Calvinists; Hooker,

by breathing spiritual and intellectual life into the new Protestant Church of England that Whitgift and others had planted in the political landscape. There is room for two heroes in this great story, although surely Hooker's is the more enduring and accessible legacy.

18. Cartwright's famous castigation of the *Book of Common Prayer* is from the *Admonition* and is answered by Whitgift in his *Defense of the Answer*. See Ayre, 326.

19. W. Speed Hill noted this delicious irony in a 1998 letter to the author.

20. Ayer, *op. cit.*, 91, 93-4.

21. John Whitgift, *A Defense of the . . . Replie agaynst Dr. Whitgift* (London: Henry Bynneman, 1574), 167. (In Lambeth Palace Library, #1574.04.)

22. The rancor between Grindal and the court went on until he died in 1583. As late as 1580, Walsingham was rebuking him for seeking relief from an assignment on the grounds that he was not a rich man. That is a "cold answer," the secretary of state said, from one who "owes" the Queen his standing as chief defender of the Reformation, as well as for "his substance." *Fairhurst Papers* #3470, f. 63. *Lambeth Palace Library*.

23. *Works* I, 40, citing George Paule's contemporary *Life of Whitgift* in Wordsworth's *Ecclesiastical Biography* IV, 387.

24. A copy of Whitgift's sermon of 17 November 1583 at Paul's Cross is in Lambeth library, 1589.1. It was first printed by Thomas Orwin in London in 1589.

25. Whitgift's letter to the queen, recounting the abuses in the Church, is reported by Walton in *Life*, 41-44.

CHAPTER 9

Appointment at the Temple

THE ANTAGONIST

Once Hooker learned that Archbishop Sandys would nominate him to Archbishop Whitgift to be Master of the Temple, he was eager to take the measure of his principal competitor for this post, Burghley's candidate: Walter Travers

The Temple Church, which Hooker entered in the autumn of 1585 in order to observe a service conducted by Travers, was modelled on the Holy Sepulchre in Jerusalem. It had been built in the twelfth century, during the reign of Henry II, by the Knights Templar, hence the name Temple Church. The Templars were knights who had sworn that it was their sacred duty to protect pilgrims in the holy lands during the days of the crusades. Later, in the fourteenth century, when the Templars were disbanded, their church and other holdings passed to the Knights Hospitaller. This religious order subsequently lost the property to the crown during Henry VIII's dissolution programme. The king then leased the buildings to lawyers, who converted them into residences, halls, and study areas—hence, the Inns of Court.

During the early history of the Temple Church and Inns of Court, the master of the Temple had been one of the most powerful figures in England. In the reign of Henry II, the master, as the chief financier of the monarchy, held the crown's money in his hands. Important decisions of State were made at the Temple in those days.

The famous Round Church, now serving as the large narthex of the Temple, had been the first part of the church building erected and was one of a number of such structures built by the wealthy and powerful medieval Templars in various parts of England. The one at Cambridge was still in use in Hooker's day. In 1185 none other than Heraclitus, the patriarch of Jerusalem, was present to consecrate the Round Church. In the following century the Templars added the choir and thereby completed one of the most unique structures in England. The nave was awe-inspiring—some eighty feet long and forty feet high. The graceful fan vaulting rising from clusters of lovely Purbeck marble columns roofed a space of ethereal beauty into which light streamed from twelve lancet windows located in the south, east, and north walls of the choir and fifteen windows to the rear in the round narthex.[1]

Just as striking as the architecture and history of the place was the congregation—the barristers, lawyers, and law students crowding into the Temple, chattering irreverently in noisy anticipation of Travers' appearance in the pulpit. These men were as different in dress and demeanour from Hooker's simple country flock at Drayton as they, in turn, had been from the usually polite students and faculty attending chapel services in their academic gowns at Corpus Christi. These lawyers and politicians were not coming to worship from the fields of husbandry or from the lecture halls and libraries of a university. Theirs was the world of power and money, of great affairs of State and commerce, and smaller, but often contentious affairs of life, and death, and property claims.

The chambers and courtrooms from which this congregation came to church were venues where men were drawn to defend and advance their lives and properties, where fortunes were made and lost, lives and careers ruined or enhanced. These were the men who drafted, interpreted, and applied the laws of the realm on behalf of clients who ranged from merchants and bankers to churches and colleges, from wealthy widows to poor orphans, from members of parliament to the queen's government itself. These were the lawyers—those lively, worldly, powerful advocates and adjudicators of the myriad rights and claims that were the marks of a society governed by laws.

The opportunity to affect the thinking of such a congregation on a regular basis was a heady prospect for any minister. Sermons given in this place, not to mention the master's informal sessions with such men, could have a greater impact upon affairs of the day than in almost any other church. No wonder the appointment of a master here was of such importance to both Archbishop Whitgift and Lord Burghley.

Hooker watched from one of the benches in the crowded church as Travers walked down the long nave toward the pulpit and then mounted it. It seemed that there would be no worship service this morning according to the prescribed form: no properly-vested minister, no opening prayers, no common confession, no absolution, nothing except Travers' sermon. Was this the reason for his popularity with these secular lawyers? With him in charge, they could avoid prescribed religious services by attending a stimulating lecture by a fiery Puritan orator.

Hooker would have anticipated that this exemplar of Calvinist radicalism might be somewhat unconventional in his liturgical performance. But, since Travers had managed to survive as *de facto* master of the queen's Temple Church for the past three years, Hooker might well have expected a higher degree of orthodoxy than this. After all, just a year ago, under the late Archbishop Grindal's commission, Travers had written a respectable tract refuting the Jesuit Robert Persons' *Epistle of the Persecution of Catholics*.

It had been only a year since Whitgift had replaced Grindal and instituted a rigid policy of enforced conformity, including a rigorous censorship of religious publications. The new archbishop was just beginning to remove preachers who refused to use the *Book of Common Prayer* and administer Holy Communion at least four times a year. Additionally, Whitgift was now requiring all ministers to subscribe to his *Three Articles* which affirmed that the queen is the supreme governor of the church, that the *Book of Common Prayer* is consistent with Scripture, and that the *Thirty-nine Articles* are the authoritative canon to be followed by all clergy in their preaching. Before long these policies would engender fierce oppositon culminating in the the infamous *Marprelate Tracts* of 1588-89, which attacked Whitgift and all bishops in a most personal and scurrilous manner, as the Puritans' rage against the archbishop reached its fever point. By that time, Whitgift would be so bedevilled by enemies that he would turn to the best minds in the Church to take up their pens to defend the established order and, indirectly, himself.[2]

Travers began his sermon.[3] "Members of the two learned and honourable societies of this house, I bid you welcome to the House of God." These opening words, Hooker would soon learn, were the beginning of the bidding prayer that recognized the proprietary rights of the two inns of court affiliated with this ancient church.

There is no surviving text of this sermon. Travers' writings of the time suggest that he may have taken as his text the seventh chapter of John's Gospel, verse 51: "Doth our law condemn any man before we have heard him, and know what he hath done?" He may have applied the words to his own case, pleading on his own behalf for no less justice from his accusers in the church hierarchy, including Archbishop Whitgift, than that which was claimed for Our Lord long ago by the "honourable counsellor" who spoke the words in John's Gospel. Travers had been serving as reader at the Temple since 1581 when he returned from Antwerp and accepted Lord Burghley's request to assist the master, Master Alvey, who was too ill to carry on his duties. Until the death of Alvey earlier that year, he had been master in all but name. Dr Alvey had been master for almost a quarter of a century, and after such a long tenure, reforms, Travers would have claimed, were badly needed when he arrived.

Among these reforms he would have counted use of the "improved version" of Holy Scripture, the *Geneva Bible* from which he had just read. This, he claimed, presented the New Testament in its purest, most accurate form—translated from the Greek by none other than the great Theodore Beza himself, and then put into English by Travers' own friend and colleague from Cambridge, Dr Lawrence Tomson, the same man who translated Calvin's sermons and fought for religious reform as a member of parliament and as secretary to Lord Francis Walsingham.

Like others in the audience, Hooker was aware that the famous Calvinist looking down at them from the pulpit this morning faced the most serious threat to his ministry since he had returned to England as

Lord Burghley's family chaplain in 1580. Whitgift had ordered total conformity to the established church discipline and already had begun removing Puritan ministers from their charges. He had recently seized and burned copies of the new edition of Travers' classic handbook for Presbyterian church organization, *The Explicatio*.

Above all, Whitgift had made it clear, as Travers and almost everyone in his congregation realized, that the increasing use of presbyterian church polity, which Travers had promoted nationally in his writings and sermons and which was now spreading rapidly in eastern England and the midlands, would no longer be tolerated. This largely secret system of church governance involved creation of the so-called "classis" (later known as a presbytery or conference of ministers and elders) as a substitute for the diocesan form of regional church government.

Whitgift also forbade the practice of each congregation calling its own minister, voting on him, and then (perhaps) sending his name to the bishop for approval. Hooker was among those who felt that this crude attempt to mix presbyterianism with episcopalianism fooled no one. What was really intended was the diminution (or elimination) of the role of bishops and an increasing role for lay leadership in the form of elders and deacons. This subversive movement, led primarily by Walter Travers, Thomas Cartwright, and John Field, was a carefully planned strategy to change radically, if not overthrow altogether, the polity of the established national Church. The new archbishop, the queen, and even Burghley, could tolerate it no longer.

Hooker would soon learn that his radical cousin had already instituted most of the features of a presbyterian system of church governance right here at the Temple Church, with the enthusiastic support of most of the lawyers and barristers in his congregation, especially those at the Middle Temple. Already, pastors, teachers (doctors), and unordained elders and deacons had begun to replace bishops, priests, and deacons in the spirit and form of Temple governance. Arguing that lay elders and deacons could administer the sacrament of Communion and oversee the faith and morals of the congregation because that was the practice in the primitive Church of the apostles, Puritans like Travers were openly flouting the polity of the church establishment.[4]

Whitgift's new orders had not only reaffirmed that the church reorganization supported by Travers was illegal, but they also proscribed so-called "prophesyings" and "exercises." These were methods widely used by advanced Calvinists to affect some of their most cherished reforms simply by changing the names of key parts of the worship service and conducting them outside the regular places and hours of worship; they provided an easy way to avoid using the *Book of Common Prayer*, wearing vestments, kneeling at worship, obeying bishops. Henceforth, Whitgift ordered, all preaching and all public worship, by whatever name, would be done only inside church walls as a part of prescribed common worship; congregations would not vote on candidates for ordination before they were presented to bishops; and individual churches would have no legitimate standing except as part of the established national Church that was governed by bishops in convocation under the headship of the queen.

Hooker's cousin continued his sermon, asking perhaps whether Dr Whitgift invoked the Holy Word as authority for his opinions about the proper forms of worship and church discipline and concluded that he could not, because, for all his reputed scholarship, he could not find in Holy Scripture any mention of bishops and surplices, kneelings, and altars, organs and established churches.

Travers went on with his talk, perhaps in a more restrained manner, supporting his main arguments against the established Church with careful references to scriptural texts. Hooker was impressed, as he had been earlier in reading Travers' works, by the careful scholarship his cousin used to support his presbyterianism. Still, his first experience hearing Travers expound his radical views from the pulpit of the Temple Church must have been a shock!

During the weeks and months following his first days in London, Hooker became increasingly familiar with the broader political scene, of which the brouhaha over the appointment of a new master of the Temple was a part. He may have spent time with Edwin Sandys' influential uncle, Miles, and learned from him at first hand of happenings in parliament and at court. Edwin himself, as well as others of Hooker's new acquaintances, provided information and insights that heightened his political sophistication. Soon he was aware of a well-organized campaign headed by Travers and a few others to subvert Whitgift's latest efforts to root out Puritanism and require conformity. It seemed that moderate members of parliament, as well as certain privy councillors and leading clergy, were being pressured by presbyterian disciplinarians inside the queen's own government, and by politically influential Puritan gentry and clergy around the country, to sabotage the archbishop's programme.

Hooker learned that a flood of pamphlets, petitions, speeches, sermons, and personal attacks were being unleashed by Travers and his compatriots. They had gone so far as to conduct a survey among ministers throughout the country, which purported to show that, if Whitgift's policies were enforced, the Church would lose many of its most talented clergy and influential laity. This public-relations campaign was aimed at the forthcoming session of parliament, scheduled to meet late in 1584 or early in 1585. Hooker now saw clearly that the appointment of Travers at the Temple was one of the most important ingredients in a carefully-conceived strategy to subvert the Church of England. With one stroke the Calvinist extremists would gain the legitimacy that would come from controlling one of the most prestigious and influential pulpits in the country, and, at the same time, they would have another important base of political operations right in the heart of national politics.

Hooker also learned from his friends that Whitgift had come under sharp attack for his recent suppression of the Puritans. Burghley had openly supported the archbishop's foes in parliament. The illegal "prophesyings" and "exercises" were defended in parliamentary speeches as effective means of training an under-educated clergy. Even some of the bishops had abandoned Whitgift on this and on other points of contention. Parliament had become a forum for attacking the established church. The queen had threatened to prorogue the Commons. In the midst of this controversy Whitgift wrote a letter to the queen urging her not to turn over any more church properties to her wealthy Protestant supporters but to keep the property for the Church, as donors had intended. He no doubt feared that if he did not speak plainly to the queen, the wealthy friends of the Calvinist reformers would seize for their own gain what little was left of the Church's wealth. He needed these dwindling resources for improved training and supervision of clergy. It was not enough to root out and punish radical dissidents if the queen would not help him to correct the abuses of which they correctly complained, especially the unacceptable presence of too many under-educated, corrupt, slovenly, and irresponsible clergy.

Whitgift was in the process of filling a number of important positions during 1584. Several sees were vacant, as well as a number of important deanships and the all-important post of master at the Temple Church. What the archbishop wanted, and what the queen wanted, was for a man of learned, discreet, and wise temperament to inhabit the Temple and bring both sound religion and good behaviour to that important congregation and, by example, to the entire city. The living attached to the post was not great, but adequate, and the opportunity for further advancement was good.

Whitgift offered the position to Hooker. Richard could expect to receive official letters patent for a life appointment from the queen by about mid-March (1585), and should take over his official duties immediately thereafter. In the meantime, he was to keep his living at Drayton Beauchamp until next fall, but would have no further duties there once he began at the Temple. Hooker accepted the offer with an altogether human mixture of pride and humility. He was a good man, but not without ambition.

Sometime shortly before his appointment at the Temple Church on 17 March 1585, Hooker left Drayton Beachamp and took up full-time residence in London. By the end of February, he had moved his few belongings out of the parish rectory at Drayton, settled into a room at the Churchmans' house on Watling Street, and begun to prepare his first sermons as master of the Temple.

There was a storm brewing in parliament. Miles Sandys was a member of Commons in this session. He had recently been dispatched by the Speaker of the House to go up to chancery court and talk the judges into rescinding a subpoena which that court had issued against the Commons. They had refused. The speaker then sent Miles to see the lord chancellor who also declined to recognize the claim of the Commons to immunity from court subpoenas. Miles was not alone among the lawyers at Middle Temple Inn and elsewhere in London who thought it imperative that the legislative branch be kept out from under the thumb of the judiciary. Separation of the two branches of government was an issue of growing importance.[6]

Of more immediate impact on Hooker's concerns was a petition, from Puritan members of the Commons to the House of Lords, urging relief from Whitgift's *Three Articles*, to which all clergy were required to conform, on pain of loss of their posts. In defending his position, Whitgift had once again enraged the Puritan firebrand Lawrence Tomson, who accused the primate of sophistry and conduct unbecoming a true divine. This was same Tomson who had been organizing support in parliament and among members of the Middle and Inner Temple Inns to pressure the queen to appoint Travers master of the Temple.[7]

All this activity, in parliament and without, amounted to little less than a well-organized strategy for limiting the archbishop's power and establishing Travers and his friends in a position to undermine the Church. The queen, Hooker learned, was so upset by this recent round of Puritan obstructionism that she planned to address parliament in person at the end of the month, about the time his appointment became known. There was no doubt that she wanted to send a message: she would support her archbishop and tolerate no more opposition to her moderate reformation of the Church. Hooker may have joined others who hoped that when the queen made her speech she would use that delicious word of hers to describe the extremists' most cherished reforms: "newfangledness." What a wonderful woman's way to dismiss all their programmes as a kind of fussy nuisance! How it must infuriate such men as Tomson, Travers, and Field that their sovereign could show such contempt for their most cherished ideas! (The queen did use the word. She said in her speech at the end of March that she was convinced that her form of church reform was God's will for England and that she wished neither to "imitate Romanists . . . nor tolerate newfangledness." There were "perils" in either extreme, she said.)[8]

News of Hooker's appointment at the Temple—and Travers' rejection—leaked out well before the assignment was official. Many, especially at Middle Temple, were not happy about it. They saw Hooker's coming as a repudiation of Travers and a victory for Whitgift.

The choice of a master had been an opportunity for the members at the inns to be directly involved in an issue that touched one of the great religious debates of the day. They were lawyers and politicians, every one, and had taken this case very much to heart. The lines had been sharply drawn for and against Hooker, even before he was to begin his work, and most were not for him.

Richard was pleased to learn that Travers had apparently taken the news of his rejection rather well. Once he learned that the queen had made her final decision, Travers stopped his campaign against Hooker. In fact, he was apparently meeting with members informally, encouraging them to welcome and support his cousin as the new master.

Perhaps, Richard thought, Mr Travers will be reasonable after all and respect the authority of the established Church. Or, perhaps, on second thought, he had merely recognized the reality of his situation and shifted ground to a more defensible position. Certainly, there was no indication thus far that Travers intended to leave his position as reader, and there had been no word as yet about removing him from that post. If he were to stay on, he would maintain full contact with residents at the inns, preach regularly, and be prepared to undermine anything Hooker said or did as master that was not to his liking.

THE ENCOUNTER

Hooker's first recorded encounter with Travers was on an early evening in late March of 1585. The place may have been a lighted corner in the ancient round "narthex." The circumstance was a meeting Travers had requested in order to welcome Hooker informally and brief him on some important matters before the new master gave his first sermon. When Travers arrived at the historic church, he was not alone.[9]

Travers began the interview by introducing the two men with him. They had been elected by the congregation to assist him in the management of the church, he explained. Hooker was shocked. Had Travers gone so far in the establishment of the forbidden presbyterian polity as to institute the practice of elected lay deacons and elders? No wonder Whitgift wanted Travers out of here.

Hooker greeted the two men with Travers politely and inquired if they had been appointed to their posts by the bishop. No, they had not. They had been chosen by the congregation to serve as "collectors" and "sidemen." Were these terms a subterfuge for the forbidden "elders" and "deacons" that Travers had advocated in his writings? Travers explained that the Privy Council had approved the use of "collectors," "sidemen," and "wardens" at the Temple long ago, ever since Alvey had been master. Their initial functions were to help with collecting alms and assuring attendance at services, but no doubt their role had expanded considerably to fill out Travers' presbyterian expectations of lay leadership.

Hooker did not wish to begin his ministry at the Temple by disturbing a practice to which the congregation had been accustomed. But, he informed Travers, they would need to seek the archbishop's approval for such significant departures from the prescribed regulations concerning church governance. Travers objected that since these men had been duly elected by the congregation, no approval from any bishop would be necessary. Bishops, he said, had no authority here at the Temple. This church was responsible only to the queen, through Lord Burghley and the Privy Council.

Master Hooker countered that it was precisely the question of whether the bishop or the congregation governed the Church that was at issue between the Church of England and well-meaning persons such as Travers who sought to replace the episcopal polity with the presbyterian discipline. It was legally the case that the queen governed here, Hooker said, but she did so through her bishops.

Travers could see at once that Hooker meant to be in charge at the Temple and that his own reforms were now in serious jeopardy. It was time for the presbyterian tactician to shift his ground. His aim, after all, was not to subvert the episcopacy, he assured Hooker, but to affect a reform that would combine the best of old ways with the more democratic congregational forms preferred by the men at the inns and, for that matter, by people throughout England.

Hooker's reputation for preferring tolerance and compromise to conflict and disorder had preceded him. But he was no fool. He knew that his cousin was not only a brilliant scholar and committed follower of Christ but also a seasoned veteran of political wars. He took Travers' measure as quickly as that gentleman had taken his. He asked Travers if he intended to stay on as reader. When he had the unwelcome affirmative response, he assured his cousin that they could work amicably together so far as he was concerned and that he looked forward to a good relationship. Perhaps Walter would help him conduct his first service tomorrow morning. He wished to follow customary liturgical practice, so far as possible, and would welcome Travers' assistance.

Travers' response was disturbing to Hooker. Walter did not expect Richard to do the morning service at all. In fact, he should take no services at the Temple until he had been properly "affirmed" by the congregation as its new master. Walter would be happy to put Richard's name before them and recommend that they give their "allowance" for him to take charge of the church. This would serve to "confirm" his appointment and "seal" his calling to preach in the Temple.

Hooker was stunned. Travers' use of words such as "affirm," "confirm," "allowance," and "seal" were code words signifying "election" by the congregation. His appointment had come from the queen. He needed no approval from those to whom he would preach and minister. He said as much to Travers. When his cousin demurred, Hooker, ever the peace-maker, relented so far as to say that he had no wish to disturb local practice on such a procedural matter and would be happy if Walter would proceed to secure the congregation's affirmation of his appointment. If Richard thought this conciliatory gesture would assuage the Presbyterian agitator, he was mistaken.

Following his meeting with Travers, Hooker was fully aware that the authorized liturgy he planned to employ at the Temple would be very different from what the congregation had grown used to under Alvey's and Travers' regimes. For those two, preaching the Word, not administering the sacraments, was the core event in worship. Richard knew that the Puritans despised the prepared homilies that were so often read out by unlearned men as a substitute for original sermons. In many respects, he agreed with them. He did not agree, however, with the Puritans' preference for extemporaneous ministerial prayers and sermons. Much better, he believed, to use the carefully prepared prayers of learned churchmen contained in the *Book of Common Prayer* than the supposedly inspired ministerial supplications of the moment. In any event, he was determined to affirm his leadership and to begin to establish a measure of orthodoxy at the Temple.[10]

At the next Sunday service, which Hooker did not attend, Travers announced from the pulpit that he had had a most satisfactory meeting with Mr Hooker and was happy to recommend that the congregation confirm him as the new master of their church. It must have been a painful deed for one who had so ardently coveted the position for himself. Certainly, it was a testimony to the sincerity of Travers' belief in the presbyterian polity that he would recommend congregational election of a man who was his rival for advancement at the Temple, and with whom he had such profound theological, liturgical, and ecclesiastical differences. But then, it was never the sincerity of either Travers or Hooker that was in doubt. What would be in question for centuries to come was the verity of their respective viewpoints, as these two gladiators, prophets respectively for Presbyteriansm and Anglicansim, wrestled for the soul of the Church of England.

NOTES

1. J. Bruce Williamson, *The History of the Middle Temple*, (London, New York: E. P. Dutton, 1924), 16-17; 92-5; generally, 3-105. See also, Hugh H. Bellot, *The Inner and Middle Temple* (London: Methuen & Co., 1902). Although it contains such errors as referring to Richard as "John" and granting him the title "doctor" (at 216 and 221), Bellot's work contains some useful information. Descriptions of the Temple Church are drawn from T. Henry Baylis, *The Temple Church and Chapel of St Ann, An Historical Record and Guide* (London: George Philip and Son, 1895), 1-40; current Temple publications; and the author's many personal visits.
2. Donald J. McGinn, *John Penry and the Marprelate Controversy* (New Brunswick: Rutgers University Press, 1966), 36-7; 168. McGinn's argument that Penry is the

sole author of the *Marprelate Tracts* is less convincing than his proposition that Whitgift "enlisted" Hooker and "assigned" him the task of defending the Church from the *Marprelate Tracts,* a commission leading directly to the writing of the *Laws of Ecclesiastical Polity*. See ix; 206-12. See also *infra*, Chapter 14, note 10.

3. There is no surviving sermon of Travers at the Temple. I have drawn for my account of this one from writings of his from this time, principally his *Supplication to the Privy Council*. See *Folger* V, 190-1 for the text.

4. For this and other details of Travers' career at the Temple, and his controversy with Hooker, the best secondary sources are William P. Haugaard, "The Hooker-Travers Controversy," *Folger*, V, Supplement I, 264-9; Egil Grislis, "Commentary," *Folger*, V, 619-26; 641-8; Knox, 65-73.

5. This is taken from Strype's account of Whitgift's letter to the queen. Strype, 340-6. See also Dent, 155-61. Whitgift's account of abuses is reported by Walton in *Works*, I, 41-44.

6. For a record of Miles Sandys' activities in the Parliament of 1584-85, see Simonds D'Ewes, *The Journals of All the Parliaments During the Reign of Queen Elizabeth* (London, 1682), 347; 353. It is sometimes difficult to determine which of the several Sandys serving in parliament in the last two decades of the century is referred to in the various journals of parliamentary proceedings. There was Miles, the brother of Archbishop Sandys, clearly the senior and most prestigious of the group—he was later to rise high in the legal profession and serve as treasurer of the Middle Temple. Then there was the archbishop's son, Edwin, who also served in one or more of Elizabeth's parliaments. Finally, there was Samuel Sandys. A close student of the parliaments has said that it "is hard, if not impossible to distinguish" which Sandys did what in which parliament. See T. E. Hartley, ed., *Proceedings in the Parliaments of Elizabeth I 1584-1589* (London: Leicester University Press, 1995), I, 397, n. 39. We are safe in assuming that the Sandys referred to in the 1585 session is Miles, since Edwin, not yet even admitted to the Middle Temple Inn, was not prepared to be in parliament before 1592, or perhaps 1589. Edwin's well-known career as an MP was to take place mostly in the next century under James I.

7. Haugaard, *Elizabeth and the Reformation*, 267. For coverage of the Parliaments of this period, I have relied, in addition to D'Ewes and Hartley, on the classic treatment by J. E. Neale, *Elizabeth I and Her Parliaments 1584-1601* (London: Jonathan Cape, 1957), esp. 58-83.

8. Cited in Haugaard, "The Hooker-Travers Controversy," *Folger*, V, 267.

9. The following details of Hooker's meetings and controversies with Travers are drawn from Travers' *Supplication* and Hooker's *Answer*. *Folger*, V, 187-210; 225-257; *Works*, III, 548-69; 570-96. See also Brook, 117. An excellent discussion of Puritan efforts to change church polity by introducing "prophesyings," "classis," "sidemen," and "wardens" is found in Paget, 63-8. He cites the Hooker-Travers conflict as a prime example of attempts to impose the presbyterian discipline, and he characterizes Travers (along with John Field) as the leading exponent of these changes. Paget describes Travers as brilliant but unable to get along well with others, and as one given to intemperate speech and behaviour, in contrast with Hooker's more moderate attitude and personality, at 56-57.

10. Hooker records his awareness of Puritan objections to the Anglican liturgy in many places, but principally in Book V of the *Laws*. See especially *Folger*, II, 113-21; *Works*, II, 118-27.

CHAPTER 10

The Great Debate Begins

For seven years of his life, between the ages of thirty and thirty-seven, Richard Hooker was an important player in the politics of the Church of England, as master of the Temple Church in London. That he never advanced beyond this position to achieve higher status and influence as a bishop, or at least dean of a cathedral, is owing to a number of conditions, including his lack of a doctorate and the fact that he was not celibate. Of greater import was what he and others would learn about his opinions on important political issues and about his personality and character during these seven years of testing in the politically-charged crucible of Elizabethan church leadership.

Even as history has obscured Richard Hooker, her muse has shrouded the "great debate" at the Temple between Hooker and Travers—surely one of the defining events in the story of emergent Anglicanism. As long ago as 1885, on the occasion of the gala celebration of the seven-hundredth anniversary of the Temple Church, sermons by the archbishop of Canterbury and the master and reader of the Temple took not the slightest note of this event or of its protagonists, arguably the two most important occupants of the Temple pulpit throughout its long history. Nor was mention made at that time of Whitgift, Burghley, Aylmer, Leicester, De Corro, Ralegh, Coke, Sandys, or the other Elizabethan figures whose formative religious and political struggles were often acted out in the Temple and its precincts. The speakers on that day in 1885 just droned on about the ancient founding of the church by the Knights Templar.[1]

To redress the balance I have reconstructed a probable sermon and church service. The sermon is presented by direct quotation, with some modernization of language and close paraphrase from Hooker's writings, especially *A Learned and Comfortable Sermon of the Certaintie and Perpetuity of Faith in the Elect*. This sermon was given at the Temple during Hooker's first months there, before the three sermons on *Justification* that were to comprise the heart of his controversy with Travers. He had actually given at least two sermons at the Temple prior to this one, but this is the first that survives.[2]

Just before the service, Hooker donned surplice, alb, and cope to signal changes in worship here at the Temple. He would use the authorized 1559 *Prayer Book* this morning, although he was aware of the Puritans' objections to that service, especially the removal in it of any condemnation of the pope, the compromise wording of the Eucharist, and the mandated wearing of cope over the surplice and alb.

Later on, but not today, he might be willing to compromise in the name of church harmony and use the 1552 *Geneva Prayer Book*, edited by the Scotch presbyterian John Knox and endorsed by Calvin himself. He was familiar with that book. President Cole at Corpus had helped write it while he was in exile at Frankfurt. It had been popular at Oxford.

Hooker, who loved music, may have decided to risk scandal as new rector of this largely Puritan congregation by arranging for a modest choral presentation. He would make it clear in this and other ways that a new day was dawning here at the Temple. We imagine four boy sopranos with the voices of angels breaking into song just before his sermon, filling the sanctuary with the glories of a William Byrd motet. "Rejoyce, Rejoyce . . . " They would sing forth in one of the finest compositions of this master of sixteenth-century English church music. Hooker was certain that Travers did not often, if ever, allow this sort of music. (Byrd was, after all, a Catholic!)[3]

The motet concluded, Richard climbed up into the pulpit. A large six-sided sounding board hanging from the ceiling over the pulpit was positioned so that this hollow wooden structure could amplify and project Hooker's rather weak voice out into the church. After putting his text on the lectern, he looked out over the congregation and began his first sermon as master of the Temple.

> That music was joyful praise to God. I am glad to begin my days with you on such notes. The Word of God read and preached out of His Holy Scriptures is surely an important foundation of our Christian life together. But ever since the earliest days of the ancient church, music has been a blessed part of our worship.
>
> My own patron, the late Bishop Jewel of Salisbury, liked to say that people singing the psalms in church was one of the first signs that the Reformation here in England was succeeding.[4]

"Whether by voice or by instrument, whether through high notes or low, musical harmony bespeaks the nature of our very souls," Hooker continued, warming to his subject.

> Music is a thing which suits all ages and stages of life, as seasonable in grief as in joy. Music has the admirable facility both to express and represent better than any other sensible means, all of the risings and fallings and turns and varieties of passion to which the mind is subject. In future, we may add instrumental music to our worship here in the Temple.
>
> I am aware that there are those who believe this is papist ornamentation. But the great prophet and psalmist David gave us not

> only the poetry of his songs but the precedent of instrumental music as well.[5]

"Speaking of David," Hooker continued,

> remember how he exhorted us to "worship the Lord in the beauty of holiness?" How fortunate we are to be able to worship in this magnificent ancient church, hallowed by the centuries of worshippers who have gone before us here. The majesty of this place provides us a special virtue, force and efficacy for prayer and worship because it helps to stir up in us devotion, holiness and actions of the best sort. Truly we are reminded that it is not only God's people who may be sanctified, but His Holy Temple as well.[6]
>
> My text for my sermon with you here at the Temple today is from one of my favourite Old Testament writers, the troubled prophet, Habakkuk. I have been preaching from this text frequently of late because I find this prophet's teachings rich in answers to questions that trouble us today, especially the issue of how we may distinguish between truth and error amidst so many conflicting religious opinions?

He read the text from Habakkuk 1:4.

> Devastation and violence confront me; strife breaks out, discord raises its head, and so law grows effete; justice does not come forth victorious for the wicked outwit the righteous and so justice comes out perverted.

"Does the prophet, in admitting the idea into his mind that God's law has failed, show himself to be an unbeliever?" Hooker asked rhetorically, and then went on:

> Because some have found it too easy purposely to distort and misconstrue what I have said in the past on this subject of faith and doubt, I will elaborate today on the question of why some people are able to keep their faith in the face of great threats to it, including their own doubts.
>
> None of us marvel that we neither recognize nor acknowledge the acts of God by reason alone, because we know that these acts can only be fully discerned spiritually. But those, like the prophet, in whose hearts the grace of God shines, who are taught by God Himself—why are they so weak in faith? Why is their assent to God's law so limited, so mingled with fear and wavering? It seems strange that they should ever think that God's law would fail them. But if we stop to think about it, such weakness of faith will not seem strange to us.
>
> When it comes to what matters most to us, it may be truly said that faith is more certain than any science. Even that which we know either by our senses or by the most infallible scientific demonstration is not as certain to us as the principal conclusions of Christian faith, provided they are grounded in what I will call the "certainty of evidence" or the "certainty of adherence."

His listeners, lawyers all, were attentive to this fine distinction. Some of them, as was the custom at the Temple, began taking notes.

> What I mean to signify by "the certainty of evidence" is when the mind assents to a proposition not because it is true in itself but because its truth is made evident or manifest to our reason. Even if something is in itself true, that will not persuade us unless it be made clearly evident to us.
>
> Thus, although it is as certainly true that there are spirits as that there are men, we are more inclined to believe in the existence of men than of spirits because they are more clearly evident to our senses.
>
> Some propositions are so evident to our minds that no one who hears them affirmed can doubt their truth—such as that a part of anything is less than the whole. But in matters of faith, we find the contrary situation. Everyone does not agree to the truth of the same proposition. This is because, unlike angels and spirits in heaven who have certainty about things spiritual by the light of their divine glory, that which we here on earth see is only by the light of grace and hence not so certain as that which we see by the strong evidence of our senses or our reason.
>
> Proofs are vain and frivolous unless they are more certain than the things they seek to prove. That is why we see everywhere in the Scripture the effort to prove matters of faith and confirm us in our beliefs by offering us evidence acceptable to our senses—our natural reason. I conclude therefore that we have less confidence about things taken on faith than about things perceived by the senses or grasped by our reason.
>
> And who among us does not have doubts about his faith at some time? I will not here recount the confessions of the most perfect of persons who ever lived on earth concerning their doubts. If I did so I would only belabour a matter well-known to every honest man of faith. The remedy for this doubt is what I just called the "certainty of adherence."
>
> What I mean here is the certainty that comes when the heart simply adheres or sticks to what it believes. This happens because we know as Christians that God's promises are not only true, but they are also good. Therefore, even when the evidence of the truth of God's promises is so small that a man must grieve for the weakness of his faith in them, he still feels an adherence to them in his heart because he has at some time tasted the heavenly sweetness, or goodness, of those promises.
>
> So it is that we will strive against all reason to hope against hope that God's promises are true. With Job, I may hold the immovable resolution that although God shall kill me, I will never stop trusting Him. Why? Not because God's law is true but because it is forever imprinted on my heart that it will be good for me, like Job, to believe in God.
>
> To be sure, our minds are so darkened with the foggy damp of original corruption that none of us has a heart so enlightened in knowledge or so firm in love of God's promise of salvation that his faith is perfect, free of doubt. If there were any such persons, they would be justified by their own inherent righteousness. There would be no need for Christ. He would be superfluous.

> Let him beware who claims a power he has not lest he lose the comfort of the weakness he does have!

Hooker continued his lecture for about thirty minutes, providing examples from Scripture to illustrate his main points. He was at special pains to demonstrate that the men of greatest faith, like Abraham, did in fact have doubts that were cured by appeals to their reason and senses. At length he reached a point in his text which he knew would be controversial.

> As for the claim of some among us that the spirit of God within us gives certain and doubt-free evidence of His truth, this is not so. It would have been, had God chosen to reveal His power through visible effects as He has in nature, with fire and the sun which inflame and lighten the world. But in His incomprehensible wisdom, God has decided to limit the visible effects of His power to that degree which seems best to Him.
>
> God provides us with certainty in all that we need to know for salvation in the life to come. But He does not give us certain knowledge to achieve perfection in this life.

"Even so, Oh God," he continued, perhaps raising his voice as if in prayer, "it has pleased You to have us feel our doubt and infirmity so that we can no more breathe than we must pray: 'Dear God, help our infirmity.'"

Hooker then continued on a different tack.

> Now I turn to the question whether by the mere thought that God had failed him, the prophet Habakkuk killed God's spirit within him, lost his faith and showed himself to be an unbeliever. This question is momentous. The peace and tranquillity of all souls depends on the answer.
>
> In order to determine whether Habakkuk's doubt, and our own, marks us as unbelievers, we need first to examine the basic difference between one who believes in God and one who does not. The doctrine that forms the sure foundation for the believer is that the faith by which he is saved can never fail. It did not fail the prophet Habakkuk and it shall not fail you. This faith is a gift from God, what Saint John calls the "seed of God" which is planted in the hearts of all who are incorporated into Christ.
>
> But our faith does not mean that we will never sin. Nor does it mean that we will never doubt God's promises. If we think that, we expect too much of ourselves. We deceive ourselves. What God's grace poured into His people does assure is that despite all sin and all doubt we will never be separated from His love or cut off from Christ Jesus. The seed of God abides forever in His children and shields them from receiving any irremediable wound.
>
> I know that there are those who will not be convinced or comforted by my argument because, like Habakkuk, they are suffering such agonies of grief over their apparently lost faith that they cannot find their true

selves within themselves. They search their hearts diligently and yet still lament for a thing that seems past finding. They mourn like Rachel and refuse to be comforted, acting as if that which does not exist does, and that which does, does not—as if they do not believe in God when they do, as if they despaired when in fact they do not.

In some such grieving persons I grant that what we have is a melancholy spirit that comes from some physical infirmity that can often be dispelled by healing the body. But there are other reasons why people become deeply depressed and seem to lose their faith. One of these is a despair that comes from deciding that others seem to have fared better in life or that they themselves were better off at some earlier stage.

A reason for this kind of despair is the false idea that people of faith will always be joyful and happy. When I am not, I must, therefore, have lost my faith. It is true that St Paul prayed for the Church at Rome, "The God of hope fill you with all joy of believing." But he did not mean by this that when we have a "heaviness of spirit" and fail to find singing joy and delight in our hearts, we have lost faith. This joy, this light, is but a separable accident of faith and not the same thing. We would not even know such delight if we did not also experience a healthy intercourse with the darkness of despair.

Too much honey turns to gall and too much joy, even spiritual joy, will make us wantons (immoral, malicious, wilful). Happier by far is that person whose soul is humbled by inner desolation than he whose heart is puffed up and exalted beyond all reason by an abundance of spiritual delight. Better sometimes to go down into the pit with one who is beholding darkness and bewailing the loss of inner joy and consolation and saying from the bottom of lowest hell, "My God, my God, why hast Thou forsaken me?" than continually to walk arm in arm with angels; to sit, as it were, in the bosom of Abraham and to have no doubt and no thought except, "I thank my God it is not with me as with other men."

No! Our God will have those who are to walk in His light feel from time to time what it is to sit in the shadow of death.

Hooker paused for a moment before continuing to read from his manuscript.

A third reason why some wrongly judge themselves to be without faith is that they base this opinion on the unreliable conclusions of their own limited rational capacities. One will have little success convincing a person who has too hard an opinion of himself that he is not so weak in faith as he feels himself to be. He will tell you he has thoroughly considered and exquisitely sifted all the corners of his heart, sees all there is within him, and knows that he no longer believes in God.

How true it is of our weak and wavering nature that we have no sooner received a grace than we are ready to fall from it; we have no sooner given our assent to the unfailing sanction of law than our very next notion is that the law is failing us. Although we find in ourselves a most willing heart to cleave inseparably to God even so far as to affirm unfeignedly with Peter "Lord, I am ready to go with you into prison and to death," yet how soon and how easily and with what small provocation we fall away when we are left to ourselves. The higher we flow, the nearer we are to an ebb when we are seen as mere men driven in the course of our own inclinations without the heavenly support of the Holy Spirit.

But the simplicity of our faith takes the naked promise of God—His bare word—and on that alone it rests. This simplicity the Serpent labors continually to pervert, corrupting the mind with vain imaginings of repugnancy and contrariness between the promise of God and those things which our senses and our experiences or some other knowledge have made obvious to us. The word of God's promise to His people is "I will not leave nor forsake you." Upon this, the simplicity of faith, Habakkuk's or ours, rests, and is not afraid.

Yet Habakkuk, beholding the land that God had set aside for His own, and seeing it occupied by heathen nations, and seeing how they ruined the land and used it for their own wicked pleasures, and beholding the Lord's own throne made into a heap of stones and His temple defiled, the carcasses of His servants cast out for the birds of the air to devour, the flesh of the innocent ones thrown out for the beasts of the field to feed upon, remembered how long and how earnestly he had cried to God to help His people for the sake of His Name as well as for their own sakes. The repugnancy between the horror that filled his senses and the unkept promise of God's law made such a deep impression on him that he did not examine the problem carefully but simply inferred from it that "The Law has failed."

So it is with us. Although we can count God's goodness to us in reconciling love by the number of hours, days, and years of our lives, if we put all these acts together they lack the force to overcome the doubt that comes from fear of losing just a tiny transitory favour from our fellows, or some small calamity. We immediately imagine that we are crossed clean out of God's book, that He does not love us but prefers strangers.

Hooker paused again before concluding.

Then, as we look at other people, we compare them to ourselves and conclude that their tables are richly furnished every day whereas ashes and dirt are our daily bread; they sing happily before the beautiful music of the lute and their children dance for them, whereas our hearts are as heavy as lead, our sighs are thick and our pulses too fast, our tears wash the beds in which we lie. The sun shines fair on them and we are hung up like bottles in the smoke, cast into corners like shards of a broken pot. Do not tell us about the promises of God! Tell those who reap the fruit of God's love. These belong not to us but to others. God forgive our weakness, but this is the way it is with us.

Well, let the frailty of our nature, the subtlety of Satan, the force of our own deceivable imaginations all be as we know them to be—ready at every moment to threaten the utter subversion of our faith. Yet faith is not really at risk.

If I remember this, that faith is never really at risk, who then can ever separate me and my God? I know in whom I have faith. I am not

> ignorant of Whose precious blood has been shed for me. I have a shepherd who is full of kindness, full of care and full of power. To Him I commit myself. His own finger has engraved this sentence on my heart: "Satan has desired to winnow you as wheat, but I have prayed that Your faith in me shall not fail." To the end of my days, therefore, I will labour to maintain the assurance of my faith like a jewel. By a combination of my efforts and by the gracious mediation of God's prayer, I shall keep my faith.

Sound Calvinist theology, except for a reference or two to the possible efficacy of works. Hooker may have taken some time at this point in his talk to explain the changes that would occur as he moved to reinstitute the authorized liturgy at the Temple. He may have asked his congregation to notice that he was wearing full vestments and had been using the authorized *Book of Common Prayer*. He may even have expressed his deep love for this beautiful book of Archbishop Cranmer's and explained that since the time of the early church Christians had worshipped God in common prayer following a pattern not unlike what was prescribed in this wonderful book. At times he felt that common prayers said together for so long must have been ordained by God Himself. In any event, here in the Temple Church, they were all under the queen's ecclesiastical jurisdiction and would henceforth follow her rules for liturgical performance.[7]

Hooker was aware that some in his congregation would agree with Thomas Cartwright that many of the forms of speech used in the *Book of Common Prayer*, such as saying at Communion: "eat thou" and "drink thou" to each particular person, rather than saying generally to everyone at once: "take, eat and drink," had been "picked out of the popish dunghill," to use Mr Cartwright's colourful metaphor. But he urged them to abandon what he regarded as rigid, intemperate, and exclusivist attitudes about the Church and its services. Simply because a practice had been used for centuries in the Roman rites and was not specifically mentioned in Scripture was no reason to abandon it. Certain rituals are followed here in England because for us they are reasonable, familiar, comfortable, pious, and not contrary to Scripture, he explained.

A further departure from ordinary practice in the Temple would be more frequent celebration of Holy Communion, a service rarely used under the extreme Calvinist régime here. Once again, his intention was not to stir up trouble, but to make plain at the outset his intent to have authorized liturgical practice installed under his leadership.

So that they would understand the spirit in which he was about to celebrate Holy Communion, Hooker no doubt explained that he stood squarely in the reformed spirit of the author of the *Prayer Book*, Thomas Cranmer, as well as other great reformers like Bishop Jewel, Dr Bucer, and Archbishop Sandys.

It was not so important, according to Hooker, to know whether the real presence of Christ's body and blood was to be found in the consecrated elements of bread and wine, by means of transubstantiation, as the Romans would have it, or by consubstantiation, as many Lutherans held. Unfortunately, too many continued to be rent with contentions over this rather unimportant issue about exactly where Christ resides in the Eucharist, when all agree that He does indeed enter the hearts of all believing participants.

Is the question of exactly how God works this miracle and exactly where Christ resides really so crucial? Hooker thought not. What was important was not how the elements were changed, if at all, but that those who receive them are, by faith, transformed through God's grace. The Sacrament is an instrument for transforming men. Christ is to be found in consecrated persons, not consecrated elements. The real presence of Christ's most blessed body and blood is not therefore to be sought in the elements, but in the worthy receiver of the Sacrament.

Hooker exhorted his congregation to meditate in silence about what they had been given in the Sacrament and to dispute less about how it worked. All should remember how few words the Apostles had ever spoken about this matter. With them, everyone should, in simple awe and gratitude, cease those curious and intricate speculations that only hinder, abate, and quench the inflamed motions of delight and joy with which we might cooperate with God as we participate in this divine grace that is extraordinarily present for us and in us in the Holy Communion.[8]

Hooker continued.

> Just a few final words before we begin the service. I want you to know that I regard the Sacrament of Communion as a means of God's grace and not merely a confirmation or seal of what He has promised in Scripture. For me, this Sacrament is as important, if not more so, than preaching of the Word. I hold that reading of the Holy Word, religious education, study, prayer, and common worship are all more edifying than preaching. You noticed, I am sure, that I placed no importance on memorizing my sermon this morning so that I might appear to be spontaneous, as many of our preachers, readers and lecturers do. I give you credit for the ability to follow my thoughts as I read them to you. In any event, God is not likely to reach you through my words so much as through the Sacrament and your own response to reading and hearing His Word.[9]
>
> Brother Cartwright and his friends, by a too strict reading of First Corinthians, chapter five, would have us exclude from our company everyone who disagrees with our opinions on each detail of worship. Are we to brand such people as "papist" and exclude them from the Communion table as the "dogs, swine, beastes, foreigners, and strangers" that Mr Cartwright says they are? I think not.
>
> God alone can know who belongs in His eternal, invisible Church. He knows who among us are not as we seem. But He does not ask us to dive

into men's consciences but rather to take one another as we outwardly represent ourselves to be. In the eyes of God they are against Christ who are not truly and sincerely with Him; but in our eyes all must be received as with Christ who are not in any outward profession or action against Him.

"Therefore," Hooker finished,

henceforth all who have not separated themselves from Christ's visible Church by their own acts of apostasy, heresy or schism will be welcome to participate in the Holy Communion services in this Temple church. In future, you need only inform me before the service of your intent to receive Communion. Unless I have strong reason to think you unworthy, I will take you as repentant of your sins and welcome you to the Lord's Table.[10]

Now Hooker came down from the pulpit and stood in front of the Communion table. He was aware from the stirring and grumbling in the benches that there was some discontent with his open invitation. Puritans were used to a more restrictive interpretation of who was and who was not worthy to receive the Sacrament. They did not approve the idea that each person could judge his own worthiness to do so. Nor did they like Hooker's rejection of the *Genevan Prayer Book*, or versions of it, which were widely used in English churches after 1584 and set the standard for Presbyterian worship. The services set forth in that book were very different from the Anglican form. They stressed the sermon, long pastoral prayers emphasizing personal sin, prayers for pardon, and lengthy readings from Scripture. When the authorized 1559 service was used, it was usually an amended form produced "illegally" by Puritan presses. These altered prayer books, more to the liking of such presbyterians as Travers and Cartwright, were probably in use at the Temple as early as 1578. They included such changes as substituting the words "minister" for "priest," "morning prayer" and "evening prayer" for "matins" and "evensong," and eliminating all the rubrics allowing private communion, baptism and the "churching of women." As Hooker was to say throughout his ministry, these changes were rather unimportant and not worth the disruption of the peace and order of the Christian commonwealth. Far more radical changes were contained in *Calvin's Form of Common Prayer*, which was in use by 1585 in many Puritan parishes in England. It is probable that Travers would have used this book had he been appointed master instead of Hooker. In fact, he may have introduced it during the month before Hooker's arrival. Although the Star Chamber suppressed the book shortly after it appeared, English editions continued to be printed abroad and used illegally in English churches throughout Hooker's ministry.[11]

Hooker opened the *Book of Common Prayer* and began the service that has been a familiar comfort to Anglicans for centuries.

> Almighty God, unto whom all hearts be open, all desires known, and from whom no secrets are hid: Cleanse the thoughts of our hearts by the inspiration of thy Holy Spirit, that we may perfectly love thee, and worthily magnify thy holy name, through Christ our Lord. Amen.

Richard continued his reading: "God spake these words and said, I am the Lord thy God, Thou shalt have none other gods but me."

He was relieved when at least some in his congregation responded with enthusiasm: "Lord have mercy upon us and incline our hearts to keep this law."

The reading of the Ten Commandments and the collect assigned for the day followed. Then Hooker read the prescribed collect for the queen.

> Almighty and everlasting God, we be taught by thy holy word, that the hearts of kings are in thy rule and governance, and that thou dost dispose and turn them, as it seemeth best to thy godly wisdom: We humbly beseech thee, so to dispose and govern the heart of Elizabeth, thy servant, our queen and governor, that in all her thoughts, words, and works, she may ever seek thy honor and glory, and study to preserve thy people committed to her charge, in wealth, and godliness. Grant this, O merciful Father, for thy dear Son's sake, Jesus Christ our Lord.

"Amen," the congregation responded.

The service proceeded through the readings of the Epistle and Gospel lessons and the recitation of the Nicene Creed. Then Hooker addressed the congregation with several announcements, reminding them of forthcoming saints' days, informing them that Holy Communion would be celebrated regularly, and that it was their legal as well as their religious obligation to participate, no less than four times a year.

Then, "Let your light so shine before men, that they may see your good works, and glorify your Father which is in heaven."

After the almsmen had collected the offering, Hooker continued with words that have rung down the aisles and into the pews and benches of Anglican churches in every corner of the globe for over four hundred years: "Let us pray for the whole state of Christ's Church," he said, turning to kneel before the table.

"Almighty and everlasting God," he read, "who by thy holy Apostle hast taught us to make prayers and supplications and to give thanks for all men: We humbly beseech thee most mercifully to accept our alms, and to receive these our prayers which we offer unto Thy Divine Majesty . . ."

Then Hooker read, "Ye who do truly and earnestly repent you of your sins . . ."

The congregation, some kneeling, but many still seated, responded in unison with common public confession:

> Almighty God, Father of our Lord Jesus Christ, maker of all things, judge of all men, we acknowledge and bewail our manifold sins and wickedness, which we from time to time have most grievously committed, by thought word, and deed, against thy divine majesty . . .

Rising from his kneeling position and facing the congregation, Hooker spoke to them the words of comforting absolution: "Almighty God our heavenly Father, who of his great mercy promised forgiveness of sins to all of them which with hearty repentance and true faith turn unto him: Have mercy upon you, pardon and deliver you from all your sins . . ."

"Lift up your hearts."

"We lift them up unto the Lord."

"Therefore with angels and archangels and all the company of heaven, we laud and magnify thy glorious name . . ."

Then, turning and kneeling again before the table, Hooker prayed on behalf of all present. "We do not presume to come to this thy table, O merciful Lord, trusting in our own righteousness, but in thy manifold and great mercies. We are not worthy . . ."

After this penitential prayer, still facing the table, Hooker stood, continuing with the service.

> Almighty God our heavenly Father, who of thy tender mercy didst give thine only Son Jesus Christ, to suffer death upon the cross for our redemption . . . Hear us . . . and grant that we, receiving these thy creatures of bread and wine, according to thy Son our Saviour Jesus Christ's holy institution, in remembrance of his death and passion, may be partakers of his most blessed Body and Blood: who in the same night that he was betrayed, took bread, and when he had given thanks, he brake it, and gave it to his disciples, saying, Take, eat, this is my body which is given for you. Do this in remembrance of me. Likewise after supper he took the cup, and when he had given thanks, he gave it to them, saying, Drink ye all of this, for this is my blood of the new testament, which is shed for you and for many, for the remission of sins: do this as oft as ye shall drink it in remembrance of me.

Following strictly the rubric of the *Book of Common Prayer*, Hooker then stood and administered the two elements to himself before turning toward the congregation and bidding them to come forward, kneel before the table and receive the Communion.

First the Bread. He said the words slowly and with notable conviction as he moved along the row of men, some kneeling and some standing, placing the wafer into outstretched hands or open mouths: "The body of our Lord Jesus Christ which was given for thee, preserve thy body and soul into everlasting life . . . Take and eat this, in remembrance that Christ died for thee, and feed on him in thy heart by faith, with thanksgiving."

And then the cup. Again slowly, with deep feeling, his voice conveyed the depth of his own faith: "The blood of our Lord Jesus Christ which was shed for thee, preserve thy body and soul into everlasting life . . . Drink this in remembrance that Christ's body was shed for thee, and be thankful."

When all who wished to do so had received the Sacrament and returned to their benches, Hooker looked out over his congregation and said in a loud voice, "Please all kneel now with me for the Lord's Prayer."

"Our Father . . ."

As the great common prayer ended with a loud "Amen," Hooker felt the presence of the Holy Spirit filling the Temple and sanctifying the worship.

"Almighty and everliving God, we most heartily thank thee, for that thou dost vouchsafe to feed us, which have duly received these holy mysteries, with the spiritual food of the most precious body and blood of thy Son our Saviour . . ." Hooker stood, certain that he was in God's temple: "Glory be to God on high," he read from the closing words of the service.

"And in earth peace, good will toward men," came the response from various parts of the church.

"Let us read together in unison," Hooker declared. And they all did, with mounting enthusiasm and volume:

> We praise thee, we bless thee, we worship thee, we glorify thee, we give thanks to thee for thy great glory. O Lord God heavenly king, God the Father almighty. O Lord, the only begotten Son Jesus Christ: O lord God, Lamb of God, Son of the Father, that takest away the sins of the world, have mercy upon us . . .

Finally, filled, no doubt, with the grace, peace, and love of God, the new master of the Temple finished the service with the familiar words of dismissal:

> The peace of God which passeth all understanding, keep your hearts and minds in the knowledge and love of God, and His Son Jesus Christ our Lord; And the blessing of God Almighty, the Father, the Son, and the Holy Ghost, be amongst you, and remain with you always. Amen.

Although he was not a fiery orator like Walter Travers, Hooker had no doubt impressed his congregation as a man of conviction and intelligence. As lawyers and students, they would have admired his keen mind and well-honed rhetorical abilities. He was persuasive. More than that, the man seemed to be in touch with the great mysteries of the historic faith of the Church. He had a way of communicating the holiness and wonder of God and Christ that went beyond what they were used to experiencing at church services. Travers' messages tended to be moralistic, argumentative, and worldly—full of dos and do nots, rights and wrongs, justification, and renewal of the spirit. There was more peace, tolerance, forgiveness, and love preached here today, mostly through a devout reading of the service. Withal, this was an experience many had not had in a long time, if at all—somehow more of a shared aesthetic transformation than a personal purification.[12]

Most of them might still prefer Travers and wish he had been named master. But now, at least, they would be eager to witness and experience what was certain to be a lively debate between the famed Puritan reformer and this surprisingly able and engaging new champion of the established Church.

NOTES

1. *Consecration of the Temple Church: Sermons Preached at the Celebration of its Seven Hundredth Anniversary* (London: Macmillan & Co., 1885).
2. See *Folger*, V, 59-82; *Works*, III, 469-81. Original copies of both sermons are in the British Library. They first appeared in print in 1612, the work of Henry Jackson of Oxford, one of the posthumous editors of Hooker's writings.
3. William Byrd (1543-1623) was the most distinguished composer of the day and teacher of such important seventeenth century musicians as Orlando Gibbons and Thomas Morally. Already active during Hooker's years at the Temple, as organist at the Royal Chapel, he was the father of the English madrigal and wrote many liturgical motets and verse anthems.
4. Drawn from Jewel's letter to Peter Martyr of 5 March, 1560, as cited in Woods, *Athenae Oxoniesis*, 386.
5. These remarks are drawn from Hooker's beautiful paean to music in Book V of the *Laws*. *Folger*, II, 151-2; *Works* II, 159-60.
6. *Folger*, II, Book V, 56-61, *Works*, II, 52-58.
7. Taken from Hooker's discussion of prayer in Book V of the *Laws*. See *Folger*, II, 113-17; *Works*, II, 118-21.
8. I have drawn this part of Hooker's remarks by quotation and close paraphrase of his words in Book V of the *Laws* on this subject. See *Folger*, II, 330-43; *Works*, II, 348-62. See also Davies, 121-22; Booty, Folger, VI, 221-3 and "A Celebration of Richard Hooker," *Sewanee Theological Review* 36: 2:186.
9. Drawn from Hooker's discussion of preaching in Book V of the *Laws*. See *Folger*, II, 87-110; *Works*, II, 84-115. See also on Puritan preaching, Horton Davies, *Worship and Theology in England 1543-1603*, (Princeton: Princeton University Press, 1970),308-16.
10. Hooker's views on the Eucharist are in Book V of the *Laws*. See especially *Folger*, II, 344-59; *Works*, II, 362-80.
11. I have taken this communion service from the authorized prayer book that Hooker would have used: *The Book of Common Prayer and the Administration of the Sacraments, and other Rites and Ceremonies in the Church of England, 1559*. I have used the copy in William Keatinge Clay ed., *Liturgical Services – Liturgies and Occasional Forms of Prayer Set Forth in the Reign of Queen Elizabeth* (Cambridge: The Parker Society, 1847), 180-98. Very few original copies remain. These may be found in the British Library, the Library of Corpus Christi College, Oxford, and the Bodleian

Library. For a contemporary account of church services at this time, see Harrison, 33-4. See, also, Davies, 275-7 and William Keating Clay, *Private Prayers Put Forth by Authority During the Reign of Queen Elizabeth* (Cambridge: The Parker Society, 1851).
12. An excellent discussion of the differences between Hooker's emergent Anglicanism and Travers' Puritanism is in Davies, 67-75.

CHAPTER 11

The Great Debate Continues

MASTER AND READER

In the early spring of 1585, as Hooker took his first steps around the grounds of the Temple and Inns of Court during the days following his maiden sermon, he might have been struck by how public his new environment was. The Inner Temple's north entrance (a beautiful door built a decade earlier) faced on busy Fleet Street just a few paces from the Strand. Although set back a few hundred feet from the street, the church itself was a gathering place all day long for a nearly constant parade of people seeking a retreat or a place for either common social intercourse or serious economic and political deal-making.

As soon as early morning worship was over each weekday, the Temple became a public meeting place similar to nearby St Paul's. In fact, the choir of the Temple was sometimes used for committee meetings of the House of Commons, as was the great hall in the Middle Temple.

Hooker would have noticed that most of the students hurrying to and fro in the Temple grounds were attired in academic gowns not unlike those mandated at Oxford—plain dark frock coats and simple round caps. He had been informed of the queen's strict dress code for law students here. No ruffles or velvet facing on the gowns and none of the much-favoured white for doublets or stockings were allowed. Even when walking outside on the city streets or in Westminster, students were forbidden to don elaborate and colourful cloaks. Only "sad coloured" gowns were permitted. For dress occasions, Spanish black was the sartorial order of the day. None of the fashionable long-curled hair—wigs or natural—was permitted. There were stiff penalties, Hooker knew, for disobeying these sumptuary rules, including fines and even expulsion. Only senior lawyers, barristers, and benchers were allowed to be within the precincts sporting more elaborate livery and long hair.[1]

The lovely Inner Temple gardens extended all the way from the south wall of that inn, along the east side of Middle Temple Hall, and down to the river. The "great garden," so called because of its impressive size and beauty, no doubt became a favourite retreat for the new master of the Temple. He would have known Shakespeare's dramatization of the legend which immortalized the red and white roses growing there. A century earlier Plantagenet and Somerset and their allies had left the noise of the inns and halls and come outside into the garden to continue their epic quarrel. "Let him that is a true born gentleman . . . from off this briar pluck a red rose for me," Plantagenet had proclaimed. "Let him that is no coward or flatterer . . . pluck a white rose from off this thorn for me," came the bold rejoinder from Somerset.[2]

A new set of stairs, financed in part by the queen herself, descended from the gardens to the water, where boats could be hired for journeys across or up and down the Thames. Richard could sit here on the wall and watch the busy river traffic coming and going along London's already ancient commercial highway. It would have provided a pleasant escape from the pressures of his duties as master and a convenient place to clear his head.

Middle Temple Hall had been built about a decade earlier immediately adjacent to Essex House—the first in a row of great mansions lining the river embankment to the west of the Temple grounds all the way down to Whitehall. The hall had been financed and planned by Edmund Plowden, Middle Temple treasurer and probably the most famous jurist of his age. In Hooker's time, this building was one of the architectural jewels of London—and remains so to this day. This grand hall served as dining room, lecture hall, classrooms, and locus of grand receptions, some of national import. Inside the vast one hundred foot-long hall, a magnificently carved oak screen stood at one end of the room and beautiful stained glass windows arched high toward the double hammerbeam ceiling that rose nearly sixty feet from the floor, the finest roof in London, Hooker would have been told. The twenty-nine foot bench-table, where senior lawyers sat, was the longest in the realm, a gift from the queen. Hewn from a single tree, it had to be delivered by floating it down the Thames from the queen's oak forest at Windsor to the Temple stairs. The smaller oak table ("cupboard"), which served as a podium for the important law lectures given twice each year, was made from timbers taken from the hatch of Sir Francis Drake's *Pelican* (later, *Golden Hind*) after the great explorer's trip around the world. Such was the grandeur and import of Hooker's new bailiwick.[3]

Unlike his predecessors, Hooker did not reside in the master's house on the Temple grounds. As Alvey's *de facto* successor, Travers had been living there for some time after Richard's arrival. The Inns, which were required to pay the salary of the master, authorized income for both Travers and Hooker, even after the latter's appointment. Travers was reconfirmed as the rightful resident of the house as late as November of 1586, some eight months after he had been removed from his post at the Temple.[4]

The rulers of the Inner Temple, always less enthusiastic about Travers than their Middle Temple brethren, showed more caution about continuing the reader's pay and benefits. Even before Hooker arrived on the scene, the word was abroad that Travers' days might be numbered. On 3 November 1584 the treasurer of Inner Temple, Nicholas Hare, ordered an audit to determine how much money might still be owing on Mr Travers' pension, with an obvious intent to clear the accounts of this man. In February of 1585, a full month before Hooker was officially confirmed as master, the Inner Temple gave Travers official notification that he would no longer receive his 20s. annual fee. Henceforth, Mr Hooker's work would be sufficient to meet the ministerial needs of the community. A reader would no longer be necessary. However, Travers' ever-faithful guardian, Lord Burghley, caused the privy council to intervene with the Inner Temple to reinstate Travers' stipend.[5]

So it was that even before Richard arrived, Walter Travers had one more reason to feel resentment. Not only did his upstart cousin have decidedly wrongheaded theological views, not only had Richard usurped his own rightful succession to the mastership of the Temple, but now Mr Hooker's presence was threatening his very livelihood. For his part, Hooker was, to say the least, highly annoyed when, taking up his duties at the Temple, he found Travers still solidly entrenched there, living in the master's house and preaching regularly. Travers was obviously a popular minister who was being cheered on by a large and loyal following of Middle Temple men who liked him personally, had supported his bid for appointment as master, and were not at all pleased with Hooker's presence among them. Furthermore, here, staring Hooker in the face, was stark evidence of the power of Lord Burghley and his Puritan allies to thwart Whitgift's efforts to rid the Church of radicals such as Travers.[6]

Thomas Cartwright had recently returned from eleven years in exile to assume joint leadership with Travers and John Field of the English presbyterian movement.[7] Perhaps this had emboldened Travers, who by this time was already a leader of the London "classis," the hub of a national presbyterian movement, within which he was the leading interpreter of doctrine and arbiter of disputes. Shortly after Hooker was installed at the Temple, there was a commotion surrounding Cartwright. He had no sooner set foot in London than Bishop Alymer had imprisoned him. Within days Cartwright was released by Burghley. Travers then joined Field and others in leading public prayers of thanksgiving for Cartwright's freedom. No doubt Travers felt the time was right for a frontal attack on Hooker at the Temple.[8]

Not only did Travers have his ally Cartwright at his side, but his ardour was further fuelled by the growing antagonism toward Hooker among Walter's followers at the Temple. The new master's refusal to bend to Travers' suggestion and follow Genevan practice had understandably incensed those who had intended all along to deny Hooker their allegiance.

Hooker must have been surprised and hurt by how quickly the opposition had escalated. At first there was some public grumbling from the Middle Temple benches during services when he used the prescribed prayers, knelt at communion, prayed for bishops, and preached anything but strict Calvinist doctrine. Such verbal opposition no doubt soon gave way to absenteeism from services. This was intolerable. Hooker warned the officers of the Middle Temple that if this were to continue he would have to inform the archbishop. Severe sanctions would be brought to bear. As the controversy over the form and style of worship services worsened, Hooker came to suspect that behind all his troubles was the subtle hand of his cousin, encouraging resistance in the name of an emerging presbyterian movement that had no intention of losing control of this important church. Ever the charming and polite colleague in infrequent personal contacts with Hooker, Travers had been increasingly strident in his attacks on the master's ideas during his regular afternoon sermons.

There was no doubt in Hooker's mind that Travers had intended all along either to convert him or unseat him. About a year later, in April 1586, in his written response to Travers' formal complaints against him to Burghley and the Privy Council, Hooker wrote that his initial "offence" in not agreeing to Travers' advice on how to "seal my calling" had subsequently

> so displeased some that whatsoever was afterwards done or spoken by me it offended their taste . . . [to such an extent that] angry informations were daily sent out, intelligence given far and wide what a dangerous enemy had crept in; the worst that jealousy could imagine was spoken and written to so many that, at length, some knowing me well and perceiving how injurious the reports were which grew daily more and more unto my discredit, wrought means to bring Travers and me to a second conference.[9]

Hooker met a number of times with Travers in mutual efforts to resolve their differences. He may also have consulted with his former mentor, John Rainolds, concerning his troubles with Travers. We know that the two were in contact about other matters at approximately this time.[10]

Not surprisingly, Travers' account of the meetings between himself and Hooker differed significantly from the latter's. In the late spring of 1585, shortly after his suspension from the Temple, Travers painted a self-serving portrait of his attitude toward Hooker, claiming, implausibly, that,

> I was glad the place [Master of the Temple] was given to him [Hooker], hoping to live in godly peace and comfort with him [but] contrary to my expectation, he inclined from the beginning but very smally thereunto, but joined rather with such as had always opposed themselves to any good order in this church . . .[11]

For his part, Hooker asserted that many of the differences between himself and Travers were actually about "silly things," which "I would rather be as loth to recite as I was sorry to hear them objected, if the rehearsal therof were not by him [Travers] wrested from me." It was Hooker's habit to describe as "silly" or "indifferent" matters which were, in fact, important enough for him to argue about. Silly they might be in God's ultimate scheme of things, but not so unimportant that Hooker would fail to insist on having his way concerning them. What was at stake here was the polity, liturgy, and theology of the Church of England, and Hooker knew only too well that these were not, in common parlance, "indifferent" matters.[12]

Throughout the rest of 1585 and on into early 1586 the relationship between Hooker and Travers did not improve but took a different direction. Earlier attempts to reconcile differences and agree on a common integrated policy for managing the Temple and conducting services ceased. In their place a policy of separate but equal prevailed.

Each man had his own service to conduct as he wished, Hooker on Sunday mornings, Travers on Sunday afternoons. The morning rite was still the principal gathering for worship, receiving the Sacrament, and preaching. But at his simple afternoon service, where the sermon was the major attraction, Travers proved himself more than Hooker's equal, drawing large, enthusiastic audiences to hear his ever-provocative anti-establishment lectures.

Before long, these morning and afternoon sermons became a running public debate between the policies and practices of a moderately reformed establishment Church and the radical Calvinists who sought to replace that Church with a new structure and a more reformed liturgy and theology. Students, lawyers, senior jurists, and members of parliament filled the Temple, Sunday after Sunday, to hear the great debate between the master and the reader. This was a better show than the monologue at Paul's Cross. Here at the Temple one could witness the great religious issues that divided the nation fought out in a public arena as two gladiators of equal strength did battle for the minds and hearts of an influential and sophisticated audience. As Thomas Fuller was to say in the next century, "the pulpit spake pure Canterbury in the morning and Geneva in the afternoon."[13]

Many of those attending these Temple debates, including men such as the fledgling member of parliament and future lord chancellor, Edward Coke, took notes throughout the sermons as carefully as they might have prepared briefs for their clients or bills for parliament. They were interested in capturing for their own use the arguments of Travers and Hooker. They also enjoyed keeping score, for this was a contest, often an emotionally charged one. How effectively would Travers, in the afternoon, refute Hooker's morning arguments?

Travers had the advantage of being the second speaker. His informers, no doubt, rushed to his quarters after Hooker's sermon to give him a *verbatim* account, whenever he had not been present to hear it himself. He had several hours to fashion a convincing rebuttal. This opportunity, coupled with his considerable oratorical abilities and his personal popularity, made Travers a clear favourite to win the competition, especially since the judges were a predominantly Puritan crowd already disposed to agree with him.

According to the earliest and most widely adopted account of the debate, written by Thomas Fuller some eighty years after the event, Hooker was not an effective preacher. Fuller said of the master that his "voice was low, stature little, gesture none at all, standing alone in the pulpit, as if the posture of his body were the emblem of his mind, unmovable in his opinions. Where his eye was left fixed at the beginning, it was found fixed at the end of his sermon." Furthermore, "His style was long and pithy, driving a whole flock of several clauses before he came to the close of a sentence. So that the copiousness of his style met not with proportional capacity in his audience . . ."

On the other hand, Fuller's informants apparently assured him, "Mr. Travers's utterance was graceful, gesture plausible, matter profitable, method plain, and his style carried with it *indolem pietatis*, 'a genius of grace' flowing from the sanctified heart."[14]

Here we have the pro-Calvinist bias of our only informant shining through brilliantly. Richard's supposed oratorical failings, even down to his "small" posture, are offered, perhaps, to suggest a "small" mind—one characterized by "unmovable opinions," no doubt as stubborn and unbending as the hated Whitgift himself. On the other hand, Fuller's favourite, the Calvinist hero Travers, is given the "graceful," "plausible," and "profitable" voice to match his "sanctified heart." Once again, Hooker is the victim of a seventeenth-century chronicler whose sources were probably biased against him. In this case, a renowned church historian too readily accepted a tradition that projected Hooker as an ineffectual cleric dominated, in this instance, not by an unscrupulous grasping woman (*à la* Izaak Walton), but by the hated high-Anglican party of the day.

In his 1585 and early 1586 Temple sermons, Hooker preached on a number of subjects, including the controversial issue of predestination. His idea that God's will for man is not absolute but conditional, because man has the freedom to disobey it and is therefore responsible for the evil he does, rankled Travers. Hooker's antagonist affirmed the predestination of man and yet exempted God from responsibility for the evil man does. Hooker found this inconsistent, while Travers, of course, cited Calvin to refute Hooker's position.

Hooker told Travers that he was tired of defending himself on this subject. He reminded his cousin that he had spoken and written often on predestination and that his ideas were well-known. He had preached on the topic openly at Paul's Cross in the presence of the bishop of London and many other church and civic leaders and had never been reproached for his ideas. Consequently, it was ridiculous for

Travers to suggest, as he had, that he, Hooker, stood alone in this matter and that both the Word of God and all the Church was ranged against his ideas on the subject of predestination.[16]

Furthermore, Hooker informed Travers, even if all the authorities in the world, including Calvin himself, were to disagree with him on this point—which they did not—Hooker's own rational faculty, which was his surest anchor in this sea of disagreement, told him that if God was not the author of the evil we do, then we must be free from His absolute predetermination to be the authors of evil ourselves.

In response, Travers informed Hooker that it was presumptuous to substitute his singular reason for the judgement of so many wise men in the Church. He said that if Richard would only pray more earnestly about this matter he would discover the error of his thinking. Hooker responded that he would consider Travers' comments and preach on the matter again in the near future. Travers warned that if Richard did so, he would put the peace of the Temple in jeopardy because so many men would then feel obligated by conscience to speak out against the master.

Another major area of disagreement in the morning-afternoon debate at the Temple was over whether faith in Scripture or reliance on human reason and ordinary sense-perception provides the more certain assurance of the efficacy of God's promises of salvation. Hooker realized that his position on this vexing question was too subtle to avoid misinterpretation, or worse, misrepresentation. His thesis was that, although Scripture contains all that man needs to know of God's revelation, God also gave man reason and sense-perception so that he could have the further assurance that seems to be required by his weak and sinful nature. Hooker never questioned the supremacy of God's Word, only the weakness in fallen man for so often needing the assurance of his own God-given reason and sense to certify what was already sufficiently revealed in Holy Scripture.

Travers, who seemed to hanker for greater clarity than Hooker in this and most theological issues, took out of context Hooker's words to the effect that "the assurance of what we believe by the Word is not so certain as what we perceive by sense." In Travers' view, "assurance of faith is sufficient beyond all human understanding." Hooker felt that his foes had oversimplified his own more subtle point in order to paint him as an opponent of the idea of the self-sufficiency of Holy Scripture.[16]

Hooker thought it sad that everything needed to be so black and white for the Calvinist extremists. In heaven we might hope for such clarity, but here on earth we must learn to live with ambiguity, tolerating one another's differences of opinion. Otherwise there would be no peace in the commonwealth.

THE ISSUES ARE DRAWN

On 1 March 1586 Hooker stood in the Temple pulpit, probably facing a full house. Word had got out that he would be preaching on matters involving Catholics. In early 1586 no subject touched a more sensitive nerve in Englishmen. Rumours abounded of Catholic plots at home and abroad to assassinate the queen, invade England, put Mary the Scot, currently under house arrest, on the throne, and restore the Roman religion. Nothing would inflame an audience more quickly than even a hint of pro-Catholic sympathy.

What he delivered was more of a lecture than a sermon. Hooker broadly defined "preaching" as including Scripture reading, homilies, and catechizing. He disdained the Puritan tendency, as he saw it, to elevate sermons as a means of salvation. All of this extemporaneous preaching of sermons and supposedly spontaneous praying was, he felt, encouraged by the illegal "prophesying" meetings. The result was to further divide the Church and nation and transform the pulpit into a platform for each preacher's personal opinion. For him, sermons were little more than the wit and emotion of the man who gave them, lasting no longer than the breath of the preacher and the attention span and memory of the audience. He much preferred the lecture or "tractate," which was carefully prepared and could be studied and meditated on for an indefinite period of time.[17]

He wished to avoid using the pulpit as a debating platform, but there was no turning back now. Although reluctant, he was in the fray and resolved to be an effective spokesman for the Church of England. At least he could try to avoid the emotional theatrics of others and appeal to the reason of his auditors with a carefully constructed argument.[18]

"This morning," Richard began his lecture, "I continue my discourse on the prophet Habakkuk who said, 'the wicked doth encompass about the righteous: therefore perverse judgement doth proceed.' But, who are the wicked? Who are the righteous? What is meant by perverse judgement?"[19]

Hooker proceeded to answer the first question by citing St Paul. The point he strove to make was that it is really none of our business first to identify and then judge and punish the wicked. Depending on what type of apparently bad persons we confront, we should either separate ourselves from them or leave them to the judgement of God. Hooker knew, even as he spoke, how uncomfortable this idea was to the more advanced Calvinists who seemed all too ready to judge those outside their community of the "elect."

> As for the righteous there neither is nor ever was any mere mortal man who is absolutely righteous in himself, void of all sin. We dare not exempt from this state of sin even the Blessed Virgin herself, though for our Lord's sake we would have preferred not to question her status if some Roman scholars had not made an issue of it.

> But even though the Church of Rome imagines incorrectly that the Mother of our Lord and Saviour was, for His honour and by His special protection, preserved clean from all sin, yet in every other aspect they agree with us that everyone has sinned, including infants, who, although they never actually offended, are defiled in their very nature as human beings . . .
>
> Indeed, there are many important areas of agreement between us and the Church of Rome. The Roman Church teaches, as we do, that God alone justifies the soul of man without any coefficient cause of justification. They teach, as we do, that Christ's merit alone brings us salvation. They teach, as we do, that man is required to act in order to apply Christ's merits or else they would have no practical effect.
>
> In all that I have said thus far, we join hands with the Church of Rome. But now let me show you where we disagree with them. We disagree about more than we agree about. Most importantly we do not hold with them that God's grace may be increased by the merit of man's good works, decreased by man's bad works [sins], or lost altogether by commission of a so-called mortal sin.
>
> This great error of the Roman Church leads to many others. For example, they hold wrongly that men may recover lost grace by such means as charitable works, application of holy water, saying of *ave marias*, crossing themselves, receiving papal blessings, utilizing the so-called sacrament of penance, taking pilgrimages, enduring fasts, and the like. This is the maze the Church of Rome lays out for her followers to tread when they ask her for the path to justification and salvation.
>
> I cannot stand here this morning and uproot this corrupt Roman structure and sift and examine the rubble for you piece by piece. But I will set alongside it the true and solid foundation and framework which God has built for our justification.
>
> In brief, God's foundation, as set forth in Scripture, is Christ alone. Only He is righteous. There is no righteousness in me whatsoever except what may come to me by God's grace through my faith in Christ. All else, as Paul says, is dung. The Roman Church errs when it says or implies that there is some inherent righteousness in man. There is none.
>
> The righteousness wherein we must be found if we are to be saved is not our own, and so we cannot be justified by any inherent quality or any work of ours. Christ alone has merited righteousness for as many as are found in Him. In Him God finds us if we are faithful. For by faith alone we are incorporated into Him.

This firm proclamation of the defining Protestant doctrine of justification by grace through faith would have pleased his listeners. Hooker continued:

> Let it be counted folly, or frenzy, or fury, or whatever, it is nevertheless our wisdom and our comfort, and we care for no other knowledge in the world but this: man sinned; God suffered; God made Himself the sin of man; men are made the righteousness.

You can see, therefore, that the Church of Rome perverts the very truth of Christ as we have it from the Apostle, when she teaches justification through some inherent grace in man.

There is, however, a second kind of righteousness. This is the righteousness of sanctification, rather than justification. In this area our good works are important. As Paul says, the "fruits of holiness" are required for this kind of righteousness. Thus when the Prophet Habakkuk talks of righteousness he means both that we may be justified by faith and so be free of sin and also that we are known to be righteous by outward signs of our holiness.

The difference between types of justification and the consequences of such difference appealed to the lawyers' love of fine points of law and close distinctions between apparently similar cases. They would have listened avidly, wanting to be sure to get this part exactly right.

Of course only God can know who these sanctified ones—these saints—are. We must assume that all who call themselves Christians are indeed saints. And we should all try to behave in a way befitting this title. We must never be proud of our holiness. The devil knows that our very virtues may be snares for us. No man's case is so dangerous as his whom Satan has persuaded that his own righteousness shall present him pure and blameless before God.

Even if we are so good as to do no evil deeds, yet we do them in our thoughts and hearts. If we never opened our mouths to utter any scandalous, offensive or hurtful word, the cries of our secret cogitations resound in the ears of God.

When we subtract all the supposedly righteous acts that we really did to satisfy ourselves or impress others, the remainder, done purely for the love of God, amounts to a small sum of good deeds.

Even prayer, the very best and holiest of our good deeds, is distracted by irrelevant thoughts, weakened by a lack of reverence and remorse, and treated by us as a burdensome task to be completed as quickly as possible.

The best things we do always have something in them which requires God's pardon. How then can we do anything meritorious which is worthy to be rewarded? The answer is, we cannot. We must acknowledge the dutiful necessity of doing our best but utterly renounce the idea that we have succeeded. We must see how far we are from the righteousness of God's law, how little fruit our faith-based justification has borne.

God knows how corrupt and unsound our best efforts are. We must put no confidence in them whatsoever. We must challenge nothing in this world because of them. We dare not call God to a reckoning as if we had Him in our debt books. Rather, our continual suit to Him is and must be to bear with our infirmities, to pardon our offences.

Hooker was out of trouble now and on safe Calvinist ground again, for a short time at least.

> Now these people of whom Habakkuk speaks, were they genuinely penitent and humble; did they strive earnestly to walk uprightly and keep God's laws? Not at all. These children of Israel were, as Isaiah tells us, a sinful and corrupt nation, laden with iniquity.
>
> And yet, so wide are the bowels of God's compassion that even when we, like the children of Israel, are laden with iniquity and treat Him with disrespect He gives us the liberty to hope that whatever punishment we may deserve we will yet be treated no worse than unbelievers and be not overcome by pagans and infidels.
>
> But the prophet Habakkuk not only complains that the righteous who call upon God have been treated badly whereas the heathen have been tolerated. He goes beyond mere complaint and breaks out from the extremities of his grief to infer that God's treatment of the righteous is perverse.

Many in his audience had felt the personal pressure of a Calvinist doctrine that assured a preordained salvation to the elect and yet seemed to require a disciplined schedule of good behavior by the saints in the midst of a thoroughly corrupt and hypocritical society that rewarded the infidels of the day. This did indeed seem a perverse judgement that God had placed on his chosen flock. How would Master Hooker resolve this dilemma for them this morning?

At this point the preacher put down the papers from which he had been reading. He looked out at the congregation and said: "Clearly there is much more that you want to hear from me on this subject and more that I would like to say to you. But that will have to wait for another day." Hooker had left them suspended at the denouement of his sermon, and now took off in a completely different direction.

> Necessity, unfortunately draws me to another stake for the time I have remaining with you this morning. Like Paul and Barnabas when requested to preach again on a subject they thought they had covered, I feel obliged to comply and to return to a subject that I talked about the last time I preached on the text of Paul's letter to the Hebrews.
>
> In that recent sermon of mine, I concluded that because the Church of Rome was so corrupted and resistant to reform, we have rightly severed ourselves from her and that even the example of our fathers in that Church cannot keep us in communion with her.
>
> Then I said something that has, as you well know, been called into question here in this Temple and elsewhere. I said: "God, I doubt not, was merciful to save thousands of them although they lived in popish superstition inasmuch as they sinned ignorantly." I ask you to mark and sift this sentence carefully to see if it is worthy of all the attention given it. If, when I have finished, you find the notion to be made only of hay or straw, I will gladly set fire to it myself.
>
> Two questions have been raised by this simple sentence of mine. First, whether our fathers, so infected with popish errors and superstitions could be saved; second, whether their ignorance is a reasonable inducement to make us think that they might be.

There is no question that the heresies of the Church of Rome are many and great, from claiming other written sources for God's revelation than the Holy Scriptures, to asserting that the bishop of Rome is head of the universal Church, to presenting the bread in the Eucharist as being transubstantiated into Christ, to worshipping images, to calling on saints as intercessors, and many other errors.

I have no doubt, nor have I ever claimed otherwise, that all those who persisted in these errors, after being admonished to abandon them, are condemned unless they specifically repented of their error. Nor have I ever said that all of our forebears in the Church of Rome were saved from damnation. I only said, and still say, that 'thousands' of them were saved by God's mercy.

It was an unfortunate error in judgement for our fathers [Roman Catholics] to follow their religious teachers and guides in the Church of Rome. But error is not heresy. And, in any event, what one man in ten thousand even understood what these doctrines meant? Surely there is a difference between those who followed and those who led. Shall we lap up all of our fathers in the Church of Rome in one condition and cast them all headlong into that infernal and everflaming lake?

If we grant that some sinners among our fathers may escape God's judgement for popish heresy, how might that be accomplished? There was only one way for them. That was to appeal to God's saving mercy. We know from Scripture that this mercy is available only to those of faith. Thus, our question must be, were any of our forebears in the Church of Rome men of faith despite their errors. The answer is, yes.

The foundation of our faith, as revealed in Scripture, is Christ the incarnate God and saviour of the world. Even if weakly held and by a slender thread, this faith may save a man despite other errors.

Richard changed the direction of his argument now, charting a course into more hazardous waters.

As I have said on other occasions, even the Church of Rome itself must be preferred to the synagogues of the Jews and Mosques of the Turks. For although Rome played the harlot worse than Israel ever did, yet she never, like the Jews, denied Christ; and so she is not quite excluded from God's new covenant in Christ.

We must think hard about this question of how many of our fathers, despite other grievous errors that they followed in the Church of Rome, ended their mortal lives uttering these words of faith with their final breath: "Christ my saviour; my redeemer, Jesus." Can we say that all such persons had failed to maintain their faith in Christ?

I do not think so. Even though it is true that the Church of Rome added works to faith as a condition of salvation, she did so only in relation to the application of Christ's merits. Never did she deny that redemption itself came from Christ alone and that He is the sole foundation of faith.

Even if I grant that the foundation of faith was overthrown when the Church of Rome added the pernicious requirements for salvation which I have already described, shall we imagine that the damage of such

> errors would so outweigh the benefit of their basic faith in Christ that even those who were never aware of these errors should be denied any hope of salvation?

Hooker now took the plunge into still deeper water. Speaking from the heart, he said:

> Is what we have here with the Church of Rome any different from the error of our Lutheran brethren who stiffly and fiercely maintain in their Wittenberg confession a similar doctrine concerning faith and works? Should we also condemn them?

Many in the congregation were amazed at what the preacher was saying. Was Hooker really comparing the followers of Luther with the hated papists? If so, as they well knew, he was close to committing treason.

> I will go still further and state that the Church of Rome, however broken and misshapen by its heresies, is still part of the Church. She has never directly denied the foundation of our faith. I do not intrude this idea upon you as some mere private opinion of mine. The best judgement of the learned men in the Church are of like opinion.
>
> I say to you: give me a man of whatever condition or estate, yea, even a cardinal or a pope, who at the extreme affliction of his life comes to know himself, and whose heart God has touched with true sorrow for his sins and filled with love toward Christ's Gospel and whose eyes are opened to see the truth and mouth open to renounce all heresy—am I still to think that because of this one error of adding works to faith such a one will never be permitted to touch even the hem of Christ's garment? And if he did so, might I never hope that Christ, in His mercy, might save him?

Hooker had now, though he may not have realized it at once, put his entire career in jeopardy.

> I tell you, I would not be afraid to say unto a cardinal or a pope in such a case: "Be of good comfort, ours is a merciful God." Let me die if ever it be proved that simply an error would exclude a pope or a cardinal from all hope of eternal life.
>
> I confess to you that if it be an error to think God may be merciful to save men when they err, then my greatest comfort is my error. Were it not for the love I bear this error, I would neither wish to speak nor to live!
>
> Alas, was such a bloody matter really contained in this simple sentence in my recent sermon expressing hope for the salvation of some of our forefathers in the Church of Rome that so many had to come down so hard on me for it?

Hooker had just uttered the most dangerous words of his ministry. Fear of Catholic invasion ran high. To even hint at mercy for the pope was not only blasphemous; in this climate, it was likely to be thought treasonable. He concluded his sermon:

> I trust that these ideas which I have been expounding are sound. Those who have attacked me because of them may well have injured my reputation. Despite that, I wish them every blessing in heaven for I have reaped much benefit from the labour they put me to in defending my position.
>
> I only regret that I had to spend so much of your time and mine in this endeavour. But because the love I bear the truth in Christ Jesus had been called into question, I dared not be silent. As for those who are the cause of all this controversy—and you well know who they are—I can only beseech them in the spirit of Christ's meekness to consider that a watchman sometimes cries 'enemy' when in fact a friend is coming. God knows that my heart is free from any unfriendly intent or meaning.
>
> Now, finally, to you my beloved who have listened to all of this, I have no further admonition than this—that you remember it is neither scandalous nor offensive in difficult cases like this one to hear differing viewpoints. If you are tolerant and open-minded you may even find comfort in a variety of opinions.
>
> And now, the God of Peace grant you peaceful minds and turn them to your everlasting comfort.

ATTACK AND RESPONSE

In his afternoon response, Travers branded Hooker a near traitor for even hinting at the pope's salvation. Richard had crossed the line into forbidden territory.

In his rebuttal sermon, Travers argued against Hooker's ideas point by point, like a lawyer. He quoted from his sermon as though he had a copy of it in front of him, enumerating what he called the serious errors in the sermon: that Hooker had said the Church of Rome was a true church, that he had said that thousands of our forefathers who lived and died in that faith were saved despite the error of joining works to faith, and so forth.[20]

Hooker had specifically forbidden Travers to refute his sermons in this public manner, at least until the reader had first discussed with him any disagreements he had with the master's ideas. But before he could vent his anger by informing the archbishop, or anyone else, of Travers' insubordination, Travers complained to the lord treasurer that it was Hooker, and not he, who had violated an agreement that the master would not dispute with the reader without prior private consultation.

Whoever, in fact, first violated any agreement to avoid disturbing the peace at the Temple by not publicly airing disagreements between "Geneva" and "Canterbury" does not much matter. There could be no keeping the lid on for long, such was the intensity of the issues involved. Still, we can appreciate Hooker's frustration over Travers' advantage in having his turn in the pulpit follow so hard on his own. Richard had to wait a full week to get back at Travers, and when he did, his opponent still accused him of breaking their peace pact.

Travers was meticulous in his refutation of Hooker's sermons. He took the master to task for his interpretation of the Roman position on faith and works. The necessity of works is not merely additional or secondary for the Roman Church, as Hooker had claimed. Rather, works were an essential part of the papalist's requirement for salvation. Travers simply ignored Hooker's subtle distinctions between types of justification.

The reader also disputed Hooker's view of the Council of Trent, claiming that the Council had made works essential to salvation and that Hooker was in error when he said otherwise. Additionally, Travers disagreed with the master's interpretation of Galatians, maintaining that the Galatian requirement of circumcision did indeed amount to going beyond justification by faith in Christ alone, which is why Paul condemned them. Travers had not missed much.

Perhaps the worst of it was that Richard's cousin totally misrepresented his comment about Lutherans. He made it sound as though it were a major theme of Hooker's sermon to lump Lutherans and papalists into one ball. Richard probably wished that he had not put that short passage in his sermon. It had probably been a delicious, but impetuous, afterthought that he had been unable to resist. Lutherans, like Catholics, he knew, differed markedly on theological questions. To be accurate he should have said that *some,* not *all,* Lutherans were as guilty as *most,* not all, papists of "overthrowing the foundation of faith," by addition of works.

Most damaging was Travers' response to Hooker's comments about the possible salvation of the pope and other Catholics. Travers said that he scarcely knew how to react to such an absurdity—that was his very word, "absurdity." Such favourable words as Hooker had spoken about the pope and the papists had not been heard in this realm since the days of Queen Mary, Travers charged. It would be up to the highest authorities in the realm to decide Hooker's fate if he failed publicly to recant these opinions about the Church of Rome.[21]

Hooker must have flinched when he heard what Travers had said to Lord Burghley on this subject. The implication that he was a traitor was all too clear. Richard could see that Walter had cleverly tied their quarrel over faith and works into the national hysteria over the threat of invasion from Catholic Spain. And, into the bargain, he had attached to that same patriotic fervour his personal struggle with Richard for mastery of the Temple Church. To support Hooker was to support Rome and Spain. To support Travers was to support queen, country and Church.

So far as we know, Hooker never publicly recanted his opinions on this dangerous subject. Regardless of the undoubted harm that his remarks and Travers' responses had done to his career, he did not change his mind on the subject of the salvation of popes and other Catholics. Corrupt she may be, but the Church of Rome was the church of our forefathers. Hooker would never renounce his faith in the promise of God's saving mercy for all who had faith in Him, regardless of their sins.

Hooker would pay dearly for these convictions. At the very least, these unrecanted sentiments about Rome made it unlikely, if not impossible, for Whitgift to promote Hooker in the church hierarchy. The bishop of Rome may have appreciated Hooker's ideas on this and other subjects, but the queen of England and her advisors probably did not.[22]

Not only did Travers refute Hooker in sermons and in correspondence to Lord Burghley, but he also orchestrated a campaign against the master throughout the Church, and even with members of parliament and the Privy Council. Travers' supporters saw to it that copies of their versions of Hooker's sermons and Travers' responses were circulated, sometimes even before Travers had delivered his remarks from the pulpit. An effort was underway to create a political frenzy at the Temple which would alarm the queen, who hated such turmoil, and lead to Hooker being ousted.

Richard had some help in counteracting this considerable political challenge to his position. Powerful and worldly-wise moderates within his circle included his domestic host, John Churchman, and the famous Sandys brothers: his patron, Edwin the archbishop of York, and Edwin's brother, Miles, leading barrister at Middle Temple Inn and prominent member of parliament. The Sandys brothers were visitors at the Churchmans, along with Richard's friend, Edwin Sandys. These were the men who supplied the political intelligence and clout that helped Richard retain his post amidst the firestorm raised by Travers and his allies over the Catholic issue. They probably advised Hooker that his best strategy was to ignore attacks for his supposed sympathy with the pope and concentrate instead on Travers' offence in disturbing the peace by openly disputing his superior on matters of doctrine. Such behaviour was directly contrary to the queen's injunction. Support for Hooker on this point could be had from all but the most rabid Presbyterians in Privy Council and parliament.

It was assumed that Travers would submit a formal complaint against Hooker to Burghley and the Privy Council. Hooker would need to respond with an answer, once Travers' objections were known. He should submit his document to Archbishop Whitgift, the proper channel, for a response. In the meantime, Richard's important friends would apprise the archbishop of the situation so that Whitgift would have time to prepare his position before Travers' patron, Lord Burghley, got to the queen.

By the time Hooker had set to work composing an outline of his charges against Travers and an explanation of some of his own statements on the issue of justification by faith and works and on the status of the Church of Rome, events overtook his pen. Travers was summarily dismissed from his post. Whitgift removed him on 23 March, before he could preach another sermon at the Temple. Within two weeks, news of his dismissal had spread by word of mouth and letter throughout the national Presbyterian network.

One such letter from Yorkshire to "godly preachers" at Newcastle-on-Tyne carried the word from a "godly gentlemen" in London that Satan himself, in the form of one "Master Hooker an Oxford man . . . teaching sundry points of doctrine savouring of a profane spirit" was "labouring to hinder the happy growth of the gospel . . ." Surely, it was a "matter of mourning that any bishop should command learned and faithful ministers [Travers] to be silent for speaking against" the ideas of Master Hooker.[23]

The speed with which Whitgift moved against Travers and the discourteous manner in which he had him ejected caused great consternation at the Temple. Even those who did not support Travers' views and were relieved to see him leave deplored the archbishop's methods. True to his reputation for arbitrary use of authority against his enemies—he could be most accommodating and even charming to his friends—Whitgift acted quickly and decisively against Travers. Almost as soon as he had learned about what he perceived as Travers' insubordination to Hooker, he had struck without warning to remove this man whom he had for so long regarded as one of the greatest threats to the peace and order of the Church of England.[24]

The congregation had gathered at the Temple on that fateful Sunday afternoon in late March, eager as usual to hear Travers' refutation of Hooker's morning sermon. As the reader mounted the steps of the pulpit, one of Whitgift's agents suddenly appeared and served him with a written injunction, signed by the archbishop, ordering him to cease all preaching at the Temple. Though everyone present was deeply shocked, Travers took it well. Cautioning the congregation to be calm, he left the church and returned to his quarters.[25]

The following Sunday, 30 March, Travers went to church in the morning and listened to Hooker's sermon, taking copious notes. Immediately thereafter he sent a letter to Burghley, no doubt at the lord treasurer's request, outlining fifteen specific charges against the master of the Temple, focusing on his three sermons on Habakkuk dealing with justification, faith and works, reason and Scripture, and his dangerous comments on the pope and the Church of Rome. Also included was reference to Hooker's oft-cited ideas on predestination.

Hooker immediately wrote a response to Travers' charges and sent it to Archbishop Whitgift. The archbishop's written reaction was somewhat ambiguous—less than completely supportive, Hooker thought. No doubt Whitgift found it difficult to deviate as far as Hooker seemed to be doing from strict Calvinist theology. Clearly, Whitgift was not pleased with any positive speech about the papalists. Still, he was generally supportive of Hooker, his criticisms apparently intended only to soften Hooker's arguments, something Richard would doubtless have done himself had he enjoyed the same advantage of hindsight.[26]

In the event, it became increasingly apparent that Whitgift was not really interested in the theological debate but was bent on removing Travers as reader at the Temple by any means available. He saw that his best weapon was one he had used earlier in his career against Cartwright and more recently to prevent Walter's appointment as master. Because Travers was not properly ordained, he had no right to serve in any English church, and that was the end of the matter.

When Whitgift presented this argument to Burghley, that gentleman told Travers to send him a brief explaining why his ordination was valid so he could use it with Whitgift. Travers did so, to no avail.[27]

When two petitions to Whitgift, through the lord treasurer, had failed him, Travers decided to appeal directly to the Privy Council in the form of an official *Supplication,* defending his ordination, explaining his personal and professional relations with Hooker, and attacking Hooker's major theological positions. This appeal was sent off in early April. Within a few days it was in the hands not only of members of the council but also of the lawyers and students at the Temple inns, the leading clerics of the Church, members of parliament, and, no doubt, the queen herself.[28]

As he prepared his *Answer* to Travers' *Supplication*, Hooker had before him a copy of that document, as well as copies of Travers' earlier petitions and his own notes on accounts by Sandys and others of Whitgift's reactions. He was especially distressed, as he reviewed these papers, by the prejudiced accounts of his ideas spread abroad by Lawrence Tomson, member of parliament and long-time secretary to the powerful Puritan statesman, Sir Francis Walsingham. Along with Burghley and Leicester, Walsingham, the queen's private secretary, was one of the most powerful men in the realm. It is likely that Tomson had been attending Hooker's sermons regularly and reporting his take on them directly to Walsingham. He may, indeed, have been the principal informant on Hooker, aside from Travers, for the Puritan political oligarchy.

Hooker knew that Walsingham and Travers enjoyed a long association. The powerful privy counsellor had come to Travers' aid when he was in trouble in Antwerp for not using the *Book of Common Prayer* in services there. Later, in December of 1584, the two men had made common cause again when Whitgift had agreed, under pressure from Leicester and Burghley, to a closed-door hearing at Lambeth Palace in order to air grievances and consider reforms in his policies as archbishop. Travers, as we noted earlier, was the principal Puritan disputant at this meeting. Walsingham had sat on a small panel of privy council members convened to hear the arguments. This two-day conference came to naught because Whitgift ignored its results. But the session did reveal Travers' continuing affinity with the secretary of state.

Walsingham was a bad person to have as an enemy. Hooker had learned recently that this master spy had established a new divinity lectureship at Oxford expressly intended to advance the more advanced brand of Presbyterian Calvinism. The man appointed to that post was none other than John Rainolds. The noose was tightening![29]

Whereas Hooker would have worried about Walsingham's ability to do him injury, he was probably angered by Tomson's interference. That spearhead for Puritan legislative activities was arguably the most radical of the more prominent and respectable Presbyterian scholars in the Commons. Richard was familiar with Tomson's writings and found most of his work far too extreme for his taste. In fact, if there was a single author, at this stage in his career, with whom Hooker was more often in disagreement than Tomson, it would be hard to say who that might be. Schooled at Magdalen, Oxford, and thoroughly "reformed" at Geneva and Heidelberg, Tomson had published, in 1576, an annotated version of the *Geneva Bible* that was preferred by most Puritans over the authorized *Bishop's Bible*. His version was far more disciplinarian in outlook than the original 1560 edition.

Tomson was an exponent of the most extreme form of the doctrine of predestination, called "supralapsarianism."[30] He was also a translator of several of Calvin's sermons. Hooker must have wondered, when he perused copies of Tomson's reports on his own recent sermons, if this radical activist had been as inaccurate in translating Calvin as he was in representing his ideas. It was not so much that the reporting itself was inaccurate as that his ideas had been ripped out of their subtle context and made to stand alone as unequivocal propositions. As for Tomson's substantive refutation of his arguments, Hooker probably bristled at the man's arrogance and his *ad hominem* argumentation. It was no proof of one's own arguments to brand one's opponent as "ignorant," or a "dissembler," or a "mere beginning student [not] well-versed" in the great writers of the past and present.

As Hooker reviewed his own and Travers' recent epistles to Burghley and Whitgift, he noted the sharp differences between them on issues of faith and works, reason and Scripture, predestination, the status of the Church of Rome. It was all there in black and white. There was not much he could add in his formal *Answere* concerning the substantive religious questions. He would need to concentrate on issues of church polity and on Travers' insubordination. He was ready to defend himself. He stacked the pile of relevant documents that he had been consulting to one side, placed a clean piece of parchment on the table, dipped his pen into a bottle of ink, and wrote across the top of the page:

> The Answere of Mr Richard Hooker to a Supplication by Mr Walter Travers to H H Lords of the Privy Counsel.
>
> To my Lord of Canterbury His Grace. My Duty in most humble wise remembered.

There was no point in sending this epistle to Burghley or the Privy Council. There would be no favourable audience for him there. As a minister of the Church, his superior was the archbishop. It was inappropriate to go around the head of the Church directly to the Privy Council, as Travers had done. A happy coincidence of propriety and politics dictated that Hooker address his appeal to his patron, Archbishop Whitgift.

Richard wrote his *Answere* quickly, possibly in a day or two. He may have had some help from young Edwin Sandys who had moved into the Churchmans' house as a long-term house guest and whose fateful collaboration with Hooker on the editing and publication of his former mentor's important writings began at about this time, in the Spring of 1586.[31]

NOTES

1. Williamson, *History of the Middle Temple*, 202, 205, 240. Daily services in the Temple were held in the morning as early as 5:30 or 6:00. It was common for students, lawyers and most other Londoners—even masters of the Temple—to begin their days earlier than most of us do today.

2. These lines are from Shakespeare's *Henry IV, Part I*, ii,iv. Like all literate people in London, Hooker was aware of the play, although it may not have been performed in London until 1592, as much as a year after he had left his post at the Temple. Shakespeare probably drew the idea for the story from his principal source for historical material, Holingshead's *Chronicles*, published in 1577, a work with which Hooker may have been familiar as well.

3. Bellot, 231, 254, 281. Michael G. Murray, *Middle Temple Hall An Architectural Appreciation* (London: Middle Temple, 1991); Joseph Dean, *Middle Temple Hall Four Centuries of History* (London: Middle Temple, 1970).

4. Charles Henry Hopwood, ed., *A Calendar of the Middle Temple* (London: Butterworth & Co., 1903), 287. The record also reports that Travers, despite his removal by the archbishop, continued to receive his pension, "til further order." See also Charles Henry Hopwood, ed., *Middle Temple Records* (London: Butterworth and Co., 1904), 24. Hooker was authorized to "have the same allowance as Mr Alvey in Michelmas Term, from every man in Commons 9d. and in Hilary and other terms, 4d to be gathered in by the Steward."

5. F. A. Inderwick, ed., *A Calendar of Inner Temple Records* (London, 1896), I, 331-3; S. J. Knox, *Walter Travers: Paragon of Elizabethan Puritanism* (London: Methuen & Co., Ltd., 1962), 6.

6. V. J. K. Brook, *Whitgift and the English Church* (London: The English Universities Press, 1957), 107; Knox, 55, 57-66, 79-80.

7. I have used the words "presbyterianism" and "presbyterian" to differentiate those advanced English Calvinists, among whom Travers was the leading spokesman, who insisted on replacing the polity of the English church with the Genevan model, from those Puritan Calvinists who urged reforms in theology, liturgy and morality within the established episcopal polity. Although I sometimes capitalize the word Presbyterian, I am aware that the denomination did not emerge as such in England until the Westminster Assembly (1643-49) and its *Confession*, during the Civil War period. John Knox's established Church of Scotland, beginning in 1560, was clearly presbyterian in form; and the strong advocacies of Travers and others during Hooker's day can have no other useful name. Most of these presbyterians, to be sure, were Puritans; but, many Puritans were not presbyterians. Many in the church, including Whitgift, Hooker, and the queen herself, accepted much of Calvinist doctrine, but they all staunchly objected to presbyterianism, which threatened the integrity of an established episcopal church polity. See Knox, 89-91; 31-2.

8. Knox, 97-9.

9. See Hooker's *Answere*, in *Folger*, V, 228-9; *Works*, III, 571-2.

10. *Works* I, 109-14.

11. See Walter Travers, *A Supplication Made to the Privy Counsel* (1586) (Oxford: Joseph Barnes, 1620), 9-10. I have used a very early copy in the British Library. The most authoritative and readily available citation is *Folger*, V, 197; also *Works*, III, 557-8.

12. *Answere*, in *Folger* V, 229; *Works*, 571.

13. Fuller, *Worthies*, I, 264; Knox, 76-8.

14. Fuller, *Church History*, III, 127-8; Walton, *Life*, in *Works*, I, 52.

15. Fuller, *op., cit.*, 128, seems to want to assure us of some evenhandedness in his treatment of Hooker. At one point, he suggests that Hooker may have been unfairly judged by some of his auditors when he "was unjustly censured for [being] perplexed, tedious, and obscure." Fuller's biographer sees his subject as a theological ally of Hooker because of the former's preference for moderation rather than the "extravagent Royalism and unrestrained Protestantism" of early seventeenth-century church politics. Fuller "belonged," we are told, "to Hooker's Church rather than to Laud's . . ." See Willam Addison, *Worthy Dr Fuller* (New York: The Macmillan Company, 1951), 275, 280.

16. Drawn from Hooker's *Answere*, *Folger*, V, 236-7; *Works*, III, 576-7.

17. Book V, (chapters 18-22), *Folger*, II, 65-110; *Works*, II, 58-115. Millar MacClure makes the point that the physical opening and reading of the Bible in the pulpit symbolized for many the connection between the sermon and the Word, and hence between the sermon and salvation itself. MacClure, 165. Unlike the sermon, which was either totally memorized from a finished composition, or, more likely, was delivered extemporaneously with some use of notes, the lecture was a polished essay read verbatim from the pulpit. The tractate was intended only for reading. A sermon might be drawn from a tractate or vice versa. See P. E. Forte, "Richard Hooker as Preacher," *Folger*, V, 660-4.

18. Travers' *Supplication*, *Folger*, V, 200. We have clear evidence that Hooker's arguments were either too subtle for his listeners or were deliberately misconstrued by them to his discredit. One unfriendly note-taker, perhaps the Puritan lawmaker, Lawrence Tomson, records in a contemporary account the Temple master's subtle argument on predestination as: "Predestination is not the absolute will of God but conditionally." Hooker's complex point about Scripture and reason is summarized as: "The assurance of things which we believe by the word is not so certain as of that which we perceive by sense." Tomson also exaggerated Hooker's position on Catholics by summarizing his argument as: "The Church of Rome is a true church and a sanctified church." British Library, *Landesdowne MS, Burleigh Papers* fol. 50; *Harleian* MS 291, fol. 183r. More readily available copies are in *Folger*, V, 283-286.

See Hooker, *Of the Nature of Pride*, *Folger* V, 309-10, *Works*, III, 507-8, for his beautiful paean to rational persuasion rooted in truths which lie beneath the emotional surface of matters. We may need to probe with our reason in order to know "not only what God doth speak but why." Izaak Walton said that "the design of his sermons (as indeed of all his discourses) was to show reasons for what he spoke; and with these reasons, such a kind of rhetoric, as did rather convince and persuade, than frighten men into piety . . . never labouring . . . to amuse his hearers, and get glory for himself; but glory only to God." *Life,* 79-80.
19. I have combined here what were actually three sermons delivered on successive Sundays from 9th to 23rd March 1586. These three, along with his sermon on predestination, were the most controversial sermons in Hooker's career. They were at the heart of the great debate with Travers that cost his cousin his job and stimulated Hooker to write *The Laws*. Collectively, the three are known as *A Learned Discourse of Justification, Workes, and How the Foundation of Faith is Overthrowne*. See *Folger,* V, 83-169 for the most authoritative text and helpful critical comments. An early copy is in the British Library: *Harley MS* 4888, fols. 92-107.
20. See especially Travers's *Supplication*, *Folger*, V, 200-1, 207-8; *Works*, III, 566-7.
21. *Ibid*., 203-4. Hooker elaborates on the Lutheran issue in marginal notes on his copy of his sermon on *Justification*. See *Folger*, V, 125, n. 1. The threat of a dire fate for Hooker over his supposedly pro-Catholic views is found in Travers' *Supplication*, *Folger*, V, 208; *Works*, 567..
22. According to Izaak Walton, the bishop of Rome did indeed appreciate Hooker. In about 1597, Pope Clement VIII purportedly read the first Four Books of the *Laws* and exclaimed in the hearing of Cardinal William Allen, who was in Italy at the time visiting the Pope: "There is no learning that this man hath not searched into; nothing too hard for his understanding; this man indeed deserves the name of an author; his books will get reverence by age, for there is in them such seeds of eternity, that if the rest [of his writings] be like this, they shall last til the last fire shall consume all learning." *Life*, 71.
23. A letter, dated 6 April 1586, from Christopher Taylour to Master Houldesworth, a minister at Newcastle-on-Tyne. *Folger*, V, 292, 261.
24. Most twentieth century students of the English Reformation are understandably biased against the rigorous enforcement of an established Church. Their sympathies, spoken and unspoken, are most often with those of our forebears who struggled against such men as Whitgift to bring us separation of Church and state and what we call "freedom of religion." In his otherwise even-handed biography of Travers, S. J. Knox cannot resist occasional outbursts in which he accuses Whitgift of "ruthless" behaviour and "extreme intolerance." See Knox, 153, 95.
25. Fuller, *Church History*, 186-7.
26. *Folger*, V, 288, 271-9; Walton, *Life*, 64-5.
27. An excellent summary and chronology of these events is Knox, 74-81.
28. Hooker, *Answere, Folger*, V, 227; *Works,* III, 370.
29. Dent, 148-9.
30. For Tomson's letters, see *Folger*, V, 283-7, 289-91.
31. Sandys' residence with the Churchmans was to be a long one. According to a court deposition given in 1613 by Philip Culme, Churchman's servant, Sandys resided there more or less permanently on three different occasions: first with a servant for about two years shortly after the death of his first wife; then for a year with his second wife, a maid, and two servants; finally, after that wife's death, for about a year with a servant. Apparently Mrs. Churchman was less than pleased with this arrangement. Sisson, 147.

CHAPTER 12

Master of the Temple

TEMPLE POLITICS

When he had finished composing his *Answere* to Walter Travers' *Supplication*, Hooker no doubt thought he had effectively expressed his complaints about Travers: that Walter had failed to consult with him before publicly airing their differences on religious issues; that his cousin had made illegal use of presbyterian forms of worship; and that Travers had been spreading abroad written charges about him before he had had the opportunity to respond to them. Hooker would have been pleased that he had gone straight to the political aspects of the dispute and shown Travers to be an insubordinate, trouble-making presbyterian extremist whose activities violated ecclesiastical regulations and disturbed the peace and order of the queen's Church.

Beyond politics, Hooker wanted to expose what he felt was Travers' hypocrisy in accusing him of abandoning his calling as a minister because he had sometimes used academic rather than patristic and biblical sources to buttress his arguments from the pulpit. Travers did the same thing when it suited his purposes, and Hooker most likely felt that it was unfair for Walter to charge him with an offense for what was common practice among learned clergy.

> I read no lecture in the law or in physics. And unless the bounds of ordinary calling may be drawn like a purse how are they so much wider to him than to me, that he within the limits of his ordinary calling should reprove that in me which he understood not, and I, labouring that both he and others might understand, could not do this without forsaking my calling?
>
> [When] I used the arguments of scholars, I trust that herein I have committed no unlawful thing. Those scholarly sources are acknowledged by grave and wise men not unprofitable to have been invented. The most approved for learning and judgement use them without blame. The use of them has been well-liked in some that have taught even in this very place before me. The quality of my hearers is such that I could not but think them of sufficient capacity for the most part to understand more than I said.[1]

A bit farther on in the text Hooker defended himself from Travers' attack on the style and content of his preaching:

> And though Master Travers be so corrupted by the city that he thinks it unwise to use any speech which savours of the schools, yet his opinion is no canon. Because his mind is already troubled, my speech seems to him like fetters and manacles; but, for others, not of his opinion, my words might have a calming effect. His private judgement will hardly warrant his bold words that the things I spoke were neither of edification or truth. They may edify some people for all he knows, and be true despite anything he says to the contrary. For it is no proof to cry "absurdities the like whereunto have not been heard in public within this land since Queen Mary's days." If this comes from him in earnest, I am sorry that his fit should be so extreme to make him speak of what he has no knowledge when he says that I neither affected the truth of God nor the peace of the Church.[2]

Hooker knew that the section of his *Answere* in which he had called for the use of reason and sense-perception as instruments for maintaining faith and criticized Travers' claim that inspiration is the only sure guide for interpreting Holy Scripture could be misunderstood. He did not mean his own solitary opinion. Rather, he had used "reason" to refer to our ability to grasp at least a small part of the divine Reason which God has for all that he does. God is not arbitrary. He has reasons for his acts and has given us the ability to understand them, at least in part. That ability is what Hooker meant by "reason." Reason is our link, although a very fragile one, to the mind of God.[3]

In his *Answere* he accused Travers of being "slippery" and "loose" in his use of sources. The arch-Calvinist was so caught up in his passion for introducing the presbyterian polity, Hooker thought, that his reason was clouded and he had become a careless scholar. Travers' citations from the great Peter Martyr were especially suspect.[4]

Reading Hooker's *Answere* today, one catches the lively spirit of this supposedly austere scholar. His anger, impatience, and wit shine through the words. He was intent on asserting the authority of his office as master and making it clear that Travers was in the wrong by spreading dissension in the face of the archbishop's explicit command not to do so. More than that, we see that Hooker had every intention of defending his moderate positions on the salvation of Catholics, the uses of Holy Scripture, and the doctrine of predestination.

Hooker was probably as gratified by the closing lines of his *Answere* as most of his readers over the centuries have been. He had a right to be pleased with himself. Rhetoric was one of his strong suits, and he was at his most persuasive when he wrote these words:

> I take no joy in striving; I have not been nuzzled or trained up in it. I would to Christ they which have at this present enforced me hereunto had so ruled their hands in any reasonable time that I might never have been constrained to strike as much in my own defence . . . But since

> there can come nothing of contention but the mutual waste of the parties contending till a common enemy dance in the ashes of them both, I do wish heartily that . . . things of small moment never disjoin them whom one God, one lord, one faith, one spirit, one baptism in bands of great force have linked; that a respectful eye towards things wherewith we should not be disquieted, make us not, as through infirmity the very patriarchs themselves sometimes were, full gorged, unable to speak peaceably to their own brother. Finally, [I wish] that no strife may ever be heard of again but this, [between] whoever shall hate strife most and whoever shall pursue peace and unity with swiftest paces.[5]

A vain hope, but a worthy one—and beautifully phrased!

There is no indication that Hooker ever received a formal reply from Archbishop Whitgift to his *Answere* to Travers' *Supplication*. Richard no doubt surmised correctly that the archbishop's failure to respond signalled that the only issue of importance to Whitgift was that Travers had not been ordained by a bishop of the Church of England and had even gone so far as to say that the very concept of apostolic succession was offensive to him. This threat to Whitgift's own authority as archbishop and to the episcopal polity in general was what rankled with Whitgift. The fact that Travers had made his appeal to Lord Burghley and the Privy Council rather than to him could not have pleased the archbishop either. The entire matter would be handled politically, with little if any reference to the theological or liturgical issues involved, or to Hooker's personal stake in the issue.

Travers had specifically addressed the ordination issue in his *Supplication* to Lord Burghley. But before he got to that matter, he had complained that he had been summarily denied the right to preach or execute any other act of ministry at the Temple or elsewhere in England without having had the opportunity to answer charges against him. Travers also averred that the punishment he had received was too harsh for any crime he might have committed. He pleaded that some "more tolerable punishment" be found. Hooker wondered if that plea for a lesser sentence was not a tacit admission on Travers' part of at least some wrongdoing.[6]

As to the merits of the charge against Travers, that he had not been properly ordained or licensed to minister in the Church of England, Hooker may have been inclined to sympathize with some of Walter's arguments in the *Supplication*. It was true, as Travers claimed, that many others who had been ordained in the Low Countries, while ministering there, were later accepted as ministers in England. It was also true, as Travers alleged, that the general practice was to accept as valid the ordination rites of reformed churches abroad. Hooker probably thought that Travers' analogy to the universal acceptance of academic degrees was especially convincing. Walter's case that his ordination had been given tacit approval by church hierarchy also had merit, Hooker may have thought. After all, Travers had been allowed to minister and preach without objection for five years at one of the most prestigious churches in England. Surely this amounted to a *de facto* acceptance of his credentials. Travers had made his case a solid one when he referred to letters to the Inner Temple from the bishop of London specifically authorizing him to preach at the Temple Church.[7]

Hooker knew, of course, as did everyone familiar with the issue of Travers' ordination, that Walter had been offered the opportunity to be ordained by a bishop in the Church of England and had refused, claiming this to be superfluous and insulting since he had been ordained already. His real reason for this blatant insubordination, Hooker recognized, was not simple obstinacy, but a deeply-held antipathy to the entire system and theory of episcopal ordination through the laying-on of hands. This was a papalist superstition insofar as Travers was concerned. Proper ordination for him was a response to a direct and personal calling from God, confirmed by a congregation of the elect.

The more Hooker thought about Travers' answers to charges that he had committed serious indiscretions by openly disputing the master's sermons, however, the less sympathy he had for his cousin. For Travers to have publicly accused his superior of error in almost all of his major pronouncements was nearly unpardonable. There was a time and a place for such disagreement, but not in the pulpit of the Temple Church almost immediately after the senior minister had preached his sermon. Clearly Hooker, and not Travers, was the aggrieved party here.[8]

WALTER TRAVERS

Even after his removal as reader, Travers remained in the Temple grounds. The Middle and Inner Temple Inns continued to pay his salary and to provide him with residence in the master's house. Since he was now free from all duties at the church, he had ample time to write and work actively on behalf of the radical presbyterian movement in London and around the country. At the same time, he could continue to stir up trouble for Hooker among the lawyers and students at the inns.

An offer from the Earl of Huntingdon of a position in a church at Leicester, well outside London, no doubt approved by Whitgift, could not lure Travers from his command-post location at the Temple. He also used his private abode on Milk Street, just around the corner from Hooker's dwelling at the Churchmans', as a base for planning and orchestrating presbyterian activities in London and around the country.[9]

In a real sense, Whitgift did not win his battle to remove Travers' influence from the Church when he had Walter ejected as reader at the

Temple. No longer tied down with parochial responsibilities, Travers now had the time and energy to lead a national movement against the archbishop. Among other activities, he worked on the revision of his *Book of Discipline,* the long-awaited "bible" on presbyterianism. This was the book that spelled out orders of ministry and all the rest of the presbyterian polity. It was a complete guide to the presbyterian form of Calvinist faith and life, a work that came close to making Travers the John Knox, if not the John Calvin, of England.[10]

For a short time after his appointment at the Temple, Hooker had received no stipend, or at least not a full payment. He was relieved when Middle Temple, always partial to Travers, finally voted to approve their share of his salary. For a while, Richard feared that they would not pay him in order to show Whitgift that, although he had the power to hire and fire, they controlled the purse strings. And yet, even as Hooker's salary was finally approved, Middle Temple authorized continued room and board for Travers. This must have annoyed Hooker more than somewhat.[11] Before the end of 1586, however, Middle Temple tired of carrying the financial burden of underwriting their champion, and cut off Travers' subsidy altogether, thereby finally ending his presence at the Temple.[12]

By early 1587 Travers had left the Temple grounds and was ensconced in his Milk Street residence in Cheapside, near St Paul's. Here, beyond the scrutiny of Hooker and the official church hierarchy, he was free to pursue his radical activities. Sessions of the powerful London classis, of which Travers was moderator, met at his house. Synodical meetings brought representatives to Milk Street from Oxford, Warwick, Northampton, and Essex. There was much coming and going of men on illegal business. Travers' house became a focus of emerging English presbyterianism, a place to meet and study his *Book of Discipline* and to plot strategies for carrying forth the principles and agendas it contained.[13]

In some ways, Hooker may have thought, life had been more comfortable for him when Travers was still at the Temple. He and his cousin had usually enjoyed good personal relations and maintained a high degree of mutual respect, regardless of their public disagreements. Unlike those quarrelsome lawyers at the inns presently so nettlesome to Hooker, Travers had been, in many respects, a kindred spirit—a college fellow and a scholar with an affinity for the life of the mind. Both had a deep commitment to religious service. Hooker was never to know that, years later, when Travers was asked by a friend what he thought of his opponent at the Temple, he had responded, "In truth, I take Mr Hooker to be a holy man."[14]

Insofar as records show, Richard and Walter never crossed paths again after Travers left the Temple. The great presbyterian completed the revision of his influential *Book of Discipline* in March of 1587. For the remainder of the century, he continued to provide effective leadership for a now declining presbyterian movement. By the early 1590s that movement was, to all intents and purposes, finished as an effective force in Elizabethan England.

A major factor in the precipitous fall of radical Protestantism was the Marprelate controversy of 1588-9, which unleashed such intemperate exponents of religious extremism upon the land that men such as Cartwright, Travers, and Rainolds were forced to take cover from the queen's wrath. Hooker was familiar with the secretly printed *Marprelate Tracts,* as was every literate person in London. These wickedly satirical broadsides aimed at the Church of England represented the last desperate attempt by Calvanist extremists to gain popular support for their cause during the sixteenth century.

Hooker did not go entirely unscathed by Martin Marprelate's sharp pen, although he was not mentioned by name. In the first of the seven tracts, reference was made to Travers' dismissal from the Temple as an example of the arbitrary folly of church authorities: "Let the Templars have Master Travers their preacher restored unto them. He is now at leisure to work priesthood a Woe, I hope."[15] Travers was mentioned in two later Marprelate pieces as well. In one, there was mention of his house on Milk Street as being a centre for illegal presbyterian meetings. After this, Travers was a marked man.[16]

In the midst of the controversy stirred by the *Marprelate Tracts*, Travers recast his earlier *Explicatio* with the publication of his *Defence of the Ecclesiastical Discipline*, in which he displayed uncompromising insistence on biblical warrant for every feature of church governance. This book, like the *Marprelate Tracts,* was secretly and illegally printed and distributed.[17]

It is surprising that during these dangerous times Travers never suffered the fate of his colleague Thomas Cartwright, who was imprisoned for such activities as conducting forbidden synod meetings, writing illegal tracts, assisting others who did the same, and encouraging use of presbyterian polity and liturgy wherever he could. Whitgift had planned to bring Travers, along with Cartwright, to trial before the church high commission. Richard Bancroft, Whitgift's chief agent for suppressing nonconformity, had secured evidence that Travers had plotted with others to encourage Cartwright to stand mute and not to cooperate with the commission's search for information about the presbyterian movement. But Travers was never tried, undoubtedly saved once again by the waning, but still significant, influence of his patron, Lord Burghley.[18] So confident was Travers in his protector that he apparently never felt it necessary to flee London or otherwise go into hiding. Even so, after 1589 he did stay out of trouble, living in quiet obscurity in London and avoiding controversy. Clearly, he had been warned to cease his radical activities or face the consequences.

Travers moved to Ireland in 1594. Here he embraced another challenge—this time one that was likely to please rather than offend the queen. In December 1591 the queen had authorized construction of the first and long-awaited English university in Ireland. A year later the new academic society, located in Dublin and named Trinity College, was ready to admit its first students. Roman Catholics in Ireland were dismayed at this development. It was obvious from the start that Queen Elizabeth would use the new college as a tool to stay the growth of political and religious resistance to her sway in this cantankerous and largely Catholic province. At last there would be an intellectual centre congenial to Reformation theology, a training-place for Protestant ministers, and a pro-English institution for educating the future leaders of Ireland.[19]

The founding provost of Trinity was Adam Loftus, the Cambridge-bred Archbishop of Dublin, an outspoken Puritan foe of Irish papalists. From the beginning, Trinity was a bastion of Puritanism, with close ties to Emmanuel College, Cambridge. Lord Burghley had been a moving force behind Trinity College and was its first chancellor. When Loftus resigned in June of 1594, the lord treasurer used his influence to have his endangered and unemployed protégé, Walter Travers, named to the post.[20]

Whitgift was delighted to have this nemesis out of the country, on assignment to fight Catholics rather than menacing the Church of England. Under Travers' leadership, Trinity might become a hot-bed of radical Calvinism, but that was a penalty Whitgift was more than willing to pay in order to watch the formidable Travers do battle with rebellious Irish Catholics. Hooker, too, probably thought it far better that his cousin use his great talents to fight papalists rather than to make trouble for the established Church at home. Undoubtedly Richard envied Walter's return to the groves of academe.[21]

Travers remained at Trinity until October of 1598, with most of his energy consumed in raising funds for the new college. He found some time to preach in the college chapel and to serve as lecturer in Latin. One of his students, James Ussher, would one day become Archbishop of Armagh, Primate of Ireland, a leading figure in seventeenth-century Irish history and a key figure in the compilation of Hooker's writings at Trinity.

Although Travers worked valiantly on behalf of the new college, even at the cost of his health and his own pocket, when he left Trinity the school was still in a financially precarious state. As an essentially English Protestant institution, it was under constant threat from rising Irish nationalism and stubborn Catholic entrenchment throughout Irish society. At the time of Travers' departure, the college, like all English institutions within the pale of Dublin and environs, was threatened by the armed forces of Irish rebels led by Hugh O'Neil, who was aided by

Spain and already closing in on Dublin in what was to be a very-nearly successful effort to overthrow English rule in Ireland.

Travers survived Hooker by thirty-five years, dying in 1635. These final decades of his life were times of intense frustration for the former leader of an important, but now dormant, movement. He lived in relatively obscure and modest circumstances, out of the public eye, too proud to receive aid from such important friends as his now famous former student at Trinity, Archbishop Ussher of Armagh. Occasionally he found a pulpit where he could preach and have an opportunity to give aid and comfort to a fellow nonconformist. In 1630, he wrote his last major work, an anti-Catholic piece entitled *Vindiciae Ecclesiae Anglicanae*.[22]

Had Travers' talent, like Hooker's, run more to writing than preaching, he might have spent his final years composing a lasting refutation of Hooker's *magnum opus,* thereby having the last word in one of the most important debates of the English Reformation. The spoken word, at which he excelled, was compelling for the moment but soon forgotten, as Hooker often said. Written words, less exciting at the moment, could endure for centuries.

THE INNS OF COURT

With Travers gone from the Temple grounds after 1586, Hooker could spend more of his time tending to his pastoral and administrative duties as master. In addition to preaching and conducting services, he was expected to supervise the general religious life of the Middle and Inner Temple Inns, enforce church attendance rules, and tend to the spiritual needs of this sophisticated and privileged congregation of lawyers.

As he settled into the routine of Temple activity, Richard appreciated how much it had in common with university life. Law students were engaged in tutor-directed studies throughout much of the day. Inns were like dormitories with impressive dining halls, much as he had known at Oxford. The semi-pastoral setting of the campus, with its broad river frontage, lovely gardens, and semi-cloistered atmosphere, was somewhat reminiscent of university life. His own weekly lecture/sermon stood, in some sense, for the required public lectures in theology at the university.

A less pleasant feature of life here at the Temple, also reminiscent of Oxford, was a student penchant for drunken and rowdy behaviour. Discipline was, in fact, much harder to maintain. The students, most of whom were from privileged families, were older, more independent, and uniformly wealthier than the Oxford undergraduates. They came here to acquire the important social graces of dancing, riding, singing, and theatre-going, as well as to study law, find entrée into the commercial and political scene in London and, if possible, find a place for themselves in the queen's government.

Away from the discipline of home or university, with the temptations of the fifth largest city in the world literally at their doorstep, many of these young men expressed their freedom in drunken brawling, whoring, and other forms of serious mischief. The area around Temple Bar on Fleet Street was no place for the unwary when the students came out to "play" at night. Within the halls, bans against such practices as possessing swords and entertaining women were difficult to enforce, especially since some of the senior barristers, including such notables as Treasurer Popham himself, had, in their own younger days, been among the principal offenders.[23]

Most of the 1,700 men who lived at the inns in Hooker's day had come straight from Oxford and Cambridge, initially to one of the eight Inns of Chancery, each housing about one hundred. They remained in a probationary status for about a year before moving to one of the four major inns of court: Middle Temple, Inner Temple, Lincoln's Inn, or Gray's Inn. As they entered the inns, which, like the commercial guilds, were often called "societies" or "mysteries," these fledgling lawyers joined a fraternity within which they would learn and then practise the craft and art of the law. In much the same manner of John Churchman's merchant taylors and other commercial companies, the inns were social groups, complete with rituals, ceremonies, and symbols that smacked of the medieval origins of the Temple itself—rich in religious and classical overtones. The lamb was the symbol of the Middle Temple, the pegasus of the Inner Temple. Each inn had its own special character. A little ditty went: "Grayes Inne for walks, Lincolns Inne for a wall, the Inner Temple for a garden, and the Middle for a Hall."[24] As a member of an inn, one was assured lifelong social contacts and economic support. The inns were a college, social fraternity, country club, civic club, professional organization, and an extended family all in one.

At the lowest level in this legal guild were the beginning probationers, the clerks and solicitors of both common and civil law. These men had not yet been admitted to appear at the "bar" (a wooden or iron rail separating the pleading lawyer, called the "utter (outer) barrister" from the judge). Since they were not yet ready to come to the bar, these men were often referred to as "inner barristers"—those kept well back from the bar. Academic life for a law student consisted of reading under the direction of a barrister who served as his tutor, attending periodic lectures and sessions of court, engaging in public legal debates called "moots"—not unlike the disputation "exercises" at Oxbridge—and doing legal research and menial tasks for one or more of the barristers.[25]

The utter barristers were themselves still only journeymen lawyers, having typically served an apprenticeship of eight years and still functioning at their appropriate level within this elaborate guild system. In another sixteen years, they might hope to become masters of the bench, often designated as "benchers." The benchers lived at the four inns, along with many of the utter barristers and assorted lesser lawyers. About two hundred members lived in each house, except for Gray's Inn, located farthest away in the country fields north of Holborn. Gray's, the most fashionable hall, and favoured by the rich, boasted over 350 members. Approximately fifteen benchers and thirty utter barristers resided in 138 living chambers at Middle Temple, along with about 150 other fledgling lawyers who could afford the cost and had friends among the benchers. Inner Temple was comparable in size.

One of the important responsibilities of senior barristers was to serve as readers (senior lecturers) in law. Their periodic lectures, a highlight in the life of the inns, were attended by all inner and utter barristers. Often a leading national jurist would deliver a lecture on a controversial parliamentary statute or a piece of pending legislation and then stay to judge a debate among the junior barristers on the bill's constitutionality. At the apex of the legal guild were the most senior and accomplished benchers, called "sargeants." These men were selected by the queen, after serving at least five years as benchers. She chose the judges and chief justices who ran her courts from among their ranks.

Presiding over each inn was a house parliament composed of senior benchers. This was the supreme governing body with authority to tax and spend, hire and fire, admit and expel, and manage all affairs of the house. Each house's chief executive officer, to whom most authority was delegated, was the treasurer, who had virtual control over the finances of his inn. Treasurers often assessed fees and spent money on their own authority. At times they also admitted students, assigned chambers, and made other such decisions, with the house parliaments serving as little more than rubber stamps.

As indication of the pre-eminence of the treasurers, each had his own special chair in the Temple Church, up front near the altar facing the congregation where he could see and be seen by all. When he conducted his first service, Hooker might have wondered at the spectacle of Sir John Popham, Middle Temple treasurer, and Andrew Grey, Inner Temple treasurer, thoroughly secular figures, seated prominently before him like great bishops, *in cathedra*. From his Oxford days, he was used to ordained academics having such place in church. But secular lawyers? That took some getting used to. Still, Hooker was aware that these two powerful men, eyeing him critically like rich employers surveying an important new employee, controlled the purse strings and shared the appointment powers here at the Temple Church. The queen and her minions might have appointed him initially to his post, but these two treasurers, along with their officers at the two inns of court, would decide how long he stayed and under what conditions.

When Hooker looked down at John Popham from the pulpit, he was eyeing a man who was one of the most promising political and legal figures in England. During his career, Popham would be speaker of the House of Commons, attorney general of England, and the jurist who presided, during King James I's reign, over both the "gunpowder plot" trial and the trial of his fellow middle templar, Sir Walter Ralegh.

Edmund Plowden, who preceded Popham as treasurer, was hardly less prestigious. He was, arguably, the finest jurist of his generation, so highly regarded that he obtained the post despite his staunch Catholicism, although his religion probably prevented Elizabeth from ever naming him a sargeant-at-law. During his six years as treasurer, Plowden made the building of the grand Middle Temple Hall his personal passion. When the edifice was completed in 1573, it became his most important monument, but not the only one. In the north aisle of the church there was an ornate altar tomb that featured a life-size reclining statue of Treasurer Plowden and served as a daily reminder to Hooker of the great man's presence. Both monuments survive to this day.

The heart of each inn was its great central hall. Often Hooker's duties as master took him from the church into the halls to attend lectures, participate in public celebrations, visit the treasurers on Temple business, or meet students for counselling sessions. Sometimes he just read or worked quietly on one of his sermons or other writings, at one of the long tables in the room.

Whenever Richard attended a formal lecture at Middle Temple Hall, given by one of the sargeants or benchers, and saw the speaker—usually a prominent national figure—standing at the grand "cupboard" in the middle of the room to read his discourse, he might well have felt out of place and ill at ease in such a politically sophisticated setting. Even so, he was stimulated by the highly charged environment. His knowledge of current political affairs and of the state of public discourse was honed to a fine edge during his years at the Temple.

Another early discovery for Hooker at the Temple would have been that the meals here at the inns were far superior to the fare he had endured for so many years at Corpus Christi College. Whenever he could, Richard probably took a free dinner with a bencher at the commons. He would have had a chair on the raised dais with the readers from where he could survey the carefully stratified seating arrangements separating each level within the guild. Food and drink were plentiful, with mutton the usual main course. Even those who sat at tables farthest removed from the dais and paid more money for poorer meals dined better than they had when they were students up at Oxbridge. As at Corpus Christi, however, manners were far from elegant—certainly nothing like the charm and warmth Richard experienced when he ate dinner at "home" with the Churchmans. Reluctant clerks waited at table here with the same lack of enthusiasm with which they changed the food-clogged rush coverings on the floor. There were pewter cups and plates, but no table linen or forks were provided. As with other favoured diners at the high table, Richard carried his own knife and fork with him and wiped his hands and mouth on the sleeves of his coat.

Hooker found dining and most other experiences more to his liking at Middle Temple than Inner Temple, probably because his closest personal attachments, with and through the Sandys family, were at Middle Temple. Nevertheless, his political and religious allies were predominantly at the other house, whose members were more frequently the favoured first-born of wealthy families. Not so bumptious as Middle Temple members, the men of this society tended to dislike the radicalism of Travers and were glad to have Hooker's temperate influence in their midst, not that Middle Temple lacked a conservative tradition. After all, the Catholic Plowden had ruled there as treasurer of the inn and the moderate Sandys' clan found it a congenial home.[26]

Before long, Hooker would have grown used to seeing many of the prominent figures of his day in his congregation and elsewhere in the halls and on the temple grounds. He had never been particularly overawed by the rich and famous, and there was no way he could gauge the future importance of those at the Temple who were not yet fully established. Edward Coke of Inner Temple was, for instance, a frequent presence at the inns when court was in session, although during Hooker's tenure his permanent residence was with his wife and children in Suffolk. Who could tell in 1586 that this promising new member of the Commons, sitting in church and taking close notes on Hooker's sermons, would soon become one of the greatest figures in all English history: attorney general, chief justice, speaker of the Commons, and author of the *Petition of Right*, *Bonham's Case*, *The Reports*, and *The Institutes of the Laws of England*—taken altogether probably four of the seven most important charters of modern constitutional government in England and America?[27]

Hooker could not know what influence, if any, his lectures and sermons had on the minds of such prospective famous men as Edward Coke. Like all writers, teachers, and preachers before him and since, he could only hope that his ideas would find fertile soil in some of his readers and listeners. He could not know, and neither can we, whether the great passion for the law that was to shine so critically for future centuries in the life and works of Sir Edward Coke was nurtured not only by what Coke learned from his legal studies at the inns of court but also from the inspiring lectures of the master of the Temple Church. What we do know is that Hooker's potential for influencing men like Coke was considerable. Hooker was a writer and speaker who, in that cynical, sophisticated, late Tudor world, had the ability to offer such powerful paeans to the majesty of law as this: "Of Law can be no less acknowledged, than that her seat is the bosom of God, her voice the harmony of the world: all things in heaven and earth do her homage, the very least as feeling her care, and the greatest as not exempted from her power, both Angels and men and creatures of whatsoever condition, though each in a different sort and manner, yet all with uniform consent, admiring her as the mother of their peace and joy."[28]

NATIONAL POLITICS

The months immediately following Travers' dismissal from the Temple in the spring of 1586 were busy times for the master. There were, for example, meetings to attend at Fulham Palace at which the bishop of London attempted to enforce the increasingly stringent regulations on clergy behaviour emanating from across the river at Lambeth Palace. At one such session, Bishop Aylmer ordered each minister to write and deliver a new sermon every week. This was no problem for Hooker. But he probably watched his colleagues squirm, some because they resented what they thought was an unwarranted intrusion of episcopal authority, others because they were plainly daunted by such an intellectual assignment, preferring to continue to read the prepared homilies.[29]

Much of the master's time was spent responding to complaints and gossip about mundane affairs at the inns. As soon as Travers moved out, Hooker probably found himself some working space in the master's house, where he could talk in private with templars and conduct the daily business that came his way. Usually there was nothing he could do but listen and sympathize. His days were filled with responding to such complaints as:

> Reductions in numbers of cook's assistants are delaying meals and making me miss religious services.
>
> Cutting back on gardeners and other servants is a foolish cost-cutting measure that we all regret;
>
> Both quantity and quality of food in commons are deteriorating badly;
>
> Penalties for missing lectures are unfairly administered;
>
> Attendance at religious services should not be required;
>
> My friend was higher on the waiting list for admission than so-and-so, who was just admitted because of political influence;
>
> My family has come on hard times. Can you find me enough money to see me through the term? I will pay it all back. I promise.

Every chaplain in every age has heard these problems and will know what Hooker's life was like better than the rest of us.[30]

A special event enlivened the routine at the Middle Temple Hall in June of 1586. Sir Francis Drake made an appearance at dinner. Drake had just returned from his amazing voyage around the world. Treasurer Popham would probably have unvited Richard to sit with him at the reader's table—the best seats in the hall—when Sir Francis made his grand entrance and delivered a gracious speech to the masters of the bench, acknowledging his own membership in the society and affirming his friendship for the brotherhood. Richard may have been introduced to the great man, shaken his hand, and had the opportunity to congratulate Drake on his remarkable feat. If he had been a participant in this historic occasion, Richard would have enjoyed the pomp, colour, good fellowship, and the best food and drink he had thus far consumed at the Temple.[31]

A somewhat unusual issue in which Hooker may also have been involved concerned the Earl of Leicester's garden. It seemed that some members of Middle Temple, whose chambers bordered on the Earl's adjoining gardens, cut doors through their rooms so they could walk out directly onto his otherwise very private property. That great man, or more likely his steward or head gardener, complained. As a result, in June of 1585, the middle temple parliament ordered the offending doorways to be walled up immediately. The outcries of righteous indignation, denial of responsibility, and refusal to comply took a year to subside. Grumblings over this campus affair could still be heard in the summer of 1586, but for his part, the Earl of Leicester had more to think about than law students walking uninvited into his garden on the Thames. The gossip at the inns about Leicester, during those waning days of 1586, turned on a far more important issue. What was the role of their rich and powerful neighbour in the intrigues at court and in parliament on the question of the fate of Mary Queen of Scots?[32]

Hooker may have gained inside information about this matter and other aspects of the high drama of politics at Westminster from his uncle, John Hooker. John, who would later write a description of the House of Commons and its procedures, was in London to attend the session of the Commons as a member from Exeter. While in town, the famous Exeter chamberlain and historian would have been eager to spend time with his now famous nephew. Their meeting would have meant even more to Richard, who had had so little contact with his family and home town.[33]

By this time, John Hooker, at sixty, was the highly accomplished manager of one of the largest and most prosperous cities in the land and, at the same time, one of England's brightest, most accomplished provincial humanists: archivist, historian, political philosopher, raconteur. John was not an intellectual in a strict sense, but he was well-read, a keen judge of human nature, and a man of vast practical knowledge. He was also a wise man, although perhaps a bit too sure of himself at times.

If, as seems likely, the two men were together in late 1586 and early 1587, Richard would have acquired some information about his father Roger's life and career in Ireland. He doubtless already knew of his father's death some years ago but would have yearned to hear more about his life. John probably told him of some of Roger's experiences managing the Carew estates in County Carlow and his exciting and dangerous life—fighting in the Butler Wars, being captured by those Kavanaugh ruffians. Richard would have been especially intrigued to learn that his father had been appointed dean of the Carew parish church at Leighlin Bridge, where he had made his home. No doubt Roger had been appointed to that clerical post after Carew pushed the Kavanaugh tribe out of the Barrow Valley. Richard realized that this appointment in the Church would not have required the sort of academic training and religious sensitivity that preceded his own selection as master of the Temple. Roger's was a "battlefield" appointment made not by the Church but by his patron, Peter Carew, who owned the church building and its properties. Roger's responsibility would have been mostly that of administrator and steward, not preacher and pastor. Still, how curious that his father had also laboured in the Church, a servant of the Lord.

When parliament reconvened on 15 February 1587, Hooker would have continued to receive regular insider intelligence about its proceedings from members at the inns and Miles Sandys, as well as from other prominent visitors at the Churchman's. His uncle John, no doubt, would have stopped by from time to time at the Temple and occasionally at the Churchman house. From these men, and from other sources, the master of the Temple kept abreast of the great events unfolding at Westminster in early 1587. Almost daily he would have heard first-hand accounts of the incredible events in the House of Commons as that body exploded with the full force of a frontal attack by presbyterian disciplinarians and separatists on Whitgift and the established Church. What Hooker and Travers had debated at the Temple just a year ago now erupted in the chambers of national decision-making. Richard might have won the war of words with Travers, but his uncle John, Miles Sandys, and other moderates now fought Travers and his friends in the bloodier battles for political power and control of the Church being waged in parliament.[34]

As early as the previous November Hooker had learned of preparations by Travers, Field, Cartwright, and their friends for this parliamentary session. The inns were rife with gossip about the pending *Survey of the Ministry* that would gather data on alleged abuses in some 2,500 parishes in eleven counties and the city of London. Copies of that report circulated freely before the end of the month and, of course, one probably found its way into Master Hooker's hands. Hooker would have been appalled by the *Survey* on two counts. First, there were so many unsubstantiated claims of abuse in clerical behaviour: idleness, absenteeism, ignorance, corruption. Secondly, the preamble to the *Survey*, in the form of a "Supplication to Parliament," called for nothing less than a complete and total change in church polity along presbyterian lines: elimination of the episcopacy, use of a

Calvinist prayer book, and a declaration that all existing church orders, canons, and customs should be abolished together with such laws as the *Act of Supremacy and Uniformity*. As Hooker read this incendiary document, he knew that if it were indeed to be presented in parliament, the event would be unique in the long history of that body. Men slipping in and out of such conspiratorial venues as Travers' Milk Street house, just a few blocks north of the Churchmans' parlour, had been hatching a revolution.[35]

John Field and his lieutenants from around the country produced a bumper crop of Puritan radicals for this session of Commons. The notorious Job Throckmorton, alleged author of the most virulent and popular Puritan literature yet printed, the soon-to-be circulated *Marprelate Tracts*, was here from Warwick. The Welsh firebrand, John Penry, another suspected author of those anonymous tracts, was present in the form of his proxy, Edward Dounlee, M.P. for Carmarthen, who would read Penry's intemperate petition in parliament. Anthony Cope was back again from Banbury, along with Sir Francis Knollys, Edward Lewkenor, Ralph Hurleston, Robert Bainbridge, and Peter Wentworth.

The two most noteworthy speeches in this session were made by Cope and Wentworth. It was difficult to believe that the two men were of the same party. Cope was so radical that even some of his allies were shocked, when they heard him speak, into seeing the dangers of carrying one's religious beliefs too far. Wentworth was just as radical but his voice seemed to be an eloquent call for the right of free speech in Commons, a call that echoed Magna Carta.

It was Cope's speech that was most troubling to men like Hooker. Cope's presentation of Field's *Survey*, along with his own resolution for virtually abolishing the present church polity and adopting a new prayer book (his so-called "Bill and Book"), surely amounted to a revolution in the making. Hooker also would have been appalled when he learned of Throckmorton's speech. This radical Calvinist was especially effective in tying both the queen's safety and liberties of Commons to the Puritan cause. In the event, Cope's bill never even came to a vote. The queen ordered that all proposals on the floor of Commons touching religion be sent by the speaker directly to her. That will be the end of them, Hooker probably thought. And so it was.

Hooker had by now probably begun to use the word "Puritan," which was gaining wider currency at about this time as a pejorative description of radical Calvinists. He would have been aware that each successive Puritan spokesman who was recognized by the Speaker of the Commons had the same supporting documents, presented similar or complementary arguments and often used identical words and phrases. Hooker would have had the impression that this was a carefully rehearsed performance, and it was just that. As Hooker knew, and no doubt observed with his own eyes, for several months there had been a steady stream of presbyterian Puritans coming in and out of Travers' house. There could be little doubt that they were in there planning a well-orchestrated strategy to accomplish in parliament the changes in church practice that they had failed to achieve in the high councils of the Church and the queen's government.

Hooker, who was to become one of history's most profound and eloquent proponents of the law as expression of both ultimate truth and human justice, was no doubt greatly interested in Peter Wentworth's powerful address, in this session of Commons, claiming the justification of fundamental law for the right of free speech in the House of Commons. Here was a moving and eloquent plea for the independent rights of the members of Commons to speak freely on any subject without fear of suppression or repression. This idea, which was to send Wentworth to the Tower, would have far-reaching implications. Did not the right to speak freely in parliament supersede the right of the queen to prevent or punish such speech, even if she were to view the speech as a threat to her well-being or that of the country at large? This question would not be resolved in Hooker's lifetime, nor was he destined to make a significant contribution toward its resolution. But he would have been deeply concerned about such issues, pondered Wentworth's speech with keen interest, and discussed its implications avidly with his colleagues and friends at the Temple and elsewhere.

For Hooker the important question raised by Wentworth was whether there was a higher natural law of reason that confirms such positive (human) rights as freedom of expression in the legislative body of a nation. Or are such supposed rights based merely on the customary practices of individual societies and so properly varied from place to place and time to time? For thinkers in a later generation, some of them drawing directly on Hooker's writings, the answer to his question was less ambiguous. They would give a ringing affirmation to the proposition, suggested by Wentworth, that the natural right to free expression was grounded in the rational laws of nature and nature's God. Hooker never did more than hint at such a translation from natural law to natural right. In doing this much, however, he was to be an important link between such medieval natural law theorists as St Thomas Aquinas and the harbingers of modern natural rights thinking such as John Locke.[35]

Of more immediate concern to Hooker and his moderate colleagues in the Church than Wentworth's claims for more freedom of speech in parliament was his linkage to the religious agenda of presbyterian radicals. Wentworth was not espousing high constitutional principles in a political vacuum. He had been closely involved with Field, Travers, Cope, and others in laying plans for an attack on the Church in this session of parliament. The timing of his call for parliamentary freedom, coming so soon after the queen had countered the Puritans' other more direct assaults on her authority, would have seemed to Hooker to be exactly what it was, part of a carefully hatched conspiracy.[36]

None of this fooled the queen. Wentworth was committed to the Tower almost immediately after his famous speech, followed at once by his co-conspirators: Cope, Lewkenor, Hurleston, and Bainbridge. Throckmorton joined them in that damp abode shortly thereafter. There was to be no political revolution, peaceful or otherwise, so long as Elizabeth Tudor was queen of England.

At first Hooker may have thought that the imprisonment of these radicals was an extreme response. On reflection, he probably decided that their real offence was not so much what they said in the Commons as the conspiracy against the Church—and the queen—that they had perpetrated as private citizens outside the houses of parliament. He, no doubt, also concluded that in such dangerous times as these the queen could hardly afford the luxury of temporizing with such men. Still, he was probably pleased that neither Whitgift's net, nor Walsingham's, had caught his cousin Walter and dispatched him to the Tower with his religious compatriots.

If the queen and her supporters thought that their swift action would silence the remaining Puritans in parliament, they were disappointed. There were loud cries for the immediate release of the imprisoned men. The new lord treasurer, Sir Christopher Hatton, calmed the situation with a masterful speech that moved most of the radicals to back away from the dangerous paths of the conspirators in their company and toward a more comfortable middle ground. Hatton was joined in his sentiments by the impressive Puritan orator, the chancellor of the exchequer, Sir Anthony Mildmay. The centre would hold.

This tumultuous session of parliament was adjourned by the queen on 23 March. John Hooker could now leave London and return home to his beloved Exeter. He did not return to parliament a second time. He was too old and tired for a repeat performance and, in any event, the Puritan-leaning leaders in Exeter who had sent him to London on their behalf did not want him to represent them again. They had wrongly counted him a supporter of the more radical Puritan ideas put forward in this session. They had misjudged their man. Although sympathetic to the Calvinist Reformation in England, as we have seen earlier, John Hooker was a pragmatist and a moderate at heart. He would have been uncomfortable, to say the least, with the radical stance of some of his religious compatriots in parliament. John would have found more congenial company among those moderates at the Temple with whom Richard had close contact, men such as Miles Sandys, who were now parting from their more extreme Calvinist brethren.[37]

Before he left the city, John Hooker may have told his nephew of the queen's message to the Commons at the close of the session. The message, delivered by means of a letter to her privy counsellor, left no doubt about where the Puritans stood, so long as this queen reigned. Elizabeth wrote:

> Tell them that Her Majesty is fully resolved, by her own reading and princely judgement, upon the truth of the reformation we have already . . . Her majesty hath been confirmed in her said judgement . . . by the letters and writings of the most famous men in Christendom . . . Her Majesty thinketh it very inconvenient and dangerous, whilst our enemies are labouring to overthrow the religion established, as false and erroneous, that we by new disputations should seem ourselves to doubt thereof. Her Majesty hath fully considered, not only of the exceptions which are made against the present reformation—and doth find them frivolous; but also of the [presbyterian] platform which is desired—and accounteth it most prejudicial to the religion established, to her crown, to her government, and to her subjects . . . Her Majesty taketh your petition herein to be against the prerogative of her crown . . .[38]

This message put a full stop, temporarily, to the Puritan and presbyterian movements in England.

Hooker's own path was now clear. He would walk with the forces of moderate reformation of the established Church, within the bounds of loyalty to the crown. He had already involved himself in enough trouble advocating a modicum of tolerance for papalists. He would not compound his problems, and those of the establishment, by making the same mistake regarding the presbyterians. Philip of Spain was preparing an invasion with a great armada of ships soon to enter the channel. What the queen needed was a stout defence of the Church from her enemies at home so that she could concentrate on meeting the threats from abroad. Whitgift was doing his best to stamp out nonconformity, but his activities had become so identified with unreasonable and arbitrary suppression of religious dissent that his credentials as a dispassionate and credible defender of the Church of England were seriously compromised.

Dean Bridges of Sarum had recently completed a written defence of the Church against the latest anonymous attack, the so-called *Learned Discourses*. Dr Bridges called his tract, *The Defense of the Government Established*, a monumental work in the somewhat tedious style of Whitgift's *Defense of the Answer* to Travers. It was at this time, in the spring of 1587, if not earlier, that Hooker resolved to turn his own mind and hand to the task of preparing a major *apologia* that would set forth the special nature and genius of the Church of England and defend her from her enemies, especially those often well-intentioned but usually dangerous reformers within her own ranks—the Calvinist extremists, Puritans and presbyterians alike.[39]

NOTES

1. Hooker, *Answere*, *Folger* V, 245. Lambeth Library holds a first edition copy printed by Joseph Barnes in 1610. *Fairhurst Papers*, #1612.41.
2. *Ibid.*, 246.
3. *Answere, Folger*, V, 255.
4. *Ibid.*, 252.
5. *Ibid.*, 256-7. This statement is similar to Thomas Cartwright's in his *Reply to An Answer*, which begins with these words: "As our men do more willingly go to warfare and fight with greater courage against strangers than against countrymen, so it is with me in this spiritual warfare, for I would have wished that this controversy has been with the Papists or with other . . . enemies of the Church . . . [rather than with a] brother . . ." See copy in Lambeth Library (1574.03), printed in 1574 by "J. S." (John Stroud), an illegal printer who decries in his Preface the "Unjust censorship" of "such good Christian writings" by the "persecuting bishops." See Pearson, 110-13.
6. Travers, *Supplication*, *Folger*, V, 190-2.
7. *Ibid.*, 192-5.
8. *Ibid.*, 195-8; 205-6.
9. Knox, 82; Paget, 63.
10. Travers completed his revision of *Disciplina Ecclesiae Dei Verbo Descripta*, popularly called *The Book of Discipline*, about a year later in March, 1587. It was the major reference and practical guide for presbyterian Puritans, used at all conferences and synods of their emerging church. Whitgift regarded it as one of the most important weapons in the Puritan arsenal. See Knox, 108-9.
11. Hooker was granted Alvey's pay on 28 June. On the same date, Middle Temple authorized partial payment to Travers. See Hopwood, 24.
12. Inderwick, 331; 333. Middle Temple stubbornly held out for Travers, continuing his support as late as November. Hopwood, 287.
13. Knox, 110. One of the many contemporary evidences of these meetings is a letter from Aylmer to Whitgift in 1589 reporting on such a gathering near Aldgate in William Barrett's house, which was attended by Robert Beale, Thomas Cartwright, Richard Gardner (preacher at Whitechapel), William Charcke (lecturer at Lincoln's Inn), and Thomas Barber (preacher at St Mary le Bow). Lambeth Library, *Fairhurst Papers*, #3470, fol. 129.
14. As late as 1591, five years after Travers' departure, Hooker purportedly complained of continued "noise," "oppositions," and "contentions" of life at the Temple. At the same time he remembered Travers as being "a good man." Walton, *Life*, 66-7. Travers' comment about Hooker is found in Fuller, *Church History*, J. S. Brewer ed. (Oxford, 1845), V, 187.
15. Cited in Knox, 116.
16. *Hay any Work for Cooper* and *The Just Censure and Reproof*, cited *Ibid.*, 117.
17. *Ibid.*, 114-15.
18. *Ibid.*, 118, 121.
19. The best account of Travers in Ireland is Knox, 124-37. See also Knappen, 472.
20. Trinity became one of the most influential Puritan colleges in the realm. Its influence was even felt outside England in the new world. Such prominent American Puritans as John Winthrop, Jr. and Increase Mather were educated there.
21. There is no evidence that while at Trinity Travers advocated presbyterianism. He seems to have been uncharacteristically loyal to the Church of England throughout his tenure there. Knox, 138.
22. We know little of Travers' life during these long final years. My account is based on his biographer's research of the rather sketchy documentation. *Ibid.*, 141-47.
23. Catherine Drinker Bowen, *The Lion and the Throne, the Life and Times of Sir Edward Coke* (Boston: Little, Brown and Company, 1956), 67.
24. Bellott, 282.

25. My accounts of the inns of court are drawn in part from two great jurists whose experiences at Middle Temple flanked Hooker's: Sir John Fortescue in the late fifteenth century and Sir Edward Coke in the early seventeenth century. Bedwell, 15, 19-20. See also Williamson, 92-5, and Bellot, 314.

26. One consequence of the difference in social complexion between the two inns was that, in Hooker's time and subsequently, more men of lasting fame passed through Middle Temple than Inner Temple. The rich, in those days of primogeniture, often rested on their wealth, contributing little of lasting historic value to society as compared with their younger siblings who had to stretch their wits and find their own paths to fame and fortune. Although many Inner Temple members in Hooker's day had noble titles, few had names that would be recognized beyond their own time.

On the other hand, Middle Temple members included such sixteenth-century notables as the jurists Plowden, Popham, and Coke and serious students of law such as John Meere of Sherborne. Many more, who would one day be famous, were not interested in the study of law so much as they were in exploiting the social and economic advantages of membership at the Middle Temple. These included the architect Inigo Jones; explorers John Hawkins, Walter Ralegh, Francis Drake, and Martin Frobisher; statesman and scholar Thomas Smith; the poet George Sandys; and Ralegh's friend, also a poet and soldier of fortune, George Gascoigne. In subsequent centuries, the list of distinguished alumni would include the diarist John Evelyn; the political philosophers James Harrington, Edmund Burke, and John Dickinson; the legal scholar William Blackstone; and the novelists Henry Fielding, Charles Dickens, and William Makepeace Thackeray.

Of interest to Americans seeking some connection to Hooker is the fact that many famous colonial Americans were to claim membership in Hooker's favourite society. In fact, it is not too much to suggest that Middle Temple was a kind of nursery for political luminaries in the new world. No fewer than five signatories of the Declaration of Independence were members, including Thomas McKean of Delaware who became the first chief justice of the United States Supreme Court. The second chief justice was also a Middle Templar, John Rutledge of South Carolina, who had been one of the drafters of the United States Constitution. The honour role of Middle Templars who helped shape the American nation also included such men as Arthur Lee and Peyton Randolph of Virginia and the colonial governor of New Jersey, William Patterson. Hutchinson, 22ff; Williamson, 71-4.

27. The others, of course, are the *Magna Carta*, the *Declaration of Independence,* and the *United States Constitution*. See Bowen, 61-9.

28. *Folger* I, 142; *Works*, I, 285.

29. Besant, 149.

30. The master's house was purchased by the inns from a Mr Roper sometime in 1585. Bellot, 202. For details of everyday events and complaints likely to have come to the master's attention, see Inderwick, 341, 335-6.

31. Hopwood, 285-86.

32. For these events see Neale, 103-45, 130. Neale's exact words, which I cannot improve, are: "Her speeches, with their moving theme—'If this cup can be taken from me'—appear against a background of irresistible argument and pressure: as a Greek tragedy with a fatal parliamentary chorus incessantly chanting Mary's doom." After much delay, obfuscation, and deception on Elizabeth's part, Mary was executed at Fotheringale Castle in Northamptonshire on 8 February 1587.

33. There is no evidence that Richard and John Hooker met while John was in London. It is almost inconceivable, however, that they did not. Late in life, John made his only extant comments about his famous relative. He said that Richard was "a notable and well learned scholar" and that his writings were a "stumbling block to many." Exeter University historian, Joyce Youings, in a private letter to the

author, says of the relationship between these two men: "It is all very tantalizing." I agree.

34. Neale, 145-65.

35. See Philip B. Secor, *Richard Hooker and the Christian Commonwealth* (Durham, North Carolina: Duke University, 1959), unpublished doctoral dissertation, 232-44, 210-17. For an argument that any connection between Hooker's thought and Locke's is spurious, see J. C. Davis, "Backing into Modernity: The Dilemma of Richard Hooker," *The Certainty of Doubt, Tributes to Peter Munz* (Victoria, B.C.: Victoria University Press, 1997), 169. Christopher Morris' summary of Hooker's political thought is still noteworthy. See his *Richard Hooker: Of the Laws of Ecclesiastical Polity* (London: J. M. Dent & Sons Ltd, 1907), xxv-xxx. See also infra., chapter 15, n. 5.

36. Neale, 154-5.

37. Miles Sandys' Puritan backing is attested to by Peter Roberts, "Elizabethan Players," in Anthony Fletcher and Peter Roberts, *Religion, Culture and Society in Early Modern Britain: Essays in Honour of Patrick Collinson* (Cambridge: Cambridge University Press, 1994), 39-40.

38. Neale, 163.

39. In a lucid analysis of a complex issue, the historian Diarmaid MacCulloch describes the twin pillars of the Catholic Church that the Reformation sought to overthrow: the papacy and the Catholic devotional life and liturgical practice based on "the power of the mass and the power of the clergy who performed it." In England, unlike the European continent, only one of these pillars was overturned: the papacy. Hence the struggle in England was far more intensely concerned with liturgy and devotional life than in Europe.

In this struggle, Hooker was the pivotal thinker in forging what was to become the Anglican Reformation of the historic English Catholic Church. According to MacCulloch, Hooker was the prophet of Anglicanism, not its defender. I agree, and have titled this book accordingly. See *The Later Reformation in England 1547-1603* (New York: St Martins Press, 1990), 1-8, 97-102.

CHAPTER 13

A Judicious Marriage

THE SECOND JOAN

For the nearly four centuries that Richard Hooker has been part of the public domain, his marriage has been maligned. This misinformation and calumny started in the mid-seventeenth century when Thomas Fuller told the world that Hooker had died a bachelor, without children. It continued with Izaak Walton's portrait of a henpecked husband cursed with a domineering mother-in-law, a homely, shrewish, incompetent, untrustworthy wife, and spiteful children. At the end of the seventeenth century, Anthony Wood described Hooker's wife, Joan, as a "clownish, silly woman, and withal a mere Xantippe"—reference to Socrates' mate, who gave her name to the prototypical ill-tempered, scolding wife. These gross misrepresentations persist into our own day when, at the base of Hooker's statue in Exeter, a tour guide intimates that Hooker was a simpleton in affairs of the heart who was seduced by a designing woman and her mother. It is far more likely that the "judicious" Hooker made a most fortunate marriage, and was a devoted, much loved husband, son-in-law, and father.[1]

When Richard and Joan first met, probably in 1584, he was an accomplished and confident thirty-year-old Oxford don with a promising future. Although he had no wealth of his own, Richard was of respectable lineage. He already had excellent connections with several of the most powerful figures in the Church and the universities. Joan, then aged about seventeen, was the oldest daughter of one of the most prominent business leaders in London. She lived with her parents, five siblings, and several servants in a grand house within sight of St Paul's Cathedral and was accustomed to the constant comings and goings of wealthy and powerful men, with their incessant conversations about the great issues of the day.

As a young woman growing up in Elizabethan England, Joan was schooled at home in the domestic arts and graces. By every means available, her parents raised her to become a dutiful wife, a producer of many children, a good manager of her prospective husband's domestic affairs, and the spiritual core of her own future family. She learned by absorbing the atmosphere of the times that her major role in life would be as a devout Christian wife and mother. Because she was the daughter of prosperous London parents, Joan received at least a smattering of the education normally reserved for male children. She was among the estimated twenty-five per cent of London girls of her day who could read and write. As such, she was exposed to some of the important religious and moral writings of the Reformation, and, at least a smattering of a few of the Greek and Roman classics.[2]

Joan's father, an enlightened and progressive man, was determined that his daughters should make good matches and be a credit to him as successful wives and mothers. He may have employed a young cleric to tutor his girls. The clergy in London were eager to spread their religious ideology among young women. In fact, it was their intention to convert women to their points of view and, by all accounts, they had some success in this effort.[3]

By the time Joan and Richard were married, on 13 February 1588, Richard, at thirty-three, was a promising cleric at one of the most important churches in London and had already achieved notoriety as the antagonist of the great presbyterian scholar and preacher Walter Travers. For her part, Joan was a mature young woman of at least twenty, ready to assume her role as the mistress of an important clerical household. The "virgin queen" of England might not approve of her major clerics taking wives, and Richard might be somewhat older than most grooms of his generation, but in no significant respect was their marriage unusual. In fact, it was typical of their day (and ours) for a professionally rising but financially struggling man to marry a younger, wealthier woman. The bachelor's experience and promise matched the young woman's energy and dowry—two necessary ingredients for her to bear many children and manage a large household.

From their first days together in 1584, Joan was probably attracted to Richard. She knew she would make an attractive mate for one of the available men who frequented her father's house. Richard would have seemed different to her from some of the rest—older, quieter, more considerate of her feelings, more attentive—a good match for her own more assertive personality.

It is fair to deduce from Joans's recorded actions later in her life, and from a discounted reliance on the aforementioned biased accounts of her relations with Richard, that she was a self-reliant, intelligent woman of high spirit. Although perhaps not a beauty, her assets were a good mind, a healthy body, a confident will. She was, no doubt, too aggressive and self-assured for some people. Her mother probably warned her about that. But Joan would have wondered how a woman was to survive in this man's world, unless she were sure of herself and what she wanted out of life.[4] The attraction was probably less instantaneous for Richard. During his first year at the Temple he had more on his mind than love and marriage. He was fully occupied with the challenge of learning his new job, while at the same time dealing with Walter Travers and his obstructionist friends. Furthermore, he was aware that matrimony would only be an impediment to further advancement in the Church.

Their courtship lasted for about a year. Since they were already living together in the same house, it was a simple and convenient matter for them to experience the lively cohabitation that preceded many, if not most, marriages in Elizabethan England. After they were married, rather little changed in their domestic routine except that they shared the same bedroom on a regular basis, and probably continued to enjoy the pleasures of a happy and vigorous sexual relationship.[5]

In the summer of 1585 Richard and Joan made their formal espousal announcement. John and Alice Churchman would have invited some friends for dinner to witness the proclamation and to assure that the espousal (engagement ceremony) was a festive occasion. Such an event was necessary to satisfy the legal and social requirements for marriage. However, Richard and his in-laws wanted a full church ceremony as well, following the traditional posting of wedding banns in church for three Sundays. Hooker believed in the sacramental nature of marriage and would be joined in that holy estate only by a minister of God using the rites of the Church of England.

As for John Churchman, he would have wanted a church wedding with a lavish reception to follow. His position, as rising master of the Merchant Taylors Guild, required nothing less. In fact he would be disgraced socially if this were not a memorable affair. He would have invited all his important friends and associates to the wedding of his oldest daughter. In addition to his colleagues at Merchant Taylors, the guest list would have included some of the most prominent people in London and in the church hierarchy, men such as the lord mayor, the treasurers of Middle and Inner Temple Inns, the dean of St Paul's, the bishop of London.

The Sandys family was no doubt well represented: by Miles, his sons William and Miles, and of course Edwin and his wife (who was ill at the time and would die within the year), Edwin's older brother Samuel and his sister Margaret, who had married Francis Evington, a prominent merchant taylor, in this very church in 1575. George Cranmer was no doubt also there with members of his family, including his younger brother William and his sisters Susannah and Dorothy. These were the two ladies who, many years later, while living with Izaak Walton, would provide Hooker's first biographer with bits of unflattering and inaccurate gossip about the young bride they watched so keenly on this happy day.[6]

On 13 February, 1588 John Churchman gave his daughter Joan in marriage to Richard Hooker in a service at St Augustine's, the family parish church next door to his house on Watling Street.[7] Richard might have hoped that Archbishop Sandys would officiate at the wedding. But the great man had retired in poor health to his family homestead in Hawkeshead, Cumbria. In 1585, shortly after Hooker's appointment at the Temple, Sandys had opened the new grammar school in

Hawkeshead and completed the new chapel in the local parish church of St Michael and All the Angels. He had financed and supervised both projects. At present he was very ill and near death.[8]

The service began with the beautiful opening words from the 1559 *Book of Common Prayer*:

> Dearly beloved friends, we are gathered here in the sight of God, and in the face of this congregation, to join together this man and this woman in holy matrimony, which is an honorable estate, instituted of God in paradise, in the time of man's innocency: signifying unto us the mystical union, that is between Christ and his church: which holy estate Christ adorned and beautified with his presence and first miracle that he wrought in Cana of Galilee . . .

It proceeded with the exchange of vows and giving of the ring, after which the minister pronounced them man and wife: "Forasmuch as Richard and Joan have consented together in holy wedlock, and have witnessed the same before God and this company . . . I pronounce that they are man and wife together. In the name of the Father and the Son and the Holy Ghost."

The remainder of the service lasted about an hour. Richard and Joan may have held hands as they heard the minister read the 127th Psalm, exhorting them to be fruitful and have children. They knelt together at the Lord's Table, recited the Lord's Prayer, then received Communion, as required of all who are married in the Church of England. They sat in the choir and listened to a short homily on marriage by the rector. Finally, they heard the prescribed passage from Paul's Epistle to the Ephesians on the subject of the duties of husbands and wives to one another.

Following the wedding, a lavish reception was undoubtely held at the Churchman's house next door to the Church. The guests making the short walk to the house would have been resplendantly attired in the highest fashions suitable to their standings as leading merchants, jurists and clerics of the city: John and his colleagues in long silk brocaded robes over their finest doublets and slops (breeches), silk stockings and leather sandals; Alice and the other women defying growing objections from Puritans to sartorial display, showing off elegant gowns of fine Italian silk, trimmed in Flemish lace, many in the latest French style with billowing sleeves and tiara-shaped black velvet hats. Inside the house, guests would have been treated to an assortment of roasts, pies, cheeses, puddings—and malmsey, the strong sweet wine from Madeira so favoured by the English of the day.[9]

MARRIED LIFE

There is no reason to doubt that Hooker found affection and emotional support, as well as some peace and joy in his marriage to Joan

Churchman. It is fair to assume that Richard and Joan were part of the trend toward a marriage based on mutual affection, in which husband and wife chose each other as mates and then clung closely to one another for mutual support and nurture in a rapidly changing and often threatening social environment.[10]

Richard had not known the sort of personal affection and intimacy that he now experienced with Joan since he was a very small boy living with his mother in Heavitree. No longer was he a lonely free-floating soul, dependent for his well-being on his own wits, the admiration and camaraderie of fellow intellectuals and clerics, and the patronage of powerful benefactors. Now he could share his deepest hopes and fears, as well the normal events of his day, with a person who was a helpmate, lover, and friend—a woman who might occasionally offer some balm to his troubled spirit and help him to achieve deeper levels of self-confidence.

On a practical level, Hooker knew that he had achieved a good marriage. He had joined one of London's leading merchant families and thus acquired a social standing to match his high post at the Temple Church. Joan's undoubtedly handsome dowry, coupled with her father's broader financial resources and political influence, assured Richard a freedom from the monetary woes that had plagued his entire life. From this point on he would feel freer to make career choices not dictated solely by financial considerations.[11]

During 1588 Richard was drawn into a plethora of small crises, some of them centering on the failure of younger members of the inns of court to attend worship services as required by the law of the land and the rules of the two inns. Many of the lawyers found the prescribed services either too romanist or too "evangelical" for their taste. Some simply resented being required to attend any religious service at all. In late June, there was an order from the Inner Temple that any member who resided in chambers or ate in commons for as little as one week must attend services at the Temple Church weekly or pay a fine to the society of twelve pence for each absence, unless he had been specifically granted permission to miss the service.[11] Hooker did not enjoy his inevitable role as enforcer of these attendance requirements and the other rules he was expected to monitor. He also disliked pursuing the culprits who occasionally stole money from the Temple poor box, or reporting students he saw wearing high boots, cloaks, or hats in town. He knew that they could be dismissed on a second breach of this rule.[13]

Richard Walter was one of a number of students expelled from Middle Temple Inn for refusing to attend church services. Since he and his friends had strong papist leanings, they may have thought that Hooker would sympathize with them. When they refused to take Communion despite several warnings, Hooker had to report them to their bench and they were expelled.[14]

Hooker may have felt some responsibility for the expulsions since his sermons seemed to support Catholics and might have prompted Walter and his fellow pro-Catholic students to think that the master would champion their cause, or at least not report them for failing to practise their religion in the prescribed Calvinist manner. At all events, Hooker did not like being put in the position of judging and condemning the religious acts of others. He was learning, however painfully, that this was the cost of being master of the Temple, or holding any position of high responsibility. He may have begun to think that this was too high a price to pay for fame and power.

Late in the spring of 1588, Joan became pregnant. As summer turned to autumn and the first hints of winter were borne on late October winds and Joan's pregnancy progressed, so did the Walter affair. That gentleman continued to absent himself from the required Communion as demonstration of his opposition to the prescribed services, while at the same time making regular entreaty for reinstatement at Middle Temple Inn. On 25 October, Middle Temple parliament ordered Walter to arrange conferences with master Hooker. Richard was to examine Walter's religious opinions and ascertain whether his beliefs were heretical or even treasonous. Only if the master certified that Walter was in conformity with established church doctrine and practice, and that he was indeed attending services, would his petition for reinstatement be considered.

Hooker had already been meeting with Walter and other nonconformists—Catholics and advanced Calvinists alike. He wished to save them from persecution by the government as well as from further discipline by their inns. The entire process was not to his liking as it required him to make the very judgements he condemned in others. Yet he had no choice but to do his best to convince Walter and others to conform.

Walter explained to the master that he believed he should be free to celebrate Communion according to whatever rite suited his conscience. The Roman Mass had been accepted here in England since time immemorial and had been the preference of Walter's family for centuries. He was a loyal subject of the queen and rejoiced in the defeat of the Armada as surely as any Englishman. But how he worshipped should be his own affair.

Such an argument tested sorely Hooker's instinct for toleration. He told the student that what he believed was between himself and God but what he practised in public must conform to the laws of England and the practice of the established Church. England was a Christian commonwealth whose prince headed the Church and whose bishops decided what kind of public religious practice would be followed by all citizens. Fortunately, the queen had drawn a wide road for her people to follow. But it was a defined path nonetheless. To allow each of us to go his own way would produce anarchy and a godless society. Surely Mr Walter could understand that?

After several conferences, Hooker made enough progress in moderating Walter's passion for the Mass that he felt comfortable making the necessary certification to Middle Temple to secure his restoration to that society. But that august body was not satisfied with the master's recommendation. Carried away with the national hysteria over the Spanish invasion, they required that Walter put in writing for the house treasurer, Miles Sandys, his "detestation of all popish religion." Walter did so, and, in February of 1589, was restored to his place at the inn. By May, he was formally reinstated as "associate to the Bench" and allowed to "sit with them at their table."[15]

Hooker no doubt hated the entire ordeal. It put into sharp focus a major dilemma of the English Reformation: how to assure freedom of conscience without weakening the authority of the Church and disrupting the social order. This was a problem much easier to solve intellectually than in real cases involving real people. The Walter episode, combined with countless similar events, taught Richard a hard lesson about himself, which he had begun to learn in his distasteful pulpit debate with Travers. He was discovering that he lacked the stomach for public leadership. Rainolds, Sandys, Aylmer, Whitgift, even Travers, were able to do what had to be done to other people in order to achieve religious goals that he often shared. He was able to make such painful decisions, but only at great cost to his sense of well-being. It hurt him too much to judge and condemn others. He was in the process of learning that his true calling was elsewhere. He would analyze, write, preach, instruct, console, perhaps even inspire; but, as soon as possible he would remove himself from the political arena.

Like other Londoners in the late 1580s, Richard and Joan lived with the normal vicissitudes of private life—in their case, a first pregnancy for Joan and daily mounting pressures at the Temple Church and inns of court for Richard—in the midst of the great public events of the day: first, traumatic fear of impending Spanish invasion, then the patriotic catharsis over national victory. The fear of, and then the salvation from, conquest by the forces of Catholic Spain formed the dramatic backdrop for the Hookers' personal lives throughout most of this period.

For the Armada victory celebration in January, 1589, London was bedecked in colourful banners, with its citizens festively attired. It was to be one of the greatest days of national celebration in all English history. As master of the Temple, Richard would have been with the official party greeting the queen as she entered the city at Temple Bar. Then he would have joined the royal procession to St Paul's, with Miles Sandys and other leading jurists from the inns of court, John Churchman and his fellow leaders of the merchant societies, and the lord mayor and aldermen of London. Hooker also would have been among the more than fifty notables with the queen at St Paul's. He heard her prayers of thanksgiving for national deliverance and then a sermon given by Bishop Pierce of Salisbury.[16]

Later, Hooker probably described to his wife all that he had seen and heard. He told her how the queen, seated in a throne mounted atop a chariot drawn by two magnificent white horses, had arrived in a grand procession at Temple Bar; how the throne was covered by a rich cloth canopy supported in the back by four columns topped with the imperial crown and in the front by two columns on top of which stood, respectively, a lion and a dragon supporting the arms of England.

He would also have related to Joan that passing directly in front of him had been members of the Privy Council and many lords and ladies of the realm, as well as bishops, the French ambassador, leading judges, and hosts of heralds and trumpeters, all dressed in their best and mounted on fine steeds. He had been impressed with the entourage of the Earl of Essex that followed directly behind the queen's footmen. As her master of horse, Essex was especially resplendent. He was followed by many ladies in waiting who were flanked by footguards bedecked in rich cloaks and carrying highly polished six-foot long combination battle axes and spears, called halberts.

Richard, no doubt, reported to his wife that he had stood only a few arm-lengths away from the lord mayor and aldermen, garbed in scarlet robes and wearing their badges of office as they gave the queen their official welcome to the city. He may have been close enough to see the mayor offer the queen the official sceptre of London and to observe her handing it back just before his honour mounted again to lead the procession into the city.[17]

The queen would have seemed old and frail to Hooker. Perhaps he had been close enough, when she knelt to pray at St Paul's, to see the age lines in her face through all the layers of white makeup. But the rest of her small frame was so gloriously cloaked in regal adornment that she appeared ageless, more a symbol than a person. Her voice, when she prayed or spoke, was clear and commanding.

Tiny Richard Hooker was born ten weeks later and was christened almost immediately at St Augustine's, on 19 February 1589.[18] Richard knew, as he held his infant son during the baptismal service, that the baby would not live long. The ceremony had more the aura of a funeral than a christening. Joan's confinement and delivery had not gone well, and when the baby arrived, he was not healthy, a scrawny bluish little thing who cried incessantly and pitifully for several hours and then only intermittently. Joan's milk came, but the baby had trouble nursing. After a few days, little Richard stopped crying but slept fitfully, his tiny body twitching occasionally in small involuntary convulsions. From time to time, he would awaken and whimper softly.

Like other couples of their day, Joan and Richard were conditioned to expect the death of children, especially infants. The poor health of mothers, primitive birthing methods, and rampant disease, especially in the city, were facts of life for them—facts that made infant mortality a common experience. Still, the realization of impending loss caused deep pain, especially for Joan. They decided to go to the family home in Enfield immediately in hopes that the better air there would revive the baby. They knew that this was a desperate remedy, especially in the dead of winter. But they went anyway. They probably hired a carrier's wagon for Joan and the baby, as neither of them was well enough to travel by horse and litter.[19]

They had travelled along the road north out of the city before. It was often crowded with elaborate carriages carrying nobility and wealthy merchants to and from their country estates in the rich farmlands, pastures, and game forests that stretched along the west bank of the Lea all the way from Tottenham to Ware.[20] The way led through Edmondton, then a small town not nearly so large or important a place as Enfield. There was a tradition that this stretch along the river from Tottenham to Enfield was a safe haven for Catholic recusants, many of whom kept illegal priests more or less hidden in their homes. The principal focus of this activity was the Arundell family, which maintained a large estate at Tottenham, as well as their famed palace on the Strand. During the early years of Elizabeth's reign, Catholics such as Sir John Arundell and his friends were fined £20 a month for not attending the prescribed Protestant services. By the early 1580s, Sir John would have been paying the crown £260 a year had the fines always been exacted.

Arundell and many of his religious compatriots in the region kept their Catholic faith and continued to harbour the priests necessary to its practice, while their sympathetic neighbours and local officials looked the other way. It was well known that there was a cottage on the Arundell grounds that was a base from which priests moved about the entire region celebrating Mass in homes of Catholic believers. Worst of all, Arundell was accused of providing a haven for priests smuggled into the country from the seminaries at Rheims. By 1585 legislation against such priests and those who sheltered them, with the perceived threat of Catholic conspiracy at home and invasion from Spain, had become draconian. The year before, while Hooker was preaching his maiden sermon at Paul's Cross, Arundell was being held in the nearby Tower, imprisoned there for helping an Oxford graduate flee to a Catholic seminary at Rheims and promising to help him on his illegal return to England as a Catholic priest. After the defeat of the Armada in 1588, Sir John had been allowed to return home. But as Hooker passed near the Arundell estate on this February morning, he would have been aware that the great Catholic lord again stood accused of recusancy and would probably be arrested soon. (Arundell died in

1590, shortly after returning from a house arrest at Ely Cathedral, where he had belatedly pledged his loyalty to the queen against the pope and other would-be foreign invaders.)[21]

When Richard and his little family finally arrived in Enfield town, they probably stopped at the lovely parish church of St Andrew to rest before proceeding on to the Churchman home. The Hookers were frequent worshippers here in Enfield, and the vicar, Leonard Chambers, and Richard may well have been friends. Although St Andrew's and the school faced onto the busy town marketplace, they were surrounded on three sides by woods and pleasant fields. This was a far cry from the sprawling, argumentative public arena of Hooker's Temple Church in London.

Baby Richard died and was buried in the cemetery at St Andrew's, after a short service for the family and a few friends probably conducted by Mr Chambers. Joan Hooker would have more children, for a while at the rate of one per year; but the pain of the loss of her first child was obviously hard to bear.[22]

By the time Joan returned to the Watling Street house in late spring she was in much better spirits. She had the demanding daily routine of a prosperous young London housewife to distract her. There was much for her and her mother to do to manage this busy household. In addition to the needs of her younger siblings, Edwin Sandys had moved in with his second wife and three servants as more or less permanent house guests. Sandys' friends, including one of her husband's favourites, George Cranmer, were also frequent visitors. And of course her father had a steady stream of personal friends and business associates staying in the house. Its convenient location and John's position in the city made the house a magnet for guests.[23]

NOTES

1. Tradition has dubbed Hooker the "Judicious Hooker" and called his marriage a dismal failure. In my view, each of the characterizations is incorrect. Certainly, his marriage was at the very least judicious, hence the title of this chapter. For the traditional story see Fuller, *Worthies*, 264; Walton, *Life*, 23-25; 90, 91-92; Anthony Wood, I, Preface, 2-3. Even Francis Paget, the late-nineteenth-century scholar who found the idea of Hooker being duped into a bad marriage inconsistent with Hooker's character as revealed in his writings, felt obliged to perpetuate the picture of a cold and unhappy marriage to a wife "not wisely chosen." Paget, 81.

2. Anne Laurence, *Women in England 1500-1760* (London: Weidenfeld and Nicholson, 1994), 165-7.

3. It is only a good guess that Joan was educated in this manner. For a perceptive analysis of the impact of the Reformation in England on the religious life of women, which concludes that the Puritans were not as successful in their efforts to woo women as most commentators have believed, see *Ibid.*, 193-213.

4. Young women like Joan Churchman, in the wealthier homes of London, served as models for the bright independent woman in such plays as Shakespeare's *The Comedy of Errors*, who "could never quite convince herself that she was inferior

to a man." Marchette Chute, *Shakespeare of London* (New York: E. P. Dutton and Company, Inc., 1964), 149.

5. Women were often the sexual aggressors in this age, which viewed sexual intercourse as a healthy, pleasurable, and even therapeutic experience for women. The already rising tide of Puritan morality would soon dampen such enthusiasm. For discussions of sexual roles in marriage during this period, see *Ibid.*, 65-68; Stone, 323-6; Fletcher, 161-2.

6. Novarr, 229-30, 270-2; Secor, *Constructing a Biography*, *op. cit.*

7. The marriage is recorded in *St. Augustines Watling Street General Parish Register 1559-1653,* Guild Hall MSS Room, MS 9535-2. See also, Sisson, 124. The church and the Churchman house were destroyed in the great fire of 1666. Rebuilt by Christopher Wren between 1680 and 1687, St Augustine's was merged with St Faith. Then it was destroyed again in the German bombing of 1941. Only the stone tower survives as a part of St Paul's Choir School. We are able to locate accurately the original church as being virtually adjacent to St Paul's Cathedral at the intersection of Watling and Old Change Streets. Although Old Change Street no longer exists, we know that it was about one hundred yards to the west of the present New Change Street. This locates the Churchman house at approximately the middle of today's New Change Street at the point where it intersects Watling Street.

8. The school, now a museum, was to be the archbishop's most enduring legacy. William Wordsworth was a boarding student there in the late eighteenth century. The poet's devotees still make regular pilgrimages to see the desk where their hero sat, after they have visited Dove Cottage in nearby Grasmere. The museum curator was delighted when this writer asked to see the Sandys' papers in the school library. "Thank God a few people are still interested in the Sandys family and not just that romantic poet," he whispered. The chapel in St Michael's is dedicated to Sandys, and many family members are buried in vaults beneath its floor. The archbishop died less than four months after the Hooker wedding, on 10 July 1588. He was survived by his wife, Cicely, six sons, including the famous poet George, Hooker's friend, Edwin, and two daughters.

9. For descriptions of dress I have consulted portraits and collections at such museums as the Victoria and Albert and works including: Natalie Rothstein, ed., *Four Hundred Years of Fashion* (London: Victoria and Albert Museum, 1985); Janet Winter and Carolyn Savoy, *Elizabethan Costuming for the Years 1550-1658,* 2nd ed. (Oakland, California: Other Times Publications, 1979); Roy Strong, *The Elizabethan Miniature* (London: Thames and Hudson, 1984).

10. Stone, 100-04.

11. Sisson, 26, 44. Sisson not only disputes the traditional view from Walton, Fuller, and Wood (cited above) that Hooker's marriage was unfortunate if not miserable, but he goes on to postulate a "suitable" and even a "happy" and "loving" marriage to Joan. He draws these conclusions not from biased contemporary sources but from an examination of chancery court records of law suits by Hooker's daughters after his death, from the facts of Hooker's life, and from Hooker's own words and actions concerning his wife and family.

12. Inderwick, 353. My characterization here of some Calvinists as "evangelicals" follows the usage of Dairmaid MacCulloch in his *Thomas Cranmer A Life*. In his masterful work, MacCulloch uses "evangelicals" to apply to those whom others have variously termed "Calvinist extremists," "puritans," "advanced Calvinists," "disciplinarians," "presbyterians." For my part, I use all of these terms at various times, as it seems appropriate. Consistency in this matter is probably not a virtue, although I would not call it a hobgoblin either.

13. Hopwood, *op. cit.*, 22-23; Bellot, 206.

14. Hopwood, *Middle Temple Records,* 298-305.

15. *Ibid.*, 300, 304-05. Miles Sandys was appointed treasurer of Middle Temple on 22 November 1588.
16. There are many excellent accounts of the Armada invasion. I like the popular account by Carrolly Erickson, *The First Elizabeth* (New York: Summit Books, 1983), 364-77.
17. My account of this famous procession is from Stow's *Annals*, 1592, quoted in Bellot, 241-242.
18. Sisson, 124, gives baby Richard's christening date as 19 February, 1589. It is given as January in *St Augustine Parish Register*, MS 8872, I. There are small discrepancies between these two sources on all the Hooker children's christenings at St Augustine's. I am inclined to favor Sisson as he had access to earlier records in the 1930s (when they were titled "St Watlings at Pauls Gate"), before Nazi bombings destroyed the parish buildings. Cicely Hooker, in fact, does not even appear in the current Guild Hall parish record, whereas Sisson found her name in the earlier St Augustine register available to him.
19. The trip to Enfield at this time is probable, since baby Richard is buried there. A. H. Dodd, *Life in Elizabethan England* (London: B. T. Batsford Ltd., 1961), 142-7 is a useful account of modes of travel at this time in and around London.
20. This account of Tudor Enfield, Edmonton, and the region along the River Lea is drawn mainly from J. Burnby, ed., *Elizabethan Times in Tottenham Edmonton and Enfield* (Edmonton Historical Society, 1995), 26. See also, Dodd, *op. cit.*, 61-65.
21. Archbishop Whitgift involved himself personally in granting permission to recusants to reside on their properties and do business in the realm on payment of "bonds" (fines). Several of his letters on the subject are preserved in the Lambeth Library, *Fairhurst Papers*, #3470, fols. 99-103, 109, 110, 113. That Whitgift was a micromanager is evident throughout his correspondence. See esp. *Ibid.*, #3470, fols. 89-115.
22. For an account of child-birthing and related matters in Elizabethan England, see Laurence, 76-82, and Stone, 51-56. That Joan was able to bear children almost annually despite the long nursing period typical at the time (two to three years), is probably owing to the fact that, like other higher class women of the day, she used wet nurses. The prevailing opinion was that nursing would spoil a mother's looks and hasten her death. Despite the urgings of religious reformers and secular humanists that women cease using surrogates and nurse their own infants, many who could afford to do so continued the ancient practice. Houlbrooke, 132-3.
23. Sisson, 28.

CHAPTER 14

Penman for the Church

THE CALL

What motivated Hooker to take up his pen and write a book that would become the definitive *apologia* for the Anglican Church? The answer to this question has long been a subject of speculation. Some have said, although no surviving documentation survives to prove it, that he was commissioned, formally or informally, by Archbishop Whitgift to write a defence of the Church. Others have claimed that Hooker was so enraged by Travers' treatment of him in their debate at the Temple that he was psychologically driven to continue the argument in print. Another view is that he wrote the *Laws* primarily for his own intellectual satisfaction. A prevailing opinion is that Hooker was commissioned by Edwin Sandys, George Cranmer, and perhaps others, to write a polemical tract to assist them in efforts to crush the Puritans through legislative action in the Parliament of 1593.

To these explanations, each of which holds part of the key to Hooker's motivation, we need to add that he was an introspective scholar who by dint of training and habit preferred to engage the issues of the day with his pen rather than with his voice. He probably learned from his tenure in the pulpit at the Temple that the public debating forum was not a congenial environment for him. He also learned that he cared deeply about the issues of the day and wanted to address them on behalf of the Church in a more coherent and lasting manner than had been done thus far.

The primary motivation for Hooker to write his great work came from within himself. It is quite unnecessary to postulate a direct commission, either from the primatial see or from Edwin Sandys and other political figures, in order to explain Hooker's decision to write *The Laws of Ecclesiastical Polity*. His love for the Church, which had nurtured him emotionally and intellectually for most of his life, his scholarly instinct to look beneath the surface of immediate arguments of convenience for important truths, his natural desire to best the famous Walter Travers and his presbyterian friends by shifting the venue for their debate from political polemic (oral or written) to a more serious intellectual ground, and his simple human ambition to make a name for himself in the Church in an arena where his talents excelled, were all drives within him conspiring and leading him to take up his pen—on behalf of his beloved Church and country, and his own inner needs for self- justification and recognition.

But was it necessary for Hooker to leave his position as master of the Temple in order to write? Surely he could find time to write, along with his other duties. Other clerics of the day did so. His wife must have raised just this question when, sometime in 1589, Richard told her that he wished to find another position. She would not have been keen about an unnecessary career change which would cost her, in one stroke, the prestige of being married to the master of the Temple Church and her desirable and convenient home at a good address in London. And why should her husband want to leave a position which assured him access to the libraries, printers, and political connections that were so important to a writer? Surely London, then as now, was the place to be for an aspiring writer—or an aspiring anything, for that matter.

Perhaps another reason Hooker wished to leave the Temple was that he no longer felt challenged now that Travers was gone and life had settled into something of an annoying routine. Perhaps he was bored. While some might find challenge in administrative detail, a man with an expansive imagination could be stifled by such tedium. Much as he had been stressed by the controversy with Travers and its aftermath, he probably missed the challenge to use his talents and energies to meet the Puritan threat and to secure his own credibility as master of the Temple. Those had been difficult years, even dangerous, but nevertheless invigorating. By early 1589 the Armada was gone, the papist conspiracies crushed, and the Puritans, with notable exceptions, in retreat. Most of the challenges in his career had waned. Now his days may often have seemed filled with routine activity.

Some of this he would not mind. He enjoyed the informal intellectual discussions at the inns on theological and legal issues. He was happy to give advice and direction to some of the younger lawyers who came to him for counsel on a variety of matters, personal and professional. He relished the opportunity to use his influence from time to time to help a gifted young man gain admission to one of the societies.[1] However, much of his daily routine involved such unpleasant administrative tasks as enforcing church attendance, listening to constant carping from die-hard Puritans at the inns about his use of established liturgical forms, and mediating disputes on matters that did not interest him.

For example, he may have been asked by Miles Sandys, treasurer at Middle Temple, to help resolve a dispute between the two inns, at about the time of the queen's procession in 1589. It was a petty issue, but important to the residents at each house. For a year or more there had been ongoing discussions about the need to repave the path from Middle Temple Gate on Fleet Street down to the river. The two societies were unable to agree on how to finance the project, so Middle Temple just went ahead on its own, had the work done, and sent a bill to Inner

Temple for its half of the cost. Not surprisingly, that society's members refused to pay since they had never agreed to the terms. They insisted that Miles Sandys meet with a delegation from their house to explain why they should share in the cost of a job they had never approved. Was this to be the stuff of Hooker's career?[2]

In addition to his desire for a more challenging but less contentious assignment, Hooker had another reason to believe that it was time to leave the Temple. He feared that his performance there might have been found wanting by the archbishop and others in authority. He worried that his perceived Catholic leanings had made him *persona non grata* at the Temple and that he would soon be pressured to leave. In the event, there may have been a fortuitous coincidence of the archbishop's desire to remove Hooker from the Temple and Hooker's own wish to repair to a quieter living where he could study and write in peace.

As it turned out, Hooker did stay on at the Temple for some time after Travers' departure in 1587. He did not leave until 1591, when he accepted largely absentee livings at Salisbury and Boscombe in Wiltshire, staying on at the Churchmans' to pursue his research and writing. It was not until 1595 that he finally left London altogether to accept a full-time residential cure in Bishopsbourne, Kent. By early 1589 Hooker's attention was already turning to what he by now regarded as the unfinished business of his debate with Walter Travers. All around him the fires of virulent Puritan extremism were flaring again. True enough, Travers had left the Temple; the Puritans' field-marshal, John Field, and their principal patron, the Earl of Leicester, had both died in 1588 (Field in March and Leicester in September); Whitgift and Bancroft had Puritan ministers on the run all over the country. But the Puritan movement was not yet dead, and the echoes of Travers and Cartwright still rang loudly in Hooker's ears.

By mid-April of 1589, with his wife back in London and now beginning to recover from the terrible trauma of the death of their son, Richard was engaged in reading a number of important manuscripts published recently as part of the ongoing debate between Puritans and the church establishment. There was the monumental work of Dr John Bridges, Dean of Sarum, entitled *A Defence of the Government Established*. Richard would have had trouble just lifting this huge 1,400 quarto-page tome from the table. Appearing in 1587 as an officially commissioned defence of the Church, it refuted line-by-line (in the style of Whitgift's earlier writing against Cartwright) a short anonymous piece popularly known as the *Learned Discourse*. That work had defended the ideas of Cartwright and the *Admonitions,* calling for careful analysis of Scripture to determine whether bishops or elders were ordained in Holy Writ.

Hooker knew that Bridges' work had been much maligned by Puritans, especially in the *Marprelate Tracts*. He may have thought parts of the book delightful, especially when Bridges punctured presbyterian icons like John Calvin. He probably recorded favourite passages for use in his own writings. One example is noteworthy: "This is but Calvin's thinking, who though he were a most excellent man, though it move many to think as he did, yet it bindeth none, but that other men may think otherwise." "Amen," Hooker thought. It was high time to stop allowing the Puritans to think that, in order to win an argument, all they need do was find support in Calvin. To be sure he is our greatest religious mentor, Hooker opined, but only a fallible human being after all.[3]

Hooker also read, at about this time, the anonymous *Defence of the Ecclesiastical Discipline*, published in 1588 in response to Bridges. This *apologia* for presbyterianism was written, Hooker suspected, by his old nemesis, Walter Travers. Another work he would have examined was Robert Some's new book, *First Godly Treatise*. He undoubtedly liked the section where Dr Some, the renowned rector of Girton parish near Cambridge, refuted the Puritan John Penry's repeated broadsides in parliament and elsewhere against the Church for having so many ministers who lacked the education to give effective sermons. Although this may be true in some cases, Some argued, it cannot matter much because it is the Holy Word and the Sacraments that are central to the service, not preaching.[4]

Hooker certainly agreed and was much pleased to see this issue stated so clearly by Some. It was time, he felt, that the Church began to insist that God's speaking and revealing Himself through His Word and His Sacraments was the essence of the liturgy—and not some clever sermon given by a minister. Preaching was a helpful aid, but the Puritans made far too much of it. There were other more important parts of divine service than emoting from the pulpit or lectern, Hooker thought—common prayer, for instance.

During this period of research and writing, Hooker would also have read John Penry's *Exhortation*, also published in 1588 as a response to both Bridges and Some. He no doubt took special note of Penry's assertion that even the best educated clergy in the queen's Church, those who knew the classics and could read and write in Greek and Hebrew, were nothing more than "ignorant ministers" if they failed to find presbyterianism in the Scripture.[5]

By far the most stimulating and distressing pieces Hooker examined at this time were the infamous *Marprelate Tracts*. Here was truly fresh material, a new style, an effective appeal to the widespread disenchantment with the corruption within the Church. Gone were the dry theological arguments of most previous debates in the English Reformation. In their place, the *Tracts* offered stinging, even vicious, crude, and violent *ad hominem* attacks on individual church leaders, presented in a lively, witty, satirical manner intended to appeal to the always popular appetite for mocking the human foibles of leaders.[6]

Over an eleven-month period, between October 1588 and September 1589, seven of these anonymous *Tracts* appeared over the name "Martin, the Evil Prelate." They were printed illegally by presses that had to be moved from one secret location to another, often just steps ahead of Bishop Bancroft's policemen. The first two were sarcastic broadsides at Bishop Bridges's *Defence*, each carrying a mocking title that began with the words, *Oh read over D. John Bridges for it is a worthy worke*. One ended its long title with the word *Epistle* and the other, *Epitome*. Taken together, they amounted to an unprecedented assault on the personal character and integrity of church leadership that went far beyond earlier attacks.

Like all literate people of his day, Hooker wondered who the author of the *Tracts* might be. The tone and style were nothing like Travers' or Cartwright's. In content, they resembled writings of the separatist radicals Robert Browne and Robert Harrison, whose works had appeared earlier in the decade. Hooker had read Browne's *Reformation without Tarying for Anie* and *Life and Manners of all True Christians*. These works argued that there should be no established religion at all and that Englishmen need pay no attention to the religious regulations of civil magistrates—including, presumably, the queen. Treason and heresy were here combined in a single idea.

A prime candidate for authorship would have been the presbyterian organizer and field-marshal, John Field, had he not died shortly before the *Tracts* appeared. Martin's personal attacks on particular church officials probably reminded Hooker that Field had been compiling a list of specific shortcoming of bishops that would provide a storehouse for just the sort of charges filling the pages of the *Tracts*. It is possible that Field's notes did find their way into Martin's work because, although Field specifically willed that his notes be burned after his death, his executors failed to do so, and his papers passed quickly into the hands of such puritan radicals as John Udall, himself accused of being Martin, and the printer Robert Waldegreve, whose illegal press produced the *Geneva Prayer Book* and other prohibited works written by Penry and his fellow Puritans. (Udall was a popular radical minister at Kingston-on-Thames who was defended not only by the predictable Puritan-lover, Essex, but also by Walter Ralegh.)

In those days, there were many other radical ministers, theologians, and members of parliament who might have crossed the line under the cover of anonymity and gone all the way to penning the radical ideas in the *Marprelate Tracts*. Hooker knew that the prime candidates for authorship were John Penry and Job Throckmorton. The Welsh radical Penry had a well-known hatred for Archbishop Whitgift. He had called the primate an "anti- Christian" known for his "hatred of the Lord" and "one of the dishonarablest [sic] creatures under heaven." Penry was hanged in 1593 on Whitgift's orders.

Job Throckmorton, cousin of the papist Francis Throckmorton, who had been executed in 1584 for his major role in a plot to assassinate the queen, was a wealthy Puritan of noble stock, related to Henry VIII's sixth wife, Catherine Parr. He caught his radicalism at Queen's College, Oxford, in the 1560s, and went on to write the 1572 Second *Admonition to Parliament*—not to be confused with Thomas Cartwright's more famous *Second Admonition*. Throckmorton later sat in parliament in 1586-87 as a leading proponent of Puritan reform. He was sent to the Tower for "lewd and blasphemous" speech but later released. He continued to be a prominent Puritan spokesman for many years thereafter, one who was widely believed to have penned at least some of the earlier *Marprelate Tracts*.[7]

In his *Laws*, Hooker shows his familiarity not only with the *Marprelate Tracts* but also with Throckmorton's writings, thereby lending some credibility to the notion that Hooker believed Job to be the author of the *Tracts*. He even used an exact phrase from Throckmorton's 1592 *A Petition Directed to Her Most Excellent Majesty:* "with whom the truth is they know not," in referring to those who supported the presbyterian discipline. That work was answered, in the same year, by Matthew Sutcliffe, Dean of Exeter Cathedral, in his *Answer to a certain Libel,* in which he specifically named Throckmorton as the author of at least three of the *Marprelate Tracts*.[8]

Whitgift commissioned Bishop Thomas Cooper of Winchester to write a response to the first of the Marprelate pieces. That work carried the typically ponderous title, *An Admonition to the People of England*. The quick response from Martin's pen had the irreverent but delicious title, *Hay any work for Cooper*, evoking the street cry of London barrel makers.

Whoever Martin Marprelate was, his work had a significant impact on Whitgift and the church leadership of the day, including Richard Hooker. These effective appeals to literate public opinion were part of the last and most extreme attempts of radical Puritans to achieve presbyterian reforms in the Church of England during the sixteenth century. The *Tracts* circulated freely through such places of influence and power as the inns of court, the universities, and parliament. They prompted as much delight and glee among those opposed to authority or neutral toward it, as they did consternation within the establishment. The queen and her archbishop saw the writings as a serious threat to the safety and stability of the realm and reacted accordingly. Udall was sent to the Tower. Penry fled to Scotland, with Cartwright not far behind him. Almost all presbyterian leaders, including Cartwright, Travers, and Rainolds, distanced themselves as quickly as they could from Martin Marprelate.

The *Marprelate Tracts* were such a provocative call to arms for those opposed to the sorts of radical change they advocated, and they coincided so closely with the beginnings of Hooker's writing of the *Laws*, that one must assume the *Tracts* played some role in Hooker's decision to write a full *apologia* for the Church. He was surely offended by the vicious, guttersnipe tone of the *Tracts* and was no doubt disappointed by the Church's official responses commissioned by Whitgift. It would simply not do to allow the archbishop and the entire church polity to be ridiculed into irrelevance!

Hooker was also aware that, although severely chastened by the queen's response to the *Marprelate Tracts*, Puritans in the session of parliament meeting in 1589 were pressing forward with their demands for major changes in the Church. The new lord chancellor, Sir Christopher Hatton, felt obliged to open the session with a strong speech against Puritan extremism. After reviewing the long history of papist offences, Hatton turned his attention to what he regarded as the fallacies in presbyterian doctrine and then directed his anger at the illegal activities of the disciplinarians. He was clearly speaking for the queen, who no one doubted had read the *Marprelate Tracts* and was infuriated by them. Hatton's speech did not prevent the Puritans from trying to get their reforms enacted. Edward Coke, Peter Wentworth, Anthony Cope, Edward Lewkenor, James Morice, Robert Beale, and young Humphrey Deavenport were all there in the Commons urging legislation to limit the power of bishops, make changes in the *Prayer Book,* and eliminate clerical pluralism. "One minister, one benefice" was their cry. But the Speaker did not even read out the more radical bills; the sensible, less radical proposals were considered impracticable, and a short parliamentary session ended with no gains for the Puritans, moderate or radical.

Hooker heard all about the parliamentary session at the inns and from Edwin Sandys and other friends and visitors at the Churchmans' house who held seats in parliament or were otherwise closely informed about deliberations in the Commons. He would have been told how old Burghley, ever the friend of Puritans, came forth in the Lords with a speech supporting the reforms, though couched in his usual cautious terms. Whitgift then spoke for the queen—in a speech that has not survived—and appeared to condemn the proposals. The reform bill got no further than a first reading, leaving the queen once more in control.[9]

Hooker was in agreement with some of the reforms advocated by the Puritans in parliament. In his writings, he condemned corruption of various sorts in the Church. He was, nevertheless, appalled by what he supposed to be the true agenda of the radical Calvinists, nothing less than the overthrow of the entire episcopal system and its replacement by a presbyterian, if not separatist, church polity. An idea that had been gestating for some time surely began to take shape in his mind at this juncture. It was an idea large enough to provide an answer both to his mounting anxiety about the future of the Church and his growing desire for a more challenging and congenial future in his own life.[10]

It is not so difficult to read Hooker's mind at this point. The Church of England could be destroyed by these constant attacks if her potential genius as a broad, tolerant, inclusive, middle way between extremes was not fully explicated. No one had adequately explained the special quality of this reformed English Church, or set forth fully how it was grounded in God's law and in the history of England. Hooker thought he knew what this Church was. But no one, including himself, had adequately held up that vision. The definitive *apologia* for his beloved Church of England had yet to be written. Certainly he had not succeeded in articulating a clear picture of it within the compass of occasional polemical sermons in his Temple debate with Travers. In fact he may have thought that the entire experience had demeaned the importance of the enduring issues raised by the Reformation in England. Sermons were not the medium for this work; nor were polemical tracts that merely refuted the attacks of the Church's opponents. What was required was a thoughtful written exposition based upon the first principles of human experience. This would be a monumental undertaking, but one that would prove ultimately to be the calling of his life. By late spring of 1589 he was well into the creation of his immortal defence of the Church and by autumn had settled into a regular daily routine of reading and composition.[11]

The first unveiling of the outline and Preface of the *Laws* was probably offered to Edwin Sandys, who was living at the Churchmans' while in London, and George Cranmer. Hooker respected the opinion of his friends, both of whom were good scholars. More importantly, they were more sophisticated and experienced than he was about the politics of religious debate in England and could give him advice on that score. Richard would also have given his father-in-law word of what he was up to. With characteristic generosity, Churchman found extra space in his crowded house for Hooker to work on his book.

Hooker's first thoughts about his project concerned his title: *Of the Laws of Ecclesiastical Polity*. His intention in the title was to suggest two important points. First, that the key issue dividing members of the Church of England was church structure and governance. On other matters, almost everyone who was not a Catholic was, as he was, a reformed Calvinist Christian. The second point he wished to make in the title was that, whatever the correct form of church polity might be, it would be discovered only by examining the fundamental laws of God and man, some of which were to be found in the customary practices of Englishmen.

Hooker's general plan was to address the issues raised by Calvinist extremists, not by rushing in and refuting them one at a time, but by first examining the nature of all truth and knowledge and then addressing the question of how we discover the right answers to any important question. Next, he would discuss in detail the types of law and which kinds govern which parts of our lives. His purpose here would be to demonstrate that it is law and not personal whim that governs all life, human and divine.

Addressing the epistemological issue—how we know what we know—Hooker planned to deal in Book Two of his work with the issue of whether Scripture is the only source of knowledge of God's law. In Book Three he would explore which forms of church governance are lawful; and in Book Four he would take up specific objections that had been made by Puritans and others against the English church polity.

He would use law as the organizing principle of his treatise. This was the best way he knew to shift the argument from the Puritan ground of self-authenticating Scripture as the source of all knowledge. With this approach he had at least a hope of reaching some lawyers and intellectuals among moderates, men with good minds who already suspected the emotional and dogmatic appeals of the extreme Calvinists. Grounding his argument in law and reason, rather than personal opinion, might give his ideas a wider appeal among influential people.

As for the more vexing practical issues of whether bishops or elders should govern the Church, the role of the crown in church governance, and whether Church and State should be separated, Hooker promised to deal with these matters in Books Six, Seven, and Eight. In Book Five he would set forth and explain the virtues of the Church of England. He would refute specific complaints, principally those of Thomas Cartwright, but would also attempt to rise above current conflicts and write in positive ways about the liturgy and theology of the English Church. He intended to demonstrate that this Church had its own distinctive character among the Christian Churches of the world and to show what its special spirit was.

Sandys and Cranmer, as we know from their later comments on Hooker's work, were generally pleased with the outline, except for what they saw as insufficient attention to immediate political threats to the Church and government from parliamentary Puritans. These two men had more interest in the Preface than other parts of the work. Parliament would be reconvening within a year or so, and they wanted Hooker to speak in his Preface directly to the issues of the day by attacking the political agenda of the Puritans, ridiculing their leaders, and generally displaying his considerable flair for political polemic.

In the event, Sandys and Cranmer were never to be completely satisfied that Hooker was partisan enough in his Preface or other parts of the work to suit their more narrow political agenda. They eventually applied enough pressure on their mentor to induce him to add a final section to the Preface in which he displayed his rhetorical skills to the fullest in the cause of refuting the extreme Calvinism of the presbyterians and separatists.

In the Preface, Hooker displayed his gift for satire when he demonstrated the way in which, in his opinion, radical Calvinists manipulated Scripture to suit their purposes and then preyed on the gullible and weak-minded with simplistic appeals to people's natural suspicions and fears of authority. He laid bare Puritan tactics, exposing Puritan uses of the Bible—how they induced people to find therein whatever suited their fancy. "They fashion," he wrote, "the very notions and conceits of men's understanding in such sort, that when they read scripture, they may think that everything soundeth towards the advancement of that [Calvinist] discipline and to the utter disgrace of the contrary."

Hooker compared the method of the Calvinist extremists, like Cartwright, with that of Pythagoras, thereby making his point very clear to anyone with a university education. In one place, he wrote words which have become a timeless attack on unsophisticated uses of Holy Scripture. He wrote: "When they and their Bibles are alone together, what strange fantastical opinion so-ever at any time entered into their heads, their use was to think the Spirit taught it them." And he went on to show what he believed to be the dangerous results of such fanaticism. His purpose was to reveal, he said, "that when the minds of men are once erroneously persuaded that it is the will of God to have those things done which is their fancy, their opinions are as thorns in their sides, never suffering them to rest till they have brought their speculations into practice."[12]

Then Hooker proceeded to puncture the Calvinist's presumption that they are specially elected by God. He said:

> After the fancy of the common sort has once thoroughly apprehended the Spirit to be the author of their persuasion concerning [church] discipline, then it is instilled in their hearts that the same spirit . . . seals them to be God's children . . . This has bred high terms of separation between such and the rest of the world, whereby the one sort are named 'the brethren,' 'the Godly' and so forth; the other, worldlings, time-servers, pleasers of man not God. . .[13]

In another passage, which no doubt pleased Cranmer and Sandys, Hooker chastised Calvinist extremists for encouraging emotion, simplicity, self-righteousness, and resistance to established authority—and for disparaging education and higher learning as aids to discovering God.

> [Let] any man of contrary opinion open his mouth to persuade them, they close up their ears; his reasons they weigh not. All is answered with rehearsal of the words of John: 'We are of God; he that knoweth God heareth us; as for the rest, ye are of the world, for this world's pomp and vanity it is that [which] you speak, and the world whose you are hears you . . .' Show these eagerly-affected men their inability to judge of such matters, their answer is: 'God has chosen the simple.' Convince them of

> [their] folly, and that so plainly that children upbraid them with it, and they say . . . 'Christ's own apostle was counted mad . . .'[14]

For Hooker, one of the most distasteful characteristics of the more advanced Calvinists was their overt opposition to learning and what he regarded as their arrogant self-righteousness about their own versions of truth. Even the two scholarly Calvinists of the more extreme stripe whom he had known well, John Rainolds and Walter Travers, seemed at times to disparage the very learning that had led them to their present opinions. Now there were the far more direct attacks on the universities and inns of court from radicals like Penry and Throckmorton. On this point, Hooker wrote:

> Neither is it altogether without cause that so many do fear the overthrow of all learning as a threatened sequel of this your intended discipline . . . seeing that the greatest worldly hopes which are proposed as the chiefest results of learning, you seek utterly to extirpate as weeds, and have grounded your platform on such propositions as do after a sort undermine those most renowned habitations . . . [of] commendable arts and sciences [the universities]. To charge you as purposely bent to the overthrow of that wherein so many of you have attained no small perfection would be injurious. Only therefore I wish that you did well consider how opposite certain [of] your positions are to the status of the collegiate societies wherein the two universities consist.[15]

He continued the same theme when he defended the importance of legal studies and described the threat he saw to civil law and courts in the Calvinist insistence on Scripture as the sole source of law.

> Your opinion concerning the law civil is that the knowledge therof might be spared as a thing which this land does not need. Professors in that kind being few, you are the bolder to spurn them . . . in whose studies, although myself have not been much conversant, nevertheless exceedingly great cause I see there is to wish that thereunto more encouragement were given, both in decisions of certain kinds of cases arising daily among ourselves and in commerce with nations abroad, whereunto that knowledge is most requisite. The reasons whereof you would persuade [us] that Scripture is the only rule to frame all our actions by are . . . [no more] effectual for proof that the same is the only law whereby to determine all our civil controversies . . .[16]

Hooker did not base all truth on formal scholarship. His appeal in the Preface to common sense as a basis for knowledge of God's will was a way of saying that truth is available to all thinking people, not just to professors and legal scholars. He made this point directly.

> The first means whereby nature teaches men to judge good from evil . . . is the force of our own discretion . . . [so that] whatsoever we do, if our

> own secret judgement consents not to it as fit and good to be done, the doing of it is to us a sin . . . Some things are so familiar and plain that truth from falsehood and good from evil are most easily discerned in them, even by men of no deep capacity. And in the same way, for the most part, are things absolutely necessary to all men's salvation either to be held or denied, either to be done or avoided.[17]

At some points in the Preface, Hooker became so satirical as to seem to be imitating the *Marprelate Tracts*, especially in his comments on John Calvin. This would have pleased Sandys and Cranmer. Perhaps they put Hooker up to it, for he was a great admirer of Calvin, whose writings he regarded as one of three pillars of the faith and worship of the reformed English Church, along with the *Thirty-nine Articles* and the *Book of Common Prayer*. All leaders of the Church, from John Jewel to John Whitgift, were in Calvin's debt, in Hooker's opinion. His quarrel was only with the Calvinist discipline and with the biblical extremism that some Puritans were trying to impose in England. The presbyterian polity might or might not be suitable for Geneva and other principalities, but here in England, Hooker believed, there was an existing ecclesiastical polity which conformed to the traditions and laws of his country.

Hooker's distinction between Calvin and English Calvinists may have been sincere, but the language with which he attacked Calvin himself in the Preface clouds the distinction.

> Divine knowledge he [Calvin] gathered, not by hearing or reading so much as by teaching others. For though thousands were debtors to him, as touching knowledge . . . yet he to none but only to God, the author of that most blessed fountain the Book of Life.
>
> Nature worketh in us all a love of our own counsels. The contradiction of others is a fan to inflame that love. Our love set on fire to maintain that which we have done, sharpeneth the wit to dispute, to argue and by all means to reason for it.
>
> Wherefore a marvel it were if a man of so great capacity [Calvin] could not espy in the whole Scripture of God [something] . . . which might breed at the least a probable opinion of likelihood that divine authority itself was the same way [as him] inclineable.
>
> All [that] . . . the wit of Calvin was able thence to draw, by sifting the very utmost sentence and syllable, is no more certain than that certain speeches there are which to him did seem to intimate that all Christian churches ought to have their Elderships endued with the power of excommunication and that part of these Elderships . . . should be chosen out from among the laity, after that form which himself had framed Geneva unto.
>
> Will you ask what should move those many learned [men] to be [blind] followers of one man's judgement . . . ? Loth you are to think that they, whom you judge to have attained as sound a level in all points of doctrine as any since the Apostles' time, should be mistaken in discipline

> [church polity]. Such is naturally our affection, that whom in great things we mightily admire, in them we are not persuaded willingly that anything should be amiss . . . Thus in every profession have too many authorized the judgements of a few. This with Germans has caused Luther, and with many other Churches Calvin, to prevail in all things. Yet we are not able to determine whether the wisdom of . . . God might not permit these worthy vessels of his glory to be in some things blemished with the stain of human frailty.[18]

In another place in the Preface, Hooker credits Calvin's deserved reputation as the author of the *Institutes* and the founder of the reformed Christian doctrine, but insists this does not make his views on church governance infallible. Those who go this far in bowing to Calvin will make him as oppressive a master as the pope once was.

> Of what account the Master of Sentences [Pope] was in the church of Rome, the same and more amongst the preachers of reformed churches, Calvin purchased; so that the perfectest divines were judged they which were most skillful in Calvin's writings. His books almost the very canon to judge both doctrine and discipline [polity] by.[19]

Now that he had his outline in hand and a draft of the Preface completed and reviewed by a few friends, Hooker proceeded to work on the rest of his opus. Even with his duties at the Temple and family responsibilities as distractions, he calculated that he could have the entire work done by sometime in late 1592 or early '93. In the meantime, there remained the vexing business of securing Archbishop Whitgift's approval for the project and along with that, a new appointment somewhere outside the Temple.

THE COMMISSION TO WRITE

In early May of 1590 Joan Hooker gave birth to a healthy baby girl who was christened on 10 May at St Augustine's church, next door—the church where Joan and Richard had been married two years earlier. The baby was named Alice, after Joan's mother, who by this time no doubt was a surrogate mother to Richard as well. Of the six children who would grace their marriage, Alice was the only one destined to have a long life.[20]

Before spring turned to summer, Richard took his wife and baby out of the heat of London for the cooler and healthier air of Enfield. Once he had his little family comfortably settled, he may have decided to stay on with them to be sure the infant was all right and to enjoy the relative peace and quiet of the country town, nicely removed from Edwin's and George's well-intended but often annoying questions, suggestions, and naggings about his writing.

At about this time Hooker probably had a meeting with Archbishop Whitgift, either on his own initiative or Whitgift's—we do not know which—to discuss his future. Any hope Hooker had for receiving a specific commission to write a defence of the Church, much less for necessary financial backing for such a project, was disappointed. The archbishop had already asked two other church leaders to undertake this work: Richard Bancroft, bishop of London, and Thomas Cooper, bishop of Winchester.[21]

Coincident with Whitgift's failure to provide official sanction for Hooker's writings, was his failure to offer the master of the Temple Church further advancement in the Church. There would be no deanship, much less a bishopric. The reasons for this decision were much the same as those that prompted the archbishop not to provide a commission for Hooker's *magnum opus*. Nevertheless, Whitgift apparently extended an informal blessing upon Hooker's project, wished him well on its completion, and asked to be kept apprised of progress. He also promised to relieve Richard of his duties as master of the Temple Church as soon as he could find a suitable living for him elsewhere, an appointment that would leave him more time for research and writing.

Throughout the remainder of 1590 and for most of the following year Richard spent most of his spare time working on his book. Whitgift had probably made available his modest library at Lambeth Palace. Here Richard found the resources he needed, the religious and pagan works of his favourites: Aristotle, Cicero, St Augustine, St Thomas Aquinas, Peter Lombard, and others, as well as more recent works by Bodin, Machiavelli, Luther, Erasmus, Calvin, Beza, and Jewel, right up to the contemporary writings of Whitgift, Bancroft, Cartwright, Travers, Stapleton, Penry, Throckmorton, Udall, and others. How much more pleasant were the hours spent reading and note-taking at Lambeth library or writing up at Enfield or at the Churchmans' house than enduring the constant hassles of his job at the Temple!

A most important support for Richard, as he intensified his work on the book during 1590 and 1591, came not from the church hierarchy but from his father-in-law, who provided Richard not only a retreat from his cares at the Temple, but also the invaluable services of his own secretary and amanuensis, the capable Benjamin Pullen. It was Pullen who, with painstaking diligence, translated Richard's hurried and often careless hand into a nearly perfect, printer-ready manuscript. When Hooker finally presented Pullen's copy of his book to the printer in early 1593, it was so beautifully and accurately done that the printer, John Windet, was able to complete the printing with unusual dispatch.

Edwin Sandys was a constant source of help and criticism throughout the long writing process. Living under the same roof allowed for efficient collaboration. Sandys was available to obtain materials from

Lambeth, read and correct drafts, discuss ideas, seek out prospective printers, and provide ready cash for buying paper, books, and other supplies. Although Richard was not always happy with his friend's criticisms, he was grateful for his support and companionship.

George Cranmer also helped by reading drafts and making critical suggestions. Like Sandys, his offerings were substantive, usually urging a more focused attack on radical Puritan opponents of the Church. Cranmer was especially keen on ensuring accuracy in citations and a high level of scholarly integrity. Together, Cranmer and Sandys urged Hooker to a more timely and polemical posture than he was inclined by temperament to assume. Richard's natural disposition was to explain, defend, and extol, rather than attack. In time, he learned to take some pleasure in tweaking the advanced Calvinists with his satirical wit—a facility that improved with practice.

One person whose opinions he especially valued during these months of writing was his old tutor and sometime friend, John Rainolds. Despite their many differences on religious questions, Richard respected Rainolds' breadth of knowledge and his talent as a writer. He also coveted the reactions of a churchman and scholar whose views were more radically Calvinist than his own. Edwin Sandys did not share Hooker's high regard for Rainolds. The arch-Calvinist Rainolds was one of the very extremists Sandys and his friends were battling against in the political arena—men such as William Cole at Corpus, and Travers, Cartwright, Coke, Maurice, Lewkenor in the Commons. Rainolds had recently been advocating at Oxford that all absentee livings in the Church end forthwith, and that there should henceforth be an emphasis on preaching over sacramental liturgies and a greater allowance for lay elders in congregational governance. He had even argued against excommunication as a punishment for heresy. On top of all that, a witness in star chamber had recently cited Rainolds for being a member of the illegal presbyterian classis at Oxford back in the 1580s. Clearly this man was no friend of either the episcopacy or the *Book of Common Prayer*, the two hallmarks of Hooker's ecclesiology.[22] Nevertheless, Hooker persisted in his desire to have his former mentor's reactions to his drafts, and, he hoped, Rainolds' approval of his work. He wished to be as fair and balanced as possible in his attacks on some of Rainolds' positions and to stay in contact with one of England's most respected theologians.[23]

During the early stages of writing, Hooker also sought the opinions of two other intellectual luminaries of the day. One was John Rainolds' successor as president of Corpus Christi, Dr John Spenser. On a number of occasions, he sent portions of his manuscript to Spenser and received critical editorial suggestions. Spenser's views were more congenial with his own than Rainolds' were—so much so that Hooker, later in life, felt comfortable naming Spenser literary executor of his estate. (The day would come when Spenser would be one of the principal editors of Hooker's writings and the author of a famous introductory epistle to the first posthumous edition of the *Laws* in 1604. Some would later go so far as to claim, falsely I believe, that Spenser had actually written sections of Hooker's book.)[24]

The other scholar consulted by Hooker in these early years of writing was Dr Robert Some, master of Peterhouse, Cambridge. Some was an outspoken Puritan, who nevertheless had broken with the extremists during the separatist controversy and had engaged in public debate with both Penry and Throckmorton. Some's *First Godly Treatise*, as we have seen, was among the works Hooker read that had stimulated him to take up his own pen in earnest. From Some, as from Rainolds, Richard would have sought the view of an advanced Calvinist to give him prior notice of likely objections to his more moderate stance on controversial issues.[25]

In April 1591 Joan Hooker gave birth to another daughter. She was christened Cicely at St Augustine's on the 21st of the month.[26] The infant was named for Edwin Sandys' mother, wife of the redoubtable archbishop of York. This name choice was further expression of the closeness of these three families: the Churchmans, the Sandys, and the Hookers. Cicely Sandys was, by all accounts and by evidence of a surviving portrait, a beautiful woman. She was also a woman of remarkable spirit and intelligence, not unusual in this age of Elizabeth I. Little did the happy parents know on this April day, that, by the time their new daughter was in her teens, they would both be dead and their Cicely would be living with her namesake. By the end of May, Joan was once again in Enfield, this time with two baby girls, well in advance of the oppressive heat and dangerous pestilence once again rampant in London.

APPOINTMENT TO SALISBURY

Richard continued to commute back and forth to London, keeping up a presence at the Temple and spending as much time as possible reading at Lambeth library and writing in his workroom at the Churchmans' house. Sometime in the middle of June, he received official word from Lambeth that he was to be made a sub-dean and canon at Salisbury cathedral. The income would be modest, but he would be out of the Temple at last and have more time to devote to his book, and to his growing family.

They would not have to move to Wiltshire. This was largely an absentee cure. Their lives would continue in London much as they had, except that he would not longer go to the Temple each day. His income would be lower. He was not, after all, to be the dean at Salisbury. A sub-dean could only expect some small rural livings in the surrounding area. The money was not of primary importance, however. John Churchman would continue to provide home and hearth.

He was appointed prebendary at Netheravon and also rector at the well-endowed parish of Boscombe, just a few miles north of the cathedral. A curate was available, or could be found, to manage the parish on a regular basis. Hooker's understanding was that the archbishop intended these appointments as a way to free him for virtually full-time work on his book.

Hooker was "presented" by the queen on 21 June and "instituted" by Whitgift on 17 July. On 23 July he was "installed" at Salisbury as a sub-dean and prebendary canon assigned to Netheravon. On the same occasion he subscribed to the *Thirty-nine Articles*. We can only speculate as to why Hooker had not previously made this subscription. The *Articles* had been official church doctrine since the Convocation of 1563. Subscription by all clergy had been required at least since the revised canons of 1571. Hooker should have sworn his allegiance when he was ordained in 1579, or when he took his living at Drayton Beauchamp in 1584, or certainly when he assumed his post as master of the Temple Church in 1585. It is unthinkable that he had refused as a matter of conscience since the theology of the *Articles* is entirely congenial with his own moderate brand of Calvinism. The likely explanation is that he did subscribe earlier but records of the event did not survive. It is probable this 1591 affirmation was merely a *pro forma* re-subscription required by the chapter at Salisbury.[27]

Hooker's new post at Salisbury was within the queen's gift because there was no bishop in residence there at the time. Whitgift had taken the first decent opening the queen had available, knowing how important it was for Hooker to leave the Temple and complete his defence of the Church in a timely manner. He wanted to give Hooker an appointment that would allow him to stay in London with his family. The appointment as a minor non-residentiary canon was probably only temporary, until Whitgift could find him a permanent cure. Hooker would not be expected to spend much time at Salisbury or Boscombe.

There is a long tradition that Hooker resided in the Salisbury close. Izaak Walton had Hooker living at Boscombe and composing the first four Books of the *Laws* while there. Elsie Smith, long-time librarian at Salisbury Cathedral, cited Hooker's oath at the time of his installation at the cathedral: "*quod in Ecclesia sarum predicta continue Residebo*," as evidence of his residence there. On the other hand Sisson was of the opinion that Hooker was never resident in Wiltshire and spent little if any time there, having always understood and accepted that this was an absentee living intended to give him leisure to study and write. Further evidence that Hooker did not live at Salisbury is the fact that he is not listed among residentiary canons at the cathedral in Le Neve's *Fasti Eccleiae*.[28] Suzanne Eward, the present librarian at Salisbury, finds "absolutely" no evidence that Hooker ever resided in the cathedral close. "In all the time Hooker was a prebendary here his name does not seem to have been listed as having been present at a chapter meeting. This surely is proof he was not resident at all."[29]

Hooker's presence at Sub-deans Court in Salisbury has been used by Georges Edelen and others to suggest he was at least sometimes in Salisbury. Chapter records show the name "Richard Hooker" present on "primo December, 1591."[30] This assignment might have been handled for Hooker by a surrogate acting in his behalf. Even if he were present, this would not have required a long stay in Wiltshire.

In July Hooker went to Salisbury for his official installation at the cathedral. As he rode across Salisbury Plain and on down toward the cathedral he would surely have recalled his visit to this area many years ago when he was just a raw youth on his way up to Oxford. How young and innocent he was then, filled with untempered awe at his first sight of the tall spire and even more overwhelmed by the towering reputation of his patron, the brilliant John Jewel. Now, nearly a quarter century later, he was returning to Salisbury, a seasoned church leader in his own right, no less in awe of this fabled place, but much better informed about how important Sarum (Salisbury) was to the history of the Church.

While at Salisbury, Hooker made his formal subscription to the *Thirty-nine Articles*, signed the chapter register, and attended the meeting at which he was installed as canon and prebendary. He was also escorted to Boscombe and introduced to the curate there. St Andrews, Boscombe was a small Norman church. The exterior stone and flint construction and the interior nave, chancel, and north transept are substantially as they were when Richard first viewed them more than four hundred years ago. Hooker was probably somewhat disappointed when he first saw the church. The edifice was not so grand as his friend Laurence Chambers' church in Enfield, which he may have coveted, nor so picturesque and pastoral as his own charge at Drayton Beauchamp a decade earlier. He had expected a grander building from the fact that the living at Boscombe had a long and distinguished history and commanded a substantial endowment. Perhaps some day, he may have thought, Whitgift would find him something better than this, a living like his earlier pastoral retreat at Drayton Beachamp, but a place close to some great cathedral and library.[31]

NOTES

1. One such occasion when a student was admitted on Hooker's recommendation is recorded in Inderwick, 357.
2. This incident is recorded in Inderwick, 360-61. Any direct involvement of Hooker in the affair is speculation on my part.
3. McGinn, 44. Hooker gave full expression to his distaste for the tendency to end debate by simple reference to Calvin in his highly satirical treatment of the famous Genevan in the preface to the *Laws*. See *Folger*, I, 3-12; *Works,* I, 127-39.

4. McGinn, 65-67.
5. *Ibid.*, 79.
6. My discussion of the *Marprelate Tracts* draws on McGinn and Neale as well as Leland H. Carlson, *Martin Marprelate, Gentleman Master Job Throckmorton Laid Open in his Colours* (San Marino: Huntington Library, 1981). See also, Dawley, 185; Collinson, *Elizabethan Puritan Movement*, 391-97, 403-04; Brook, 125-38. Copies of Whitgift's original depositions against printing "Martins Libelees," as he called them, are in the Lambeth Library, *Fairhurst Papers,* #3470, fols. 105-106.
7. Differences of opinion about authorship of the *Tracts* continue to the present day. Walter Travers, who is mentioned in the *Tracts*, is one of many suspects. McGinn, 167-8, makes a case for Penry. Carlson, 303-305 disagrees, going so far as to disparage McGinn's scholarship. His candidate, and mine, is Job Throckmorton. Collinson says that Throckmorton is "almost certainly" Martin. *Elizabethan Essays,* 243. Cartwright's authorship of the Second Admonition is also in doubt. Pearson asserts that many of Travers' contemporaries, including Hooker, did not ascribe authorship to Cartwright. Pearson, *op. cit.*, 74.
8. See, Carlson, 120.
9. For the best account of this parliament, see Neale, 216-31.
10. That the *Marprelate Tracts* were an important stimulus for Hooker's writing the *Laws* is not a new idea. Although differing in many respects, two recent commentators on the history of the *Tracts*, McGinn and Carlson, agree that they were an important factor in Hooker's writings. McGinn goes the farthest in insisting that Hooker specifically refutes the *Tracts* in his Preface to the *Laws*. I am inclined to agree. I am less certain about McGinn's speculation that Whitgift directly "assigned the task to Hooker" of responding to Martin, although I think a plausible case can be made that Hooker was among those like Bancroft, Bridges, Some, Cooper, and Sutcliffe who were "enlisted" by Whitgift at various times to aid in his own defence against the Puritan extremists. McGinn, ix; 206-12.
11. The most succinct argument among modern scholars for Hooker's place as the premier formulator of the "Anglican mind" is Patrick Collinson's comparison of Hooker's writing as the "one work of genius" amongst many "tedious and uninspired writings in emergent Anglicanism." Hooker, Collinson believes, set the definitive benchmark against which Puritanism is to be measured: his affirmation and their denial of the principle that a citizen of the State and member of a Church are one and the same. The argument that Hooker conceived the idea to write the *Laws* as an outgrowth of his debate with Travers and without any specific commission or involvement by Whitgift, was implied by Walton and has found continued acceptance down to our own day, though Sisson makes a case for the contrary view that at least the early books of the *Laws* were a collaborative effort authorized and supervised by Whitgift. No doubt Whitgift approved and encouraged the project, but Hooker had sufficient motivation and strength of character to proceed on his own initiative and to press his own agenda for what should be in the work. And, I find it most unlikely that Whitgift helped compose the work. Bauckham argues that the doctrinal differences between Hooker and Travers have been exaggerated and that Whitgift did not approve of Hooker's performance at the Temple, or of his Catholic-leaning views, sufficiently to commission him officially to write a defence of the Church. I find this view persuasive as a partial explanation for Hooker's leaving the Temple and not being offered a higher position or an official commission to write the *Laws.* The Archbishop's views on some subjects were actually closer to Travers' opinions than Hooker's.

See Collinson, *op. cit.*,, 22, 103, 294, 315, 430-31; Bauckham, 50. Another compelling argument along similar lines is Diarmaid MacCulloch, *op. cit.* A contrary view, that the English Reformation was essentially completed long before Hooker wrote, is offered by Rosemary O'Day, *The Debate on the English Reformation* (London:

Methuen, 1986). Her fascinating conclusion is based on an assessment of the religious ideas and practices of working clergy rather than policies at the high levels of Church and state. For the argument that Hooker might well have conceived the idea to write the *Laws* without any specific commission or involvement by Whitgift see, e.g., Hill, *Studies*, 129-30. Sisson, 45-49, makes the case for the view that the project had Whitgift's support and "blessing". He also cited Chancery Court records to suggest that Whitgift was one of a number of "eminent persons" who saw Hooker as a "deputed spokesman of the church." 4-6; 145.

12. *Folger*, I, 16, 44; *Works,* I, 147-8, 185.
13. *Folger*, I, 18; *Works*, I, 151.
14. *Folger*, I, 19-20; *Works*, I, 153-4.
15. *Folger*, I, 39-40; *Works*, I, 178-9.
16. *Folger*, I, 41; *Works*, I, 180-1.
17. *Folger*, I, 12-13; *Works*, I, 143.
18. *Folger*, I, 3, 10, 26-27; *Works*, I, 128, 138-9; 162-3.
19. *Folger*, I, 11; *Works*, I, 189.
20. Sisson, 124. *St Augustine Parish Register* gives Alice's christening date as January, 1590. Alice lived to be 61 and died on 20 December 1649. None of the other three girls lived beyond the age of 22. The two boys died in infancy.
21. There is no hard evidence as to who initiated Hooker's move from the Temple Church. It could have been Whitgift as much as Hooker himself. Or some intermediary might have spoken to the archbishop on Hooker's behalf, or to Hooker on the archbishop's behalf. Nor is there evidence that Whitgift actually gave prior approval for the writing of the *Laws* or of a personal meeting between Hooker and Whitgift to confirm his new appointment. Nevertheless, the circumstantial evidence makes a compelling case for Whitgift's awareness of and at least tacit approval for Hooker's project. Izaak Walton offers the same view by putting into Hooker's mouth a long appeal to Whitgift for a quiet living where he might write his opus. *Life*, 66-8.
22. Haugaard, "The Preface," *Folger*, VI.I, 52-3, describes Rainolds as "the most prominent Puritan theologian" at Oxford. See also Gibbs, *Folger* VI.I, 307.
23. That Hooker maintained a friendship with Rainolds and corresponded with him about the *Laws* and other matters is clear from Cranmer's notes to this effect on a MSS copy of Book VI and other references to their correspondence. See *Folger*, III, 112; *Works*, III, 111-112.
24. Hamlett Marshall, a posthumous editor of a sermon by Spenser, made this claim in 1605. See Haugaard, *op. cit.*, 57, n. 119. Spenser's wife, Susannah, made the same claim to Hooker's biographer, Izaak Walton. Novarr, 268-272, discredits this idea. Although unsubstantiated and discredited, these stories probably contain an element of truth that Hooker may have consulted rather extensively with Spenser.
25. George Cranmer refers to Some's apparent review of some early parts of the *Laws.* See *Folger*, III, 112. We have no hard evidence on the nature and extent of his influence on Hooker.
26. Sisson, 124.
27. See John Le Neve, *Fasti Ecclesiae Anglicanae 1541-1857*, compiled by Joyce M. Horn (University of London Institute of Historical Research, 1986), 60. For an excellent analysis of the history and impact of the *Articles*, see Haugaard, *Elizabeth and the English Reformation*, esp. 233-234, 257.
28. Walton, *Life*, 68-69; Elsie Smith, "Hooker at Salisbury," *Times Literary Supplement*, 30 March, 1962, 223; Sisson, xiii, 45-46; Le Neve, *Fasti Ecclesiae,* x.
29. Miss Eward disabused the author of a cherished notion, which he doubtless has shared with many other Hooker followers, that Hooker's residence in the close at Salisbury was supported, if not confirmed, by the fact that the sub-dean's house at 18 The Close, near St Anne's Gate, bore the name "Hooker House." Miss Eward's

predecessor as cathedral librarian had stated flatly that Hooker was "allocated" a house in the close and there wrote the first four Books of the *Laws,* using the cathedral library for resource material. In fact, says Miss Eward, the Hooker name was merely affixed to the old sub-dean's residence some years ago by a tenant probably filled with wishful thinking. It has no historical standing. The current tenant has removed the sign. (Private letter to author, 10 July 1996).

Edelen "Chronology," *Folger*, VI.2, xxiii-xxiv, relies on records in chapter Act Books at the cathedral which he believes placed Hooker at the installation of Bishop Coldwell and at Sub-dean's court in 1591. Haugaard relies on this evidence to indicate that Hooker may have spent a significant amount of time in Wiltshire during these years. Examination of cathedral records by Suzanne Eward and her archivist assistant, Pamela Stewart, reveals that far from attending Coldwell's installation, Hooker was among those chastised for not doing so! The oft-cited folio which Edelen believes named Hooker as present, (15r, Book 16, *Peruddocke*), is only a list of those ordered to attend. Another list shows his name among those who were cited as being "contumacious" for failing to do so. Other chapter records show that, indeed, because of the negligence of such as Hooker, there was no quorum present for the election and proxies had to be appointed to secure enough votes to elect Coldwell. See "Dean of Chapter Records," *Presses*, 10, PRO Trowbridge, Wiltshire, and *Press IV*, "Procuritoria," 2 Dec., 1591, for letters of the dean of the chapter, John Bridges, naming persons as proxies for the election and for related materials. See also Box in the cathedral library.

30. See *Subdeans Act Book*, 1589-1596, D4/3/2, fol 6, Wiltshire Public Records Office, Trowbridge.

31. I am indebted to the Rev. Geoffrey Davies, vicar at Boscombe when I first visited there in 1986, for giving me an historical tour of the building and showing keen interest in the question of Hooker's possible residence there. Davies showed me an early edition of Hooker's *Laws* kept carefully under lock and key in a chest near the back of the nave as evidence of the "Hooker tradition" at Boscombe, if not of the great man's actual residence there.

CHAPTER 15

Of the Laws of Ecclesiastical Polity

It is impossible to know with certainty exactly when the eight books of the *Laws* were written. It is most likely that by the autumn of 1591, shortly after his appointment at Salisbury, Hooker had completed a first draft of most of the work, although Book VI may not have been finished in draft before 1593.[1] Hooker's own notes, as well as those of Edwin Sandys and George Cranmer, argue for completion of that book not before late in that year at the earliest. As he reviewed the manuscript of his book, Hooker had input from a number of friends and associates, most notably Edwin Sandys, who was often resident with Hooker at the Churchmans' house during these years.[2]

BOOK I

Sandys, like most others who have ever read Book I, would have been impressed immediately by Hooker's treatment of the origins and types of law, and by his grounding of all human institutions, divine and human, in the reasonableness (lawfulness) of heavenly and divine ordinances. Clearly Hooker's writing in Book I ranks with the finest theoretical treatments of law and civil society. His exposition of the reasonableness of law, and his demonstration of how obedience to it is connected to God's rational purposes, is probably unparalleled in English writing. Not only does Book I serve as a superb introduction to the rest of the *Laws*, but it is in its own right a complete treatise. If Hooker had written nothing more, his place as a premier political philosopher would have been assured by this treatise.

At the beginning of Book I, Hooker warned that some hard intellectual work on the part of his readers would be necessary to discover the legal foundations of the English system of government. His book would not be another facile treatment of present-day issues, but a serious exploration of the origin and nature of law and government. Hooker would address enemies and friends alike in a tone they were not accustomed to. He would speak with the voice of an Aristotle, Cicero, St Augustine, St Thomas, St Paul as a philosopher of life, not a mere quibbler in the current religious debates.

Hooker defined law in such a broad way as to identify it with the order, harmony, and reasonableness of all creation and not merely what could be enforced by a powerful ruler. He sought to provide a basis for distinguishing lawful from unlawful acts of rulers and subjects alike. The distinguishing characteristic of a law was not the sanctions behind it, but the reasonableness of its commands. He asserted that the purpose (object) of a law, properly named, is virtue, goodness, the well-being of those upon whom it acts. Law is whatever reason defines as goodness and requires that we pursue. If a precept has been assented to in a commonwealth for a long time, there is a presumption that it is reasonable and hence a true law. Law is reason embodied in custom. In this sense, virtue, custom, and reason are all clues to the presence of law. If an ordinance promotes virtue, conforms to custom, and appeals to the common sense of our reason, it is probably a law.

The contrary claim of some followers of Calvin that all law comes from God and that God revealed his law only in Scripture is an error, according to Hooker, because this opinion fails to account for the fact that so many laws, rightly defined, are not to be found in Scripture. The Puritans err on several other points as well. For one thing, they oversimplify God's law for humankind by identifying it solely with God's will. One of Hooker's most brilliant strokes in Book I was to affirm that God's very nature may be seen as the *reason* (law) that defines his own working, not merely his *will*.

God, so far as we will ever know him, *is* the reasonableness of all things, including himself. God, for Hooker, is an not arbitrary and wilful creator and judge, but a reasonable and so lawful creator. We know him because he has given us the faculty of reason enabling us to see his nature, *i.e.*, his goodness—which is to say, his reasonableness. In a broader sense, God's full nature, for Hooker, is ultimately mysterious because he often acts in ways that human reason cannot fathom. Still, so far as God acts in the world, and especially toward humankind, he usually does so in a manner that is lawful, in that it conforms to the reasons for which he created humankind and the universe in the first place.

Some Calvinist extremists err further, according to Hooker, by insisting that only what can be found in Scripture is a basis for human law. In this they limit God's means for revealing his nature and his commands. To the contrary, Hooker said, God shows himself to humankind in his natural laws, through his acts in human history, and in the mind of human beings—as well as in Scripture. The Bible is but one source for our laws, and even the Bible cannot be understood except through the exercise of reason. The Puritans' claim that the religious practices of the Church of England are invalid because they are not specifically sanctioned in Scripture is facile and unconvincing, so far as Hooker is concerned. Scripture is, of course, a complete and sufficient guide in the matters for which God gave it to us, namely matters of salvation. But even here, reason is required to fathom its meaning. Furthermore, this is a special sort of reason which is expressed not in each individual person's private opinion—even if that person is Calvin himself—but in the corporate judgements of the Church, over time.

An important part of Hooker's theory of law in Book I is his distinction between changeable and unchangeable laws. That distinction helps to explain why laws governing civil society may differ according to time and place but laws affecting our salvation and the working of nature and the universe are immutable. For Hooker, the Puritans were wrong in insisting upon one universal form of church government and practice for all Christians—which would be, of course, whatever polity they happened to prefer, most likely the presbyterian form. By casting this debate on the higher ground of the nature of law, Hooker illumined what for him was the answer to the vexing issue of what was the correct church polity, namely that while some matters are eternally fixed by God's immutable wisdom, others are left for humans to determine according to wider and more varying standards of reasonableness. Church governance and practice fall into this latter category.

In Book I, Hooker went so far as to suggest that those who thought they could find in Scripture all the law they needed for every individual and social contingency were demeaning God's true purposes in Holy Scripture:

> [A]s a man whose wisdom is in weighty affairs admired would take it in some disdain to have his counsel solemnly asked about a toy, so the smallness of some things is such, that to search the Scripture of God for the ordering of them were to derogate from the reverend authority and dignity of the Scripture, no less than they do by whom Scriptures are in ordinary talk very idly applied unto vain and childish trifles.[3]

Both in its broadest reach and in each small aspect, Hooker's grasp of law in Book I is the genius of the entire work. For him, law was the creative force of the universe. He tried to show how all existence: divine, angelic, natural, supernatural, human, national, international, religious and secular, is related in one vast, ordered, reasonable, system of law. Law is the origin, the explanation, and the creative force for good in life. Law is the end toward which all things tend. It is the wisdom of God, the foundation of human society, the dictate of reason, the instrument of virtue. Hooker's famous summary cannot be improved upon or heard too often.

> [O]f law there can be no less acknowledged, than that her seat is the bosom of God, her voice the harmony of the world: all things in heaven and earth do her homage, the very least as feeling her care, and the greatest as not exempted from her power; Angels and men and creatures of what condition soever, though each in different sort and

manner, yet all with uniform consent, admiring her as the mother of their peace and joy.[4]

Building upon his theory of law, Hooker suggested the beginnings of a theory of government that incorporated the notion of popular sovereignty recently enunciated by the French philosopher, Jean Bodin, himself drawing on a strong medieval strand of thought. Like Bodin, Hooker insisted that all legitimate political power comes originally from the community and may return to it again under certain dire circumstances. He speaks of a social compact whereby power was first transferred from the people to a government, perhaps a monarch. Such notions were later used to justify rebellion against kings. Is this where Hooker was headed—toward a modern theory of consent and revolution, *à la* John Locke and Thomas Jefferson?[5] Certainly not! Hooker meant only that, as Aristotle said, we are all political animals by nature and cannot live in isolation outside society. Since selfishness puts us at war with one another in an ungoverned society, we form civil governments to maintain peace and provide the order necessary for our general tranquillity. Only in this general and theoretical sense did Hooker speak of popular sovereignty and social compact.

Still, Hooker did seem to do more than merely hint at the proposition that government rests upon the consent of those governed and that there is, therefore, some prospect of recalling an unjust ruler and returning to the natural state of popular sovereignty. But, he made it clear that once a government was established, the presumption was that it thenceforth had the tacit consent of the people even though they did not actually approve its particular laws or deeds. Hooker's ideas in this area were not fully developed. He moved cautiously from a general theory of popular sovereignty and social compact into the dangerous ground of practical politics—a ground inhabited by real kings who were apt to be uneasy with opposition to their rule from those who claimed some original right to make their own laws. These were dangerous times, and such ideas as this could be easily misconstrued. When he expanded on some of these notions in Book VIII, Hooker, as we shall see later, waded still farther into these troubled waters.[6]

BOOK VI

Edwin Sandys' enthusiasm for Hooker's discussion of law and politics in Book I did not extend to his mentor's views on courts and their jurisdiction in Book VI.[7] He agreed with Hooker's assertion of the appropriateness of church-court jurisdiction in matters touching church governance, Sacraments, preaching, and like matters. He also concurred that bishops were the proper recourse in religious disputes, because, as Hooker said in citing Ignatius, bishops bear the image of God and Christ. But Sandys could not countenance Hooker's tendency to expand the Church's legal jurisdiction into areas where there was an overlapping with civil courts. Performing marriages, probating wills, interpreting testaments, managing estates, and the like belonged properly in civil courts, in Sandys' opinion. Common and civil law, not canon law, should apply in such matters.

Hooker, on the contrary, wrote in Book VI that there was a long and valid tradition of church jurisdiction in these cases. Sandys' position, he felt, only gave comfort to presbyterians like Matthew Sutcliffe, who was then advocating that consistory courts of lay elders and clergy should have wide jurisdiction over matters of social and religious behaviour. Those radical Calvinists would love to make common cause with civil lawyers like Edwin Sandys as part of their strategy to overturn the authority of the established Church. They had even advocated placing the queen under the jurisdiction of their consistory courts. How could Sandys and other friends of the established Church fail to see the danger in promoting jurisdiction for non-church courts? Furthermore, Hooker said, there was danger in expanding secular courts because civil lawyers had a tendency to pursue their own personal gain rather than justice, whenever money was to be made out of a case. Civil judges should pay more attention to curbing the greed of lawyers and less time trying to extend their jurisdiction over church matters. All things considered, this was no time to allow civil courts to breach the historic separation between religious and secular legal jurisdiction. Where there was ambiguity or overlapping, it would be best to resolve the matter in favour of ecclesiastical jurisdiction.

Sandys' major disagreement with Hooker over Book VI had to do not with court jurisdictions, but with Hooker's views on the subject of confession and penance. Although Edwin shared Hooker's anti-presbyterianism, he never liked it when his mentor seemed to stray too far in the opposite direction and embrace what he regarded as such Romish practices as confession, absolution, excommunication, and oaths of conformity. He failed to see, in any event, what these practices had to do with the major subject of Book VI, which he took to be the jurisdiction of church courts.[8]

In fact, Hooker specifically condemned the "sacrament" of penance, the Catholic emphasis on private confession, and the idea that works of penance were a condition for absolution. His general emphasis was on public (corporate) confession and God's loving grace. Nevertheless, he did assert a connection between penance and church-court jurisdiction. In a general sense, the two were related because each had to do with the question of jurisdiction and so with legitimate authority. In so far as it controlled the matter of penance, the Church had jurisdiction over the inner spiritual lives of people. In so far as it controlled matters of moral behaviour, through its courts, the Church had jurisdiction over the external lives of people as they lived them out in society. The question of where jurisdiction lies was a key issue in both instances.[9]

If the church courts had extensive jurisdiction in matters of personal and social behaviour, Hooker felt, this would make it clear that the Church had the power to punish for a wide range of transgressions. It mattered that people have some fear of church courts because of the importance of penitence to their salvation. What separates man from God is his sin. Therefore, how we get rid of sin is the key to our spiritual health. This we do by repenting. Why do we repent? In part, at least, because of fear: fear of God's wrath, fear of public disgrace, fear of the punishments meted out by the courts. True enough, this fear is no excuse for requiring acts of penance which enrich the coffers of the Church, as it does for the papists. It is also true that the assurance of God's free, forgiving love at the end of this painful process of penitence mediates our fear. But without the foreknowledge, and so the fear, of having to make an outward public show of penitence in Church, the full healing grace of Christ through his body, the Church, might not be available.

In other words, Hooker argued here that faith in God leads the wrongdoer to fear his wrath and, at the same time, the wrath of the Church, even as he trusts in God's love for those who repent their sins within the body of the Church. And, since repentance is the one avenue that sinners have back to God, the Church's courts must have a hand on the instruments of worldly judgement and punishment which lead men to penitence. For Sandys, as perhaps for us, Hooker's logic here is somewhat strained. What we are left with is advocacy of an expanded legal jurisdiction residing in the Church, in part out of a desire to frighten people into repenting so that they will then be able to accept God's free gift of forgiveness. What Hooker seems to be arguing is that anything that helps sinners to repent, including a fear of the Church's penalties, is a good thing. If the Church could only condemn and not inflict penalties, then fear-leading-to-repentance might be absent. This is not unlike the Catholic "imperfect contrition" based on fear of hell rather than love of God, but much more subtle than the pope's selling indulgences. But was it less damaging to the freedom of the repentant soul? Perhaps not.

What is clear from Hooker's discussion of penance in Book VI is that he was seeking a middle ground between what he believed was the essential truth in the Catholic doctrine of penance and what he also believed was the validity of the reformed affirmation of man's freedom to sin and repent and God's freely given grace in his offer of forgiveness to the penitent sinner. While Hooker's connection between penance and an expanded jurisdiction for church courts is so pragmatic as to seem at first blush duplicitous, his intention is to insist on the importance of maintaining a visible and effective presence for the spiritual life—repentance and forgiveness—within the legal structures of a Christian commonwealth.

Sandys was so annoyed with Hooker's discussion of penance and court jurisdiction in Book VI that he managed to prevent publication of large sections of the Book when he had the opportunity to do so after Hooker's death. Clearly the entire matter was a source of serious contention between the two men.[10]

BOOKS II, III, IV

Discussions with his readers about the first four books of the *Laws* were less contentious than those about the Preface and Book VI. Book I, as we have seen, was a triumph and no doubt regarded as such from the outset. The central theme of Book II was that Puritans err when they view Scripture as the only law for man and that this insistence reveals their cramped and unphilosophical view of life, not to mention a serious epistemological dilemma. It was Hooker's intent in this Book to refute Thomas Cartwright's negative argument from Scripture that, because the English church polity was not found there, it must be discontinued. The disciplinarians were far too extreme in their use of Scripture, Hooker said. They would insist upon its approval for every minuscule part of life, even as to whether people should use rush or straw to cover their floors. As the Apostle Paul taught us, God's great wisdom is revealed in many ways, including his glorious work in nature, our human experiences with him, the exercise of our reason, by personal inspiration, and through his Holy Word.[11]

Hooker agreed that Scripture was the final authority regarding the purpose for which it was intended, namely, our salvation. In other areas, unless Scripture specifically forbids it, we may act according to standards of truth as revealed to us by God in other ways. In any event, the meaning of Scripture is rarely self-evident. Hooker seems to be infuriated by the popular idea that any ordinary person's opinion was valid as to the meaning of God's Word. He wrote, in Book II, that such an idea,

> being once inserted into the minds of the vulgar sort, what it may grow unto God only knows. Thus much we see, it has already made thousands so headstrong even in gross and palpable errors, that a man whose capacity will scarcely serve him to utter five words in sensible manner blushes not in any doubt concerning matters of Scripture to think his own bare YEA as good as the NAY of all the wise, grave, and learned judgements that are in the whole world: which insolency must be repressed, or it will be the bane of Christian religion.

Hooker thought that it was rare for the meaning of Scripture to be self-evident. The authority of the Church and its scholars was necessary to interpret the Holy Word. If we must choose between the biblical interpretations of that time-honoured authority, the Church, and the opinion of some rebellious ministers dressed up as so-called "Disciples of God," the choice for Hooker was obvious.[12]

In Book II Hooker made one of his rare specific mentions of a person who had been important in his personal life, in this case his early patron, the Calvinist icon John Jewel. Hooker took offence at Cartwright's use of Jewel as an authority for some ideas with which he disagreed. The bishop of Salisbury, he said, was "the worthiest divine bred in Christendom for the space of some hundreds of years," and he simply would not have him misquoted in this way.[13]

In Book III, Hooker continued the argument that Scripture does not ordain any particular form of church governance and that consequently the disciplinarian Calvinists were wrong in attacking the English church polity. Scripture provides a broad outline for the spiritual, invisible church: one body, one Lord, one faith, one baptism. But in this visible world of ours, the Bible is largely silent as to the details of church polity, leaving us free to design our own outward forms of church government and practice. If Scripture comes close to mandating any particular discipline, it is probably not the one advocated by Cartwright and his followers. Sandys was pleased that Hooker referred by name to such Calvinist foes as Thomas Cartwright. That would help him and his allies in their parliamentary contest with the Puritan extremists. Sandys and Cranmer were always happy when Hooker illustrated his general points by reference to current political issues and personalities, and wished that he would do so more frequently.[14]

Hooker tried in Book III to expand the definition of church polity beyond matters of governance and orders of ministry to include common prayer, ceremonial practices, baptismal and eucharistic rites. There was more at stake in the conflict with Calvinist extremists than the choice between bishops and elders. To explain his ideas, Hooker appropriated and enlarged a concept that quickly became a hallmark of his *apologia* for the Church. This was the distinction between matters essential to salvation and those things, such as forms of church governance and liturgical practice, that were "indifferent" to salvation. The former were prescribed in Scripture and universally applicable. The latter were important, but not essential, and might appropriately differ from time to time and place to place according to the varying traditions of Christian communities.

Humans are to use their God-given reasoning power to understand and evaluate these "indifferent" matters of church polity and liturgy, even as they use their minds to interpret Scripture in order to understand what is necessary to salvation. In each case, reason is the key. We never escape the need to use this marvellous facility. Hooker said that he marvelled at the ingenuity of those biblical literalists who used their reason so willingly when disparaging reason's authority to understand the word of God and yet denied its efficacy in discovering God's will.

In one of the most important and memorable parts of Book III, Hooker made his plea for tolerance within the "visible" Church here on earth. Nothing better characterizes this premier Anglican than his insistence that men have no business judging one another as to who is and who is not a true Christian. To God alone belongs this right. Hooker affirmed that all, including Roman Catholics, who profess one Lord, one faith, one baptism are members of the Church, no matter how much they sin, so long as they continue in that profession of their faith.

Living a life of "moral righteousness," "hope", "charity," "faith," and "love" is important to salvation and membership in the "invisible church" of God. But here in the Church on earth, all that is required is outward profession of faith in Christ. Hooker wrote "If by external profession they be Christians, then are they [members] of the visible Church of Christ . . . although they be impious idolaters, wicked heretics . . ."[15]

This was a powerful, if largely unheeded, message of reconciliation to a national Church torn by internal dissension.

Edwin Sandys enjoyed Hooker's biting comments at the place in Book III where his mentor described what he regarded as the "utter conceit" of those who thought there was no Church at all "until Martin Luther invented it." Clearly, Hooker had a more modest view than many of his colleagues as to what the Reformation had accomplished. He also castigated by name Calvin and John Knox who, as he saw it, were so "crazed" in their hatred of Roman Catholics that they refused to baptize Catholic children. The Calvinist extremists, he said, were masking their dangerous and radical attitudes about the Church of England behind their hateful attacks on Romanists. This might fool some, but Hooker was not deceived about what he believed was their true intention which was to overthrow the established Church. This was the kind of writing Sandys liked to see from his friend.[16]

In Book IV, Hooker made his case for the Church's right to use or discard romanist or reformed ceremonies and practices as it saw fit. It was only natural (reasonable) for English people to prefer Catholic practices since their fathers had been raised in that Church. In any event, as he had shown in Book III, these were matters "indifferent," to be determined by reference to the customs of each country's own national Church. Throughout Book IV, Hooker used Scripture to prove his points as he refuted Thomas Cartwright's criticisms of the established Church, one at a time. Hooker may have found this sort of writing tedious. But it was characteristic of religious debate of the day, and he knew it would please Sandys and Cranmer because it lent itself to isolating particular political issues.

Hooker's anguish over the religious intemperance of his day emerges with special eloquence in Book IV. He despairs over an age in which "zeal has drowned charity," and skill in argument has "quenched meekness" of spirit. He bemoans the fact that, as he sees it, Calvinist extremists cannot find more important things to occupy their time than quibbles and quarrels over church ceremonies. He argues that what really bothers Puritans and disciplinarians is that church authorities do not seem to hate Catholics enough. Surely the burden of proof is not on the Church of England to defend its traditional polity and ceremonies but upon those who would have the Church change. Their mere "methinketh," he said, should have no credence before the established wisdom and authority of the Church of England.[17]

PRESSURE FROM FRIENDS

Throughout the remainder of 1591 and all of 1592, as Hooker continued the task of completing and revising the *Laws*, he reviewed suggestions from his readers, including, in addition to Sandys and Cranmer, John Spenser, John Rainolds, Lancelot Andrewes, and Robert Some.[18] George Cranmer proof-read many pages of the manuscript, notably Book VI. George was a stickler for detail, often finding places where Hooker had been careless in citing sources or criticizing particular word choices, and pointing out grammatical errors. He was, in many respects, Hooker's severest critic. For example, he did not like the phrase "obligatory declaration" in Book VI because he thought it failed to communicate Hooker's meaning that if someone disobeyed the law they would be punished. Why didn't Hooker just say what he meant? In another place, Cranmer pointed to the need for a parenthesis around a phrase and, in another, a sentence that began "Towards thyself" he thought was poorly written.[19]

Hooker's ego was probably bruised by these criticisms, but he knew that he needed some help with his grammar and composition. He was no doubt aware of his tendency to be a bit lazy about citations. He was so familiar with his authorities that it was a great bother to check them all for accuracy. At some of their sessions, Cranmer went so far as to correct Hooker's Greek. He even suggested that his mentor insert long sections of historical material that he had researched and written himself. Hooker may have taken offence, especially at some of George's substantive suggestions, and told him so. He would not soften his views on the jurisdiction of church courts, nor would he eliminate the section on penance. It was not necessary to remind him that Dr Some had said he wished for more perspicuity in his style, or that John Rainolds would be able to verify some of his citations. He could remember those painful items quite well by himself, thank you![20]

Edwin Sandys continued to talk with Hooker about revisions in the *Laws* during these years when Sandys was frequently in residence at the

Churchmans. Sandys tended to be gentler than Cranmer with his complaints and suggestions, perhaps mellowing as he grew older. Edwin usually began his objections with friendly phrases like, "Probably" or "It seems to me that" or "I think." His recommendations for change, although fewer and often more gently proffered than Cranmer's, were no less substantive. He continued to press the issue of church versus civil court jurisdiction, and specifically challenged Hooker to show why cases involving marriage, bastardy, and estate settlement should be decided in religious courts. He also worried about what he regarded as Hooker's carelessness in citing sources, and urged Richard to quote directly from Travers, Cartwright, and other opponents more frequently and more directly throughout the work. Unless Hooker set forth the exact references he was refuting, his work would lack integrity. Edwin went so far as to tell his mentor that, for his own good, he should be more careful about "bare narrations" that were neither quoted nor credited. He knew that Hooker had a great storehouse of knowledge in his head but urged his friend to be more precise about his sources.[21]

In the spring of the year, Joan had good news for her husband. They would be parents again before winter, and there was no reason not to expect another healthy baby. They would all go up to Enfield to escape the dangers of London in the summer. Richard could write there as well in the city. If the newborn were a girl, they would name her Jane, for her mother. If a boy, it would be John, for John Churchman. (The supposition that the namesakes chosen were Richard's mother and uncle is unlikely.) In the event, Jane Hooker was baptized at Enfield on 1 October 1592. Hooker was thirty-eight years old. This was his third daughter in as many years.[22]

Meanwhile, pressure was mounting on Hooker to have his book ready for publication by the end of the year. The treatise was needed, as Sandys and Cranmer repeatedly reminded him, to serve as a reputable tract to counter anticipated Puritan attacks on the Church in the forthcoming parliament. Puritan radicals were already gearing up for the session, scheduled for early 1593. It was clear that James Morice, Edward Coke, Walter Ralegh, and others would press for legislation to overturn or at least restrict Whitgift's regulations on clerical conformity. Even the queen's cousin Sir Francis Knollys, who had been senior privy counsellor in attendance at every session of Commons since the queen's ascension, was rumoured to be leaning toward supporting Morice's well-known antipathy to episcopal abuses.

It was obvious to everyone coming into and out of the Churchmans' house in the autumn of 1592 that, even in the wake of the infamous *Marprelate Tracts* and with the imprisonment of many key Puritan leaders, including Thomas Cartwright, who had been released just a few months ago after spending a year and a half in Fleet Prison, and the death of their field captain, John Field, the Puritans had no intention of retreating. In fact, the recent death of John Udall, the separatist minister from Kingston—whom Ralegh and other staunch Puritans had saved from the executioner only to see him die while being released—seemed further to inflame the radicals. Events were at a high pitch. It was rumoured that John Penry, a suspected candidate for authorship of the anonymous *Marprelate Tracts*, was on his way back from Scotland where he had fled to escape arrest. If Whitgift were to catch him, Penry might be tried and executed before he could find his way into the halls of parliament.

The atmosphere would have been especially charged around the table at the Churchmans' these days because Edwin Sandys would be in the Commons this session. He had a keen interest in assuring that Hooker's book speak directly to the issues likely to be debated there. Even more importantly, Edwin's uncle Miles, now treasurer at Middle Temple and one of the country's most prominent jurists, had been sitting in every session of the Commons since 1563 and was bound to have a major role in this one as a defender of the Church from the radicals. Hooker's colleagues wanted his book to be in Lord Burghley's hands before the parliamentary session began. If Burghley could be moved to at least a neutral position by Hooker's eloquence, that would be a help. No doubt the archbishop would appreciate Hooker's assistance in this enterprise.[23]

Extreme positions on the radical Calvinist wing were held by Henry Barrow (c. 1550-93) and Robert Browne (c. 1550-1633) who, as we shall see, sought separation from the established Church and the autonomy of each and every congregation, the first as a means to a spiritual democracy, the second on the grounds that any idea of church order was completely corrupt. In addition, Anabaptist refugees from the Low Countries, refusing to admit that infant baptism was true baptism, were a further separationist threat.[24] To be useful in the forthcoming parliamentary debate, Hooker's book would need to address the relationship of the Barrowists and Brownists to the mainline disciplinarian Puritans. If Hooker could make Burghley see that the natural consequence of continued leniency toward his Puritan friends and their presbyterian discipline was to aid and abet the heresy and treason that almost everyone admitted was evident in Browne and Barrow, then legislation might be passed to curtail presbyterianism, as well as Brownism and anabaptism. There was a real danger to be confronted here, Hooker's friends believed. If presbyterianism, with its emphasis on lay supremacy and weak central authority in the Church, were to take hold, it seemed inevitable that the next step would be congregationalism with its elimination of all establishment in religion. Next to go would be royal headship, the episcopacy, and, finally, the entire ideal of England as a unified Christian commonwealth. What remained would be a complete separation of Church from State, with the Church consisting of nothing more than a collection of individual congregations run largely by an uneducated laity.

No doubt, logic was stretched in this effort to demonstrate the necessary connection between the presbyterians and such sects as the Brownists. Nevertheless, Hooker agreed that a relationship did exist, even if it was not an inevitable one. And, logic aside, in the world of real politics the connection was highly probable, if not inevitable. That was why legislation was necessary to curtail, or even outlaw, the presbyterian discipline.

The part of Hooker's book that was most likely to be read right away by Burghley and others in parliament was the Preface. They would be too busy to bother with the rest. Their attention would have to be captured in these early pages of the book. The Preface already had a polemical tone, as Hooker had no doubt intended from the outset, although to make a specific case that the acts of the Barrowists and Brownists were directly attributable to the activities of the Calvinist extremists had probably not been part of Hooker's original purpose. But now there was the prospect of including a ban on activities by presbyterians and separatists as part of a bill outlawing Catholic recusancy, a law that was sure to be popular. Would Hooker be willing to make the necessary changes in his Preface to help in this effort? Yes, he would try to do so. But he would not compromise his principles or descend to the gutter with Martin Marprelate. Nor would he compromise the basic integrity of his book, which was, in his view, a single piece, argued from general principles to particular cases, from the first part to the last. He had made his purpose clear in the outline and Preface, and would not destroy the unity and symmetry of the work by inserting narrow polemical attacks where they did not fit into the overall design.

He showed his friends the place in the Preface where he had made this intention explicit. "Thus have I laid before you the brief of these my travails . . . the whole entire body whereof being [so] compact, it shall be no troublesome thing for any man to find each particular controversy's resting-place, and the coherence it has with those things, either on which it depends, or which depend on it."[25]

But at the end of the day an exasperated Hooker finally succumbed to pressure and added the desired polemic, a short piece that was quite out of keeping with the tone and content of the rest, as a kind of addendum. Here, at the very end of the Preface, he felt, this bit of political arguing would do the least damage to his intentions for the book as a whole.[26]

HELP FROM FRIENDS

The Preface and first four Books of the *Laws* were completed and ready for the printer before the end of 1592, shortly before the opening of the 1593 session of parliament. Now its author faced the daunting task of finding a publisher. This would not have been a problem had his work enjoyed the *imprimatur* and financial backing of the archbishop. But Hooker had no such backing. His work had never been officially commissioned, although, as we have seen, Whitgift had approved the project and found Hooker the livings necessary to support himself while writing.[27]

The archbishop had many claims on his increasingly limited resources and probably thought that if Hooker's work was worthy, a printer would run the risk of absorbing costs of production against expected income from sales. In any event, Whitgift was not relying on Richard's book. He had recently encouraged a number of more prominent figures to defend the Church. The Dutch theologian, Adrian Saravia, had just come out with his defence of the episcopacy. Thomas Bilson, soon to be bishop of Winchester, and Richard Bancroft, the formidable bishop of London, would soon publish major defences of the Church as well.[28]

For the next several weeks Hooker worked closely with John Churchman's able servant and secretary, Benjamin Pullen, as that able amanuensis transcribed his untidy manuscript into a beautifully-written copy, ready for the eyes of the most exacting printer. Richard knew many printers from his years of browsing through their bookstalls around St Paul's and on Fleet Street. He visited several of them with his manuscript. He went, for example, to John Bill's shop in Paul's Churchyard. Bill had a good location, and sales of his books usually went well. From Bill, as from others, he received a polite but negative response. Seeking a fuller hearing, he went to his best hope—his cousin, John Windet, whose Cross Keyes press was down near Paul's wharf. He had probably never met Windet but would have known of his prominent fellow-Devonian and certainly that he was the son of his Aunt Anne, one his father's five sisters.

Windet told him that it would not take long to print the manuscript because it was written in one of the finest hands he had seen. Unfortunately, there was little market for theological works these days. A few years ago, about the time of the *Marprelate Tracts*, interest in religious conflict was high and he could have expected to sell almost anything like this back then. Even now, a work attacking the Church might do quite well, but not one that defended the establishment. Hooker's book was just too great a financial risk, cousin or no.[29]

Hooker may have protested that, with parliament meeting again in a few months and the prisons filling up with separatists, interest in religious books would quickly return. Windet was not moved by such arguments. The fact was that this was a long book, with eight separate parts projected. Windet probably advised his cousin to sell his book to a printer who would do the entire work in instalments. That way, if all copies of the first printing were not sold, they could be used in future editions that would include later parts of the work as they were completed. Yes, Windet would be glad to enter into such a contract, but could not risk his own money because he could not see a market for the book sufficient to return a profit in a reasonable period of time. Richard was undoubtedly shaken by this response. Like all writers who have laboured for years to complete a major work, he had become so immersed in his subject that he came to believe instinctively and uncritically in its merit. To learn now, near the end of his long travail, that very few would be interested in reading what he had written must have been almost too much to bear.[30]

He then approached the Company of Stationers Hall. He had passed the impressive edifice a thousand times on his way to and from the Temple Church and knew how powerful this guild of printers was. Members were granted by the government a monopoly on book making. No work could be published in England without their approval. From here, terms of printing were carefully regulated, and from here agents were sent to find and destroy the illegal presses printing banned books such as the *Marprelate Tracts*. Illegal books were carried into the Hall and burned in the kitchen. For any writer in Hooker's time, this was a place to be reckoned with. He asked to see William Norton, the master of the printer's guild. He probably knew Norton personally and told him of his difficulty finding a printer. He no doubt explained that the archbishop was aware of his work and had encouraged him in it and that there was an urgency about having the book produced in time for the meeting of parliament early next year. He had the manuscript in hand in a fair copy but had been unable to find any member of the Stationer's Company in the churchyard or on Fleet street willing to undertake the work.

Norton told Hooker what he had already heard from Bill, Windet, and others. Despite Hooker's fine reputation as master of the Temple Church, there was simply no market just now for theological writings. Still, if the archbishop had agreed to underwrite the cost, there should be no trouble finding a printer. Whitgift's failure to do so could only demonstrate that even he knew that a book of this sort needed to be subsidized.[31]

Norton advised Hooker to seek a financial patron to assume the risk of publication. He stressed that he was talking about risk, not certain loss. He believed, in fact, that given Hooker's reputation, the book probably would sell, but slowly—too slowly for a commercial printer to make a decent return. For someone who could afford a small return over a longer time, this was not a bad prospect. Of course, such a person would need other motivations than making money. These motivations might be fear or dislike of religious zealots and purifiers; political ambition; desire to win favour with the archbishop; love of the established Church; friendship for Hooker himself.

It was important to find a patron at once and get the book into print as quickly as possible, not only to have it ready for Burghley's eyes before parliament met, but also because, as Norton undoubtedly informed Hooker, other works, very like his in purpose, would be published in the near future. Richard Bancroft, the bishop of London, who was Whitgift's right arm and probable successor, was about to come out with two such books.[32]

Hooker turned to his friends, including Edwin Sandys. Sandys in fact had several motivations for acting as Hooker's patron: friendship for his former tutor, sympathy with most of his moderate religious views, a desire to influence Burghley and others in Commons, and the financial wherewithal to await a long-term return on his investment or to absorb a loss, if necessary. So it was that Sandys stepped forward at a critical moment in Hooker's life and became a friend indeed. Without his timely assistance, the *Laws of Ecclesiastical Polity* would probably never have seen the light of day.

Sandys proposed that Hooker entrust him with Pullen's copy of the manuscript and he would see what terms he could obtain out on the street. Then he would calculate a fair return for himself on his investment and a reasonable payment to Hooker as author. When he had done all this, the two men would reach a final agreement and proceed with the publication. Hooker was so overjoyed that his book would soon be published that he did not concentrate much on the details. His overriding desire was to see that as many people as possible read the book. He urged Edwin to make his calculations so as to assure a low selling price so that the work would be affordable, even if this meant that he made little or nothing out of it himself.[33]

Early in the new year Sandys explained to Hooker the details of a tentative arrangement he had worked out with John Windet for printing the book. Windet would produce an initial run of 1,200 copies at a cost for printing and design of £52, which Sandys would pay. The printer would guarantee the same cost per page for Book Five when that was ready. The total should run to about £125. Edwin would save some money by supplying the paper himself. He could obtain about 150,000 sheets, enough for this and future editions, at something less than 8s. per ream. Sandys figured the total cost for the first four books at £100.4s., and for Book V £136.16s., a total investment of some £237. He viewed this financial outlay as an expression of support for Hooker but also as an investment. Most of the receipts from sales would come to him, since Windet would be paid his costs in advance. With luck and patience, Sandys believed he could make a decent return. He and Windet agreed on a sale price of 2s.6d. a copy for each Book. That may not have been as low as Hooker wanted, but it was a moderate price.

Under the rules of the Stationer's Company, the book had to be registered as belonging to one of their members, in this case John Windet. Windet agreed informally (illegally?) that Sandys would be guaranteed most of the sales receipts for himself, while the printer would retain rights to only a small sum to cover his costs for selling the book and for an additional profit. All rights to the book's earnings, other than those reserved to Windet, belonged to Sandys, since it was he and not Hooker who had the contract with the printer.

As a gesture of good faith, Edwin paid Hooker £10, in advance, for the Preface and first four Books. As soon as the rest was in Windet's hands, which he assumed would be soon, he would pay Hooker another £40—£20 for Book Five and £20 for the final three. The author's total payment was therefore to be £50, more than twenty percent of the receipts from sales necessary for Sandys to break even on his investment. This arrangement probably seemed fair to Hooker. Edwin was putting up the money and assuming the risk, although he also stood to get most of the gain if the book were to be a commercial success. Hooker felt that the real gain was his. At last, his book would be published!

In the event, Sandys' total investment in the first five books, including his payments to Hooker, was to reach about £278—probably as much as £20,000 ($35,000) in today's currency—a tidy sum even for a large book of some 125 folio sheets. Sandys eventually received a return on his investment, although sales were slow. By 1597, when Book V was printed, Windet had more than enough copies left of the original sheets for a new printing of the enlarged work. By 1611 the original copies of Book V had been sold. After 1611 the work sold more briskly. But Sandys shared in none of those profits. When Windet died in 1610 his apprentice and successor, William Stansby, reneged on Windet's agreement with Sandys and made a healthy return on subsequent editions of the book, without repaying Sandys for his costs in producing some of them. We do not know how many copies of the original edition were sold but may reasonably estimate that Sandys made a profit on the first edition of not more than £90, which he lost on later editions due to Stansby's dishonesty. (Strictly speaking, Stansby was within his legal rights because Windet's original agreement with Sandys was in violation of rules of the Stationers Company, which stipulated that sole rights to the work should be vested in the printer.)[34]

On 29 January 1593 John Windet entered into the official Register of the Company of Stationers in London his rights to "The lawes of ecclesiastical policie *[sic]* Eight bookes by Richard Hooker." Hooker had sent a fair copy to the archbishop a few weeks earlier so that Whitgift would have time to review the work and approve its hurried publication. The Stationers register, therefore, carries the necessary words: "Aucthorized *[sic]* by the lord archbishop of Canterbury his grace under his hand."[35]

Windet set about at once to produce the book. As he had little time before parliament convened, he hired two additional compositors to assist him and his apprentice, William Stansby. With Pullen's clear copy from which to work and Hooker's help in proof-reading the pages, the task was done in about six weeks, too late for the opening session of the Commons but probably in time to be used by Miles Sandys and his colleagues before serious legislative business began in mid-March.[36]

On 13 March Lord Burghley received one of Hooker's personal printed copies of the *Laws*, sent to him by the author with a letter attached. The letter was not a dedication. If there had been a dedication, it would have been to Whitgift. Rather, what Hooker sent to Burghley, who had never done any good thing for him but, to the contrary, had consistently championed his foes, was merely an acknowledgment of Burghley's great influence in parliament, in the hope that he might read and be influenced by his book. The letter said, in part:

> My duty in most humble manner remembered . . . I must in reason condemn myself of over-great boldness for thus presuming to offer to your Lordship's view my poor and slender labours: yet, because that which moves me so to do, is a dutiful affection in some way to manifest itself [that] . . . I am in that regard not out of hope that your Lordship's wisdom will the easier pardon my fault, the rather because my self am persuaded that my faultiness had been greater, if these writings, concerning the nobler part of those laws under which we should live, should not have craved with the first your Lordship's favourable approbation, whose painful care to uphold all laws, and especially the ecclesiastical, has by the space of so many years so apparently showed itself . . . Wherefore submitting both myself and my simple doings unto your Lordship's most wise judgement, I humbly take my leave. London, the xiiith of March 1592 [old style]. Your Lordships most willingly at commandment. Richard Hooker.[37]

When parliament convened in February, plague was already beginning to spread in London. More than 10,000 people died in the city that year, including the lord mayor and three aldermen. This devastation was exacerbated in 1594 by the start of five years of alternating drought and fierce rainstorms. The resulting poor harvests produced widespread poverty, food riots, and rampant crime throughout the country. 1593 was the start of a difficult period of sickness, death and social unrest—all accompanied by runaway inflation—that lasted until the end of the century.[38]

As soon as he had sent a copy of his book off to Burghley, Hooker and his family left the infested city for Enfield. He had done his part in the great anti-Puritan crusade and now was content to let his politically astute friends chart the course of events in parliament. They would keep him informed via the messengers who traversed the route to and from Enfield almost daily. He had more important matters on his mind now as he made his way north with Joan and the girls. He was worried about his wife. She was pregnant again. This was the fifth time in as many years. These early months were the most risky. Richard knew he had been little comfort during the frantic effort to get his book published. Now he could relax and devote himself for a while to his family.

He soon received word from London about the proceedings in parliament. Edward Coke, now the queen's Solicitor General, had been named Speaker in the Commons for this session. He opened the session with the Speaker's request for the Common's traditional privileges—freedom from arrest, freedom of speech, and so forth. These were granted by the queen, with some guarded remarks from her representative about care in the interpretation of "free speech." A warning had been delivered before the session with the example of Peter Wentworth, who had earlier written intemperately against the queen in the style of John Knox of Scotland and then pressed for a bill requiring Elizabeth to make a decision on her successor. He had been arrested on the orders of the Privy Council and sent to the Tower (where he died in 1597).

James Morice, that perennial Puritan spokesman, had put forward a bill that would restrict several of Whitgift's regulations requiring conformity of the clergy, basing his case on English common law and citing the Magna Carta. He was supported by Sir Francis Knollys from the Privy Council and Henry Finch, MP for Canterbury, among others. Robert Cecil, old Burghley's son and heir-apparent, said he admired Morice's bill but, since the queen had expressly opposed his ideas, his proposal could not stand. Coke delayed matters long enough for the House to run out of time. The queen summoned him and gave him a message to deliver to the House the next day. No debate on Morice's bill could take place, and once again a potentially troublesome session had been manipulated by the queen. Morice was forcibly removed from the Commons and placed under house arrest in the home of Sir John Fortescue. Before the session was over seven members, including the moderate Puritan Robert Beale, were under house arrest.

To Hooker, the most important news from parliament concerned the bill requiring obedience by the queen's disloyal subjects. The original intent of the bill was to clamp down on Catholics who failed to attend church services at least monthly and anyone who harboured recusants. One provision went so far as to prevent the daughter of a recusant father from having a dowry, and another would remove children of recusant parents above the age of six from their homes. Puritans feared that the vague language of the bill would allow Whitgift to apply it not only to romanists but to nonconforming Puritans as well, unless they were specifically excluded from its coverage. This was in fact exactly what the bill was intended to do and why, therefore, it did not include a specific exclusion for any nonconformists. Miles Sandys' speech on 17 March contained a powerful argument for allowing the bill to apply to Barrowists, Brownists, and all other nonconformists, as well as Catholic recusants. Miles drew his comments directly from Hooker's Preface to the *Laws*, where blame had been laid for these extremists at the door of the Puritan disciplinarians. Hooker's book had been finished in time to be helpful.

Later Hooker learned that the bill advocated by Edwin and Miles had failed even to be presented. A somewhat milder measure was presented, which would make traitors of anyone attempting to convert people to illegal religious practices. This bill was designed to get at those who owned and ran illegal presses and writers of heretical and treasonous tracts. Miles had spoken in favour of this measure as well. Even Burghley had ventured forth to support the idea, reluctantly no doubt. Perhaps Hooker's Preface had influenced him. Walter Ralegh had spoken against the bill. This would not endear him to the queen, Hooker knew. The arch puritan, Henry Finch, was vicious but effective in his attack on the proposal. No one in England would be safe from such a law, Finch said.

Toward the middle of April Hooker had news of the end of the session. Parliament had adjourned on the 10th, after the worst aspects of the bill—worst no doubt from Hooker's point of view, not Edwin's—had been removed. The legislative result of all this debate was two separate laws, one against Catholics and one against Protestant separatists, both of which were harsh but less severe than the earlier proposals. Under their provisions, persons refusing to attend church services could be imprisoned and, if they continued to stay away for as long as three months, might be banished from the country. Although enforcement depended on the attitudes of judges, this was the first time legal penalties in a specific law which was directed explicitly against Puritans had been enacted into law. (The recusancy laws of the 1560s had applied to *all* recusants without distinction.)[39]

The Hookers probably stayed away from unhealthy London for much of the rest of the year. Margaret was born sometime in the summer or autumn. She was named for Edwin Sandys' sister, the wife of Francis Evington, a family friend who would one day be master of John Churchman's merchant taylor's company and a trustee of Hooker's estate. Never had the ties between the Sandys, the Churchmans, and the Hookers been so strong as on the day Margaret was baptized.[40]

During 1594, the Hookers probably remained out of London as much as possible, although by late 1593 the plague had spread as far north as Enfield. Joan would have remained in Enfield while Richard travelled from time to time to Salisbury and Boscombe. He may have preached several times at St Andrew's, visited his colleague Nicholas

Fuller at nearby Allington, and spent some time reading and revising Book V of the *Laws* in the library at Salisbury Cathedral.

Toward the end of the year a messenger brought a letter to the Churchmans' house informing Richard that he would be moving to Kent. The word he had was that William Redman, rector at Bishopsbourne and Barham, had been named bishop of Norwich, and his living, which was the queen's to give, was vacant. Richard told Joan that the rectory at Bishopsbourne was large and comfortable—and only three miles from Canterbury Cathedral!

NOTES

1. On the dating which I follow, see Haugaard, *Folger*, VI, Pt. I, 40-43; 51. Hooker himself implied that he had the book completed in draft by early 1593 and needed only to make revisions, when he wrote in the Preface to that edition: "I have . . . thought it at this time more fit to let go these first four books by themselves, than to stay both them and the rest, till the whole might together be published." In 1597, at the end of the first edition of Book V, he wrote: "Have patience with me for a small time, and by the help of Almighty God I will pay the whole." For a discussion of alternative theories, see W. Speed Hill, "Hooker's Polity: The Problems of the 'Last Three Books,' " *The Huntington Library Quarterly*, 34:320.

2. Sandys' home base at this time was apparently in York, although he actually resided much of the time at the Churchmans' in London. He still held a prebend at York and had married a local girl named Southcote in 1590, shortly after the death of his first wife. The couple, with three servants, moved in with the Churchmans on Watling Street for about a year but then resettled in York some time in 1591, shortly before the second Mrs Sandys died. See Sisson, 28, 147. The original Sandys' family homestead was at Hawkeshead, between Lakes Windemere and Coniston. Archbishop Sandys was born there sometime between 1516 and 1519. His sons, including Edwin, grew up in Worcester, London, and York when their father was resident bishop in those sees. (Sandes Hotel still exists in Worcester on land once owned by the eldest son, Robert.) The family roots remained at Hawkeshead. Toward the end of his life in 1588 the bishop returned frequently and founded the Hawkeshead Grammar School, which the poet, William Wordsworth, attended in the late eighteenth century.

3. *Folger*, I, 132-3; *Works*, I, 275. All references to Book I in this section are drawn directly from Hooker's words. *Folger* 55-142; *Works,* 195-285. Gibbs has an excellent analysis of Book I in *Folger*, VI, Pt. I, 81-124.

4. *Folger*, I, 142; *Works*, I, 285.

5. *Folger*, I, 95-105; *Works*, I, 239-46. Hooker may have been aware of Bodin's 1576 work, *Six Livres de la République,* although he never cites it. The two men had much in common. Like Hooker, Bodin (1530-96) was an advocate of religious toleration who saw limited monarchy as the best form of government. Bodin served as representative to the Estate General from Blois and also as chief lawyer to the king of France. He died of the bubonic plague in 1596.

John Locke's debt to Hooker's tentative notion of a social contract as a basis for his own full-blown and highly influential doctrine of popular consent was appropriately acknowledged by Locke in his 1690 work, *Two Treatises of Civil Government*. Locke (1632-1704) was a natural-rights philosopher whose ideas influenced Thomas Jefferson in the *Declaration of Independence*, forging thereby a tenuous intellectual link between Hooker, the penman of the Church of England and Jefferson, the penman of the American Revolution. The distinguished nineteenth-century historian Henry Hallam went so far as to affirm that Hooker's thinking on the social contract "absolutely coincided with that of Locke." See

Hallam, *The Constitutional History of England,* (London: John Murray, 1846), I, 214-19. In a recent article, J. C. Davis argues convincingly against making too much of such connections between Hooker and modern political theories. See Davis, *op. cit.*

6. For Hooker's discussion in Book 8, see *Folger*, III, esp. 331-56 ; *Works*, III, esp. 340-67.

7. The portion of Book VI dealing with church and civil courts has not survived. What remains of Book VI is Hooker's tract on penance. We are able to reconstruct the missing part of Book VI from Hooker's *Autograph Notes, Folger*, III, 463-94, and Sandys' and Cranmer's notes on Book VI, *Ibid.*, 105-40.

8. This discussion of Hooker's treatment of penance in Book VI is drawn from Gibbs, *Folger*, VI. Pt. I, 249-308; P. G. Stanwood, *Folger*, III, xix-xxvi. See Peter Marshall, *The Catholic Priesthood and the English Reformation* (Oxford: Clarendon Press, 1994) for a discussion of penance and absolution as practised by Roman Catholic priests in England up to the ascension of Mary Tudor.

9. Davis, *op. cit.*, 173. See Lee W. Gibbs' commentary on Book VI in light of the recent discovery by P. G. Stanwood of Hooker's *Autograph Notes, Folger*, VI, Pt. I, 252-3, 260-61, 295-301, 306, esp. n. 79.

10. There has been much speculation about the fate of this section of Book VI. Sisson, 98, 101-107, suggests that Sandys' disagreement with Andrewes on this issue, at the time when these two men and Dr Spenser (Hooker's friend and the literary executor of his estate) were making a posthumous examination of Hooker's manuscripts, led to Sandys' complicity in delaying publication of Book VI, or possibly even adulterating the text to alter Hooker's intent. Sisson refers to Sandys' "negligence or worse fault" in this regard. Evidence of Sandys' disagreement with Andrewes is found in Interrogatory #25 in the 1613 chancery trial, when Dr Spenser is asked to testify concerning this doctrinal dispute between Sandys and Andrewes. Sisson, 152-3.

Spenser, who knew the truth of the matter, refused to answer the question on the grounds that his answer could be of no help to the complainants in the case. But he did say, in his Preface in the 1604 edition of the *Laws*, that Hooker had "perfected" Book VI (and VII and VIII) before he died and they were later "spoiled" by "evil disposed minds." *Works* I, 93; Sisson, 99-106, 144, 153. Haugaard, and Gibbs (Folger, VI, Pt I; 40-43; 46-50; 255-61) are among scholars who agree that the entire work was finished, at least in draft form, by early 1593 and that revisions were made later. Stanwood (*Folger* III xx-xxii, xxvi), holds that the last three books were not composed until after 1593. Haugaard's chronology of events in *Folger*, VI, Pt. I , 51 is helpful. Georges Edelen holds with Spenser's contemporary statement that whatever loss or adulteration there may have been occurred after and not before Hooker's death. *Ibid.*, 249, n. 2. Because Hooker nowhere indicates that penance as such will be discussed in Book VI, most scholars believe that, although he did in fact write all that is found in Book VI, he did not intend it to be part of the *Laws*. Others, however, contend that there is a connection between Hooker's stated subject for Book VI (church jursdiction) and penance because the "power of the Keys" to forgive sins is the surest evidence of church jurisdiction. This is the view I share. See A. S. McGrade, "Repentance and Spiritual Power; Book VI of Richard Hooker's *Of the Laws of Ecclesiastical Polity,*" *Journal of Ecclesiastical History* 29 (Apr. 1978), pp. 163-76.

11. Francis Paget, *An Introduction to the Fifth Book of the Laws of Ecclesiastical Polity* (Oxford: Clarendon Press, 1899), 104; Haugaard, *op. cit.*, 129-133. See Books II and III of the Laws, *Folger*, I, generally 169-207, esp. 170, 191-2, 207-9, 144-8; *Works*, I, 335-6, 286-300; 352-4..

12. *Folger*, I, 183, 184-6; *Works*, I, 327, 328-30. In a recent article, the editor of the Folger edition of Hooker's works, W. Speed Hill, analyzes Hooker's use of Scripture as a text which Hill thinks Hooker believed (understood) by "textual faith" to contain and convey God's Word, but which, for Hooker, still required man's

rational faculties to be grasped. In this sense, Scripture, though not self-evident in its meaning, does, through reason, transmit the Word of God to man. Hill's conclusion is not only a useful insight into Hooker's understanding of the sense in which God's truth was *in* Scripture, but also a ringing affirmation of the possible truth contained in all texts to which people repair for meaning, including Hooker's own text, *The Laws of Ecclesiastical Polity*. Contemporary literary analysts, Hill believes (and I agree), ignore such possibilities in those texts to which readers become "attached" at deeply personal and "quasi-devotional" levels at the price of overlooking one of mankind's earliest and most enduring attachments—to literary texts. See Hill, "Scripture as Text, Text as Scripture: The Case of Richard Hooker," *Text, An Interdisciplinary Annual of Textual Studies* (Ann Arbor, Michigan: The University of Michigan Press, 1996), 9: 93-110; esp. 95, 107, 109-110.

13. *Folger*, I, 313-14; *Works*, I, 170-71.

14. Hooker may have added a polemical section at the very end of Book III, just before it went to press in early 1593. See Haugaard, *op. cit.*, 138-9, and Paget, 106-20.

15. *Folger*, I, 194-8; Works, I, 338-42.

16. *Folger*, I, 201, 202-03; *Works*, I, 345-6, 347-8.

17. *Folger*, I, 272-4, 276-80, 288-93, 299, 332-5;; *Works*, I, 417-18, 425-32, 433-8, 477-9; Paget, 120-2.

18. Extant letters from Hooker to Rainolds are evidence that the two men were in contact during this period. The letters, one of which was written from Enfield, contain references to Churchman's servant, Benjamin Pullen, and to Henry Parry and other colleagues at Oxford. In one letter Hooker says that, while at Enfield, he is in regular contact with London. *Works*, I, 109-14.

19. Cranmer was a fine scholar, well equipped to challenge Hooker on matters of substance as well as grammar and composition. See letter concerning his scholarship written by John Rainolds. *Ibid.*, 106-8.

20. This is drawn from Cranmer's and Sandys' *Notes* on Book VI, in *Folger*, III, 107-30. These notes were probably not written until 1593. *Ibid.*, xxx. The originals are in the Corpus Christi College archives, MSS 295, 1-18.

21. *Folger*, III, 130-40.

22. St Andrew's Register, cited in Sisson, 125.

23. This discussion is drawn from a number of sources. The best of these are the summary and analysis by William Haugaard in *Folger*, VI, Pt. 1, 27-61, and Sisson, xiv, 4-5, 45-78. I follow Haugaard's opinion that Whitgift was among those "eminent persons"—referred to but not named, in the 1613 chancery trial to settle Hooker's estate—who pressed Hooker to complete his work in time to be useful in the 1593 Parliament. Haugaard, 54; Sisson, 145.

24. On Barrow, Browne, and Anabaptists, see the respective entries in *Oxford Dictionary of the Christian Church* (3d ed. 1997), with bibliographies.

25. *Folger*, I, 36; *Works*, I, 173.

26. Haugaard, *op. cit.*, 46-50, 60-61. It is obvious that the original Preface ends with chapter vii. Chapters viii and xix contain the polemical material as a kind of addendum. Haugaard notes, as evidence, Hooker's otherwise inappropriate statement at the end of chapter ix, that "with us contentions are now at their highest float." Hooker knew this to be a gross overstatement. By this time the Puritans were in retreat and controversy had largely subsided. All that was at highest float were the concerns of the Sandys and their allies about the upcoming debate in parliament.

27. I follow Sisson's opinion that the book was rushed to print to be ready in time to support the *Conventicle Act* (restraining Puritans) in the parliament of February-April, 1593 and that it had the approval of Whitgift. I do not agree with Sisson that Hooker's entire career from the time of his appointment at the Temple had been calculated by the archbishop to make him the "deputed spokesman for the church."

Sisson, xiii-xiv, 4-5, 45-49, 145. Haugaard is closer to the truth in his contention that, although Whitgift may have encouraged the project, the primary motivation was Hooker's own. Haugaard, *op. cit.*, 54.

28. Adrian Saravia (1531-1613) was a prominent Dutch theologian who settled in England. His *Diverse Degrees of Ministers of the Gospels* (1591) claimed divine institution for the episcopacy. Saravia would soon become Hooker's closest friend and confidant. See *infra,* chapters 16 and 17. Thomas Bilson (1547-1616) published *The Perpetual Government of Christes Church* in 1593 on a similar theme. He was later Bishop of Winchester. Bancroft wrote two similar works in 1593. See below, note 32.

29. Sisson, 50, 52.

30. *Ibid.*, 52, for the court record containing the contemporary recollection of John Spenser that Hooker was "dismayed" and "melancholy" over his failure to find a publisher.

31. *Ibid,*, 48-50.

32. Bancroft's two works appeared anonymously in 1593. They were: *Survey of the Pretended Holy Discipline*, a personal attack on Calvin's tactics in Geneva, and *Dangerous Positions and Proceedings*, in which he ridiculed the presbyterian discipline in Scotland and Geneva in an attempt to show that presbyterians were openly seditious. Both works were more polemical and less philosophical than Hooker's *Laws*. See Brook, 146-7.

33. Evidence of Hooker's attitude in this regard is found in the testimony of Sandys' servant Eveleigh that Hooker himself insisted on a lower price for Book V than the printer's guild preferred because he wished to sell more copies. Sisson says that for Hooker the book was never a "commercial" venture but a "crusade." *Sisson*, 68.

34. *Ibid.*, 53-60, 68-74.

35. Edward Arber, ed., *A Transcript of the Company of Stationers from 1554-1640* (London: Privately Printed, 1875), II, 625, 295.

36. Hill, *Folger*, I, xxix-xxx; Sisson, 64. Both agree that the work was printed sometime before the copy was sent to Burghley on 13 March. For a convincing argument that printing took more time than the three weeks suggested by Edelen, (*Folger*, I, 369-71), see Mark Bland, "The Appearance of the Text in Early Modern England," *Text II* (1998), 120, n. 3. Bland also suggests that the choice of a simpler title-page design and use of folio and English Roman type rather than quarto and Blackletter, were intended to make Hooker's book appear more as a literary work than a theological tract and hence more appealing to moderates, if not Puritans. As Hooker's cousin, Windet, Bland feels, was probably sympathetic toward Hooker's effort to win over some of the more advanced Calvinists to his ideas. *Ibid.*, 119-21.

37. *Works*, I, 116-17.

38. Neale, 335-6.

39. *Ibid.*, 241-323, esp. 287-291. See also Haugaard, *op, cit.*, 27-61.

40. Sisson, 44, n. 1; 165, n 1.

CHAPTER 16

Pastor of Bishopsbourne

LIFE IN THE COUNTRY

In January of 1595, thanks to Archbishop Whitgift, Richard Hooker found his heart's desire: a peaceful living in the lovely countryside just south of Canterbury. Here he would live comfortably, raise his family away from the clamour of London, minister to a manageable parish of God's English people, and pursue his scholarly interests. He had realized the dream of many a cleric with an intellectual bent: to preach and administer the sacraments, tend a portion of Christ's flock, and have time to read and write.

There has always been speculation as to why this distinguished Anglican never rose higher in the Church that he more than anyone else was to set on its true and lasting course. Many explanations have been attempted: that he was married; that he did not have a doctorate; that he was in ill-health; that his opinions on Catholics and on the doctrine of predestination were not appreciated by church authorities; that he had failed, for whatever reasons, to stay the course at the Temple Church; that he lacked sufficient ambition to press his own case for promotion. There is validity to each of these explanations. To them I would now add another: Hooker was happy, perhaps delighted, with his appointment at Bishopsbourne and sought nothing more. By this time in his life, after those tumultuous years in London, he knew himself well enough to be contented with this opportunity to combine scholarly work with the life of a country pastor.

What could be better? The great library at nearby Canterbury cathedral—far superior to that at Lambeth or the Temple—was available for his continued work on his *apologia* for the Church. Old friends and congenial colleagues could visit him here. Safely removed from the hectic pace and foul plagues of London or Oxford, he could enjoy some leisure and have time for the joys and pains of a more secure family life. Best of all, he could practise what mattered most to him: the daily life of priest, comforter, preacher, and shepherd for his congregation of country people.

It would have been difficult to find a more idyllic place to settle in all of England. Bishopsbourne was (and is) a pretty little village nestling in the bosom of the Elham Valley. The valley falls gently down from the old Roman road between Canterbury and Dover. This road (today's A2), just a quarter of a mile up the path from Hooker's new church, was old Watling Street which ran, in theory, all the way from Churchman's house in London to Hooker's home here at Bishopsbourne.

Fields dotted with grazing sheep, brightened by patches of wild flowers, and delineated by occasional stands of beech trees, presented the harried Londoner with a bucolic setting for his new life. Hooker's Bishopsbourne came complete with the small Neilbourne Stream running intermittently southward through the town centre and farm lands spotted with substantial red brick houses and great black barns poking their roofs up behind the church steeple—and all of this only a short five miles from Canterbury Cathedral.[1]

Hooker's appointment here apparently became effective on 7 January 1595. The post was the queen's to give, as had been his other two major appointments, at the Temple and at Salisbury. No doubt Elizabeth acted on the recommendation of her archbishop who was fulfilling a promise to find Hooker a suitable living where he might finish his writings.[2]

For some years before and after Richard's tenure at Bishopsbourne, the living at St Mary's was attached to the chapter at Canterbury. His immediate predecessor, Dr William Redman, had been archdeacon at the cathedral when he was given the living here. Hooker's successor, Dr Charles Fothersby, was also to be archdeacon simultaneously with his appointment at Bishopsbourne, becoming dean of the chapter in 1615. No doubt Whitgift encountered some resistance at Canterbury when he gave Bishopsbourne to someone like Hooker who was not a chapter member. An added problem was that Richard would be a full-time resident rector which meant that most, if not all, the income from the living would be consumed by his salary. To lose such a tidy sum from the coffers of the chapter would meet with disapproval from the canons, who would otherwise have had most of that money to distribute among themselves. For his part, Whitgift was pleased to add Hooker to his growing list of well-educated and devout clerics who truly resided in their cures and ministered regularly to the parishioners in their charge.[3]

When Richard and Joan moved into the rectory, they were making their first real home together. And a large house it was, with twelve rooms plus separate bakehouse, washhouse, stables, and barn. Joan had come into her own at last as mistress of a substantial household. Her father would have made certain that the furniture and household items loaded into carts for shipment from London were more than adequate to fill his daughter's new home.[4] Among the luxuries of this rather affluent London family were nine large carpets, several valuable "turkey cushions" (richly-coloured wool-piled imitation velvet cushions) intended to make seating more comfortable and at the same time offer a social statement to guests of the now famous new rector of Bishopsbourne, and a beautiful cupboard covering, called a "darnix." More substantial items included a large table, eight good stools, a cupboard, a plate cabinet, a set of andirons, and a large walnut chair—all for the parlour. The chair was one of Hooker's prized possessions. Walnut was still rare in England.[5]

In the hall they placed another long table, a number of shorter stools, a settle, and a smaller cupboard. Upstairs, Hooker's study and small adjoining parlour held a square table, several "presses" (armoires), two trestle beds and a number of hampers holding his books and manuscripts. By the time they had finished moving in, the six bedchambers on the upper floors were filled with beds, truckles, feather mattresses, rugs, curtains, cupboards, and chairs. The largest chamber, above the parlour, held the biggest bedstead and a substantial wood-panelled chest containing Joan's treasured linens: some twenty tablecloths, dozens of napkins, towels, and—a great luxury in those days—a pair of bedsheets. The windows in most of the bedchambers were draped with green sage curtains. Joan felt fortunate indeed to have so much of this fine cloth—a blend of wool and silk resembling serge—and enough rods to hang the curtains on. Many trunks and wainscotted boxes arranged along the walls and under the windows held the pillows, bolsters, and blankets that made life comfortable for this prosperous clerical family.

Dr Redman had left the kitchen, buttery, wet and dry larders, bakehouse, washhouse, barn, and stables well furnished. These accoutrements, including cheese presses, butter churns, large kitchen utensils, andirons, scales, kettles, kneading troughs, pumps, a few saddles, bridles, and the like, went with the living and were passed on from one rector to the next. An ample supply of wheat, barley, oats, and podder (green vegetables), a few chickens, hogs, cows, and two geldings were also on hand to see the new occupants through the rest of the winter. Still, Richard and Joan found it necessary to supply some tables, chairs, presses, and cupboards of their own in order to complete the furnishing of these working parts of the homestead.[6]

The parish clerk, Sampson Horton, was probably the first person to give Hooker a complete tour of the church building. We have Walton's account of Sampson bowing his head, tipping his cap, and barely raising his eyes to meet those of his new master. Over the years the relationship between rector and clerk was correct but cordial.[7]

St Mary's was an ancient foundation. The building had been erected about 250 years earlier to replace a smaller structure that had been on the spot since Saxon days. The tower had been last repaired over a hundred years ago. The first thing that caught Hooker's eyes as he stepped into St Mary's was probably the floor—lovely small medieval tiles spreading out over the entire expanse of the church. The floor was older even than the tower. The pride of St Mary's were the famous medieval paintings of scenes depicting death and resurrection. One showed the martyrdom of St Edmund, the East Anglian king who had been killed by the Danes, accurately depicted with arrows piercing his body. Another displayed the fictitious tale of St Nicholas resurrecting three boys who had been murdered by a butcher who used children as his meat supply. In this scene St Nicholas was depicted as a tall figure in bishop's robes blessing the three naked boys in the pickling tub. Turning round to look above the doorway, Richard would have seen an armed giant, nearly twice the size of any of the other painted figures on the walls. The huge man, clothed only in a knee-length cape, was in the act of striking his lance into the body of a smaller kneeling figure. In addition to the lance, the giant bore many other weapons, including three daggers coming out of his mouth and two large swords on each side of his head. The small kneeling figure had his palms extended toward the viewer.

There were still more wall paintings. At the west end of the nave was a startling depiction of the resurrection. At the top of this painting was the Angel of Death with a chain extending down into hell, with the souls of the saved and the damned strung out along the length of chain. These souls were of all sorts: kings, archbishops, common people—all contorted in horrible writhings. At the bottom stood a figure on a tomb flanked by two angels. Hell was portrayed as a wide-open jaw with sixteen molars and curved canine teeth. On the wall in the south nave St Michael was weighing souls in a scale of good and evil. On one side of the scale was a small kneeling figure, hands clasped in prayer; on the other side were heads of several of the damned being pulled downward by a small demon. A little to the right of St Michael was a lovely painting, more peaceful than the others, of four holy women at the tomb of Christ.[8] How different this was from the stark simplicity of the Temple Church in London or any other church Richard had served! How had the marauding Puritans ever missed this place? Was there a church left in all England with such religious art on its walls?

Hooker probably never quite got used to the wall paintings, with their emphasis on judgement, damnation, death, and hell. Although he was certainly no Puritan when it came to church decorations, he was no papist either. These paintings may have been, for him, too reminiscent of the superstition and terror that sometimes had been used before the Reformation to frighten Christians into submission to the Church.

In the weeks and months that followed, Hooker spent much of his time in the church conducting services, meeting with his curate and clerk, and pursuing his own private meditations and prayers. He no doubt came to appreciate many of the fine features of the building, aside from the startling wall paintings. There was, for example, the stained glass in the windows high over both sides of the chancel and in the south window. The church also had an impressive hammer-beam ceiling and an ancient stone baptismal font. Hooker must have come to regard St Mary's as a very special place—a holy place—where he felt especially close to God.

At Bishopsbourne, evening would find Richard at home with his family, no longer off at some meeting at the Temple Church, the Inns of Court, or Lambeth Palace. He led family devotions before supper like any good husband and father of the day, using his well-worn copy of Henry Bull's *Christian Prayers and Meditations*: "All things depend upon thy providence, O Lord to receive at thy hands due sustenance in time convenient. Thou givest to them and they gather it: thou openest thy hand, and they are satisfied with all good things."[9] When they had finished their meal, Richard probably handed Joan his copy of Bull and, like a proper Elizabethan wife, she would read: "We render thanks unto thee O Lord God, for the manifold benefits which we continually receive at thy bountiful hand; not only for that it hath pleased thee to feed us in this present life, giving unto us all things necessary for the same, but especially because thou hast of thy free mercy fashioned us anew, in an assured hope of a far better life, the which thou hast declared unto us by thy Holy Gospel."[10]

A likely source for Hooker's evening devotion was John Woolton's *The Christian Manual*, a compendium of pithy sayings from classical and contemporary writers as well as from Scripture. We may imagine him, at the end of the evening, his last candle burning low, kneeling by his bed and praying: "Merciful Lord, keep me in prayer, fasting, study, and meditation that I better may hear Your voice and know Your will and speak Your mind." Then, still on his knees, he would reach over for his Woolton and read a favourite prayer:

> . . . even as all things are now hidden by the means of the darkness which thou hast sent over the earth, so thou wouldest vouchsafe to hide and bury all our other sins, which this day or at any time heretofore we have committed against thy Holy commandments. And as now we propose to lay our bodies to rest, so grant the guard of thy good angels to keep the same this night and fore evermore. And when or whensoever our last sleep of death shall come, grant that our bodies may rest both temporally and eternally to thy glory, and our joy, through Jesus Christ our Lord. So be it.[11]

Much as Hooker relished his new life as an obscure country parson, he could not escape his past. There is a tradition that Hooker was an impoverished holy man to whom religious pilgrims journeyed to pay homage at Bishopsbourne. This idea was spawned by Walton, who could never resist the temptation to sanctify Hooker—perhaps in a conscious effort to create Anglican saints to replace some of the Catholic ones. There is no warrant at all for picturing Hooker as a poor holy man. Rather, at this time in his life, he was no more or less than a scholar who was well-known to a select group of other scholars, highly-placed clerics and politicians as a somewhat unassuming writer and preacher who had made controversial statements during a brief tenure at the Temple in London and was now in the process of completing a major defence of the Church of England. His life had been quietly productive, with occasional flashes of controversy to season its passage. Almost nothing about him justified Walton's famous characterization of him during these years at Bishopsbourne:

> the innocency and sanctity of his life became so remarkable that many turned out of the road . . . to see the man whose life and learning were so much admired; and alas! as our Saviour said of St John the Baptist, 'What went they out to see? a man clothed in purple and fine linen?' No, indeed; but an obscure homeless man, a man in poor clothes, his loins usually girt in a coarse gown . . . stooping, and yet more lowly in the thoughts of his soul.[12]

A more accurate portrait of Hooker comes from the president of Corpus Christi College, Dr John Spenser, who characterized his friend as "a true humble man" of a "mild and a loving spirit" and "a soft and mild disposition"—a man ill-suited to his contentious post at the Temple. Yet, Spenser says, dissensions in the Church eventually "made his heart hot within him and at length the fire kindled," which provoked him to his great defence of the Church. Spenser wrote that Hooker preferred a "quiet private life" and "neither enjoyed nor expected any the least dignity in our church."[13] Francis Paget, a close student of Hooker's writings, decided that he was a "shy man" who was "by temperament inclined to deference."[14]

By this time in his career he had obtained a national, even international, reputation from the publication of the early books of the *Laws* and from his highly visible tenure at the Temple as the cleric who had stood up to the formidable Walter Travers. Consequently, there probably were frequent visitors to Bishopsbourne, breaking the rural calm. Some were old friends from Oxford and London. Others came to discuss theology and politics and to take the measure of this unassuming defender of the queen's Church who seemed to aspire to nothing more than a quiet country living—highly uncharacteristic in this aggressive, grasping age.

Although he was undoubtedly pleased by visits from such friends as Edwin Sandys, George Cranmer, Bishop Andrewes, and Adrian Saravia (the new canon at Canterbury who soon became a close friend), Hooker discovered that his real joy was ministering to the everyday needs of the people of the parish: visiting their homes when they were sick, being present at times of personal and family crisis, administering Communion, or making uninvited house calls simply to offer friendship and support. The people of the parish soon came to respect, and perhaps even to love, this gentle scholar in their midst.

Walton provides a credible and attractive example of his ministry and his personality. It seems that, following each Rogation Sunday church service, Hooker led his small flock on a trek out of the churchyard eastward to Watling Street, south along the old road toward Dover, then turning west in about two miles to traverse the border of Kingston. He chatted amiably with his parishioners throughout the walk, enjoying especially the chance to converse with the younger families in his flock. He strolled along, staff in hand, listening to problems and complaints, giving personal advice, gently exhorting his parishioners to maintain their parish rights and liberties by this physical delineation of their rightful territory and, withal, simply enjoying the congenial annual outing with his extended family.[15]

In addition to pastoral duties, Hooker probably enjoyed his preaching at Bishopsbourne more than any he had done before. Here he was not trying to win debating points with sharp Puritan opponents or to defend his right to hold on to a post. His sole aim was to preach the saving gospel of Christ to country people whose lives were beset not so much by great issues of State as by the mundane fears, temptations, and hardships of life. He soon became comfortable using homely rural examples to make the gospel understandable to farm families. One of his sermon themes was the relationship between God's promises and human responses. One Sunday, when he wished to illustrate the lesson that God rewards those who bring him their treasures, he used the familiar words of Solomon in Proverbs, chapter 3: "Honour the Lord with your wealth as the first charge on all your earnings; then your barns will be filled with plenty and your presses (vats) break with the store of sweet wine." Was the lesson here that our bellies must first be filled before we serve God, Hooker asked his congregation from the pulpit?[16]

> No. But it is true that the cares and needs we have in this world are the greatest obstacle which keeps our minds from aspiring to heavenly things. Therefore, this promise is made to assure us that the best way to satisfy our needs is to first honour God. God will not allow those who honour Him to be worse off because of their service to Him than they otherwise would have been.

Alert to the trap of suggesting that good works could earn God's favour, Hooker quickly added: "This does not mean that our service of good works earns us such generosity at God's hands. That He rewards His servants comes not from worthiness of our deeds but from His goodness."

The question of how to be assured of God's favour was central to the concerns of simple people whose lives were constantly beset by the hardships of disease, early death, uncertain harvests, the rampant inflation of the day, which brought ever-rising prices for necessary goods, and the general uncertainty and stress of living in an era of rapid social and political change. Generally, Hooker's counsel to his troubled flock was for them to have a patient and peaceful spirit, use common sense, follow the advice of wise Christian leaders, and trust that God in his own way and in his own time would reward those who were faithful to him.

Lest his people think that God was interested only in their making donations to the Church, Hooker preached often on the more important offering, prayer. One of his most beautiful sermons on any subject was an explanation of Matthew, Chapter 7: "Ask, and it shall be given to you; seek, and you shall find; knock, and it shall be opened unto you. For whosoever doth ask shall receive; whosoever doth seek shall find; the door unto everyone which knocks shall be opened."[17] He began this sermon with the Scriptural reading, and then continued:

> In these words we are first commanded to 'ask,' 'seek,' and 'knock;' secondly, promised grace sufficient to each of these tasks. Of this asking, or praying, I shall not need to tell you either at whose hands we must seek aid or to remind you that our hearts are those golden censers from which the fume of this sacred incense of prayer must ascend.
>
> Against invocation of any other than God alone in our prayers of asking, if all other arguments should fail, yet this bar might suffice: that whereas God has in Scripture delivered us so many patterns for imitation when we pray, yea framed ready to our hands all suits and supplications which our condition on earth may at any time need, there is not one, no not one to be found, directed unto such as angels, saints, or any, saving God alone.

Hooker knew he must do all he could to rid his congregation of their inclination to venerate idols, especially the saints. He rarely lost a chance to warn them that God alone was to be the object of their prayers. He looked down at his congregation and continued:

> Fervency and humility are the proper attitudes to bring to our prayers of asking. Our fervency shows us to be sincerely affected towards what we crave; but that which must make us capable therof, is a humble spirit.
>
> Asking is easy, if that were all God did require. But seeking requires labour on our part, a work of difficulty. When we lack mature judgement we are apt to join our prayer with neglect of necessary labour. If we seek the counsel of those who are wise in these matters we will learn that the labour involved in seeking God is the keeping of His commandments.
>
> You see now what it is to ask and seek. The next duty is to 'knock.'

Following his usual mode of developing an argument in logical fashion, Hooker continued:

> There is always in every good thing which we ask, and which we seek, some main wall, some barred gate, some strong impediment or other objecting itself in the way between us and home; for removal whereof, the help of stronger hands than our own is necessary. So knocking is required in regard to hindrances, lets, or impediments, which are doors

shut up against us, till such time as it please the goodness of Almighty God to set them open.

Many are well contented to ask, and not unwilling to undertake some pains in seeking; but when once they see impediments which flesh and blood judges to be invincible, their hearts are broken. So it was with Israel in Egypt: they asked for and sought their liberty with great alacrity; but at length they came to knock at those brazen gates, the bars whereof they had no means to overcome, so they had no hopes to break asunder. Mountains on this hand, and the roaring sea before their faces, then all the forces that Egypt could make coming with as much rage and fury as could possess the heart of a proud and potent and cruel tyrant. Is this the milk and honey that had been spoken of? Is this the paradise in description whereof so much glossing and deceiving eloquence had been spent?

But God opened the door for the people of Israel when Moses did his part by knocking. Soon, however, some of the sons of Jacob stopped seeking or knocking, preferring a life of ease even at the price of slavery. Issachar was one of these, chastised by his father as one who 'though bonny and strong enough for any labour, doth notwithstanding sit still like an ass under all burdens; he shall think himself that rest is good, and the land pleasant; he shall in these considerations rather endure the burden and yoke of tribute, than cast himself into the hazard of war.'

We are for the most part all of Issachar's disposition. We account ease cheap, howsoever we buy it. And although we can happily frame ourselves sometimes to ask, or endure for a while to seek; yet loth we are to follow a course of life, which shall too often hem us about with those perplexities of knocking, the dangers whereof are manifestly great.

But of the duties prescribed of asking, seeking, and knocking, this should suffice. Now we turn to the promises which God has made in response to our prayers. These promises are of good things to come in the future. But they will come to us not merely by our asking, seeking, and knocking but by God's own means which are not to us altogether probable or likely. Thus He keeps us from the idleness of resting too easily in confidence in His goodness toward us or in our offerings to Him. He knows too well how quickly we would claim the credit for His grace.

Hooker concluded his sermon:

We will never fathom the circuit or the steps of His divine providence. We can only be astonished by His means of keeping His promises to us and exclaim with the Apostle Paul: 'O the depth of the riches of the wisdom of God! How unsearchable are his counsels, and His ways past finding out.'

Let it therefore content us always to have His word for an absolute warrant; we shall receive and find in the end; it shall at last be opened unto you: however, or by what means, leave it to God. Let there on our part be no stop to asking, seeking and knocking and the bounty of God we know is such, that He grants over and above our desires. Saul sought

> an ass, and found a kingdom. Solomon named wisdom, and God gave Solomon wealth.
>
> Let us sing with the psalmist who said of the Lord's servant: 'He asked for life, and thou givest him long life, even for ever and ever.' Our God is a giver. And He better knows than we the best times, and the best means, and the best things, wherein the good of our souls consist.

The longer Hooker ministered at Bishopsbourne, the more keenly he realized the need for God's saving love amidst the often difficult lives of ordinary people. Theological debate on issues of predestination, the precise nature of Christ's presence in the Eucharist, whether Catholics were irrevocably damned, and the question of which was the proper church polity seemed remote, if not irrelevant, to the needs of a grieving mother who had lost another infant child, a farmer with a failed crop, a vagrant begging at the rectory door for food and shelter. These situations called for the Church's saving message of hope, peace, mercy, love—not moralistic recrimination, proclamations of God's judgement on the wicked, or some kind of insistence on separating the elect from the damned. It was not that Hooker lost interest in the great theological issues of the day, but only that he found them less relevant in his life as pastor to rural working people than they had seemed in the intellectually-charged atmosphere at Oxford or the political cauldron at the Temple.

Preaching sermons of comfort and hope, and caring directly for people's spiritual needs through counselling in church or visiting in their homes often took precedence in his daily routines over revising the last Books of the *Laws*. When he did write, his passion was for polishing Book V, where he turned his keen mind to questions of worship, prayer, preaching, music, and the great ceremonies of the Church that brought meaning, joy, and comfort to ordinary people: Holy Communion, Baptism, prayer, confession, marriage, funerals, "churching" of women after childbirth, special festival days. These were the aspects of life in the Church he relished exploring in his sermons and writing, not only because they challenged him intellectually but also because they intersected his everyday experience as a pastor.

On more than one Sunday he sought to comfort his congregation by explaining why and how it was that good things in life often are preceded by or even grow out of failure, disgrace, pain, suffering, and death. No doubt he discovered that few messages fell on more eager ears than those that saw hope in despair and good coming somehow from that constant dread companion of all their lives—death.[18] A favourite sermon theme was Hebrews, Chapter 2, verses 14-15. One Sunday he began his sermon by reading the passage:

> The children of a family share the same flesh and blood; and so he too shared ours, so that through death he might break the power of him

> who hath death at his command, that is, the devil; and might liberate those, who through fear of death, had all their lifetime been in servitude. (*The New English Bible*, 1961)

Then he continued:

> The very centre of Christian belief, the life and soul of Christ's Gospel, rests in this: that by ignominy, honour and glory is obtained; power [is] vanquished by imbecility; and by death salvation is purchased.

He went on to explain how the Jews, who had longed for and prophesied a messiah, failed to accept Christ as the anointed one because he came not as a king but as one who would die foolishly and in shame. Even the Apostles made this mistake at first, he explained.

> It was not until Christ was dead, raised, and ascended to his Father that the right understanding of the ancient prophecies came to light. Until then, they never imagined that death was the means by which such great things would be accomplished. It was in this sense that the Apostle referred to the Gospel as a mystery, hidden since the beginning of the world, concealed from all former ages, and never opened until when it was revealed to the Saints of God.

He then posed the great conundrum of Christian faith and, simultaneously, the horrible dilemma of his people's lives—the relationship between death and life:

> But why did the Son of Man, who had the power to create and sustain the world need to die to deliver man when he could have done so simply by commanding it? If we enter into the search for what God intends to reveal to us, we can find a thousand testimonies to show that the whole scope of Christ in the work of our deliverance was to display the treasures of His infinite love, goodness, grace and mercy. Our deliverance He could have accomplished without His death. But that was insufficient to express His love for us; and so, "Behold," He said, "I lay down my life for them."

Now Hooker proceeded to explain why the only bar to Christ's promise of salvation was a person's explicit rejection of or contempt for this freely offered divine gift of a life of eternal peace and joy. He was echoing and expanding upon his sermons at the Temple and his writings in Books III and IV of the *Laws* where he had come close to espousing the Arminian doctrine of universal tolerance, love, and salvation. Though no Pelagian, he also sought to limit what he saw as the debilitating over-emphasis on original sin in so much of the Calvinism of his day. Here in this setting the idea that all of his flock could be saved from their pain and suffering somehow seemed right, despite the reservations about this which still lingered from his early indoctrination in Calvinist doctrine, and, dare he think it, despite the authorized doctrine of predestination in the *Thirty-nine Articles*. He continued:

> If anyone is deprived of deliverance, the fault is his own. Let no man therefor dig the clouds to look for secret impediments to his salvation. Let not the subtlety of Satan beguile you with fraudulent expectations and drive you into such labyrinths and images as the wit of man cannot enter without losing itself.

Hooker may have caught himself here before actually naming what labyrinth of Satan he had in mind: that tortured doctrine of double predestination so dear to John Rainolds and other advanced Calvinists. He saw clearly now just how injurious such an idea could be to the lives of ordinary people struggling for hope and meaning in their lives, threatening them with eternal separation from Christ's love through no apparent fault of their own. How false such a notion was to the spirit of Christ and to the words of Scripture! Still, there was no need this morning to cause controversy by attacking a sophisticated doctrine that few in his congregation knew or cared about.

He went on:

> The only fatal bar which closes the door to God's saving mercy is man's wilful contempt of the grace offered to him. Upon this sure foundation let us therefore build: Christ died to deliver us ***All.*** You have the plain expressed words of our Lord and Saviour inviting ***All*** 'to come unto him who labour.' You have the blessed Apostle's express assertion that Christ has by his death defeated Satan, to the end that he might deliver ***All*** who are held in bondage.
>
> Urge this idea upon yourself, God cannot deny Himself. And He preaches deliverance by His death to ***All*** [author's emphasis].

He had expressed what he had come fully to believe, that all who openly professed Christ's name could be saved by his grace and find hope in his love and care for them. If this be heresy to some, then so be it. He had learned from experience here as a country pastor what he had suspected all along to be the truth about Christ and his good news—that all who called on his name might have hope of salvation from fear, suffering, and death.

He continued, turning his attention now to a constant concern of his people, their fear of death:

> Death considered in itself is an enemy. Because death has as yet the upper hand against all, conflict with it is naturally feared. And they who speak of it from a merely natural sense can only decide that it is all terrible. But there are many factors which can abate the fear of death. For example, one who despairs of life or lacks patience with it or has had

enough of its troubles and tribulations may be content to have them ended in death. Or, with Aristotle, one may say that like birth, death is beneficial to the state of the world. Birth stops death and death eases the ways for new births. We should be content to give place to others by our death even as in birth we succeeded those who died before us.

But the truest weapons we have to strike back against the natural terrors of death are first the submission we owe to God's will, at whose commandment our readiness to die shows that we are called as His sons, and not as servants.

As sons we may take possession of our inheritance with joy. Those who lived as sons are blessed. The pains they suffered here are now ended; the evil they did is buried with them and their good works follow them. Their souls are safe in the hands of God. Not even their bodies are lost, but laid up for them.

He had spoken from the heart about some of his deepest personal convictions and undoubtedly believed he had given hope to his people while reaffirming his own faith. More than once he would be asked by members of his parish to elaborate further on why it was that God would allow such terrible sufferings among the faithful who came to services each Sunday, prayed regularly, and tried earnestly to believe that they would receive the gift of eternal life. The common sense of the matter seemed to be that God was breaking his promises and rejecting rather than loving his children.

Hooker tried to explain, in personal counselling sessions and in sermons, that there were, as he saw it, two forms of God's rejection of man. The first was indeed a complete and total rejection, but the second was a rejection that served only as a trial or test of faith. While Hooker often implied that all people were saved, when pressed he became a Calvinist again and would say that God may have marked off some as unworthy vessels of his favour. But he did not accept the extreme Calvinist doctrine of double predestination. This was the belief that God had selected which people would be saved and which would be damned even before he had created men and women and given them the freedom to reject his grace. While Hooker would not limit God's power to predetermine individuals to damnation, he found this to be a useless doctrine to dwell upon. He preferred the idea that God does not forsake those who are truly born of him, and that all who call on his Name are likely to be counted among those who may be saved by his grace.

Hooker taught that God never totally foresakes his own, even though, from time to time, he tests his children severely by turning his wrath upon them. He cited Isaiah as an example, where the prophet says, "For a moment in anger I hid my face from you for a little season; but with everlasting mercy I have compassion for you, says the Lord, your Redeemer;" and Jeremiah saying, "I shall make an everlasting covenant with them that I will never turn away from doing them good," and John saying, "He loved his own to the end."

Hooker also taught his people that, although God may seem to reject mankind, even his own son, Jesus Christ, he never abandons a person completely, only partially and only for a time. Even then, only the body and those lower parts of a person's nature, wherein the passions and emotions reside, are cut off. Our intellects, our souls, the parts of us where reason, wisdom, judgement, and the light of God's truth shine are not extinguished.

We are to remember, Hooker taught, that God gave Job's body over to be tormented by Satan; but his life, his soul, was spared. In the case of our Lord and Saviour, Satan and his imps were permitted to use whatever malice they could invent to inflict on Christ's body: "They wounded his eyes with the spectacle of scornful looks, his ears with the sound of heinous blasphemies, his taste with gall, the feeling throughout his body with such torture as blows, thorns, whips, nails, and spear could breed, until his soul was finally chased out like a bird." So terrible was his suffering that there is no reason to wonder why he cried out to God with such despair, "My God! My God!" And who, Hooker asked, can hear this mournful cry of Christ today and not feel that his own soul has been "scorched without leaving a single drop of the moisture of joyful feeling?"

When Christ cried out, "My God, my God, why have you forsaken me?" his words, the force and vigour of his speech showed clearly that he had already "clasped God with indissoluble arms" and that God was already "abiding in the fortress—the very pinnacle and turret of Christ's soul." And so it is with us, Hooker taught, if we call out to God with such fervour in the midst of our own despair.

As to why God went to so much trouble and allowed his creatures to cause themselves so much grief in order to love them fully, Hooker had no easy answer to offer. He thought the best response to questions about the workings of God's awful intelligence was an amazed silence.[19]

ADRIAN SARAVIA

Shortly after Hooker's arrival at Bishopsbourne he began to enjoy the company of Dr Adrian Saravia, a renowned Dutch theologian who had recently been named a canon at Canterbury. That the two men were kindred spirits and soon became friends is attested to by Walton and its likelihood corroborated by Keble. There is no need to doubt this relationship. The two men had so much in common that they would have been mutually attracted.[20]

Adrian Saravia (1523-1613) was the most prominent Dutch theologian living in England during Elizabethan and Stewart times. Although a leader in the Calvinist Church in the Netherlands, Saravia gradually became convinced that the episcopal polity in England was preferable to the presbyterian organization. He was highly favoured and generally supported by Leicester and others in Elizabeth's court and also by Archbishop Whitgift. His most famous book, *Of the Diverse Degrees of Ministers of the Gospel*, was published in England in 1591. Released while Hooker was still at the Temple, the book was an immediate sensation for its claim that God himself had established the rule of bishops in the Church and that therefore their authority was *ius divinum*. Hooker would have known that this treatise was part of an ongoing debate between Saravia and Theodore Beza, Calvin's successor at Geneva. In 1592, Beza wrote a *Response* to the *Diverse Degrees* on behalf of Calvinists everywhere who saw Saravia's ideas as a frontal attack on their presbyterian discipline. Travers and Cartwright were particularly incensed by Saravia. Recently the Dutch anglophile had responded to Beza in his *Defence*, thereby establishing himself as the apologist *par excellence* for the English episcopacy.[21]

Whitgift did not commission Saravia to write either *Diverse Degrees* or *Defence*, although he encouraged the writings. The clever archbishop used the Dutchman as he had Hooker, enjoying the benefit of his defence of the Church without running any political or financial risk. Hooker and Saravia probably found common ground not only in many of their shared views on religious issues but also in their respective opinions of the *modus operandi* of the Machiavellian archbishop of Canterbury. Despite the mutual interests and opinions that drew these two brilliant defenders of emergent Anglicanism into a growing friendship, there was much that distinguished them. Saravia, a generation older than Hooker, had risen rapidly in the church hierarchy and was a far more sophisticated and worldly figure than the pastor of Bishopsbourne.

Still, the two men had some experiences in common. Both had been at Oxford, Saravia for a shorter time and with less academic distinction. Both had had differences with Hooker's mentor, John Rainolds. In 1588 Saravia had quarrelled with Rainolds about a tract written by the Oxford scholar Hugh Broughton, *A Conceit of Scripture*, in which Broughton had attempted to reconcile historical chronologies with the Bible. Rainolds had taken offence at the piece and attacked Broughton more fiercely than the occasion warranted. Archbishop Whitgift interceded and asked Saravia to moderate the dispute on his behalf. After looking into the matter, the Dutchman advised Whitgift to side with Broughton against Rainolds. Saravia decided that Broughton's effort to reconcile history and tradition with Scripture, although flawed in the execution, was commendable in principle. It was no doubt comforting for Hooker to discover in his new friend a person who had successfully bearded his formidable Calvinist mentor.

Hooker and Saravia found other areas of agreement. One was on the question of predestination. Back in 1590 Whitgift had asked Saravia to draft an assessment of a controversy over the doctrine of predestination that had begun when William Barrett preached a sermon at Cambridge criticizing the views of Luther, Calvin, Beza, and Peter Martyr on this subject. As a long-time Calvinist, Saravia could hardly dispute God's predestination of all human acts. Yet he was troubled by the consequent idea that human beings are morally unaccountable for their actions. So he defended Barrett's opinion that God, despite His prior *knowledge* of all that men may do, leaves them free to make their own choices.[22]

Hooker was wrestling with the same problem, and reaching much the same conclusion, in his forthcoming Book V of the *Laws*. In fact, discussions with his new friend may have helped Hooker to clarify his opinions as the two scholars shared insights and authorities on this most troublesome issue of their day. Hooker would have described for Saravia his Paul's Cross sermons and subsequent debate with Travers at the Temple and been reassured when Saravia confirmed his own opinion that while God knows all, he does not hinder personal freedom to choose good or evil. Hooker was supported also by Saravia's opinion that a possible consequence of human freedom is good works as an evidence of faith. None of these issues was a simple matter of black and white, the two men agreed. Above all, one must keep an open mind and adopt the broadest possible position on issues like these.[23]

During their visits to one another, at Bishopsbourne and Canterbury, the friendship ripened. Hooker soon learned that his new friend was a master at collecting multiple church livings, usually paying scant attention to any that involved pastoral and preaching duties. Saravia had been rector at Tatenhill, north of Birmingham, for eight years while he was simultaneously a prebendary at Gloucester. Apparently he had spent little time at either place. Now that he was a canon at Canterbury he still retained the other posts and was also rector at Lewisham and at Great Chart in Kent. Sitting right here in his parlour, Hooker had a living example of the abuses of multiple livings and absentee clergy which the Puritans rightly attacked and the Church laboured to reform.[24]

Did Adrian have a moral problem accepting positions that he never really filled? Would he be able to meet any of the rector's obligations at Great Chart and Lewisham, much less Tatenhill and Gloucester Cathedral, and still attend chapter meetings at Canterbury? No doubt the two men discussed the issue. Richard, after all, had taken largely absentee posts at Salisbury Cathedral, Boscombe, and Netheravon so that he could spend time in London writing his book. Both men knew they were part of a serious problem. They may have comforted one another that there was no other realistic way for the Church to compensate its officials and scholars except to continue the regrettable practice of absentee livings. Guilt, like misery, loves company.[25]

BOOK VII

In their frequent meetings during the final years of Hooker's life, the older scholar was especially helpful in the shaping of Book VII of the *Laws*, which dealt with the episcopacy. Richard had this Book, along with Books V, VI, and VIII, in good draft form as early as the spring of 1593, before coming to Bishopsbourne. Publication had been delayed because Sandys and Cranmer wanted him to make changes—and Sandys, after all, was paying the costs of publication. Saravia may have helped him refine Book VII so that it became the most polished of the final three.[26]

Hooker would have been at first surprised that a long-time Calvinist like Saravia could be so supportive of the episcopacy. In fact, it had taken the Dutch theologian some years to abandon the presbyterian polity. When he did so, it was primarily out of a conviction that what was appropriate as a form of church government in Geneva, Zurich, or Leiden was not necessarily applicable in England. Each country had its own traditions when it came to ecclesiastical polity. There was no single form sanctioned by Christ. There could and should be variety. The longer he had lived in England, the more Saravia had come to believe that what worked best here was the time-honoured system of episcopal governance, not elders and deacons.

Furthermore, when he was in Holland, teaching at Leiden and serving as rector of the university there, many of Saravia's colleagues never thought him sufficiently orthodox in his Calvinism, especially on major issues such as predestination and the nature of Christ's presence in the Eucharist. He had always protested that he was a good Calvinist, but perhaps he had never been dogmatic enough. How Hooker identified with this problem! He had had similar experiences with orthodox Calvinists such as Rainolds and Travers.

Saravia went so far in his support of the episcopacy as to say that if there were indeed a single best form of Church governance, it would be rule by bishops. His reading of Scripture taught him that there was a difference between the Apostles and other ministers. His reading of history made it clear to him that in theory and practice there had always been a gradation of ecclesiastical authority among clergy, with bishops, patterned on the twelve Apostles, at the top. Over many years, he eventually reached the conclusion that Christ himself had probably chosen the episcopal form as best for his Church. But he drew a distinction between the general matter of who governs the Church and the narrower issue of how ministers are made. One might in theory hold that a call to the ministry comes from God and then is received and validated in many different ways, including election by a congregation, and yet at the same time maintain that supreme authority in the Church belongs to bishops, not congregations with their elders and deacons. By this theory, Saravia's ordination in

Holland was valid in the Church of England so long as he fully accepted the authority of English bishops over him.

This was fine in theory but as a practical matter, if bishops did not have the power to ordain ministers, then any other authority they had was greatly diminished. Saravia insisted that he was talking only about foreigners ordained in their own countries and then coming, at the sufferance of English bishops, to serve as ministers in the Church of England. In no way would legitimacy of foreign ordination apply to Englishmen who were ordained abroad and then claimed admission to the English clergy solely on the strength of such ordination. A man like Hooker's nemesis Walter Travers, who openly defied episcopal authority in his own Church by refusing to submit to its authority over him in the matter of ordination, had no legitimacy in the Church and was, in fact, little short of committing treason.

As the two men shared experiences and opinions on the subject of ordination, they agreed that how ordination occurs is not a matter of ultimate importance touching salvation. The form might vary according to a country's traditions and customs, so long as it was done in a reverent manner, acknowledging that a call to ministry comes from God and that the Church, by whatever means, merely confirms God's choice. They also agreed about the important functions and duties of bishops in governing the Church: to build up the faith, train and nurture the clergy, maintain a decent and orderly religious behaviour among the people, manage the properties and money of the Church wisely, and in every way bring honour and glory to Christ by reflecting His goodness and grace in their own lives.

The two men did not agree on Saravia's assertion of the divine authorization of the English espicopacy. The Dutchman went too far for Hooker when he claimed that Christ himself had set bishops over his Church. Hooker did not think it possible to know God's will so definitively on such a secondary issue as this, one clearly not essential to salvation. Also, he thought Scripture to be not nearly so definitive on this question as his friend did. Hooker was willing to concede that the order of bishops might have been divinely established, but not that it was definitely so. In Book VII, he went so far as to say that it was due to "divine instinct" that the Apostles began this "sacred" regimen of bishops. He also claimed that the institution had the authority of tradition, having been with the Church in some form or another for more than fifteen hundred years. He was aware, however, that congregational approval of new ministers was often a part of the process in the early Church. On balance, Hooker preferred a common sense position affirming only that there was at least as good a case to be made out of Scripture for episcopal polity as for the presbyterian form and that the English preferred their system of bishops because it was reasonable and conformed nicely to their history and traditions. He would rather just let it go at that. He was not inclined to be pressured into saying more than he believed about the origins of bishops' powers merely because such a statement might be politically advantageous to the Church establishment. Characteristically, Hooker's defence of episcopacy rose above the polemic of the day and found voice in such lofty expressions as: "A most certain truth it is that churches and cathedrals and the bishops in them are like mirrors in which the face and very countenance of apostolic antiquity remains ever to be seen, not withstanding of the alterations wrought by the passage of time and the course of events. For the defence and maintenance of them we are most earnestly committed to strive, even as the Jews were for their Temple and the High-Priest of God therein."[28]

For his part, Saravia probably found Hooker's views on the episcopacy timid. Bishops of the day needed unequivocal support from scholars such as Hooker and himself. Bishops were in a difficult position, caught between the crown, on whom they depended for appointment and support, and their clergy, who screamed constantly for more independence. The real intention of troublemakers such as Travers and Cartwright in their quibbling over the liturgy was to gain freedom from bishops and eventually to overturn the episcopacy altogether. One need only take a good look at the Second *Admonition* or at Cartwright's *Reply* to Whitgift's *Answere* to see that this was the case.[29]

Hooker agreed with his friend that many presbyterians had ulterior motives when they attacked church ceremonies. Their true aim was to topple bishops and, perhaps, kings as well. Richard had said as much in the opening lines of Book VII. For his part, Saravia approved Hooker's laying bare the strategy of the radical Puritan campaign, which was to mount a three-pronged attack against the traditional pillars of English society: the nobility, the courts, and the Church. The radical Calvinists and separatists were too clever, Hooker said, to strike directly at either the nobility or the judges and lawyers, so they pretended to make common cause with these two groups against the weakest branch of the commonwealth, the Church, and especially the bishops. The Puritans cynically urge that the nobility will grow richer and the courts will gain broader jurisdiction as the established Church declines in power. So-called reformers strike their axes at the weakest branch first, while making the claim that the sap from that wound will flow freely into the other two branches. A nice metaphor.[30]

In Book VIII, Hooker went still farther and warned that some of the Protestant extremists meant to strike against the monarchy itself. For the present, they deferred to the queen for political advantage, but their true intent was to ease her out as soon as possible.[31]

Withal, there was ambivalence in Hooker's attitude to the episcopacy. His advocacy, in Book VII, of good livings, titles, retinues of attendants, handsome estates, special social and legal privileges, and large financial endowments for prelates may be taken as indication that bishops, if not divinely ordained, were the next thing to it. Hooker justified such wealth as a practical aid to social cohesion in a commonwealth where bishops, like judges, scholars, and ministers of state, required the financial independence and social status that would engender the public deference necessary to maintaining the general well-being of the community. Such outward signs and tokens of office signify to everyone the importance of a social hierarchy within which each person may find his own place, and so his own peace and safety.[32]

Having said this much for the status of bishops, Hooker assured Saravia that, as he saw it, the true measure of good bishops was not that they be rich and titled. A bishop must be a wise and careful shepherd of Christ's flock. Hooker was dismayed by the abuses committed by too many bishops of the day, and said so forthrightly. He enumerated the travesties of prelates who carelessly ordained their clergy, corruptly bestowed church livings, and held parish visitations to see what extra income they might glean from them. Rather than instructing and supporting their ministers, some bishops continued to engage in the foul system of encouraging multiple livings beyond the legitimate needs of the recipients of them.[33]

Defending bishops was always difficult for Hooker. On the one hand, he was aware that the Calvinist extremists exaggerated episcopal abuses for their own gain as they "gaped after spoil" with their "gleeful attacks" on the supposed wealth of prelates. At the same time, he recognized that many objections were justified. A system so riddled with corruption and abuse was difficult to justify. The injury that issued from defects in the episcopal system of the day was exceedingly great. If bishops did not begin deporting themselves in a proper manner, they would never be respected. The Church at large would be the loser. It was imperative to put the episcopal house in order before it rotted from within.[34]

Saravia may have warned Hooker, as the two reviewed drafts of Book VII, that his friend was coming dangerously close, at one place, to pointing an accusatory finger at the queen as the one responsible for abuses in the Church. This was where he wrote that despite all the pressures upon "her royal majesty" to appropriate church wealth for her own use, "her sacred majesty" has given her word not to seek or allow "gain by pillage" of the Church. Though not saying the queen was at fault, merely using the words "pillage" and "her royal majesty" in the same sentence could be misunderstood. Queen Elizabeth's propensity to acquire whatever she laid her hands on, in the Church or anywhere else, was so well-known that even to raise the issue could cause trouble for Hooker.[35]

In the final analysis, Hooker insisted on the need to support bishops and their financial independence even if they were sometimes corrupt. In his view, it was a mistake to rob them of their wealth because that was the same as robbing Christ. He wrote in Book VII that "even if bishops were all unworthy, not only of [their] living, but even of life, yet what hath our Lord Jesus Christ deserved, for which men judge him worthy to have the things that are his given away from him unto others that have no right unto them? For at this mark it is that the head lay-reformers all aim."[36]

Furthermore, it made no practical sense to plunder the Church. The gain to the State would be much less than the loss because "no one order of subjects whatsoever within this land bears the seventh part of what the clergy bears in the burdens of the commonwealth." Each year, Hooker claimed, the government took some £26,000 from church revenues. All the world could see that the Church had fallen to a low ebb as a result. It was deplorable! "To rob God, to ransack the Church, to overthrow the whole order of Christian bishops . . . what man of common honesty can think it . . . lawful or just?" Hooker asked.[37]

Hooker was overwrought by what he saw as the weakening of the Church through the systematic despoiling of its wealth by the government and the consequent corrupting of bishops. But there was another side of Hooker as well, perhaps the less practical, more spiritual, side, as when he said, on the same subject: "After all, if in the end those of us who labour in the Church are reduced to begging for alms, we will be no worse off than our ancestors who worked before us to guide people to salvation."[38]

BOOK V

During his time at Bishopsbourne, Hooker published his most enduring contribution to the Anglican tradition: his explanation and defence, in Book V of the *Laws*, of the faith and practice of the Church of England. No other treatise has had a more profound influence on the spiritual life of Anglicans. In Book V Hooker gave the Church he loved its most complete and inspirational *raison d'être*. He completed in this Book the formulation of the basic spirit of Anglicanism, begun by Archbishop Cranmer fifty years earlier in the *Book of Common Prayer*. Hooker brought Cranmer's book to life, giving it meaning for clergy and lay people as well as countless writers and scholars outside the Church.[39]

Because Hooker was a reluctant, if effective, political polemicist, his heart was always in Book V, the least political part of his treatise. Influences by outside persons, such as Sandys and Cranmer, had little if any impact on this portion of the *Laws*. Archbishop Whitgift, to whom Book V is dedicated, may have helped to shape some parts of the work, and trusted theologians whom Hooker respected, such as Adrian Saravia and Lancelot Andrewes, may have made suggestions. But, excepting some of his sermons and tracts, Book V of the *Laws* is as pure and undiluted an expression of Hooker's thinking on the subjects he cared most deeply about as we shall ever see.[40]

Book V reads, in parts, as though it were written for the ages. Nothing done by Jewel, Whitgift, Bancroft, or any other apologist for emergent Anglicanism, is comparable. Hooker went far beyond mere refutation of criticisms of the Church by such Puritans as Thomas Cartwright. He offered a positive justification for the entire worship service: why Anglicans prefer prescribed common prayers to what they often regard as either the minister's personal catharsis, or worse yet, just so much quasi-sponateous babble; how and why Anglicans use the psalms and litanies; their joy in church music, beautiful sanctuaries, and appropriate clerical vestments; why sermons are so much less important to them than prayer and the sacraments. As long as there is a Church of England and a world-wide Anglican community, Hooker's Book V will endure as the most important *apologia* for those Churches. Only Anglican writers who came after Hooker and drew directly from his treatise would match or surpass his brilliance.

Hooker's reflections in Book V on prayer are especially noteworthy as examples of the enduring influence of this part of the *Laws* in shaping one of the main pillars of Anglican religious thought and practice. Prayer, he believed, was the very *raison d'être* of the Church. "Is not the name of prayer usual to signify . . . all the service that ever we do unto God?" In one place, he wrote of how prayer can come in many forms: "Every good and holy desire, though it lack the form, has, notwithstanding, in itself the substance, and with him, the voice of prayer, who regardeth the very moanings, groans, and sighs of the heart of man." In another place, he explained succinctly some of the conditions that must prevail for a prayer to be efficacious: "first the lack of that which we pray for; secondly, a feeling of want; thirdly an earnest willingness of mind to be eased therein; fourthly, a declaration of this our desire in the sight of God . . ."

He repeatedly made it clear that for prayer to work, the supplicant must first believe in God's mercy and acknowledge dependency on God. He always emphasized the primacy of faith and the sovereignty of God as keys to prayer.[41]

When Cartwright objected to the "prayer for deliverance from all adversities," solely on the ground that he could find no warrant for this kind of prayer in Holy Scripture, Hooker did not spend much time "quibbling" with "T. C." but went right to the heart of why he thought it was beneficial to have such general prayers for deliverance from future calamities, as well as from those that presently afflicted people, whether or not these prayers were set forth in Scripture:

> To think we may pray unto God for nothing but what He has promised in Holy Scripture we shall obtain is perhaps an error.
>
> Prayers are unto God most acceptable sacrifices because they testify we desire nothing but what comes by His hands; and our desires we submit with contentment to be over-ruled by His will.

Hooker was making the point here that it is good to pray to God for what there is no foreknowledge of because that is a way of demonstrating total reliance upon God. Hooker elevated the argument with Cartwright and others from a bickering over what Scripture does and does not mean to a rational discussion of the relationship between faith and prayer.

Common (corporate) prayer has always been a hallmark of Anglicanism. Hooker explained that it was preferable to private prayers because, when God's people gather as a community to worship, their single voice rises to God with an assurance, a worthiness, a shared judgement, and a public consensus which soars beyond the private petitions and thanksgivings of each individual believer.[42]

When he defended the Church's common prayer "for the salvation of all believers," Hooker was treading on dangerous ground. In that age of strident anti-Catholicism, a general prayer of this kind was easily construed as including the hated papists within the folds of its entreaty to God. But Hooker insisted on emphasizing God's love for all his children and God's likely response to all who called upon him in faithful prayer. This is a theme that shines throughout all Hooker's writing and marks his Anglican heirs with the sign of Christian tolerance and inclusiveness to the present.

> Christian charity thirsteth after the good of the whole world . . . [because God's] ***desire***, is to have ***all*** men saved, a work most suitable with His purpose who gave Himself to be the price of redemption for ***all*** . . .
>
> [C]oncerning the state of ***all*** men with whom we live . . . we may till the world's end . . . always presume that . . . there is hope of everyman's forgiveness . . . And therefore charity which hopeth all things prayeth also for ***all*** men [author's emphasis].

Perhaps Hooker's most beautiful paean to prayer is at the beginning of his discussion of the topic in Book V.

> "Between the throne of God in heaven and his Church upon earth . . . if it be so that Angels have their continual intercourse, where should we find the same more verified than in those two ghostly exercises, the one Doctrine, and the other Prayer? For what is the assembling of the Church to learn, but the receiving of Angels descended from above? What to pray, but the sending of Angels upward? His heavenly inspirations and our holy desires are as so many Angels of intercourse and commerce between God and us."[43]

Another of Hooker's lasting contributions in Book V is his treatment of the sacraments, especially the Eucharist. His resolution of the argument about the presence of Christ in the elements has endured within the Anglican community over the centuries. In the midst of the terrible disputes between transubstantialists, consubstantialists, and those who saw the Sacrament as a mere symbol or token of some mysterious act of God, Hooker said simply that we shall never know in what form Christ is manifest in the sacramental elements any more than we can know in exactly what way God is incarnate in Christ. But Christians do believe that Christ is incarnate in the Sacrament just as God is incarnate in Christ, even though they cannot know how this works. The doctrine of Incarnation has been a key to Anglican understanding of the Eucharist and other miracles of God ever since Hooker made it so. He insisted that the Eucharist is not, as the Puritans said, a mere symbol or naked sign intended to teach something about Christ. Rather, sacraments are "heavenly mysteries" and "visible signs of invisible grace," a grace so real and present that it actually "worketh salvation."[44]

But how are we to be certain that the Sacrament "worketh salvation?" Not by debating the issue, said Hooker, but by experiencing God's grace through the act of *participating* in the Eucharistic liturgy. When we "participate" in Christ's incarnation in the Eucharist, as we are supposed to do on a regular basis, God makes his "glorious presence" known to us and "delivereth into our hands that grace available unto eternal life." As we are co-mingled in the Eucharist with Christ, we participate in his resurrection. What happens within the renewed life and spirit of the believer as he participates in this act of Communion with Christ is our surest evidence of Christ's real presence, not what does or what does not happen to the elements of bread and wine.[45]

Consequently, Hooker says, we should not concern ourselves with the unanswerable question of exactly *what* or *who* is present in the elements of the Eucharist. The elements "contain *in themselves* no vital force or efficacy, [and] they are not physical but *moral instruments* of salvation, duties of service and worship, which unless we perform as the Author of grace requireth, are unprofitable . . ." It is our "performance" that makes the miracle work. If we do not faithfully receive the Sacrament, if we do not participate with God and Christ as partners in this holy transaction, then there is no Holy Communion, no Eucharist. Our participation in this liturgy is indispensable to the process of Christ's incarnation in us.[46]

This "participation" is mutual. We and Christ possess each other in the Eucharist.

> Participation is that mutual inward hold which Christ has of us and we of him, in such sort that each possesses the other by ways of special interest, property and inherent copulation.[47]
>
> For does any man doubt but that even from the flesh of Christ our very bodies do receive that life which shall make them glorious at the later day, and for which they are already accounted parts of his blessed body? Our corruptible bodies could never live the life they live, were it

not that they are joined with his body, which is incorruptible, and that his is in ours as a cause of immortality.[48]

Book V is a storehouse of what was to become Anglican doctrine. So much of it shows Hooker's common sense approach to complex theological issues, as well as his gift for soaring prose, the sort that loses precision as it gains altitude but endures at lofty heights. For example, on the always complicated issue of the Triune God—the Trinity—he wrote:

> The Father as goodness, the Son as wisdom, the Holy Ghost as power do all concur in every particular, outwardly issuing from that only glorious Deity which they all are. For that which moves God to work is goodness, and that which orders his work is Wisdom, and that which perfects his work is Power. All things which God in their times and seasons has brought forth were eternally and before all times in God, as a work unbegun in the artificer, which afterward he brings into effect. Therefore whatsoever we do behold now in this present world, it was enwrapped within the bowels of divine Mercy, written in the book of eternal Wisdom, and held in the hands of omnipotent Power, the first foundations of the world being as yet unlaid.[49]

Hooker wrote much in Book V about the nature of the Church. Once again, the doctrine of Incarnation was at the core of his thinking. Anglicans since Hooker have uniformly defined their Church as the Body of Christ in the world. For Hooker "Body of Christ" was not a cold doctrine. This Body was a community filled with love and mutual support for its members. It was a living body of loved and loving believers. The humanity of Hooker is never more evident than when he speaks of the Church, his own true mother:

> The Church is to us that very mother of our new birth, in whose bowels we are bred, at whose breasts we receive nourishment.
>
> We are . . . in God through Christ . . . from the time of our actual adoption into the body of his true Church, into the fellowship of his children. For his Church he knows and loves, so that they which are in the Church are thereby known to be in him. Our being in Christ by eternal foreknowledge saves us not without our actual . . . incorporation into that society which has him for their Head, and makes together with him one Body . . .
>
> God made Eve of the rib of Adam. And his Church he framed out of the very flesh, the wounded and bleeding side of the Son of man.[50]

Hooker completed his editing of Book V during his early years at Bishopsbourne. It was published in 1597. By then he had finished the final three Books as well, although Book VIII still needed more work. Sandys and Cranmer were still pressing him to include additional specific refutations of the Barrowists and Brownists, references to the

Marprelate Tracts, and an attack on atheists. Some of this political material he eventually agreed to include. Even Book V has a polemical cast at some points. But for the most part, in this fifth Book he had written an apology for the Church that rose above contemporary politics to a higher ground from which it would illumine the life of Anglicans for centuries.[51]

NOTES

1. In a recent essay, Collinson speculates that one reason why Hooker might not have aspired to higher posts was that his fortunate marriage removed the financial need to do so. I agree. I also agree with Collinson that Hooker probably antagonized some in the church hierarchy who might have advanced his career, by his refusal to be more pointedly political (less ambiguous) in his defence of the religious establishment. See "Hooker and the Elizabethan Establishment: in McGrade, *Hooker and Christian Community*, 166.

For descriptions of Bishopsbourne by twentieth-century admirers see Arthur Mee, *Kent* (London: Hodder and Stoughton, 1936), 49-50; Frank Entwisle, *Abroad in England* (London: André Deutsch, 1982), 18-20; 37-40. Watling (Wattle) Street was one of the four main Roman roads in Britain. The others were Guithelin, Ermine, and Icknield. (The latter makes a well-known appearance in the opening pages of Thomas Hardy's *Jude the Obscure*. See Harrison, 443.)

2. Walton says that the queen gave Hooker, "whom she loved well," this "good living of Bourne" with effect from 7 July 1595. Walton, *Life*, 69. The correct date is 7 January 1595, Edelen, *Folger*, VI, Pt. 1, xxiv; Sisson, 45. It would appear that Hooker also served as rector of the church of St John the Baptist in nearby Barham, which was larger than Bishopsbourne in those days and still is today. The list of rectors for St John's shows Hooker listed for 1594-95, and then no one in the post until 1600. Apparently, Bishopsbourne was the principal church in the Elham Valley in Hooker's day. It was closer to Canterbury and had a fine rectory. Hooker's ministry at Barham was probably non-stipendiary.

3. Walton and Keble agree that Hooker held no other benefices while at Bishopsbourne. See *Works*, I, 70 and n. 41.

4. Unfortunately, Hooker's rectory was demolished in 1954 to make way for a private house. As recently as 1936, the historian Arthur Mee (*op. cit.*) visited the very room where Hooker studied and reported that he could look out of the window and see, as Hooker had, the 250-foot-long yew hedge that for centuries has been known as the "Hooker hedge" and, just beyond the hedge, the west side of the lovely church of St Mary the Virgin. Alas, this grand, well-furnished Hooker homestead with its fine ceilings of moulded black oak beams, the only home he ever had to call his own, is no more.

5. These and other details of the layout and furnishings in Hooker's Bishopsbourne house are drawn from Rosemary Keen, ed., "Inventory of Richard Hooker 1601," *Archaeologica Cantiana* (Ashford, Kent: Heidley Brothers, Ltd., 1957), LXX, 231-6.

6. At the time of his death five years later, the value of Hooker's goods and chattels was appraised by Robert Rose and Edward Slater at £613.7s., including books and book hampers at £300 and a small amount of cash, clothing, and plate. This was a substantial inheritance for his wife and children. *Ibid.*, 231.

7. Walton and Keble record the polite relationship between rector and clerk. They also tell us that Sampson so admired his master that when, in the middle of the next century, he discovered that one of Hooker's successors was planning to introduce a Puritan form of liturgy at St Marys, he served his beloved master's memory by refusing to participate. The bare tale is Walton's; Keble did the research

and gives us the clerk's name and some facts about his life. See Walton, *Life*, 78-9 and Keble in *Works*, 79, n. 1

8. These historic wall-paintings, which were probably but not certainly there during Hooker's tenure, are currently being uncovered and, one hopes, restored. See Peter Austin and Tom Organ, *Report on the Conservation of the 14th Century Wall Paintings,* 1995. (Available as an unpublished research paper from the Reverend Alan Duke, at St Mary's, Bishopsbourne.)

9. This widely-used manual for private devotions was first published in 1570. At a time when private prayers and devotions were not prescribed by the Church but left to individual preference, a collection like this was useful. Bull was a Fellow at Magdalen, Oxford, who collected his devotions from various clergymen over many years. See Henry Bull, ed., *Christian Prayers and Holy Meditations* (Cambridge: The Parker Society, 1842), and William Keating Clay, ed., *Liturgies and Occasional Forms of Prayer Set Forth in the Realm of Queen Elizabeth* (Cambridge: Cambridge University Press, 1847), 30: 54.

10. Clay, 55.

11. *Ibid.*, 53.

12. Walton, *Life*, 77.

13. *Works*, I, 122.

14. Paget, 204.

15. Walton, *Life*, 80-1.

16. What follows is a faithful rendering, with some paraphrase and modernization, of Hooker's *Sermon Fragment on Proverbs 3, Folger* V, 414-17.

17. What follows is a faithful rendering, with some paraphrase and modernization, of portions of Hooker's *Sermon on Matthew 7:7, Folger* V, 385-94.

18. What follows is a faithful rendering, with some paraphrase and modernization, of portions of Hooker's *Sermon Fragment on Hebrews 2:14-15, Folger* V, 402-13.

19. The foregoing is drawn by faithful rendering with some modernization of portions of Hooker's *Sermon Fragment on Matthew 27:46, Folger* V, 399-401.

20. See Walton, *Life*, 74-77; *Works,* 74, notes 1, 2, 3 and 4; 75, n.1. In recent years two Hooker scholars have expressed similar views, noting especially Saravia's probable influence on Book VII of the *Laws*. See McGrade, "Introduction to Book VII," *Folger*, VI, Pt. I, 336 and James Cargill Thompson, "The Philosophy of the Politic Society," in Hill, *Studies in Richard Hooker*, 69, n. 26.

21. A fine copy of the original English edition, printed by John Wolfe in London, is in the Lambeth Library. A good treatment of his life and thought is Willem Nijenhuis, *Adrianus Saravia (1523-1613)* (Leiden: E. J. Brill, 1980).

22. Nijenhuis, 131-3; 71-74.

23. *Ibid.*, 71; 132-3.

24. Saravia was conscientious about attending chapter meetings during his six years at Canterbury. But after being named a canon at Westminster in 1601, he spent most of his days in London. He took Lancelot Andrewes' stall when Andrewes was named dean at Westminster. *Ibid.*,110-11; 115-16; 130.

25. *Ibid.*, 133.

26. Letters from Sandys and Cranmer and their notes on Hooker's drafts show that Hooker probably had this work in draft form by April of 1593. For a full discussion of problems associated with dating the last three Books, see McGrade, "The Three Last Books and Hooker's Autograph Notes," *Folger*, VI, Pt. I, 235 and William Haugaard, "Introduction to the Preface," *Ibid.*, 41-46.

27. See *Folger* III, 149-53, 169-99; *Works* III, 145-9, 167-200 for Hooker's description of the duties and powers of bishops.

28. This quotation is from *Folger*, III, 184; *Works*, III, 183.

29. McGrade, *op. cit.*, 311-26 has a good discussion of these issues.

30. *Folger* III, 145-6, 344-6; *Works* III, 141-2, 354-6.

31. *Folger* III, 213-216, 168-172, 147-148; *Works* III, 155-68, 217-19, 166-8, 143-5. James I was to raise Hooker's and Saravia's concerns to the level of national policy early in the next century. His experience as a child and as monarch in Scotland had taught him well to be wary of the political danger inherent in Calvinist extremists. At the Hampton Court Conference in 1604, which gave birth to the so-called King James version of the Bible, the new king uttered his famous, "No Bishop, no King" remark, signaling his fear that if presbyterian discipline was permitted in England that would spell the end of the monarchy. "I will harry them [presbyterian Calvinists] out of this land," thundered the king. And he did. They fled by the thousands to colonial America where they established their own style of religious and political intolerance in New England.
32. For Hooker's extended case for privileges of episcopal office, see *Folger* III, 264-89; *Works* III, 274-302.
33. *Folger* III, 293-8; *Works* III, 306-10.
34. *Folger* III, 299-300, 308; *Works* III, 312-13, 321-2.
35. *Folger* III, 306-7; *Works* III, 320.
36. *Folger* III, 290-1; *Works* III, 1: 302.
37. *Folger* III, 307-11; *Works* III, 321-5.
38. *Folger* III, 311-12; *Works* III, 324-5.
39. A definitive comparison of the ideas of Cranmer and Hooker has yet to be written. In an excellent recent biography of Cranmer, Diarmaid MacCulloch says that the great archbishop was "far from being an Anglican." However, Cranmer's long feud with the arch high-churchman, Stephen Gardiner, makes him seem, by contrast, more evangelical than in fact he was, just as Hooker's conflict with extreme Calvinists makes him seem more Catholic than he was. I believe that the two men shared, broadly speaking, a preference for Lutheran rather than Calvinist strands of the Reformation in England, i.e., a reformed Catholicism based on established national churches governed by princes and bishops, with prescribed forms of worship and biblically based theology. MacCulloch, *Thomas Cranmer a Life*, (London and New Haven: Yale University Press, 1996), esp. 264, 617.
40. It is reasonable to suppose both that Hooker saw Book V as a defence of *The Book of Common Prayer*, and that Whitgift had an interest in the completion of Book V, saw advanced drafts, and may have sought to influence some parts of it. See Booty, "Commentary of Book V," *Folger*, VI, Pt.I, 192-3. Certainly, Hooker was familiar with Whitgift's earlier controversy with Thomas Cartwright (TC) and was probably influenced by his sarcastic treatments of Cartwright's criticisms of the Prayer Book liturgy. For examples of the sort of writing Hooker would have admired in Whitgift and that he may have emulated in parts of Book V, see John Whitgift, *A Defence of the Ecclesiastical Regiment in Englande defaced by T. C. in his Replie against D. Whitgift* (London: Henry Bynneman, 1574), 133. (Original copy in Lambeth Library.)
41. *Folger* II, 110, 189-92; *Works* II, 115, 200-3.
42. *Folger* II, 111-121, 198-9; *Works* II, 116-127, 202, 209-10.
43. *Folger* II, 110, 203; *Works* II, 115, 214-15.
44. *Folger* II, 207-9; *Works* II, 219-22.
45. *Folger* II, 244-8; *Works* II, 255-9. I am indebted to John Booty for highlighting the concept of "participation" in Hooker's doctrine of the Eucharist. See Booty's "Commentary on Book V," in *Folger*, VI, Pt. I, 197-8.
46. *Folger* II, 246-7; *Works* II, 257-8.
47. *Folger* II, 234; *Works* II, 245-51, 219-22.
48. *Folger* II, 241; *Works* II, 251-2.
49. *Folger* II, 236-8; *Works* II, 247-8.
50. *Folger* II, 239-40; *Works* II, 249-50.
51. Hooker refers to a "politic use of religion" by unbelievers who follow the lead of such "wise malignants" as Machiavelli, whose *Discourses* he cites. This section on

atheism may have been one of the additions to Book V that he was urged to write. *Folger* II, 25-26; *Works* II, 21-22. Booty, *Folger*, VI. Pt. I, 187-93. Cranmer and Sandys made strong suggestions for changes and additions in both style and content of most of the Books of the *Laws*. Their notes on an early draft of Book VI, which is now in the archives at Corpus Christi College, give evidence of this fact. More evidence on the process of writing the last books is seen in the notes made by Hooker on his copies of the last three books, first discovered by P. G. Stanwood at Trinity College, Dublin, in 1974. See *Folger* III, xx-xxxvi.

CHAPTER 17

The Final Years

By all accounts, Hooker was never physically vigorous. His rather early death at age forty-seven may have been the consequence of unhealthy living conditions he endured at Oxford and the numerous plagues he survived in London. The emotional stresses of his career at the Temple and continual harpings by Sandys and Cranmer to revise his *magnum opus* did nothing to improve his constitution. Although his spirits revived in Bishopsbourne, his body did not.[1]

His frail physical nature was not helped by trips to unhealthy London to visit Joan's family, to discuss his book and other church business with friends and colleagues, and to attend special family celebrations. One such special occasion was the christening at the family church of St Augustine's of his and Joan's fifth child, her first live birth in four years. This happy event took place on 21 June 1596. Little Edwin Hooker was named either for Richard's former patron, the late Archbishop Sandys, or for the archbishop's son, Richard's patron and friend, Edwin—or both. Once again, there was the prospect of a male heir to carry Hooker's name into the next generation.[2]

Edwin Sandys was not present for the christening as he was at the time on an extended journey on the Continent with George Cranmer. Close friends since their days together at Corpus Christi under Hooker's tutelage, these two men travelled in Europe together for more than two years, visiting political and religious leaders. The trip was to be formative for Sandys' reputation as a religious thinker in his own right, for it led him, unwittingly perhaps, to spread some of Hooker's ideas on to the international stage. As a result of his trip, he wrote an influential treatise, not published until 1605, entitled *A Relation to the State of Religion*, reissued in 1629 as *Europae Speculum*. In this work, in the spirit of his mentor, Sandys recommended reconciliation among the reformed Christian Churches of Europe. His debt to Hooker's ideas is clear in the book's opening words:

> Having now almost finished the course of travel, and coming to cast up (as it was) the short account of my labours, I shall here endeavour briefly to relate what I have observed in the matter of Religion . . . in those Western parts of the world, their divided factions and professions and differences in matters of faith, and their exercises of religion, in government ecclesiastical, and in life and conversation, what virtues in each kind emanate, what eminent defects. Moreover, in what terms of

opposition or correspondence each bindeth with other, what probabilities, what policies, what hopes, what jealousies are found in each part for the advancing therof: and finally, what possibilities and good means for uniting, at least wise the several branches of reformed professions.[3]

Sandys and Hooker could not agree on revisions in Books VI, VII, and VIII before Sandys' departure for Europe in 1596, and so those Books were not included with Book V in the forthcoming 1597 edition of the *Laws*. Edwin was still baulking at Hooker's treatment of the courts and religious penance in Book VI, and found his support of the episcopacy in Book VII and royal headship of the Church in Book VIII not sufficiently fervent. Hooker was disappointed by this reaction. The entire work was probably now completed to his satisfaction.[4] Nevertheless, he continued to labour at revising parts of the *Laws*, although with decidedly less enthusiasm. With Sandys and Cranmer out of the country for an extended time and Joan safely delivered of his new son, Hooker worked to prepare Book V for publication. It was ready by early 1597 and printed later that year. Thereafter, he largely abandoned further work on the last three Books.[5]

Hooker hoped the words of his dedication of Book V to Whitgift would not seem to lack sufficient deference. Perhaps he should have invoked God's blessing on Whitgift personally and not merely on "all who fear" God. He disliked the excessive flattery that so often characterized book dedications and could not bring himself to imitate it. He trusted that his reference in the dedication to the "scurrilous" and "immodest" writings of Martin Marprelate, and his assertion that the true intent of Martin and his friends was not religious reform but overthrow of the episcopacy, would satisfy the archbishop's appetite for political engagement. Perhaps he should not have referred so pointedly to the need for reform in the Church; but he was confident the archbishop would approve his closing words referring to their common mother, the Church—that great body they had both laboured so hard to defend: "That God which is able to make mortality immortal give her [the Church] such future continuance as may be no less glorious to all posterity than the days of her past rule have been happy to ourselves . . . In which desire I will here rest, humbly beseeching your Grace to pardon my great boldness and God to multiply his blessing upon them that fear his name."[6]

Hooker had little time to celebrate the appearance of Book V in print before terrible tragedy struck. In July of 1597, his son Edwin died, little more than a year old. Joan had taken the baby up to Enfield hoping the change in air would help. In mid-July Richard was summoned north to bury his second son in the Churchman family area of the St Andrew's churchyard, next to his little brother Richard.

Returning to Bishopsbourne, Hooker sought comfort for his grief by ministering to his flock. He probably found it especially restorative to console a member of his congregation who had recently lost his wife. He told the widower and his children: "When the Apostles and disciples grieved at the death of our blessed Saviour, he reassured them that he would never leave them, but be with them till the end of the world. 'Where I am, you shall be. My peace I give you. Let your hearts be not troubled.' No less has he promised you in your grief." As to why one's beloved family members should be taken by God, when so many who are less worthy are blessed not only with long life but also with great prosperity and good health, Hooker replied to the grieving husband, and all who have faced similar tragedy:

> We can never fathom the ways of God. But do not imagine that those blessed in this life with riches and other good fortune are happy and contented. If they seem happy, theirs is a vainly imagined felicity. In fact, they are often anxious and without contentment, lacking any peace of mind and spirit.
>
> We must be patient in our grief. Patience is the virtue that can sustain us until the worst of the pain is gone. In the meantime, take comfort in the chorus of praise we sing for your beloved, as we have for all the saints departed this life in the fear of God. Within the bosom of our Saviour's Church you and I can both take our comfort.

As for the fear of death engendered by loss of loved ones:

> There is no disgrace in being afraid. Let no one tell you that because Christ promised salvation it is a sin to be afraid of death. Fear is a natural feeling. But we are blessed, you and I, because we know where to take our fears. We run headlong into the Church, the body of Christ, where we will surely find Grace to overcome our terrors and then be comforted by the assurances of our Saviour.

Hooker spoke to the grieving parishioners not only in comforting generalities. From the pulpit, he assured the man that his wife would be missed by all members of the little church family, who admired and loved her.

> Before I say too many words and bring more wounds than comfort to your spirit, allow me to say a little about this virtuous gentlewoman in our parish who lived a dove and died a lamb. She was an example to all of us with her hearty devotion towards God, tender compassion to those in need, motherly affection to servants, kindness to friends and a mild disposition toward all. To women she was a model of rectitude, with her quiet tongue, except when duty required her to speak out, and of patience, even in the midst of her own pain.[7]

Adrian Saravia visited Bishopsbourne frequently during these final years of Hooker's life. The two men would have talked of many things, but principally church politics, from the broad issues covered in Books VII and VIII of Hooker's opus, to the latest political controversies in the Church. The peripatetic Saravia brought his friend fresh news from London. They probably talked animatedly, for example, on cold winter afternoons in early 1598 about the recently concluded session of parliament. Saravia would have reported that most of the members in Commons were newcomers. With Knollys, Wentworth, and Morice all dead since the last session, and Robert Beale absent, there were no big guns for the Puritan party. Most of the issues those days were social and financial, not religious. The recent famines and food riots across the country had prompted a long debate on proposed legislation to limit enclosures, return pastures to tillage, assist the poor, prevent soil erosion, and prevent people from leaving rural towns for the cities. These were matters of more immediate import to the people of Hooker's parish than the religious issues that had dominated recent sessions of parliament. Francis Bacon had led an effort on behalf of major legislation for poor relief, establishment of new hospitals, and tougher penalties for theft and vagrancy. Most of this failed to survive to any significant extent in the House of Lords. As for the Puritans in Commons, they seemed completely whipped. A few of them, led by Henry Finch, raised the old issue of clerical abuses. That came to little result because the queen quickly intervened and promised, in her inimitable fashion, that she would look into the matter.[8]

As experienced men of the Church whose careers had been defined by the religious controversies of the age, Hooker and Saravia must have spent many stimulating hours together during the closing years of the century in the relative peace and calm of Bishopsbourne discussing not only immediate political issues but also their respective ideas on broader theological and eccesiological questions. Hooker's recently published Book V was grist for their mill. It was reassuring to Richard whenever a man of Saravia's experience and erudition spoke admiringly of his work, as the older man undoubtedly did now, concerning the place in Book V where Hooker explored the relationship between the *Book of Common Prayer* and the civic virtue of citizens. Prayers spoken in common, within God's House, were not mere petitions to the Almighty, but the common voice of the whole people ascending in prayer to the Redeemer. When Hooker wrote that these prayers were the basis of the moral strength of the English as a people, he was doing much more than merely responding to Cartwright's pesterings about whether one should stand or kneel at prayer, how long the service should be, and where the sermon should be placed in the order of the service.

For Hooker, the Prayer Book played a central role in the relation between religion and civic virtue. Prayer Book usage was the essential means whereby the commonwealth might achieve its intended end: a happy life, well lived, protected against wickedness and malice, and enlightened as to the nature of public duties, both religious and civic. No private extemporaneous prayers, such as the Puritans advocated against the Prayer Book, could ever hope to perfom this great civic function of uniting a whole people of God in an act of public common worship.[9] He proclaimed this general theme of the integral relationship between common religious worship and civic virtue in the opening pages of Book V: "True religion is the root of all True Virtues, and the stay of Well-Ordered Commonwealths . . . Let Polity acknowledge itself indebted to Religion; godliness being the chiefest top and wellspring of all true virtues . . . So natural is the union of Religion and Justice, that we may boldly deem there is neither, where both are not."[10]

This theme was made more even explicit in Book VIII where Hooker made the point that Church and state together make a single society, a Christian commonwealth. This was the heart of Hooker's political philosophy and Saravia would have applauded it. Both men believed that there was no one in the Church of England who was not at the same time a citizen of the English commonwealth, or any member of the commonwealth who was not also a member of the Church of England. Citizens exercised their civic duties as members of the commonwealth and their religious duties as members of the Church. But in all things they were members of a single Christian commonwealth of England. For all their protestations to the contrary, what many of Calvin's disciples in England were trying to do was separate Church and State, the Brownists and Barrowists being at least forthright in this error.[11] But what of the fact that there had been a Christian commonwealth for centuries under the headship of the pope? Had Protestants not fractured that unity with their reformation of religion? Hooker's response was that, to the contrary, in those commonwealths where the Bishop of Rome held sway, there were in fact two separate societies: a church, which he rules, and a civil society ruled by a secular prince. In this realm of England, however, there was but one society: a true Christian commonwealth headed by only one ruler, a sovereign queen.[12]

This raised the dangerous question of what recourse there would be if a monarch like Queen Elizabeth were sinful and corrupted the Church with her decisions. A most perplexing issue! For his part, Hooker followed the lead of the influential thirteenth-century English jurist Henry Bracton who had said that the monarch in England had absolute powers only under the law—never above it. Hooker wrote rhapsodically on this subject:

> Happier that people whose law is the king in the greatest things, than those whose king is himself their law. Where the king guides the state

> and the law the king, that commonwealth is like a harp or melodious instrument, the strings whereof are tuned and handled all by one.
>
> I . . . commend highly their wisdom by whom the foundations of this commonwealth have been laid . . . [who assured that] no person or . . . cause [would] be unsubject to the king's power yet . . . the power of the king over all and in all [is] limited [so that] unto all his proceedings the law itself is a rule . . . "*Lex facit regum.*"[13]

Furthermore, unrestrained, royal power over the Church is, in some societies, granted originally by the whole people who make up the body politic. That transfer of power is assumed to be ratified immediately by God. Different societies make this original grant of their God-given authority to a variety of political institutions, including, as in the case of England, to a monarch. So long as the king rules, there is no authority within the realm superior to him in matters both religious and civil.

Saravia, a proponent of the idea of divine institution of church leadership, might have wondered if Hooker really intended to say that God, on his own authority, could not appoint a king as a ruler. Must all civil power derive first from the people over whom it was to be exercised? The question would have given Hooker the opportunity to show this continental Calvinist his extensive knowledge of the Bible. He was as aware as Saravia that there had been many kings of ancient Israel who were anointed directly by God as his lieutenants on earth. However, nowhere in Scripture did it say that all monarchs would have this authority. It was clear to Hooker that in Christian commonwealths like England kings had their authority to rule only from the people. Once established, however, the king ruled thereafter by divine right, since the people's action had been intended by God all along. The same pertained to kings who gained power by conquest and to those who did so by inheritance.[14]

Did Hooker mean to say that, although the power of monarchs came originally from the people of England, once given, it was transferred irrevocably and could never be reclaimed even if the king should violate their trust? Almost, but not quite. It was Hooker's position that just as the head of a person, although superior to the body, is totally dependent upon it, so the power of the monarch was always dependent upon the sovereignty resident in the body politic. Despite this dependence, the head holds absolute sway over the body unless it is severed from it. In that unlikely case, the body politic may help itself to what was originally its own. All power then reverts to the body which must find a new head. Like the case of a man dying without heirs, his estate reverts by escheat to the lord of the manor.

Hooker was frankly ambivalent on the thorny issue of whether, when the prince abused his authority over them, the people had a right to reclaim their original power by overthrowing him. The answer was yes and no. Yes, if the compact by which political power was originally transferred from a society to a monarch prescribed reasons and methods for removing him. Even then, there must be a tradition of acquiescence by the king in such provisions. No, if there is no prior constitutional method described in the compact that first created the government. After all, the people formed government in the first instance because their facility for disagreement prevented them from living peacefully together in a natural and ungoverned state. Thus, in theory there was a right to unseat an unjust king, but in practice this was a highly circumscribed right, one not quite justified in Hooker's political philosophy.[15]

In Book VIII, on the matter of the king's headship of the Church, another issue emerged—that of the role of the clergy in limiting the monarch's authority. After all, there was a long tradition in England of shared governance of the Church. Although the king appointed bishops, for example, and had a voice in approving church law, these acts were rarely consummated without the initiative and approval of the higher clergy or the Church Convocation. Certainly, the king ought never to act as a judge in a court, especially a church court. The most Hooker was willing to say about such royal power was that no important ecclesiastical decision might be made without the king's consent.[16] This was a far cry from the authority over the Church soon to be claimed by the first Stewart king of England and arguably too restrictive a view of royal headship of the Church for Saravia, who might also have taken issue with Hooker's idea that parliament, with Church Convocation annexed to it, constituted the supreme law-making body in the realm. If the king was below the law, and the parliament (and Church) made the law, where did that leave the prince? In responding that the king was an essential part of the legislative body, Hooker seemed to be severely limiting the monarch's authority.

Hooker admitted that he was propounding a difficult doctrine. When he spoke of parliament as the supreme law-making body, he was not viewing it as a simple legislature concerning itself with such matters as the regulation and sale of "leather and wool" but, at its fullest reach, as a high court of parliament which pronounces and enforces through its various parts the many types of law—constitutional and statutory, civil and ecclesiastical—that rule the land. The supreme among the parts of the high court of parliament is the king. But he may never alter any law or statute of parliament nor dispense with any legal contract or title, because his power has derived from the ancient common law of the body politic. He is like "a watchman" or agent of the public welfare who always has at heart the best interests of his subjects. If he should act otherwise, he is not king at all but a tyrant.[17]

It is not surprising that it was to be many years before these sentiments of Hooker's ever saw the light of day, and then only during a time when anti-royalist sentiments were in the ascendancy. In the current reign, his comments on royal authority were not likely to please the queen. He was far too qualified in his support of the monarchy to suit Elizabeth, much less her probable successor, the King of Scotland. Perhaps Sandys had done him a favour after all in resisting publication of his last three books.

Whenever he went into the sanctuary of St Mary's to pray alone, but especially on Sundays at the services of common prayer, Hooker may well have given thanks for his beautiful, hallowed church building. In the recently published Book V of the *Laws* he had attacked the Puritans for complaining that the established Church made too much of church buildings and other outward signs of God's presence. They were wrong: all that is done in praise of God should correspond to the power and majesty of the God we worship. This correspondence between our inner spiritual lives in God's presence and the outer world in which we must make our way, we express in the beauty and majesty of our church buildings, rituals of worship, attire of clergy, and all the outward forms of our praise.[18]

The so-called purifiers of our religion say we should keep our sanctuaries bare of all adornment so as to imitate what they call the "nakedness of Jesus" and the "simplicity of the gospel." But where has God anywhere said that he wishes to dwell in a beggarly fashion and take pleasure in being worshipped nowhere save a poor cottage? Through all history, men of faith have praised God by making their temples of worship their most glorious buildings. It is true that God cares most for our inner spiritual affection toward him. But surely he must also approve a cheerful affection in us, one which regards nothing too beautiful or dear to be expended in the furniture of our worship of him? Grand church buildings serve as a witness to the world of God's almightiness, whom we seek to honour with our most lavish outward expressions of his power and glory.[19]

The same logic applies, Hooker said, to all of the outward signs of worship: celebration of special saints' days, the naming of Churches for saints—like his own St Mary the Virgin—the wearing of the surplice, kneeling and standing and sitting at different parts of the service, using the sign of the cross. These have been practised by long tradition of the Church in England as seemly expressions of our praise for God and not out of desire to imitate the Roman Church.[20]

What upset Hooker most about the Puritan attacks on the forms of worship was the need to answer them at all. What the Church of England practised was only what had long had the sanction of reason and custom. The Church chose to follow the "gray hairs" among its members because the aged are apt to have more experience and wisdom in such matters. People are perhaps slow to change their worship without some urgent necessity to do so; there is no virtue in innovation for its own sake. Those who seek change in these matters often do so out of disregard for tradition, shallow thinking, and inexperience.

For Hooker the authority of the established Church in all such matters was sufficient warrant for the religious practices he defended. And to those such as Thomas Cartwright who asked why we hang such judgements on the Church's sleeve, Hooker replied that, as Solomon said, two heads are better than one, or, in other words, the opinion of the historic Church ought to be sufficient to shut the mouths of those who, with nothing but the authority of their own interpretation of Holy Scripture, bark against our traditional religious forms and practices.[21]

The Puritans, he felt, had too many petty complaints about the Church's beautiful religious practices. To show the Puritans for the petty nitpickers he believed they were, he enumerated some of the items they would overturn the entire Church in order to change: praying after rather than only before the sermon; allowing for private baptism by lay persons in the face of imminent death; maintaining the custom in wedding ceremonies of "giving away the bride": blessing a wedding ring and using phrases such as "with my body I thee worship"; using a few time-honoured words in baptism and funeral services that do not come from Scripture; conducting services of thanksgiving for the safe delivery of women from the perils of child birth—and the list goes on.[22]

It grieved Hooker that the Puritans should "bite at these matters" which, though important, were, he felt, hardly worthy of such attention. Surely these wise men have been given, by God's grace, both wit and learning for better purposes.[23]

Perhaps what offended him most among the many attacks upon forms of worship was what he saw as Puritan carping at the use of music. Our very soul responds to music, finding there the harmony which defines its nature, he wrote. In musical harmony, the image and character of both virtue and vice may be perceived, while the mind is being delighted. Music touches the divine within us. It is a thing that delights people of all ages and in all conditions of life. Music is "as seasonable in grief as in joy." Music, he said, has that most "admirable facility to express and represent to the mind, more deeply than any other sensible means, the very standing, rising and falling, the very steps and inflections, the turns and varieties of all passions whereunto the mind is subject." More than that, music can initiate these movements of our minds and souls.[24]

Hooker also expressed one of his favourite complaints: the disciplinarians' long sermons. How they loved to preach! For them, the sermon was the be all and end all of worship—more important than the blessed sacraments, common prayer, even than reading from Holy Scripture—and yet the sermon was merely one man's opinion, after all.[25]

When all else has been said, the central exercise of worship must always be prayer, and most especially common prayer. All that we do in our service is prayer. And what is prayer? It is that blessed intercourse between us and God that pleases God and saves our souls. It is that conversation in which we seek help and God instructs and saves us.[26]

Early in 1598 Hooker received a long letter from George Cranmer. He probably had hoped to have news about George's trip with Edwin Sandys to France, Italy, and Germany. Instead, the letter contained no more than an essay on how Puritanism had declined as a major threat to the Church and why university scholars should stick to basic theology and stay out of politics. And, of course, there was the inevitable advice on what he should do to improve his book, namely discredit the Puritans still further by tying them to the radical Brownists, Barrowists, and even atheists, and by insisting that the true aim of such people was not to reform but to overthrow the established polity of the Church. Nothing much new here beyond what Cranmer had urged in the past.[27]

By this time Hooker had undoubtedly decided that he had gone as far as he intended in incorporating such suggestions. If George and Edwin wanted more changes, they would have to find another author or write their own tracts. Hooker had some pride, after all, and had collaborated on this work about as much as he intended to. Still, as he looked at some lines he had marked in George's letter, he reflected that Cranmer had taken his measure accurately when he said that he suspected that Richard would rather assume the best about his Puritan foes than associate them with either John Browne or Henry Barrow. Those two men and their followers were not loyal English Calvinists but blatant separatist congregationalists. Hooker knew Browne's *Reformation Without Tarrying for Any*, published back in 1582, with is stark advocacy of separation of Church from State and each congregation from the others. Browne had established the first Congregationalist church in Norwich, which he later moved to The Netherlands. Despite his radicalism, he had taken orders as an Anglican priest and had become Master of St Olave School in Southark. He was a thoroughly unstable man, Hooker may have thought.

Richard probably remembered Henry Barrow somewhat more sympathetically. Barrow had been infected with radical Puritanism while a student at Corpus Christi, Cambridge, and then gone on to Grays Inn, only to abandon the law to follow Browne. Richard no doubt shuddered when he recalled Bishop Aylmer's cruelty to Barrow in 1593. It had been the talk of London at the time. The bishop had Barrow tried on one day, convicted on the next and then tied to the gallows tree. At the last minute, by prearrangement, a reprieve arrived—the worst kind of mental torture. About a month later Barrow was hanged anyway.[28]

When they returned from Europe toward the end of 1598 Cranmer and Sandys probably stopped at Bishopsbourne to visit their mentor, enquire about his health, check progress on the last four Books of the *Laws*, and recount their experiences abroad. Cranmer, now thirty-three, was much matured as he regaled Hooker with tales of "godless politics" in France and the limitations on speech against the State in the Senate of Venice. Hooker would have been pleasantly surprised by the cosmopolitan tone of his friends and gratified to hear some of his own ideas come back to him, now enlarged and enriched by his former students as they tried them out on the larger European stage.[29]

Neither Cranmer nor Sandys any longer had a strong interest in the remaining portions of Hooker's book. The need to combat Puritans was not urgent. On a personal level, Cranmer was now largely preoccupied with his plans to obtain a post in Ireland. He had been frustrated in this a number of times, but was intent on being posted there soon. For his part, Edwin also had other projects in mind. He was now keenly interested in foreign exploration and commerce and would have talked excitedly with Hooker about prospects for planting a colony in the new world of the Americas and about playing a role in the forthcoming government of King James, once the old queen was gone. Like George, Edwin's scholarly interests were becoming international in scope, focusing on reconciliation within the Church through inter-denominational Councils.[30]

Hooker was to live for only two more years, just barely into the seventeenth century. These were years filled with the routines of a country pastor and punctuated by visits from old Oxford and London friends, occasional trips to London and Enfield, and many hours of reading and contemplation. His own growing library, augmented by visits to Canterbury, supplied all that he needed.

Late in 1599 he was jolted by one of the worst shocks of his life. An anonymous tract that specifically attacked his book appeared under the title, *A Christian Letter of certaine English Protestants, unfeigned favourers of the present State of Religion, authorized and professed in England; unto that Reverend and learned man, Mr R. Hook. Requiring resolution in certaine matters of doctrine (which seem to overthrow the foundation of Christian Religion, and of the church among us) expresle contained in his five books of Ecclesiastical Pollicie*. Adrian Saravia may have been the first to bring Hooker a copy of the work and tried to soften its blow. By this time, Saravia's was well acquainted with his friend's sensitivity to criticism and possibly told Hooker that now that his work had been attacked in print, he had finally arrived as a great writer. He should now write his "defence," and later, a "reply" to the "answer," and so on.

The speculation was that the anonymous piece had been hatched at Cambridge. A group of fellows there had been upset with what they saw as the threat of Arminianism in Hooker's writings. That old predestination issue continued to plague him. A prime candidate for actual authorship of *A Christian Letter* . . . was Andrew Willet, who was rapidly gaining a reputation as one of the most learned writers among the Puritans. He had a church just outside Cambridge where he kept in close touch with Puritan friends. Although he professed loyalty to the Church of England, Willet kept his senses alert for hints of papism, opposition to predestination, or any smell of Arminianism. Some would count him as not the most extreme of Puritans, perhaps somewhere in the middle of that group.

But why, Hooker wondered in anguish, would they accuse him of undermining the established Church when it was these very Cambridge radicals from whom he was defending the Church? The clear answer was that Hooker had frightened his foes into action. They were worried about his attack on them because it was so different from what they had endured until now from defenders of the established Church. No one had ever so systematically torn apart their discipline and laid bare their true intentions. The Puritans and presbyterians had to take him seriously and so had chosen to say that it was he, and not they, who undermined the true Church. This, Hooker thought, was a lame ploy on their part and would convince no one. Saravia would have advised Hooker not to fret about *A Christian Letter*. He should just sit down and write his reply to it. But fret Hooker did. Why would they not let him alone on this issue? He had said time and again that he was neither an Arminian, rejecting all idea of God's predestination, nor a Pelagian, denying original sin. Furthermore, he had advocated neither universal salvation (though he had certainly come close to it) nor salvation through works. He had said only that it is commendable to pray for the salvation of all people and that the sinning we do is not God's responsibility but our own.[31]

At first reading, Hooker found what he regarded as serious errors in the line of reasoning in *A Christian Letter*. What seemed to have bothered the author of the *Letter* most about Hooker was that he had dared to oppose Calvin and that he was too scholarly in his mode of writing. If these were their weightiest objections to his great tome, they were desperate indeed. For the rest of the year and on throughout much of 1600 Hooker worked frequently on his response to the *Letter*. He also no doubt occasionally did some revising of the last three Books of the *Laws*. His steadily failing health prevented him from completing either task. When he had a good day and his old spirit revived, he probably preferred to work on his answer to the *Letter* because that work had challenged both his credibility as a scholar and his integrity as a person.

Hooker's initial responses to the *Letter* were visceral. He wrote out some of them passionately in the margins of his copy of the tract. The author, he felt, was attacking him "without eyes for he seems not to perceive the bare meaning of the Church's most basic teachings and doctrines. I think his godparents have much to answer to God for not seeing that he was better trained in his catechism class." At a place where he was criticized for a ponderous writing style, Hooker wrote: "How this asse runs, kicking up his heels as if a summerfly had stung him." In another place, Hooker advised the author to go "read some good catechisms." In another, he wrote in anger, "Ignorant Asse;" in still another, "You lie, sir."[32]

Eventually he came to see, possibly with help from the older and, in this instance, more dispassionate Saravia, that there was substance to some of the points in the *Letter*, and that these deserved thoughtful replies. After all, there were twenty-one separate objections to some of Hooker's most cherished positions on virtually every subject, especially his views on free will, grace, predestination, and the Sacraments. Still, the more Hooker read the tract the angrier he became. The author of the *Letter*, whoever he was, was far more personal in his attacks on Hooker than Walter Travers ever had been. He went so far as to accuse Richard of hypocrisy for trying, as he said, to reinstitute popish religion under the guise of attacking Puritan extremists. He accused Hooker of "hoodwinking" his readers, of "beguiling" and "bewitching" them with a "popish brew," of "lulling them to sleep" with his rhetoric while he undermined the Church.[33]

Despite his pique, Hooker may have granted, with reluctance no doubt, that the author of the *Letter* had hit upon a clever stroke in twisting to his own purpose Hooker's opening metaphor about dreams at the beginning of the *Laws*. Hooker had written that he would not "through silence permit things to pass away as in a dream." Like a distorted echo, the *Letter* mimicked and mocked Hooker with these words: "When men dream they are asleep, and while men sleep the enemie [Hooker] soweth tares, and tares take root and hinder the good corn of the Church before it be aspied. Therefore wisemen [Willet and friends] through silence permit nothing to pass away as in a dream."[34]

In time, Hooker cooled down and penned a tract which might have served as either part of a response to the *Christian Letter* or as a preamble to the final three books of the *Laws*. A few sample passages from this work reveal the state of his thinking about religious conflict during these final months of his life.

> Contention arises, either through error in men's judgements or else disorder in their affections. When contention grows by error in judgement, it ceases not, till men by instruction come to see wherein they err, and what it is that did deceive them. Without this [learning and teaching] there is neither policy nor punishment that can establish peace in the Church.

> I had rather bewail with secret tears than public speech the contentions and strife of our times.

> You are not ignorant of the "Demandes," "Motives," "Censures," "Apologies," "Defences," and other writings which our great enemies

> have published under colour of seeking peace, promising to bring nothing but reason and evident remonstrance of truth. But who seeth not how full gorged they are with virulent slander and immodest speeches, tending much to the disgrace [and] nothing to the disproof of that cause which they endeavour to overthrow?
>
> But however sober and however sound our proceedings be in these causes, all is in vain which we do to abate the errors of men unless their unruly affections be bridled. Self-love, vain-glory, impatience, pride, impertinence, these are the bane of our peace. And these are not conquered or cast out except by prayer.[35]

Hooker probably continued working on his reply to the *Letter* until the time of his death. It was more important, he would have felt, to use his waning energy to complete this major defence of his apology for his beloved Church than to do any further editing of the last three books of the *Laws* which had been by now altered to his satisfaction, needing only a propitious time for publication. That the last three books were completed by the time of Hooker's death is attested in several ways. John Keble, Hooker's nineteenth-century editor, cites Lancelot Andrewes' letter to Dr Henry Parry at Corpus Christi, Oxford, just a few days after Hooker's death, implying that Hooker had finished the books. John Spenser, who published an edition of the Laws in 1604, said in his preface, "To the Reader," that Hooker "lived till he saw them completed . . . and hastened death upon himself, by hastening to give them life." Spenser went on to make the unsubstantiated claim that "some evil disposed minds, whether of malice or wicked blind zeal, it is uncertain . . . by conveying away the perfect copies, left unto us nothing but certain old unperfect and mangled drafts, dismembered into pieces . . ." (*Works* I, 123). Izaak Walton reported, in the Appendix to his life of Hooker, with even less reliability, that Spenser's wife (Walton's aunt, and sister of George Cranmer), who was his principal source, had told him that her husband had completed Hooker's remaining fragments himself. Walton would have us believe that what we have today of the final books is at least as much Spenser's work as Hooker's. Walton also tells the totally false story of Joan Hooker's complicity in allowing certain Puritan ministers into her husband's study to destroy and carry off his writings and how, when later questioned by Whitgift at Lambeth, she confessed and was found dead (of guilt?) the next morning in her bed. Hallam calls Walton's story one that "gossiping compilers of anecdote can easily accumulate." Samuel Coleridge was to characterize the tale as politically motivated: "In short, it is a blind story, a true Canterbury tale, dear Isaac!"[36]

In his study at Bishopsbourne Hooker gathered up his earlier tracts and sermons written on predestination, grace, and the sacraments, as well as relevant parts of the fifth book of the *Laws*. Drawing on materials he had used long ago in his *Answere* to Travers' *Supplication*, he nearly completed his response to the attacks against him on the predestination question. He also managed to put forth some of his answer to criticism of his positions on the sacraments and grace before his energy gave out. Unfortunately, his answer to the *Christian Letter* was still incomplete and in rough form when the end finally came, although his notes have survived as eloquent testimony to his humanity—and as adequate antidote to Izaak Walton's portrait of the perfect man. In the original copy of the *Christian Letter* in the Corpus Christi College archives we can still see in Hooker's clear and strong hand—with more decisive strokes of pen than is usual in his extant writings—angry words such as "corrupt" and "false." More important than Hooker's marginal notes for a grasp of the content of his intended response to the *Christian Letter* is an incomplete manuscript in which he addresses at length the substance of some of the major attacks on his ideas. While there is nothing really new in this tract, it seems to have been written as a new piece in response to the *Letter*. It is entitled (by Keble) *Fragments of an Answer to the Letter of Certain English Protestants*. In its original form in the Library at Trinity College, Dublin, it is entitled, *A Treatise by Hooker on Grace, the Sacraments, Predestination, Etc.*[37]

During the last months of his life Hooker was too weak to continue his pastoral and priestly duties, much less to complete any revisions in Books VI to VIII. He could only hope that among his friends there would be someone who would see that his unpublished works were edited and published. His wish was to be fulfilled. Almost immediately upon news of his death, his friends and colleagues, most of whom would soon become leading lights in the Church, rushed to secure and then later to edit and publish his writings. Principal among these executors of his literary estate were John Spenser, a fellow and soon to be president at Corpus Christi; Henry Jackson, a Corpus fellow assigned by Spenser to edit several of Hooker's sermons; Nicholas Eveleigh, steward to Sir Edwin Sandys who had been a fellow at Corpus with Hooker and would soon be a chaplain to the queen and then successively bishop of Winchester, Worcester, and Chichester; and Lancelot Andrewes, prebendary at St Paul's, who would one day be dean at Westminster and then bishop of Chichester, Ely and Winchester. Of course, Edwin Sandys was still involved as a principal executor of Hooker's estate.

As the end of his life drew near, Hooker no doubt prayed that someone would come forward to provide the response to *A Christian Letter* that he had been unable to complete himself. Shortly after his death that prayer was answered when Archbishop Whitgift commissioned Dr William Covel, a fellow at Queens College, Cambridge, to answer the *Letter*. In 1595, Covel had written his own defence of the Church, entitled *Polimanteia*, in which he called Hooker a "defender of true religion". Covel's defence of Hooker's *Laws* appeared in 1603 under the title, *A Just and Temperate Defence of the Five Books*. Comparing this work with Hooker's notes toward his own response to the *Letter*, it is clear that Covel's work fell short of what Hooker would have accomplished had he lived to write his own reply. In fact, Covel did little more than quote Hooker's own words from the *Laws* to defend him. Still, Covel did say in his *Defence* that Hooker's book was "incomparably the best that ever was written in our Church."[38]

According to Izaak Walton, Hooker's declining health had been made worse by a trip to London in the early autumn of the year. He reports that on the river ride between London and Gravesend Richard contracted a fever from which he never recovered. Another of his improbable and unsubstantiated tales is that Sandys and Cranmer had to go to court to clear Hooker of a false charge of "trepanning" (the entrapping of an unwary person in order to cheat them) in which he and George Cranmer were allegedly involved. The only apparent value of this yarn is that it gave Walton yet another oportunity to extol Hooker's virtue in forgiving the dastardly Puritans who had so wrongly accused him.[39]

His health was undoubtedly failing before this time. The disastrous medical treatments of the day, combined with his own apparent penchant for religious fasting, only hastened the end. Walton attests that Hooker's life at Bishopsbourne was one of "constant study, prayers and fasting." Although I have tried to show that Hooker did not live the life of a pious monk, I see no reason to doubt that fasting and prayer were part of his regular routine, since we know from his writings that he believed in the importance of penitential offices. As he neared death, he no doubt increased these exercises in penance, as well as his private confessions with Saravia. His death at forty-seven was well before what counted as "old age" at the time. A contemporary authority reports that at sixty, a man was just entering the "aged" category. Not until about that age would one be saluted with: "God speed you well."[40]

As he prepared to die Hooker took comfort that his prosperous father-in-law would see to the needs, comfort, and long-term financial security of his wife and children. It was a reasonable surmise, but not to be. Within a year of Hooker's death, John Churchman was plunged into financial ruin with disastrous consequences for Joan Hooker and her children.

Joan was to be criticized for re-marrying so soon after Richard's death, but it is possible that he had advised her to find another husband when he was gone. His girls would need the protection of a father. Joan was still young and Richard would leave her a dowry sufficient for her to make a good match. Under the terms of the will, Joan, as his "beloved wife," was to be his sole executor and principal remainder beneficiary. John Churchman and Edwin Sandys had agreed to be general overseers of the estate. Richard bequeathed £100 each to Alice,

Cicely, Jane, and Margaret as dowries to be paid at their marriages. In the event of the death or failure to marry of any of the girls, the others would share the forfeited amount. His other bequests were few: £5 to the poor at Barham parish, 50s. for the poor at Bishopsbourne, £3 for a new pulpit at St Mary's. (After Hooker died and as Joan was preparing to remarry, an inventory of household goods, including Hooker's books, was made. The estimated value came to over £500. This, coupled with payments from Sandys on Hooker's book, when completed, would make a decent dowry for Joan.)[41]

On 20 October 1600 Hooker's will was registered. From that time on he was confined to his bed. On the first day of November Saravia was pleased that he sat up and looked somewhat revived, after he had spent some time watching silently by his friend's bedside while the dying man ate nothing and said nothing, apparently in a semiconscious state.[42] Able to converse briefly, Hooker asked his friend to hear his final confession and give him the Sacrament when his time came. He would like a simple funeral service following the rites in the *Book of Common Prayer*, with burial in the churchyard at St Marys. No, he did not want to be buried in London, nor did he want word of his death sent to London until after he was interred. Would Adrian see to these details?

The next day Saravia found Hooker worse than he had left him and tried to awaken him before it was too late. Richard opened his eyes and whispered to his friend that it was time to administer last rites. Adrian heard his brief confession. Hooker said simply: "I commend and bequeath my immortal soul to God's merciful care."[43]

Saravia could tell that Hooker was slipping away. He quickly withdrew the host from his case and forced it between his friend's lips. "This is my Body . . ."

About a week later Philip Culme, Churchman's apprentice, dismounted in Hooker's stable, ran up to the rectory, and banged hard on the front door. When Joan Hooker answered he explained at once that her father and mother were on the way down from London and had sent him on ahead to see to her needs. Assured that Mrs Hooker had everything under control, Culme then explained his other errand concerning the safekeeping of her late husband's manuscripts. Joan directed the messenger to Richard's study. Philip mounted the stairs and soon began to fill his cloak bag with a treasure.[44]

NOTES

1. See Walton, *Life,* 77, 84; John Spenser's Preface to the *Laws, Works,* I, 123.
2. The conclusion is fair that little Edwin was named for the archbishop, or his son, or both. Like others in their day, Richard and Joan named their children for family members and close friends. *St Augustine Parish Register*, MS.8872.1; Sisson, 124.

3. Quoted from one of the three 1605 editions in the British Library. The book appeared in several subsequent printings including a lovely little 3" x 5" leather bound edition of 1638, also in the British Library. For a full discussion of Sandys' trip to Europe, the resulting treatise, and the probable influence of Hooker and his thought see Rabb, *op. cit.,* 18-20, 21-46. For a useful discussion of the intellectual relationship of Sandys and Hooker, see H. R. Trevor-Roper, *Renaissance Essays* (Chicago: The University of Chicago Press, 1961), 103-20. I agree with Deborah Shuger that Sandys' book was, in fact, a "political complement" to Hooker's *Laws*, not only in its support of church councils but also in its astute analysis of the inner workings of church leadership élites as they strove with varying degrees of success to influence the general populace. See Shuger's "Societie Supernaturall: The Imagined Community of Hooker's *Laws*" in McGrade, *Richard Hooker and Construction of Christian Community,* 312-14.

4. For analysis of Sandys' disapproval of parts of Book VI and related matters, see McGrade, *Folger* VI, Pt. 1, 236-44; Gibbs, *Ibid.,* 49-71; Sisson 99-102, 127-56. At the end of the printed copy of Book V in Windet's 1597 edition, entitled *Of the Lawes of Ecclesiastical Politie Eight Bookes by Richard Hooker*, which in fact included only the Preface and first five Books, Hooker wrote these words: "To the Reader. Have patience with me for a small time and by the help of almighty God I will pay the whole." There can be little doubt that he was ready with the last three books at this time and was disappointed that they were not published.

5. Book V first appeared in 1597 in a printing by John Windet that included a reissue of the first four Books. Books VI and VIII did not appear for another fifty-two years, in 1648, from the printer Richard Bishop. In the British Museum copy, what appears to be a 226 page volume contains only 202 pages because pages 124-48, where Book VII was obviously intended to have been inserted, are missing. Bishop expresses regret on the title page at having been unable to secure a copy of that Book, which did not appear for another fourteen years when Bishop John Gauden of Exeter brought out an edition of all eight Books, the first ever, in 1662.

6. *Folger* II, 8; *Works* II, 9.

7. This is a summary of (rather than a quotation from) Hooker's *Funeral Sermon: A Remedy Against Sorrow and Fear, Works* III, 643-53; esp. 648-9; *Folger* V, 367-77; esp. 373..

8. Neale, 325-67.

9. *Folger* II, 111-19; *Works* II, 116-24. See John E. Booty, "Commentary on Book V," *Folger* VI, Pt. I., 196-7.

10. *Folger* II, 16-17; *Works* II, 13-14.

11. *Folger* III, 319-20: *Works* III, 329-30 and generally 328-40. See also Philip B. Secor, *Richard Hooker and the Christian Commonwealth*; Booty, *op. cit.*, 201-4; McGrade, *Folger* VI, 337-49.

12. *Folger* III, 329-30; *Works* III, 340.

13. *Folger* III, 341-2; *Works* III, 352-3, and generally 342-53.

14. *Ibid.*; *Folger*, 316-28, 33-36; *Works*, 327-38m 44-6.

15. *Folger* III, 338-9; *Works* III, 350. Unlike Luther and Calvin, Hooker did not have a notion of separation of religious and secular authority to serve as a basis for a full-blown theory of resistance to unjust rulers. His emphasis of human reason and free will was rooted more in the medieval Thomistic and Aristotelian theories, than in the Augustinianism that undergirded more radical Protestant political thought. See Arthur P. Monahan, "Richard Hooker: Counter Reformation Political Thinker," McGrade, *Richard Hooker and Construction of Christian Community*, 203-217. For a contrary view that sees Hooker as decidedly not a Thomist, see W. J. Torrance Kirby, "Richard Hooker as Apologist of the Magisterial Reformation in England," *Ibid.*, 219-33.

16. *Folger* III, 393-4, and generally 385-413; *Works* III, 404-5 and generally 396-419. See also Hooker's *Autograph Notes*, *Folger* III, 491, 493, 496.

17. *Folger* III, 401-9; *Works* III, 408-16.
18. *Folger* II, 33-4; *Works* II, 29-30.
19. *Folger* II, 56-60; *Works* II, 52-5.
20. Hooker's treatment of these issues is found in Book V: Chapter 12 (dedication of church buildings); Chapter 29 (vestments); Chapters 30 and 65 (signs, gestures and kneeling); Chapters 59-72 (festivals and saints).
21. *Folger* II, 34-5, 38-40; *Works* II, 30, 33-5.
22. Book V: Chapters 29-48m 68-75. Hooker's annoyance about attacks on these "indifferent" practices may actually have been directed not so much at his ostensible foe, Thomas Cartwright (T. C.) as at his erstwhile mentor and colleague, John Rainolds. For an intriguing analysis, which I find plausible, that suggests a serious breach between Hooker and Rainolds, see Collinson, *op. cit.,* 156-160, esp. 159.
23. *Folger* II, 165; *Works* II, 175.
24. *Folger* II, 151-152; *Works* II, 159-160.
25. See generally Book V, Chapters 21 and 22 in *Folger* II, 83-110; *Works* II, 84-115.
26. *Folger* II, 110; *Works* II, 115.
27. Cranmer's letter is dated February, 1598. As Keble suggests, Hooker may have asked Cranmer for his suggestions after receiving a copy of the recently published Book V of the *Laws.* I think it more likely that Cranmer's advice was unsolicited and perhaps even unwelcome. The letter is reproduced in *Works* II, 598-610, esp. 598, n. 2. For helpful commentary on the letter, see Paget, 218-21.
28. *Ibid.*, 604-5. See F. J. Powicke's two works: *Robert Browne Pioneer of Modern Congregationalism* (London: Congregational Union of England and Wales, Inc., 1910) and *Henry Barrow and the Exiled Church of Amsterdam* (London: Congregation Union of England and Wales, Inc., 1900). See also Christopher Morris, *Political Thought in England,* esp. 165.
29. *Works* II, 605, esp. n. 2; 608; Paget, 221, n. 1.
30. Sandys showed little interest in Hooker's writing after his tutor's death late in 1600. In 1601 Sir Edwin acquired a country house in Kent, the home of his—and Hooker's friend George Cranmer, who had died recently in Ireland. Rabb, 47-8. Cranmer had finally received his commission and gone to Ireland as secretary to Lord Governor Mountjoy in 1600. He died there in 1601, as we have seen, in a military skirmish with Tyrone's forces, on the way to the decisive battle of Kinsale. Sandys went on to a distinguished career in the next century under James I, serving in the Commons, receiving a knighthood, serving as treasurer of the Virginia (London) Company, helping to plant a colony in Virginia where he advocated representative government, writing *Europa Speculum* (1605), an important work on reconciliation of the Christian Churches of Europe. See W. B. Patterson, "Hooker on Ecumenical Relations: Conciliarism in the English Reformation," in McGrade, *op. cit.*, 288-99 for an analysis of the conciliar movement in England, with special attention to Hooker's view in Books I and IV of the *Laws* that the English parliamentary system might be applied on a world-wide basis through international church councils.
31. Hooker's own copy of *A Christian Letter*, with his marginal notes preparatory to writing a response, written in 1599, is in the Corpus Christi College Archives: Fulman MSS 1682, 215b. Hooker writes defensively of Books I to V: "As learned as any of the realm . . . saw them and read them . . . before they ever came to your hands." Readily available copies of Hooker's notes are in the British Library; *Folger* IV, 1-79; *Works* II, 537-97. In my treatment, I have followed the commentaries of Keble in *Works* I, xvii-xxvii, Paget, 208-18, and Booty, "Introduction," *Folger* IV, xxii-xlviii. Booty notes that, although Willet denied authorship when accused of it by Richard Parks in 1607, such denials were common at the time and need not be taken at face value. Typical examples of Hooker's denials of the major charges made against him in *A Christian Letter*, especially the charge that he rejected

predestination, are in *Autograph Notes, Folger* III, 462-538, esp. 523, 524, 529, 531, 532. Paget, 207-10, believes that it was because Hooker's defence of the Church was regarded by Puritans as the most effective to date that they unleashed such a strong attack on him.
32. *Folger* IV, 22-42. Paget follows William Covel's 1603 response to *A Christian Letter* and speculates that the tract caused Hooker such anguish "that it was not the least cause to procure his death." Paget, 207.
33. Drawn from various places in Hooker's notes for a reply to *A Christian Letter*. See also Paget, 210-11.
34. *Folger* IV, 6.
35. Taken from a tract, probably written by Hooker, entitled *A Discovery of the Causes of the Continuance of these Conditions Concerning Church Government, Works* III, 460-1, 464; *Folger* III, 455-9. Keble doubted it was Hooker's work. Works III 461, n.2. But P. G. Stanwood believes the piece was written either as a free-standing essay or as a preamble to the last three books of the *Laws. Folger* III, 453. See also Rudolph P. Almasy, "'They are and are not Elymas': The 1641 '*Causes*' Notes as Postscript to Richard Hooker's *Of the Laws of Ecclesiastical Polity,*" McGrade, *op. cit.*.,183-201.
36. *Works* I, 91-4, 123. Hallam, *op. cit.* H. N. Coleridge, ed., *The Literary Remains of Samuel Taylor Coleridge* (London, 1838), III, 19-20.
37. Corpus Christi College archives, Fulman papers, MSS 1682, 215A. More readily available copies are in the British Library and *Folger, op. cit.* For the incomplete manuscript see Keble, *Fragments of an Answer to the Letter of Certain English Protestants*. In its original form in the Library at Trinity College, Dublin, it is entitled, *A Treatise by Hooker on Grace, the Sacraments, Predestination, Etc.* See *Folger* IV, 81-97, 99-167; *Works* I, xxv-xxvi; II, 537-97.
38. A handwritten copy of Covel's *Just and Temperate Defence* is in the Corpus Christi archives, No. 1682, 215A. See *Folger* IV, xliv-xlv.
39. Keble discredited this story with the note that such a crime did not even exist in Hooker's day. Walton, *Life,* 82; 82, n. 2.
40. Walton, *Life,* 84. Harrison, 449.
41. A copy of the original will, possibly in Hooker's hand, is in the archives of the Archdeacon's Court at Canterbury Cathedral, PRC 32/38, f. 291. A more readable printed copy is in *Works* I, 89-91, n. 1. The will was "proved" on 3 December, a month after his death, when Joan appeared in person to give her oath before the commissary general in Canterbury.
42. Walton, *Life*, 85.
43. I have drawn these words from Hooker's will.
44. Exactly what Culme gathered up to take back to London has long been a matter of dispute because it raises the question of the extent to which Hooker had "perfected" the last three books of the *Laws*, which did not appear until decades later—and then in varying degrees of completeness. The best summary discussions of the fate and the content of the last three books are by Gibbs and McGrade, *Folger* VI, Pt. I, 249-383; more generally see Haugaard, *op. cit.*, 1-80.

EPILOGUE

Richard Hooker's Legacy

A few days after Hooker's death, the long saga of the fate of his writings began—one of the most important and intriguing bibliographic adventures in literary history. Most of what is known of this tale is implicit in chancery court records of early-seventeenth-century lawsuits involving Hooker's daughters and the executors of his estate and contained in random comments by various of his literary executors.

9 November 1600
Home of John Churchman, Watling Street, London

John Churchman received the sad word of Richard's death from Henry Parry, who had heard the news from Lancelot Andrewes at St Paul's Cathedral next door. These two men, friends and supporters of Hooker, wanted someone to hurry down to Bishopsbourne right away to protect Richard's papers lest they fall into the hands of unfriendly Puritan extremists who disliked his writings.[1]

Summoning his trusted steward/apprentice, Philip Culme, Churchman gave instructions to that gentleman that he was to leave straight away for Bishopsbourne, see to Joan's welfare and assure her that her parents would arrive shortly. If Philip saddled a good horse and left before supper he could catch a Thames barge and be at Gravesend in three hours. From there, riding through the night with several stops to rest his mount, he would be in Bishopsbourne by dawn.[2]

John also entrusted Culme with an urgent mission. As soon as he had satisfied himself as to Mistress Joan's welfare, Philip was to go upstairs in the rectory to Mr Hooker's study and fill a cloak-bag with all of the manuscripts he found there. It was feared, Churchman confided to his servant, that some of these papers would be, or perhaps already had been, either stolen or adulterated or both. Culme was to return to his master with the cloak-bag with all haste.[3]

Late Spring 1601
The Churchmans' House in Watling Street

John Churchman ushered three important guests into the parlour of his great house in Watling Street: Dr John Spenser, president of Corpus Christi, a trustee of Hooker's will and soon to be named chaplain to King James I; Dr Henry Parry, distinguished Oxford scholar, soon to be made bishop of Worcester; and Edwin Sandys, Hooker's friend, patron, confidant—a prominent lawyer, parliamentarian, author, and a long-familiar figure in the Churchman household. Accompanying Sandys was his former classmate at Corpus Christi College, now his steward, Nicholas Eveleigh.

The four men watched eagerly as Culme carefully removed each of the tied manuscripts and individual sheets from the bag and placed them in front of them. They may have sensed that they were actors in some important drama, but they could scarcely imagine how momentous this occasion was to be for the life of their Church.

For the next several hours they worked assiduously, sorting and inventorying Hooker's precious writings. The Preface and first five books of his *magnum opus*, *Of the Laws of Ecclesiastical Polity*, had been published some years earlier, Books I-IV in 1593, and Book V in 1597. Their interest today was focused on the long-awaited final three books, as well as any sermons, letters or fragments that Culme might have found in Hooker's study.

They discovered that what existed of Books VI and VII was fairly polished, needing only minor editing. Book VIII was in fragmentary form, clearly incomplete, with portions apparently missing. Then there was an assortment of sermons and tracts that looked promising. When they had finished glancing through the papers, they decided that Sandys, who had been closest to Hooker during his life and had, in fact, made editorial suggestions during the writing process, should do a careful sorting of the manuscripts before the group met again to decide what to do with the papers. It was also decided that Lancelot Andrewes, whose opinions Hooker had respected, should be added to their little editorial group.[4]

Sometime later in 1601
The Churchmans' House in Watling Street

When the small group met again they parcelled out portions of Hooker's unpublished manuscripts for further editing preparatory to publication. Lancelot Andrewes, though unable to attend the meeting, was assigned the task of editing some of Hooker's sermons. Henry Parry agreed to help with that work.

Dr Spenser took the manuscripts of the still unpublished last three books of Hooker's work and agreed to bring them into readiness for printing. Books VI and VII seemed to be in rather good condition although VI was apparently missing a section toward the beginning. What they had of Book VIII might need considerable work.[5]

Surprisingly, Edwin Sandys, who had been so closely associated with the writing and publication of the early parts of the *Laws*, was not much interested in taking a direct hand in the process of preparing his friend's remaining writings for posthumous publication. Not many years earlier it had been important to Sandys to use Hooker's writings as part of a strategy for defending the Church from Calvinist extremists. But now that threat was largely gone and Sandys had other interests. The archbishop's son, with his keen interest in church affairs and domestic politics, was well on the way to becoming Sir Edwin Sandys with interests in international religion, politics, and trade—interests that would soon reach as far afield as the new world in America.

Nevertheless, Sandys' long-standing affection for his former teacher and friend would keep him interested in promoting Hooker's reputation and his writings. But the lion's share of work fell to John Spenser, who agreed to see the last three books of the *Laws* as well as several of Hooker's sermons, through to publication as soon as he could, given his heavy responsibilities as a college president.

The meeting at Churchman's house no doubt included conversation about Hooker's former student and friend, George Cranmer, grand-nephew of the martyred archbishop Thomas Cranmer and a close associate with Edwin Sandys in advising Hooker during the writing of the *Laws* a decade earlier. Cranmer would have been among the small group involved in sorting and editing Hooker's papers had he not recently gone to Ireland as secretary to Baron Mountjoy, the new lord governor during the final phase of Queen Elizabeth's ongoing campaign to rid that troubled country of foreign Catholic influence.

Before conversation at the Churchmans' had gone far, Sandys would have informed the group of the tragic news he had just received from Ireland. His friend, George Cranmer, was dead, killed fighting alongside Lord Mountjoy while on the way to meet the Spanish force at Kinsale. An English soldier standing near Cranmer during the skirmish had nearly shot the accursed Tyrone, killing the man standing beside him instead. Tyrone had a thousand lives.[6]

January/February 1616

The scene now shifts to court proceedings some years later. We hear Sir Edward Coke, now attorney general, pronounce in Star Chamber that John Churchman and his son Robert had defrauded their creditors in an effort to conceal their assets. This set the stage for the frustration of Hooker's daughters as they sought to recover money from their father's estate that had been entrusted to Churchman.

The war in Ireland ruined John Churchman completely. O'Neil's submission in 1603 had been purchased at the high price of Lord Mountjoy's devastation of Irish property, destruction of inventories, ruination of trade, and consequent *de facto* invalidation of contracts with London merchants such as John Churchman. John's efforts to save his homes in London and Enfield had failed.

"Churchman v. Bradshaw," Star Chamber
Attorney General Sir Edward Coke Presiding

We find the charges of the plaintiff, Churchman, in this case to be vexatious and without merit, to wit:

that, on 8 June 1605, the defendant Bradshaw in company of the Sheriff of Enfield and twenty armed men caused a "riot" when they forcibly invaded the Churchman home at Enfield, assaulted Robert Churchman and terrorized his wife Anne and sister Mary, both women being pregnant and in mortal danger of being killed by the invaders, and further that, John Churchman transferred title to his house at Enfield to his son Robert in satisfaction of a bond pledged in 1599 to Richard Benyon of Coxhall as surety for the 600 pound dowry paid by that gentleman at the marriage of his daughter Anne to said Robert Churchman, and further

that, Peter Bradshaw, a major creditor of said John Churchman, used bribery to influence members of a fact-finding commission appointed by the court to determine if said John Churchman had transferred title to his home and lands at Enfield to his son Robert in order to keep it out of the hands of his creditors, including said Bradshaw.

To the contrary, this Court reaffirms its earlier decision in this matter and finds that, as deposed by Bradshaw and confirmed by the commission, the following are the true facts in this case:

that John Churchman attempted to defraud his creditors, including Bradshaw, by transferring title to his house and lands at Enfield to his son Robert after he knew he was bankrupt, and further

that there is no credible evidence that Bradshaw used bribery to influence the findings of the commission, and further that Robert Churchman was the cause of the so-called "riot" at the Churchman house when he attempted to strike the sheriff and provoked that person to draw his sword in response when he came peaceably to order to have the house vacated and forfeited in payment of debts of John Churchman, and further

that, throughout this matter, Robert Churchman has been a villain trying in every way to avoid his legal responsibilities, whereas his father John has shown remorse for any wrongdoing which his hard circumstances may have led him to commit, as evidenced by the deposition of the defendant Peter Bradshaw in which he stated that John Churchman, his London neighbour, told him that, to wit:

he was ashamed to look any honest man in the face because he had dealt so badly and dishonestly with his loving neighbours, and wished that

> there were [a] law to take away his life for dealing so dishonestly, and wished that he might be laid in some dark dungeon where he might never see honest man again in the face.[7]

December 1609
Dean House, Home of Ellen and John Huntley
Chipstead, Surrey

In the meantime, some years earlier Hooker's daughters had become the legal charges of John Huntley. This new guardian was doing his best to retrieve all the money he could for the three young women.

Hooker's three surviving daughters, Alice, nineteen, Cicely, eighteen, and Margaret, sixteen, had moved in with Huntley and his mother, Ellen, in 1607 after previous residences in a succession of temporary "homes" during the decade since their famous father's death. At first they had lived at Stone Hall, Wincheap, in Canterbury, where they were crowded in with stepbrothers and stepsisters in their stepfather's house. Then, when their mother died in early 1603, the girls were moved into the Churchmans' house in London until their grandfather was forced to sell that house to pay creditors. Next, Cicely went to live with her namesake, Cicely Sandys (Edwin's mother), while her sisters stayed with their uncle Robert at the Churchmans' country house in Enfield for a short time until creditors took that house as well. After that, their aunt, Elizabeth Stratford Churchman, had taken Alice and Margaret to live with her for a while before John Huntley became their legal guardian and moved all three Hooker daughters into his house. (John was their late mother's cousin—the son of their grandmother's sister, Ellen.)

Huntley knew that the difficulties in unlocking the girls' inheritance had all begun with their mother's disastrous marriage to Edward Nethersole just months after their father's death. It probably bothered him that his cousin, Joan Hooker, had married that scoundrel Nethersole right there in Richard's parish church at Bishopsbourne. Nethersole and his heirs had wasted no time in stealing Joan's inheritance—a legacy from Richard valued at some £1,000.

On the other hand, Huntley could scarcely blame Joan for marrying Nethersole. She had needed a husband to protect her daughters and their inheritance. Nethersole was a good "catch" at the time—one of Canterbury's leading citizens, the mayor back in 1590, and soon to be a city alderman again. Joan Hooker had struck a good bargain in her marriage contract—or so she must have thought. The agreement bound her new husband to provide for her daughters until they were either eighteen or married and to double their £400 legacy from their father and safeguard half of Joan's own £700 dowry as a further inheritance for the girls. Nethersole had posted a bond for the contract. Who was to know that he never intended to keep his word?

The Hooker daughters' financial woes had been compounded when their wealthy grandfather and principal supporter, John Churchman, had lost almost all of his property and other assets to his creditors back in 1605. Huntley could only be glad that the girls' grandmother, Alice, had not lived to see the ruination of her once proud and prosperous husband.[8]

There were three legal avenues available to them. First, there was the Nethersole estate. Here is where Joan Hooker had been wronged. Next, there was Joan's brother, Robert Churchman. It was high time, Huntley believed, to put pressure on his cousin to make good on the £400 his father still owed his granddaughters. Finally, there was the matter of what, if anything, Sir Edwin Sandys might be liable for in connection with alleged profits from the sale of Richard Hooker's writings.

Hooker's *Laws of Ecclesiastical Polity* was selling fairly well after a slow start. Alice Hooker felt strongly that some of Sandys' profit on these sales should be coming to her and her sisters. On the other hand, Cicely, who had been living with Sandys's mother, may have been aware that Sir Edwin had actually made little if any money on the book sales. In any event, Sandys' contract with the printer probably made no allowance for payments to Hooker's heirs.

At the very least, Huntley believed that the young women should seek sworn depositions from persons with knowledge about the sale of their father's book, as well as from those involved in Nethersole's treachery. But the best first course of action would be to seek what was due his charges from their own family—the Churchmans. Huntley knew that the girls' uncle, Robert Churchman, was willing to make good on as much of his deceased father's obligation as possible.

John explained to the Hooker daughters what they must do to secure the £400 legacy that Richard had left them in trust with their grandfather, to be paid, if necessary, for living expenses and then to serve as a dowry when they married. John Churchman had posted an £800 bond with Dr John Spenser, President of Corpus Christi College, and Anthony Stratford, the girls' uncle—the two men appointed in Hooker's will as trustees—as a guarantee that Churchman or his heirs would pay the legacy when the girls came of age. Robert Churchman should now be deposed, required to stop procrastinating, and made to pay his nieces what was due them from this part of their legacy.

It would take years of work in the courts to unravel this tangled web, Huntley knew. There would be suits and countersuits, not only in chancery but in star chamber as well. His mother, the girls' great-aunt, would have to be prepared to pay the court costs and stay the course. It would be expensive.

John Huntley must have been exultant when he told Hooker's daughters of his first success on their behalf. Their uncle, Robert

Churchman, had agreed, without any court order, to pay £300 of the total £400 owed to them by their grandfather, providing the late Anthony Stafford's brother made good on the remaining £100 (plus £40 interest), which Robert claimed he had paid over to Anthony.

The lord chancellor himself, Sir Thomas Ellesmere, handed down a decision ordering Stafford to make this payment when that gentleman had refused voluntarily to do so because, as he claimed, he had never received the £100 from Robert Churchman in the first place. The court also appointed a new trustee for the estate, the master of the Merchant Taylor's Company, Francis Evington. As a member of the Merchant Taylors, he had close associations with the Churchman family. He was also the brother-in-law of Sir Edwin Sandys, long a guardian of Hooker's interests.

Sometime in 1612, almost twelve years after Hooker's death, the full £430 inheritance he had intended for his daughters was recovered, thanks to the generosity of Ellen Huntley, the effective work of John Huntley, the somewhat reluctant and belated good will of Robert Churchman, and the legal system of England.[9]

It took an additional three years for the nasty business of the Hooker girls' suit against their nefarious stepfather, Edward Nethersole, to yield judicial remedy.

13 January 1613
Chancery Court, London
Huntley Home, Chipstead, Surrey

> Masters in Chancery hereby order that in pursuance of an order of the court dated 25 November 1612 and pleadings and answers subsequent thereto, Thomas Nethersole, son and heir to Edward Nethersole, is obligated on behalf of his deceased father to pay one hundred pounds to each of the plaintiffs, Alice, Cicely, and Margaret Hooker, which was legally due them under the terms of their deceased mother's marriage contract with said Edward Nethersole.
>
> Furthermore, it is ordered that Zachary Evans, to whom Nethersole had transferred goods with intent to defraud plantiffs' deceased mother, must pay the plaintiffs twelve pounds and two sets of armour with gauntlets to be chosen by them out of three in his possession, and, further, that Richard Wood, who had entered into bonds to secure Nethersole's estate, is also liable to the plaintiffs for thirty-five pounds to be paid by the end of next month.[10]

John Huntley would have announced the results of the suit against Nethersole and his agents to Alice, Cicely, and Margaret Hooker with much satisfaction. In addition to whatever the suits of armour might fetch, they would receive £247, a compromise settlement to be sure, but nevertheless an amount the judge had thought fair, given the complicated nature of the Hooker-Nethersole litigation.

The story of the armour was probably of special interest to the young women. The gist of it was that Thomas Nethersole's son-in-law, Zachary Evans, had swindled both Thomas and his father Edward (Joan's husband), with the result that there was no money left for Thomas to make good on his debt to the Hooker girls, even though he had lands valued far in excess of what he owed them.

At the trial, William Dalby, a merchant taylor in London and friend of John Churchman, testified that Evans received valuable personal property from Edward Nethersole before Joan Hooker had married him. He then deeded this property in order to defraud Joan by reducing assets with which to honour his obligations under the marriage contract. Among those goods was a chest containing three sets of armour. The judge decreed that Hooker's daughters were entitled to two of these as partial payment for what Nethersole owed them.[11]

All three of the young women undoubtedly thought that now at last they would have sufficient money to be independent or to use as a dowry to attract a husband. Alas, both Cicely and Margaret died shortly after these fortuitous decisions in Chancery Court, Cicely at twenty-one and Margaret at twenty.

Some years later, probably in 1618, Alice was supposedly betrothed to one Thomas Langley, a London stationer. Huntley claimed that he paid over her inheritance to Langley as a dowry. In fact, it appears that Alice was never formally betrothed. Certainly she never married. What Huntley paid Langley became lost in complicated sales of encumbered land. In 1623 and 1624, Alice sued her guardian to recover her inheritance. She probably never did. She died on 20 December 1649, aged fifty-nine, still unmarried and living at John Huntley's house. She may have lived on with Huntley because she had no other significant means of support.[12]

June 1614
Home of John Huntley, Chipstead, Surrey

Alice Hooker's final effort to claim her full inheritance was her contention that Sir Edwin Sandys owed her money from the sale of her father's now-famous book.

She had assumed all along that Edwin Sandys had made a decent profit. As Richard Hooker's sole heir, it seemed unfair that she should be living as a poor dependent woman when her father's one-time friend, the rich and powerful Sir Edwin, reaped more money than he needed from these book sales. Surely there must be relief from such an unfair situation.

The court depositions showed that Hooker had, in effect, signed over his rights to the book and its profits to Sandys long before his death. Sandys had, as we have seen, financed the project at a time when no printer in London would do the work without prepayment of all costs.

Not only did Sir Edwin provide all of the financial underwriting but he also paid Alice's father for the rights to his book in advance: £10 for the first four books of the Laws in 1593 and £20 for Book Five in 1597. In addition, he had given Richard a few complimentary copies for his own use. Sandys had agreed to pay £20 for the last three books, as soon as her father finished them.

Nicholas Eveleigh, one of Sir Edwin's stewards, who had been with Hooker and Sandys at Corpus Christi College, swore to all this in his court deposition. In effect, Hooker had sold his rights to the book to Edwin Sandys in order to get it printed at all. He had had no choice. It was either that or see the ideas he cared so passionately about go unpublished. Edwin was indeed his friend and, in this matter, his salvation. According to the court testimony of William Norton, master of the Stationers Company, there was simply no market for such a book at the time. He had been approached himself and had said no.

Alice protested that Sandys' motives were not so pure. She would have learned from her mother and others in the family that Edwin Sandys and George Cranmer, her father's former students and long-time friends, were constantly urging him to change his ideas to suit their politics. She may have believed that Sandys paid for her father's book because he wanted to promote his own political ideas back in 1593 when Sandys was battling against the religious separatists in parliament.

Huntley told Alice that whatever Sandys's motives—and they were probably mixed—he did put forward the money, take the risks, and at the same time pay her father a fair sum up-front without any assurance of recouping anything on his investment. Whether Sandys did in fact earn any money on his investment is a matter of conjecture. The best estimate, Huntley would have felt, was that Sir Edwin had recouped his original investment and perhaps made a small profit. According to the court testimony of John Bill, a leading printer of the day, the 1593 and 1597 editions eventually sold out. The 1604 and 1611 editions did well also. Sir Edwin may have seen some modest return from the first two editions.[13]

Could more profit have been made if the book had been priced higher? Perhaps. But depositions showed it was probably Hooker who had insisted on a low sales price. Apparently the author wanted to be sure his ideas were affordable to as many readers as possible. Right or wrong, the decision on price was most likely his and not Sir Edwin's or that of the printer, John Windet.

Although the editions in 1604 and 1611 did quite well, they made no money for Sandys because they were produced by John Windet's successor, William Stansby, who claimed they were new editions and that consequently Sandys had no claim on income from their sale. Stansby kept all the profits for himself on the grounds that the rules of the Stationers Company stipulated that, failing any explicit contract with the author of a book, the printer/publisher had sole rights to the work. Still, Stansby was morally if not legally bound to honour Windet's agreement with Sandys. When deposed in these chancery trials, Stansby lied and said he had no knowledge of any such agreement, despite the fact that he had been Windet's close colleague (as his apprentice) and would have been privy to all such arrangements. Even when William Norton, head of the powerful Stationers Company, appealed to him to honour his predecessor's agreement with Sandys, Stansby refused.

Worst of all, Huntley informed Alice Hooker, Sandys had planned to share any profits from the sale of the later editions with her, not because he was obligated to do so but out of his long-time affection for her father. In effect, Stansby had swindled not only Sir Edwin Sandys but Alice Hooker as well.

12 December 1664
Izaak Walton's House: Paternoster Row, London

We now move forward to the time of the restoration of the English monarchy following the Puritan Commonwealth of Oliver Cromwell. High-church Anglicans rule the Church of England and are seeking a founding hero to legitimate their cause.

In 1664 Walton was a septuagenarian who might reasonably hope at this stage of life to rest on his laurels as one of the most respected—even revered—scholars, authors, and churchmen of his day. But the archbishop of Canterbury had been persistent. He simply would not take no to his request that Walton, the author of biographies of such church notables as John Donne and Henry Wooten—as well as a work on fishing *(The Compleat Angler)* that would one day immortalize him—should sit down and write an authorized life of Richard Hooker.

Walton had long had an interest in Hooker and had even thought seriously at one time about writing his biography. Without Archbishop Gilbert Sheldon's insistence, however, he probably would not have done it so soon after his wife's death. He just felt too old and tired to do another book.

The archbishop knew how to win a man to his cause. About two years ago, following Rachel Walton's death, the persistent Sheldon had presented Izaak (for a minimal cost of only forty shillings a year) with a forty-year lease on a fine new house in one of London's best streets, Paternoster Row. Now, when he was not living at the episcopal palace at Winchester with his patron and friend, Bishop George Morely, or enjoying extended stays with the bishop of Salisbury or other friends in the Church, he was here on Paternoster Row happily mingling with other clerics and scholars among the book publishers, writers, mercers, and silk and lace sellers whose shops lined this avenue just north of St Paul's churchyard.

Walton had taken the archbishop's broad hint and done his bidding. He had written a life of Hooker and done some of it right here in his beloved new home—the house Sheldon had "given" him for doing the job—just a few steps away from the old Churchman house on Watling Street where, eighty years earlier, his subject, Richard Hooker, had lived, loved, and done some important writing of his own.[14]

The project had taken a lot out of Walton. Sheldon had pressured him to complete the task quickly. Ever since the archbishop had been promoted from London to Canterbury a year ago, he had sought to re-establish the full prerogatives of the Church after the long Puritan interregnum, an agenda applauded by the restored monarchy and the neo-Laudian church leadership. Part of Sheldon's strategy was to secure the mantle of Richard Hooker as the premier apologist for his conservative preferences for episcopal church government, traditional liturgy, and royal supremacy. Thomas Fuller had spoken highly of Hooker recently in his *Worthies of England* as a "great champion" of the established Church against schismatics and separatists during earlier times of crisis. Sheldon wanted that tradition of high praise for Hooker continued and enlarged.[15]

Never mind that Hooker's positions on the episcopacy and kingship were non-ideological and often intentionally ambiguous. Never mind that Hooker's ideas had been used in the past to support diverse viewpoints on these and other subjects. His standing was so high that it would be desirable to resurrect his persona, sanctify his writings, and elevate his reputation as the premier theologian and guide for the Church.

The problem with the Hooker strategy, as Sheldon and Walton both knew, was that there was already an unattractive (and unauthorized) life of Hooker in the field. It had appeared in 1662 from the pen of that decidedly low-church bishop of Exeter, John Gauden, author of a sycophantic paean to Charles I, *Eikon Basilike*, and a fraudulent remonstrance to Cromwell which he had falsely claimed to have made on behalf of the Church. Now Gauden was trying to ingratiate himself with Charles II by dedicating his *Life of Hooker* and his enlarged edition of the *Laws of Ecclesastical Polity* to the new king.

Sheldon and his party did not like Gauden's edition because they did not like Gauden. But they had more substantive complaints. Gauden had printed, for the first time, the long-suppressed (or just missing) Book VII, containing Hooker's unacceptably ambiguous treatment of the sanctity of apostolic succession and royal headship of the Church, and his moderate—not to say presbyterian—position on orders of ministry. The archbishop was also displeased by Gauden's inclusion of new materials from Book VIII in which Hooker said that kings were bound by the law and not above it.[16]

The archbishop had also told Walton, perhaps disingenuously, that what really bothered him about Bishop Gauden's Life of Hooker was his disparagement of the character of this great man. Walton would have agreed that Gauden's descriptions of Hooker were less than flattering. It did not help Hooker's reputation as a hero of the Church for Gauden to say that the great man's character was marred by a sense of personal inadequacy and distrust of others, that he had not been much liked or respected by his fellow students and professors at Oxford, that he had been chastised by Archbishop Whitgift for his role in the debate with Walter Travers at the Temple Church in London, and that, as a kind of punishment, he had been stuck away by the Church in obscure livings.

Sheldon may have told Walton that he thought Gauden would never have been made a bishop in the first place had he not successfully curried favour with the king. The archbishop would see to it that Gauden never got his coveted promotion to Winchester. In the meantime, he was counting on good Izaak to correct Gauden's errors concerning Richard Hooker and give the Church a portrait showing that great man worthy to be the founding authority of the Anglican Church.[17]

On this December day in 1664 Walton returned home from his short walk across St Paul's churchyard from Stationers Hall where he has just officially registered his *Life* of Hooker for publication. He had finished the work only two months ago. Sheldon had read the manuscript quickly and fixed his *imprimatur* by the end of October. Two weeks ago Izaak had completed writing his dedication to his friend, Bishop Morley. The task was finished at last.

As he contemplated the process of doing Hooker's *Life*, he reflected on the helpful biographical tidbits about Hooker he had received over the years from Archbishop James Ussher of Armagh, Thomas Morton, Bishop of Durham, and John Hales, his historian friend at Eton, before they all had died earlier in the century. Their testimonies and those of other friends and associates had helped him to correct many of the factual errors in Gauden's *Life*, especially those affirming Hooker's bachelorhood, his weak performance at college and the poor reception of his debates with Walter Travers at the Temple Church.

However, the old man was probably not altogether satisfied with his *Life* of Hooker. His subject's trail had been cold. Hooker, after all, had been dead for more than sixty years. Walton knew that some critics would fault his sources. He was also well aware that he had filled in blanks in the Hooker narrative with long and often extraneous material about other better-documented figures of the day, especially Archbishop Whitgift.

Walton may also have been cognizant that his aging memory was less than reliable as a source for some of the personal anecdotes about Hooker that he had included in the biography. He no doubt hoped that his recollections of conversations overheard so long ago were still accurate. It had been nearly forty years since he and his wife, Rachel, were living here in London, with Rachel's widowed mother, Susannah Cranmer Floud and her sister (Rachel's aunt), Dorothy Cranmer Spenser, boarding with them. Walton had known their brother William Cranmer in those days as well. He could recall hearing the two widows and their brother discuss childhood memories of Richard Hooker, and the second-hand accounts they had had from their deceased brother George Cranmer, Hooker's student, friend, and literary collaborator.

Aunt Dorothy had been married to John Spenser, a close friend and disciple of Hooker who later became a trustee of Hooker's estate, one of the early editors of his writings, and president of his Oxford *alma mater*, Corpus Christi College. As Walton remembered it, Dorothy had had no use for Joan Churchman Hooker and her family and had seemed to regard Hooker's marriage to Joan as a most unfortunate event.

Dorothy's husband had been deposed in those ugly lawsuits brought by Hooker's daughters, after their father's and mother's deaths. John Spenser must have brought home to Dorothy some sordid tales about Joan Hooker, her unreliable father, untrustworthy brother, and money-grubbing daughters. Still, Walton may have thought, perhaps he should not have relied so much on the biased tales of his aunt.

Those Hooker trials had created a minor scandal in London for more than ten years, Walton recalled. Aunt Susannah gossiped often about how scandalized her family (the Cranmers) and their friends were by the attacks in these court cases on the reputations of good people who had admired and helped Hooker, especially their friends, the Sandys. According to her, Joan Hooker and her girls were nothing but a pack of greedy, grasping, ungrateful women, tainting Richard Hooker's memory and unworthy of his name.

To Walton, Hooker must indeed have seemed a saint to have endured the abuse of such a shrewish wife as his aunts had painted Joan Hooker to be. The aged writer probably doubted that he had significantly overstated his characterization of Hooker as simple, trusting, dove-like, inspired, and saintly. In all events, Archbishop Sheldon wanted a hero for the Church and Walton had provided just that!

Izaak assumed that his readers would understand that his purpose as biographer was not simply to record facts but to provide in his subject a moral pattern, an example for good living. His little anecdotes about Hooker as a caring son, a diligent and pious student, an inspired preacher, a long- suffering husband and father, a beleaguered defender of the faith, and a man who worked himself to death in defence of Walton's beloved Church of England were intended to reveal a higher truth than mere fact. When he put pious speeches into Hooker's mouth, Walton was confident that his readers knew these were not to be taken literally but as expressions of the highest aspirations of

Christian faith emanating from the heart of one of the founding spirits of Anglican Church.

He may have had some genuine misgivings, however, about one portion of the biography. He had repeated uncritically his Aunt Dorothy's claim that her husband John Spenser had actually written large segments of the last three books of Hooker's *Laws* as well as her story about Mrs Hooker's complicity in the destruction of some of Richard's manuscripts by Puritan scoundrels. Supposedly, Joan had let one Mr Charke and another Puritan minister from Canterbury into her husband's study at Bishopsbourne before his body was even cold. She had then been summoned to testify before the Privy Council as to the fate of Richard's writings. She confessed her wrongdoing and died the next day. Divine retribution—but totally untrue!

Walton probably put these stories in his biography of Hooker—some of them had been recounted by Spenser and Gauden before him—not so much because he trusted his aunt's veracity, or his own memory, or the accuracy of those who had printed them before now, but because they supported the opinion of the Archbishop—and his own—that the last three books, as published by Gauden, with their questionable views on the episcopacy and related matters, were not authentic Hooker. Surely these books had been tampered with by Puritans and low-churchmen. The true Richard Hooker would not have been so ambiguous (or open-minded) on such important issues. Would he?[18]

NOTES

1. Dr Henry Parry (1561-1616), a fellow at Corpus Christi College with Richard Hooker, chaplain to the queen and bishop of Winchester in 1607 and Worcester in 1613 (after Hooker's death), was a friend of both Andrewes and Hooker. Lancelot Andrewes (1555-1626) was also a kindred spirit, clerical colleague, and friend of Hooker. During the 1590s, while a prebend at St Paul's Cathedral, Andrewes was notable as one of the finest preachers in London. His sermons at St Paul's, in opposition to extreme Calvinism, paralleled Hooker's own efforts just down the street at the Temple Church. A graduate of the Merchant Taylor's School in London, a fellow and the master since 1589 at Pembroke Hall, Cambridge, Andrewes went on, after Hooker's death in 1600, to become one of the leading lights of the Jacobean church. He served as dean of Westminster Cathedral, bishop of Chichester, Ely and Winchester, general editor of the authorized version of the Bible and, withal, a brilliant scholar and stirring preacher. On 7 November 1600, just five days after Hooker's death, Andrewes wrote to Parry, after apparently being frustrated in his efforts to contact Sandys and Cranmer, to express his concern over the fate of the manuscripts at Bishopsbourne, and asked Parry to contact John Churchman. His letter is reproduced in *Works,* I, 91-2, n. 1. The original is in the Bodleian Library, MS Rawlinson D.404, f.112r. See also *Works,* I, 123; 91-2, for John Spenser's accounts of the fate of Hooker's works.

2. A fast horse could make the forty-odd miles along the Dover Road from Gravesend to Canterbury in well under eight hours. From there it was only three miles south to Bishopsbourne. See Ridley, 80-83 and Harrison, 401.

3. Taken from the depositions of Philip Culme in Chancery Court, 3 November 1613, in Sisson, 146-47.

4. See Chancery Court depositions of Robert Churchman and John Spenser, February 1613, *Ibid.*, 149-53, 92-5.

5. *Ibid.* It would seem that the sermons, except for the sermons on Jude which were kept by Sandys' steward, Nicholas Eveleigh, found their way into Spenser's hands as well. Spenser later employed a fellow at Corpus Christi, Henry Jackson, "to put together the various fragments of Hooker's works." Jackson, according to the nineteenth-century college president and historian Thomas Fowler, displayed "indefatigable energy" in this task and eventually was able to publish several sermons as well as Travers' *Supplication* and Hooker's *Answer*.

According to President Fowler, Jackson was a jealous and cynical man who never appreciated how fortunate he was to have been sponsored by Spenser in such an important project. (Graduate assistants of any era might be inclined to greater sympathy for Jackson.) Thomas Fowler, *The History of Corpus Christi College* (Oxford: Clarendon Press, 1893), 173-4.

The most authentic copies of the *Sermon of Justification* and of Hooker's *Answer* to the *Supplication* are in the Library of Trinity College Dublin, ms 118; 119, and The British Museum (Harleian MS 4888) and of the *Sermon on Faith in the Elect* in the Corpus Christi College archives MS 288. Hooker's drafts of Books VI and VIII, also in Trinity College Dublin, were in the hands of Lancelot Andrewes and Bishop James Ussher of Armagh in 1648 when they first appeared in print. See Richard Bishop's "To the Reader," in his 1648 printing of the *Laws*. See *Folger*, III, IV, V for copies of Hooker's sermons, tracts, and later books as well as for the most authoritative analysis and discussion of their printing history.

6. This incident is recorded by our major eyewitness source for much of the period, Fynes Moryson, in his 1663 work, *Pacta Hibernia: A History of the Wars in Ireland, The Itinerary of Fynes Moryson* (Glasgow: James MacLehose and Sons, 1907), II, 341.

7. *Churchman v. Bradshaw, et. al.*, Sisson, 178, generally, 174-79.

8. Alice Churchman died in early September 1601, at the height of her husband's fortune and influence. Joan Churchman Hooker Nethersole died in 1603.

9. *Hooker v. Churchman and Stratford*, Sisson, 157-60, 40. Under the prevailing rule of primogeniture, the first son (or daughter) would normally inherit most of the estate. But in Kent, where the Hookers lived, the law of gavelkind prevailed. This meant that all sons (or daughters, if there were no sons) would inherit equally. It is probable that Hooker intended this result. See Harrison, 172.

10. *Hooker v. Evans, et. al.*: Sisson, 170, 161-69. 40-1.

11. *Ibid.*; also, 40-2.

12. *Hooker v. Huntley, Ibid.*, 171-73; Sisson, 30, n.1..

13. *Hooker v. Sandys, Ibid.*, 127-56, 66-78.

14. Novarr, 227-28.

15. Fuller, *Worthies*, 264; Novarr, 200-07.

16. Novarr, 211-22.

17. *Ibid.*, 223-25.

18. Walton has been correctly discredited in these stories and in many other parts of his biography. See esp. Sisson, 80-8; Novarr, 268-75; *Works*, I, ix-xi.

Bibliography

OF WORKS CITED

ADDISON, WILLIAM. *Worthy Dr Fuller*. New York: The Macmillan Company, 1951.

ALEXANDER, J. J. "Ancestors of John Hooker". *Devon and Cornwall Notes and Queries*, 1936-37. 19. 222.

ALMASY, RUDOLPH. "They are and are not 'Elymas': The 1641 *Causes* Notes as Postscript to Richard Hooker's *Of the Laws of Ecclesiastical Polity*", A. S. McGrade, ed., *Richard Hooker and the Construction of Christian Community*. Tempe, Arizona: Medieval & Renaissance Texts and Studies, 1997.

ALYMER, JOHN. Letter to Whitgift. *23 November 1589. Lambeth Palace Library: Fairhurst* Papers, MS 3470, fol. 129.

(ANON.) *A Christian Letter of certain English Protestants, unfained favourers of the present state of Religion, Authorised and professed in England: unto that Reverend and learned man, Mr. R. Hoo. Requiring resolution in certain matters of doctrine (which seem to overthrow the foundation of Christian Religion and of the church among us) expresslie contained in his five books of Ecclesiastical Policie*. 1599. Corpus Christi College, Oxford. MS 215b; *Folger*, IV, 6-79.

(ANON.) *Consecration of the Temple Church: Sermons Preached at the Celebration of Its Seven Hundredth Anniversary*. London: Macmillan & Co., 1885.

ARBER, EDWARD, ed. *A Transcript of the Registers of the Company of Stationers of London: 1554-1640 AD*. II: 625. 295. Privately printed in London, 1875. British Library. Contains John Windet's entry for the first four Books of Hooker's Laws on 29 January 1593.

AUSTIN, PETER AND TOM ORGAN. *Report on the Conservation of the 14th Century Wall Paintings*. Available as an unpublished research paper from St Mary's Church, Bishopsbourne, Kent, 1995.

AVIS, PAUL. *Anglicanism and the Christian Church*. Minneapolis: Fortress Press, 1989.

AYRE, JOHN, ed. *The Sermons of Edwin Sandys, D.D.*. Cambridge: The Parker Society. III, 1841.

——————, ed. *The Works of John Whitgift, D.D.*. Cambridge: The Parker Society. III, 1853.

BACKUS, IRENE. "Laurence Tomson (1539-1608) and Elizabethan Puritanism," *Journal of Ecclesiastical History*. 28. No.1. January, 1977.

BAIKIE, JAMES. *The English Bible and Its Story*. Philadelphia: J. B. Lippincott Company, 1925.

BAILEY, HENRY. *Salisbury Cathedral Library*. Salisbury Cathedral, 1978.

BAUCHAM, RICHARD. "Hooker, Travers and the Church of Rome in the 1580's." *Journal of Ecclesiastical History*. 29, 1978.

BAYLIS, T. HENRY. *The Temple Church of St. Ann, An Historical Record and Guide*. London: George Philip and Son, 1895.

BEDWELL, C. E. A. *A Brief History of the Middle Temple*. London: Butterworth & Co., 1909.

BEIR, A. L. AND ROGER FINLAY. *The Making of the Metropolis: London 1500-1700*. London and New York: Longmans, 1986.

BELLOT, HUGH H. L. *The Inner and Middle Temple*. London: Methuen & Co., 1902.

BESANT, WALTER. *London in the Time of the Tudors*. London: Adam & Charles Black, 1904.

BLAND, MARK. "The Appearance of Text in Early Modern England, *Text, An Interdisciplinary Annual of Textual Studies*. II. Ann Arbor, Michigan: The University of Michigan Press, 1998.

BOGGIS, R. J. E. *A History of the Diocese of Exeter*. Exeter: William Pollard & Co., Ltd, 1922.

BOOTY, JOHN E. "A Celebration of Richard Hooker." *Sewanee Theological Review*. 36:2, 1993.

————. "Introduction: Book V." *Folger Library Edition of the Works of Richard Hooker*. VI, Pt.I.

————. "Hooker and Anglicanism." *In Studies in Richard Hooker: Essays Preliminary to an Edition of His Works*. W. Speed Hill, ed. Cleveland and London: The Press of Case Western Reserve University, 1972.

————. *John Jewel as Apologist for the Church of England*. London: SPCK, 1963.

————. "Richard Hooker, Anglican Theologian." *Sewanee Theological Review*, 36:2, 1993.

————. "The Quest for the Historical Hooker." *The Churchman*. 80, 1966.

BORER, MARY CATHCART. *The People of Tudor England*. London: Max Parrish and Co., Ltd, 1966.

BOWEN, CATHERINE DRINKER. *The Lion and the Throne, The Life and Times of Sir Edward Coke*. Boston: Little Brown and Company, 1956.

BRAUDEL, BERNARD. *The Structures of Everyday Life*, I. New York: Harper & Row, 1981.

BRAYLEY, W. AND H. HERBERT, *A Concise Account Historical and Descriptive of Lambeth Palace*. London: S. Gosnell, 1806.

BRIGDEN, SUSAN. *London and the Reformation*. Oxford: Clarendon Press, 1989.

BROOK, V. J. K. *Whitgift and the English Church*. London: The English Universities Press, 1957.

BRUCE, JOHN AND THOMAS PEROWNE, eds. *The Correspondence of Matthew Parker*. Cambridge: The Parker Society, 1853.

BULL, HENRY, ed. *Christian Prayers and Holy Meditations*, 1556. Cambridge: The Parker Society, 1842.

BURNBY, J., ed. *Elizabethan Times in Tottenham, Edmonton and Enfield*. Edmonton: Edmonton Historical Society, 1995.

BURNETT, DAVID. *Salisbury, The History of an English Cathedral*. London: The Compton Press, Ltd, 1953.

BYRNE, MURIEL ST. CLARE. *Elizabethan Life in Town and Country*. 1925. Gloucester: Alan Sutton, 1987.

CANNY, NICHOLAS. *The Elizabethan Conquest of Ireland*. New York: Harper & Row, 1976.

CARLISLE, NICHOLAS. *A Concise Description of the Endowed Grammar Schools in England and Wales*, I. London: Baldwin, Cradock & Joy, 1818.

CARLSON, LELAND H. *Martin Marprelate Gentleman Master Job Throckmorton Laid Open in His Colors*. San Marino: Huntington Library, 1981.

CARLTON, CHARLES. *The Court of Orphans*. Leicester: Leicester University Press, 1974.

CARTWRIGHT, THOMAS. *A Reply to an Answere made of M. Doctor Whitgifte Aganste the Admonition to the Parliament By T. C.*. 1574. Lambeth Palace Library: 1574.03.

CHANDLERY, P. J. *The Tower to Tyburn*. London: Sands & Co., 1924.

CHARTIER, ROGER, ed. "Passions of the Renaissance." *A History of Private Life*, III. Cambridge: Harvard University Press, 1989.

CHILDE-PEMBERTON, WILLIAM S. *Elizabeth Blount and Henry VIII*. London: Eveleigh Nash, 1913.

CHURCH, R. W., ed. *Hooker Of the Laws of Ecclesiastical Polity*, Bk.1. Oxford: Clarendon Press, 1896.

CHUTE, MARCHETTE. *Shakespeare of London*. New York: E. P. Dutton and Company, Inc., 1964.

CLAY, WILLIAM KEATINGE. *Liturgical Services Liturgies and Occasional Forms of Prayer Set Forth in the Reign of Queen Elizabeth*. Cambridge: The Parker Society, 1847.

——————. *Private Prayers Put Forth by Authority During the Reign of Queen Elizabeth*. Cambridge: The Parker Society, 1851.

CLIFTON-TAYLOR, ALEC. *The Cathedrals of England*. Norwich: Thames and Hudson, 1967.

COLLINSON, PATRICK. *Elizabethan Essays*. London: Hambledon Press, 1994.

——————. *The Elizabethan Puritan Movement*. London: Methuen & Co., 1967.

——————. *The Religion of Protestants: The Church in English Society 1559-1625*. Oxford: Clarendon Press, 1982.

CORPUS CHRISTI ARCHIVES. *Liber Admis 1517-1646; Liber Magni* (Unnumbered folios).

COVEL, WILLIAM. *A Just and Temperate Defense of the Five Books*. London, 1603. Corpus Christi College Archives: Fulman MS #1682, 215.E.1.15 a ff..

COYLE, SANDY, ed. *The Herbs and Flowers of a Shakespeare Garden*. The Herb Society of America, 1983.

CRANMER, GEORGE. *Concerning the New Church Discipline, An Excellent Letter, Written By Mr. G. Cranmer to Mr. R. H.*. *c*1592-3. *Works*. II.

——————. *Notes Upon Mr Hookers Sixt Book*. Corpus Christi College, Oxford. MS 295, fol 3, 1.

CRESSEY, David. *Birth, Marriage, and Death: Ritual, Religion, and the Life Cycle in Tudor and Stewart England*. Oxford: Oxford University Press, 1977.

CURTIS, EDMUND. *A History of Ireland*, 6th ed. New York: Barnes and Noble, 1950.

CURTIS, MARK. *Oxford and Cambridge in Transition 1558-1642*. Oxford: Clarendon Press, 1959.

DARLEY, GILLIAN AND ANDREW SAINT. *The Chronicles of London*. London: Weidenfeld and Nicolson, Ltd, 1994.

DAVIES, HORTON. *Worship and Theology in England 1534-1603*. Princeton: Princeton University Press, 1970.

DAVIS, J. C. "Backing into Modernity: The Dilemma of Richard Hooker." *The Certainty of Doubt, Tributes to Peter Munz*, 157-179. Miles Fairburn and W. H. Oliver, eds. Victoria, B. C.: Victoria University Press, 1997.

DAWLEY, POWELL MILLS. *John Whitgift and the Reformation*. London: Adam and Charles Black, 1955.

DEAKIN, Q. E. "John Hooker's 'Description of Excester': A Comparison of the Manuscripts," *Devon and Cornwall Notes and Queries*. 104; 121.

DEAN, JOSEPH. *Middle Temple Hall: Four Centuries of History*. London: Middle Temple, 1970.

DENT, C. M. *Protestant Reformers in Elizabethan Oxford*. Oxford: Oxford University Press, 1983.

DEVON RECORDS OFFICE. *Roger Hooker's Interest in Tin Works and His Debts*. H.H.3.55, fol. 39; 57 fol. 148.

————. *Richard Hooker's Grants from the City of Exeter*. Act Book 4, 1581-1588.

D'EWES, SIMONDS. *The Journals of All the Parliaments During the Reign of Queen Elizabeth*. London, 1682.

DICKENS, A. G. *The English Reformation*. rev. ed. Glasgow: Fontana Press, 1967.

DODD, A. H. *Life in Elizabethan England*. London: B. T. Batsford, Ltd, 1961.

DODWELL, C. R. *Lambeth Palace*. London: Country Life Limited, 1958.

DORAN, SUSAN AND CHRISTOPHER DURSTON. *Princes, Pastors and People*. London and New York: Routledge, 1991.

DOUGLAS, C. E. AND W. FRERE, eds.. *Puritan Manifestoes*, 1907. London, 1954.

DOWLING, THADY, ed. *Annals of Ireland*. Dublin: R. Butler, 1849.

DUNCAN, C. D. "Public Lectures and Professorial Chairs," James McConica, ed., *The History of the University of Oxford,* III. Oxford: Clarendon Press, 1986.

ECCLESHALL, ROBERT. "Richard Hooker and the Peculiarities of the English: The Reception of the 'Ecclesiastical Polity' in the Seventeenth and Eighteenth Centuries." *History of Political Thought,* 2.1. January, 1981.

EDELEN, GEORGES. "A Chronology of Richard Hooker's Life," W. Speed Hill, ed, *The Folger Library Edition of the Works of Richard Hooker*, VI. Cambridge and London: The Belknap Press of Harvard University, 1990.

————. "Hooker's Style," W. Speed Hill, ed., *Studies in Richard Hooker*. Cleveland: The Press of Case Western Reserve University, 1972.

————. *The Description of England* (1587). William Harrison, ed. New York: Dover Publications, 1994.

EDWARDS, DAVID L. *Christianity: The First Two Thousand years*. London: Cassell, 1997.

ELTON, G. R. *England Under the Tudors*. London and New York: Routledge, 1974.

ENTWISLE, FRANK. *Abroad in England*. London: André Deutsch, 1982.

ERICKSON, CAROLLY. *The First Elizabeth*. New York: Summit Books, 1983.

FALLA, TREVOR. "Heavitree." *Discovering Exeter*. Exeter: Exeter Civic Society, 1983.

FARR, EDWARD, ed. *Select Poetry Chiefly Devotional of the Reign of Queen Elizabeth*. Cambridge: The Parker Society, 1845.

FLETCHER, ANTHONY AND PETER ROBERTS, eds. *Religion, Culture and Society in Early Modern Britain Essays in Honour of Patrick Collinson*. Cambridge: Cambridge University Press, 1994.

FLETCHER, J. M. "The Faculty of Arts," James McConica, ed., *The History of the University of Oxford,* III. Oxford: Clarendon Press, 1986.

FORTE, E. P. "Richard Hooker as Preacher." *Folger*, V.

FOWLER, JOSEPH. *Medieval Sherborne*. Dorchester: Longmans, 1951.

FOWLER, THOMAS. *The History of Corpus Christi College*. Oxford: Clarendon Press, 1893.

FREEMAN, EDWARD A. AND WILLIAM HUNT, eds. *Historic Towns*. London: Longmans, Green & Co., 1906.

FULLER, THOMAS. *The Church-History of Britain from the Birth of Jesus Christ until the Year MDCXLVII*, III. London: John Williams, 1665.

————. *The History of the Worthies of England*, I. London: J.G.W.L., 1662.

GAUDEN, JOHN. *The Life & Death of Mr. Richard Hooker* in *The Works of Mr. Richard Hooker . . .* London: J. Best, 1662.

GIBBS, LEE W. "Introduction to Book VI." *Folger*. VI.I.

————. "Theology, Logic and Rhetoric in the Temple Controversy between Richard Hooker and Walter Travers." *Anglican Theological Review*, 65.2. 1983.

GOSART, ALEXANDER B., ed. *The Spending of the Money of Robert Nowell*. Blackburn, Lancashire. Printed for private circulation. Townley MSS, 1877. British Library 2.326g.19.

GREENSLADE, S. L. "The Faculty of Theology," James McConica, ed., *The History of the University of Oxford*, III. Oxford: Clarendon Press, 1986.

GRINDAL, EDMUND. *Letter to Walsingham with Response*. 2 and 17 September 1580. Lambeth Palace Library: Fairhust Papers, 3470, fol., 63.

GRISLIS, EGIL. "Commentary," *Folger*, V.

————. "The Hermeneutical Problem in Richard Hooker." *Studies in Richard Hooker: Essays Preliminary to An Edition of His Works*. W. Speed Hill, ed. Cleveland and London: The Press of Case Western Reserve University, 1972.

HAIGH, CHRISTOPHER, ed. *The Reformation Revised*. Cambridge: Cambridge University Press, 1987.

HALLAM, HENRY. *The Constitutional History of England*, 5th ed., I. London: John Murray, 1846.

HAMMER, CARL I., JR. "Town of Oxford," James McConica, ed., *The History of the University of Oxford*. III. Oxford: Clarendon Press, 1986.

HARRISON, WILLIAM. *The Description of England* (1587). Georges Edelen, ed. New York: Dover Publications, 1994.

HARTE, WALTER J., ed. *An Account of the Seiges of Exeter, Foundation of the Cathedral Church and Disputes Between the Cathedral and City Authorities by John Vowell alias Hoker*. Exeter: Muniment Room. James G. Commin, 1911.

————. ed. *Exeter City Muniments*, 52. Devon and Cornwall Record Society.

————. *Gleanings from the Common Place book of John Hooker, relating to the City of Exeter (1485-1590)*. Exeter: Wheaton & Co. (no date).

————. *John Hooker's Description of the citie of Excester*. Exeter: Devon and Cornwall Record Society, 1919.

———— with J. W. Schopp and H. Tapley Soper, eds. *Office of Arms Chart 1597*. (Showing "Joan" as wife of Roger Hooker.) Exeter City Muniments, 52.

HARTLEY, T. E., ed. *Proceedings in the Parliaments of Elizabeth I 1584-1589*, I. London: Leicester University Press, 1995.

HASTINGS, ROBINSON, ed. *The Zurich Letters 1558-1579*. Cambridge: The Parker Society, 1845.

HAUGAARD, WILLIAM P. *Elizabeth and the English Reformation*. Cambridge: Cambridge University Press, 1968.

————————. "The Hooker-Travers Controversy." *Folger*, V.

————————. "The Preface." *Folger*, VI.1.

————————."Books II, III, IV." *Folger*, VI.I.

HEADLAM, CECIL. *Oxford and its History*. London: J. M. Dent & Sons, 1926.

HIBBERT, CHRISTOPHER. *The English A Social History 1066-1945*. New York: W. W. Norton, 1987.

———————— AND BEN WEINREB, eds. *The London Encyclopedia*. London: Macmillan, 1983.

HILL, W. SPEED. *The Doctrinal Background of Hooker's Laws of Ecclesiastical Polity*. Doctoral Dissertation. Harvard University, 1964.

————————, gen. ed. *The Folger Library Edition of the Works of Richard Hooker*. 7 vols. 1977-1998. Vols. I-V: Cambridge, Massachusetts and London, England: The Belknap Press of Harvard University; Vols. VI and VII: Binghamton, New York and Tempe Arizona: Medieval & Renaissance Texts and Studies. (Cited in this bibliography as Folger.)

————————. "Hooker's Polity: The Problem of the 'Last Three Books'," *The Huntington Library Quarterly*. 34, 1971.

————————. *Richard Hooker A Descriptive Biography of the Early Editions: 1593-1724*. Cleveland and London: The Press of Case Western Reserve University, 1970.

———————— ed., *Richard Hooker Works: Index of Names and Works*. Tempe, Arizona: Medieval and Renaissance Texts & Studies, 1998. [Published as vol. VII in *Folger Library Edition of the Works of Richard Hooker*.]

———————— ed., *Studies in Richard Hooker: Essays Preliminary to an Edition of His Works*. Cleveland & London: The Press of Case Western Reserve University, 1972.

————————. "The Evolution of Hooker's Laws of Ecclesiastical Polity," *Studies*.

————————. "Scripture as Text, Text as Scripture: The Case of Richard Hooker," *Text, An Interdisciplinary Annual of Textual Studies*. 9. Ann Arbor, Michigan: The University of Michigan Press, 1996.

HINTON, EDWARD M. *Ireland Through Tudor Eyes*. Philadelphia: University of Pennsylvania Press, 1935.

HOBHOUSE, CHRISTOPHER. *Oxford As it Was and As it is Today*. London: B. T. Batsford, Ltd, 1939.

HOOKER, JOHN. *A Catalog of the Bishops of Excester, with the description of the Antiquitie, and first foundation of the Cathedrall Church of the same*. London: Henry Denham, 1584. Also, Bk.2, 1584. Exeter: Devon Records Office

————————. *Common Place Book*. In Walter Harte, ed. *Gleanings from the Common Place Book of John Hooker*. Exeter: Wheaton & Co. (no date).

————————. *The Description of the Cittie of Excester, Colected and Gathered by John Vowell alias Hooker gentleman and Chamberlain of the same Cittie*. London: Blackletter, 1559; 1571; 1580 in British Museum General Catalogue of Printed Books. London, 1964, CCL, 2430; 1587 in Holinshed's Chronicles. 1600 in Devon Record Office. Exeter City Archives. Book 52. Also in Harte, ed. *John Hooker's Description of the citie of Excester*. Devon and Cornwall Record Society, 1919. Pt. II.)

————————. *The Discourse and Discovery of the Life of Sir Peter Carew*, John Maclean, ed., *John Hooker's The Life and Times of Sir Peter Carew* (1584). London: Bill & Daldy, 1857.

————————. *New Year's Gift List of 1584*. Vernon Snow, ed., *Devon and Cornwall Notes and Queries*. 140; 161.

——————. *Order and Usage of the keeping of a parlement in England*. London: John Allde,1572. In Vernon F. Snow. *Parliament in Elizabethan England, John Hooker's Order and Usage*. Hartford: Yale University Press, 1977.

——————. *A Pamphlet of the Offices, and Duties of everie particular sworne Officer, of the Citie of Exeter*. London: Henry Denham, 1584.

——————. *Synopsis Corographicall of the Province of Devon*. Exeter: Devon Records Office. c. 1600. fol. 116.

HOOKER, RICHARD. *The Answere of Mr. Richard Hooker to a Supplication Preferred by Mr. Walter Travers to the HH. Lords of the Privy Counsell*. 1586. Trinity College, Dublin: MS 119; *Folger*, V.

——————. *Autograph Notes*. Trinity College, Dublin. MS 364, ff. 69-84; *Folger*, III.

——————. *Autograph (Marginal) Notes on A Christian Letter*, 1599-1600. Corpus Christi College, Oxford: MS 215b; *Folger*, IV.

——————. *The Causes of the Continuance of These Contentions Concerning Church Government*. Trinity College, Dublin: MS 774, fol. 56; *Folger*, III.

————. *The Dublin Fragments on Grace and Free Will, the Sacraments, and Predestination*. Trinity College, Dublin: MS 121; *Folger*, IV.

——————. *The First Sermon Upon Part of St. Jude*, c.1582/83. *Folger, V.*

——————. *Of the Laws of Ecclesiastical Polity: Books I-IV*, 1593; *Book V*, 1597; *Books VI, VIII,* 1648; *Book VII*, 1662. *Folger*, I-IV.

——————. *A Learned and Comfortable Sermon of the Certaintie and Perpetuitie of Faith in the Elect*, 1585. Corpus Christi College, Oxford: MS 288; *Folger*, V.

——————. *A Learned Discourse of Justification, Workes, and How the Foundation of Faith is Overthrowne*, 1586. Trinity College, Dublin: MS 118; *Folger*, V.

——————. *A Learned Sermon of the Nature of Pride*, 1585/86. Trinity College, Dublin: MS 121; *Folger*, V.

——————. *Letter To the worshipful my verie loving friend M. D. Rainolds at Queens College in Oxford*. (undated). Corpus Christi College, Oxford archives. MS 303, fol. 208.

————. *Notes Toward a Fragment on Predestination*. Trinity College, Dublin: MS 364, fol. 80; *Folger*, IV.

——————. *A Remedie Against Sorrow and Feare delivered in a funerall Sermon*, 1595-1600. *Folger*, V.

——————. *The Second Sermon Upon Part of St. Jude*, c.1582/83. *Folger*, V.

——————. *A Sermon Fragment on Hebrews 2.14-15*. *Folger*, V.

——————. *A Sermon Fragment on Matth. 27-46*. Trinity College, Dublin: MS 774; *Folger*, V.

——————. *A Sermon on Matthew* 7.7. Trinity College, Dublin: MS 774; *Folger*, V.

——————. *A Sermon Fragment on Prov. 3*. Trinity College, Dublin: MS 774; *Folger*, V.

——————. "A Pension to Richard Hooker," 21 September 1582. *Act Book 4 1581-1588*: 399. Devon Records Office.

——————. *Richard Hooker's Will*. Archdeacons Court, Canterbury Cathedral. PRC: 32/38, fol. 291.

HOOKER, ROBERT. *Robert Hooker's Will*, 1534. Devon Records Office: H.H.3-55, fol. 93.

HOOKER, ROGER. *Witness to Challoner's Will*. PRO, London: PCC47, Bakon: 375.

——————. *Interest in Father's Tin Works*. Devon Records Office: H.H.3.55: fol. 39.

——————. *Debts Recorded*. Devon Records Office: H.H.3.57: 148.

——————. *Letter from Ireland*. John Maclean, ed., *John Hooker's The Life and Times of Sir Peter Carew* (1584). London: Bill & Daldy, 1857.

—————— Possible listing on the Devon Muster Role. Howard, A. J. and Stoate, T. L., eds. *The Devon Muster Roll for 1569*. Almondsbury, Bristol, 1977.

HOOKER, ZACHARIE (ZACHARY). *Will of Z. Hooker*. 1643. Charles Worthy, Esq., *Devonshire Wills: A Collection of Annotated Testamentary Abstracts*. 124. London: Bembrose & Sons, LTD., 1896.

HOPE, VYVYAN AND JOHN LLOYD. *Exeter Cathedral*. Audrey Erskine, ed. Exeter: Dean and Chapter of the Cathedral, 1988.

HOPWOOD, CHARLES HENRY, ed. *A Calendar of the Middle Temple*. London: Butterworth & Co., 1903.

——————, ed. *Middle Temple Records*. London: Butterworth & Co., 1904.

HOSKINS, H. G. *History of Devon*. Tiverton, Devon: Devon Books, 1992.

——————. *Two Thousand Years in Exeter*. Chichester: Phillimore & Co., Ltd, 1960.

HOULBROOKE, RALPH A. *The English Family 1450-1700*. New York: Longmans, Inc., 1984.

HOWARD, A. J. AND T. L. STOATE, eds. *The Devon Muster Roll for 1569*. Almondsbury, Bristol, 1977.

HUTCHINSON, JOHN. *A Catalog of Notable Middle Templars*. London: Society of the Middle Temple, 1902.

INDERWICK, R. A., ed. *A Calendar of the Inner Temple Records*. London, 1896.

INGRAM, MARTIN. *Church Courts, Sex and Marriage in England 1570-1640*. Cambridge: Cambridge University Press, 1987.

JEWELL, JOHN. *Zurich Letters*, I. Hastings Roberts, ed. Cambridge: The Parker Society, 1845.

KEBLE, JOHN, ed. *The Works of Mr. Richard Hooker*. 3rd.ed., 3 vols. Oxford: Oxford University Press, 7th ed., 1887.

KEEN, ROSEMARY, ed. "Inventory of Richard Hooker, 1601." *Archaelogia, Cantiana*. LXX. Ashford, Kent: Headley Brothers, Ltd, 1957.

KENDALL, R. T. *Calvin and English Calvinism to 1649*. Oxford: Oxford University Press, 1979.

KER, N. R. "The Provision of Books," James McConica, ed., *The History of the University of Oxford*, III. Oxford: Clarendon Press, 1986.

KERR, JESSICA. *Shakespeare's Flowers*. New York: Thomas Crowell & Co., 1969.

KIRBY, W. J. TORRACE. *Richard Hooker's Doctrine of Royal Supremacy*. Studies in the History of Christian Thought. Vol. 43. Brill Academic Publishers, 1997.

KNAPPEN, M. M. *Tudor Puritanism*. Chicago: Chicago University Press, 1939.

KNOX, S. J. *Walter Travers: Paragon of Elizabethan Puritanism*. London: Methuen & Co., Ltd, 1962.

LAKE, PETER. *Anglicans and Puritans? Presbyterianism and English Conformist Thought from Whitgift to Hooker*. London: Unwin Hyman, 1988.

LAMB, CHRISTOPHER. *The Parish Church of St. Andrew Enfield*. Gloucester: The British Publishing Company Limited, 1968.

LAURANCE, ANNE. *Women in England 1500-1760*. London: Weidenfeld and Nicolson, 1994.

LE BAS, CHARLES WEBB. *The Life of Bishop Jewel*. London: J. G. & F. Rivington, 1835.

LEE, SIDNEY, ed. *Dictionary of National Biography*, V, XXVII. New York: Macmillan, 1891.

LE NEVE, JOHN. *Fasti Ecclesiae Anglicanae 1541-1857*. Compiled by Joyce M. Horn. London: University of London Institute of Historical Research, 1986.

LEWIS, C. S. *English Literature in the 16th Century Excluding Drama*. Oxford: The Clarendon Press, 1954.

LITTLE, BRYAN. *Portrait of Exeter*. London: Robert Hale, 1983.

LOACH, JENNIFER. "Reformation Controversies," James McConica, ed., *The History of the University of Oxford*, III, 363-96. Oxford: Clarendon Press, 1986.

McADOO, HENRY R. *The Spirit of Anglicanism*. New York: Charles Scribner's Sons, 1965.

McCAFFREY, WALLACE T. *Exeter 1540-1640*. 2nd edition. Cambridge: Harvard University Press, 1975.

MACLEAN, JOHN, ed. *John Hooker's The Life and Times of Sir Peter Carew (1584)*. London: Bill & Daldy, 1857.

MacCULLOCH, DIARMAID. *The Later Reformation in England 1547-1603*. New York: St. Martins Press, 1990.

———. *Thomas Cranmer, A Life*. New Haven and London: Yale University Press, 1996.

MACLURE, MILLAR. *The Pauls Cross Sermons*. Toronto: University of Toronto Press, 1958.

MARSHALL, PETER. *The Catholic Priesthood and the English Reformation*. Oxford: The Clarendon Press, 1994

McCONICA, JAMES, ed. *The History of the University of Oxford*, III. Oxford: Clarendon Press, 1986.

McGINN, DONALD J. *John Penry and the Marprelate Controversy*. New Brunswick: Rutgers University Press, 1966.

McGRADE, A. S. "Introduction to the Last Three Books and Autograph Notes." *Folger*. VI.I, 233-47, 309-83..

———, ed. *Richard Hooker and the Construction of Christian Community*. Tempe, Arizona: Medieval & Renaissance Texts & Studies, 1997.

———, ed. *Richard Hooker of The Laws of Ecclesiastical Polity*. Cambridge: Cambridge University Press, 1989.

———, AND BRIAN VICKERS, eds. *Richard Hooker Of The Laws of Ecclesiastical Polity*. New York: St. Martins Press, 1975.

MEE, ARTHUR. *Kent*. London: Hodder and Stoughton, 1936.

MELLOR, HUGH. *Exeter Architecture*. Chichester: Phillimore & Co., Ltd, 1989.

MILNE, J. G. *The Early History of Corpus Christi College*. Oxford: Basil Blackwell, 1946.

MILTON, ANTHONY. *Catholic and Reformed The Roman and Protestant Churches in English Protestant Thought 1600-1640*. Cambridge: Cambridge University Press, 1995.

MONAHAN, ARTHUR P. "Richard Hooker: Counter Reformation Political Thinker," A.S. McGrade, ed., *Richard Hooker and the Construction of Christian Community*. Tempe, Arizona: Medieval & Renaissance Texts & Studies, 1997.

MOORMAN, JOHN R. H. *A History of the Church in England*, 3rd ed. Harrisburg, Pennsylvania: Morehouse Publishing, 1980.

MORGAN, IRVONWY. *The Godly Preachers of the Elizabethan Church*. London: The Epworth Press, 1965.

MORRIS, CHRISTOPHER. *Political Thought in England: Tyndale to Hooker*. London and New York: Oxford University Press, 1953.

——————. *Richard Hooker Of the Laws of Ecclesiastical Polity*. Everyman's Edition. London: J. M. Dent & Sons, Ltd, 1907.

MORYSON, FYNES. *The Itinerary of Fynes Moryson*, II. Glasgow: James MacLehose and Sons, 1907.

MUNZ, PETER. *The Place of Hooker in the History of Thought*. London: Routledge & Kegan Paul, 1952.

MURRAY, MICHAEL G. *Middle Temple Hall, An Archiectural Appreciation*. London: The Middle Temple, 1991.

MYERS, JAMES P., ed. *Elizabethan Ireland*, A Selection of Writings by Elizabethan Writers in Ireland. Hamden, Connecticut: Anchor Books, 1983.

NEALE, J. E. *Elizabeth I and Her Parliaments 1584-1601*. London: Jonathan Cape, 1957.

NIJENHUIS, WILLEM. *Adrianus Saravia (1523-1631)*. Leiden: E. J. Brill, 1980.

NOVARR, DAVID. *The Making of Walton's "Lives"*. Ithaca: Cornell University Press, 1958.

O'BRIEN, CONOR CRUISE AND MARIE. *The Story of Ireland*. Englewood Cliffs: The Viking Press, 1968.

O'DAY, ROSEMARY. *The Debate on the English Reformation*. London: Methuen & Co., Ltd, 1986.

ORME, NICHOLAS. *Education in the West of England 1066-1548*. Exeter: University of Exeter Press, 1976.

——————. *Exeter Cathedral as It Was 1050-1550*. Exeter, Devon County Council: Devon Books, 1986.

OSSORY, JOHN. "The Father of Richard Hooker." *The Irish Church Quarterly*, V. 6. Dublin, 1913.

OXFORD UNIVERSITY. *A Concise Guide to Colleges of Oxford University*. Oxford, 1992.

——————. *New Illustrated History of Oxford*. Oxford, 1993.

PAGET, FRANCIS. *An Introduction to the Fifth Book of the Laws of Ecclesiastical Polity*. Oxford: Clarendon Press, 1899.

PAM, DAVID O. *The Rude Multitude, Enfield and The Civil War*. Edmonton: G. G. Laurence & Co., 1977.

——————. *The Story of Enfield Chase*. Enfield Preservation Society, 1984.

PARKER, MATTHEW. *Correspondence*. John Bruce and Thomas Perowne, eds. Cambridge: The Parker Society, 1853.

PARRY, H. LLOYD. *The Founding of Exeter School*. Exeter: James G. Commin, 1913.

PEARSON. A. F. *Thomas Cartwright and Elizabethan Protestantism 1535-1603*. Cambridge: Cambridge University Press, 1925.

PITMAN, H. D. GERALD. *Sherborne Observed*. Sherborne: The Abbey Press, 1983.

——————. *The Church of St. Mary Magdelen at Castleton*, revised edition. Published by the church, 1975.

PORTER, H. C. *Puritanism in Tudor England*. Columbia: University of South Carolina Press, 1971.

————. "Hooker, the Tudor Constitution, and the Via Media," W. Speed Hill, ed., *Studies in Richard Hooker: Essays Preliminary To An Edition Of His Works*. Cleveland and London: The Press of Case Western Reserve University, 1972.

PORTER, ROY. *London, A Social History*. Cambridge: Harvard University Press, 1995.

POWICKE, F. J. *Robert Browne Pioneer of Modern Congregationalism*. London: Congregational Union of England and Wales, Inc., 1910.

————. *Henry Barrow and the Exiled Church in Amsterdam*. London: Congreagational Union of England and Wales, 1900.

PRIDHAM, T. L. *Devonshire Celebrities*. London: Bell & Daldy, 1869.

PRINCE, JOHN. *The Worthies of England*. London: Longman, Hurst, Rees, 1810.

PROCKTER, ADRIAN AND ROBERT TAYLOR. *The A to Z of Elizabethan London*. No. 122. London Topographical Society, 1979.

QUENNELL, MARJORIE AND C. H. B. *A History of Everyday Things in England, 1500-1799*, 7th ed., V. II. London: B. T. Batsford, Ltd, 1945.

QUINN, DAVID BEERS. *The Elizabethans and the Irish*. Ithaca: Cornell University Press, 1966.

RABB, THEODORE K. *Jacobean Gentleman Sir Edwin Sandys, 1561-1629*. Princeton: Princeton University Press, 1998.

RAINOLDS, JOHN. *Oratio in Laudem Artis Poeticae* [*circa* 1572]. Intro. by William Ringler. Princeton: Princeton University Press, 1940.

RAPPAPORT, STEVE. *Worlds Within Worlds: Structures of Life in Sixteenth Century London*. New York: Cambridge University Press, 1989.

REECE, SUSAN. Research Notes, card 3539. Exeter: The Devon and Exeter Institution.

RIDLEY, JASPER. *The Tudor Age*. London: Constable and Company, Ltd, 1988.

RINGLER, WILLIAM. *Stephen Gosson*. Princeton: Princeton University Press, 1942.

ROBISON, HASTINGS, ed. *The Zurich Letters*, 1. Cambridge: The Parker Society, 1845.

ROSE-TROUP, FRANCES. *The Western Rebellion 1549*. London: Smith, Elder & Co., 1913.

ROSENBERG, ELEANOR. *Leicester Patron of Letters*. New York: Columbia University Press, 1955.

ROTHSTEIN, NATALIE, ed. *Four Hundred Years of Fashion*. London: Victoria and Albert Museum, 1985.

ROUTH, C. R. N. *Who's Who in Tudor England*. London: Shepherd-Walwyn, 1990.

ROWSE, A. L. *Court and Country: Studies in Tudor History*. Athens, Georgia: The University of Georgia Press, 1987.

————. *Oxford in the History of the Nation*. London: Book Club Associates, 1975.

————. *The Elizabethan Renaissance The Cultural Achievement*. New York: Charles Scribner's Sons, 1972.

————. *The England of Elizabeth*. London: Macmillan and Co., Ltd, 1950.

ST AUGUSTINES WATLING STREET. *General Parish Register* 1559-1653. Guild Hall Mss. Rm., Ms. 9535, 2.

SALGADO, GAMINI. *The Elizabethan Underworld*. Stroud: Alan Sutton Publishing, Ltd, 1992.

SALISBURY CATHEDRAL. "Penruddocke." *Chapter Act Book*, 16.15r.

————. *Sub-deans Act Book*, 1589-1596. D4/3/2,fol.6r, Dec.1,1591. Wiltshire Public Records Office, Trowbridge.

————. *Box 34*, Dec.30,1591. "Letters patent of John Coldwell. . ."

————. *Press IV*. "Procuratoria." Dec.2,1591. "Letters of John Brydges. . ."

————. *Sub-deans Act Book 1589-1596*. D/4/3/2,fol.6. Trowbridge: Wiltshire Public Records Office.

————. *Dean of Chapter Records, Presses 1,2, 4*. Trowbridge: Wiltshire Public Records Office.

SANDYS, SIR EDWIN. *Notes of Mr Hookers Sixt Book*. Corpus Christi College, Oxford archives. MS295, fol.3, 1.

————. *A Relation to the State of Religion: and what Hopes and Pollicies it hath been framed and is maintained in the severall states of the westerne parts of the World*. London, 1605. British Library, C.110e12. (Also published as *Europae Speculum* . . .)

SARAVIA, ADRIAN. *De Diversis Ministrorium Evangelii Gradibus . . . [Of the Diverse Orders of the Ministers of the Gospel . . .]*. London: John Wolfe, 1591. (Lambeth Library 1591.29.)

SAVOY, CAROLYN AND JANET WINTER *Elizabethan Costuming For The Years 1550-1580*, 2nd.ed. Oakland, Cal.: Other Times Publications, 1979.

SCHOFIELD, JOHN. *The Building of London from the Conquest to the Great Fire*. London: British Museum Press, 1984.

SCHOPP, J. W. AND H. TAPELY SOPER, eds. With Walter J. Harte. *Office of Arms Chart of 1597*. Exeter City Muniments, 52.

SEAVER, PAUL S. *The Puritan Lectureships, The Politics of Religious Dissent, 1560-1662*. Stanford: Stanford University Press, 1970.

SECOR, PHILIP B. *Richard Hooker and the Christian Commonwealth*. Unpublished doctoral dissertation. Duke University, 1959.

————. "In Search of Richard Hooker: Constructing a New Biography." McGrade, Arthur Stephen, ed., *Richard Hooker and the Construction of Christian Community*. Tempe, Arizona: Medieval & Renaissance Texts & Studies, 1997.

SHUGER, DEBORAH. "Societie Supernaturall: The Imagined Community of Hooker's Laws, A. S. McGrade, ed., *Richard Hooker and the Construction of Christian Community*. Tempe, Arizona: Medieval & Renaissance Text & Studies, 1997.

SISSON, C. J. *The Judicious Marriage of Mr. Hooker and the Birth of "The Laws of Ecclesiastical Polity"*. Cambridge: Cambridge University Press, 1940.

SMITH, ELSIE. "Hooker at Salisbury." *Times Literary Supplement*: 233. March 30, 1962.

SNOW, VERNON F. *Parliament in Elizabethan England, John Hooker's Order and Usage*. Hartford: Yale University Press, 1977.

————. "John Hooker's Circle: Evidence from his New Year's Gift List of 1584." *Devon and Cornwall Notes and Queries*. 140; 161.

SOPER, H. TAPELY AND J.W SCHOPP. eds. With Walter J. Harte. *Office of Arms Chart of 1597*. Exeter: City Muniments, 52.

STONE, LAWRENCE. *The Family, Sex and Marriage in England 1500-1800*. New York: Harper and Row, 1977.

STOW, JOHN. *A Survey of London*. Stroud, Gloucester: Publishing Ltd, 1994. (Reprint from 1603 ed.)

STRONG, ROY. *The English Renaissance Miniature*. London: Thames and Hudson, 1984.

STRYPE, JOHN. *Historical Collections of the Life and Acts of John Aylmer, Lord Bishop of London in the Reign of Queen Elizabeth* (1700). Oxford: Oxford University Press, 1821.

———. *The Life and Acts of the Most Reverend Father in God, John Whitgift, D.D.* London, 1718. (British Library copy: BL 490.1.5.).

STURGESS, H. A. C., ed. *Register of Admissions to the Honourable Society of the Middle Temple,* I. London: Butterworth & Co., Ltd, 1949.

THOMPSON, W. D. J. CARGILL. "The Philosopher of the 'Politic Society': Richard Hooker as a Political Thinker." W. Speed Hill, ed., *Studies in Richard Hooker: Essays Preliminary To An Edition Of His Works*. Cleveland & London: The Press of Case Western Reserve University, 1972.

TORRANCE, W. J. "Richard Hooker as Apologist of the Magisterial Reformation in England." A. S. McGrade ed., *Richard Hooker and the Construction of Christian Community*. Tempe, Arizona: Medieval & Renaissance Texts & Studies, 1997.

TRAVERS, WALTER. *Disciplina Ecclesiae Dei Verbo . . . et Anglicanae Ecclesiae . . . Explicatio (Book of Discipline)*. 1587. In Francis Paget, *An Introduction to the Fifth Book of Hooker's Treatise of the Laws of Ecclesiastical Polity*. Oxford: Clarendon Press, 1899.

———. *A Supplication Made to the Privy Counsel by Mr Walter Travers*. 1586. British Library: Harleian MS 4888; Lambeth Library, Fairhurst Papers: 3470, fols.82-87; Folger, V, 187-210.

TREVOR-ROPER, HUGH. *Catholics, Anglicans and Puritans*. Chicago: University of Chicago Press, 1987.

———. *Renaissance Essays*. Chicago: University of Chicago Press, 1961.

TYACKE, NICHOLAS. *Anti-Calvinists and The Rise of Arminianism 1590-1640*. Oxford: Clarendon Press, 1987.

WALTON, IZAAC. *The Life of Mr. Rich. Hooker, The Author of those Learned Books of the Laws of Ecclesiastical Polity*. London: Richard Marriott, 1665.

———. "Preface to the First Edition of the Life of Hooker." John Keble, ed. *The Works of . . . Mr. Richard Hooker: With An Account of His Life and Death by Isaac Walton*, 3rd ed. Oxford: Oxford University Press, 1845.

WEINSTEIN, ROSEMARY. *Tudor London*. Museum of London, 1994.

WESCOTE, THOMAS. *A View of Devonshire in MDCXXX*. Exeter, 1845.

WHITGIFT, JOHN. *A Defense of the Ecclesiastical Regiment in Englande defaced by T. C. In his Replie against D. Whitgift*. London: Henry Bynneman, 1574. (Original in Lambeth Palace Library: 1574.04.)

———. *Letters*. Assorted correspondence: 1587-94. Lambeth Palace Library: Fairhurst Papers, MSS 3470, fols. 89, 99-103, 109-113, 115.

———. *Notes on the Hooker-Travers Controversy*. 1586. Lambeth Palace Library: Fairhurst Papers, 2006, fols. 6-15; *Folger* V.

———. *Sermon at Paul's Cross*. 1583 Lambeth Palace Library: 1598.22.

WILLIAMSON, J. BRUCE. *The History of The Middle Temple*. New York: E. P. Dutton and Company, 1924.

———. *The Middle Temple Bench Book*, 2nd ed. London: Chancery, 1937.

WILSON, H. B. *The History of the Merchant Taylors Schools*. London, 1812.

WINSTANLEY, WILLIAM. *The Honour of Merchant-Taylors*. London, 1668. (The British Library.)

WOOD, ANTHONY. *Athenae Oxonienses, An Exact History of all the Writers and Bishops Who Have Had Their Education in the University of Oxford,* 1691-92. V.I. Philip Bliss, ed. London, 1813.

WOOD, REGINALD. *Sir Walter Ralegh, Gold Was His Star*. Lewes, Sussex: The Book Guild, Ltd, 1991.

WOOLTON, JOHN. *The Christian Manual,* 1576. (Parker Society Edition). Cambridge: Cambridge University Press, 1851.

YOUINGS, JOYCE. *Sixteenth Century England*. Harmondsworth, Middlesex: Penguin Books, Ltd, 1984.

————. *Tuckers Hall Exeter*. Exeter: The University of Exeter Press, 1968.

Index